FINAL VOYAGES

Kermit "Kit" Bonner

TURNER PUBLISHING COMPANY
412 Broadway
P.O. Box 3101
Paducah, KY 42002-3101
(502) 443-0121

Turner Publishing Company Staff:
Project Coordinator: Julie Agnew Thomas
Designer: Lora Ann Lauder

Library of Congress
Catalog Card Number: 1-56311-289-2
ISBN 978-1-63026-934-0

Additional copies may be purchased directly
from Turner Publishing Company.

This publication was compiled using available
information. The publisher regrets it cannot assume liability for errors or omissions.

Photo: The USS Wakefield *after the disaster on September 3, 1942, when a fire broke out that threatened
the crew and several hundred troops being carried.
The* Brooklyn *was able to come alongside and help
rescue over 800 men. The ship was nearly burned out,
but was later renovated. The training and skill of the*
Brooklyn's *crew saved the day.*

TABLE OF CONTENTS

DEDICATION

"Final Voyages" is dedicated to all men and women who have served in or are currently part of the United States Naval Service. It is also dedicated to my father, Lt Commander Kermit H. Bonner Sr., USN (Ret), a fine naval officer; my mother Edna Bonner, who always had faith in me; and my son Kermit III, who also served his country in the United States Army.

Thanks to my wife Carolyn and my daughter Catherine for encouraging me in this effort.

INTRODUCTION

Final Voyages is pictorial chronicle of twenty five warships of the United States Navy which were active during the Twentieth Century. They performed in war, in peace and a few saw extensive service in allied navies. Each has a story to tell. Many are well known, yet some have moved quietly through history in the wake of more famous ships and events. Final Voyages is the story of the known, the unknown, the famous, the infamous. It is a story about the navy.

Ships such as the aircraft carrier *Enterprise* and the heavy cruiser *San Francisco* fought with distinction and their achievements were the subject of continuous media attention. Others such as the light cruiser *Helena* and the heavy cruiser *Salt Lake City* fought valiantly in one major engagement after the other, but were never accorded the public acclaim they so richly deserved. By comparison, ships such as the light cruiser *Boise* were given a disproportionate share of credit for the efforts of others. Some never had a chance such as the battleship *Oklahoma*, lost through lack of foresight, or in the case of the *Langley* just plain incompetence which sentenced her to death just to satisfy international protocol.

Ships such as the destroyer *Ward* will be forever known for a singular act, that of firing the first shot of World War II. Likewise the light cruiser *Concord* will be remembered for firing the last shot. Ironically, both ships were relics of an era gone by, yet one would signal the beginning and the other the end of the most violent confrontation in the history of mankind. In between the two shots a modern navy fought a modern war.

The light cruiser *Milwaukee* will be known as the sole major warship lent to the Soviet Union, and sadly, upon her return was called the "filthiest ship in the United States Navy". The peasant navy of communism had not yet learned the use of soap and water as part of a five year plan. But, balanced against the deplorable condition of the *Milwaukee*, the light cruiser *Brooklyn* would be furnished loving care for nearly half a century by her new owners, the Navy of Chile.

Others such as the destroyer escort (high speed transport) *Belet* (later the Mexican ship "*California*") would be lost due to ineptitude and foolish pride, yet her crew would be saved. In contrast, the destroyer *Brush* would eventually end her days as part of the navy of Taiwan, yet one of her American crews would be lost due to ignorance and arrogance. One ship, the destroyer *Blakeley* would eventually sail as the combination of two ships and emerge as an engineering triumph, while another, the destroyer *William D. Porter* would nearly kill the leader of the free world, but in her own death spare every man of her crew.

Final Voyages is the saga of the great, the pathetic, the tragic, and even the humorous. It is a story about the ships of United States Navy and how they ended their days. It is also the story of a navy that no longer exists, a steel pre-microchip navy manned initially by professionals and later by amateurs turned professional. A navy that is slowly slipping out of focus into history.

-Kermit H. "Kit" Bonner

The USS *Arkansas*, the *Pennsylvania*, the *Saratoga*. The stories of these celebrated ships, and dozens of their more- or less-famous sisters, unfold in *Final Voyages*, an affectionate chronicle of their "lives" and times. The reader will witness kamikaze attacks, weather sea changes in naval policy and procedures, and watch as some of these battleships, cruisers and destroyers go to their final rest at the bottom of the sea.

This book has been a true labor of love for author Kermit "Kit" H. Bonner. In reading his accounts of the ships' varied fates, his devotion to these great gray ladies is undeniable. Hundreds of one-of-a-kind photos provided by Mr. Bonner illustrate the proud heritage of these former rulers of the waves, as well as the men who sailed them.

These ships and their gallant crews helped keep America free, sometimes making the ultimate sacrifice in payment for that precious gift. Some of the more fortunate battleships, cruisers and destroyers that sail through these pages survive today as public museums, testaments to the work that continuing democracy entails. Turner Publishing Company is proud to salute them all, and to present *Final Voyages*.

Sincerely,

Dave Turner

Dave Turner
President, Turner Publishing Company

The Enterprise at sea in August 1944 after being thoroughly modernized and painted with a new camouflage scheme. She fairly bristles with new 40mm quad mounts for AA defense.

FINAL VOYAGES

CHAPTER I

THE DESTROYERS

USS *Belet*, DE-599, APD-109, MEXICAN DESTROYER, *California* "ANATOMY OF A SHIPWRECK"

Just after 0800 on January 16, 1972, while steaming southward along the California coast, the Mexican destroyer, *California*, formerly the USS *Belet*, APD-109, EX DE-599, ran aground nine miles north of Ensenada, Mexico. Stranded just off Point San Miguel, she became a total loss within five days.

THE APD - FAST TROOP TRANSPORT

The *California* was originally built and commissioned by the U.S. Navy on June 15, 1945, as the USS *Belet,* DE-599, and was later converted to a high speed troop transport, APD-109. The *Belet* was built by the Bethlehem Steel Company at Hingham, Massachusetts where she was laid down on January 26, 1944, and launched on March 3, 1944. She was one of 50 *"Rudderow"* class escort destroyers hurriedly built during World War II and converted to the highly successful APD. These ships were not retrofitted for their troop transport role like the older "Wickes" class four stack destroyer, but were modified during construction. The Navy had experienced great success with the use of fast troop transports in the south Pacific and in 1943 ordered 100 of the new DE's converted to APD's. With a 160 plus man complement of marines or soldiers plus light equipment, singularly or in company with other APD's, these ships could seize small islands or make surgical landings wherever needed. Of course, the APD was not limited to carrying combat ready marines, but also carried UDT (frogmen), coast watchers, intelligence agents or anything or anyone else that the Navy required.

She displaced 1400 tons, was 300 feet in length and had a 37 foot beam. Powered by two Foster-Wheeler boilers, her turbo electric engine could drive her at 24 knots. She mounted a single enclosed 5 inch/38 caliber gun forward and a AAA battery of 20/40MM, however her main battery was her ability to transport and deliver up to 162 combat ready men at critical points. She carried up to four midships mounted landing craft (LCVP's) for this purpose.

Her first Captain was Albert P. Merrill, who had just been relieved as the commanding officer of the USS *Edward C. Daly*, DE-17. Known to his officers as being somewhat fastidious, he was able to assemble an effective crew and wardroom. Many of the crew had been transferred from the destroyers, *Rowan*, *Fred T. Barry* and the *French*, a destroyer escort, yet it was a typical late wartime complement of veterans and new arrivals. Soon after commissioning, the new APD sailed for Key West for sound training. She then went through rigorous training for her combat role as a fast troop transport on the West Coast. At the end of her abbreviated training period, she arrived in Port Huenenme, *California* and embarked her passengers, 160 marines and their officers.

The *Belet* was on her way to war, and all knew her mission was to land her troops on the Japanese mainland for the assault that was estimated to cause upward to a million casualties. As the ship and her anxious crew passed eastward of Wake Island, they heard the news of two bombs being dropped on Hiroshima and Nagasaki. The atomic bomb had spared the *Belet*, and the war ended shortly thereafter. She proceeded onward to Japan, however, and eventually became a port director unit near Wakayam, Japan. Boredom replaced anxiety, and the crew and officers wanted only to return home. Finally, in late 1945, the order came to return to the U.S. for decommissioning and mothballing. She was placed in reserve by her second and final American naval captain, Lt. Cmdr. Hitchcock.

Moored in reserve at Jacksonville, Florida for nearly a quarter century, she was selected and purchased by the Mexican Government in December 1969, along with five other APD's. She was assigned to Acapulco as her home port, where her duties were typically patrol, and qualifying naval cadets from the Vera Cruz Naval Academy. Her spacious troop compartment made her ideal for carrying cadets, and she was carrying 18 when she met her end.

HARD AGROUND, CONFUSION AND INACTION

Dotted with small inlets and coves that have sandy or mud bottoms, the stretch of water from San Diego along the western Baja California coast to Ensenada, Mexico is well traveled, and has a minimum of navigational hazards. There is a beacon at Point San Miguel, and charts clearly show rapid shoaling from an average of 200 fathoms to 35 fathoms within 1000-1500 yards from the beach. There are no significant sub surface obstructions such as wrecks, reefs or rocks, and the nearest island is just southwest of Ensenada. The *California* was a relatively modern warship reconditioned in the U.S. prior to transfer, and had the minimum standard navigational aids (e.g. radar, RDF, fathometer, and so forth) required for safe cruising. The story of her unexpected, yet tragically typical

The USS Belet, *DE-599 just before her launching on March 3, 1944. She was converted to fast attack transport (APD) halfway into her construction as a "Rudderrow" class destroyer escort. The APD's had proven their value time after time in the south Pacific, and the destroyer escort hull format was perfectly adapted to this new variant.*

The Belet *shortly after being launched at the Bethlehem Steel Company's yard at Hingham, Massachusetts. Tugs will usher her to a fitting out basin where she will be converted to an APD over a fifteen month period.*

The Commanding Officer
and Wardroom Officers of the

U. S. S. Belet

cordially invite you to a reception
to be held in the
Bachelor Officers' Quarters
Hingham, Mass.
following the commissioning ceremony
5:30 to 7:30 p. m.

R.S.V.P.

Lt. Cmdr. Phillip Merrill, the Belet's *prospective commanding officer issues the traditional invitations to relatives, dignitaies and guests to celebrae the commissioning of his new ship on June 15, 1945.*

The officers and men stand at attention as the commissioning pennant is hoisted formally inducting the USS Belet *into the U.S. Navy. In the background, APD 114, USS* Walter S. Gorka *has been launched a scant three weeks before the Belet's commissioning date of June 15, 1945. Neither would see any World War II experience.*

The former United States Navy fast attack transport USS Belet, *APD-109, now the Mexican destroyer and fleet flagship* California *lies broached to just north of Ensenada on January 21, 1972. She has run aground five days previously, and all efforts to free her had failed.*

loss is not unlike that of many others on the California coast including the seven American Destroyers lost on September 9, 1923. They ran aground at Point Arguello, just north of Santa Barbara.

The *Delphy, S. P. Lee, Young, Nicholas, Woodbury, Chauncey,* and *Fuller,* sleek and graceful modern four piper destroyers, followed one another onto the rocks off Point Arguello in a dense fog. Steaming at 20 knots, and inadvertently off course, a navigation error combined with negligence cost 22 lives in the worst peacetime naval loss in U.S. Naval history. As these ships were firmly driven and wedged into the rocks, there was no possibility of salvage. The remains of these ill fated destroyers were eventually worn down by wind and sea, until no reminder, save written history, exists. The loss of these destroyers in many ways, parallels that of the *California.*

The *California* encountered a thick fog off of the coast, and for one reason or another touched sandy bottom within 200 yards of the beach while making moderate speed in the early daylight hours of January 16, 1972. The combination of events that caused this stranding has never been fully explained to the public. Yet there was the fog, the same type that engulfed the seven American destroyers nearly 70 years earlier. The *California* had adequate navigation equipment, but apparently it played no effective role in preventing this loss. More significant than the circumstances that caused the grounding were the events that transpired over the next five days. These events provide a vital clue as to why this fine ship was first stranded and conclusive evidence as to why she was eventually declared a total loss.

JANUARY 16 1972, SUNDAY, 0810

The *California*, carrying 80 regular crew, and 18 naval cadets, while steaming down the coast, struck a gently shoaling sandy shelf approximately 200 yards from the beach. This area was just below a point called Punta San Miguel nine miles north of Ensenada, Mexico. As she slid onto the sandy bottom, she broached with her port side parallel to the beach. She quickly be-

came firmly gripped by the sand. Breakers began mercilessly crashing against her starboard side, and she was progressively rocked and pushed toward the beach. The crew and cadets remained aboard the stranded destroyer, which by now was listing to port by 8-10 degrees.

Efforts were made to back her off, but to no avail. She radioed the Ensenada Naval Station for assistance. Tugs were promised. At first it was reported that she had dragged her anchor, thus causing the grounding, but this account was later changed, and the accident was attributed to the fog. There was even a short lived rumor that the fuel lines had become clogged, thus causing engine failure. At this point, however, there was no plausible explanation available to the public.

JANUARY 17, 1972, MONDAY, 1330

After a day and a night of being pounded by the surf, the destroyer had now been pushed to within 100 yards of the beach, and early afternoon low tide exposed her entire stern. The crew and cadets, now unsure of what to do, still remained with the ship. Power was being maintained to enable the pumps to cope with a number of minor leaks that were multiplying due to the ship's up and down movement on the bottom. Aside from hundreds of well wishing American and Mexican sightseers now lining the cliffs surrounding the small cove, no practical assistance had arrived. A line was finally secured to the beach which allowed limited rubber raft traffic, but that was the extent of any rescue operation.

JANUARY 18, 1972, TUESDAY, 0900

Fog had again descended on the marooned ship, yet small tugs from Ensenada had arrived. Also, the USS *Molana* ATF-106, and the USS *Gear* ARS-34 were standing by. Supplementary pumps were sent out to the *California* to cope with increased flooding, especially in the engineroom, but getting a line on her from seaward was virtually impossible. The seas continued to buffet her without abatement, and efforts to move her were minimal. Some of the breakers were reaching the height of her funnel, and

the force of the sea was acting as a hammer slamming her bottom on the many small rocks now underneath her.

JANUARY 19, 1972, WEDNESDAY, 1400

Assistance was finally requested from the U.S. Navy, and divers responded from the USS *Gear*, and made a survey of the ship's condition. It was confirmed that many of her key compartments were flooded, and that the ship had now moved onto a jagged rock ledge that was punching new and larger holes in her with each successive swell. The sickening, and almost unnatural noise of the hull grinding on the rocks could be heard for miles, even on the rescue ships anchored several hundred yards out. To the crew who still remained aboard, the noise was unbearable, and particularly terrifying to the young cadets. A line was eventually attached from the salvage ship, but by this time, the surf was so severe, that there is little hope of pulling the stricken destroyer free.

JANUARY 20, 1972, THURSDAY, 1400

The crew and cadets, save three, abandoned the *California* as the water hit the boilers causing them to explode. The fuel lines had already become contaminated, and the engines had ceased to function. Fortunately, no one had been seriously injured, and an orderly evacuation took place at low tide. The crew carried their belongings in boxes above their heads, and waded ashore. Several of the crew that were interviewed spoke of their four day ordeal as being a living nightmare. The Captain could not be found near the ship or in Ensenada for comment, yet one of the officers stated that he was "serene" about the decision to abandon. There was no further comment, except official regret at the loss.

EPILOGUE

The ship settled further, and most hull level compartments were flooded by the end of the week. The motion of the ship on the rocks literally ground up the bottom of the hull. By the

January 23, 1972, the California *is damaged beyond any hope of redemption and has been abandoned. Her captain has disappeared, and only the tourists are left to mourn her loss.*

The USS Blakeley, *DD-150, just after commissioning in May 1919. She would have to wait nearly a quarter century to make her mark in naval history.*

An aerial photograph of the Blakeley *shortly after her bow was blown off by a torpedo fired by a German U-boat in the Caribbean. Six men were killed, but immediate and effective damage control prevented the loss of the ship.*

following Saturday, January 22, 1972, she was fully abandoned, and only a few guards were left camped on the beach amidst rafts and orange life preservers. They remained to prevent independent salvage, and looting. There was also the munitions and other military hardware to be removed.

By the end of 1972, the *California* was a dismembered skeleton on the sands. The cause of this disaster was attributed to the fog that has been, and continues to be a killer of many ships on that coast. However, of the ships that have been stranded, the *California* had the best chance for escape. Unlike her seven predecessors who, in 1923, were lodged among jagged rocks, and without power, the *California* was aground on sand, and had power for four days. Had assistance been requested immediately from the nearby San Diego Naval Base, then the *California* may have been salvaged. Unfortunately, the delay of three days caused her to become firmly embedded on the rocks within 100 yards of the beach. Her loss was more appropriately due to poor communication, indecision, misplaced pride, and as always with any disaster of this nature, a lack of respect for the sea.

USS *BLAKELEY* DD-150
"TRIUMPH OF ENGINEERING"

The USS *Blakeley*, DD-150 was one of many World War I assembly line destroyers built to counter the German U-Boat threat. As the U.S. entered the war late, the *Blakeley*, like many of her sisters never saw combat. She was launched on September 19, 1918, and not placed in commission until May 8, 1919, six months after the Armistice.

The *Blakeley* was a "four piper or flush decker" a design unique to the U.S. Navy. She displaced 1154 tons, carried a main battery of four 4 inch/50 cal guns and twelve 21 inch torpedo tubes in four triple mounts. She could make 35 plus knots, and was a sight to see at full power. Many still consider service aboard one of these ships as the best training ground for destroyer sailors as they demanded much from their crews and required a high degree of seamanship. Life aboard was harsh but rewarding. Creature comforts were at a premium, and today's sailor lives in more luxurious accommodations than the captain of a four stacker.

MILITARY BUDGET CUTS AND DRAW DOWNS HAVE A LONG HISTORY

Unfortunately, the Navy faced extreme draw downs and budget cuts in the immediate period after World War I, and many of these graceful ships practically sailed from launching to mothballs. The *Blakeley* was no exception, and although she was an active unit of the Atlantic Fleet for three years, on June 29, 1922 she went into reserve at the Philadelphia Navy Yard. Coincidently, a sister ship, the USS *Taylor*, DD-94, which had her beginnings at the Mare Island Naval Shipyard on the other side of the U.S., was placed out of commission during the same month in Philadelphia. The *Taylor*, or at least part of her would figure prominently in the future of the *Blakeley*.

The Navy attempted to keep as much of the destroyer force active as funds would permit by using rotating crews and providing minimal upkeep. The ships were used for a number of different tasks such as being part of the "rum runner" enforcement fleet of the Coast Guard. They were also used as remote control targets and for experimental purposes such as carrying a scout plane. This was short lived. Unfortunately, most found their way into various "red lead row" reserve anchorages, the most famous being the San Diego Destroyer Base. The *Blakeley* was one of those selected and sealed for a decade long period of inactivity.

For ten years, the *Blakeley* rusted and provided a home for sea birds, but in 1932 and up through 1937 she was active again in the Scouting Fleet. Laid up for a second time in 1937, she emerged again in 1939, and was recommissioned. She joined the fast expanding Neutrality Patrol in the dark uncertain period known as "short of war". Her area of operation was the Caribbean where she escorted troop transports and provided general convoy protection. At the same time, a sister destroyer, the *Taylor* had been decommissioned and was being used as a training hulk for damage control parties at the Philadelphia Navy Yard. She now held the inglorious designation of Damage Control Hulk No. 40.

THE OLD DESTROYER SURVIVES A GERMAN TORPEDO

On May 25, 1942, the *Blakeley* was steaming just off Martinique when at 0850 she altered

A crude wooden bulkhead is fitted over the damaged area just forward of the superstructure. It almost looks as if a tin can had been bent around a wooden frame, but this temporary measure held until something more substantial could be installed. The damaged destroyer was only allowed a short period of time for emergency repairs and medical assitance alongside the Vichy French carrier, Bearn, anchored at Martinique.

The Blakeley, *in the left background, has been prepared to receive the bow of a decommissioned sister, the USS* Taylor. *The* Taylor *had been given the ignominious role of damage control hulk sporting the number 40. The bow portion of the* Taylor *had already been severed and was being moved toward the* Blakeley *via heavy shipyard crane. A large audience had gathered to watch this rather peculiar event in naval architecture and shipbuilding.*

course to investigate a sound contact. It was quickly determined that the contact was bogus and probably a school of blackfish. Just as the ship was again settling down on her previous course, a submarine launched torpedo hit her between frames 18 and 24 about four feet below the water line. The impact was so great that the forward 60 feet of the tin can was blown off, and there was immediate and real concern about her survival. Within minutes however, a well trained and disciplined crew brought the ship back under control, and after a short period of adjustment, the helmsman was able to set a course for the harbor of Fort de France which was fortuitously nearby. The ship was steered with a combination of rudder and varying shaft speeds, and what was seemingly impossible was accomplished. Within four hours after being hit by the U-Boat's torpedo, the *Blakeley* was securely moored to the starboard side of the impounded French carrier, Bearn. Sadly, six men died and twenty one were wounded during the attack. The loss might have been much higher had the officers and crew of the *Blakeley* not responded with such skill and determination to save their ship.

The *Blakeley* was initially fitted with a crude, but effective timber bulkhead to cover the bow area blown off and a rather peculiar looking anchor was fashioned from a truck axle and differential housing. But they worked, and she was able to make her way from Fort de France to San Juan, Puerto Rico, where a steel stub bow was attached for the eventual trip back to the Philadelphia Navy Yard. A question arises at this point about the logic of the Navy making such an effort to save an obsolete ship that had been heavily damaged. The reason is simple; it was mid 1942, and the U.S. was fighting for its very existence, and every destroyer, even a partial one, was worth it's weight in gold.

TWO SHIPS BECOME ONE

Throughout the summer months of 1942, the *Blakeley* and her sister ship *Taylor*, now Hulk

No 40, shared the same drydock. An engineering miracle was about to take place, as the bow section of the *Taylor* was removed and judiciously grafted onto the *Blakeley*. It was a perfect fit, and by September 1942, the *Blakeley* resumed her duties, a new ship with the latest weapon and electronics systems. Interestingly enough, the anchor detail was now able to anchor the Blakeley from the bow of the *Taylor*!

The residual 255 feet of the *Taylor* went back to her duties as Hulk No. 40, and was subsequently scrapped in August, 1945. She had served her country in more ways than could be expected.

The *Blakeley* spent the balance of her wartime career back in the convoy escort business with the exception of two short deployments in the Atlantic, one of which entailed hunter-killer duty. Her final duty was in New London where she was assigned the task of training submarines to avoid destroyers. This final duty was a bittersweet irony considering her experience in May 1942!

She was decommissioned at the Philadelphia Navy Yard on July 21, 1945, and sold for scrap on November 30, 1945. She earned one Battle Star for convoy service, but moreover, she earned the respect of all those who witnessed her triumph against the sea, and the subsequent engineering achievement that makes the U.S. Navy and it's destroyer force the finest in the world.

USS *BRUSH*, DD-745
"A BRUSH WITH DEATH"

The USS *Brush*, DD-745 was one of hundreds of World War II built destroyers turned out in assembly line fashion. Designed prima-

The bow of the Taylor *is just about connected to the* Blakeley, *and the fit looks perfect. Destroyers of any kind were worth their weight in gold during the critical see-saw period in mid 1942, so anything was possible.*

rily for the Pacific conflict, these 2,200 ton *Sumner* class destroyers were considered expendable, and not expected to survive in mortal combat more than 90 minutes. Yet, the *Brush* and most of her sisters would serve the U.S. Navy and those of our allies for many decades to come. Armed with six 5 inch 38 caliber guns and an impressive array of anti-ship torpedoes and anti-aircraft weapons, the *Brush* and others like her were sent to fight the Imperial Japanese Navy and air force in that country's last dying gasp in the waning months of World War II. The *Brush* was launched on December 28,

December 23, 1943, launching day for the new destroyer, USS Brush, *DD-745, at the Bethlehem Steel Yard on Staten Island. She was christened by eight year old Virginia Perkins, granddaughter of Dr. Charles Francis Brush. The* Brush *was one of the 2,200 ton* Sumner *class big destroyers designed for Pacific combat. Cynics coined them 90 minute wonders because that was their anticipated life expectancy when swarm attacked by determineed Kamikazes. The* Brush *lived a long, yet peculiar life.*

1943, built by the Bethlehem Steel Corporation in Staten Island, New York. She was commissioned on April 17, 1944, and immediately sailed for the Pacific.

She would fight through the rest of World War II and earn five battles stars for combat worthiness during her cruise. She would again fight in the Korean Conflict where she would strike a mine that did substantial damage to her hull and killed thirteen of her crew. The *Brush* would be awarded an additional four battle stars for service during the "forgotten war". The rest of her career from the Korean War through mid 1969 would be spent in training, escort and other duties typically assigned to most destroyers in the Western Pacific.

The *Brush* was never upgraded under the FRAM (Fleet Rehabilitation and Modernization Program), and spent her entire career in her original configuration as an Allen M. Sumner class destroyer. She was eventually stricken from the Navy Register on October 27, 1969, and sold to the Republic of China (Taiwan) on December 9, 1969. She was renamed *Hsiang Yang*, and armed with Hsiung Feng anti-ship missiles in place of after five inch twin mount. To this was also added a quadruple Sea Chaparral launcher for MIM-72 Surface to Air Missiles.

The former USS *Brush* and five sister destroyers spent the next 15 years in patrol and interdiction roles, and finally on January 1, 1984, she was decommissioned and sold for scrapping at a local ship breaker. For nearly forty years the *Brush -Hsiang Yang* provided valuable service to two nations, yet one incident that occurred in early 1947 nearly went unrecorded. That incident had a progressively profound and tragic effect on 300 young sailors.

ANXIOUS TO GET HOME

It was 7:30 on the morning of February 27, 1947, when the *Brush* and two other destroyers swept into the deep blue waters of Kwajalein Lagoon located in the heart of the South Pacific. The *Brush* was on her way home to San Francisco, and most of the youthful crew of recent enlistees was anxious to get on with their lives outside of the navy. The three ship formation was alone except for a group of broken and scarred warships anchored together just inside of the lagoon. These abandoned battleships, cruisers, and carriers once represented the pride of many navies, and had been left there to rust and slowly sink after being used for "atomic bomb" target practise. The crew of the *Brush* lined the rails staring at the ghost fleet, but they would soon be moored within 100 yards and have five days to gaze at them. The other two destroyers anchored some distance from the *Brush* further in the lagoon.

Kwajalein is typical of hundreds of lagoons surrounded by sandy islands with swaying palms and balmy breezes. Unfortunately, it was one of the first sites used to dump American nuclear waste, and the last sight that many of the *Brush*'s crew saw as relatively healthy men. Incredibly, within 30 years, all but a few of the crew would be dead, some suffering hideously for years, and others just quietly dying. None really knowing why or how.

Ted Dvorak, one of the survivors, has suffered from chronic fatigue, diabetes, coronary and nervous disorder since the early 1950's when he was summarily retired from the Navy due to disability. The reason for his retirement was simply given as anxiety reaction, but he and his few

remaining shipmates now recognize that the cause lies with the five day stay in Kwajalein lagoon. Over the years, the evidence has continued to mount as Dvorak and other crewmen were found to have large skin lesions containing toxins of an unknown origin. In other instances, five former crewmen died of colon cancer in New Orleans within one year, and other crewmen still living, such as Quenton Miller have had various cancers since 1966. But the most compelling testimony occurred when Dvorak began a large scale effort to locate his shipmates.

In 1985, Dvorak, nostalgic to reunite with his former shipmates and form a "Ship's Reunion" group began a worldwide search for all former *Brush* crewmen, and in particular his shipmates of 1946-48. Astonished, he soon discovered that 270 of his original 300 man crew could not be located. He continued his search, and began to find that many had died at early ages, some as young as 40. Some died of natural or accidental causes, but the majority were lost before they reached age 50. By comparison, he was able to contact 70% of the crew who served on the *Brush* prior to the 1947 visit to Kwajalein. Digging deeper, he located nearly 90% who came aboard after the incident were alive. Today, the USS *Brush* (DD-745) reunion organization lists 900 former crewmen from the ship, but only 20 from the Kwajalein visit.

He then began a search for information through the unconnected caves of the Federal government. Beginning with the Navy Department, he covered a lot of ground including the Veterans Administration, Defense Department, National Archives, and the Nuclear Defense Agency. He was repeatedly told that it was sheer coincidence and that there was no proof that nuclear radiation had affected his shipmates. He was also informed that as long as the sailors had not boarded the ships of the target fleet, then there was no problem with radiation. Undaunted, he finally turned to his old friend, the late Les Aspin, then a Congressman from his local district. Aspin was successful in verifying that the *Brush* had stopped at Kwajalein Atoll in February 1947, and that the remainder of the nuclear target fleet was anchored there in close proximity. He could not obtain any further information, and the question of whether the exposure to the radioactive target fleet caused the premature deaths of Dvorak's shipmates continued to go unanswered.

OPERATION CROSSROADS AND THE ATOMIC BOMB TESTS

World War II ended with the formal surrender of Japan to the Allies on September 2, 1945. The abrupt capitulation was due to the massive destruction caused by Atomic weapons used on the cities of Hiroshima and Nagasaki. The Atomic Age had come, and although the war was over, the U.S. Navy was not satisfied with the gruesome evidence available in Japan nor even that gathered in New Mexico as a result of the world's first nuclear detonation test. The Navy needed to respond to it's critics that the "bomb" made navies obsolete and admirals unnecessary. Consequently, the congress was convinced to spend $125 million to allow seventy three target ships to be subjected to atomic explosions. Approval from congress was as much due to pressure from the Navy as well as morbid curiosity about the outcome. After all, some predicted that a hole in the bottom of the ocean would result, and all of the seas would disappear into the core of the earth! No one really believed it, but national security was at stake. Besides, it was a perfect opportunity to demonstrate to a controlled audience of world leaders what destructive power the U.S. was now capable of exercising. Just as funding from the congress was being obtained in Washington, 2,500 miles away on the west coast, Ted Dvorak and a new crew of 17-21 year old sailors were being assigned to their first ship, the USS *Brush*. The previous crew of wartime veterans had gone back into civilian life, unscathed except for their memories.

The site selected for the tests was Bikini Lagoon in the Marshall Islands, just 250 miles north of another lagoon, Kwajalein. As to the bombs, the first, affectionately known as "Gilda" would be dropped from a bomber using the now orange painted battleship *Nevada* as a bullseye, and the other weapon would be detonated 100 feet under the water. It was known as "Betty", and together the two detonations and the resulting tests would be known as Operation Crossroads or the Bikini Atoll Atomic tests. 42,000 men, 22 women, 1 dog, 200 pigs, 200 goats, and 4000 laboratory rats sailed in over 200 ships to Bikini Atoll with the express purpose of preparing and anchoring 73 target ships composed of older warships from the U.S., Germany and Japan. They also set up thousands of items such as coke bottles, footballs, baseball bats, cots, vehicles and various foodstuffs to see the effects of the two nuclear blasts. The preparation work began in January 1946, and continued unabated for six months. In Washington D.C., a dwindling group of dedicated anti-bomb protesters marched daily in front of the White House, but their slogan, "Crossroads is the wrong road" was ignored. Protests by animal protection societies were repeatedly met with the statement, "these animals will give their lives for humanity"! Few in government were interested in denying a victorious military the opportunity to test it's latest weapon.

On July 1, 1946 all of the targets were ready and testing equipment prepared. At 0900, "Gilda" was dropped from an Army B-29 bomber and exploded over the target fleet. Although it was a loud, violent explosion with the now familiar bright flash and mushroom cloud, it was considered a great disappointment by the media, congressional, and senate members watching from 18 miles away. The world did not end with a chain reaction explosion, nor did the ocean swallow the target fleet! After the explosion, the mushroom cloud quickly dissipated in the wind, and most of the fleet was still afloat. Even the orange colored bullseye ship *Nevada* was upright with only minor damage, and some of the bright color still visible. "We paid $125 million for that?" a senator from Oregon loudly demanded. A relieved congressman called it, "just a big firecracker". Within 10 hours, research teams entered the lagoon and examined all of the target ships. They found far less severe destruction and radioactivity than anticipated. Even one goat was alive on the *Nevada*!

"Betty" was made ready for the second test. This bomb was suspended 100 ft under a test ship, just above the bottom of the lagoon.

This would be the first underwater detonation, and many were hoping for a better show or at least that the dreaded "atomic bomb" would live up to it's reputation. At 0825 on July 25, "Betty" did her stuff, and within a millisecond, a 6,000 foot geyser a half mile wide rose out of the lagoon taking with it warships, one billion tons of water and sand, and eventually the lives of many innocent observers. The difference between "Gilda" and "Betty" was immediately obvious to all. Dense highly radioactive water vapor and debris covered all of the remaining target fleet and drifted down on the helpless observers, who now could only think to man their battle stations. They immediately took what limited precautions that were known to escape radiogenic poisoning. As panic grew among the project leaders, extensive attempts were made to cleanse the target fleet of the plutonium residue by hosing and scrubbing them, but the radiological safety director, Colonel Stafford Warren quickly concluded, "some of the most important ships had many lethal doses deposited on them which are retained in crevices and other places." He later warned the Project Director, Admiral W. H. P. Blandy, that "plutonium is the most poisonous chemical known and it is an insidiously toxic in very minute quantities". "The target ships would remain dangerous for an indeterminate time thereafter" Based on this and growing fears for the safety of personnel at the target site, further testing was suspended and

One billion tons of water and ocean bottom are sucked five times higher than the World Trade Center by the explosive force of the second Bikini Atomic test. The spreading water vapor cloud contaminated everything and everyone within ten miles.

Bikini atoll was abandoned within three weeks. All documents related to decontamination efforts became classified just as a precaution against future litigation.

In spite of the presence of unplanned overwhelming radioactivity, and a lack of knowledge on how to deal with the problem, Operation Crossroads was declared a success. "Betty" took most of the credit. Within weeks, Bikini lagoon was just a vacant radioactive nightmare, and the thousands of sailors, civilians, and what was left of the test animals left for the U.S. The remaining ships were towed to Kwajalein lagoon for further examination and study. By late 1946, those too "hot" with radioactivity were anchored end to end near some rocks at the lagoon entrance. The remainder were brought to San Francisco for additional testing and scrapping. A few of the most radioactively deadly ships were scuttled in deep water outside of the lagoon in early 1948. One was the old battleship *Pennsylvania*, sister ship to the *Arizona*, now a memorial in Pearl Harbor. The *Brush* would tie up closest to this and other "glowing" hulks.

A Dead Fleet Beckons

For five days in February-March 1947, the crew of the *Brush* baked in the hot sun within rock throwing distance of the Bikini test fleet. They fished for and ate sharks, swam and sun bathed. As there was no water barge available to provide drinking water, the *Brush* took on 14,000 gallons of the still waters of the lagoon, and converted it to fresh water. The crew was told that the burned and charred ships had survived atomic bombs at Bikini. There was no order to stay off of the ships, nor any precautions against radioactivity given the crew of the *Brush*. Sailors are natural souvenir hunters and they explored the old hulks and brought back such items as a ship's wheel, brass name plates, and so forth. Clift Wentworth, then a ship's boat coxswain, ferried some of the officers back and forth from the wrecks, but the *Brush* had no geiger counter or radiation detection equipment. After all, what couldn't be seen was not dangerous! Several hundred photographs were

taken, but these were later confiscated by the officers and destroyed. The *Brush* left for Pearl Harbor and the west coast on March 3, 1947.

Most of the 300 members of the 1946-48 crew of the *Brush* were discharged before and during 1948, and went their separate ways. When the Reunion Committee began it's search in 1985, only 30 who were aboard at Kwajalein could be located, and now in 1994, only twenty remain.

In 1946, later in 1985 and even now, the Navy refuses to accept any responsibility, nor even discuss the issue other than in very general non committal terms. Obtaining any information is like pulling teeth, and all questions are being referred to such agencies as the Veterans Administration and Defense Nuclear Agency. Yet the available evidence now strongly suggests that the *Brush*'s crew was accidently subjected to dangerous and ultimately lethal doses of radioactivity from the residual Bikini atoll target fleet.

American Chernobyl

Author and attorney Jonathan Weisgall of Washington D.C., now recognized as a leading expert on Operation Crossroads has described it as "America's Chernobyl". His book, "Crossroads", published by the Naval Institute Press places the responsibility for anecdotal incidents such as that with the *Brush*'s crew squarely on the shoulders of the U.S. Government. As the legal counsel to the displaced Bikini Islanders, he has also assisted the Committee on Natural Resources, chaired by Rep. George Miller of the San Francisco's East Bay's 7th District. This committee has oversight authority on the Marshall Islands, and is formally investigating the effects on those who were exposed to the testing at Bikini Atoll. Among other issues, it has considered mounting evidence that the government failed to provide adequate safety precautions for those involved during and after the tests.

There is no proof of a secret, sinister attempt by an uncaring government to subject humans to radiation, but all of the signs point to an dreadful accident compounded by pure ignorance. At the time, scientists, the Navy, and

congress were uninformed, and could not predict the future effect of the "bomb". Why one person survives and another dies is still much of a mystery. The most common misconception was that only direct exposure should cause any harm. Precautions were almost non-existent, and the crew of the *Brush* was unaware as to what had happened when they drank the distilled lagoon water, compared souvenirs or just simply spent hours staring at the old ships. Death and illness from an invisible killer was inconceivable to the young crew of the *Brush* as well as the people of that generation. Even today, it is difficult to establish what is considered a lethal dose of radiation. A rough measure used by most agencies and experts is 600 Roentgens or "rads", yet far less has been known to cause radiogenic illness and death. A "rad" is the common measure used to determine exposure to such things as x-rays, sunlight, and so forth. What can be tolerated varies with each human being and circumstance, and no government agency is willing to commit to a number or dosage due to fear of litigation. According to Weisgall, a tolerance level of .1 roentgen per day in 1946 has now been lowered by a factor of 365 for the general population. In other words, what as considered safe in 1946, has now been determined to be 365 times over the safe limit! The number of "rads" that the *Brush*'s crew absorbed will never be known, but apparently it was sufficient to cause a higher incidence of illness and premature death that is typically associated with over exposure to radiation.

Unknown to Dvorak, in 1986, pressure from the Federal Government's General Accounting Office caused a 10 year study to begin on the effects of nuclear blast testing on exposed observers or into today's governmentspeak, "downwinders". The study, being conducted by the Defense Nuclear Agency, Commission on Nuclear Blast Testing, is in it's eighth year and a report will not be issued until 1996. The study was initiated because the GAO suspected that radioactive metering devices being used in the early days of nuclear bomb testing were improperly calibrated. Perhaps, 450, 300 or even 250 rads would cause illness and death, and maybe not immediately, but a decade or more later. The Commission is reviewing the cases of over 200,000 observers that were potentially exposed to nuclear blasting including those in Nagasaki and Hiroshima. This is small compensation to Dvorak and his shipmates, but it is an acknowledgement that the government is now vitally concerned about the long term effects of overexposure to ionized radiation. Unfortunately, the study results will not be available until a half century after the *Brush*'s visit to Kwajalein Lagoon J. Robert Oppenheimer, known as the father of the Atomic Bomb once wrote, "When the time has run and that future has become history, it will be clear how little we today foresaw or could foresee". Unfortunately, by the time all of the investigations and government studies are completed, a generation of unknowing nuclear bomb testing victims may not be alive to hear a formal confirmation of this frightening, but ignored prediction.

The U.S. Navy destroyer, Brush, *as she looked during World War II and her visit to "dead fleet" in February 1947. Her crew was an unwitting victim of nuclear "friendly fire."*

Left: The USS Livermore, *DD-429, on July 30, 1949, for which the* Livermore/Gleaves *class of pre-World War II destroyer was named. The* Hobson *was one of 66 ships built in this class. Unfortunately, this photo of the* Livermore *shows her in a rather embarrassing position. She is hard aground having been stranded the night before off Cape Cod carrying 300 reservists on a summer cruise. Reserve training was not supposed to include grounding and refloating. she was refloated that afternoon. In August 1961 she was broken up. Right: The new destroyer,* Hobson, *steams up the Cooper River to the Charleston Navy Yard where she was built with care and attention to quality.*

USS *HOBSON*, DD-464, DMS-26
"LOST AT SEA"

There are defining moments in the life of each individual as well as every ship. The defining moment for the USS *Hobson* was at 2221 on the night of April 26, 1952, 700 miles west of the Azores in the Atlantic. It was at that moment that the *Essex* class aircraft carrier, USS *Wasp*, CV-18 collided with the ill fated destroyer minesweeper with such force that she was sliced in two. The *Hobson* had crossed from port to starboard in one of the many task force evolutions called for during maneuvers, and it was her last as well as the tragic end for 176 of her crew. Within four minutes, both halves of the ship sank, leaving 61 oil soaked souls to be rescued. The 61 had unknowingly joined an elite group of survivors which included the 32 who escaped from the overturned *Oklahoma* at Pearl Harbor, and those who escaped the sinking cruiser *Helena*, lost at Kula Gulf nine years earlier.

The loss of the *Hobson* and 176 of her crew was the worst peacetime disaster in U.S. Naval history, and although the ship will be forever remembered for this accident, there were other events in her eleven year life that must never be forgotten.

A CHARLESTON NAVY YARD DESTROYER

The Navy's Bureau of Construction and Repair authorized a series of destroyer designs during the 1930's that began with the Farragut class and culminated with the *Fletcher's*. The class just prior to the *Fletcher* was the *Gleaves/Livermore* of which the *Hobson* was a member. This popular class had the largest number of destroyers (66) next to it's successor, the *Fletcher's*, and served in all theaters of World War II. Seven of the *Gleaves/Livermore* class were built by the Charleston Navy Yard, Charleston, South Carolina.

The *Hobson* was launched on September 8, 1941, barely three months before the Japanese attack on Pearl Harbor. She was sponsored by Mrs. R. P. Hobson, widow of Rear Admiral

HOBSON'S CHARACTERISTICS

LOA: 348' 3"   LWL: 341'   Beam: 36' 1"
Depth: 19' 7"   SHP: 50,200   Speed: 36.5 kts
Endurance: 5,250 miles @ 12 knots/3,620 miles @ 20 knots
Main bat: 4 5"/38 cal dp/Mark 37 director
Torpedo Tubes: ten 21 inch   AA'bat: 40mm/20mm
Compl: 14 officers/262 crew   ASW: 2 DC tracks

Hobson a Spanish American War Medal of Honor winner. Admiral Hobson had died just five years before the commissioning of a ship that would carry his name through several major naval engagements during World War II. The urgency of war caused the yard to accelerate construction and fitting out schedule's, and the *Hobson* was commissioned on January 22, 1942 with Lt. Commander R.N. McFarlane assuming command. Although the yard had begun to turn out assembly line ships as other shipyards on both coasts, no ship was built with less than the highest quality. The *Hobson* was no exception, and Captain McFarlane made a point of complimenting the yard on their hard work and the obvious quality that they built into his new ship. Interestingly, like many of her sisters she was materially changed from her original design by the foresightedness of the Chief of Naval Operations. He knew that AA defense would be paramount in the imminent war that would be fought in the Pacific. The addition of a heavier AA battery would prove valuable in the hard years to come.

Like all *Gleaves/Livermore* class DD's, the main battery for the *Hobson* was originally planned as that of five 5 inch/38 cal DP guns arranged in an A, B, aft (C), X and Y format. This was altered for a number of the Gleaves/Livermore class due to the obvious lack of short range AA capability, so the *Hobson* was built with two aft mounted twin 40MM bofors mounts/directors and four 20MM orleikons in

lieu of C turret. Other than this life saving alteration the *Hobson* shared characteristics with the balance of the *Gleaves/Livermore* class (see chart above.)

The *Hobson* also shared something else in common with her sister destroyers and for that matter nearly every ship of the fleet, and that was a navy that was increasingly dependent on citizen sailors. The *Hobson* had her share of "old salts", but she also had a large complement of "boots" straight from the Charleston Navy Yard barracks. These boots would become veteran seamen within a few months, and many would participate in more naval battles than any other naval sailors in the history of sea warfare. To a man, none would ever let their shipmates or the ship down.

The *Hobson*, like virtually every ship being commissioned on the east coast headed for Casco Bay, Maine for extensive shakedown and training exercises. For almost six months the ship and her crew became acclimated to each other and formed that special bond that makes for an efficient fighting unit.

THE *HOBSON* ENTERS THE COMBAT ZONE

On July 1, 1942, the *Hobson* sailed for the Gold Coast of Africa as an escort for the carrier *Ranger*, a ship that the she would accompany periodically during the war. The *Ranger* was carrying a cargo of 72 P-40 fighter aircraft to augment Allied forces in North African theater.

An Army Airforce P-40 fighter plane leaves the deck of the carrier, Ranger, *on its way to a staging area and eventually the North African theater. The other AAF pilots look on anxiously as they know their turn will come soon. The* Ranger *transported 72 of these fighters on this trip and many more on other occasions. No Army pilots crashed on takeoff, but all gained a healthy respect for the naval aviator.*

The USS Hambleton *DD-455 and the USS* Rodman *DD-456, about to slide down the ways on September 26, 1941 at the Federal Shipbuilding and Drydock Co. Yard in Kearny. Both were sister ships to the* Hobson *and would figure prominently in her life. The* Rodman *would be there to the last, and rescue several of the crew from the* Atlantic *after* Hobson *collided with the carrier* Wasp *on April 26, 1952. The* Rodman, *like the* Hobson, *was converted to a DMS and was sold to Taiwan in July 1955. The* Hambleton, *also a DMS convert, was stricken in July 1971 and expended as a target.*

In a rather unorthodox move, Army pilots flew the aircraft from the *Ranger*'s deck to staging areas for employment against Rommel's Afrika Corps. All were safely launched, and the AAF pilots learned through experience that Naval Aviators are a special breed. The *Hobson* acted as plane guard and escort, and the mission was successful and uneventful. On August 5, the task force returned to the U.S., and the *Hobson* was detached for further training off the coast of Norfolk and Newport.

For the next few months and until being selected as one of the units of the Center Attack Group of Western Attack Force (North African landings), the *Hobson* was involved in intensive training exercises, and in October 1942, acted as escort to a convoy to Bermuda from Norfolk.

Operation Torch, as the multi-prong attack on the North African coast was called was to be the most significant amphibious assault in the war to date, and marked the allied move from a defensive posture to one of aggressiveness. It was none to soon for the European allies, especially the Soviets who daily were calling for a second front to reduce the pressure of the German Wermacht on their homeland. The Western Task Force under the overall command of Rear Admiral H. Kent Hewitt, was divided into three groups, each with a major objective on the Moroccan coast. The Center Attack Group was to attack Fedhala, just 15 miles north of Casablanca. This target area was unusually active and during the landings, ships such as the light cruiser *Brooklyn* and heavy cruiser *Augusta* destroyed not only shore batteries, but a Vichy French cruiser and destroyers which attempted to interfere with the assault.

The *Hobson* was detailed to act as screen for the carrier *Ranger* and provide ASW protection. This was especially important as the waters around the landing area seemed to be alive with Axis submarines and many transports were sunk or seriously damaged before escort vessels could drive the intruders away. The *Hobson* by a trick of fate escaped being the target of a torpedo when

one of her sisters, the *Hambleton* DD-455 relieved her. The *Hobson* was detached for refueling, and the *Hambleton* took up station as escort to cargo transports anchored offshore of Fedhala. Foolishly, the *Hambleton* was also ordered to anchor, thus disabling any prospect of avoiding torpedo attack as her captain later bitterly pointed out. The *Hambleton* survived the attack, but was seriously damaged.

The *Hobson* was finally detached from the North African theater and returned to the U.S. for additional training and repair. Shortly thereafter she again joined the *Ranger* to make an anti-submarine sweep in the western Atlantic. On March 2, 1943, she was able to rescue the survivors of the torpedoed British freighter, SS *St. Margaret*. Two women were among those saved after several days drifting in an open lifeboat. The Atlantic sea war spared nobody.

In August of 1943, the *Hobson* joined with the Royal Navy for a series of operations, however, prior to her arrival in Scapa Flow, she escorted the *Queen Mary* in a high speed run from Great Britain to Canada. The *Mary* was carrying Prime Minister Winston Churchill to Quebec for an allied conference.

Throughout the summer and early fall of 1943, the *Hobson* in company with her old fighting companion, the *Ranger*, worked with the British Home Fleet in guarding convoys to the Soviet Union. On October 3, 1943, just before dawn, the *Ranger* launched a strike of 20 Dauntless divebombers (SBD) accompanied by eight Wildcat fighters (F4F) to attack shipping in the Norwegian port of Bodo just south of the Lofoten Islands. The raid was successful as six troop/cargo transports totalling 23,000 tons were sunk and many others damaged. Operation Leader,

as it was named, was a success and the Germans could no longer depend on having Bodo raid free.

The *Hobson* continued in her escort/support role with elements of the British fleet up through December 3, 1943. It was a tribute to the crew of the *Hobson* and her builders that she behaved so well in the roughest part of the most treacherous ocean, the North Atlantic. She did an admirable job and although Great Britain was our closest ally, it was still difficult for an American warship to work under British command. The ship and her crew remained is U.S. waters through late February 1944, with a bonus time extension due to engineering problems, but unknown to the crew, her test in combat was yet to come.

U-BOATS AND A PRESIDENTIAL UNIT CITATION

On February 26, 1944, the veteran destroyer joined one of the deadliest formations conceived by the Allied navies - the hunter killer group. For years, the allies had fought the German U-Boat wolf pack strategy with a sheep dog mentality. The convoy's, faced with a highly organized and coordinated wolf pack concentration, were shepherded by escort ships that would try to intervene and protect the helpless merchantmen. The best that could be done was being done, but shipping losses mounted. This would soon change for a number of reasons, and the hunter-killer approach was one of the positive efforts initiated to curb the U-Boat menace. With the huge number of escort vessels coming out of American and Canadian yards and the advent of what the British dubbed the "Woolworth carriers" aka CVE's, the Allies could now develop and implement aggressive operations against the U-Boat. The *Hobson*, fresh from ASW training, joined the USS *Bogue*, CVE-9 and other escorts to locate and destroy Axis submarines. It was a wolf pack in reverse, and the U.S. Navy held all of the trump cards such as improved ASW equipment, air reconnaissance, and effective tactics.

In less than three weeks, one of the *Bogue's* patrol planes spotted an oil slick which was coming from the U-575 which was running submerged. The *Hobson* was taking on fuel, and very nearly cut the lines in order to get to the slick area. As it was, the engineering plant was strained, yet she arrived in time to depth charge the contact and help force it to the surface. Gunfire from the *Hobson* and a destroyer escort finished the job. What sets the American sailor above all others occurred next as the *Hobson* rushed to rescue 17 survivors. This operation was then completed and the destroyer could return home, but not before rescuing a downed Canadian patrol plane pilot. The pilot was very near death, consequently, the *Hobson* was ordered to proceed to Casablanca where medical facilities would save him. They were also able to relieve themselves of their 17 reluctant but secretly relieved prisoners. They would be a part of the 10% of the German Kriegsmarine underseas force that would survive the war. By all standards the U-Boat force had the highest mortality rate of any naval force, whether Allied or Axis. Unknowingly, the *Hobson* had a date with destiny in the same general area just over eight years later when she would join the U-575.

For her work as a member of the Bogue hunter-killer group and the extraordinary effort made to successfully locate and sink the U-575, the *Hobson* and her crew were awarded the Presidential Unit Citation.

THE GREAT CRUSADE - INVASION AT NORMANDY

The *Hobson* next returned to the U.S. for a minor yard period, but the talk everywhere was of something big that was about to happen. On April 21, 1944, she sailed as an escort for an ammunition ship and others on their way to Belfast. She arrived at Plymouth, England on May 21, 1944 just two weeks before the Normandy invasion. The crew was indeed surprised to see the extent of shipping, supplies and men in the area and quickly guessed that a major amphibious operation was about to occur. She went through rigorous training in shore bombardment and inshore boat landing coordination. The ship was sealed during this period and no one was permitted ashore, even to visit the former English summer resort of Torquay close to their area of operations. The crew was advised that there would be an invasion, but where and when was kept confidential. Finally on June 3, Captain Loveland, already a well respected leader informed them of the exciting yet frightening role they had been assigned. In essence, the *Hobson* was expendable. She was detailed to lead the first wave of landing craft to Utah beach due to her shallow draft. She was to defend her charges with gunfire and by simply being a large target.

The "longest day" was best summed up by Robert Burgin, Machinist Mate 1st who kept a diary of each moment of June 6, 1944. At the time, those who wrote of the event had no idea that fifty years, and probably 100 years later it would mean so much to the world to know what happened on that day.

The ship had been at General Quarters since 2030 on June 5, 1944, and the crew was anxious to carry out their mission. As a precaution many of the crew are now wearing or keeping close all of their most treasured possessions such as rings, photographs and so forth. If they were to die, then at least it will be in the company of worldly goods most dear to them. By 0100 the ship had been underway for some time and was closing the landing area with hundreds of other ships of all shapes and sizes. The shore bombardment units such as the battleships *Texas* and *Nevada* remained further out, and the transports and guide ships such as the destroyers *Hobson*, *Herndon*, *Corry* and *Fitch* inched closer to the beach. The ship moved slowly across the channel, frequently at 6 knots to maintain station with other ships. Flares were often seen ahead, and word came down that paratroops had landed in France. Finally, chow was served which consisted of two ham sandwiches, coffee and a Baby Ruth Bar. At 0300 the *Hobson* arrived within 10,000 yards of her objective. The attack was about to commence.

For the next few hours the target area was saturated with bombs, gunfire and rockets. Over 120 tons of bombs were dropped on the Utah Beach defenses and thousands of 14 inch, 8 inch, and 5 inch shells followed. The area was so dark with gunpowder smoke that vision was impaired, and the men choked on the fumes. The ship vibrated continuously from shore bombardment concussions, and as the *Hobson* drew closer to her goal which was just over 4,000 yards from the beach, the fear and terror that grips the soul in combat rose to almost unbearable proportions.

At 0630, the first wave of troops began to hit the beach, and the *Hobson* along with her sister ships poured salvo after salvo into their assigned targets. The destroyers were not unopposed in their effort as many shells were being returned from German positions, yet none hit the *Hobson*. Suddenly, the *Corry* was hit hard. It was assumed that she had been hit by a German shore battery, yet it was later determined that she had struck a mine. She had less than 50 minutes to live.

Keeping up a heavy fire on the beach, the *Hobson* and *Fitch* went to rescue survivors from the *Corry* which at 07:20 split in two and sank. The *Hobson* continued firing until early afternoon when she was relieved by the USS *Butler*. She had expended every 5 inch round available, and at 1430 sailed for Plymouth. For the *Hobson*, the "longest day" was over. When they arrived, they found out that no orders had been issued for their ship beyond June 6, 1944. It had been assumed by the invasion planners that the *Hobson* and the other guide destroyers would have suffered the same fate as the *Corry*. That too had been kept secret.

For the next two weeks, the ship patrolled near the Normandy coast, but the war had moved inland, and what had been the gates of hell, now was a vast supply dump that resembled an anthill. The old destroyer performed another service which was a precursor to modern late 20th Century warfare, and that was to electronically jam German glider bomb frequencies to prevent target acquisition. This accomplished, she sailed southward to Cherbourg.

The Allies required a suitable harbor for the massive supplies that would be required to move the armies across France and into Germany. Normandy was a temporary stopgap, and the logical choice was Cherbourg, France. The battleships *Texas* and *Arkansas* opened fire on their target areas on June 25, 1944, and quickly came under fire from the beach. The *Hobson* and *Plunkett* intervened and laid a covering smoke screen that helped obscure the old battleships, and enabled a safe retirement from the area.

Her next operations included convoy escort and the final assault on France from the Mediterranean - the landings in Southern France. She acted as an inshore gunfire spotter for the battleship *Nevada*, and as the troops went ashore, she provided gunfire support. Aside from periodic convoy escort duties, the role of the *Hobson* in the European theater was drawing to as close, and on November 10, 1944, she arrived back at her builders yard in Charleston.

CONVERSION TO DMS-26 AND THE PACIFIC ORDEAL

The crew of the *Hobson* had been through the ringer having fought submarines and participated in the greatest invasions in the history of warfare, and when the order came to convert the decorated destroyer to a minesweeper, many were upset. After all, a destroyer is a destroyer and a minesweeper, well, it's just a minesweeper. This feeling would soon change, and just before Christmas, 1944, she sported sweep gear and was minus her after most 5 inch turret, torpedo mounts, and some of her ASW armament. Fortunately, she alone among the 24 converted destroyers, was armed to the teeth with two quadruple 40MM mounted aft, and additional 20mm forward and aft. This anti-Kamikaze retrofit would help save her life. She was ordered to the Pacific to participate in what was to be her last operation of World War II, the invasion of the Japanese held Okinawa.

Throughout early 1945, the new DMS moved westward through the Panama Canal to San Diego and on to Ulithi. On March 24, 1945, she and a number of other minesweepers began the massive task of mine removal in the intended invasion route. It took seven days. Periodically, the minesweeping force was attacked by Japanese aircraft, a new experience for the *Hobson*. During this operation an old four stacker was hit by a Kamikaze, the most potent weapon of the war to date, and almost unstoppable. Again, the *Hobson* was considered expendable.

On April 16, the invasion of Okinawa had been underway for two weeks, and the *Hobson* was ordered to replace the *Mannert L. Abele* DD-733, a modern 2200 ton Sumner class which had been sunk. The *Hobson* was now a radar picket destroyer which meant she was also to serve as an outer target for incoming Kamikazes. Better to sink a DD than a carrier!

Accompanied by the *Pringle* DD-477, the ships kept a watchful eye on the sky, but true to form, the Kamikaze just seemed to appear, and just before 0900 multiple aircraft appeared from out of nowhere. One hit the *Pringle* amidships and there was a violent explosion. She quickly became a fiery inferno and sank. The *Hobson* had her hands full and shot down one and then another, but the second released a delayed action bomb which detonated between the stacks and caused considerable damage to the forward engineroom. The plane's engine hit just aft of stack number two and went through the deckhouse doing major damage below. A fire began, and the starboard engine went dead, yet the old destroyer kept up heavy fire against the other attackers. During this short but interminable time, she also rescued 136 of the *Pringle's* crew. This also included shooting sharks that repeatedly approached the struggling swimmers. Before it was over, three more suicide planes were destroyed and the *Hobson* was able to move off toward Kerama Retto, a temporary anchorage that seemed to be the aid station for the many ships hit by Kamikazes. It also became the graveyard for many.

In her last furious fight for survival she lost four men, three of which died instantly in the engineroom, and the fourth when he was pinned by the plunging aircraft motor. The ship limped back to Norfolk, a journey of 10,000 unassisted miles. On June 15, 1945, she entered the Norfolk Navy Yard, just as another fellow traveler, the new APD-109, USS *Belet* was being commissioned. Japan surrendered as the *Hobson* was undergoing repairs. The war was over for the *Hobson*. She was awarded six battle stars for service. She earned them all the hard way.

Post War Service And The Night Of April 26, 1952

By early 1946, the *Hobson* was again in the minesweeping business and for the next few years operated off the east coast and the Caribbean. These years, in comparison to those of the war were uneventful. In June 1950, another war started. The North Korean armed forces invaded the South, and the United Nations was drawn into this conflict. The training schedule for the *Hobson* intensified, but she saw no service in this war. Unfortunately, the destroyer minesweeper was proven ineffective in the Korean waters, and they were replaced by more economical smaller units. The *Hobson* now operated in the Atlantic and provided plane guard and screening utility to carrier operations. On the night of April 26, 1952, she was working with the USS *Wasp* CV-18, 700 miles west of the Azores in that role.

The *Hobson* was a member of a task force under the command of Rear Admiral H. B. Jarrett was on it's way to the Mediterranean. It consisted of the carriers *Wasp*, *Palau*; cruisers *Worchester* and *Baltimore*, two submarines, one oiler, and of course the ever present screen of 15 destroyers. On April 25, the *Hobson* had been refueled by the oiler *Pawtachuck* and on the 26th, assumed station on the port quarter of the *Wasp*.

Destroyers that screen carriers are in harm's way during flight operations as they must keep station constantly regardless of the weather or any rapid position changes by the carrier. In daylight hours, a competent careful destroyer captain has a lookout keep the carrier under continuous surveillance to anticipate any move. Often a shift can occur without warning due to changing flight conditions, and the priority is the safety of the carrier's flight crews. A course change begins often before the voice order is heard aboard the escorting ships.

On one destroyer, a Lt. (jg) with the best luck for anticipating carrier course changes was posted to watch the rudder of the carrier. He could detect a disturbance around the rudder and almost always predicted a course change. Carrier captain's were often unaware of the problems faced by escorting destroyers, but the law of the sea held that the tin can stayed clear, but on station. A carrier captain had more to worry about than his escorts. So it was on the night of April 26, 1952, but as with all tragedies, there were a number of factors that came into play. And, also with all tragedies, no one will ever really know what really happened, because the one man who made the decisions, Captain William J. Tierney died within moments of the collision. He could not swim.

Early in the evening of April 26, at approximately 2000, the carriers had launched a night training strike which was due to return just before 2300, but the events that would lead to the tragedy had begun on the 25th. Captain Tierney, recent to sea command had received a letter from the fleet commander exhorting him and all other escort ships to more efficient and effective maneuvers when alongside the carriers. It amounted to a peptalk type memo and was not directed at anyone in particular, but Tierney obviously took

The Hobson *in her Destroyer-Minesweeper configuration. She is now DMS-26, yet still a destroyer and packs a punch to prove it. She shot down four incoming Kamikazes in her last wartime action and survived a midships bomb hit. Her 10,000 mile journey back to the Norfolk from the Kerama Retto on a none to reliable engineering plant was a triumph.*

In one of the most famous photographs ever taken Harold Brooks, Chief Electricians Mate, jumps from the bow of the dying destroyer to pipe hanging down from the carrier Wasp. *He did not get his feet wet, but 176 others were not so fortunate as they went down with the two halves of the ship.*

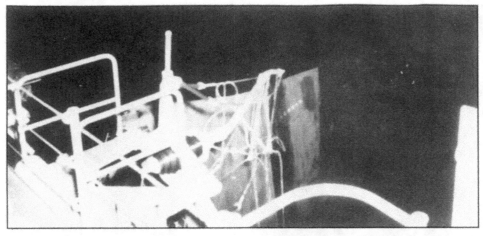

This is probably the last image of the Hobson as her bow passes down the side of the carrier Wasp. Both sections of the ship that had been sliced in two sank within four minutes of impact. Captain William Tierney of the Hobson could not swim and went down with the forward half. His last words were, "someone did not change course" in response to a question asked by a sailor who was abandoning ship.

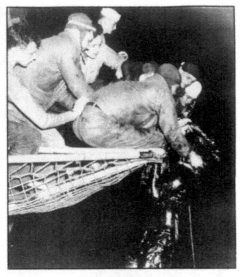

James McIntyre of the Hobson is hauled aboard the Wasp by plane handlers. The oil covered the sea around the sunken ship to a depth of six inches and made survival many times more difficult.

it to heart and wanted to make a good impression. He was not unpopular with the crew and had attempted to bring a greater spit and polish attitude to the aging destroyer. This was not resisted, but like any change, it was talked about. On the following day, the Captain rehearsed the crew in the "Williamson turn", invented and named by a World War II destroyer escort captain. It was an effective way of quickly retrieving a man overboard as it would bring the ship back to her original track and avoid the long outboard turn used in the past.

The evening watch found Lt. William A. Hoefer, the executive officer with the conn and in control of the ship. She was steaming at 24 knots out of a possible 28 knots with the steam provided by the on line boilers. She was 3,000 yards off of the starboard quarter of the Wasp, and the sea state was moderate. Captain Tierney, who was also on the bridge, observed that the Wasp's aircraft would be returning to the carrier soon and anticipated that the carrier would have to turn into the wind, probably at 250 or 260 degrees. Hoefer watched as the captain began to outline his plan for maneuvering ahead of the carrier and coming up on the port quarter as his new station. A sister ship, the Rodman, DMS-21 would move to the starboard side. Concerned, Hoefer, who had been aboard for 16 months turned the conn over to Lt. Donald Cummings, and began discussing the intended evolution with the captain. He pointed out the potential problem of both ships being a position of a head on collision, and within minutes the discussion escalated to a heated argument. Hoefer relented and strode out to a bridge wing to cool off. As he walked out he instinctively turned the radio receiver down a notch.

INCREASE SPEED TO 27 KNOTS, COURSE 260 AND "EXECUTE"

Aboard the Wasp, course and speed change instructions were issued, and Lt. Robert T. Herbst had the conn. The ship's captain, Burnham C. McCaffree was also present and awaiting the eminent recovery of the incoming flight. Herbst called for right standard rudder and ordered flank speed. He also looked for the red running lights of the Rodman and

Hobson and satisfied himself that they were also beginning the evolution.

Aboard the Hobson, Captain Tierney reassumed command by ordering instructing the helmsman, "right standard rudder" and to steer 130 degrees. Unfortunately the elements of fate began to conspire against the destroyer. The glass on the port pelorus was fogged thus preventing an accurate bearing on the carrier. The surface search radar aboard the Wasp had failed. The wind shifted and the Captain McCaffree decided to alter his intended course from 260 to 250 degrees. Since heading into the wind is virtually an absolute for aircraft recovery, the change was fully warranted. The Wasp notified the Hobson of her course change, but no one is certain that Captain Tierney heard the message because none of the bridge personnel heard it. Tierney had also failed to inform his staff of his plan for taking station, so they could not anticipate and in essence assist in the operation. Suddenly, the captain ordered full left rudder, and within 30 seconds ordered a full right rudder. Not really certain of Tierney's intentions, Hoefer became alarmed and advised that the ships were on a potential collision course. It wasn't indecision as Hoefer suspected, and the truth dawned on him. The Hobson was executing a "Williamson Turn", and in theory, it would put the ship in the right position. Unfortunately, too many factors had to be present for the move to succeed, and when the carrier changed direction to 250 degrees, the result sealed her fate. Indecision now replaced planning on the bridge and staying out of the way of the fast approaching carrier became paramount. At this moment left full rudder was ordered on the Hobson as Tierney had decided to race ahead of the Wasp. It was too late, and aborad the carrier, Lt. Herbst told his captain, "we're in trouble". Captain McCaffree then ordered, "all back emergency", and although this was the proper command, the dye had been cast. For a moment, it looked as if the Hobson would successfully escape. First the bow, then the bridge and the number one stack crossed in front of the carrier, but then there was a grinding crash, and the Hobson was hit. Aboard the Wasp orders were quickly issued to light ship, man lifeboats, and call out the fire and rescue party away. The Hobson had been split apart.

The aft section drifted along the side of the Wasp, and the forward half temporarily lodged in the bow of the carrier. Aboard the Hobson, it sounded like a grinding noise, and for 176 men, it was one of the last noises they heard. The ship was dying, yet 61 men would now begin their fight for survival.

ORDEAL AND SURVIVAL

The aft part of the ship would sink first, yet some men did escape. Walt Byers, a radarman 2nd was asleep on the lowest of three tier bunks, and felt a large bump. Startled, he and others in the aft berthing compartment slowly began to awaken, but time was short. Byers hit the deck and found himself in waist high water with 6 inch of fuel oil on top. He and a shipmate, Ernest Niskala along with a few others raced to the hatch leading to the main deck, but it would not open. Fortunately, the scuttle (an inner hatch) was freed, and the men were literally shot out of the hatch by the force of water and air escaping. Forty men of the 61 saved escaped from this hatch and found themselves thrashing around in the water with the huge bulk of the carrier looming over them. Aboard the carrier, lines were being lowered and rafts dropped over the side. Unfortunately, one set of double liferafts hit a party of five men who were never seen again.

The water was covered with a thick glutinous mass of fuel oil that made survival nearly impossible, but it was happening. Men were being rescued by boats from the Rodman and Wasp, and men were being hauled up by lifeline. One man, James Mcintyre, in no uncertain terms, loudly told his would be rescuers to throw down two lines as he weighed 240 pounds!

Another survivor, Chief Electrician Harold Brooks was able to grab a pipe hanging from the Wasp just as the Hobson began her descent. He never got wet, and his jump to safety was captured by a photographer aboard the Wasp.

Of the personnel on the bridge, eleven out of thirteen were saved including Lt. Hoefer, yet the captain was lost.

For several hours the area was combed for

Whaleboat number 2 is hoisted aboard the Wasp with a few survivors from the Hobson. The crew of the Wasp and the destroyer, Rodman, showed their humanity on many occasions that night as they risked their lives to save their fellow seafarers.

This USS Wasp, CV-18, an Essex class carrier. Some 90 feet of her bow was lost due to the collision, and to prevent flooding, she was backed nearly 1,200 miles to Graveshead Bay, New York. The captain of the Wasp, Burnham C. McCaffree was found faultless for the collision.

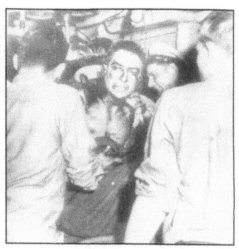

An unidentified survivor aboard the Rodman. Choked with oil in cold waters wearing skivvies only, it was a miracle that any men survived. The look on this man's face tells the whole story of his ordeal.

USS *WARD*, DD-139, APD-16
"FIRST TO FIGHT"

Every war has begun with an act of overt aggression, and World War II was no exception. To some, the Second World War actually began when the destroyer *Rueben James* DD-245 was lost on October 31, 1941, or to others when the gunboat *Panay* was sunk by the Japanese in 1937. Still others theorize that World War II began on the day after the Armistice was signed ending World War I simply because certain issues were yet unsettled. But, there is no doubt that the first true shot bringing the U.S. into war was fired by the USS *Ward*, DD-139 at 0645 on December 7, 1941 just outside of the entrance to Pearl Harbor. The shot from the old destroyer's number one 4 inch/50 caliber mount was in response to an overt act of aggression by an Imperial Japanese two man midget submarine. The craft was attempting to penetrate the harbor defenses and attack the U.S. Navy's battle fleet as part of an overall air and undersea attack. The midget submarine attacks were dismal failures, but the one engaged by the *Ward* set off a chain of events that heralded a new chapter in the greatest military conflict in human history.

The *Ward* hit the submarine in the conning tower with it's second shot from mount number three on the starboard side of the galley deckhouse, and finished the job with several depth charges set at minimum depth. It was a sure kill, but no one would believe it even when the message was forcefully relayed to Fourteenth Naval District headquarters. You would think that "We have attacked, fired upon and dropped depth charges upon a submarine operating in defensive sea area", would prompt an immediate response, but message was logged and began it's way up through the bureaucratic maze that was the U.S. Navy. There had been too many previous sightings and depth charge attacks, so a report of a submarine was viewed with a jaundiced eye. Especially that of a broken down old destroyer, manned by midwestern reservists and a captain with less than 10 hours command experience. Just under 90 minutes later at 0755 the navy of pre-Pearl Harbor attack days would

additional survivors, but the morning revealed only some wreckage and an oil slick to mark the worst peacetime tragedy in U.S. Naval history. During the early morning hours the wind had increased to 25 knots and the seas rougher, so any further search was ruled out. The *Wasp* began her trip back home. It was necessary for the carrier to back the entire distance to Graveshead Bay to avoid taking on water from her crunched bow. The helmsman experienced great difficulty steering the ship, and on a few occasions, she yawed around in a great circle before returning to some modicum of control. When the weather finally calmed to the point where an inspection could be made of the damage, it was discovered that the gash was 90 feet in length and 15 feet in depth. Incredibly, the *Wasp* was also trailing 600

feet of anchor chain and an 81 foot section of hull plating. It was no wonder that steering was so difficult.

Fault finding in government service is a lengthy process, and the collision of the *Hobson* and the *Wasp* was no exception. After detailed testimony, it was ultimately determined that Captain Tierney was at fault. It was speculated that he decided too late that his original plan was incorrect and in making a course correction, the problem was compounded. We will never really know.

The long and illustrious voyage of the *Hobson* was over. She had done more than her share for the country that she had served so well. She will always be remembered not only for her tragic end, but also for her contributions in war and peace.

A *final photograph of the survivors of the* Hobson *tragedy. This was taken aboard the* Wasp *shortly before she arrived at Gravesend, New York.*

The brand new destroyer, Ward, *on the builders ways at the Mare Island Naval Shipyard. She took seventeen days from keel laying to Launching. This shows her on the tenth day. After over 100 years of faithful service to the U.S. Navy, this shipyard was ordered closed in 1997 for reasons of economy.*

COMMON SPECIFICATIONS

LOA	314' 4"	SHP	24,610
LWL	310" 0"	Speed	35 + knots
Beam	31' 11.5"	End	3,800 miles @ 15 kts/2850 miles @ 20 kts
Depth	20' 7.75"	Main batt	4 4inch/50 cal sp
Displ	1,149 tons	Torpedo tubes	12 (4x3) 21 inch
AA Batt	3 inch/23 cal	ASW	2 D.C. Racks/Y-guns
Complement	Captain/7 officers/10 petty officers/114 crew		

The Ward *on the 14th day after keel laying. Shipfitting crews worked triple shifts and over 275,000 rivets went into her construction.*

change forever. The Japanese Navy would see to that.

THE USS *WARD* DD-139 - A FOUR STACK, FLUSH DECK DESTROYER

The *Ward* was one of 267 flush deck, four stack destroyers commissioned as the result of World War I building programs. The Navy had observed the war in Europe, and quickly determined that it was wholly inadequate as a world contender. Consequently, in 1916, the Congress was convinced to provide funding for a massive naval building program over the next three fiscal years. The real growth came in the destroyer class, yet most were not completed until long after the war ended. Some sailed virtually from commissioning to inactive reserve to the shipbreakers. The era of the "assembly line, disposable ship" had begun.

The design selected was that of a flush deck, four stack ship, armed with twelve torpedoes, and four surface (single purpose) 4 inch/50 caliber guns. Anti-submarine capability was an afterthought and included a crude hydrophone apparatus, stern mounted depth charge tracks and Y-guns. Anti-aircraft defense was equally unimpressive and consisted of a 3 inch/23 caliber gun and later a few water cooled 50 caliber machine guns. After all, the designed purpose of this destroyer class was for fleet duty and torpedo

attack. Ironically, only one successful torpedo attack would ever be launched, and the primary purpose of these ships would be everything but classic fleet work.

The lead ships were known as the "*Wickes*" or "*Clemson*" class and although the quality of individual ship construction varied from shipyard to shipyard, the following common specifications of the flush deckers were as in above chart.

Of special note was the power plant installed in these ships. Some observers have mused that the four piper destroyer was just a tight fitting shell around two very powerful engines. These were oil fired Parsons Turbines that could develop up to 26,000 plus horsepower, and in some ships, 37 plus knots. The engineering plant was divided into a high pressure turbine for maximum speed and a cruising turbine for 20 knot or less economical speeds. They were connected to high pitch three blade propellers via two shafts housed in tubes lined with lignum vitae, the hardest wood known to man.

Combustion Engineer or Normand boilers provide 250 pounds of steam and there were vertical airlocks for entrance to the fire rooms. The firerooms were sealed, and the airlocks prevented a flashback. The ships derived electrical power from two 250 kilowatt direct current generators. Underway, these ships were menacing and powerful. They were a beautiful sight and embodied early 20th Century warship design, but

they were too late for one war and too antiquated for the next.

The *Ward* was a cookie cutter version of the class, yet her birth was marked by something different from all of her sisters. She was built in 17 days from keel laying to launching, which when you consider that the average destroyer was taking six-ten months to build, was remarkable. She was built at the Mare Island Naval Shipyard in Vallejo, California, and the short building period has been attributed to the clever planning of the yard's master shipfitter, Irish born J. T. Moroney. Moroney used pre-fabrication tech-

The infamous "red lead fleet" of inactive destroyers at the San Diego Destroyer Base. For nearly 20 years the Ward *gathered barnacles and seagull droppings before being freed to fulfill her destiny.*

The Ward *tethered to the* Chew, *a sister offshore patrol unit in the quiet days before the attack on Pearl Harbor. Most of the fleet had been painted in the new navy blue color scheme.*

niques and began assembling various sections on the ways. Combined with the efforts of 18 riveting gangs working around the clock, the ship touched the water just 17 days after keel laying. To this day, shipyards have been hard pressed to duplicate this feat.

The *Ward* was commissioned on July 24, 1918, but the Armistice ending World War I had been signed long before she took up her duties as flagship of Destroyer Squadron 18. Aside from various training exercises and a role as plane guard for the around the world flight of the Navy's NC-4 seaplanes in May, 1919, the *Ward* accomplished nothing out of the ordinary. On July 21, 1921, she joined dozens of her sisters in reserve to become part of "red lead row" at the San Diego Destroyer Base. As the years wore on, the ships became havens for sea birds and were virtually forgotten. Occasionally, one or two were brought out of mothballs, cleaned up, repaired and sent to sea on one assignment or another, but most just sat and rusted.

Finally, nearly two decades later on February 10, 1941, the *Ward* came out of retirement. She was the last of the old four stackers to emerge, and unfortunately, had been stripped of everything usable by other ships that had recommissioned ahead of her. Ironically, the *Ward* became the ultimate beneficiary of previous wholesale looting, because she was given new equipment. By late February, 1941, she left the base with a new coat of paint, new equipment and a new crew. She was still obsolete, but from a miles under keel standpoint, she was factory fresh. It was almost as if she was a time capsule from another era, manned by a futuristic crew, most of which were reservists from St Paul, Minnesota. As they would find out, life aboard a four stacker was far different than in most modern ships.

FOUR PIPERS WERE NOT LUXURY HOTELS

These ships were conceived for fighting, and not comfort. They were also designed for the professional sailor who is supposed to be used to hardship. The citizen sailor of the early 1940's reluctantly acclimated themselves to the four

stackers, and many longed for the day that they would meet their Navy recruiter in a dark alley!

The staterooms for the officers were small, the heat rarely worked, and air conditioning consisted of porthole scoops and electric fans. They did have a wash basin in each room, but the wardroom shared a common shower facility. Mess attendants were assigned to keep the staterooms clean and neat, and the food was often very good, especially when fresh vegetables and dairy products were available. The captain, executive officer and engineering officer had individual staterooms, but they were small. Moving down the chain, the Chief Petty Officers had their own country and a central table surrounded by bunks. They also had upright lockers to hang their uniforms. Portholes and wind scoops like the commissioned officers were also CPO luxuries.

At the bottom of the food chain, the enlisted men had the worst or most spartan quarters on the ship. Men could either stay in their bunks (better than hammocks), or sit at a center table. While sitting at the table, bunks had to raised. During heavy weather, their clothing became sodden due to six-ten inches of sea water sloshing around on the deck. Sailors quickly learned to beg, borrow or buy empty 25 pound coffee cans from the cooks in order to seal their belongings against flooding.

While in the Aleutians, North Pacific or North Atlantic, men off watch would go to bed with regular and winter underwear, dungarees, two pair of socks, two blankets and a pea coat. For amusement they could scrape ice frost from the inside bulkheads. In the tropics, it was too hot to sleep below decks, so most found a vacant spot topside for their mattresses. Rain was not appreciated. Shoes and clothing would become mildew rotten if not kept clean and dry.

Food was prepared in the galley deckhouse between stack number's two and three. Side by side 4 inch/50 caliber deck guns were bolted to the roof of this deckhouse. The food was considered good, but his depended on the ship, the buying skills of the mess department, and ultimately the cooks themselves. All in all, life was bearable but better conditions would have been preferable. Interestingly, comparing yesterday's primitive standards to today, most destroyer sail-

ors were fiercely loyal to their ships and shipmates. Living conditions was not the most important factor in a destroyerman's makeup. Benefits such as a more tight knit crew, and far less of big ship navy culture and petty rituals were enticements that made the little ship navy attractive.

It was under these conditions, that the *Ward* resumed her role as a fleet destroyer in the newly formed Pacific Fleet. By early March, 1941, she arrived in Pearl Harbor and took up her duties as a rotating member of the offshore patrol with her sisters, *Allen* DD-66, *Chew* DD-106, and *Schley* DD-103. Aside from various and diverse assignments that were important but in the backwaters of fleet operations, these destroyers patrolled off of the entrance to Pearl Harbor where security was very tight. It was on the evening of Saturday, December 6, 1941, that the *Ward* had the duty, and with a new commanding officer, Lt. William W. Outerbridge. For the next several hours, the old ship, a new crew and a captain new to command would defend the harbor locked battle fleet from submerged intruders.

THE *Ward* GOES TO WAR

The *Ward* began her patrol sequence late on December 6th, and for several hours all was routine like any other patrol. At approximately, 0342 however, a message was intercepted from the Condor, a small minesweeper, "sighted submarine on westerly course speed five knots". Further questioning by the *Ward* gained little information, and a search proved fruitless. As the *Ward* had gone to general quarters, everyone was now wide awake, so Outerbridge decided to let them sleep through reveille. For the next hour and a half, little happened until the cargo auxiliary USS *Antares* AG-10 towing a 500 ton barge appeared and began heading for the entrance to Pearl Harbor. While observing the *Antares*, things began to happen, and at 06:00 Herbert Raeubig, Sm 2nd, the duty helmsman thought he saw something between the barge and the *Antares*, something he had never seen before. By this time, Lt. Oscar Goepner, the gunnery officer and OOD saw it and was joined by Howard Gearin, quartermaster of the watch. At first, it was thought that a buoy was caught in the tow line, but it soon became obvious that it was a miniature conning tower. Outerbridge was now present in his pajamas, and general quarters was again sounded. Even a patrolling Catalina PBY got into the act and was circling the object.

Lt. Hartwell Doughty, the executive officer joined the crowd on the bridge and asked, "what are you going to do?" Outerbridge, with competing feelings about a career being cut short if he was wrong, yet instinctively knowing what to do, announced that he would open fire as soon as the *Ward* was ready. She was ready almost immediately, and Outerbridge was taking no chances. He accelerated to full speed, and at 300 yards ordered the guns to commence firing. Mount one missed with it's shot, but came close. Mount three hit the conning tower directly, and the sub began to dive. The *Ward* was preparing to ram, but cruised over the target dropping four depth charges set at 100 feet. The low tech method of signalling the ASW crew to drop charges by using the steam whistle on the number one stack worked fine. It blew four times, and there could be no doubt now that they had sunk the sub.

It was 0653, and an hour remained before the main air assault would begin. The message relayed to the 14th Naval District informing higher authority that the *Ward* had attacked, fired upon and dropped depth charges on a submarine outside the entrance to the harbor fell on deaf ears, and the air attack by the Japanese proceeded with complete surprise. A number of reasons have been cited for the effectiveness of the surprise attack. Probably the most believable was that it was considered unbelievable - in other words, it couldn't happen here. Pearl Harbor was considered impregnable and no foreign power would have the audacity to attack without warning.

The *Ward* continued on it's patrol, and shortly after the attack on the midget submarine, she was called upon to drive a sampan from the restricted area by firing rifle shots at it. Next, a sonar contact was made and the *Ward* made another depth charge attack. No sub was seen, but by this time, there was considerable noise and activity going on near Ford Island in Pearl Harbor. The Japanese air raid was underway, and the *Ward* soon was drawn in as one of the attacking aircraft attempted to bomb her, but missed. The only defense the old destroyer had against air attack was her 3 inch/23 caliber AA gun, and it misfired several times. Her 50 caliber machine guns were equally useless as the water jackets were corroded with salt and the barrels quickly overheated. The only remaining defense was to maneuver at high speed. This she accomplished and no further attacks were made. This was fortunate as the only other planes that came in range were stray Army B-17's coming in from the West Coast.

The rest of the day was spent picking up additional depth charges from Pearl Harbor, topping off her fuel tanks and returning to her patrol area. The reality of war was visibly driven home as the young crew and her captain looked at the destruction of Battleship Row and Pearl Harbor in general. An uneasy fear settled in. By the evening of December 7, she was instructed to join a pickup task force sent to look for the Japanese attackers. What they would have

accomplished had they encountered Admiral Nagumo's force is debateable.

For the next several months, the *Ward* was employed as a convoy escort, local submarine patrol and provided training assistance to the Submarine Forces, Pacific. She also had surface and air search radar installed by the Pearl Harbor Navy Yard. Even with updated electronic equipment, she was no match for the modern Fletcher class destroyers that were joining the fleet in increasing numbers, so a new role was being envisioned for her and several other four stackers. In September, 1942, Captain Outerbridge, who had won a Navy Cross for his action on December 7, was relieved by a Lt. Commander Robert H. Wilkinson. Outerbridge was a favorite with the crew, and there was a special bond with the crew that has continued for decades. They had shared something that few men will ever know.

THE OLD DESTROYER BECOMES A NEW AUXILLARY PERSONNEL DESTROYER (APD)

A new kind of war was being waged in the Pacific that called for island hopping and lightning strikes against an enemy that was entrenched in one jungle or one island after another. The traditional frontal assault of concentrated air and sea bombardment followed by a massive coordinated landing of thousands of troops was necessary for heavily defended objectives. However, not all operations required that kind of resource commitment. The fast well armed shallow draft transport whether alone or in tandem with others was an ideal solution. The best candidates for conversion to the Auxiliary (later Armed) Personnel Destroyer (APD) were the four stack destroyers of World War I. They were plentiful, easy to convert and could be back in action quickly. The *Ward* entered the Puget Sound Naval Shipyard on Christmas eve, 1942, and emerged on February 11, 1943 as an APD.

The conversion consisted of removing boilers number 1 and 2 along with stacks 1 and 2. The old forward boiler/firerooms became a troop berthing space, and small surgical operating room was also built in, unique to the *Ward*. Other work including removal of her torpedo tubes and all of her 4 inch/50 caliber guns. A new battery was installed that consisted of three 3 inch/50 caliber DP guns, five 20mm AA guns and four depth charge "I" guns. Actually her main battery now consisted of four landing craft (Higgin's LCPR's) suspended on four gravity type davits (two to a side) that would transport up to 200 troops to any landing site selected.

The *Ward* had now joined a growing number of four stackers that had been converted to APD's. As the war progressed, the APD came to mean "all purpose destroyer" as these ships were called upon to perform nearly every task conceivable. They carried mail, supplies, Army and Marine Raiders, Fiji Island scouts, casualties to the rear, 55 gallon drums of aviation and other fuels, as well as UDT teams and coast watchers. Some APD's boasted, "you call, we haul". They also provided ASW escort, anti-air defense, but their main role was that of transporting troops to landing areas, and providing gunfire support as needed. The *Ward* was no exception, and her first task was running 1000 bags of much needed mail to Pearl Harbor. From there she sailed for the South Pacific where she would fight her way to the Philippines and eventually to Leyte and Ormac Bay where she would meet her rather ironic, if not surreal ending.

The *Ward* became a fixture in the South Pacific and carried such luminaries as Colonel Carlson's famous Marine Raiders. She operated in and around the islands near Guadalcanal, Bougainville, Cape Glouchester to Green Island where she struck a submerged coral pinnacle and lost a propeller. The crew anticipated being returned to the West Coast or at Pearl Harbor for

The Ward *loading troops for an assault on Cape Sansapor, July 30, 1944. The boat crews on the APD's were among the best small boat handlers in the Navy.*

The destroyer has just been hit by a Kamikaze amidships. The plane hit her on the port side, but the engine lodged in the starboard side. The engine can be identified as the flowing area at the waterline. The Ward has less than 30 minutes to live.

The destroyer O'Brien begins her rescue and firefighting effort. Water streams can be seen from another rescue ship in the foreground. William Outerbridge was captain of the O'Brien and was ordered to sink the Ward as a menace to navigation. The Ward sank at 11:30 that morning.

The crew of Gun Number 3 that successfully hit the conning tower of the midget submarine. They only fired one shot, but that was enough.

yard time, but the war had moved far enough forward that a floating drydock was available. The ship was too important to be released. Through 1943 and into 1944 the old destroyer made landing after landing and carried literally thousands of troops on the long road back to the Philippines. Most of the passengers were good natured and the APD's made a point of providing good food and accommodations because they knew that the troops might not have such luxuries for several weeks or months. For this the troops were grateful, and few bad words were said about the Navy, at least the APD Navy.

MacArthur's commitment that he would return was carried out by the men of ships like the Ward. This kind of fighting was hot, dirty, highly dangerous and at times nearly unbearable. There was nothing romantic or glorious about the kind of war waged by the Ward, her crew and the troops and other passengers she delivered. But, it took ships like her to win and in the end that was all that counted. It was not all work as the APD's were periodically spared for some brief

rest periods, but this too was dangerous. Bypassing large enemy concentrations as the Allies made their way to the Philippines meant that rear areas could be dangerous. Swimming and beach parties were occasionally reminded of enemy presence as snipers interrupted sun bathing and barbecues. Of course, the Japanese were not the only ones who put a damper on recreational activities. After one operation, the boat crews discovered that the floor boards of the Higgin's boats made excellent surfboards, and soon APD's were towing them around for the crew's enjoyment. This was shortlived because an Admiral with no sense of humor steamed into the area aboard a cruiser and put an end to the surfing competition. It was back to beach parties and drinking warm beer.

This war winning island hopping strategy brought the veteran destroyer to December 6, 1944. The place was Ormoc Bay off the island of Leyte in the southern Philippine chain. The task was to deliver four heavily armed companies of the Sixth Army Rangers onto the island.

DEATH OF A SENTRY

By early morning, December 7, 1944, all of the army Rangers were safely ashore and the Ward was detached for anti-submarine patrol between Leyte and Ponson Islands. It was not from below that harm would come, but from above. Shortly before 1000 twelve Japanese twin engine bombers accompanied by four fighters arrived and began attacking the ships in the immediate vicinity. It was initially looked like a classic torpedo attack, but quickly changed to a Kamikaze raid. The Kamikaze had become the most dreaded weapon of war faced by the Allies. A determined pilot baked in religious fervor would dive his loaded plane into a ship, preferably a large aircraft carrier or fully loaded transport. Accuracy was more important than life, and to sacrifice one's life for the Emperor assured a place in heaven. Against this fanaticism was arrayed carrier combat air patrols, and sailors manning AA guns who wanted to live. Such was the situation faced by the Ward and others on the morning of December 7, 1944. The destroyer Mahan DD-364 was hit first at a dis-

tance of seven miles from the Ward. In one of the most vicious Kamikaze attacks to date, the Mahan was hit by three planes and was quickly turned into a fiery inferno. An abandon ship order was reluctantly given as all power systems failed, and the flames fanned by the destroyer's high speed got completely out of control.

Knowing her turn in the barrel was next, the Ward immediately began evasive maneuvers by fishtailing or swinging back and forth at full speed. This was designed to throw off the suicide minded pilot's aim. At five minutes before ten o'clock, three planes headed for the twisting destroyer, and began long slow dives toward her. The first two were disabled by AA fire and smashed into the sea in front and behind her. The third plane hit it's mark and slammed into the Ward's port side amidships. The engine continued through the fortuitously vacant troop area and lodged in the starboard side shell plating.

The old ship had been mortally wounded, and despite all efforts, it was a lost cause. The engines had been disabled, and with no power, firefighting equipment was useless. Other ships such as the APD Crosby and minesweeper Scout were joined by the destroyers O'Brien DD-725 and minesweeper Saunter to help fight fires and ultimately rescue the crew of the Ward. By 1024 it was obvious to all that the ship was doomed. Captain Farwell, who had been Ensign Farwell, an assistant engineer on the Ward three years earlier, ordered, "All hands, prepare to abandon ship". The men left the ship in an orderly fashion and were rescued by ships standing by. Farwell was taken aback as he boarded the O'Brien and was greeted by Captain Outerbridge. It was almost inconceivable that at this moment that men who had shared one of the most important events in history should again be reunited. It defied logic and explanation and will go down as one of the most bizarre coincidences in history.

The O'Brien was ordered to sink the Ward with gunfire, and the first salvo hit her magazine and a tremendous explosion occurred. At 1130, she slipped stern first into her grave. Both Farwell and Outerbridge could not resist the urge and tears filled their eyes. Shortly thereafter they returned to a safer anchorage in San Pedro bay, and the Ward's crew began their trek back home.

Epilogue

The USS *Ward*, DD-139, APD-16 earned six battle stars for service in World War II, and a Navy Unit Commendation. She spent her entire wartime career in battle, and even had she not been the sentry that sounded the alarm at Pearl Harbor, she would have had a every credible career as a fighting ship. She is remembered today by the First Shot Naval Veterans.

The First Shot Naval Veterans was formed in St Paul, Minnesota from which most of the Ward's crew had originated and was instrumental in acquiring Mount Number 3 (4 inch/50 caliber gun) that had fired the shot that struck the conning tower of the midget submarine on the morning of December 7, 1941. The one that started it all. It is now located on the Minnesota State Capitol Grounds as a monument.

The names of the gun crew are:

E. J. Bukrey	A. Domagall
C. W. Fenton	H. P. Flanagan
Joe Fluegal	Donald Gruening
R. H. Knapp	K. C. J. Lasch
R. B. Nolde	J. A. Peick

One only has to look a photograph of the guncrew taken shortly after the Pearl Harbor raid to see the obvious - youthful innocence with a purpose. Unfortunately for the Axis powers, there was an entire nation made up of people just like those who manned gun number three on that fateful morning.

USS *William D. Porter*, DD-579 "The Saga of the *Willie Dee*"

From November 1943 until her bizarre loss in June 1945, the American destroyer, *William D. Porter* was often met with various clever greetings whenever she entered port or joined naval ships. Until 1958, the significance of the expressions, "don't shoot, we're Republicans!" or, "what happened to the fish that got away?" and the USS *William D. Porter* DD-579, was almost a cult secret of the U.S. Navy. The Navy kept a lid on this incident until it was discovered by a Miami News reporter covering the destroyer crew's annual reunion in 1958. The Pentagon reluctantly confirmed the story, yet to this day, little official comment has been made by the Navy who would prefer not to discuss it. You see, a half century ago the "*Willie Dee*" as the *W. D. Porter* was nicknamed had accidently fired a live torpedo at the battleship *Iowa* on November 14, 1943 during a practice exercise. If this wasn't bad enough, the *Iowa* was carrying President Franklin D. Roosevelt, Secretary of State Cordell Hull and all of the country's World War II military brass to the "big three" conference in Teheran. Roosevelt was to meet with Stalin of the Soviet Union and Churchill of Great Britain, and had the *Porter's* successfully launched torpedo struck the *Iowa* at the aiming point, then the last 50 years of world history might have been quite different. Fortunately, the *Porter's* warning caused the *Iowa* to evade the speeding torpedo, and events carried on as we know them.

The Problems Begin

The USS *William D. Porter*, DD-579, was one of many Fletcher class, high bridge destroyers built during World War II. They were powerful and menacing ships. They mounted a main battery of five DP 5 inch/38 caliber guns and an assortment of 20mm and 40mm AAA guns, but their main armament consisted of ten fast running and accurate torpedoes that carried 500 pound warheads. This destroyer was placed in commission on July 6, 1943, under the command of Commander Wilfred Walter, a man on the Navy's career fast track.

In the months before she was detailed to accompany the *Iowa* across the Atlantic in November 1943, the *Porter* and her crew learned their trade, but not without experiencing certain mishaps that were to set the stage for the "big goof". Actually, the mishaps began when she was mysteriously ordered to escort the pride of the fleet, the new 63,000 ton battleship, *Iowa* to North Africa. The night before they left Norfolk, the *W. D. Porter* successfully demolished a nearby sister ship when she backed down along the other ship's side and with her anchor, tore down railings, life rafts, ship's boat and various other formerly valuable pieces of equipment. The "*Willie Dee*" merely had a slightly scratched anchor, but her career of mayhem and destruction had begun!

The next event was just 24 hours away. The four ship convoy which consisted of the *Iowa* and her secret passengers along with the *W. D. Porter* and two other destroyers was under strict instruction to maintain complete silence. As they were going through a known U-Boat feeding ground, speed and silence were the best defenses. Suddenly a tremendous explosion rocked the convoy, and all of the ships commenced anti-submarine maneuvers. This continued until the *W. D. Porter* sheepishly admitted that one of her depth charges had fallen off of the stern and detonated. The "safety" had not been set as instructed. Captain Walter was watching his fast track career becoming sidetracked.

Shortly thereafter, a freak wave inundated the ship stripping everything that wasn't lashed down and a man was washed overboard, and never found. Next, the engine room lost power in one of it's boilers, and along with everything else that had happened, the Captain had to make reports almost hourly to the *Iowa* on the *Willie Dee's* difficulties. At this point, it would have been merciful for the force commander to have detached the hard luck ship and sent her back to the Norfolk.

The morning of November 14, 1943 dawned with a moderate sea, and pleasant weather. As the *Iowa* and her escort were just east of Bermuda, and the President and his guests wanted to see how the big ship could defend herself against air attack, the *Iowa* launched a number of weather balloons to use as anti-aircraft targets. It was exciting to see over 100 guns shooting at the balloons, and the President was duly proud of his navy. Just as proud was Admiral Ernest J. King, the Chief of Naval Operations, large in size, and by demeanor, a true monarch of the seas. Disagreeing with him meant the end of a naval career, yet up to this time, no one knew what firing a torpedo at him would mean!

Just When Things Couldn't be Worse

Over on the Willie Dee, Captain Walter watched the fireworks display with admiration, and envy. Thinking about career redemption, and breaking the hard luck spell, the Captain sent his impatient crew to battle stations, and they began to shoot down the balloons that the *Iowa* had missed and had drifted into the *Porter's* vicinity. Down on the torpedo mounts, the crews watched, waited and prepared to take practice shots at the big battleship which even at 6000 yards, seemed to blot out the horizon. Lawton Dawson and Tony Fazio, Torpedomen, were among those responsible for the torpedoes, and ensuring that the primers (small explosive charge) were installed during actual combat, and removed during practice. Dawson, unfortunately forgot to remove the primer from torpedo tube number three. Up on the bridge, a new torpedo officer ordered the simulated firing, and commanded "fire one, fire two, and finally, fire three". "There was no "fire four", as the sequence was interrupted by a whoooosssshhh sound that was the unmistakable noise made by a successfully armed and launched torpedo. Lt. H. Seward Lewis who witnessed the entire event later described the next few minutes as what hell would look like if it ever broke loose! Just after he saw the torpedo hit the water on it's way to the *Iowa*, and some of the most prominent figures in world history, he innocently asked the captain, "did you give permission to fire a torpedo?" Captain Walter uttered something akin to, "Hell no, I, I, iii, aaa, IIIII————whatttttt?" Not exactly in keeping other famous naval quotes such as John Paul Jone's, "I have not yet begun to fight" or even Farragut's, "damn the torpedoes, full speed ahead", although the latter would have been appropriate.

The next five minutes aboard the *Willie Dee* consisted of everyone racing around shouting conflicting instructions, and attempting to warn the *Iowa* of imminent danger. First there was a flashing light warning about the torpedo, but in-

A torpedo like that fired by the Willie Dee *just about to hit the water. With a speed of nearly 50 mph, it can destroy a target miles away with its 500 lb. warhead. There is still some debate as to whether the* Iowa *would have been sunk by the torpedo, but fortunately, it did not happen.*

The Fletcher *class destroyer,* William D. Porter, *at rest in the Pacific in early 1945. These were graceful, yet powerful warships upon which victory in the Pacific was dependent.*

Houston's *LCS 86 comes alongside the* William D. Porter *as she is slowly sinking by the stern. The rescue effort was flawless, a tribute to the officers and men of the* Porter *and the LCS.*

dicating the wrong direction, and next the *W. D. Porter* signalled that she was going in reverse at full speed? There was strictly enforced radio silence, but finally it was decided to notify the *Iowa*. The radio operator on the destroyer yelled, "Lion (code word for the *Iowa*), lion, come right. The *Iowa* operator more concerned about improper radio procedure, requested that the offending station identify themselves first. Finally, the message was received and the *Iowa* began turning to avoid the speeding torpedo.

Meantime, on the *Iowa*'s bridge, word of the torpedo firing had reached FDR, who only wanted to see, and asked that his wheelchair be moved to the railing. His loyal secret service body guard immediately drew his pistol as if he was going to shoot the torpedo! The *Iowa* began her evasive maneuvers, yet trained all of her guns on the *William D. Porter*. There was now some thought that the *Porter* was part of an assassination plot! Within moments of the warning, there was a thunderous explosion just behind the battleship. The torpedo was detonated by the wash kicked up by the battleship's increased speed, and the crisis was over as well as some careers. Captain Walter's final utterance to the *Iowa* was in response to a question about the origin of the torpedo, and the answer was a weak, "we did it".

Shortly thereafter, the brand new state of the art destroyer, her ambitious captain, and seemingly fumbling crew were placed under arrest and sent to Bermuda for trial. It was the first time that an entire ship and her company had been arrested in the history of the U.S. Navy. The ship was surrounded by Marines when it docked in Bermuda, and held there for several days as the closed session inquiry attempted to find out what happened. The outcome was delayed for a couple of days until torpedoman Dawson finally confessed to having inadvertently left the primer in the torpedo tube which caused the launching. Just after the torpedo left it's tube, Dawson had thrown the primer over the side to conceal his mistake. The truth was eventually pried out of him, and the inquiry drew to a close. The whole incident was chalked up

In a classic, and never to be forgotton image of the naval war in the Pacific, the life of the William D. Porter *is ended. Her death was as strange as her life. Her crew watches from LCS 86 as the bow of their ship is about to disappear under the surface. Emotions were mixed, but there was sadness.*

to an incredible set of circumstances, and placed under a cloak of secrecy. The Navy then behaved like my mother when one of the kids had done something wrong, even though it was an accident. She would tell my father, "just don't stand there, punish someone!"

Captain Walter, and several other former *William D. Porter* officers and sailors eventually found themselves in obscure shore assignments, and Dawson was sentenced to 14 years hard labor. President Roosevelt intervened however, and asked that no punishment to meted out as it was an accident.

IN THE DOG HOUSE

The destroyer next found herself in the upper Aleutians on patrol. It was probably thought that this was as safe a place as any for the destroyer

and those around her. Before being reassigned to the another area in the Pacific, she accidently, but of course, successfully lobbed a 5 inch shell into the front yard of the American base commandant. Joining other ships off of Okinawa, the *Porter* did distinguish herself by shooting down a variety of Japanese aircraft, and reportedly three American planes! She was generally greeted by, "don't shoot, we're Republicans", but the crew of the *Willie Dee* had become used to the ribbing. However, the crew of a sister ship, the USS *Luce* was not so polite in their greetings because the *W. D. Porter* accidently riddled her side and superstructure with gunfire.

On June 10, 1945, the hard luck ship met her end. A Japanese "Val" bomber constructed almost entirely of wood and canvas slipped through the defenses and as it has very little metal surface, it was not unlike our present day stealth planes. It did not register on radar. It was a fully loaded Kamikaze, and it headed for a ship near the *Porter*, but just at the last moment veered away and crashed alongside the unlucky destroyer. There was a sigh of relief as the plane sunk out of sight without exploding, but unfortunately, it blew up underneath the destroyer, and opened up her hull in the worse possible location.

Three hours later, the last man, Captain C. M. Keyes slid down a line to the waiting deck of LCS 86. His first remark upon greeting Captain *Houston* of the rescue ship was, "There goes my ship, and me without a dime in my pockets". Keyes was referring to a previous sinking and was aware of the difficulty in dealing with naval finance officers. He would later go on to complete a distinguished career of 30 years, yet the Porter would forever be a part of his life.

Moments later, the ship that almost changed the face of world and national politics slipped stern first into 2400 feet of water. Miraculously, not a single soul was lost in this sinking. It was almost as if the ship that had been so unlucky chose to let her patient and valiant crew live. The saga of the *William D. Porter* was over.

Every so often the crew of *Willie Dee* gather and remember the ship they served on. They remember the good times, and as the years pass, the torpedo incident has become one of amusement and notoriety, rather than the heart wrenching embarrassment they endured in November 1943.

L to R: Tony Fazio, H. Seward Lewis and Paul Hudson, survivors of the William D. Porter *and witnesses to the "fish that got away" during their 1958 reunion. It was from this reunion that the news got out about the accidental torpedo launching.*

CHAPTER II

THE CRUISERS

USS *BOISE* CL-47 "THE ONE SHIP TASK FORCE"

The USS *Boise* CL-47 was a light cruiser of the *Brooklyn* class and one of the seven units built during the mid 1930's as an answer to the Japanese "*Mogami*" class cruiser. Interestingly, the Mogami's, which were initially armed with fifteen 6 inch guns were rearmed as eight inch heavy cruisers prior to World War II, consequently, the *Brooklyn* and half sister *St. Louis* class were in response to a ship that never was. It did not matter, because the history of each of these ships is steeped in glory and achievement far beyond the dreams of their designers in the Navy's Bureau of Construction and Repair. These cruisers successfully fought everything from battleships to kamikazes in the Pacific to tanks and radio controlled bombs in the Mediterranean and Atlantic. Of these cruisers, the *Boise* had one of the most spectacular careers. She fought not only in the Pacific, but in the Atlantic and Mediterranean. She was the only member of the class to accomplish such a feat. She also helped dethrone an Argentine legend, Juan Peron when she fired at shore targets that forcefully helped to end his dictatorship in 1955. But, the *Boise*, nearly wasn't the *Boise*. During her early 1930's construction, a group of local pastors from the city of *Boise* strenuously objected to a cruiser, an engine of war, being named after their city. Cruiser number 47 or Newport News Shipbuilding hull number 361, was now to be named *Idaho Falls*, but in the nick of time, a congressional delegation and Idaho's governor prevailed and the new ship was named the *Boise*. But, the name of the ship is unimportant compared to the accomplishments of her crew, one captain in particular, and the lifelong devotion of a fine lady. Herein lies the real story of this magnificent, graceful, but lethal warship.

THE OPPORTUNITY OF A LIFETIME - FOR A YOUNG MIDWESTERN GIRL

Salome "Sal" Springer Clark was the twenty two year old daughter of Idaho's governor-elect,

Salome Clark, the daughter of the Governor-elect of the state of Idaho poses with flowers and a bottle of Snake River water just prior to christening her ship, the USS Boise, CL-47.

An excellent view of the stern of the cruiser USS Boise. They were the first cruisers built by the U.S. Navy with a square or bobtail stern. Just forward, the lower part of the aircraft hanger can be seen. It could accommodate up to four SOC scout aircraft, and the excessive vibration of the propeller shafts under this area never materialized.

28

H-361-#27
4-1-36

The Boise *begins her slide into the water amid cheers from many well wishers. Salome Springer Clark would follow the life and times of this cruiser. She always considered it her ship.*

A new light cruiser, Boise, *leads a column of ships from the east coast to join the recently formed Pacific Fleet. Many of thse ships would shuttle back and forth from the Atlantic to the Pacific dependent on the international situation. The* Boise *would flight in both oceans and in the Mediterranean.*

Barzilla Clark and was chosen to christen U.S. Navy cruiser number 47 as the USS *Boise*. It came as a complete surprise to this young civil service worker that she had been invited by the Secretary of the Navy to help launch one of the Navy's most technologically modern warships.

A telegram was received by the family asking for either the governor's wife or daughter to perform the age old christening ceremony, yet Sal's mother was ill and her older sister had just been married. The task fell to Salome who had never seen an ocean nor traveled far from *Idaho Falls*. She was not even sure what a cruiser was, and certainly had no idea how a ship was launched.

In early December, 1936, she traveled by train to Newport News, Virginia, to the launching site and there she first saw the *Boise* on the builder's ways. On December 3, 1936, she would help launch this ship, but in the days preceding the ceremony, she attended a number of functions leading up to the christening. There were tea's, parties and receptions, all new to a midwestern girl who had never been east of the Idaho state line. Yet, she had not forgotten her roots, and on the appointed day, she duly christened the new cruiser with a bottle of Idaho's own Snake River water in lieu of the more traditional champagne. As the cruiser began it's accelerating slide into the James River, she told the crowd of thousands, "I hope the *Boise* will sail successfully in years to come, and I will continue to watch her career with interest". This was no idle comment, as she did just that. All ship's sponsors have expressed their appreciation for the honor, but Salome Clark took it more seriously than most. To her, being as part of the history of this great ship was a life pivoting event.

She watched for every news item involving the *Boise*, and when her ship was damaged during the Battle of Cape Esperance, she led the effort to sell war bonds to provide money for her speedy repair. She maintained a scrap book of the history of her ship as she called it, and was present when the ship was transferred to the Argentine Government in 1952. She was later invited back to the Newport News Shipbuilding and Drydock Company when the new Los Angeles class attack submarine USS *Boise*, SSN-

764 was christened. Where ship's named *Boise* are concerned, Salome Springer Clark was not far away.

Sal Clark, later Mrs. Salome Clark Springer had a love affair with a light cruiser that spanned nearly a half century. She was a devoted advocate, and to her, the *Boise* was always her ship. Her attachment was never more evident than when she learned that her ship had been broken up for scrap in Brownsville, Texas in 1981. She was proud to have been a part of the ship's history, but regretted the method by which the ship's life was ended.

THE USS *BOISE* - A *BROOKLYN* CLASS LIGHT CRUISER

The *Boise* was one of seven ships designed as *Brooklyn* class light cruisers. These were revolutionary ships for a number of reasons, but primarily due to the arrangement and type of armament as well as location of their aviation units. They could carry up to four scout seaplanes in an covered hanger aft. Their sterns were square, and often they were called "bobtail" cruisers. Some even made the mistake of calling them "hollywood cruisers", but blackeyes and split lips put an end to that reference. The armament that the *Boise* and her sisters mounted set them apart from any other like ship in any navy.

They mounted fifteen 6 inch/47 caliber semi automatic guns arrayed in five turrets. Three were forward, with turret B in a superfiring position. Two were aft with turret X in a superfiring position over Y. The guns were fed with semi fixed ammunition which consisted of a 32 pounds of high explosive housed in a brass cartridge used to fire a high capacity (H C) or armor piercing (AP) shell. The high capacity projectile weighed 105 pounds and the armor piercing, 130 pounds. The relative light weight of the ammunition allowed the gun to be hand served rapidly, and short sustained firing rates were as high as 12 - 15 shells per barrel per minute. It was no wonder that these ships were known as "machine gun cruisers"!

The basic strategic concept was to acquire a target and using a ladder effect, smother it with hundreds of shells in a short period of time, or

at least immobilize the target. Concept and reality diverged greatly in practise.

The Brooklyns' were beautiful and graceful ships. They were the last pre-World War II big light cruisers built. They had almost a yacht-like quality, and were immediately recognizable. They displaced 11,581 tons (13,000 plus) wartime, were 608 ft overall length with a 62 ft beam. Aside from her main armament, the *Boise* and her sisters carried eight 5 inch/25 DP guns (four to a side in the waist, and a variety of 1.1 inch/50 caliber anti-aircraft batteries (later 20mm/40mm).

The *Boise* like most of her sisters was upgraded with new electronics and a superstructure alteration during mid World War II. The Boise's came after the October, 1942 Battle of Cape Esperance. However, her silhouette was unmistakable, even to her end in 1981.

The *Boise* was built by the Newport News Shipbuilding and Drydock Company and would share the fitting out basin with two other ships destined for fame, the carriers *Enterprise* and *Yorktown*. She was laid down on April 1, 1935, launched December 3, 1936 and finally commissioned on October 3, 1938. It took three and one half years from keel laying to commissioning, but in the pre war period, this was not unusual. Her construction was not only of benefit to the Navy, but to the economy as well. Thousands of idle shipyard workers went back to work building cruisers like the *Boise*, and the $238 million spent on this program by President Roosevelt was a shot in the arm to the depression crippled shipbuilding industry, not to mention unemployed workers.

Her commissioning Captain was B. V. McCandlish, and like most ships built on the east coast of the U.S., she spent time in Casco Bay, Maine ironing out her engineering problems, which were few. She then went on an extended shakedown cruise to South Africa. She was carrying the U.S. ambassador to that country. While in port, she rendered a 21 gun salute to South African officials who were being ferried out to the ship. They had not been informed of the salute and when the 3 pounder saluting gun began firing, many of the dignitaries jumped out of the launch or fell to the floor boards in fear. The country's president had his top-hat blown off. The top-hat incident not withstanding, the ship and her crew were welcomed and treated quite well.

Back in Norfolk, the *Boise* made minor repairs and calibrated her machinery. In mid 1939, as a unit of Cruiser Division 9, she was supposed to be one of the major units to participate in the World's Fair in New York, yet the increasing Japanese threat in the Pacific precluded this and she sailed westward through the Panama Canal to become part of the Pacific Fleet. Shortly after she left, sisters *Brooklyn*, *Phoenix* and *Honolulu* joined her. All became part of a vastly enhanced Pacific battle force now based at Pearl Harbor, T. H., and the object lesson was not lost on militarists now heading the Japanese government. The proximity of the U.S. Pacific fleet to the growing Japanese sphere of influence was alarming, and later served to crystallize thinking that would result in the attack on Pearl Harbor.

The *Boise* operated with the Pacific Fleet from May 1939 until November 1941, and at one time served as the flagship for Commander Cruisers Battle Force, Rear Admiral Husband Kimmel. Kimmel would later take the brunt of responsibility for the losses sustained by the Japanese air attack on Pearl Harbor on December 7, 1941. He would be forcibly retired from the Navy and later die a broken man. Many now regret the folly of blaming this man solely for this tragedy, but in December, 1941, punishment was the order of the day.

McCandlish was relieved as captain by S. B. Robinson on August 28, 1940, and was her commanding officer when the war broke out. Many considered, "S. B. " as he was called behind his back, an old stick in the mud, yet he lived to be 101 years old and was quite a dancer into his early nineties. Maybe he didn't hit his stride until after leaving the *Boise*.

THE *BOISE* GOES TO WAR - AS PART OF A FORGOTTON FLEET

The *Boise* had been a frequent visitor to most ports along the West Coast and Hawaii, yet on November 18, 1941, she would steam to Manila, Philippine Islands as escort for five troop laden transports to augment the American garrison under General Douglas MacArthur. One of the persistent legends that is still believed today by some was that this convoy passed the Japanese task force bound for Pearl Harbor. This like so many other myths, is just that. The *Boise* and her charges passed several hundred miles from the fast moving Japanese force, and their paths never crossed.

The *Boise* arrived in Manila on December 4, and rather than returning to Pearl Harbor, the war caused her to become a unit of the Asiatic Fleet. Admiral Thomas Hart prevailed on the Navy Department to have the *Boise* assigned to his command and his request was granted. After all, the *Boise* was a modern warship with state of the art weapons and above all, radar. She was manna from heaven and was not going to escape. The Asiatic Fleet was a haven for ships, officers and enlisted men who were not really part of the East Coast naval establishment. The ships were obsolete or obsolecsing such as the

The Boise *at anchor just before the war engulfed her. She is still painted in a light grey color with her decks and bright-work shining. Just after the war began, she was immediately painted dull grey. Beauty was a peacetime luxury no longer practical and even dangerous.*

four pipers, *John D. Ford*, *Stewart*, and *Edsall*; the ancient light cruiser *Marblehead* and the heavy cruiser *Houston*.; ammunition and torpedoes were defective; and many of the officers were not considered proper for the straight laced crowd at Pearl Harbor. The unspoken rule, run a ship aground - next duty, the Asiatic Fleet was not entirely unfounded.

One of the more humorous stories told and retold by China sailors seems to sum up the prevailing opinion of the Asiatic Fleet. The gunboat Ashville patrolled the Yangtze River ostensibly to protect American lives and property, and as the years wore on, the officers and men gradually allowed the Chinese servants and helpers to take over the non military operations of the ship. At the end of one of her forays up river, she was unable to locate a buoy for mooring, and the captain ordered the anchor dropped. An amazed crew watched as the anchor bobbed to the surface! The Chinese crew had sold the iron anchor for scrap years before, and replaced it with one made of wood and painted it to resemble the original. Such was the Asiatic Fleet.

The *Boise* found herself as part of a fleet forgotten by the mainstream naval establishment. This fleet would have survived in the previous war, but was ill equipped and trained for the one the Japanese forced on them. On December 7, a Saturday on that side of the world, the *Boise* was now on her way to Cebu, where she was to pick up the SS *Gertrude Kellogg*, a merchantman, and escort her to Honolulu, T.H. The mission was canceled when on December 8, at 0500, a message was intercepted from Pearl Harbor, "Air Raid Pearl Harbor, this is no drill". Within minutes the ship was accelerating to 30 plus knots, and the crew went wild with rumors. Finally, the truth began to seep in, and Hart's message to his command, "Japan started hostilities, govern yourselves accordingly", became the order of the day. But who would the *Boise* attack? Or what would attack her?

One of the first items necessary to change

the *Boise* from her peacetime appearance to that of a warrior to was to paint everything dull grey. The popular and efficient first lieutenant and damage control officer, Lt. Cdr Freddie Bell began the task immediately. He was forcibly convinced of the necessity to paint the beautiful holystoned teak decks when one of the SOC scout plane pilots informed him that he could see the gleaming ship for miles, also visible to the enemy. Khaki uniforms were now necessary, so most of the tropical white's were boiled in coffee to at least make them look light brown. This was not the best idea, because they came out mottled, and would have been embarrassing had they been seen by the Japanese!

The first real combat opportunity presented itself on December 10. While steaming in company with the *Houston*, *Marblehead* and escorting destroyers (newly formed Task Force 5 under Rear Admiral William A. Glassford), she detected several surface targets at 25,000 yards. All turrets were trained on the targets, and challenges made. There was no response, and the force commander elected to vacate the area rather than tangle with half of the Japanese Navy. Husbanding forces may have been prudent at this early stage of the war, but many of the crew did not understand this. The U.S. Navy had just sustained it's worst defeat, and refusing combat was a concept not appreciated by a revenge hungry crew.

As December wore on, and the *Boise* was assigned to escort merchantmen escaping from Manila, she intercepted a Vichy French liner, the Marshall Joffee which was attempting to return to occupied France. She was boarded, and prize crew took her in hand.

For the next five weeks, the *Boise* escorted Allied ships in their escape from the Japanese onslaught. She at one time or another was in the *Celebes Sea*, *Balikapan*, *Soerabaya*, *Darwin* and *Makassar*, all which would be successfully attacked by Japanese aircraft over the next few months. The Allied forces were retreating to-

Edward J. "Iron Mike" Moran. Annapolis class of 1917, he was a consummate athlete and a dynamic leader. He retired as a Rear Admiral in 1947, truly an honorable man.

Captain Moran's cabin aboard the Boise *after it was peppered with shrapnel during the Battle of Cape Esperance. This damage was not nearly as great as that done to the forward part of the ship late in the 27 minute battle.*

ward Australia, and the pitiful few ships available were not going to stem the Japanese tide. The Allies needed carriers, and a hundred ships like the *Boise*.

On the evening of January 20, 1942, she was in company with the *Marblehead*, and destroyers of DesRon 20 when the task force was ordered to prepare for a night surface action against suspected enemy invasion forces heading toward Balikpapan. In the early hours of the following day, January 21, she touched bottom on an uncharted reef in the Sape Strait, and did sufficient damage to warrant being ordered out of the formation for repair. Glassford transferred his flag to the *Marblehead* and proceeded. The *Boise* changed course for Tjilatjap, Java for a more extensive examination of the damage. Bell and his damage control team sealed off the flooded compartments, but the damage was serious. While in Tjilatjap, the crew was overwhelmed by the perspective of the Dutch people of Java. They knew that time was short and soon their home would be occupied by an army whose reputation for cruelty and butchery was well known. It was difficult for American bluejackets to think of little children and women being left to the mercy of a military machine that did not hold to the western beliefs of compassion and forbearance. Balanced against this, the *Boise's* crew was relieved, albeit with some guilt that they would escape the fate of Japanese occupation.

Her fuel and 5 inch/25 cal ammunition were transferred to the *Houston* where it was put to good use in the coming days against repeated air attacks. In fact, the *Houston*, now with non defective ammunition was able to evoke gratitude from many a merchant captain when defending them from Japanese air attack. During a particularly heavy attack, one captain said it all with, "look at that bastard go!"

Edward J. "fighting Mike" Moran, her pug faced, popular executive officer relieved the conservative S. B. Robinson as commanding officer,

and she began her odyssey to find an unoccupied drydock. Moran gave definition and personality to the *Boise*. He was a consummate athlete, having been offered a contract with the Boston Red Sox baseball team after graduating from Annapolis in 1917. He had a great heart for others and ran a tight ship. His son, Moore, who adored his father said that his favorite quote was, "when you play, play hard, when you work, don't play at all". Iron Mike was a perfect match for the *Boise* at this time in naval history. His first job was to see that his ship was again combat ready. This would prove more difficult than originally anticipated.

She limped to Colombo, Ceylon where there was no facility available. She then left for Bombay, India, where a harassed port captain forcibly told Moran that he would have to wait his turn, at least the *Boise* wasn't sinking and others needed the drydocks more than she did.

There were a number of refugees in Bombay, having escaped the Japanese. They had little money, but did have some very expensive jewelry which they gladly traded for American greenbacks at greatly reduced rates. It seemed as if the whole world had turned upside down. Finally, the *Boise* was allowed drydock time, and

her damaged plates were removed and literally straightened by hand. Of course, the repair work was interrupted by a shipyard worker strike, and the Boise's crew had to do most of the work. On April 4, 1942, she departed Bombay for Melbourne, Australia, but was diverted to Mare Island Navy Yard for further repair and improved radar. She was fitted with SG radar, a vast improvement over the SC sets generally available to most of the larger fleet units. As the modernized cruiser was leaving San Francisco Bay, Lt. Al Fox, an assistant communicator was invited to observe how the new radar installation worked. He was greatly impressed when the scope showed the Bay Bridge in distinct detail at a significant range. SG radar would figure prominently in the future of the U.S. Navy in the south Pacific, but at this point was only available to a limited number of ships. Unfortunately, few knew how to operate and get the most from this system, and even fewer understood it's potential. The Japanese had no radar at this time.

The *Boise* left San Francisco in late June, 1942 and headed for the South Pacific where she escorted convoys and carried out other related assignments.

Back at Midway Island on July 29, 1942,

she was assigned a rather interesting task that would end in tragedy. She was to steam toward the Japanese home islands and when within 500 - 600 miles distant, she was to launch her SOC scout aircraft for an attack against the offshore Japanese early warning picket line. A feint attack was designed to divert attention from the impending attack on Guadalcanal. On August 5th, she launched two SOC's to make the feinted attack but also to confirm intelligence reports of two Japanese light cruisers in the immediate area. After some hours, it became evident that the two aircraft were lost, and the *Boise* had to retire at high speed. It was a difficult choice for Moran, and the aviators were never heard from again. It is uncertain as to the value of this operation, but the landings on Guadalcanal were successful.

STREET FIGHTING AT SEA - THE BATTLES TO HOLD HENDERSON FIELD

To date the *Boise* had not been where the fighting was and to cap it all, was embarrassingly damaged by running aground. The crew was poor spirits, but if any captain, crew and ship was due for a victory, it was the *Boise*. It would be an curious set of circumstances that would thrust this unblooded warship into the first major surface battle that would also result in a sorely needed victory for the Allies.

The battle for Guadalcanal, actually the focus of Allied efforts to defeat the Imperial Japanese Navy in the Pacific can be described in many ways, all bad. It was a violent, terrifying seemingly never ending campaign with results measured in blood and death rather than ground gained. Casualties on land and at sea for both sides were frightful. The sea battles that were fought in this area were the most terrible and savage in naval history. Guadalcanal was not a geographical location, it was an emotion.

The naval battles around the Solomon Islands were not planned for nor foreseen in any pre-war training by the U.S. Navy or that of it's adversary, the Imperial Japanese Navy. All classes of ships fought everything from aircraft to surface forces to submarines, and often simultaneously. It was violent, bare knuckles hand to hand combat, but at sea between battleships, cruisers and destroyers, and it was a rare event when the forces were evenly matched on a ship to ship basis. Ironically, combat at sea resembled that occurring on land between Marines and the crack Japanese troops sent to kill their opponents and eventually evict the survivors. Many of the battles took place at night to avoid air attack, and the results were frequently overestimated by both sides. If the total of claimed sinkings by both sides had been accurate, by January 1943, neither would have had so much as a whaleboat left in their warship inventory.

Even the climate and waters surrounding the islands were inhospitable. It was humid, hot, malaria ridden and the rain came in buckets. Fungus grew on untreated shoes, and clothes quickly rotted. Disease was rampant. The sea was infested with sharks, having been fed by the dead of Solomon Island natives as part of their burial ritual. Shipwrecked sailors who escaped shark attack faced any number of other dangers from strafing aircraft to unsympathetic Japanese

Army fanatics who took no prisoners. All in all, the region was considered hell on earth. It was a peculiar place for a showdown, but retaining it was crucial to both sides who now had to restructure their very global warfighting strategy. Whoever triumphed in the year long savage ordeal to follow would win the war in the Pacific. It was that important.

Soon after the Allies landed on Guadalcanal August 7, 1942, the first of many naval battles took place in the early morning hours of August 9th. In order to protect the tenuous hold the Marines now had on the beachhead and former Japanese airfield, the Allied naval force made a wide deployment north and south of Savo Island, just over 10 miles from Cape Esperance. Guarding the north entrance to the channel were the heavy cruisers, *Vincennes, Quincy* and *Astoria* with supporting destroyers *Helm* and *Wilson*. The south entrance was patrolled by the heavy cruisers *Chicago*, and HMAS *Canberra* and *Australia* with U.S. destroyers *Patterson* and *Bagley*. Just after 0130, a fast moving column of seven Japanese cruisers and one destroyer commanded by Rear Admiral Gunichi Mikawa came roaring toward the south entrance at over 25 knots. The firepower available to this force was formidable and included 52 fire and forget "long lance" torpedoes, 34 eight inch and numerous 5.5 inch, 5 inch and 4.7 inch guns. The ships were manned with determined men, and although they had no radar, they had excellent night vision equipment, were highly disciplined, and knew the general disposition of the force opposing them. They also had the element of surprise because the picket destroyer *Blue* did not notice this force speeding by her at less than 1,000 yards range. She had made her routine turn away from them just as they passed, and lookouts failed to look astern. Of course had the *Blue* illuminated the enemy, she would have been fired upon by over 50 guns and immediately destroyed. Considering the eventual outcome, her warning would have made little difference.

The Japanese force which included the heavy cruisers *Furutaka* and *Aoba* swept into the channel undetected and launched torpedoes at dark but distinct Allied targets at about 0140. Gunfire soon followed and the *Canberra* was left sinking and the *Chicago* immobilized with a part of her bow blown off. Just over 30 minutes later the incredibly unscathed attack force met the ships of the northern outpost. In the ensuing melee, the Japanese force was able to throw the American guard into a turmoil and sink all three cruisers standing guard. The *Astoria* and *Vincennes* sank within an hour and the ailing *Quincy* slipped under the following day. Mikawa had scored a major victory over Allied forces, although he had failed to destroy the transports, his main objective. Not only were four cruisers lost, but so was hope. The Marines guarding Henderson Field as the former Japanese landing strip was now known and the sailors on the surviving ships became uneasy and skeptical of being able to preserve their slim gains, let alone mount a successful campaign. Even with radar the American Navy had failed to intercept this raiding force. Could our navy defeat the IJN in the South Pacific? We had succeeded at Midway, but could our surface forces defeat them

on their terms and in their backyard? There was some doubt now, especially about the fighting caliber of on site Allied naval leadership.

Over the next two months, there were carrier versus carrier battles, and an almost routine nightly brawl between light forces of both navies. The channel adjacent to the contested area of Guadalcanal became known as Ironbottom Sound in recognition of the many ships that littered and would litter it's bottom. The Allies and Japanese attempted to supply ground troops nightly and both agonized for their efforts. Japanese destroyers known as the "Tokyo Express" ran supplies and troops to the Japanese Army while heavier units bombarded Allied positions with deadly regularity. American APD's (four pipers converted to high speed transports) attempted to supply the desperate marines and suffered severe losses. There was no lack of desperation or courage on either side.

Against this backdrop of confusion, doubt and anxiety, the *Boise* and other cruisers were thrown into the contest to keep the Marines on Guadalcanal. Another showdown was in the offing, and it was to take place on night of October 11, and the early morning hours of October 12, 1942. It would be fought in the same general area of the previous August 9 humiliation just off Cape Esperance. Although it was unspoken, it was a do or die proposition for the Allies, and in particular, the U.S. Navy.

THE BATTLE OF CAPE ESPERANCE - 27 MINUTES OF GLORY

Authors Note: There have been a number of accounts of this battle, and frankly, I share the view of Charles Cook, Captain, USN (Ret) whose book, "The Battle of Cape Esperance" presents the facts to date as he was told and he could substantiate. There is much controversy over many aspects of this battle, not the least of which was the ultimate outcome. Like Cook, I will present what I have found including Japanese sources and official USN records corroborated by eyewitnesses. Remember, there was no precedent for the night battles being waged in the waters around the Solomon Islands, and most nights were murky and the eyes played tricks on lookouts and observers. Radar was in it's infancy and one of it's most common failings was it's tendency for target pips to vanish for any number of reasons, and rarely when they were actually sunk. Each side had a reputation for over estimating success and speaking softly of failure. Add the overwhelming need for an American victory and you have an adequate foundation upon which to base your own conclusions. These are not excuses, but the reader needs to have a familiarity with the territory before judging the right or wrong of certain actions.

Preventing reinforcement of the Japanese garrison and the nightly bombardment of the Marine positions around Henderson Field were the major tactical objectives of local surface forces. The overall strategic objectives were to retain the toehold on Guadalcanal and prevent the Japanese from expanding their lines of supply and communication or severing the Allied lines between Austral-Asia and North America. A line had been drawn in the sand, and one or the other would lose. It was that simple!

Admiral Mikawa who had earned his reputation just two months earlier at the Battle of Savo Island entrusted the October 11 - 12 troop reinforcement and support force to his cruiser division commander, Rear Admiral Aritomo

Goto. With the way events were unfolding, to Mikawa, it was just a matter of time before the Americans were driven out. This mission was considered routine. Goto was not of the same caliber as his superior, Admiral Mikawa. He would soon die for his complacency. Goto commanded a force of five ships designed to provide point cover for a reinforcement operation. The Second Infantry Division was to be landed in concert with it's equipment and supplies. Goto's support force consisted of the heavy cruisers *Aoba*, *Kinugasa* and *Furutaka* which were accompanied by destroyers *Fubuki* and *Hatsuyuki*. Goto flew his flag in the *Aoba*.

The heavy cruisers were of the *Furutaka* class built in 1923-24, and modernized in 1938-40. They mounted six 8 inch guns in three twin turrets, four 4.7 inch guns, and most importantly, 12 of the dreaded 24 inch type 93 "long lance" torpedoes. These torpedoes more than leveled the playing field and offset the advantages of the U.S. Navy's rapid fire 6 inch guns. The type 93 torpedo could outdistance gunfire and were uncannily accurate. These cruisers could steam at 34.5 knots, and like their counterparts were lightly armored (1 inch belt). They too were "thinclads".

The destroyers were built between 1927-28, and were modernized in the mid 1930's. They were armed with six 5 inch guns, and nine 24 inch long lance's. Maximum speed was 34 knots and they were protected by shell plating only. They were the world's first destroyers with enclosed gun mounts. Neither the cruisers or destroyers had any sort of radar, and had to rely on night vision equipment and lookouts with superb acuity. The Japanese force boasted eighteen 8 inch guns, twelve 5 inch, and twelve 4.7 inch guns. They also could bring up to 54 torpedoes into action.

Balanced against this force would be an American column (TF 64.2) consisting of the heavy cruisers *San Francisco*, *Salt Lake City*, light cruisers *Helena* and *Boise* supported by destroyers *Duncan*, *Farenholt*, *Buchannan*, *Laffey*, and *Macalla*. The cruisers were armed with 8 inch and 6 inch weapons, and the destroyers with 5 inch and 21 inch torpedoes. The American force mounted nineteen 8 inch guns, thirty 6 inch guns, and fifty-two 5 inch guns. The force also carried up to 25 torpedoes. The force was commanded by recently promoted Rear Admiral Norman Scott who had made life a living hell for those around him until he was assigned sea duty. He was described as conservative and a good planner. He began exercising his force long before the battle by practicing night maneuvers and developing certain tactics. One of his unspoken, but well known axioms was that captains should think for themselves and attack when the opportunity arose.

Scott was aware that a sizeable naval force which probably included cruisers was coming down the slot toward Guadalcanal. Information received late on the afternoon of October 11, caused him to deploy in a position to intercept this force late that night off Esperance. He formed a column formation with three destroyers in the van the *San Francisco* (flag), *Boise*, *Salt Lake City* and *Helena*, and the remaining two tin cans bringing up the rear. By sunset general quarters had been sounded and the force settled down to wait. He launched SOC's from the flagship, *Boise* and *Salt Lake City* just after 2100. The *Salt Lake City* lost her aircraft due to an internal fire which was seen for dozens of miles. In fact, lookouts on Goto's ships saw the light in the far distance but wrongly assumed that it was a friendly light? The first of many mistakes.

The ships steamed at 20 knots just off Cape Esperance for the next 2-1/2 hours receiving poor and confusing reports from circling scout planes. The SOC's were excellent as gunfire spotters but left much to be desired as nightwatchmen. Just after 2330, the Scott ordered a countermarch that would turn the entire column, but also necessitated that the three leading destroyers turn and race parallel to the cruiser column to resume their lead position. Just as they came racing alongside at 30 knots, both *Helena* and *Boise* began to track five distinct targets that were certain to be the enemy. *Boise* reported them as "bogeys" and both ships queried the flagship for permission to fire. Confusion really mounted when they were answered with a "Roger" to their requests. This term meant not only message received, but also commence firing. *Helena* and *Boise* opened up with all guns on rapid fire at 2346. Just prior to pressing the firing keys, bridge personnel on both light cruisers could see Goto's force with the naked eye. Captain's Moran and Hoover (*Helena*) wondered aloud whether Scott wanted them to board the Japanese ships prior to shooting at them! Moran was innocently asked which target to fire at, and he replied, "Pick out the biggest, and commence firing". The *Boise* did just that. Just after the light cruisers opened fire, *Salt Lake City* and *San Francisco* opened up firmly accompanied by the five destroyers. The destroyer Duncan in a courageous if not reckless move took it upon herself to break formation and charge the Japanese column. Scott was nearly beside himself with rage and concern about his command disintegrating into a general melee, and the *Boise* and *Helena* mistaking the three parallel moving U.S. tin cans as the Japanese. He did not have the benefit of SG radar and there was no danger until the *Duncan* charged at the oncoming Japanese line. Scott yelled for a cease fire at 2350, yet relented a minute later. That temporary slackening of well aimed fire hurt the American chance for complete victory. Moran was absolutely incredulous that an order of this nature was issued. Throwing away an obvious advantage was simply out of the question, and in any event, Hoover and Moran kept up a firing pitch that must have spat out projectiles at the rate of 150-180 per minute per ship. *Boise* later reported that she fired 800 six-inch and 500 five-inch shells. They were literally smothering the Japanese column with multicolored shells splashes and hits. Both captains later complained that the rapid firing of their forward three turrets caused flash blindness and they had to rely on others for intelligence.

Goto's force was caught completely by surprise and he was mortally wounded in the first exchange. He was thoroughly unprepared for what he received and as proof his guns were trained fore and aft, and crews were not at battle stations. Many of his officers thought that the trailing reinforcement group was firing blindly, so he refrained from immediately opening fire. It was Savo Island in reverse, and Scott had literally crossed the "T", the most desired and sought after naval maneuver possible. Unfortunately, he was unable to exploit it's full potential. Confusion, lack of radar intelligence and fear for the three destroyers erased his chances for a smashing victory.

In all, the *Aoba* would take 40 hits before escaping at high speed. The *Furutaka* and destroyer *Fubuki* were not so fortunate as they were literally blown to pieces with multiple shell hits. The *Fubuki* sank at 0012, just 26 minutes after the engagement had been opened. This was a sweet revenge for the U.S. Navy as it was the *Fubuki* which had alerted a superior cruiser force as to the location of the *Houston* and Australian cruiser *Perth* on the night of February 28, 1942. The remnants of the ABDA command were attempting to escape through the Sunda Strait when they were intercepted, shot to pieces and sunk. The few survivors that escaped being machine gunned in the water were tortured until war's end in the most inhumane of the Japanese prisoner of war camps.

Furutaka lasted less than three hours and sank at 0248. The other destroyer and the heavy cruiser *Kinugasa* escaped unscathed, and along with the mauled *Aoba* made their turn to uncross the "T". Their aft turrets and torpedoes began to make life miserable for the *Salt Lake City* and *Boise*. Just after midnight, a reverse of fortune occurred.

Kinugasa opened fire with her 8 inch guns and torpedoes were launched. Moran, knowing what a long lance could do, was quick to swerve his rapidly moving cruiser out of harm's way, and skillfully avoided being hit from below. Luck abandoned the *Boise* shortly thereafter. She was out of the column formation and anxious to resume the battle, she switched on a searchlight to illuminate a nearby target. The wounded *Aoba* and still untouched *Kinugasa* took her under fire using the searchlight as a bull's eye. At 7000 yards the Japanese aim was excellent and the *Boise* was hit at least seven times by high caliber shells. She was hit in the most crucial location, the forward 6 inch magazine - for most ships, this would have been fatal. It was fully expected that she would vaporize like HMS *Hood* or the USS *Arizona* when hit in similar locations. She would have, had the fire spread, but a twist of fate saved the cruiser. One of the shell hits opened the hull to the sea, and this accidental flooding reduced the fire hazard to that manageable by the damage control teams. The *Boise* also owed her continued survival to the *Salt Lake City* which valiantly pulled alongside to block further Japanese fire. The burning gases and explosions erupting from turrets 1 and 2 threatened to destroy the entire ship, and very nearly did, but Moran's Irish heritage and it's good fortune prevailed, yet 104 men and 3 officers were consumed by the fires and gases. By 12 minutes after midnight, it was all over. What was left of the Japanese formation was fleeing.

The *Boise* would fight another battle that night and that was one of damage control. When Moran was first apprised of the damage, his concern was for the men and not the ship. This was the mark of a great commanding officer. For nearly three hours her damage control teams worked miracles by shoring up bulkheads and using everything available to plug holes. They

An unexploded 8 inch shell jammed in the armor plate of the barbette of turret number one.

Another view of the scorecard painted on the bridge of the Boise. Two heavy cruisers, one light cruiser and three destroyers, claimed sunk.

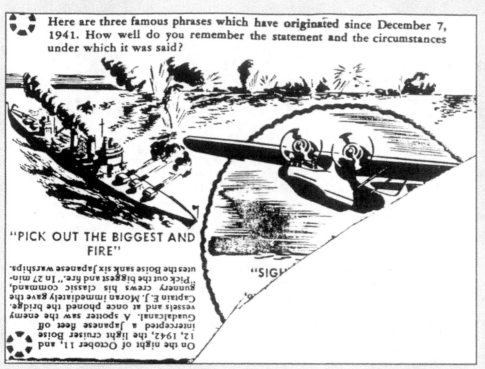

A Wheaties cereal guessing game using Moran's then famous words, "pick out the biggest and fire".

Battered Cruiser Boise Christened By Idaho Falls Girl

News of the U.S.S. Boise, light cruiser, which miraculously survived a sea battle in the Solomon island zone, recalls to Idaho Falls residents the christening of the vessel by Mrs. Al Springer, Boise, formerly Salome Clark, daughter of former Governor and Mrs. Barzilla Clark, of Idaho Falls.

News of the survival of the ship is contained in today's war bulletins, printed above in this column.)

Mrs. Springer smashed a bottle of Snake river water against the keel of the trim fighting craft in January, 1936, a few days before her father was inaugurated governor.

Mr. Clark said: "My daughter—all of the family for that matter —has always been interested in the fortune of the Boise. She told me she would watch with interest what the Boise would do in this war. Apparently, she is giving a good account of herself against the Japs."

Newspaper article regarding the Boise being christened.

Cruiser Boise Barely Missed Being Named Idaho Falls

Tribune Intermountain Wire

IDAHO FALLS, Idaho—Here is something, which would be a big honor to Idaho Falls now, that few, if any, of the residents know about.

The U S S cruiser Boise, which was placed in the halls of fame last week after having sunk six Japanese war vessels in a battle in the south Pacific, came mighty close to being named Idaho Falls.

Former Governor Barzilla W. Clark of Idaho Falls, whose daughter, Mrs. Salome Klinger of Boise, christened the ship in the New Jersey shipyards, made the revelation Wednesday. He said Idaho's congressional delegation almost changed their minds upon recommending the name "Boise" after pastors of churches there had objected.

The former governor and his daughter were "plenty anxious" to have the name "Idaho Falls" selected. "But, of course, Boise is the capital and so the name was better," Mr. Clark said.

The ship was christened with water from Snake river, which the former local girl dipped out of the forebay of the municipal power plant, and carried in a bottle across the United States. "Salome insisted on taking the water out just before it went into the generators," Mr. Clark said. "She said if it had enough potential power to turn those large turbines, it should be 'strong water' for a salty battleship."

Newspaper article regarding the Boise almost being named Idaho Falls.

Crew of the Boise *pose for a picture showing that their ship destroyed six Japanese warships. These innocent pictures and the publicity that accorded all of the glory to the* Boise *did not set well with the Navy Department or the crews of the ships that were also at Cape Esperance.*

A memorial and dedication service being held aboard the newly repaired USS Boise. *A plaque has been cast out of bronze that commemorates the 107 killed at the Battle of Cape Esperance. The plaque is now part of a monument in the City of Boise at Julia Davis Park.*

worked with the full knowledge that at any time the ship would erupt in fiery destruction. This was the true victory for the *Boise* at Esperance. Just before 0300 she rejoined Task Force 64.2 whose officers and men were incredulous that she was still afloat.

ESPERANCE SCORECARD

Both sides were quick to announce victory. The Japanese claimed that they sank two enemy heavy cruisers. The American Navy claimed four heavy cruisers and four destroyers. Scott innocently thought that he had engaged ten plus ships and had sunk at least six of them. This was understandable as the eyes played tricks and radar would also show ships disappearing from screens for any number of reasons. Hits on ships at their extreme ends were mistaken for two ships being hit and sunk.

In reality, the Japanese lost the heavy cruiser *Furutaka*, probably sunk by the combined efforts of the *Boise*, *Helena* and *Salt Lake City* at the outset of the engagement. The destroyer *Fubuki* was literally assassinated by the combined fire of the entire American force seven minutes into the engagement. The *Aoba* was raked with 40 hits from the Scott's cruisers, yet was able to escape at high speed. The cruiser *Kinugasa* was hit twice and the destroyer *Hatsuyuki* received only minor damage. The entire force would have been annihilated had radar been trusted and the column movement of Scott's force been different.

The Americans lost the destroyer *Duncan* which was probably hit by errant shells from fellow ships. The *Boise* was hit hard but survived and the *Salt Lake City* was hit three times by 8 inch shells. But, victory is not merely measured in ships sunk, but in lessons learned and enforced changes in enemy planning and morale. For Scott, the *Boise* and her sister ships, it was a major victory. The seemingly invincible Japanese navy could be defeated on our terms rather than their's. The Allies had radar, and it's use could only improve chances for ultimate victory. The bluejackets of the U.S. Navy again proved that they were willing to fight to the death in this struggle, and could win.

The *Boise* was detached and ordered to the

U.S. for a prolonged period of repair and renovation. As the west coast shipyards were fully occupied, she was diverted to the Philadelphia Navy Yard, arriving on November 19 1942. Her number one turret was still pointing to starboard as it had been when it was hit by an eight inch shell that jammed it's training mechanism. She and her crew were greeted by cheering mobs of wellwishers including the Chief of Naval Operations, Ernest J. King. He and Captain Moran surveyed the damage and priority was given to her immediate repair and return to sea. An old friend, Salome Clark Springer, the *Boise's* sponsor upon hearing that her charge had been damaged, led the effort in Idaho to sell $3 million worth of war bonds to pay for the repair work.

Unfortunately, a reporter from the Philadelphia Inquirer newspaper noticed the scorecard painted on the bridge depicting two heavy cruisers, one light cruiser and three destroyers being sunk at Cape Esperance. Several pictures were taken with the crew pointing to the scorecard, and a feeding frenzy of propaganda began. "The One Ship Fleet or Task Force" was born in the mind of the media, and even Wheaties cereal boxes had the phrase, "pick out the biggest" on the reverse flap as part of a famous victory slogan contest. The truth became a casualty and due to security rules, the *Boise* was accorded the honor of sinking six ships and the efforts of now deceased Admiral Scott, the *Helena*, *San Francisco*, *Salt Lake City* and the five destroyers were lost in the wake of the media's need for a good yarn. Ironically, five months after the battle, the media would hear the same claims from the crew of the *Salt Lake City*. They too sank six ships that night! It was not until after the war that historians printed the facts, yet the legend of the "One Ship Task Force" still lives in some quarters. The fact that the *Boise* was not responsible for sinking six ships and in reality was part of a force that dispatched two enemy ships does not diminish the valiant efforts of her crew to willingly fight and later demonstrate super human efforts to save this gallant ship. The *Boise* and her crew at Esperance won a great victory and unknowingly stemmed the tide of Japanese victory. After the Battle of Cape Esperance, Japan would never smile again.

REPAIR, RENOVATION, AND RETURN TO BATTLE

During her period in the Philadelphia Navy Yard, the *Boise* received what would be the standard upgrade for ships in her class. Her bridge was cut down and opened for greater visibility and control. She lost her armored conning tower, had her electronics upgraded, and her anti-aircraft battery was intensified with 20mm and 40mm guns. She was now a modern cruiser and able to fight not only surface ships but aircraft as well.

"Iron Mike" Moran was also relieved and given a promotion to Commodore, the Navy Cross and command of PT boats in the South Pacific. He felt uneasy about this new assignment, as if it was some form of punishment for what had occurred at Cape Esperance, but being navy, nothing was ever said. He remained a Commodore until war's end and retired from active service in 1947. He was given a graveyard promotion to Rear Admiral, and spent his retirement years traveling the globe. He died on Easter weekend 1957 in Paris, France. Moran was an honorable man proven many times over, but most forcefully when he was offered $30,000 by the Saturday Evening Post for his story about the real truth of the Battle of Cape Esperance and he declined. His reason, he did not want to hurt those who were still living with the truth.

The *Boise* finished her yard time in late March 1943, and immediately went into refresher training under the command of Captain Hewlett Thebaud. By June 8, 1943, she was on her way to the Mediterranean to fight the other two members of the Axis powers, Germany and Italy.

For the next six months she would earn a reputation for excellence in gunfire support like her sisters *Savannah*, *Brooklyn* and *Philadelphia*. She became the scourge of the Italian and Sicilian coasts continuously in demand by the army to disrupt German and Italian supply lines, tank formations and troop concentrations. She expended thousands of 6 inch and 5 inch rounds against targets day and night, with a high degree of accuracy. This was a role never envisioned for these light cruisers, that of gunfire support to land troops. It eventually emerged as one of

Like many of her sisters, she has been given a facelift that includes improved electronics, open bridges, and many 20mm/40mm antiaircraft guns spotted all over her. She would need every close in weapon system available to fight her new enemy, the high speed aircraft.

The Boise acts as a very heavily armed attack troop transport as she carries 788 troops of the British First Airborne Division to accept the surrender of the Italian Naval base at Taranto. The operation came off without major incident, although a minelayer (HMS Abdiel) was sunk at the mooring where the Boise was to have been stationed.

most important functions of the rapid fire light cruiser.

Her gunfire support mission was interrupted on September 7, 1943, when she was detached to serve with British 12th Cruiser Squadron. Captain Thebaud at first thought that he was in hack as the message detaching him was somewhat curt, but he soon found out that he was to help capture and secure the Italian naval base at Taranto, thus denying it to the Germans. Now the *Boise* became the most heavily armed fast attack transport in naval history. She was loaded down with British First Airborne Division numbering 788 ground troops that composed a rather rum group known as "Popski's Private Army". Her aft hanger was packed with jeeps, motorcycles, field artillery and other equipment. The ground force would assault the objective with force if necessary. It was quite a force that approached Taranto. It included the battleships *King George V* and *Howe* as well as a number of cruisers and destroyers. No chances were being taken. As the force approached it witnessed the end of an era as the main body of the proud, but "cardboard navy", began leaving with guns depressed fore and aft. It was over for the Italian Navy.

The *Boise* still had some luck left to her because in a quirk of fate, she elected to tie up at another mooring other than that selected for her. The British minelayer *Abdiel* took her place and was sunk during the night by a contact mine.

The *Boise* resumed her station on the gunline off Salerno on September 12. She was to replace the *Savannah* which had been severely damaged by a radio controlled glider bomb with a warhead of some 3,000 pounds. The *Savannah* should have been blown up, but like her sister, the *Boise* which was hit in the same general area a year earlier, flooding caused by the hit, prevented a massive explosion. Both ships owe their continued existence to fortune, cartridge powder containers, and superb damage control.

On September 25, she received a new skipper, Captain John S. Roberts, as the war had moved inland toward Rome, the *Boise* was detached and sent back to the U.S. for reassignment.

BACK TO THE PACIFIC AND HER LAST TOUR

The much decorated and well worn cruiser left for the South Pacific on December 6, 1943, and was back in warm water on December 30, as part of what had become known as MacArthur's Navy. In September 1942, when it was conceived, it consisted of 5 cruisers, 8 destroyers, 20 submarines and 7 small craft. It was not a navy, not even a group, but considering the relative importance of MacArthur's command at that stage of global strategic thinking, it was more than enough. Eighteen months later, Macarthur's Navy had swollen to being the third largest Navy in the World. Here the *Boise* would fight until the end of the war, and become a favorite place for MacArthur to view his successes and victory.

In January 1944, she became part of the 7th Fleet and specifically, a unit in Admiral Russell "Count" Berkey's Task Force 75. Berkey's command usually consisted of the light cruisers *Phoenix*, *Boise* and *Nashville* with a destroyer screen. This force would remain in tact and slowly shoot up everything on the coast of New Guinea. This force was invaluable to the ground forces engaged in some of the bloodiest fighting in World War II. They fought their way up the New Guinea coast providing gunfire support for landings at Madang-Alexishafen (January 24 - 25); Humboldt Bay (April 22); Wakde-Sawar (April 29 - 30); Wakde-Toem (May 15 -25); Biak (May 25 - June 10); Noremfoor (July 1 - 2); Cape Sans (July 21 - August 31); and finally the occupation of Morotai (September 1 - 30). These campaigns were hot, sultry and miserable. The stench of rotting jungle, dead men and destroyed war materials were ever present. It was another form of hell on earth.

The war took a new turn now as MacArthur was ready to fulfill his promise to the Philippine people and the world that he would return, and return he did, beginning at Leyte in the southern half of the 7,000 islands that make up the Philippine chain. The *Boise* was right in the middle of this, and like the Supreme commander, was returning to where she too was forced to leave just under three years earlier.

The *Boise* participated in the invasion of Leyte on October from October 20-24, 1944, and in company with Australian cruisers, fired on targets continuously. She used 3,400 six-inch, and 1,750 five-inch shells during this four day bombardment. On October 25, however, she would fight one more, and her final ship to ship engagement.

PEARL HARBOR/SAVO ISLAND REVENGE - THE BATTLE OF SURIGAO STRAIT

Some would say that the entire Pacific war was in revenge for the Japanese attack on Pearl Harbor, but one battle seemed to capsulize the U.S. Navy's avenging spirit. Primarily, because it was fought by some of the victims that were damaged or sunk on December 7, 1941. This battle however also marked the end of an era of capitol ship versus capitol ship. The world would probably never witness this kind of warfighting again. It would pass into history and join medieval longbow and pike warfare as well as well as the Roman Turtle formation. The *Boise* was part of this last hurrah.

By late 1944, the Imperial Japanese Navy had lost most of it's aircraft strength in a number of disastrous air battles with the U.S. Navy's ever increasing carrier strength. Similarly, IJN surface forces had been whittled down by the fighting in the southwest Pacific and American submarines had done their part. The IJN had one last gasp available to throw the invaders out of Leyte, and prevent the eventual onslaught against their home islands. In addition, the loss of access to the east indies oil fields would in and of itself be sufficient to destroy the empire. It had to be all out gamble. Against previous public information policies the Emperor and the people of Japan were informed of the gravity of this situation. For this one last effort, the IJN amassed virtually all of their naval might and remaining fuel supplies for a desperate three pronged attack on the landing force. One would consist of planeless carriers to draw Halsey and his heavy units northward away from the landing area.

Another would bring on the heaviest units of the fleet (63,000 ton) monster battleships *Yamato* and *Mushashi* from the west and the final thrust from the south. It was hoped that either the western or southern forces or both could approach Leyte without being decimated by air power, and disrupt the landings. The plan very nearly succeeded.

The Allied defense and the Japanese southern attack force that would fight in the strict confines of the Surigao Strait consisted of:

Allied: Vice Admiral Jesse B. Olendorf
Battleships: *Mississippi, Maryland, West Virginia, Tennessee, California, Pennsylvania*
Heavy Cruisers: *Louisville, Portland, Minneapolis, HMAS Shropshire*
Light Cruisers: *Denver, Columbia, Phoenix, Boise*
Destroyers: 27 US and 1 Australian

Japanese: Vive Admiral Nishimura
Battleships: *Fuso, Yamashiro*
Heavy Cruiser: *Mogami*
Destroyers: 4 ships

This force was backed up by another under the command of Vice Admiral Shima that consisted of two heavy cruisers, one light cruiser and four destroyers.

In the early morning hours of October 25, 1944, Olendorf's surprise package was ready for the desperate Japanese southern force that was moving into the Surigao Strait. PT Boats would sound the alarm and fire torpedoes as the enemy approached, and as they came further into the trap they would be assaulted by a swarm attack of destroyers launching torpedoes. The main event would take place when they met the central body consisting of older by effective battleships guarded on each flank by cruisers who would put paid to any stragglers.

The *Boise* guarded the right flank, and as she watched the end of an era in the early morning, her turn came just before 0400, and she went to rapid fire on the battleship *Yamashiro*. She was quickly instructed to conserve shells and fire slowly and deliberately. A light wind kept the gun smoke off the bow area, and the captain and many crew were able to witness their handiwork. Soon, their adversary turned out of range and disappeared. In the end, the Japanese lost the battleships *Fuso* and *Yamashiro*, heavy cruiser *Mogami*, and most of the rest of it's primary and support force. The Imperial Japanese Navy ceased to exist. The Allies did not lose a single ship. This was also the swansong for the all gun warship, yet the final burial would not occur for several years. The outcome for the other two forces was even worse, and the Imperial Navy was no more.

A DISTINGUISHED PASSENGER AND THEN IT IS ALL OVER

Captain Roberts suffered a heart attack in November, and he was temporarily replaced by Cmdr. Thomas Wolverton, the executive officer, and former damage control officer at Cape Esperance. Wolverton claimed that much of his success in saving the ship that

A tired and weary ship that has expended over 20,000 rounds of ammunition and sailed 500,000 miles comes home. The Boise *may have had a slow start, but after she got going, there was no stopping her.*

THE OFFICE OF THE MAYOR
CITY OF BOISE,
State of Idaho

PROCLAMATION

WHEREAS, during World War II, America was called to defend freedom both for the United States of America and throughout the world; and

WHEREAS, in the United States Navy the American fleet was comprised of many great ships and sailors; and

WHEREAS, the people of Boise, Idaho in whose honor the U.S.S. Boise was named, are proud of the men who served in the defense of our country; and

WHEREAS, the courage, imagination and daring shown by the exceptional crew on board the U.S.S. Boise make the citizens of Boise proud to pay tribute to those gathered today;

NOW, THEREFORE, be it resolved, that I, Dirk Kempthorne, MAYOR of the City of Boise, Idaho, declare September 26, 1987 as

U.S.S. BOISE CREW MEMBER DAY

in commemorating this reunion and further declare that all flags in the city be flown, not at half mast, but at full mast to proudly demonstrate the living memory of a great ship and her entire crew;

AND FURTHER, that this city administration will diligently seek the commissioning of a new U.S.S. Boise so that the distinguished service of the ship bearing this name shall be the inspiration for a new era in naval pride and history under the flag of the United States of America and the banner of the U.S.S. Boise.

IN WITNESS WHEREOF, I have hereunto set my hand on this the twenty-sixth day of September, in the year of our Lord nineteen hundred eighty seven.

Dirk Kempthorne
MAYOR OF BOISE, IDAHO

The City of Boise Idaho has not forgotten its namesake and honors its former crew with a proclamation.

night was due to Freddie Bell's training. Wolverton was relieved by Captain W. M. Downes on December 6.

Just over a month after assuming command, Captain Downes received a rather interesting visitor. Officer's stewards mate 2c, Estaneslas Bandong had left the ship on December 3, 1941 to visit his relatives in Manila, and couldn't catch up with the *Boise* until January 11, 1945. He was not charged with being awol! His career had been on hold for 37 months until his country changed hands again.

From the successful conclusion of what became the Battle of Leyte, the *Boise* provided support and escort to various amphibious landings moving up the Philippine chain. In January 1945, and again in June 1945 Douglas MacArthur toured his command aborad what was becoming one of his favorite ships, the *Boise*. He was an honored guest and was well respected and liked by the crew. After disembarking their favorite passenger, the *Boise* headed for home, and the war's end found her just completing repair and refitting at the Long Beach Naval Shipyard. She was assigned to be part of the Navy Day ceremony in New York during October. She was given a heroes welcome. She and her crew of veterans had earned the undying gratitude of free men and women everywhere.

Her final duty was that of bringing homesick, GI's back from Europe as part of the Magic Carpet Operation. She eventually arrived back in Philadelphia in early 1946, and after a period of preparation, she was mothballed and laid up in reserve with her sisters *Brooklyn* and *Philadelphia*. She was decommissioned on July 1, 1946. She had been in service for just under eight years and had earned eleven battle stars. She helped to sink three combat ships and was credited with shooting down seven attacking aircraft. She also fired nearly 20,000 five and six inch shells at dozens of targets. Without her excellence in gunfire, many soldiers and marines would not have survived the war.

With all of the new cruiser construction during the war, and all of the lessons learned from the past war, the *Boise* and her sisters were now obsolete, and barring a major conflict, would probably never fly the Stars and Stripes in combat again. But, that did not mean the *Boise* would never put to sea again.

A New Lease On Life - ARA "*Nueve De Julio*" Of Argentina

As part of the Mutual Defense Assistance Program with several major nations in South America, the U.S. agreed to sell six major warships to Brazil, Argentina, and Chile at two per country. The large surplus of high quality warships in the American inventory was quite attractive as the price, 10% of the original price plus renovation costs. Selected were six light cruisers of the *Brooklyn - St. Louis* classes. Two each were provided to the major powers of South America as much out of equity as to preserving a crucial balance of power. It would not do to have one nation as a super power in the region.

Brazil was sold the *St. Louis* and *Philadelphia*; Chile received the *Brooklyn* and *Nashville*, and Argentina acquired the *Boise* and the *Phoenix*.

*Mrs. Salome Clark Springer, is again present as the ship she has cherished changes hands.
The Boise now been sold to the Argentine Navy and will be renamed the "Nueve de Julio".
The Argentine Navy was ecstatic about this acquisition and that of sister ship, Phoenix. As
the 9 de Julio, the old cruiser will serve the Argentine Navy for nearly thirty years.*

The ship's bell and memorial plaque removed before the Boise *was sold to Argentina. A monument was built in Julia Davis Park in honor of these mementos of a great fighting lady and her brave crew.*

The arrangement was made in 1950 - 1951, and the average price was $7.8 million.

On a cold day in March, 1952 the USS *Boise* CL-47 hauled down the Stars and Stripes and the Argentine colors were raised. Present at the formal transfer were representatives of both governments and staff from the Philadelphia Navy Yard. Also present was Salome Clark Springer, and prospective Argentine commanding officer, Captain Nestor P. Gabrelli. She became the *Nueve de Julio*, named after the day of Argentine independence.

Salome, who had wished the cruiser well just 14 years before again waved as the cruiser began service in the Navy of Argentina. The City of Boise withdrew three items before the ship left on April 5, 1952. The ship's silver service, bell and the plaque commemorating the dead from the Battle of Cape Esperance were placed in Julia Davis Park in Boise.

The Argentine Navy was elated at having such warships as the *Phoenix* (ARA *General Belgrano*) and *Boise* (9 *de Julio*) as flagships in their fleet. Both were used extensively for patrol and flag showing throughout the hemisphere. Sadly, the *General Belgrano* was sunk by a British submarine during the 1982 Falklands/Malvinas War. There were nearly 400 men killed in the torpedo attack, and an uneasy peace still exists between these two nations.

The 9 *de Julio* served as flagship and was based out of the large naval base at Puerto Belgrano on the southern coast of Argentina. During the period of 1952-1955, there was great civil unrest in Argentina as see saw governing bodies literally dismembered the country. President Juan Peron, formerly an army colonel/dictator was a known opponent of the Navy, yet highly popular due to his outward support of the workers and his charismatic almost saintly wife, Eva Duarte (Evita). Soon after her death on 1952, his grasp on the country's leadership began to falter, and by 1955 he was fighting for his political life.

The old cruiser now went back into combat on the side of the revolutionaries against the loyalists supporting Peron. In the summer of 1955, she fired her 6 inch guns at various loyalist military and commercial targets along the coast as well as an important oil refinery at Mar del Plata.

The Brooklyn's *keel is laid at the New York Navy Yard on March 15, 1935. She would be a part of two navies for nearly 57 years, and serve both the United States and Chile well. Admiral Ingersoll presides over the ceremony.*

Her massive bombardment is one of the catalysts that causes Peron to flee to Uruguay in exile. Fascism had again been defeated.

The following year in 1956, there was an accidental collision with the *General Belgrano*, but repairs were carried out on both ships and they were operational within months. For the next several years, the 9 *de Julio* was used for training, patrol and exercises with visiting allied naval forces. She received some minor electronic updating and now carried two helicopter in lieu of her old SOC biplanes.

By the late 1970's her active service days are over and she became a spare parts ship for the *General Belgrano*. In 1981, the old girl was sold to Consolidated Andy, a scrap firm in Brownsville, Texas. She has served two navies with distinction and pride for a total of 43 years. It was fitting that her final resting place would be back in her country of origin. Part of her lives however, in the hearts of her former crewmen and the proud citizens of Boise, Idaho, who still remember this ship with a plaque and photograph in the Idaho State House. Also, children play near the ship's bell and the honor role of her dead. This area remains unblemished, a place of reverence.

USS *BROOKLYN*, CL-40
"THE LAST SURVIVOR"

Ships, like their crews have souls, individuality and live through series of events that make up their history. They can leave a legacy of positive achievement or disaster. The USS *Brooklyn*, Cl-40, (Chile's Crucero O'Higgins) is known for it's exceptional achievement and endurance. She carried her crews, American and Chilean, through war and peace, providing a safe sanctuary, yet also as a fighting platform for the enforcement of the better convictions and beliefs of mankind.

As a fighting unit of the U.S. Navy, her assignments ranged from successful salvage and rescue, to providing accurate fire support for determined allied troops against the Axis. If there is one individual who most epitomized the character and spirit of this fine warship, it had to be Captain, later Vice Admiral Francis C. Denebrink (1896-1987). Initially, one of the *Brooklyn's* peace time executive officers, and later her captain in war, this popular and respected officer still commands the affection of many who served with him. As with the ship that he loved so much, Admiral Denebrink demonstrated the same qualities of endurance and outstanding achievement.

CONSTRUCTION, LAUNCHING, FITTING OUT AND COMMISSIONING

The light cruiser, USS *Brooklyn*, numbered Cl-40 by the Navy Department, and the namesake of a seven ship class, was laid down on March 12, 1935, at the U.S. Navy Yard at Brooklyn, New York. It would be just short of twenty one months before her hull would slide down the greased ways into the East River on a blustery November 30, 1936. On that day, in a ceremony that lasted a mere 15 minutes, she would be christened by Miss Kathryn Lackey, the daughter of Admiral F. R. Lackey, a native of Brooklyn, New York. The traditional bottle of champagne was duly smashed against her straining hull, and she began her angled glide down the ways. As she touched the waters of the East River, the cheering of hundreds of well wishers died out however, the efforts of the citizens of the Borough of Brooklyn would never be forgotten. It was they who prevailed upon the Navy Department to name this new, almost futuristic warship after their city, Brooklyn. It was also they who carried out a massive public bond drive campaign to secure the monies necessary to build and equip this ship. This was accomplished even as the U.S. was reeling from worldwide depression, and still in the early stages of economic recovery. Finally, it was the citizens petition that caused this ship to be built in the Brooklyn Navy Yard. In a sense, the USS *Brooklyn* was the property of the citizens of Brooklyn, yet on permanent loan to the U.S. Navy.

The Navy Yard at Brooklyn, New York was no stranger to illustrious warships, as many had begun their careers on the builders ways as unconnected wood and steel beams being shaped into fighting ships. The first was the ship of the line, the USS *Ohio*, launched on May 30, 1820, and the 51st was the *Brooklyn*, Cl-40. Significantly, two other ships built earlier in this yard would serve as rallying points for American patriotism. Each would serve their country well, but only at war's opening gun. They were the USS *Maine*, launched on November 18, 1890, and the USS *Arizona*, launched on June 19, 1915. Although the *Brooklyn* was launched some 22 years after the USS *Arizona*, she, her seven sisters, and two half sisters of the *St. Louis* class would spend four years avenging her death.

For ten months, the new cruiser underwent the final stages of construction, including the installation of her modern five triple barrel 6 inch/ 47 caliber gun turrets. In essence, this armament was her reason for existence. In addition to her armament, the superstructure was completed, funnels were mounted as well as the full installation of the aviation unit.

During the ten month fitting out period, additional crew began to appear and take up residence at the Receiving Ship (USS *Seattle*). There was a core of experienced hands assigned to the *Brooklyn* in the months just prior to her commissioning however, nearly 20% of her plank owning crew were assigned directly from boot camp, primarily from the Naval Training Station Center in Newport, Rhode Island. This was the case with men such as Layton W. McCabe and Paul K. Ramsey, whose first ship out of boot training was the *Brooklyn*. Ramsey would later demonstrate his skill as a coxswain while assigned to launch #2 which carried equipment and personnel during the frantic rescue of 33 of the marooned crew of the submarine *Squalus*. He still recalls his service as a *Brooklyn* boat coxswain as one of the more exciting periods of his naval service.

Finally, the day of her commissioning arrived, September 30, 1937. The ceremony was brief, conducted by Captain Jonas P. Ingram, in the absence of the Navy Yard commandant. Cap-

Miss Catherine Jane Lackey does the honors at the christening of the Brooklyn *on November 30, 1936.*

The new 10,000 ton cruiser, Brooklyn, *slides down the ways at the New York Navy Yard on November 30, 1936. She was the namesake of seven light cruisers that were financed by an executive order of President Roosevelt. The $238 million in funding allowed for an expansion in the Navy and provided needed employment for thousands of depression era men and women.*

The Brooklyn *shortly after being commissioned. Her tall fore and main masts would be shortened and radar would be added; but for now, crow's nest had to suffice for detection of enemies.*

tain William D. Brereton, Jr. USN, assumed command. It was none to soon for world events were becoming more intolerant with each passing day. In the far east, the Japanese Army was cutting a swath of misery and death, as it was about to enter Nanking, China. On the other side of the globe, the stain of Naziism was firmly entrenching itself, even in the homes of the German people. The German civil courts had now ruled that children could be forcibly removed from their parents, if Nazi ideals were not routinely taught at home!

A further six weeks were necessary for the new cruiser to conduct her engine and power trials. Engine trials were completed on December 8, 1937, however, there was still to be a lengthy period devoted to extensive post commissioning modifications. After her period in the yard, she sailed for Guantanamo Bay, Cuba for an in-

tensive period of drills, indoctrination, and exercises to enable her to become a viable unit of the fleet.

During this period, world events were shaping the future of this pristine cruiser, and some, quite close to home. Of particular note, were the actions being taken by the Navy Department to prepare for the war that all professional military men, diplomats, and savvy politicians knew was coming. Following on the authority of the Vinson-Trammel Act of 1934, or the "naval expansion bill", President Roosevelt, in early 1938, encouraged congressional passage of acts necessary to vastly increase naval armaments, and formalize "neutrality". Neutrality, enforced by arms!

In June 1938, the *Brooklyn* joined with her sisters, the USS *Savannah*, Cl-42 and the USS *Philadelphia*, Cl-41 as part of the three ship

IF YOU CAN'T guarantee to put me on the cruiser Brooklyn I'll go into the army.

A popular cartoon in New York about men who wanted to sail on ships named after their hometown.

considered a welcome relief when she, and her sisters were ordered to New York to participate in the formal opening of the World's Fair scheduled for April 30, 1939. By the opening of the Fair, the Atlantic Squadron had now laid claim to Cruiser Division 8, as well as several other more modern warships. The Squadron now consisted of 30 plus warships, and it's role was changing to meet the more ominous needs of the day.

On the day the Fair formally was opened, the Atlantic Squadron, under the overall command of Rear Admiral Alfred Johnson, sailed into a misty New York Harbor. The USS *Honolulu*, Cl-48, and the *Brooklyn* were already in port as the line of ships slowly steamed in, led by several destroyers. One of the destroyers in the line was the *Rueben James*, later sunk by a German submarine on October 31, 1941. She was destined to be the first casualty of a war, that was yet undeclared, but very real. The *Savannah* led the cruisers of the Atlantic Squadron up the Hudson.

It was a golden opportunity for the American people as well as many foreign visitors to see the latest in American naval might. It had been five years since such a large number of ships had congregated in the harbor, and the city was justifiably proud of their navy and its' men. Thousands of visitors toured the ships. Visiting hours were between 1-5 daily, and the *Brooklyn*, accessible from the 96th Street landing, was quite popular. The crews and the officers of the assembled ships were entertained ashore at various functions, and all agreed it was quite a liberty port! 12,500 sailors versus New York City!

Thoughts of war were temporarily placed on hold as the wonders of the future were taken in by millions at the exposition. The theme of the fair was dedicated to, "Peace and Progress". For the crew of the new cruiser this respite was shortlived as a tragedy was unfolding in nearby waters that would require the services of this cruiser and her crew.

THE *SQUALUS* DISASTER AND THE *BROOKLYN*

At 1530 on May 24, 1939, the *Brooklyn* was instructed to immediately leave the Brooklyn Navy Yard, put to sea and head for a position five miles south/east of Isle of Shoals, Hampton Beach. This was just off the coast of New Hampshire, near the Naval Station at Portsmouth. The cruiser was to act as operations control vessel for the rescue of 59 crew marooned aboard the sunken USS *Squalus*, a modern 1,450 ton, 310 foot submarine just recently launched in September 1938. William W. Smith was now captain of the *Brooklyn*, having just assumed command six days prior from Captain Brereton.

The *Squalus*, commanded by Lieutenant O. F. Naquin, had left Portsmouth for a routine test run early on May 23, and was accompanied by a sister submarine, the USS *Sculpin*. After diving, and not surfacing according to schedule, a yellow metal canister was seen floating near the location where the *Squalus* was known to be operating. The canister, resembling a lobster pot, according to several local fisherman, was actually a combination communication and location marker for a downed submarine. The *Sculpin*

Cruiser Division 8, under the direction of Rear Admiral Forde A. Todd. Admiral Todd flew his flag in the USS *Philadelphia*, whose commissioning actually predated that of the *Brooklyn* by one week. This new division carried out training, training and more training.

Within three months, however, on September 6, 1938, another major change in naval organization was announced by the Chief of Naval Operations (CNO), Admiral William D. Leahy. The *Atlantic Squadron* was formed, and Admiral Todd was later appointed to command this new seven cruiser, seven destroyer squadron. Initially, the Squadron was composed of older ships such as the battleship *New York* and a number of recommissioned four piper destroyers. Publically, this force spent much of its time and energy in training, but was actually the precursor to the Atlantic Fleet. The Squadron's origin was found in President Roosevelt's instruction to the CNO to assemble a temporary force to patrol the Atlantic from Newfoundland to South America. When advising his Cabinet of this action, Roosevelt stated, "if some submarines are laying there and try to interrupt an American Flag and our navy sinks them it's just too bad...." The tone had been set! The intended purpose of the *Atlantic Squadron* was to protect American shipping and lives in the Atlantic. It also demonstrated, to those who were watching, the seriousness of American intent in defending her interests.

The *Brooklyn* remained as an integral part of Cruiser Division 8 which was later augmented with a sister ship, the USS *Nashville*, Cl-43. Throughout the early months of 1939, the *Brooklyn*, as part of Cruiser Division 8 conducted gunnery drills and other operational exercises. It was hauled in the marker, and quickly established contact with her sister, now lying on the bottom 240 feet below the surface. Unfortunately, before Lt. Naquin, of the *Squalus* could make a full report, the telephone line went dead. However, it was known that the *Squalus* had sunk as the result of a faulty valve and the crew's quarters as well as the after torpedo compartment were flooded.

Assistance was summoned, and submarine rescue ship, the USS *Falcon*, began it's journey to the wreck site. At 2145 on that same day, a message tapped in morse code was received by oscillograph from the sunken *Squalus*, "Condition satisfactory, but cold". Time was running, and the air was becoming progressively more foul.

The initial rescue plan called for raising the entire submarine, however this was quickly discarded due to time and logistics factors. The time remaining for crew survival became the most critical consideration. A diving bell and a proficient team were needed. Fortunately, both were available.

At 1530 on May 24, 1939, the cruiser, docked at the Brooklyn Navy Yard, was given emergency orders to sail at once for the wreck site and transport 3,000 feet of needed air hose. Most commanding officers have the luxury of some time to become accustomed to their ship, but for newly appointed Captain Smith, this was not possible. As night fell, the *Brooklyn* cast off, and at high speed made her way through fog, and moderately heavy seas to the site. The urgency of her mission was so great that she left many crew members ashore. Although local radio station interrupted their programming to broadcast a plea to *Brooklyn's* sailors to immediately return to the ship, many never made it. Some had to take the train up the coast, and go by boat out to the ship. Two sailors hitched a ride on one of the tugs escorting the cruiser out of the harbor, and jumped aboard at the last minute, but for all others, it was too late.

She arrived near the site at noon on May 25, 1939, and took up station as the operations control ship. "The seas around the wreck were rough", according to Coxswain Paul Ramsey, so only the number two launch was lowered and used during the operation. Ramsey would later witness many of the 33 survivors being brought up by the Falcon's diving bell. The bell, a new development in submarine rescue work, could only carry a limited number of passengers, and it took four trips to the *Squalus* to bring up all 33 survivors. Ramsey described them as gray faced, haggard and near death, but they had lived. There was no media coverage of the of the survivors emerging from the bell, and when the reporters learned of this, they were quite upset. Several crew members of the *Brooklyn*, who had been graciously hosting the correspondents listened to complaints for three days.

By the end of day on May 26, 1939, the 33 had been rescued, and the fate of the remaining 26 had been sealed. Aside from providing assistance to the rescue, the *Brooklyn* acted as a floating media center for nearly 50 correspondents and reporters who were covering the story. Fortunately, the USS *Sacramento* relieved her on May 28, 1939, and she left the area and her guests behind.

A series of original newspaper photos dealing with the Squalus *disaster.*

THE *BROOKLYN* SAILS FOR THE PACIFIC

Just after the *Squalus* rescue, the *Brooklyn* and the balance of Cruiser Division 8 sailed for the Pacific via the Panama Canal in June 1939. On the trip along the Mexican coast, the crew encountered a rather violent storm that left many with their heads in the "head". The Pacific Ocean was not as peaceful as it was supposed to be! The *Brooklyn* was to remain in Pacific waters until mid-1941, when she would return to the Atlantic. Stops were made in Long Beach, California, San Francisco for the opening of the Golden Gate Exposition, and Portland, Oregon for "Fleet Week". At about the time World War II began in Europe, the *Brooklyn* entered the Puget Sound Naval Shipyard in Bremerton, Washington, for needed repair and overhaul.

Until early 1940, the cruiser embarked on a number of cruises off of the West Coast. She operated with the Battle Force in various maneuvers and fleet exercises (problems), often returning to Long Beach, California. By mid-1940, Cruiser Division 8 had moved 2400 miles westward, and was operating out of Pearl Harbor, T H. Much of the fleet remained in Hawaiian waters from this point onward, thus sending an obvious message to the Japanese government. Training, drills and more exercises, proclaimed the "Brooklyn Dodger", the ships newsletter.

The summer of 1940 was spent exercising out of Pearl Harbor, and in the fall, the *Brooklyn* returned to the West Coast for upkeep. In January, 1941, she returned to Hawaiian waters, and encountered a severe storm while in transit. The Brooklyn's length to beam ratio of 10 to 1 did not help matters much. A change of command took place on February 3, 1941, when Captain Ellis P. Stone relieved Captain Smith. Captain Stone had an extensive breadth of experience when he assumed command of the cruiser. He had served in destroyers, battleships, and recently had been the Naval Attache in Paris, France.

A few days after Captain Stone took command, a secret message directed the *Brooklyn*, in company with her sisters, *Savannah, Philadelphia* and *Nashville* to transport Marines and equipment to Midway. This was done to reinforce this outermost island of the Hawaiian chain against the growing probability of attack by the Japanese. The marines were landed by launch from the cruisers as there was no available docking. The reinforcements would prove crucial just over a year later in the Pacific War's pivotal Battle of Midway. But reinforcing Midway was just one among many indications that war was coming. General Quarters was called often, and training was primarily directed at war preparation.

There remained one more major operation that the *Brooklyn* would participate in while assigned to the Pacific Fleet, and that was the extremely popular March, 1941 visit to Samoa, New Zealand, Australia, Fiji, and Tahiti. It would be not be foolish to say that most men join the navy with ports like this in mind. Few if any, would join if the recruiter promised visits to Murmansk or Sitka! The cruise to these ports is still talked about in glowing terms.

With war imminent, the Pacific command was loathe to let several of it's major fleet units abandon their rigorous training schedule for what amounted to a well intentioned goodwill visit sponsored by the State Department. The diplomats prevailed. The lucky ships were the cruisers, *Chicago, Portland, Brooklyn* and *Savannah*, escorted by Destroyer Squadron 3.

Every port the ships visited caused celebration. Our allies down under had felt neglected by the free world, and the visit by an American Squadron of modern warships confirmed that they were not forgotten. Each stop was characterized by dances, marches, bands, and welcome speeches. The trip was a tremendous success, and actually enhanced training.

THE *BROOKLYN* JOINS THE UNDECLARED ATLANTIC WAR

On May 20, 1941, the Pacific days for the cruiser came to end as she, with other heavy units such as the battleships *Idaho, New Mexico* and *Mississippi*; cruisers *Philadelphia, Nashville, Savannah* and several destroyers, were reluctantly ordered to augment the Atlantic Fleet. Admiral William "Bull" Halsey was incredulous at the loss of these ships, but demands on the Atlantic Fleet for convoy escort and military occupation of various locations overrode his blustery objections. Not until 1952, would the *Brooklyn* again cruise Pacific waters, and then under Chilean colors as the *Crucero O'Higgins*.

Under secret orders, she sailed for the Atlantic. Most of the ships selected to transfer were already at sea when the word was passed that they would be changing stations. Wives could not be notified, as there was a blackout on all communication during the month's time it would take to make the trip. Even letters written while in transit were to make no reference to any ship movements. Even as the ships departed Guantanamo Bay on the last leg of the journey, speculation ran rampant as to where they were headed. Morning General Quarters was now

routine, and many men slept and remained closer to their battle stations than in lazier days. Bermuda, Boston and Norfolk were the favorites, but as she continued up the eastern seaboard, the weather became colder and the fog thicker. It was Boston!

German submarines were wreaking havoc in the Atlantic, and new phases such as "short of war", "Neutrality Patrol", and "convoy" became commonplace in Atlantic Fleet jargon. There was to be no rest and the first major mission while assigned to the Atlantic Fleet was in the making.

After pressure by Great Britain on the Icelandic government, the U.S. was allowed to relieve the 15,000 British Empire troops protecting Iceland. A reinforced brigade of marines under the command of Brigadier General John Marston, USMC, and a squadron of patrol planes were the first contingent of American forces. Transporting this force was a convoy made up of 23 ships, including the *Brooklyn*. It was designated Task Force 19, under Rear Admiral David McD. LeBreton, and arrived in Reykjavik, Iceland on July 7, 1941. The German intelligence service, which was surprised by the occupation, was in shock and had much to explain to Hitler for this miscalculation. This was the first American Naval task force to embark on an expeditionary mission on this undeclared, but very real war. Men on the *Brooklyn*, as well as the other ships of the force, were warned to shoot at any enemy (German) craft above, on or below the surface if they came within range. There were incidents, particularly as the force neared Reykjavik. Many depth charge were dropped by escorting destroyers, but no kills were confirmed. The pitiful evidence of raiding German submarines seemed to be everywhere as wreckage, rafts and life boats were sighted. This was just the beginning. For the *Brooklyn* and her crew, who a few weeks before were basking in Hawaiian sun, the change to bitter fog laden cold waters with death and destruction just a torpedo wake away was dramatic.

The odor of cod fish pervaded everything in the immediate area of Reykjavik, and was commented on none to kindly by American sailors. Quickly, the city of Reykjavik was dubbed, "Rinkydink"! The cold and miserable terrain, and peculiar people of Iceland were gladly tolerated in view of the significant strategic gains made by the allies. Germany was denied this all important location in geo-military strategy, and the allies now could extend patrols further than ever before. It was a bargain at twice the price!

The carriers *Wasp* and *Yorktown*, both destined as Pacific war casualties, often operated with the *Brooklyn* from the Azores to the main base at Bermuda. This was known as the *Central Atlantic Neutrality Patrol* which operated out to 30 degrees West longitude. It was composed of Carrier Division 3 (*Ranger, Wasp* and *Yorktown*), and as of July 15, 1941, Cruiser Division 8 (*Brooklyn, Nashville, Philadelphia*, and *Savannah*). Cruiser Division 8, no stranger to prominent flag officers, was now commanded by Admiral H. Kent Hewitt, who would later gain fame in the North African and Italian campaigns. The cruiser patrolled the central Atlantic in order to protect allied shipping from any form of

enemy attack. There were periscope sightings, and a phantom German cruiser which turned out to be a British battleship, HMS *Rodney*. Each day brought some new challenge, and as the ship was operating under war time conditions, the transition that was shortly to take place did not cause much difficulty. The anticipation that the crew felt was akin to that which football players feel in the minutes between the coin toss and the kickoff. Finally, after just returning from gunnery practice to Hamilton Harbor, Bermuda, the anticipation was over. The Japanese had ended it with a surprise attack on the Naval and Army bases in Pearl Harbor on December 7, 1941.

Wilbur Davis, an exuberant sailor, who wore out the sleeve on his jumper by sewing and ripping off his gunner's mate crow recalled that rumors abounded, and the following day, the *Brooklyn* hurriedly left for Martinique with the carrier *Wasp*. This, to prevent the Vichy French warships stationed there from actively entering the war on the side of the Axis. A settlement was soon reached and a confrontation avoided. The French ships which included an aircraft carrier *(Bearn)* and one of the fastest cruisers in the world, the *Emile Bertain*, never played a more significant role than creating anxiety over their proximity to Allied shipping lanes. Interestingly, the *Emile Bertain* would later work hand in glove with the *Brooklyn* during the Operation Anvil, the landings in southern France in August, 1944.

She steamed for New York for the addition of short range anti-aircraft guns and general repairs. She claimed a submarine kill on her way back to the U.S. Many onlookers swore that a torpedo just missed her stern as the ship's spotter aircraft (SOC's) were dropping bombs on the target. The war that everyone had expected had now begun.

THE *BROOKLYN* FIGHTS FOR FREEDOM

For the first several months, the *Brooklyn*, now armed with additional 20mm AAA, and carrying nearly 2,000 more tons in additional weight since her launching in 1937, escorted convoys across the Atlantic. Now using heavy escort forces including cruisers and battleships, convoys were getting through with little or no loss at this early stage of American involvement in the war.

These were the early days, days of learning and gaining experience. The *Brooklyn* had fallen into an important routine of escorting fast convoys across the Atlantic. On June 12, 1942, a new Captain reported aboard. He required no orientation, as he had recently been her executive officer. Captain Francis C. Denebrink relieved Captain Stone. It was rare in the Naval Service for a former executive officer to come back as a ship's captain, but it did happen, much to the appreciation of those who had served with Captain Denebrink previously. Always a stickler for proper procedure, timeliness, and training, these traits would save the lives of 1500 men less than three months later. Denebrink was not a man to remain aloof from the men of his ship, and often chatted with them. He showed genuine interest, and it was appreciated.

The USS *Wakefield*, AP-21, formerly the SS *Manhattan*, one of the three largest (24,289 tons) American Merchant Marine ships converted to troop transport, was in a fast convoy returning from England in early September 1942. Task Force 38, which included the *Brooklyn* provided the escort. The *Wakefield* was crowded with civilian construction workers and counting her crew, she was carrying 1,500 men. On September 3, she caught fire, which quickly spread.

Not content with simply creating an effective fighting unit, Captain Denebrink had requested that the *Brooklyn* also be designated a rescue ship in the event of a major disaster. The officers and crew made thorough preparation for a contingency they hoped would never happen. This was fortunate for the 1500 men aboard the *Wakefield*. As soon as she indicated her plight to the Convoy commander, the *Brooklyn* and destroyer USS *Mayo* were granted permission to come alongside the burning ship and affect the rescue. Everything had already been thought of, including extra bedding, medicine and toilet facilities. The *Brooklyn's* crew was on top of this problem from the outset. The *Mayo* took off 247 passengers, and the cruiser quickly rescued nearly 800 more. At the request of the *Wakefield's* captain, the rescue ships backed off to allow the remaining 400 plus crew on the burning ship to bring the situation under control. In less than 30 minutes, it was obvious that the fire could not be conquered, and the *Brooklyn* was asked to return for the balance of the crew. Forty-five minutes later, the *Wakefield's* captain left the ship as the last one rescued. Miraculously, not one man lost his life. The rescue was an unqualified success. The reason was obvious, the planning by the cruiser's leadership and crew. A rescue of this magnitude, in waters known to harbor enemy submarines, was nothing short of magnificent. Captain Denebrink was later awarded the Navy and Marine Corps Medal for this achievement.

The *Wakefield*, still burning, was towed to Halifax and beached. She burned steadily for eight days, yet even with all the superstructural damage, she was repaired and returned to service within two years.

After this incident, the *Brooklyn* began to make preparations along with her sisters, *Savannah* and *Philadelphia*, for one of the most important convoys of World War II, and the beginning of the Allied offensive. The month selected was November 1942. The place was North Africa, in a place called Morocco.

THE *BROOKLYN* PITCHES WHEN IT IS TIME TO "PLAY BALL": *OPERATION TORCH*

It was time for the American Navy in the Atlantic to take the offensive. The days of defensive operations had come to an end, and for the Axis, *Operation Torch* signified the beginning of the end. The light cruiser *Brooklyn* and her sisters would play a decisive role in the North African invasion.

The Allies had been reeling from one Axis victory after another. Pearl Harbor, Singapore, Dunkirk, and Tobruk were just a few sites where the Allies had experienced defeat. Hitler's armies were knocking on Moscow's door, and for 18 months the Soviet Union had been subjected to the horrors of war, Nazi style. A second front was repeatedly demanded by Stalin, and the Allies knew that they must accommo-

date an ally who, virtually alone, was desperately trying to hold off the German war machine. A significant amphibious landing on the European coast was not considered a viable option at this stage of the war, so another location had to be selected. Criteria for determining the initial point for an allied assault centered on three major needs. First, the protection of the Suez Canal was vital to preserve this important supply line; secondly, a foothold was required that by it's proximity would enable a firm stepping stone into Europe; and finally, something valuable enough to the Axis as to cause a substantial political and military commitment. North Africa was ideal, so a joint operation was planned for an attack against Morocco (American force) and Oran and Algiers (joint American and British force). It is at this point that political theory met with military reality. An amphibious force had to be rapidly assembled, trained, protected, and transported several thousand miles across a rough ocean that was submarine infested. Admiral Henry K. Hewitt, and General George S. Patton, both who would figure prominently in the war years to come, were chosen for the command roles in the attack on Morocco, and the *Brooklyn* would become an important element of the overall allied plan, to be coined *Operation Torch*.

The overall plan called for three separate attacks on the North African coasts. The Center Naval Task Forces would assault and capture Oran; the Eastern Naval Task Force would attack Algiers, and the Western Task Force would attempt the capture of Casablanca. This was to be the first Anglo-American amphibious operation, and the largest in the war to date.

The strategic assignment of the American Western Task Force (TF 34), carrying 35,000 green troops, was to assault and capture Casablanca and it's valuable harbor through a series of landings. The landing sites chosen were Safi, Fedala, Mehdia, and Port Lyautey, all on the Moroccan coast. The coast was inhospitable with it's rocky shores and coupled with a treacherous ocean, the landings would be precarious at best. In addition to natural barriers and emplaced shore batteries, the area was defended by units of the French fleet. The potential opposing force consisted of the *Jean Bart*, a modern battleship, light cruisers, and the large high speed destroyers that the French Navy had built during the treaty years.

Units of the Western Task Force starting from the Eastern Seaboard of the U.S. met a various locations in the Atlantic. The *Brooklyn*, *Savannah* and *Philadelphia* with a destroyer screen left from Norfolk and at sea, awaited the balance of the Task Force approximately 450 miles off of the east coast. When the force assembled, Ensign Ray Wasarhaley's fears of the unknown were somewhat mitigated as he watched major elements of the Atlantic fleet form up. Most ships were manned by reservists going into their first real combat. In fact, over 30 officers and half of the cruiser's crew had never even been to sea. Yet, there was an aura of confidence even in view of General Patton's derisive remarks that the Navy would probably screw up and deliver the landing force late to the wrong beach. The Navy proved him incorrect.

Secrecy was stressed as Allied forces were

uncertain as to French reactions to landings. The obsession of secrecy was so great that even the garbage was sunk en route and bilges could only be pumped at night to prevent detection. Fortunately the trip over was reasonably uneventful despite all of the media hype about the landings being in Casablanca even before the Task Force sailed. There were a number of submarine sightings, but no ships were successfully attacked.

As the fleet approached the Atlantic coast of Africa, it split into three groups. The *Brooklyn* and the heavy cruiser *Augusta* comprised the fire support group of Task Group 34.9, the Center Attack Group, the largest of the task force, and charged with the capture of Fedhala, and the subsequent occupation of Casablanca from the rear.

The initial concern of the *Brooklyn* and the balance of the force were the large caliber shore batteries in and around Cape Fedhala, particularly those of Batterie Fort Blondin at Sherki (Chergui). On November 8, 1942, eleven months since the European Axis declared war on the U.S., the assault began. Captain Denebrink had set the tone a week earlier when he informed the crew that this was to be a "killing affair". The sober realization that effective leadership, discipline and accurate gunnery were the elements that would prevent death and destruction to the landing force and the *Brooklyn* herself set in. At 0400 the assault began with the first wave, and opposing fire commenced quite by accident from a French corvette that found herself among the transports. Quickly, the French ship was subdued by the fleet minesweeper USS *Auk*, AM-57, but the die was cast. Shortly after 0500 and the force observed French searchlights trained first upward and then targeting on the transports. Soon thereafter, the shore battery at Chergui opened up on the assault force, and the USS *Murphy*, DD-603 responded. Taken under fire, she requested assistance. It was time for the *Brooklyn* to "Play Ball". Steaming in from her patrol area, and launching a Seagull for spotting, the *Brooklyn* commenced firing. In an 85 minute period, she fired over 750 rounds of 6 inch. During that last few minutes, she confirmed the rumor that the U.S. Navy had "machine gun" cruisers. During this bombardment, she disabled the offending battery, firing a shell every 6.7 seconds! Shortly after the light cruiser's rain of fire began, the spotter aircraft simply cautioned, "No change, No change". The French soon discovered that speed was not the major advantage in cruiser design, but the quality of the main battery.

By 0800, the task group became aware of another enemy threat in the form of it's navy, both surface and sub-surface, emerging from Casablanca harbor. The *Brooklyn* just happened to be in an intercept position to prevent the sortie from harming the transports.

The Allied covering force charged with protecting the landing force became preoccupied with reducing the battleship *Jean Bart* to rubble, and were unable to respond to the sortie of lighter forces. Consequently, the *Brooklyn* and her heavier consort, the *Augusta* met this new threat which consisted of the *Primauguet*, a light cruiser, two destroyer leaders and five destroyers. This enemy force which was directed to exit Casablanca Harbor and dash up the coast to break up the landing, mounted eight 6 inch guns, over two dozen 5 inch caliber guns and 40 plus torpedoes. This was a formidable force, yet the *Brooklyn* and *Augusta* in company with destroyers *Wilkes* and *Swanson* were able to thwart the attack and drive the French force into the waiting jaws of the covering force. Witnesses on the transports and aboard both French and American warships were impressed with the terrier like quality demonstrated by the light cruiser. Reducing the range by steaming at full speed toward the enemy force, she opened up with her main battery and by 0900, the French were retiring to Casablanca harbor. Within 20 minutes, the *Brooklyn* and *Augusta* had driven off the attacking French force, and the covering group had begun it's pounding.

Just as the *Brooklyn* returned to her assigned patrol area near the transports, she was attacked by a submarine, the French *Amazone,* which fired five torpedoes. Observers aboard were truly thankful for Captain Denebrink's decision to sharply turn 90 degrees to the port. They then watched the torpedoes pass harmlessly down the starboard side. Had Captain Denebrink chosen to turn in a different direction, then this narrative would just be coming to an end.

As Captain Denebrink had his hands full in dodging torpedoes, a second attack by French destroyers was quickly brewing. The cruiser *Primauguet* in company with several destroyers reopened the surface engagement at about 1010. The *Brooklyn* and her partner, the *Augusta* began repelling the attackers with concentrated fire from their main batteries. These two cruisers were performing some rather fancy footwork, and at the same time hurling 8 inch and 6 inch shells at the attacking force. During this engagement, the lucky cruiser received her one and only hit of the war, a 5 inch shell fired by a destroyer which turned out to be a dud. At about 1045, it struck the main deck and bounced off, wounding six men. In exchange, the *Brooklyn* shot the French destroyer *Boulonnais* to pieces, and was the major contributor to the destruction of the cruiser *Primauguet*.

A third surface attack by three smaller French ships materialized in the early afternoon, but they too were routed and driven away from the transport area by the *Brooklyn* and *Augusta*.

The Naval Battle for Casablanca ended with this final sortie. The light cruiser earned high marks for her performance, including the praise of a little known writer, Samuel Elliot Morison, who was riding her during the day's work. At battle stations for nearly 16 hours, the crew of the *Brooklyn* broke up three enemy naval attacks and prevented a major shore battery from disrupting the landing force. She fired nearly 2,400 six-inch shells, and was complimented by Admiral Hewitt for her aggressive and determined spirit.

Few commands ever participate in a sea battle, let alone three victorious attacks in one 24 hour period. This was to be one of the finest hours for this ship and her dedicated crew. The cruiser never shirked her duty, and charged in without regard for anything except her mission.

The *Brooklyn* was soon to exchange places with the USS *Cleveland*, CL-55, a successor design to the *Brooklyn/St. Louis* class. She was low on ammunition and the *Cleveland* was fully loaded. On November 9, 1942, the *Brooklyn* moved to assume escort duty for the carriers, but the battle was not yet over. She would still shoot down a French fighter, and dodge many real and suspected submarine attacks.

Aside from being low on ammunition, she was also quickly running out of fuel oil, so it was necessary for her to refuel as soon as possible. She put to sea to rendezvous with a tanker, but heavy weather prevented it. Worse still, her bridge windows had been blown out by continuous firing, and as she was virtually out of fuel, her buoyancy caused a sickening movement that affected many of the crew who had just begun to acquire their sea legs.

Finally, she was ordered to put back into Casablanca Harbor and fuel from a tanker now stationed there. This she was able to do on November 13, and the crew was able to get a motionless nights sleep.

Within a week, the *Brooklyn* was now on her way back to the U.S. as a battle hardened and scarred veteran. In transit, she encountered one of the worst storms in modern history, and Thanksgiving Day, 1942 was prepared from dehydrated, frozen and canned foods. However, success had been realized in her first major combat test, and Allied victory in North Africa was assured. Another of the *Brooklyn/St. Louis* class cruisers had proven their worth, many times over.

The ship arrived at the Brooklyn Navy Yard on December 1, 1942. Minor repairs were made and many of the crew enjoyed a richly deserved liberty. Just before Christmas, however, she was ordered back to Casablanca to provide heavy escort for a convoy.

Nearly all convoys were escorted by cruisers or battleships to prevent attack by the capitol ships of the German Navy. A standing policy in the German Navy, fortunately discovered by the Allies early in the war was put to Allied advantage. The German surface fleet refrained from attacking heavily guarded convoys simply due to a fear of being damaged. Convoys were safe

from surface attack even with the smallest cruiser or oldest battleship in company. The very presence of a cruiser of the *Brooklyn* class was sufficient deterrent to a German surface attack. In fact, the first question often asked was, "is there a cruiser present?" If the answer was affirmative, then the attack was postponed.

The *Brooklyn* was forced to return to New York due to engine troubles early in the trip over. After repairs were made, she was to escort three convoys to Casablanca during the period December 1942 through June 1943. During this period, she was to receive a new commanding officer to relieve the respected and well liked Captain Denebrink. Captain Humbert V. Ziroli, who learned his trade as the executive officer of sister ship, *Philadelphia* assumed command on February 14, 1943.

The *Brooklyn* would be a vital participant in the next major offensive of the European campaign, and that was the naval and amphibious attack on Sicily during the period July 10-14, 1943. Prior to the next invasion, coined *Husky,* there was training in Casco Bay, Maine, and next a month's overhaul at the Philadelphia Navy Yard. She had minor alterations that improved her air defense capability. By early May 1943, she sported additional 20MM guns, and an improved fire direction system. Slowly, she and her sisters were being retrofitted based on war experience, primarily centering around the need for a saturation close in defense system against high speed aircraft.

The role of the cruiser was changing by default from the more romantic ideal of a commerce raider destroyer and fleet scout to amphibious assault fire support and task force anti-aircraft protection. Cruisers that relied upon the 50 caliber MG or 3 inch/50 cal gun to fight 300 mph plus aircraft were easy prey for concentrated air attack as experiences in the early months of the war would tragically prove. The *Brooklyn/St. Louis* class, as yard time and periods that they could be spared from front line service, were being rearmed with 20mm and 40mm as well as improved fire control systems. The concept of AAA guns mounted in galleries for concentrated

The Brooklyn *shortly after her first overhaul in early 1943. She now sports many 20 mm antiaircraft guns and the one of the early radar installations. Her bridge is still pre-war vintage, yet she now has life rafts on all of her turrets as a precaution.*

The Brooklyn *after her final wartime refit. Her conning tower is gone and her superstructure has been reduced by a deck level. She also has 40 mm guns in tubs in addition to 20 mm guns. Her bridge is now open to facilitate antiaircraft defense, and she was the look of a modern World War II light cruiser.*

defense came into vogue and was most prominent on the heavier units of the fleet.

OPERATION HUSKY, PUNCTURING THE SOFT UNDER BELLY OF EUROPE

The lexicon of the Twentieth Century would be sadly lacking were it not for the contributions of Sir Winston Churchill, war time prime minister of Great Britain. It was he that coined the term "soft under belly of Europe", referring to the suspected weakness of Germany's Axis partner Italy, in repulsing an assault by Allied forces. Unfortunately for the Allies, Germany came to the rescue of her faltering partner soon after the Allies launched their first major seaborne attack against the continent of Europe. The operation to attack Sicily was not considered easy, but after the successes in the African Desert, the Allies were counting on a dispirited Italian response, and maybe even trapping a substantial part of the German Armed forces.

Gathering in and around Oran Harbor in North Africa, over 2,500 vessels designated to carry, escort or support 250,000 troops prepared for the attack on Italy. Facing this sizeable force was an estimated 370,000 combined Italian and German troops. And, as with the previous invasion of North Africa, secrecy was only in the mind of the planners. All attempts to prevent the enemy from knowing the destination of the forces gathering in Oran Harbor were dashed by such things as junior officers passing out maps of Sicily and tour guides for the assault troops.

The *Brooklyn*, in her first visit to the Mediterranean was part of a primary fire support group that included the new *Cleveland* class light cruiser, the USS *Birmingham*, CL-62 and nine destroyers. Task Force 86, designated Joss or Licata was to provide fire support for U.S. Army assault units under the command of Major General Lucian K. Truscott. This was the left flank of the overall operation.

While under the overall command of Rear

Admiral Richard L. Connolly, the fire support unit of which the veteran cruiser was a member was under the control of newly promoted Rear Admiral Lawrence Dubose. Admiral Dubose had just been advanced in grade after his successful command of the USS *Portland*, CA-33 during her many bitter and violent night clashes with the Japanese in and around Guadalcanal.

The major objective for the Joss Force was to take and hold the port and airfield facilities at Licata. By early morning on July 10, 1943, the *Brooklyn* was on station and ready to fulfill her role. As usual, the trip from Oran to the landing site was through some of the roughest storms on record, but the crew of the *Brooklyn* had been seasoned for this. Promptly at 0430, the command was given, and the staccato bark of multiple 6 inch guns interrupted the peace of the night, and the battle to take Sicily and eventually all of southern Europe was on.

Of course, the *Brooklyn* and her counterparts were not free to amble back and forth across the assault line and fire at targets of opportunity. The Italian and German Air Forces threw their entire weight into disrupting the landings, and several times the cruiser was near missed by bombs. On the evening of the 11th, the night was lit up by flares dropped by attacking German bombers, and her luck nearly ran out as she was near missed and the *Birmingham* was strattled. By July 13, the pre-selected targets had been dealt with, and the *Brooklyn* was asked to visit shell fire on targets requested from ground forces including those at Agrigento. The old SOC's were kept busy spotting, and the accuracy of fire was outstanding. Interestingly, the designers of the *Brooklyn/St. Louis* class probably never envisioned a role such as concentrated fire support for such graceful ships. It didn't really matter however, as there are many foot soldiers alive today thanks to the support provided by the *Brooklyn* and others of her kind.

The *Brooklyn* was a lucky ship, and brought her crew through this action safely. One of her

crew, L. M. Robbins, looked back nearly 50 years and told me it was like a dream. Even though there were multiple air raids, and the ship accidently ran afoul of an Allied minefield on the last day of her participation in the initial assault, she came through unharmed.

On the 14th, she and her sisters, *Boise* and *Savannah* left for Algiers, and within a month, she was back in home port, New York. Two days after her arrival in New York on August 15, 1943, the Sicilian campaign ended in Allied victory. The New York visit was not to last, as she was soon recalled to the Mediterranean and was later detailed to replace the *Savannah*, which had been seriously damaged by a German glider bomb on September 11, 1943. The *Brooklyn* as part of Task Group 81.5 under Admiral Lyle A. Davidson would provide needed fire support for the Salerno Operation.

Captain Ziroli was relieved on October 11, 1943, and was succeeded by Captain Robert W. Cary, just off a sister ship, the USS *Savannah*. The damaged *Savannah* had made her way to Malta for temporary repairs, and would now be sent back to the U.S. for a major repair and overhaul job. Captain Cary had distinguished himself well during the crisis that befell the *Savannah* in early September when a glider bomb plunged through turret #3 and exploded just above the keel in the magazine.

With the Sicilian campaign wrapped up, the *Brooklyn* spent her time in various in theater roles such as escorting the new fast battleship, USS *Iowa*, BB-61 which was carrying a greatly aged President Roosevelt to the Teheran Conference. As she was about to wrap up the year, her crew entertained many children of beleaguered Malta, and a even today reports persist that the Christmas Tree that decorated the festivities was stolen from under the nose of the Island Governor.

ANZIO (*OPERATION SHINGLE*), SOUTHERN FRANCE (*OPERATION ANVIL*) AND HOME

The *Brooklyn* had become one of the premier fire support ships in the European Theater of operations and could always be depended on to locate and destroy targets. The landings at Anzio, which were nearly a disaster for the Allies were in part successfully prosecuted due to the cooperative can do spirit of the cruiser and a never say die crew. The assault on the Anzio-Nettuno area became a stalemate as allied forces were virtually pinned down on the beachhead. The whole purpose of a landing force quickly exploiting a flanking maneuver was thwarted by the determined resistance of crack German troops. In short, the Allies had a potential Dunkirk in reverse on their hands. *Operation Shingle* was in trouble.

On January 22, 1943, the landings began, and within a few short days, nearly 70,000 troops with over 750 field guns and tanks began slugging it out with the opposing forces. Captain Cary was overall fire support group commander (Task Group 81.8), and he came inshore through hostile minefields to deliver artillery assistance on call. The other half of his group, HMS *Penelope*, another six inch gun light cruiser was unfortunately sunk less than a month later by the submarine U410. L. M. Robbins well remembers the crew of the *Penelope* sharing it's gin with her American visitors from the *Brooklyn*. His last visit was on the night that preceded her tragic loss that resulted in over 80% casualties.

However, not only were the German ground forces formidable, but the air was filled with enemy fighters and bombers that rendered the area a living hell. The night only brought more enemy air attacks on the roadstead and the ships struggling to avoid being hit. Each night was punctuated with the erie lights of parachute flares and explosions. The *Brooklyn's* luck held, and she was finally relieved on February 9. On her last day, she fired 950 six inch shells. She was wearing out the barrels of her guns. Leaving Anzio was just fine with Lane Kohan, who had the dubious honor of being assigned to the masthead lookout (crows nest) on the foremast during an enemy air attack. An ME-109 literally flew under him at 50 feet above sea level. Almost in slow motion, he could look down on the pilot of the 300 mph fighter plane. That did it!

The tired cruiser sailed for Tunis, North Africa and embarked Rear Admiral Lyle A. Davidson. He was transferring his flag to the *Brooklyn* from the USS *Philadelphia*, CL-41 which would in rotation, take up continued fire support duties.

The cruiser was to return to the Anzio area and provide rotational fire support well into May 1943, and finally on May 26, the last shot was fired. The "Mighty B" had acquitted herself well, and had broken up a number of enemy concentrations. Her exclusive specialty was the ability to hit targets protected by gullies and ravines. These targets were difficult, if not impossible to hit with land based artillery fire. Her spotting aircraft, whether her own Seagulls or Piper Cubs of the Army expressed amazement at the accuracy and devastation of her fire.

Captain Cary had been temporarily relieved by Captain F. C. Layne until a formal transfer took place on April 12, 1944. It was on this date that Captain F. R. Dodge assumed command. Captain Dodge saw the *Brooklyn* through the victorious, but costly end of the Anzio campaign.

Less than a month from the end of *Operation Shingle, Operation Overlord*, the assault across the English Channel on Hitler's Fortress Europe at Normandy had begun on June 6, 1944. In tandem with *Operation Overlord* was *Operation Anvil* which was the assault on Southern France. The *Brooklyn* would fight her last battle as a unit of the U.S. Navy in the Cannes/Toulon area as part of Task Force 87 or the Camel Force. She would be in the finest company as she was joined by battleship *Arkansas*, heavy cruiser *Tuscaloosa*, light cruiser *Marblehead* as well as a number of Free French units.

On August 15, 1944, the *Brooklyn* began the bombardment of the playground of the rich. The bombardment group opened fire at 0730 guided by the cruiser's venerable SOC's. Fire support continued through the day as the *Brooklyn* and her consorts destroyed enemy pillboxes and other military targets. Within a week the Army under Major General Alexander M. Patch had advanced over 140 miles into the interior of France, and the German defenders were abandoning their weapons. The war was far from over, but *Operation Anvil*, also known as the poorest kept

secret of World War II was a complete success. On the her final fire support mission, she leveled enemy defenses on the shoreline of the La Napoule Gulf. The shooting war was over for this battled hardened ship.

Prior to steaming for home and a much needed overhaul and modernization, the *Brooklyn* carried Vice Admiral Hewitt, the American architect of naval victory in the Mediterranean, on a tour of recently established American Naval bases. Finally, on November 21, she departed the area and arrived in New York on November 30, 1944, 15 months away from home.

OVERHAUL AND MODERNIZATION

The *Brooklyn* was now nearly eight years old. Still modern by normal naval standards, but times were not normal. The *Cleveland* class light cruisers had virtually eclipsed the *Brooklyn/St. Louis* class and although they had three less six inch guns, they more than compensated with twelve 5 inch 38 caliber guns and improved fire control. The *Brooklyn* had some catching up to do, consequently she entered the Brooklyn Navy Yard for a face lift. Improvements and alterations took the form of adding blisters for greater stability; replacing the conning tower; adding 40mm mounts; and lowering the forward superstructure by a deck level; and adding improved visibility through the use of an open bridge area. The experience of the USS *Savannah* indicated that not only would the addition of blisters improve stability, but would also add needed longitudinal strength to the hull. Improved fire control apparatus and radar electronics were also added in anticipation of being transferred to the Pacific area and having to deal with the Japanese air threat.

She had entered the yard under the temporary command of Commander Herbert F. Eckberg, and when she emerged on April 12, 1945, she was under the command of William F. Fitzgerald. The war was over before any forward assignment came, and until October 30, 1945, the *Brooklyn* spent her time in training and preparation for something novel, being the first major ship mothballed. She also became the first ship of an newly created fleet, the 16th or Inactive fleet. Captain Fitzgerald, late of the *Brooklyn* became the commanding officer of the *Philadelphia* group of the Reserve Fleet.

Decommissioned on January 30, 1946, she was now silent except for a maintenance crew and rested alongside Pier A of the Philadelphia Navy Yard. Sporting four well earned Battle Stars, she became just another warship among the many in the yard as it filled up with dozens of ships that no one seemed to notice any longer.

REDEMPTION AND SALE TO A GRATEFUL OWNER - CHILE. THE *BROOKLYN* FINDS A NEW HOME AND A NEW NAME, THE *O'HIGGINS*

Six U.S. Navy cruisers were to be sold to three South American countries that had petitioned the U.S. to sell modern warships. The end of the Second World War found the U.S. Navy with a vast surplus of relatively modern warships. Six of the *Brooklyn/St. Louis* class were selected for overhaul and renovation for their new owners. The

Chilean and American officers survey the sleeping cruiser. The Chilean's have already hoisted their flag on the mainmast. They are standing just forward of the hanger cover. The aft hanger and square stern of the Brooklyn/St. Louis *class light cruisers were hallmarks of these great ships.*

ex USS *Boise* and USS *Phoenix* were sold to *Argentina*, the ex USS *Philadelphia* and USS *St. Louis* went to Brazil and the USS *Nashville* and USS *Brooklyn* were sold to Chile. All were sold for 10 percent of their original price plus the cost of renovation or about $7.8 million. The Mutual Defense Assistance Program agreed to by each nation provided the legal vehicle, and obviously by selling two each to the three major South American powers, a balance of power was maintained.

The *Brooklyn* was sold to Chile on January 9, 1951 when that country's flag was hoisted on June 30, 1951, she was formally commissioned in the Chilean Navy as the Crucero *O'Higgins*. She became a unit of the cruiser fleet under Vice Admiral Immanuel Holger, and was joined later that year by the *Nashville*, now the Crucero *Prat*. The *O'Higgins* had been reconditioned for her new owner at the Philadelphia Navy Yard and arrived in Chilean waters in January 1952.

The Chilean Navy was at a low ebb when the two light cruisers were added to their inventory. Their naval forces were not merely obsolete, but in a state of constant disrepair and unavailability. Few of the ships were capable of mid 20th Century warfare, even to a limited degree. Antisubmarine and antiaircraft defense capability was virtually non existent. The two light cruisers were Godsend's to this nation. The *O'Higgins* and *Prat* were more to the Chilean people than two grey hulled obsolecsing cruisers, they were a symbol of the revival of Chile as a Southern Hemispheric power. These ships would dominate the Pacific coast of South America for decades to come, and the citizens of Chile knew it. Neither ships would ever fire their guns in anger, but the Navy now had the teeth to back up any international political moves made by their government. In general, both ships operated up and down the coast from their base at Talcahuano conducting patrols and showing the flag. They also participated in various multi national naval maneuvers, and often old sailors aboard American warships were surprised to see ghosts from the past war suddenly appear from

The former USS Brooklyn, *now the Chilean Crucero* O'Higgins *alongside a dock at the Chilean Naval Station at Talcahuano. She had been the pride of the Chilean Navy for over 40 years and served as its flagship for many of those years.*

The Brooklyn/O'Higgins *being towed in company with another vessel destined for scrapping in India. She is riding high on her final voyage.*

over the horizon in the form of the cruisers *O'Higgins* and *Prat*.

It was not until 1960, that the Chilean Navy did more for the citizenry than represent them at sea. In the early morning hours of May 21, 1960, an 8.2 scale earthquake that lasted 81 seconds hit southern Chile. It was followed by a tidal wave that compounded the damage done by the quake. The men from the *Prat* and *O'Higgins* as well as others from the naval forces ashore assisted in rescue and providing food and medical attention to the thousands of people injured and made homeless by the disaster. The cruis-

ers were now truly a part of the landscape and national fabric.

For years thereafter, the *O'Higgins* continued with patrol duties and acted as the flagship of the navy. Many career naval officers and others who selected private industry or government service owed their initial training to their experiences aboard this cruiser. Most of the flag officers that are or have been Naval Attache's in Washington D.C. were brought up on the aging cruiser as cadets. She had become a national institution, but by the mid 1970's, she was getting old and cranky. On August 12, 1974, the

old cruiser unfortunately hit an uncharted pinnacle in the Smith Canal near the islands of Angelotti. The sharp rock cut a jagged hole approximately 75 meters in length which flooded the boiler and engine rooms. For all intents and purposes, the *O'Higgins* was finished as a warship and was now only of value for spare parts for the *Prat*. But, she was not just any warship, she was more to the people of Chile - she was a symbol of strength and vitality. It was decided that an all out national effort would be made to rebuild her.

There were other forces at work during this period beyond that of the charity of the citizenry, however. Argentina was always seen as a potential enemy, and in 1978, when the *O'Higgins* was rebuilt better than new, tensions intensified over the ownership of a series of islands near the Beagle Canal. The simple fact that the *O'Higgins* was again a viable military weapon was an influence in the successful resolution of the difficulties. In addition, there was obviously some hard feeling with the U.S. which had refused to assist the Chilean Navy in it's effort to rebuild the *O'Higgins*. This was peculiar especially in view of the Chilean government's refusal to allow Soviet warships the luxury of using their naval facilities as a Pacific base. But, international politics often makes no sense.

The Chilean Navy enlisted the help of many artisans and university students to help redesign and modernize the old ship. Most of the damaged or worn parts had to be designed and hand forged. The entire country more or less contributed in spirit or actuality to rebuild this ship and by 1978, she was back in action. She was modernized to the extent that she was again fully capable, but as a 1940's vintage warship. This was a triumph for a nation and one of it's proudest moments.

The *O'Higgins* would serve the people of Chile for another fourteen years and end her days as an active unit on January 14, 1992. This was nearly 40 years to the day from the date she sailed into her country's home waters for the first time. The farewell address was given by Vice Admiral Jorge Llorente Dominguez and many a tear was shed as the flag was hauled down for the final time. With the passing of the *O'Higgins* (*Brooklyn*), the world also saw the end of the all gun cruiser era which had only lasted a scant century.

On October 7, 1992, the cruiser was sold to the Income Ship Trade Company of India to be towed away for scrapping. She was sold for approximately $1 million by a cartel of former Chilean Naval Officers who had purchased her from the Navy.

An important era in naval history had past - she was the last survivor of that era.

USS *CONCORD* CL-10
"LAST TO FIGHT"

The USS *Concord* CL-10 was one of the ten "Omaha" class light cruisers built as the result of the 1916 naval expansion program. Also included in the three year congressional appropriation were 267 four piper destroyers and two battlecruisers. The battle- cruisers would eventually become the celebrated aircraft carriers, *Lexington* CV-2 and *Saratoga* CV-3. The Naval

The new Omaha *class light Cruiser, USS* Concord *CL-10, at William Cramp and Sons Shipyard in Philadelphia, PA, on October 13, 1923. She will be commissioned on November 15, 1923 and Captain O. G. Murfin, USN, will be her first skipper. The two most obvious reasons for her obsolescence, even at this point, are her broadside six inch guns and four stacks.*

The Concord *anchored in Port Sudan during her first major cruise after commissioning and shakedown. The time is April 1924, and cruisers like the* Concord *were often used as a means of flag showing and enforcers of American diplomacy.*

Arms Limitation Treaty penned in Washington D.C. in 1922 would later ensure the temporary suspension of international capitol ship construction, but left the door open for aircraft carriers such as the "*Sara*" and the "*Lady Lex*".

THE FIRST BATTLE - ON PAPER AND WITHIN THE NAVY DEPARTMENT

The *Concord* and her sisters were built over an eight year period from the 1916 congressional authorization through the commissioning of the last of the class, the Memphis CL-13 on February 4, 1925. The lengthy construction period for this class reflected a national anti military and arms mood, yet there was another more direct cause. Argument, dissention and disagreement in the Navy Department, and in particular, the Bureaus of Construction and Repair, and Engineering caused unreasonable and costly delays. Added to the original design, the class was burdened with fore and aft twin 6 inch/53 turrets, supplementary torpedo mounts and underwater communication and hydrophone equipment. This overloaded a design that was already top heavy and ungainly. It also caused a slight loss of speed from the intended 35 plus knots to just under 35 knots. The class experienced other problems such as being crammed too full of heat producing machinery which caused the interior crew spaces to resemble an oven in the tropics. A steel deck also contributed to the problem of heat retention. As construction eventually materialized into a ship, more complaints were registered.

The *Omaha's* were wet ships and when sharply heeled would ship water over the main deck, flooding the torpedo mounts. The anti-aircraft battery of short range 3 inch/50 caliber open mounts was inadequate and more of a sop

to air attack fearmongers than an effective obstacle to air attack. One of the class, the USS *Marblehead* CL-12 would regretfully find this out in the one sided duels with Japanese bombers in and around Java in early 1942. The fearmongers were right.

Worst still were the comments of foreign naval observers who expected the U.S. Navy to produce a modern competitor. The *Omaha's* were called Victorian, archaic and quaint. They were the last warships of any navy in the 20th Century built with a broadside battery. The *Omaha's* simply were outclassed and in actuality obsolete at birth. The intended roles of this class as destroyer leader and advance scouts for the gun battle line never materialized. Radar and the airplane consigned them to lesser occupations. Interestingly, however, those who served aboard them ignored the stated pitfalls of the class and were fiercely loyal. The *Omaha's* were fast, and there are claims that the *Concord* was able to make 37 plus knots for many hours without breakdown while in the Japanese infested North Pacific. A handy advantage when trying to avoid searching bombers and other warships. As to the crowded crew conditions, most "*Conk*" as the *Concord* was

nicknamed crewmen remember her as clean, sleek, and a pleasure to serve in. So much for official criticism.

The *Concord* shared basic characteristics with her nine sisters (see chart above).

The *Concord* was laid down on March 29, 1920 at the William Cramp and Sons Shipyard in Philadelphia, Penn. She was launched on December 15, 1921 with Mrs H. Butterick as her sponsor, and commissioned nearly two years later on November 3, 1923. Captain O. G. Murfin was assigned as her first skipper.

THE INTER-WAR YEARS

After her initial period of shakedown and righting minor builder mistakes, the new cruiser embarked on a flag showing trip to the Mediterranean and the near east. Like most of the battle force she was first assigned to duty in the Atlantic and was a frequent visitor to the Caribbean where she periodically called at Panama, Guantanamo Bay and other of the more or less notorious flesh pot ports. Of course, a bluejacket's pay of $21 month didn't go very far, but it was enough to relieve the tedium of spit and polish training and the ever present rituals

---

CONCORD'S BASIC CHARACTERISTICS

Displacement 7,100 tons LOA 555' 6"
Beam 55' 4.5" Boilers 12 Yarrow (265psi)
SHP 93,045 Speed 34.92 knots
Endurance: 4,970 miles @ 20kts/7,080 miles @ 15 Kts/8,460 miles @ 10 kts
Complement: peacetime 29 officers/429 enlisted
Complement: wartime 64 officers/750 enlisted
Main battery: 12 six inch/53 caliber guns/torpedoes
Anti aircraft battery: initially four 3 inch/50 caliber
Wartime AA battery: 20mm/40mm

---

observed by the Navy's pre-war commissioned officer hierarchy.

In 1924 and into 1925, the cruiser spent time in Pacific and Hawaiian waters as the Flagship of the Commander Destroyer Squadrons, Scouting Fleet. At long last she was actually employed in the role that her designers envisioned when they planned her a decade earlier. She operated out of Pearl Harbor when it was in it's infancy as the future bastion of the Pacific. Often, the *Concord* could be found in the Lahaina Roads off Maui, and she and her sisters would participate in attacks from the sea on the islands. War gaming was an annual affair and was codified as a Fleet Problem. One of the theoretical problems called for an air assault on the fleet in Hawaiian waters. Prophetically, the attacking forces prevailed.

In late 1925, she returned to the Atlantic and with other major fleet units was reviewed by President Hoover on June 4, 1927. From then on and until the beginning of World War II, the *Concord* was on a see saw schedule of assignments in the Atlantic and Pacific. During this same period a whole series of modern light cruisers began joining the fleet, the *Brooklyn/St. Louis* class, and the now nearly 20 year old *Omaha's* found themselves being pushed further in the background of naval operations.

The *Concord*, along with the rest of the U.S. Navy was on a virtual war footing from April 1, 1940, and she was based out of Pearl Harbor. She and the rest of the fleet began intensive training in anticipation for what everyone over the age of 10 knew was about to happen. The only questions were where, when and how. The why and the who were known - the Imperial Japanese Navy would respond to continued Roosevelt Administration demands to cease war like activities and the cold blooded murder of Chinese and Indochinese civilians!

A DESTINY FINALLY FULFILLED

World War II found the *Concord* in San Diego just about ready for an extensive shipyard overhaul. This meant that she would be fitted with 1.1 inch AA guns, surface and air search radars and Mark 51 AA gun directors. Later, the cranky 1.1's would be replaced by centerline 40mm Bofors and strategically placed 20mm AA guns.

By early February 1942, the modernized cruiser emerged from her overhaul and began a series of convoy escort and patrol operations that took her from the Society Islands to Bora Bora and ultimately back to the western South American coastline. This done, she embarked the now retired Rear Admiral Richard E. Byrd on a special assignment to investigate a variety of islands in the southeast Pacific. The trip began on September 5, 1943 and ended on November 24. Byrd, no stranger to adventure, was appointed by the President to determine the ultimate usefulness of a number of locations for military bases and postwar commercial aviation potential.

Unfortunately, the *Concord* suffered her first and only major catastrophe when a gasoline explosion killed 22 men including the ship's executive officer. Apparently, gasoline fumes had accumulated in several lower compartments and were ignited by a breaker switches on the rudder motors. A bomb could not have done more damage, yet the entire ship would have been vaporized had the explosion reached the 5000

The Concord *shortly after being modernized. She has lost her high fore and main masts, and her forward observation tower has been enlarged and enclosed.*

The Concord *passing through the Panama Canal in January 1932. She and other fleet units were on their way to the now traditional wargames in the Hawaiian area. A number of sailors are sitting on the railing of the port searchlight platform admiring the view, and probably cursing the humid heat.*

A Berliner Joyce OJ-2 seaplane is launched from port catapult of the Concord *while in route to Pearl Harbor in early 1932. In 1935, the* Concord*, along with most major fleet units, would have SOC-1's in their aviation units.*

A swimming party in Guantanamo Bay for the crew. Often warships would allow recreation such as swimming, but the ever present fear of sharks made a rifle armed lookout essential.

A stunning view of the stern of the USS Omaha at high speed. When these ships would pull out the stops, they could really move–a beautiful sight.

The Concord and her sister, the Omaha, take on fuel oil from the tanker Neches just before the dawn of World War II.

In an ironic twist, the local Japanese citizens welcome the American fleet to Maui in 1930.

One of the many streets in Honolulu where a sailor on liberty could spend his money. Most were clip joints, but it was the only game in town.

Clarence Weskamp, gun captain of the aft 6 inch/53 caliber turret when it fired the last salvo during World War II. The shots were fired at shore targets in the Kuriles.

The gun crew that fired the last shot. Most went on to civilian life and successful careers in business, industry and government. Unknowingly, on that August night in 1945, they forever gained a place in history.

gallons of aviation fuel and depth charge racks that were just above the storage area. The ship was severely damaged, yet Admiral Byrd refused to cancel the expedition. The dead were buried at sea and the journey was continued, even at half speed. The *Concord* limped into Balboa, Panama for a two month repair job, and by March 1944, she was back in action and on her way to the frozen north. Some of her sisters, *Trenton* CL-11 and *Richmond* CL-9, had already been in the North Pacific for several months. This area of naval operations was very little publicized, and the heroes of the north went virtually unnoticed in the wake of other more media grabbing events. However, a definite military objective was achieved by these old cruisers and others of Task Force 94, North Pacific Force. American soil was protected against future Japanese invasion, and the enemy's homeland was made insecure by repeated sea strikes and heavy bombardments. Coming within a few thousand yards of the Japanese homeland had a debilitating effect on civilian morale.

Finally, the aging cruiser would carry out her designers and builders wishes. She would fight other ships and bombard shore bases. She would also fight another enemy and that was bad weather on a scale unknown by her crew. 100 knot winds nicknamed "williwas" and incessant cold, wet fog were constant companions, and any luckless crewman falling overboard met death within minutes. The sea was just above freezing at 35 degrees.

In all she made ten strikes against shipping and shores bases on the Kuriles and other close islands. The first visit was on June 13, 1944, when she successfully bombarded Matsuwa To. Next she bombarded military and industrial installations on Paramushiru. After a brief overhaul at Mare Island Naval Shipyard she was back in the Aleutians on November 21, 1944.

For the next several months in company with other older and seasoned cruisers and destroyers,

she successfully attacked local shipping and shore targets. The attacks were almost routine: a fast run in, rapid bombardment and swift retirement. Praying for the mariner's nightmare, fog was a common pastime on the way out. This was the only true protection against Japanese bombers.

Ice flows were the next hazard and further operations against the Kuriles were delayed until late June 1945. Even in view of problems of ice, fog, and island fortifications, the *Concord* and accompanying destroyers penetrated the Sea of Okhotsk and sank four cargo vessels. There would be one further raid by the *Concord* in mid July, when she bombarded Suribachi, just 200 miles from the Japanese home island of Hokkaido. This was too close for comfort for the veteran cruiser, but she and her companions escaped unscathed.

Victory was in the air as the Allies had already defeated the Germans in Europe, and the Army Air Force and Navy carrier aircraft were bombing everything of value on the Japanese mainland. There would be one last attack by the *Concord* as a unit of the North Pacific Task Force under Rear Admiral J. H. Brown, Jr. This attack would forever establish a place for the *Concord* in U.S. Naval history.

THE LAST SALVO OF WORLD WAR II

The *Concord*, now under the command of Captain C. A. Rumble, also commanded a task group built around the cruiser. This group on the way to her designated target of Paramushiru, located a group of fishing trawlers and sank all six of them. Two hours later, the group moved into position with Admiral Brown's main force of two other light cruisers and nine destroyers. As the *Concord* lined up to begin her bombardment, crew members speculated on when the Japanese would surrender; it was no longer a case of if, but when. It was 2006 on August 12, 1945.

For the next twenty minutes all ships in the formation fired at military targets and commercial fishing cannery on the island. The range was 9,000 yards. Just before 2030, the bombardment ceased. Clarence Weskamp, the after centerline 6 inch gun turret captain noticed that the recoil liquid was overheating, and ordered a temporary cease fire to allow for cooling. By this time, all ships had quit firing. Westkamp contacted the gunnery officer for instructions because the guns were still loaded and ready to fire. The gunnery officer ordered the turret to fire the shells in the barrels, and two minutes after the task force had ceased fire, silence was broken by the *Concord's* after turret. It was approximately 8:30, and the last salvo of World War II had been fired. It had been fired by a light cruiser from another era, and ironically, the first shot of the war had been fired by a destroyer (*Ward*) of the same vintage. In between, a modern war had been waged and won.

Upon achieving this landmark, the *Concord* again began to recede into history. She entered Ominato, Japan as part of the occupation force and witnessed the shame of a defeated enemy. The Japanese military legacy was one of triumph at Pearl Harbor in 1941 and now, in 1945, children begging for the *Concord's* garbage while she was anchored in Japanese home waters.

She left Japan and sailed for the Philadelphia Navy Yard via Pearl Harbor, and the Panama Canal. She was decommissioned on December 12, 1945 and sold for scrap on January 21, 1947. Her after turret, however, was removed on January 12, 1946, and now awaits display at the Smithsonian Institute. Other ships, including a number of submarines laid claim to firing the last shot, but the Navy Department has formally credited the *Concord* with that honor. The ship that was obsolete at birth will forever be remembered for her contribution to peace and victory in the greatest war in the history of mankind.

The new 10,000 treaty cruiser slides down the ways at the Brooklyn Navy Yard on August 29, 1939 - a scant few days before the Second World War would begin. The Helena was the last of the treaty cruisers and had less than four years to live.

The Helena in a prewar photograph. She like the other cruisers of the day were not only built for speed, but for aesthetic appeal. She was a beautiful example of American craftsmanship.

USS HELENA CL-50
"THE FIGHTENIST SHIP IN THE U.S.N."

A BROOKLYN CLASS HALF SISTER

The USS Helena, CL-50 was one of two light cruisers built as half sisters to the seven ship Brooklyn class big light cruisers. The other was the USS St. Louis, CL-49. Both distinguished themselves in war and peace, and today both ships quietly lie at rest in several hundred fathoms, one in the South Pacific and the other in the South Atlantic. The Helena met her end violently on July 6, 1943, the victim of Japanese destroyer launched "long lance" torpedoes, while the St. Louis died peacefully on August 24, 1980. The "Lucky Lou" or Brazilian Navy Tamandare had been a flagship in Brazil's navy for over 25 years and was being towed to Hong Kong for disposal when she developed a leak (probably through her shaft housings) that caused her to slowly roll over and sink. She now rests in the mid South Atlantic and the Helena in the Pacific in Kula Gulf.

The Helena class was slightly different from the seven ship Brooklyn class in they were armed with four twin mount 5 inch/38 caliber guns spotted on either side of the forward and after superstructures. The secondary battery was the first use of the Mark 29 dual purpose mount that was fully enclosed with splinter plate. It also marked the first use of the soon to be popular 5 inch/38 caliber gun aboard a light cruiser. The Brooklyn's were armed with the 5 inch/25 caliber in eight open mounts situated amidships. Both would prove formidable to the enemy, but the 5 inch/38 caliber gun would quickly supplant the 5 inch/25 caliber as the weapon of choice.

Another design difference was that the aft superstructure was located right behind funnel number two, whereas in the Brooklyn's, the secondary superstructure was situated much further aft. Essentially, however the Helena was a big

light cruiser cut from the same cloth as the Brooklyn's. They were all flush deck ships with the distinctive five turret arrangement where three triple barrel turrets were located forward and two aft. The number two 6 inch turret superfired over turrets one and three. All had a square stern which has become the style for most U.S. Navy cruisers in the late twentieth century, and they were the first to house up to four scout aircraft in a fantail hanger. While the Brooklyn class would be the father of the Baltimore class heavy cruisers, the Helena class would become the precursor to the war built Cleveland class of light cruisers

The Helena class was distinguished by characteristics listed in the chart above.

The Helena was a beautiful ship that had graceful but menacing qualities. She was all business as anyone who has ever seen her will testify. Even the few photographs that are available give ample evidence of her lethal nature - a street fighter of the sea. Although her career was cut short in mid war, she and her crews accomplished outstanding battle feats, and would truly rate the nick name, "the fightenist ship in the U.S. Navy". Like a true fighter she went down with all guns blazing, but not before earning seven battle stars (the hard way) and the first Navy Unit Commendation awarded by the Secretary of the Navy for conspicuous service and valor.

HELENA'S CHARACTERISTICS

Displ: 10,000 tons (actual 11,790)
Beam: 61' 7"
Speed: 33.04 knots (trial)
Endurance: 7690 miles @ 15 knots
Main Battery: 15 six inch/47 guns
Secondary Battery: 8 five inch/38 cal dp
Draft: 25' 10"
Boilers: 8 express/high temp (700 deg)/high pressure (565 psi)
Machinery: geared turbines turning four shafts

LOA: 607' 4"
SHP: 101,079
Fuel: 2036 tons
Compl: 82/1134
AA: 1.1/20mm/40mm
Deck: teak over steel

PRELUDE TO WAR

The Helena was launched on August 27, 1939, just days before the beginning of the Second World War. She had been laid down on December 9, 1936 at the New York Navy Yard and was funded by the Vinson Trammel Act (H R 6604) of 1934. Of course, by the mid 1930's, the handwriting was on the wall, and President Roosevelt in opposition to many pacifists began a program to strengthen the U.S. Navy. Without his foresight and that of others, ships like the Helena might never had been built, and the Imperial Japanese Navy might even today be the navy that roams the Pacific unchallenged.

The new cruiser was christened by Miss Elinor Carlyle Gudger and named for the city of Helena, Montana. She was commissioned a mere three weeks later, on September 18, 1939, with Max B. Demott as her first captain.

Until late December 1939, she went through a variety of sea trials and minor repairs were made in preparation for her shakedown cruise to South America. On December 27, 1939, she left a cold and snow covered Norfolk for Buenos Aires, Argentina where it was a summer. After an abbreviated stop at the Guantanamo Naval Base, she arrived at Buenos Aires on January 22, 1940. The crew was allowed liberty in this port as well as in Montevideo, Uruguay where the *Helena* arrived on January 29, 1940.

All of South America seemed to be talking about the recent naval battle that had taken place just off the River Platte. Royal Navy and Commonwealth Cruisers *Ajax, Achilles* and *Exeter* had run the German pocket battleship, *Graf Spee* to earth in a gun battle that raged for several miles. The battle began in the early morning hours of December 14, 1939 and continued as the *Graf Spee* which was a merchant ship raider retreated up the 100 mile length of the River Platte to Montevideo. As this was a neutral port, the *Graf Spee* was allowed to remain only for 72 hours. On December 18, she left the port and shortly thereafter disembarked her crew. A tremendous explosion followed as over 20,000 sightseers watched her being scuttled. Hitler was not about to let the pride of the German Navy be destroyed by British warships lying in wait just outside of Uruguayan territorial waters.

The *Helena* slowly cruised by the *Graf Spee* or what was left of her in late January 1940, scarcely a month after she had been scuttled. It was at once sobering to see a major warship destroyed, but it was also comforting to know what a modern well handled cruiser could accomplish. Soon the *Helena* would also be fighting overwhelming odds that would include some of the most powerful battleships yet built. The crew of the *Helena* met and drank with the German sailors who had been stranded in Montevideo. The crew of the *Graf Spee* was not allowed any personal possessions when they left their ship, and they were virtually homeless, so several rounds were bought by the crew of the American cruiser. There was no animosity between crews, after all, a seaman is a seaman, no matter what navy. Captain Demott allowed the crew to visit the fire burned hulk in the ship's boats, an experience never forgotten.

In mid February, 1940, the *Helena* left for the U.S., again via Guantanamo Bay. For the next several months, the *Helena* was in training on the east coast, and running additional trials. Finally, in September, she began her journey to the Pacific. After transitting the Panama Canal in late September, she arrived in San Pedro on October 3, 1940. She would never return to the Atlantic as her life's work would be in the Pacific.

On October 21, 1940, she arrived at Pearl Harbor and took up her duties as part of the U.S. Pacific Fleet. Slowly over the last several months, major units of the fleet had been moved from San Pedro to Pearl Harbor as a show of force to deter the Japanese in their Pacific rim ambition. The militarists in Japan were quick to note the increased number of modern American warships coming and going in the mid and western Pacific and registered one complaint after another with the State Department. It was an ironic twist that Japan accused the U.S. of so much sabre rattling when her own long range destiny included the domination of the Pacific, preferably through the use of deadly force. The *Helena* spent time in gunnery exercises and fleet maneuvers. Interestingly, the training would be of little real value as the textbook concept of cruiser deployment and use would end up on the cutting room floor at 0755, December 7, 1941.

The cruiser Helena *is decked out for visitors after her trip to South America. Her forward 5 inch/38 caliber twin mount is turned to starboard, and her two gun directors just above the bridge are prominent.*

"AT LEAST WE'LL BE ALONGSIDE THE DOCK, I JUST HATE WAITING FOR A BOAT"

The *Helena* was scheduled for routine maintenance and was allowed a place of honor alongside 1010 dock (named so because it's length was 1,010 feet) rather than being anchored out in the harbor like her sister, the light cruiser *Phoenix*. The down side was that the ancient minelayer *Oglala* would be moored outboard, but at least the location was convenient to downtown Honolulu transportation. Happily for all concerned, the old minelayer wasn't carrying any mines. Normally, the flagship of the U.S. Pacific Fleet, the battleship USS *Pennsylvania* was moored alongside 1010, but on Saturday night, December 6, 1941, she was in drydock with a couple of tin cans, the *Cassin* and *Downes*, so the berth was free to the new light cruiser and her ancient friend.

Saturday nights in Honolulu on the eve of World War II were consumed by movies, dances, drinking and simply being ashore. There was always a sea of white hats on Hotel Street, and it was always tough getting served at the Royal Hawaiian, especially for junior officers. Things would change in the social climate as well as that of the military, and in just a few hours. The history of the *Helena* and how generations would view her as a fighting ship would also change.

THE DAY EVERYONE DREADED BUT KNEW WAS AT HAND - DECEMBER 7, 1941

Dawn on the 7th of December was heralded by a few low clouds, but a magnificent sunrise quickly illuminated Pearl Harbor and the boats and launches that crawled like water beetles from one anchorage to another. It was another beautiful day in paradise, and the crew of the *Helena*, at least those who were aboard began to get around for breakfast and the prepare or the day's muster and liberty. At 0755, the Japanese Imperial Navy broke the calm with a massive attack on the anchorage, and surrounding military installations. Their primary targets were the aircraft carriers and battleships. The 175 attacking planes of the first wave found none of the former, but eight of the latter. The entire attack plan was built around neutralizing the main elements of the U.S. Pacific Fleet.

Months before in a quiet anchorage in Japan, senior officers of the Imperial Japanese Navy had reluctantly agreed to a plan whereby American military might could be incapacitated for at least long enough for the Empire to secure vitally needed natural resource holdings in the East Indies. Once the oil reserves held by the Dutch in what is now Indonesia were captured, a deal would be struck with the U.S. After all, a nation whose military might was reduced to that of a second rate power would gladly accept the conditions of an armistice. Besides, it was the manifest destiny of the Empire of Japan to rule the Pacific and ensure that she no longer was viewed as less than a super power. Although unspoken, there were also certain racial overtones to the decision to engage the U.S. in war. In 1924, U.S. Immigration laws severely limited immigration from the orient, which included the Japanese along with the Chinese and Koreans. To be included with other oriental races was an insult not forgotten.

Based on the lessons learned from the Great Britain's Royal Navy carrier launched attack on the Italian fleet at Taranto in 1940, the planners of the Pearl Harbor raid prepared their own design. With certain exceptions, it was tactically brilliant. The attacking force concentrated on ships and aircraft and neglected permanent installations such as the shipyard repair facilities, submarine base and fuel oil reserves. This would cost them dearly as well as their underestimation of the American people and their resolve to win out over any odds. They also miscalculated the industrial resilience of the U.S. Whereas their naval and military forces were numerically superior after the attack, this advantage was only temporary. The Japanese could not replace lost warships as quickly as the U.S., and this above all would seal their doom. They began and ended the war with their first team, yet the U.S. was able to field another more powerful first team within 18 months after Pearl Harbor.

The surprise attack was designed to occur on a Sunday morning, just after dawn and consist of torpedo, dive and high level bombers supported by fighters in two waves. Six first line carriers would deliver a 350 plus plane attack from a position 200 miles to the northwest of Pearl Harbor. It worked.

The attack began at 0755 with a bomb being dropped on the ramp on Ford Island immediately followed by "kate" torpedo planes swooping in on the anchorage at main deck level dropping specially designed shallow running torpedoes. These were aimed at ships in battleship row and others either moored in locations thought to be reserved for carriers and other capitol ships. Ironically, the *Helena* and *Oglala* were tied up in the area normally inhabited by the fleet flagship, *Pennsylvania*, so they received attention early in the attack as a torpedo plane mistook the two as being more important that they were. Rear Admiral W. R. Furlong was on the quarterdeck of the *Oglala* and first noticed the unusual air activity. He quickly deduced that the fleet was being attacked by Japanese aircraft, and signalled all ships to sortie. On board the *Helena*, moored inboard, a lookout recently assigned to the Asiatic Fleet and familiar with Japanese aircraft markings identified the attackers immediately and warned the OOD to sound the alarm. Other officers and crewmen were also becoming aware of the situation and within seconds they all heard, "general quarters, man your battle stations". This produced the desired effect, and men began to make their way to their stations, but in the professional tradition that this cruiser was to establish from the outset, they moved purposefully and without paralyzing excitement. Of course, the crew of *Helena* had to deal with an unanticipated hazard, and that was a torpedo hit that occurred at 0758.

Three minutes into the raid, a lone torpedo bomber, looking for the *Pennsylvania* successfully launched a torpedo that slammed into the cruiser's hull amidships blowing a large hole under the waterline and flooding an engine and boiler room. Quick thinking and effective damage control established water tight integrity and preserved the ship. She could not sortie as instructed, and for a few seconds her ability to defend herself against other attackers was in doubt as the wiring to the 5 inch and 1.1 inch AA guns had been severed. However, by 0800 her guns were on line and firing due to superb

damage control and a shift from main power to that of an emergency diesel generator.

The *Oglala* did not fare so well. The torpedo detonated in the hull of the light cruiser, but also started the plates of the ancient minelayer. She began to leak from a hundred openings, and just before 0845 private contractor tugs working nearby were asked to assist the old ship and she was moved around to the stern of the *Helena*. Furlong asked for submersible pumps from the *Helena*, but it was too late, and the minelayer capsized just after 1000. To their credit, the *Oglala*'s gunners continued to fire at the attackers until the ship actually heeled over. Some say the old girl actually died of fright, but her crew was the soul of courage.

The *Helena* began to furiously duel her attackers and was eventually credited with shooting down six aircraft. Her 5 inch mounts fired 375 shells during the battle and the 1.1 inch and 50 caliber guns were firing continuously, keeping the attacking aircraft at bey. None would brave her intense AA barrage, although it was reported that one 5 inch mount manned by Marines forgot shells and were firing powder charges only. It didn't matter because with the exception of some random strafing, the *Helena* was unharmed except for the surprise torpedo. The 5 inch gunners were so intent that one gun captain jumped out of the turret and yelled at bridge personnel on the *Oglala* to get out of the way as his mount would be firing in close proximity at incoming attackers. The officers, including Admiral Furlong vacated the bridge immediately. After all, the Helena's gunners were not letting anything get in the way of protecting their ship. In typical wartime exaggeration, Japanese observers stated during their debriefing that the *Helena* and *Oglala* were struck by no less than five torpedoes.

At the end of the two hour battle, Captain R. H. English (later Rear Admiral) was more than satisfied with his crew. They had performed in a quiet determined fashion. The wounded who lined the decks covered with purple ointment to lessen the effect of burns were cared for, and the injured cruiser made ready for the next attack.

It never came, but shortly after the sunset, she and every other ship that had operating guns opened fire on what was suspected as enemy aircraft. It turned out to be carrier planes from the *Enterprise*.

The day was over, and the cleanup and repair began. The *Helena* was not damaged nearly as badly as many of the other ships, and her crew was anxious to get in the war. The cruiser was placed in the still incomplete drydock number 2 on December 10, 1941, where plates were welded over the damage just sufficient to enable her to make passage to the Mare Island Naval Shipyard. Her four 1.1 inch AA mounts were also removed to be installed on sister cruisers, *Honolulu* and *Phoenix*. The value of effective AA defense had been reinforced on December 7.

PERMANENT REPAIRS AND BACK TO THE FIGHT

The *Helena* spent the first few months of 1942 being repaired and modernized at the Mare Island Naval Shipyard. The refit included improved radar which when used and trusted was invaluable. Unfortunately, during the earlier stages of the war in the Pacific, maximum advantage of radar was not taken. The superstructure of the ship was also altered based on Captain English's very real complaints about the lack of all around visibility from the bridge. The enclosed bridge and pilot house did not afford her captain the ability to fight his ship against air attack. This was true of all the *Brooklyn/Helena* class. As a consequence, the yard reduced the existing structure by removing the conning tower and built a large open bridge. A sister ship, the cruiser *Boise* would also have a similar modification made in the same yard.

The *Helena* also received 20mm and 40mm mounts in various locations including one quadruple 40mm on pedestals located amidships on the port and starboard sides. This installation would become common on all future cruisers.

With her repairs complete, the *Helena* left San Francisco and the U.S. for what would be the last time in July 1942. She pointed her bow

The Helena *moves out of Mare Island Naval Shipyard on her way back to the South Pacific in July 1942. She has been modernized with 20 mm/40 mm antiaircraft guns and the latest surface search radar (SG). When she joined the fighting around Guadalcanal, she was the most modern heavy ship available.*

The date was July 6, 1943, and the time was approximately 2 AM. The place was Kula Gulf, and the Helena has just fired her last salvo at a force of ten Japanese destroyers bent on supplying troops ashore - the "Tokyo Express". What the photographer saw with his camera, the Japanese torpedo battery operators also saw at about 2,000 yards range. The new 24 inch "long lance" torpedo could not miss, and the Helena was hit by four. She sank within ten minutes.

toward the South Pacific and during the summer of 1942, she provided escort to various convoys and carrier groups operating between Espiritu Santo and Guadalcanal.

On one of her forays, the *Helena* was escorting the *Wasp* CV-7 when the carrier was struck by three submarine launched torpedoes on September 15, 1942 from the Japanese I-19. She became a fiery inferno, but her's were not the only troubles. The battleship *North Carolina* was also hit by a torpedo launched by the I-15 and the destroyer *O'Brien* was reduced to a wreck by another torpedo launched by the same submarine. The *Helena* was able to help rescue over 400 survivors and transport them to safety at Espiritu Santo, and the transports carrying vitally needed Marine reinforcements got through to Guadalcanal three days later, but at a high cost. The loss of the *Wasp* reduced American carrier strength to an all time low, and even in view of the victory at Midway, and 4,000 new American faces on Guadalcanal, the issue was again in doubt. The Marines on Guadalcanal were barely hanging on. Night after night they were subjected to aerial and sea borne bombardment and the days were not much better. It was literally hell on earth. It was for ships like the *Helena* to provide relief.

The Guadalcanal Survival Battles

Most historians and all who were present in the Solomons in late 1942 thru mid 1943 agree that a series of the most bloody and violent naval battles recorded took place in order to retain a small piece of real estate on Guadalcanal. The prize was Henderson Field, so named for a Ma-

rine major who died at Midway. The Japanese were the first tenants yet were forcibly evicted on August 7, 1942 by Marines who landed on Guadalcanal and at nearby Tulagi, Gavutu, Tanambogo and Florida Islands.

Within two days, the Japanese retaliated with a swift naval attack on ships guarding the Marine foothold. A task force commanded by Admiral Mikawa consisting of seven cruisers and one destroyer swept into what would become named Ironbottom Sound and attacked the surprised Allied patrol force and ultimately sank the American cruisers *Astoria*, *Quincy*, and *Vincennes* as well as the Australian cruiser *Canberra*. The cruiser *Chicago* was also damaged by a torpedo hit in the August 9 attack. Thus began the see saw struggle over who would occupy Guadalcanal and hold the airfield. These battles were horribly violent and typical western ethics were cast aside in favor of the most base of all human emotions. The Allies set aside their humanity in order to defeat an enemy who had demonstrated a complete lack of respect for human decency. It was war to the finish, and the American Navy was not about to lose. The next major engagement would include the *Helena* and would takes place on October 11-12, 1942 for a period of 34 minutes. She was now commanded by Captain Gilbert C. Hoover, who as skipper of the cruiser, would win two gold stars signifying his second and third Navy Crosses.

The Allied defeat at the Battle of Savo Island on August 9, had a demoralizing effect on the naval and ground forces in the Solomons. The Marines fully expected to be withdrawn from Guadalcanal, and the area surrendered to the

Japanese. Nightly the Japanese Navy ran supplies and reinforcements to there own beleaguered forces on the filthy disease ridden insect haven area of contention. Destroyers selected for their speed and armament were regrettably substituted for the cargo ships that had been lost to unrelenting American air and naval activity. The Japanese called it the rat run, but to the Americans it became known as the "Tokyo Express" and was almost a scheduled shuttle for the Imperial Japanese Navy. It had to be derailed, and soon. For this task, Rear Admiral Norman Scott was called upon to pull together remaining American cruiser and destroyer strength to intercept and turn back the now confident IJN.

Scott, a sailor from the old school with an aggressive spirit, was able to weld and train a group of cruisers and destroyers into a cohesive force capable of night combat. Up until this point, the Japanese owned the night and conducted their most successful operations in the dark. The Allies, at first leery of the seemingly unstoppable IJN finally realized that with training and daring, coupled with faith in radar, they could win. Scott, while not an advocate of radar, was able to train his ships and instill some confidence in their crews. On the night of October 11-12, his training, the skill and bravery of cruiser and destroyer crews plus a lot of luck would provide a much needed victory over a seemingly invincible foe.

Esperance: Radar Detects The Enemy But Is Not Trusted

The *Helena* was provided with the new SG surface search radar as was the light cruiser *Boise* who along with the heavy cruisers *San Francisco* and *Salt Lake City* accompanied by the destroyers *Duncan*, *Laffey*, *Farenholt*, *Buchannan* and *McCalla* comprised Scott's Task Force 64. The other cruisers were still relying on the older less capable SC surface search radar. This force was about all that could be spared for close in guard duty, and almost as a prophesy of the future was a pickup squad of whatever was available. They might face battleships, heavy cruisers or simply destroyers. The size and composition of the night's opposing force was immaterial, the American Navy would fight anything set against them, but now on their terms.

The Japanese were confident that soon they would again have their property back and the Allies would be forced to leave. Accordingly, Admiral Mikawa of Savo Island fame sent Admiral Aritomo Goto who had earned his reputation by successfully seizing Guam and Wake Island from Marine defenders to shoot up the Marines on Guadalcanal. Goto would command a veteran group of three heavy cruisers (*Furutaka*, *Aoba*, *Kinugasa*) and two destroyers (*Hatsuyuki* and *Fubuki*). All of these ships were first line caliber, yet did not have radar. All carried the 23 inch "long lance" torpedo with sufficient tubes to make life very dangerous for any column of Allied warships foolish enough to get within lethal range. The bombardment group would divert Allied attention from a reinforcement group that consisted of two seaplane carriers (*Chitose* and *Nisshin*) pressed into service as troop transports accompanied by four

The first group of oil soaked survivors are retrieved by the destroyers Radford *and* Nicholas.

The sunken cruiser's men lined the rail of the first rescue ships.

destroyers. This group would land 700 plus army troops and their equipment. Then the troublesome Marines would be dealt with, and the Japanese plans for advance could get back on schedule.

Scott, in flagship *San Francisco* received word of his opponents on the afternoon of the 11th, and ordered his force to accelerate to 29 knots in order to put them in position just off Cape Esperance when Goto arrived. It was to be Savo Island in reverse. For several hours Task Force 64 patrolled waiting for the Japanese to either appear or additional word from prowling aircraft. Shortly before 2200, scout aircraft were catapulted from the *San Francisco* and *Boise*. The *Helena* was not informed to launch, so dumped her aircraft over the side to alleviate the danger of fire. One of the SOC's from the *Salt Lake City* caught fire due to faulty flares and had to be jettisoned. The light was visible for miles, and lookouts on Goto's flagship, the *Furutaka* saw the flickering in the distance. They quickly attributed it to a signal from friendly forces ashore. This was a big mistake.

Aboard the American ships, nerves were raw as the night wore on, yet aboard the Japanese ships which were closing fast, there was little concern. Standard procedure was being followed and the ships were not at general quarters, another major error. Finally, at approximately 2325, the *Helena* saw the enemy illuminated on her SG scopes. The target seen at a range of 27,700 yards was moving toward Task Force 64 and within minutes would form the base of a classic "T", the most desirable position in naval surface warfare. At this rate, Scott would cross the "T" and in theory could anni-

hilate them without sustaining much in the way of counter fire.

Captain Hoover in the *Helena*, did not inform the flagship of the oncoming enemy force for several minutes and at that time other surface search radars began to see what the *Helena* had seen. But, it was still unbelievable. A column countermarch was ordered and the ships began their evolutions when the *Boise* and *Helena* both reported targets. Confusion reigned due to poor communication.

At 15 minutes till midnight, gunners and bridge personnel were certain that an enemy force was moving toward them and now at 5,000 yards. The SG radar was not lying, and it was time to do something. Hoover requested permission to open fire with the standard "interrogatory roger" signal. This was misinterpreted by the flagship, and Hoover received an affirmative "roger" in return. Scott thought Hoover was merely asking if a previous message had been received. Within seconds all fifteen 6 inch guns and four of the 5 inch guns let loose and commenced rapid fire which astonished both the Japanese and American flagships. There was confusion, but within seconds the *Boise* did likewise as did the balance of Task Force 64.

The Japanese flagship, heavy cruiser *Furutaka* was raked with six inch fire from the *Helena* as was the destroyer *Fubuki*. The *Helena's* guns literally tore these ships to pieces as was promised by the ordnance designers of the 6 inch/47 caliber gun. All of the other ships joined in and for several seconds there was almost an uncontrolled melee. Fearing that some of his destroyers might be the target of his

unleased pit bull cruisers, Scott called for a temporary cease fire at 2347, but within a minute allowed unrestrained firing to resume. The battle would last for another 33 minutes with short lulls.

The *Boise* was badly mauled and the *Salt Lake City* received some hits, but the worse damage occurred on the destroyer *Duncan* which later sunk due to being hit numerous times by Japanese and American shells. The Japanese lost the cruiser *Furutaka* and the destroyer *Fubuki*, and the balance of the now dead Admiral Goto's force retired. The *Aoba* had suffered 40 hits and the *Kinugasa* was not undamaged. It was decisive victory for the Americans and a badly needed spirit lift for the Marines and sailors on and around Guadalcanal. Although the Japanese were able to land the reinforcements, no longer was the IJN considered invincible by either navy. Scott and his ships had reversed a very dangerous trend. It was not the beginning of the end, but it was a beginning. The cruiser *Helena* contributed mightily to this encounter. Her quick thinking captain and well disciplined crew did the job they were sent to do, and with great honor and valor. Unknowing to many of the crew who were to perish some eight months later, they would not receive credit for their efforts until historians fully analyzed the battle reports and the over anxious media propaganda was corrected after the war's end. Contrary to the reports in late 1942, there was no "one ship task force". The battle at Cape Esperance was a joint venture spearheaded by the *Helena* and her brave crew.

ROUND TWO: THE NAVAL BATTLE OF GUADALCANAL, NOVEMBER 12-15, 1942

Cruiser strength was dwindling in the South Pacific. The October Battle of Cape Esperance resulted in the light cruiser *Boise* and heavy cruiser *Salt Lake City* being ordered out of the theater for major repair. Both sides were losing cruisers and destroyers at an alarming rate and not just to night surface action. Daily air attacks and the ever present threat of submarines took their toll. The U.S. Navy had won a victory at

Cape Esperance, but Japanese were far from convinced to give up Guadalcanal.

After the Battle of Cape Esperance, the *Helena* patrolled in the Solomons area and out to the relative safety of Espiritu Santo, but there was little safety there as well. On the night of October 20, the tired cruiser dodged several torpedoes and again survived, but she was quickly using up her nine lives.

The upcoming Naval Battle of Guadalcanal would consume most of her remaining luck, but she would survive. She and three other ships would be the only units combat capable after this battle. Nine others would fall victim. November was to be the month of destiny for both sides as each side decided to make a supreme effort to bring victory. In early November the Japanese successfully landed troops and equipment at Koli Point on Guadalcanal and within days the *San Francisco*, *Helena* and destroyer *Sterett* shot up their positions. The *Helena* expended 1,000 high capacity 6 inch shells alone in this bombardment. Those aboard could literally see Japanese soldiers running for their lives and it was a small wonder that any survived the devastation created by the bombardment ships. Shore bombardment by either side was highly destructive and rendered troops and equipment unfit, not to mention the affect it had on morale.

No matter what the Allies would do to prevent the Japanese from wholesale reinforcement, they seemed to get ashore every night somewhere near the American positions. Incredibly, the IJN was able to land nearly 70 destroyer loads of troops and equipment in the week between November 2 and November 9. Clearly, something had to be done to stem the tide.

In early November, transports loaded with equipment and fresh troops left Espiritu Santo for Guadalcanal. Included were the basics, food and ammunition. Both were in short supply and Marines ashore had been supplementing their meager diet with captured Japanese food stocks. The Japanese were not even this lucky. Two groups of transports made their way to Guadalcanal under heavy escort consisting of cruisers *Helena*, *Portland*, *Atlanta* and *Juneau*. On November 12, 1942, the first stirring of a major showdown occurred as the transports, which were being unloaded came under heavy air attack. The anti aircraft gunnery discipline was excellent, and the damage was minimal. The *San Francisco* was hit aft on her director by a disabled Japanese plane that elected to commit suicide, but other than that, there was little overall damage. As the transports were almost unloaded, it was decided that they should break off, and the escort forces would deal with enemy ships that had been identified in a growing number of aircraft reports. The Japanese had enough of the inconclusive type of naval warfare occurring around Guadalcanal and was ending a major bombardment force to literally finish off Henderson Field and put the Americans in flight. If Admiral Hiroaki Abe's advanced force of two battleships, one heavy cruiser, and fourteen destroyers ran into any surface opposition, it would be dispatched on sight and the bombardment would go ahead as planned. As there was no real air superiority on either side, Abe was confident that he could deal with anything the Allies might throw against him. His raiding group

included the battleships, *Hiei* and *Kirishima*, light cruiser *Nagara* and fourteen heavy destroyers. Their total armament consisted of the following:

Weapon	Number
14 inch guns	16
5.5 and 6 inch guns	39
4.7 and 5 inch guns	69
Torpedo Tubes	126 of which 104 are 24 inchLL

Although the Japanese force did not have adequate surface search radar, they did have over 100 "long lance" torpedoes which could travel up to eleven miles at 49 knots or 22 miles at 36 knots. This weapon also packed nearly twice the destructive force of the contemporary American 21 inch torpedo. Ranged against this fast moving group (30 knots), Rear Admiral Daniel J. Callaghan (Uncle Dan) had a pick up team of five cruisers of various capability and eight destroyers. They could bring the following armament to bear against the Japanese:

Weapons	Number
8 inch guns	18
6 inch guns	15
5 inch guns	90
Torpedo Tubes	72 - 21 inch

The American 21 inch torpedo was still considered satisfactory by many commanders. This was unfortunate as in many cases it proved to be defective due to faulty exploders. In any event, even if the Navy's torpedo was effective, the Japanese far outnumbered the American force sent to prevent it's intended bombardment of Henderson Field. It was for Callaghan and his group to accomplish something that most naval planners would have never expected to be possible. Callaghan carried his flag in the heavy cruiser *San Francisco* while Rear Admiral Norman Scott, victor of the earlier Cape Esperance struggle, was riding in the light cruiser *Atlanta*.

Callaghan arrayed his ships in a single column led by destroyers *Cushing*, *Laffey*, *Sterett*, and *O'Bannion*. Next came the cruisers *Atlanta*, *San Francisco*, *Portland* and *Helena*. Bringing up the rear were the destroyers *Aaron Ward*, *Barton*, *Monssen* and *Fletcher*. Unfortunately, ships with the most sophisticated radar were not in the lead. The *Helena*, equipped with the latest and most efficient surface search radar was in the center of the column. It was apparent that lessons had not been learned from the Battle of Cape Esperance. In addition, the formation was a single column selected mainly because precedent had been set at Cape Esperance.

As the ships moved into the darkness of November 12, it became obvious that a major fleet action was in the offing. The crew of the *Helena*, eating a supper consisting of an apple, sandwich and candy bar listened intently to Captain Hoover as he provided current information on the composition and probable location of the enemy force. He also made it quite clear that at all costs the Japanese were to be prevented from hitting Henderson Field. For the *Helena* and the other twelve ships, it was the top of the ninth with two outs in a losing ball game. They were expendable.

Friday the 13th was to be given reinforced emphasis because just before 0130, the *Helena* began tracking two large blips that could only be an enemy formation approaching the American column. The combined approach speed was in excess of forty knots and within minutes they would be upon each other. The *Helena* made all preparations necessary for an engagement including disposal of her scout planes and dumping many gallons of highly flammable aviation gas over the side. All other ships had done likewise and were as ready as could be expected for what was to follow.

The Japanese battleships were in column formation surrounded by a semi circle of destroyers out front as a screen. Admiral Abe was not anticipating any formal opposition to his missions and did not issue surface battle plans. However, his sailors were prepared for a bombardment, and were standing ready to open fire. There would be no repeat of Esperance this night. Interestingly, his heavy caliber gun magazines were laden with high capacity shells designed to cause maximum damage to people and equipment. This was a blessing in disguise because American heavy cruiser armor was sufficient to protect them from serious hull damage, but topside crews would literally be slaughtered.

Without adequate radar, Callaghan had to rely on the *Helena* and destroyer *O'Bannion* for up to date information and communications being what they were coordination proved to be awkward and difficult. This would prove fatal for many ships and men. The delays and lack of sustained reliance on radar caused the American force to move close enough to the onrushing Japanese that they could literally see the American lead destroyers with the naked eye. Admiral Abe was not anticipating a major surface engagement, but by 0142, on November 13, 1942, he knew that it had been thrust upon him, and he reacted shortly thereafter. Eight minutes later at less than 2,000 yards, the Japanese illuminated their opponents with search lights and opened fire. The cruiser *Atlanta* was the first to be chewed up.

Aboard the *San Francisco*, with surprise lost, Callaghan ordered that all ships commence firing, "odd ships to port, even ships to starboard". Within minutes, the waters which had already experienced so many clashes, were again filled with racing torpedoes and the flashes of gunfire could be seen for miles. A general melee followed as ships fought individual duels with one another, but it was an uneven fight. The *San Francisco* took 45 hits, many of a major caliber and her captain, Cassin Young and the well liked and respected Admiral Daniel Callaghan were killed. Admiral Scott on the *Atlanta* was also killed. The *Helena* attempted to avenge the *Atlanta* by firing furiously at the destroyers and cruiser *Nagara* that had taken the thin skinned AA cruiser under fire. The range dropped to 2,300 yards or about 1-1/2 miles. For the next quarter hour the *Helena* shot at everything that she encountered with every gun available. Her 6 inch guns took a ship that was decimating the *San Francisco* and her five inch twin mounts went after a destroyer. Even her 40mm antiaircraft guns made a contribution as they chased a light cruiser out of range.

Incredibly, the Japanese turned northward just

Nearly 400 survivors on the Radford *are transferred to the* Helena's *sister ship, the* St. Louis, *in Tulagi Harbor. The crew of the* Helena *will never forget the men of the* Radford *and* Nicholas *for their concern and bravery to stand by fellow seamen.*

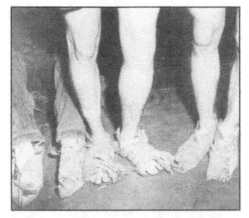

After drifting ashore on enemy infested Vella Lavella, many of the 150 plus survivors had to resort to any kind of clothing to move into the jungle and escape searching Japanese patrols. None were found and all made it safely back. The coastwatchers and loyal natives saved many a life while endangering their own.

Rescued survivors relax on Guadalcanal prior to their trip back to the U.S.A. The survivors would leave in thirty days.

after 0200 and began a slow withdrawal. The battleship *Hiei* had been badly mauled as had several destroyers. The battleship *Kirishima* had been hit, but was still combat capable. Callaghan's force had done it's work, but at a huge cost.

When the smoke cleared, only the *Helena*, *San Francisco*, and *Juneau* accompanied by destroyers *O'Bannion, Fletcher* and *Sterett* were capable. But that in itself is a misnomer. The *San Francisco* was badly hurt and had lost several score officers and men, including Admiral Callaghan and Captain Young. The *Juneau* was barely able to make 15 knots due to torpedo damage. Captain Hoover assumed command of the remaining ships and the slowly moved toward the safety of the New Hebrides. As the ships were limping away, the wounded *Juneau* was hit by a submarine launched torpedo that destroyed her in one huge explosion. Witnesses aboard the *Helena* watched in horror as entire 5 inch mounts were flung hundreds of feet in the air. Captain Hoover signalled a circling Army Air Force B-17 to notify Admiral Halsey's headquarters to send help to the few survivors of

Juneau, but by the time a rescue attempt was made, only ten of the ship's company survived. Unfortunately, Hoover was relieved of his command of the *Helena* soon after because Admiral Halsey felt that he had derelict in not doing more, and initially, the B-17 report was not received. Hoover was later reinstated, but the crew of the *Helena* felt slighted by Halsey's rash decision.

SCORECARD

Over the next two days, the battle would rage on until Japanese ultimately lost the battleships *Hiei* and *Kirishima* as well as destroyers *Akatsuki* and *Yudachi*. Many hundreds of Japanese sailors perished rather than be rescued, and not a few were executed by American naval gunfire. Chivalry and human rights concerns had no place off Guadalcanal.

On the other side, the U.S. Navy lost the AA cruisers *Atlanta* and *Juneau*. They had no business participating in a sea battle with battleships no less. But in war, you work with whatever resources are available. The heavy cruisers *Portland* and *San Francisco* were badly damaged. The *Portland* had been hit by a torpedo in the stern which disabled her steering gear and the *San Francisco's* main deck had been turned into a charnel house. The *Helena* was relatively untouched except for minor splinter damage, and one casualty, but it was the destroyers that suffered most. The *Barton, Monssen, Cushing, Laffey* and later the *Preston, Walke* and *Benham* found their way to the bottom of "ironbottom sound". The remaining destroyers were generally unhurt, but overall the casualties on the American side were horrendous. But, in probably the bloodiest and most terrible sea battle of the late 20th Century, the American Navy had withstood uneven odds and prevailed.

KULA GULF - WHERE FORTUNE FINALLY TURNED AWAY

The *Helena* had been living a charmed life since her first battle damage at Pearl Harbor. To come through the Battle of Cape Esperance and Bloody Friday (November 13, 1942) virtually untouched was nothing short of amazing.

For the next several months following the Naval Battle of Guadalcanal, the veteran cruiser bombarded one enemy held position after another in the Allied drive up the Solomons chain. In January 1943, she pounded New Georgia and was often in company with sister ship *St. Louis* and half sister *Nashville*. She fired literally thousands of 5 and 6 inch rounds at enemy troop concentrations and shore installations. She was one of the premier ships to use the Mark 32 proximity influence fuse which would become a standard in the future. The battle between aircraft and ship was still uneven, but the proximity fuse leveled the playing field somewhat. She even assisted in the destruction of a Japanese submarine RO-102, and any effort in this direction was helpful. The waters where American ships operated were infested with Japanese submarines.

Task Group 36.1 under Rear Admiral Walden Ainsworth consisted of old teammates, light cruisers *Honolulu, St. Louis* and *Helena* screened by destroyers *O'Bannion, Radford, Jenkins* and *Nicholas*. They had just provided concentrated bombardment at Vila-Bairoko and late on July 5, 1943, the Tokyo Express was detected making a run to reinforce troops on Munda.

Ainsworth instructed his force to accelerate to 29 knots and they headed for a showdown with three groups of Japanese destroyers which were headed into Kula Gulf down the slot. The Japanese were no longer bat blind and one of the destroyers, the *Niizuki* now carried radar. Rear Admiral Teruo Akiyama led the group of destroyers of which three were being used for support

Safe as they leave Espiritu Santo for home. For many of the survivors, this will be their last combat assignment, but a few would find their way back to the violence of the South Pacific.

and seven were carrying supplies and troops. The American force outclassed the Japanese force in medium caliber guns, but the Japanese destroyers were carrying the 24 inch torpedoes which more than compensated for the disparity in gun firepower. At 0140 on July 6, the battle actually began with Ainsworth's force detecting the Japanese transports at about 25,000 yards. A column formation was assumed and the cruisers and destroyers headed at 25 knots to make the interception. Seventeen minutes later at 0157 the *Helena* and others let loose at the Japanese formation. The Japanese had not been fooled however, as they had detected the American force almost an hour earlier and Admiral Akiyama had already made his dispositions. His flagship, the luckless *Niizuki* was immediately hit and sank within two minutes. Unaffected, the other Japanese destroyers launched their "long lances" set at high speed, and the die was now cast for the *Helena*.

The *Helena* had opened fire just before 0200, but was not using flashless powder. It made a perfect aiming point for Japanese torpedomen, and the waters became alive with streaks. Ainsworth's cruisers fired rapidly at the Japanese ships to the tune of 2,500 shells in five min-

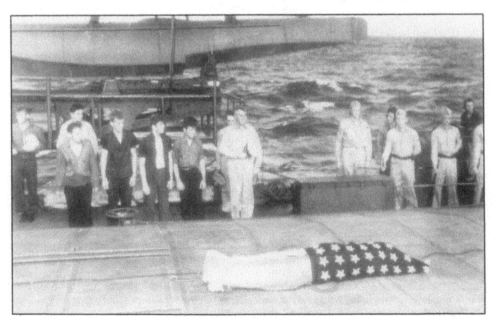

On the hanger door of the St. Louis, all turn out to pay tribute to one of the final victims of the Kula Gulf sinking. In all, the Helena *lost 168 of her 1,000 plus crew. Sometimes just being part of something is the highest level of importance a human can aspire. Being a member of the* Helena's *crew was one of those rare honors.*

utes. The *Helena* was hit seven minutes after opening fire at 0203 by a torpedo just forward of turret 2. Within three more minutes she was hit amidships just under the number two stack by two more torpedoes. She was also struck by a dud torpedo near her stern, but it failed to detonate. It would not have mattered as she was mortally wounded and with a broken back she jackknifed and sank six minutes later at 0210. Her bow remained afloat and pointed upward in a macabre fashion.

Captain Charles P. Cecil who had replaced Captain Hoover called for abandon ship and the crew abandoned with discipline and honor. Many of the crew had prepared for this day, and had sewn money, cigarettes and knives into their life jackets. Hundreds of men were able to successfully get off the sinking ship and various groups of swimmers and those on rafts were organized for the rescue effort that was sure to come. Shortly after, the destroyers *Radford* and *Nicholas* began fishing men out of the oil slickened waters. By 0617, the *Radford* and *Nicholas* had retrieved 745 *Helena* survivors and then beat it back to Tulagi. Volunteers were left in four whaleboats to locate and rescue some of the survivors that had drifted out of the immediate area.

Captain Cecil and 80 survivors were picked up two days later by destroyers *Gwin* and *Woodworth* just seven miles from Rice Anchorage.

Up to 200 clung to the upturned bow of their beloved ship and were later assisted by a passing four engine navy liberator that dropped inflatable rafts. Two days later they straggled ashore on Vella Lavella. This group now down to 165 men armed themselves with whatever local coastwatchers could provide and evaded Japanese patrols until rescued by APD's *Dent* and *Walker* which were escorted by a number of destroyers. By July 16, all but 168 of the *Helena's* crew had been rescued and were on their way home via Espiritu Santo. Many rode on their sister ship, the *St. Louis*. It was like being home for the last trip.

The survivors of the USS *Helena* went on to other ships and stations, but none would ever forget the valor and courage that became second nature to the operations of this gallant cruiser. She was truly the "fightenist ship of the U.S. Navy".

THE USS *MILWAUKEE*, CL-5 "FROM RUSSIA WITH LOVE"

In 1916, the Congress of the U.S., under pressure from President Wilson and events in Europe provided for the construction of a modern navy which included a massive number of destroyers and ten scout cruisers spread out over the following three fiscal years. The class of scout cruisers, taking nearly nine years to build was named after the lead ship, the USS *Omaha*, CL-4. Ostensibly designed to scout ahead of the traditional battle line and fight ships of like size and class, or provide protective support to destroyers during their attacks, these roles never materialized. The airplane eclipsed the need for fast scout cruisers, and the introduction of radar eliminated this function entirely. Accompanying destroyers in a planned and well coordinated torpedo or gunfire run never became a reality either, except on paper.

The old cruiser, Milwaukee, *stranded off Eureka, California on January 13, 1917. She had been attempting to help Submarine H-3 which had drifted aground on Samoa Beach on December 14, 1916. While using her 24,000+ horsepower to pull the submarine off the sand, she too became stranded. No lives were lost, but dignity and pride suffered mightily. The submarine was later refloated by cutting a channel through the sand to open water. The* Milwaukee *was broken up by wind and waves, a hopeless loss!*

THE MILWAUKEE - A LIGHT CRUISER OBSOLETE AT BIRTH

The U.S. Navy attempted to imitate the more modern light cruisers being built by the major European navies, but the length of time used to build the class and endless argument and disagreement within the Naval hierarchy over various plan alterations conspired against the *Omahas'*. By the time the lead ship was commissioned on February 4, 1923, so many changes had been made, the *Omaha* and later her sisters were dubbed obsolete at birth. Foreign naval observers described the class as Victorian and archaic. The navy completed the remainder of the class, but later improvements did little to prevent them from leaking nor make them habitable for their crews. The crews roasted in the summer and froze in the winter. There was insufficient living space for a peacetime crew let alone one swollen by wartime requirements. Insulation was virtually non existent, and the heat produced by too much machinery in too little hull space made these ships very difficult to operate or serve in. They were also the last warships built by any nation with a broadside battery. In short, there was very little to recommend them. However, they did serve a purpose, and while most of the *Omahas'* were consigned to the backwaters of World War II, and quickly scrapped just after the war, one, the USS *Milwaukee* outlasted them all. Even if it was under the red star of the Soviet Union.

The USS *Milwaukee*, CL-5, was launched on March 24, 1921, and commissioned on June 20, 1923. She was built by the Todd Dry Dock and Construction Co. in Seattle, Washington, and to her crew she will always be remembered as the *"Millie"*. She was initially armed with twelve 6 inch/53 caliber guns, four 3 inch/50 caliber AA guns and deck mounted torpedo tubes. In addition she was equipped with the most advanced hydrophonic depth sounding equipment available. It was put to good use during her shakedown cruise

In one of her first roles after being commissioned, the Milwaukee, *along with sister* Detroit, *acted as floating communication stations for the U.S. Navy's newest dirigible ZR-3, which was flying the Atlantic during October 1923.*

to the Australia in the late summer of 1923. She was able to bring back substantial data on the Pacific and its ocean bed while in route.

In April, 1924, shortly after her return from Australia, her crew went ashore in Tamalapa, Honduras to protect American lives and property during one of the many popular revolutions within the "banana republics" of Central America. For several days, gunfire was exchanged with the rebels, and although lives were lost on both sides, American interests were preserved.

The Milwaukee *is again called upon to assist U.S. around the world flyers by stashing spare parts and fuel in certain locations on Labrador. Here on July 19, 1924, she is moored next to a stores ship taking on supplies. This view shows the two starboard side 3 inch/50 caliber AA guns that would prove ineffective against any but the slowest aircraft.*

The Milwaukee *enters drydock for a much needed overhaul and cleaning on August 16, 1927. Her overlapping radio communications top masts and wiring are much in evidence.*

Three months later on July 19, she left for northern waters to carry supplies and fuel to various bases in Labrador to help prepare for the "round the world" flyers, and again in October she acted as a mid ocean communications link for another test of flight endurance. This time she was accompanied by a sister, the *Detroit* CL-8 as they assisted the Navy's latest dirigible, ZR-3 in one of it's maiden flight. The speed and endur-

The Millie *in 1936, after being modernized. Her masts have been shortened, and the bridge structure has been improved and expanded. This particular view shows the starboard side 6 inch/53 caliber broad side guns that marked this class as a throwback to pre World War I days.*

ance of these cruisers made them indispensable for these type of assignments.

Changing gears again, in October 1926, the *Millie* again responded to adversity when she came to the rescue and assistance of the hurricane ravaged Isle of Pines in the Caribbean. The crews of the cruiser and another naval ship, the *Goff*, spent days working tirelessly to provide food, medical attention and restore power and telephone service to the island.

Generally, the *Milwaukee* spent the balance of the inter-war years assigned to duty in the Pacific. In early 1938, she embarked on a flag showing trip to many far eastern ports to demonstrate the resolve of the U.S. to the increasingly bold Japanese military regime. The ruling military hotheads of the Japanese government had just allowed, and perhaps even encouraged the sinking of the gunboat *Panay* in the Yangtze River. The lesson was not overlooked, but was not forceful enough to convince the Japanese militarists to avoid war with the U.S.

WORLD WAR II AND THE *MILLIE*

The *Milwaukee* was in the New York Navy Yard undergoing overhaul when the Japanese attacked Pearl Harbor on December 7, 1941.

Captain Forest B. Royal, for whom a Gearing class destroyer was later named, hastened the overhaul and she was on her way to the Caribbean by the end of December. During those early years of the war when victory was longed for, but uncertain, the cruiser was assigned convoy and patrol duty. Her operating area was from South American ports across the Atlantic narrows to Africa and along South and Central American coastal routes. The *Milwaukee*, with her sisters *Omaha*, *Cincinnati*, and *Memphis* provided the muscle for the "banana fleet" as the force that operated in South American waters was affectionately nicknamed. The vigilance of these cruisers and supporting destroyers with Allied air patrols virtually eliminated the Axis submarine menace in the region. It was during this period in May 1942 that the *Milwaukee*, with the destroyer *Moffett*, helped to rescue the crew of the torpedoed Brazilian freighter, *Commandante Lyra*. After saving the crew, a determined boarding party from the

cruiser was able to prepare the smoldering ship for tow back to Brazil.

Later, in November, 1943, the cruiser in company with sister *Omaha* intercepted the German blockade runner, *Annaliesc Essenberger* and assisted by the destroyer, *Somers* compelled the Nazi crew to scuttle and burn her. The *Milwaukee* rescued 62 crew and transported them to Brazil for imprisonment.

FROM SPAM TO BORSCHT - TRADED IN MID SEASON

The now twenty year old cruiser left the South Atlantic area for New York and a much needed overhaul. The overhaul only lasted eight days and the lower decks were rife with rumors about the future. For once, no one was right! On February 27, 1944, she left New York as part of a major convoy bound for Great Britain and finished the trip in Scapa Flo. Here speculation was laid to rest as several landing craft pulled alongside and unloaded Soviet and American bilingual petty officers and officers. The *"Millie"* was being offered to the Soviet Navy as part of a compromise agreement to forestall "Uncle Joe" Stalin from taking the now idle Italian Fleet. Arrangements had been agreed to by Churchill, Roosevelt and Stalin at the Big Three Conference in Teheran. The British were contributing a battleship, the aging *Royal Sovereign*, eight destroyers, four submarines and 40,000 tons of merchant shipping. The U.S. provided the cruiser, the *Milwaukee*.

Six days was allowed for a shakedown and familiarization period for the new owners, and then it was on to Murmansk as part of a large convoy. The trip was not without incident as several submarine and air attacks had to be beaten off, but the cruiser and convoy arrived unscathed. As the convoy was negotiating its way into Murmansk, the *Milwaukee* was detached and entered the harbor. Here the rest of the Soviet crew boarded her and a further period of intense training ensued. What struck the crew of the *Milwaukee* was the obvious attention to every detail on the part of the Soviet crew, and the nagging habit they had of demanding an accounting for every single item on the equipment inventory. There was no shore leave for the

Soviet naval personnel line the deck aft as the veteran cruiser enters American territorial waters. The lettering on the hull is cyrillic and identifies the ship as the "Murmansk".

A Soviet seaman stands watch on the fantail of the ship he is about to leave. It is not known if there were any women serving as crew members aboard the cruiser, but it was common on most Soviet warships. It has taken nearly fifty years for the U.S. Navy to follow suit.

U.S. Navy personnel at the Philadelphia Navy Yard inspect flea infested cushions in the old cruiser's wardroom. The Murmansk, not the Milwaukee, was dubbed the "filthiest ship in the Navy."

American Bluejackets except for a brief trip to a hill overlooking the harbor for the ship's photographer. He was to take picture of the ship being transferred just in case the Russian's claimed otherwise later. On the other hand, missing shore leave in Murmansk was not a major disappointment given the restrictions on travel and the lack of recreational opportunity. On April 20, 1944, Averill Harriman, U.S. Ambassador to the Soviet Union arrived aboard the old cruiser, and in a brief ceremony, turned the ship over to the Soviet Navy. The Stars and Stripes was replaced by the Hammer and Sickle, and the *Mil-*

waukee became the *Murmansk*. Later there would be much grumbling by the U.S. Congress as the transfer of this ship was done secretly and not without consultation. There were no congressional hearings, and some complaints were registered with the Navy Department.

The only bright spot for some of the *Milwaukee's* crew was watching their Soviet counterparts maneuver the ship. As they were leaving on a British aircraft carrier, they watched the veteran cruiser ram a dock, and the Kingfisher scout plane was catapult launched while the ship was alongside the dock and very

nearly crashed. As the bluejackets left for home, most wondered whether they would ever see the old ship again, or more to the point, would she survive the new ownership? Although the Soviet Union and the U.S. were allies, the *Milwaukee's* crew remembered that they had to travel a greater distance to ensure friendly relations, a condition that seems to have endured as a prerequisite of our two nations' continued peaceful relationship.

The *Murmansk* made a number of patrols and escorted convoys along the north European coast until the war ended. From 1945 to 1949, the record of her service is sketchy due to Soviet secretiveness.

BACK TO THE USA

On March 8, 1949, she was brought back to the U.S. and turned over to the U.S. Navy. The 800 member Russian crew never touched American soil as they were transferred to the waiting transport ship, *Molotov* and whisked back to the motherland. More evidence of the "cold war" that was heating up! Once more the venerable old ship flew the stars and stripes, but her age and her material condition ruled out any future except the ship breakers. All of her nine sisters had gone before her, and she was the last. As the old cruiser was being inspected by her original owners, Commander Roland Blockson, of the Fourth Naval District bitterly remarked that she was the "filthiest ship he had ever seen". The "peasant navy" of Russia apparently did not know what soap and water were for, and let the old ship deteriorate. She was rusting, corroding, and unsanitary. The ancient four stack cruiser was quickly sold to American Shipbreakers, Inc. of Wilmington, Delaware for $148,000 and towed off on December 10, 1949. Before leaving she was cleaned up in order to make the trip in style. No great lady should face

Soviet transport, Molotov, *removes the crew of the* Murmansk, *and quickly sails for home. No crew members were permitted to set foot on United States soil. The incident was reminiscent of the Royal Navy's 18th century practise of not allowing crews to leave ship while in port for fear of losing men.*

The veteran cruiser, Milwaukee, *now no longer needed by the U.S. Navy, is nevertheless cleaned up and flying the Stars and Strips. Now decommissioned, the old cruiser heads for Wilmington, Deleware where she will be scrapped. She was sold for $148,000 to American Shipbreakers, Inc. and broken up in early 1950.*

Workmen install one of the twin barrels in turret number one. Only the Pensacola *and the* Salt Lake City *were armed with ten eight inch guns in a 2 - 3 - 3 - 2 format. All heavy cruisers built after the* Salt Lake City *were armed with nine eight inch guns in three triple turrets.*

her end without dignity and pride, and the staff of the Philadelphia Navy Yard made sure she was prepared and suitably honored. She was the last of the *Omaha* class, and like her sisters never carried out the mission for which they were designed and built.

All, however, served their country with distinction in peace and war. Many a cruiser sailor serving on the ships such as the *Oakland, Wilkes Barre, Cleveland,* and *Philadelphia* owed their training to experience gained in the *Omahas'*. This was a priceless contribution, especially during the first months of World War II. If you could make it on the *Milwaukee* or one of her nine sisters, you met the definition of "cruiser sailor".

THE USS *SALT LAKE CITY* CA-25
"FAITHFUL TO THE END"

WASHINTON/LONDON NAVAL TREATIES - BLIND MAN'S BLUFF

The USS *Salt Lake City* CA-25 and her sister, the *Pensacola* CA-24 were the U.S. Navy's first attempts at cruiser construction under the mandates of an international treaty. The agreement, known as the Washington Naval Arms Limitation Treaty was concluded in Washington D.C. on February 6, 1922, and set certain standards for warship numbers, tonnage and firepower. The unstated but real agenda of the treaty sought to limit naval strength by an expansionist Japan, and at the same time allow a nearly bankrupt Great Britain freedom to recover from the financial devastation of World War I. What it actually accomplished was to further enrage Japan and cause her government to falsify it's tonnage reports as well as causing Italy and France to fudge on their building programs. Great Britain still went broke, and the U.S. ended up with some very substandard ships, only made effective by good crews, disciplined training, and pure luck. To add insult to injury, the agreement also established a ratio of allowable naval tonnage per country, and

each country not accorded the highest or a 5 was slighted in the international community, apologies and rationale not withstanding. The U.S. was at 5, Great Britain 5, Japan 3.5, and France and Italy 1.75. Germany, bound by the Treaty of Versailles, was not included. Politics and shrewd negotiation had replaced rational naval theory, and a generation of treaty bound ships would end up fighting each other in the next war. For all intents and purposes, the Washington Naval Treaty and it's followup conference in London in 1930 were exercises in political control over the military with smoke and mirrors.

Established naval doctrine prescribed that warship construction should demonstrate and protect national interests or at the very least maintain technological and fleet size parity with other nations. The Naval Treaties as they became known and ultimately vilified just caused another hoop for naval designers and architects to jump through. In the case of the Japanese and Italian naval staffs, they simply lied when they promised compliance with the treaty limits. The Japanese *Mogami* class cruiser touted at below 10,000 tons was actually over 12,000 tons and would ultimately be armed with eight inch guns. The Italians were not as good at falsifying their claims as the Japanese who at least had the good sense to keep international inspectors at arm's length. The 63,000 ton battleships *Yamato* and *Mushashi* were obviously over any limit, but the construction of these ships proves beyond any shadow of a doubt that the Imperial Japanese Navy was not about to be hampered by a western treaty. She had other military aims and a paucity of thin shelled, under armed warships would not serve her international ambitions.

The U.S. Navy followed the precepts of the treaties, and from 1927-39 built eighteen heavy

The Salt Lake City *shortly before her formal commissioning ceremony. Her distinctive bulbous bow is evident as is the lack of any real armor belt. She was a "tinclad," but fought well in World War II.*

cruisers using the 10,000 ton upper limit. They were politely known as the treaty cruisers. Less charitably, they were dubbed, "thinclads, tinclads, guns on eggshells", or in the case of the Italian Navy, "cardboard cruisers". The treaties also caused another rather interesting phenomenon, the cruiser became a quasi capitol ship, and all navies now had to rely on this class as their primary surface combatant. The U.S. Navy would have this repeatedly demonstrated in the 1942-43 sea battles for the conquest of Guadalcanal. The quest for naval planners now centered on cramming a power plant capable of sustained high speeds, eight inch guns, torpedoes, anti aircraft defense, and some modicum of armor protection at less than 10,000 tons. Compromise was mandatory, and what emerged during the late 1920's and early 1930's would set the stage for the early, and actually most of the Pacific surface warfighting.

The Japanese elected to falsify most of their claims, and built cruisers that were heavily armed (guns and torpedoes), top heavy, fast, yet relatively unprotected. The Italians and French both sacrificed heavy armament and virtually all armor protection for speed, hoping that 37 plus knots would keep their cruisers out of harms way. The Italians were mistaken. The British chose a number of different plans, mainly designed to protect their trade routes, but they too sacrificed armor protection for endurance and speed.

The U.S. Navy's Bureau of Construction and Repair studied the issue carefully, and prepared a number of design schemes before actually settling on the *Salt Lake City* and *Pensacola* as their first offerings. They did not want a repeat of the troublesome *Omaha* class, so something entirely new was built, after compromise and argument. Much attention was given to the Royal Navy's *Hawkins* class cruisers that approached 10,000 tons and mounted 7.5 inch guns. In fact, the *Hawkins* became the stepfather of cruiser construction under the Naval Treaties. Great Britain was willing to sacrifice almost anything except their new *Hawkins* class cruisers built just after World War I. American designs followed the 10,000 ton, 8 inch main armament mold for the next two decades, and the *Salt Lake City* was the first offering.

THE FIRST AMERICAN TREATY CRUISER - THE *SALT LAKE CITY* CA-25

Although sister ship, *Pensacola* CA-24 was laid down nearly six months before the *Salt Lake City* (June 19, 1927), sponsored by Mrs. Helen Budge, was launched first on January 9, 1929, and also commissioned first on December 11, 1939. Both were authorized in 1924 along with six other heavy cruisers, but the congress only provided funds for the first two to begin in the FY 1926 building program. For all intents and purposes, the *Salt Lake City* was the first treaty cruiser built for the U.S. Navy, and interestingly, she and her sister were first designated as light cruisers (CL), and it was not until the London Naval Conference that the difference between heavy and light cruisers was established based on main armament size. A heavy cruiser mounted 8 inch guns, and a light cruiser, six inch.

The *Salt Lake City* was built at the New York Shipyard in Camden, New Jersey by a subdivision of the yard, the American Boveri Electric Company. She was named in honor of the capitol city of the 45th state, Utah. Keeping within the 10,000 ton limit strained not only the designers, but the builders. Most cruisers had a 10:1 ratio of length to beam, but not the *Salt Lake City*. She was 570 feet long at the waterline with a beam of 65 feet, or a 8.7:1 ratio. Weight had to be saved, and even her freeboard was cut down to save tons. A rather odd nose-like bulbous bow was fitted to keep her relatively dry in a seaway, but that addition was only partially effective. Her hull and superstructure caused her silhouette to resemble a swayback horse, and she became known as the "swayback maru". Looks are deceiving however.

When completed, the *Salt Lake City* and her

<table>
<tr><td colspan="2" align="center">*SALT LAKE CITY'S* CHARACTERISTICS</td></tr>
<tr><td>Displacement: 10,000 tons</td><td>LOA: 585' 6"/LWL: 570'</td></tr>
<tr><td>Beam: 65' 3"</td><td>Draft: 22' loaded</td></tr>
<tr><td>SHP: 107,746</td><td>Speed: 32.78 knots</td></tr>
<tr><td>Endurance: 7,020 miles @ 15 knots</td><td>Protection: Belt 2.5 inch</td></tr>
<tr><td>Main Arm: Ten 8 inch/55cal guns</td><td>Torpedoes: Six 21 inch</td></tr>
<tr><td>AA Battery: Four 5 inch/25 cal dp</td><td>Close In: 50 cal/1.1 inch</td></tr>
<tr><td colspan="2">AA battery later upgraded to multiple 20mm/40mm guns in 1942.</td></tr>
</table>

Show girls from a broadway review join bluejackets in an impromptu dance routine. Life aboard a cruiser was not always this pleasant, but it was interesting!

sister Pensacola suffered from a weak sternpost and serious vibration. Both ships rolled very sharply and in a chop, a snap roll could cause the radio mast to break off. This happened to the *Salt Lake City* in 1931. Of greater concern was the ability of these ships to deliver accurate gunfire given the unstable platform caused by rolling. Bulges were later added to reduce the rolling. Being light ships, both were damaged when a broadside was fired. The vibration severed fittings and caused structural damage. The *Salt Lake City* and her sister had some rather serious problems to resolve before becoming active contributing members of the fleet.

Even the crew space allotment was reduced from what was usual on later cruiser classes, and as habitability was becoming a major issue in the Navy, overcrowding was a problem. This became critical when her crew swelled from 41 officers/612 enlisted in peacetime to 81 officers/1,054 enlisted in wartime. This was partially resolved with the removal of the torpedoes, tripod main mast, and so forth to reduce weight.

The *Salt Lake City*, although not the designed

prototype (*Pensacola*) had the characteristics listed in the above chart.

Captain F. L. Oliver assumed command on December 11, 1929, and the new cruiser left Philadelphia on January 20, 1930 for her first cruise to determine what had to be repaired or corrected. Aside from the fact that she was a brand new cruiser type, she was also the first major ship of the U.S. Navy to be commissioned in two years. In the ever changing world of the naval armaments race, this was a long time. The *Salt Lake City* began an intensive shakedown exercise off the Maine coastline and immediately problems appeared that required correction, such as a weak sternpost, and a dangerous tendency to roll. During her main battery firing tests, a three gun salvo would cause excessive vibration which had a negative impact on the director and fire control systems. Of course the severity of the rolling also called into question her stability as a gun platform. The rolling was mollified by the adding anti-rolling tanks and enlarging her keel bilges. These were teething problems that would later be corrected, and the ship embarked on her first major cruiser on February 10, 1930 to Cuba, and later to Rio de Janiero, Brazil in a

Looking aft from the foretop, her four 5 inch/25 caliber guns can be seen. Later, the Salt Lake City would have four more 5 inch guns mounted and numerous 20mm/40mm antiaircraft weapons.

Anti rolling bilges are fitted to the Pensacola *as it was soon discovered that both the* Salt Lake City *and her sister rolled dangerously, up to 40 degrees.*

flag showing effort. The parties thrown in honor of the *Salt Lake City* and her crew are still remembered along with the difficulty maneuvering the ship through the fog created by a rum hangover!

Returning to the American naval bastion at Guantanamo Bay, Cuba on March 31, 1930, she officially joined Cruiser Division 2 of the Scouting Force. She was designated a heavy cruiser (CA-25) on July 1, 1930 as a result of the mandates of the London Naval Treaty that separated the heavy and light cruiser by the main armament size. With a ten eight inch gun main armament, there was no question that the *Salt Lake City* was a heavy cruiser.

For the next eighteen months, she operated with Cruiser Division 5 off of New England, and in early 1932, she joined with other heavy cruisers *Louisville* and *Chicago*, and headed for the West Coast. After numerous exercises, she was permanently assigned to the Pacific Fleet. For the next several years she operated out of San Pedro ranging the west coast from San Diego to Bremerton. In July 1934, she spent some time at the Puget Sound Naval Shipyard receiving her first major refit which included the addition of 50 caliber machine guns on her fore and main masts. By 1937, she would have landed her torpedo tubes, had her main fire control director enclosed at her foretop, and increased her freeboard. From 1937 up through 1939, she was a unit of the Pacific Fleet and most of her assignments were of a routine nature. She was also rearmed in February 1941 with four quad 1.1 inch close in weapons for air defense. These were vital for the war to come, and even these would be replaced by 20mm/40mm AA. She did visit Wake Island during the last remaining months of peace, and was detached to visit Brisbane, Australia in August 1941. This was done to show the Aussies that we were in support of them, a lesson not lost on the ever watchful Japanese. On December 7, 1941, she was at sea, just returning from escorting the carrier *Enterprise* to Wake Island. The "*Big E*" had just flown off a

12 plane Marine squadron of Wildcat fighters to establish air defense for the tiny atoll. The fact that the task force would not hit Pearl Harbor on Saturday night was a big disappointment for the crew of the *Salt Lake City*. There were several scheduled dances, and even one where the swing bands from various battleships would compete in the "battle of the bands". The *Arizona* almost won the honors that Saturday night, which would have been the last victory for this gallant but doomed ship. As dawn broke to clear skies, the main event was about to happen.

THE *SALT LAKE CITY* GOES TO WAR - THE EARLY DAYS OF HIT AND RUN

The *Salt Lake City* would have been among those who reluctantly received the unannounced visit of 359 attacking Japanese aircraft on the morning of December 7, 1941. A storm and a fueling problem aboard the cruiser *Northampton* combined to make the Task Force commander, Vice Admiral William "Bull" Halsey decide to enter Pearl Harbor later on December 7, rather than attempting to transit through the mine field and defensive sea area outside the harbor on the evening of the previous night. Success in sea warfare is as much due to circumstance and planning as fortune. Had the *Enterprise* and her task force entered and secured on December 6, history might have been quite different. Both would probably have been moored facing outboard near the USS *California*. Both would have been perfect targets for torpedo attack.

The ship's crew's listened with absolute horror and rage as they heard the blow by blow description of the two hour defeat of the U.S. battle force bottled up in Pearl Harbor. At dusk, the force slipped into the blazing, oil blackened hell of Pearl and quickly refueled. They left as the sun was rising, echoing Halsey's sentiment that "soon the only place Japanese would be spoken would be in Hell!".

The *Salt Lake City* went sub hunting for the next three days, and although they were certain that they had hit one of the many I Boats that lie in wait for escapees from Pearl Harbor, there was no confirmed kill. They did avoid torpedoes as evidenced by the tell tale tracks passing down their port and starboard sides. For the next few days, the *Salt Lake City* as part of Task Force 8, guarded the approaches to Oahu, and prepared for the abortive attempt to relieve the dwindling marine defenders on Wake Island. In one of the war's more regrettable decisions, the relief force was recalled and the island fortress surrendered on December 23, 1941. Men wept at the prospect of leaving fellow fighting men to their fate, and one disgruntled pilot dubbed the episode, "the battle of the yellow races" as a commentary on the cowardly order to abandon the rescue attempt.

For the next several weeks and until February 1, 1942, the *Salt Lake City* operated in and around the area adjacent to Midway, and later Samoa. The purpose was convoy escort and keeping communication and supply lines open. On February 1, 1942, the question, "where is our navy?" was answered as Admiral Halsey in commanding a task force built around the *Enterprise* made as surprise assault on the Marshall Islands. The demonstrated purpose was to knock out sea-

plane reconnaissance, but strategically, the Navy was showing the Imperial Japanese Navy that none of it's far flung bases was immune from attack. The *Salt Lake City*, as part of a group that included the cruiser *Northampton* and destroyer *Dunlap* separated from the main force and at 0715, Admiral Raymond Spruance ordered the bombardment to commence on targets of opportunity in the lagoon and those on Wotje Island. The bombardment would last 97 minutes at ranges from 30,000 to 11,000 yards. The ancient SOC gunfire spotter planes from the cruisers kept the eight and five inch guns on target, which was no little accomplishment. The Japanese had camouflaged their main installations quite well, and only by close observation, could they be detected.

The Japanese were somewhat taken by surprise, and reacted slowly to the assault. The *Salt Lake City* opened fire just before the *Northampton* and has been unofficially credited with firing the first salvo on Japanese held territory. Wotje had been under military development for nearly ten years and the *Enterprise* kept opposing aircraft from interfering with the work of the marauding cruisers, and the results were good. Much damage was done, including sinking and immobilizing cargo vessels in the lagoon. Although Wildcat fighters from the *Big E* kept the skies relatively clear of Japanese aircraft, the *Salt Lake City* and USS *Northampton* came under air attack later during the shore bombardment, yet the *Salt Lake City* emerged unscathed. At noon, the cruisers rejoined the main force and began retiring out of range of land based Japanese aircraft that were sure to come. They did, late in the day, but were successfully beaten off.

These were dark days for the navy. The Japanese octopus of expanding conquest was quickly engulfing all it touched, and seemed invincible. The small quick moving task force built around the *Enterprise* and accompanied by cruisers such as the *Salt Lake City* provided hope.

From the Marshall Islands she sped to a date with Wake Island, two months too late, but in any event on February 24, she laid down a heavy bombardment on the new occupants, the Japanese. At a range of 16,000 yards, the *Salt Lake City*, *Northampton* and destroyers *Maury* and *Balch* fired their main armament against targets being coordinated by the six SOC scout planes hovering over the atoll. Actual battle damage results were disappointing, primarily due to the use of armor piercing shells rather than the more appropriate high capacity bombardment shells. The SOC's made a minor contribution by dropping 100 pound bombs on various targets, but overall the raid was not as successful as it could have been.

From there, her force went to carry out air attacks on Marcus Island on March 4. The *Salt Lake City* did not participate in a shore bombardment at Marcus, this was a strictly an air affair.

The ultimate hit and run raid was about to take place in April, 1942, and the *Salt Lake City* would participate. It was the brainchild of Admiral E. J. King and his air operations officer, Captain (later Vice Admiral) Donald Duncan. Duncan discussed it with "Hap" Arnold, Chief of the Air Corps, and Lt. Colonel James Doolittle

One of the few photographs of four treaty cruisers moored together. From the stern of the Pensacola which is in the midst of a change of command ceremony on December 30, 1931, the cruisers Chicago, Salt Lake City and Northampton can be seen in New York harbor. The Chicago and Northampton would be lost in the desperate battles to retain Guadalcanal.

The newest cruiser in the U.S. Navy is commissioned on December 11, 1929. She cost the taxpayers $13,675,833.00, a paltry sum by any standard today, yet she would prove to be worth every cent.

In a classic shot photographed from her sister, Pensacloa, the Salt Lake City has her main battery trained to port. She is followed by another treaty cruiser, the USS Chester.

The Sale Lake City in Australia. Note the rather peculiar camouflage pattern of a false bow wave.

The 1.1 inch antiaircraft guns fire at Japanese bombers sent from enemy held bases in the Marshall Islands. The Salt Lake City and Northampton shot down two of the attackers.

was selected to lead the attack. In short, a carrier was to transport 16 specially equipped B-25 medium bombers to a point close enough the Japanese home islands so they could be launched on a one way mission to bomb various industrial centers such as Tokyo, Kobe and Ngoya. The damage to actual war production would be negligible, but lowering the morale of the Japanese and improving that of the Allies was worth the risk.

Training for the attack began in early 1942 at Elgin Field, Florida under intense secrecy. Only volunteer crews were selected, and the aircraft had to be in perfect condition. They were given instruction by naval aviators on how to get a plane the size and weight of the fully loaded B-25 off a plunging wind swept carrier deck. Within weeks, the pickup squadron was ready and flew to Alameda Naval Air Station where from 10,000 feet they saw what looked like a postage stamp size flattop moored next to the base. It was to be their new home for the next few days. It was the USS *Hornet*. Of course, there had been a test to see if B-25's could successfully launched from a carrier. While finishing her shakedown cruise in the Caribbean, two Mitchell's were launched and when they failed to crash, the plan was given thumbs up. The *Hornet* then made a dash through the Panama Canal and arrived in Alameda just in time to meet her new Army squadron. On April 2, 1942, the force sailed for "Shangri la," where President Roosevelt late contended from which the raid originated.

On April 13, the *Hornet* rendezvoused with the *Enterprise* and various other support ships including the *Salt Lake City*. The *Enterprise* would provide total air cover as the Hornet's deck was fully covered with Doolittle's B-25's. All went well until the morning of 18th, when a Japanese picket boat was discovered nearly 700 miles from it's homeland. The *Salt Lake City* and the *Vincinnes* both identified them, and the light cruiser *Nashville* smothered the target with 6 inch shells. But, it appeared that the cat was out of the bag, so the launch order was given. At a range of 668 miles from Tokyo, Doolittle led his group off the *Hornet* beginning at 0725. The north Pacific was rough and stormy that morning, but all sixteen aircraft made it.

The lead plane piloted by Lt. Colonel Doolittle leaves the plunging deck of the carrier Hornet.

After the successful launch, Task Force 16 headed back to Pearl Harbor, arriving on April 25, 1942. The visit was shortlived as the force was ordered to sail to the southwestern Pacific to reinforce the *Yorktown* and *Lexington* in the clash that was about to take place in the Coral Sea. The Allies had now drawn a line in the sand, and the Japanese were to advance no further. A lot of blood and ships would be lost, but the line would hold firm, although sometimes shaky.

She arrived too late to have a material affect on the outcome of the Battle of the Coral Sea which was fought over May 7-8. The carrier *Lexington* was lost, but so was the Japanese light carrier *Shoho*. Also sunk were the destroyer *Sims* and fleet tanker *Neosho*. The Japanese sustained some damage to their fleet carriers *Zuikaku* and *Shokaku*. On balance, the Allies suffered greater material losses, but on a strategic level, the Japanese advancement into Port Moresby on New Guinea was blunted. The lifeline between the U.S. and Australia was not severed.

The *Salt Lake City* was deployed near Australia as the *Enterprise*, *Yorktown* and *Hornet* went northeast to meet the new threat at Midway. The *Salt Lake City* was to act as a last line of defense should the emerging clash at Midway become a defeat for American Naval Forces.

It was not fortunately, and on June 4-7, American Naval forces in what became the pivotal battle of the Pacific war destroyed four top line Japanese carriers and their irreplaceable experienced air groups. The *Yorktown* was also lost, but another line in the sand had been drawn, and the Japanese would advance no further. It was a stunning victory for Admiral Raymond Spruance, a former cruiser commander who just three months earlier was directing the bombardment of Wotje Island by the *Salt Lake City* and the *Northampton*.

IRON BOTTOM SOUND AND THE NAVAL BATTLES FOR GUADALCANAL

The *Salt Lake City* was to now join a rather exclusive club that included anyone and everyone who fought in the bloody and horrible battle to hold the vermin, disease infested piece of dirt known as Guadalcanal, particularly, that little strip of acreage the that encompassed Henderson Field. Whoever retained control of the airstrip commanded the sea lanes between the U.S. and Australia and had a toehold for northward advancement. For several months, it was the most valuable piece of real estate on the face of the earth.

One of the SOC pilots holds a homemade bomb destined for anything Japanese. It is named for one of the more popular captains of the cruiser, Ellis Zacharias, who commanded her in the early fretful days of the Pacific war.

The Pensacola and Salt Lake City rest after four years of sustained combat in the Pacific. They are being prepared to participate in atomic tests known as "Operation Crossroads" in July 1946.

The Japanese had begun a small airstrip in the early summer of 1942, and by accident it was discovered by a B-17 flying a low level reconnaissance flight. This information and all that it meant did not go unheeded by the Allied high command, and a maximum effort was to be made to eject the current tenants and finish the facility for Allied use.

The *Salt Lake City* was assigned to the carrier *Wasp* as an escort to oversee and protect the initial landings on Guadalcanal and Tulagi. The landings began on August 7, and with the exception of stiff ground resistance on Tulagi, the landings went generally unopposed. The Japanese even left their uncooked daily meal for the onrushing Marines who crept up on their new airfield. It was too good to be true, and with most too good to be true situations, it wasn't. The Japanese still had a sizeable air force and navy available, and they were not about to give away important real estate.

The *Wasp* kept the carriers *Saratoga* and *Enterprise* up to air strength by ferrying planes, and at the same time provided a limited combat air patrol over the beachhead. Unfortunately, just over a month after the landings, the *Wasp* fell victim to a Japanese submarine. The *Salt Lake City* rescued many survivors. For the *Salt Lake City*, her days as an escort were about to end, and she would join the traditional battle line in some of the most grueling ship to ship battles fought in any war.

The Allies had just suffered a major setback on August 9, when a fast moving surface force of cruisers and destroyers under Admiral Mikawa swept around Savo Island and within minutes, decimated a Allied force of four heavy cruisers (*Astoria*, *Quincy*, *Vincennes*, and the Australian *Canberra*). The pride of two navies and the ability to defend the worried Marines on Henderson Field now rested in what would become known as "ironbottom sound".

Pressure from Cincpac, MacArthur and everyone who had a voice in Allied military politics began to mount. The Allies could ill afford to suffer another defeat such as the Battle of Savo Island, and they did not have unlimited resources, especially cruisers.

THE BATTLE OF CAPE ESPERANCE - THE USN MAKES A COMEBACK

The recent loss of the carrier *Wasp*, the four cruisers in August and the constant harassment of the Tokyo Express by night was getting on the nerves of the defenders. The Japanese were winning, and they seemed almost unstoppable. Both sides were hemorrhaging military strength, and big losers were the Allies. It was within this context that Mikawa, the victor at the Battle of Savo Island sent in his deputy, Admiral Aritomo Goto with a force of three heavy cruisers (*Aoba*, *Furutaka*, *Kinugasa*), eight destroyers, and two seaplane tenders loaded to the gunnels with troops and equipment. The Bombardment group consisted of the three heavy cruisers and two destroyers that would precede the reinforcement group. A sound plan and very little opposition was expected.

Unknown to the Japanese, Admiral Norman Scott flying his flag in the heavy cruiser *San Francisco* had been conducting night maneuvers with cruisers *Salt Lake City*, *Boise*, and *Helena* in concert with five destroyers from destroyer squadron 12. Both navies would converge late in the evening of October 11, 1942, and for 27 minutes would exchange gun fire and torpedoes.

On the evening of October 11, Scott brought up his column on a northeast course just four miles above Cape Esperance. In line ahead were the destroyers *Farenholt*, *Duncan*, *Laffey*, cruisers *San Francisco*, *Boise*, *Salt Lake City* and *Helena*. The rear of the column was guarded by the destroyers *Buchannan* and *McCalla*. The lead elements of the Japanese force, the three cruisers flanked by destroyers *Fubuki* and *Hatsuyuki* were steaming on a course that would unexpectedly allow Scott the rare advantage of "crossing his opponents T", thus enabling his entire broadside to engage the enemy.

Like all plans of mice and men, none are perfect. The *Salt Lake City* launched one of her SOC's for night spotting, and a flare caught fire and caused the plane to burn out of control after being jettisoned. So much for secrecy. On the other hand, the Japanese mistook the burning SOC (nearly fifty miles away) as a land signal from friendly forces. Having the capability of early detection and warning was crucial to success, and the *Helena* and *Boise* had improved surface search radar and discovered the Japanese force nearly 25 minutes (2325) before they opened fire at 2346. Scott, on the *San Francisco*, had no such improved radar, and was not apt to depend on the reports being given him by near frantic captains on other ships. By this time, the opposing forces were nearly at point blank range. Finally the *Helena* and immediately afterward, the Scott's other ships opened fire with all guns that could seek out even a suspected target. For a short period, it was a general slug fest

The Salt Lake City *firing on shore targets. She is unofficially credited with firing the first salvo at Japanese held territory on Wotje.*

What the Salt Lake City *looked like as she retired during the now famous Battle of the Komandorskies. All main battery guns were trained aft and firing as quickly as they could be served. She fired 832 rounds of 8 inch.*

with the American's dishing out the most pain and misery. Scott, however, was concerned that his cruisers were actually abusing his destroyers, and ordered a cease fire. Within a minute the cease fire order issued at 2350 was rescinded, and the general melee continued. The Japanese lost the destroyer *Fubuki* within minutes as she was virtually annihilated by 8 inch, 6 inch, and 5 inch shells. The cruiser *Furutaka* was also fatally mauled by multiple shell hits primarily from the *Salt Lake City*, *Helena*, and *Boise*. Although the *Aoba* was also struck some forty times, but managed to escape.

The *Boise*, moving out of the column to avoid torpedoes switched on her searchlight to illuminate a target, and became the hunted. She then came under violent attack by the now retiring *Aoba* and *Kinugasa* who pumped seven heavy caliber shells into her, one of which hit her forward magazine. This should have caused her to vaporize, but another below the water line hit permitted the immediate and fortunate flooding of the areas in danger. The *Boise* also owes her survival to the bravery of Captain Ernest J. Small who placed the *Salt Lake City* in front of the fire being directed at her by the retiring Japanese force. For this, the *Salt Lake City* sustaining three major hits.

By 20 minutes after midnight on October 12, the battle was over, won by the Americans. There were mistakes on both sides, but the bravery and tenacity of the American bluejacket was proven, and no longer would the Japanese own the night. The worst was yet to come, but at least the playing field had been leveled. The Japanese could be beaten at sea.

The *Salt Lake City* was damaged sufficiently to send her back to Pearl Harbor for a four month overhaul and repair period. She had also lost five men who were buried at sea shortly after the battle. After Esperance, the Japanese would begin a long retreat back to their homelands. Unfortunately, wartime censoring did not allow the *Salt Lake City* to claim her just due for many months, but history now gives credit where credit is due.

The Aleutians And The Battle Of The Komandorskies - My Speed Zero

The *Salt Lake City* had just barely mended her wounds from the successful Battle of Cape Esperance, when she was ordered to join Task Group 16.6 under the command of newly promoted Rear Admiral Charles H. "SOC" McMorris who flew his flag in the ancient light cruiser, *Richmond*. McMorris had recently held command of the USS *San Francisco* at Cape Esperance, but was relieved just prior to the running battle of November 12-15, 1942 which very nearly sank his former ship. He was familiar with the *Salt Lake City* and appreciated her assignment to his task group. A heavy cruiser of the caliber and fame of the *Salt Lake City* was always a welcome addition to any fighting unit. However, McMorris was under no illusion that his group and many of the ships consigned to the Aleutian campaign were considered first line. Complicating matters further, many of the men were newcomers to the Naval service as those who were experienced were being assigned to the new cruisers of the *Cleveland* and *Baltimore*

class. But, you do the best you can with what you have.

McMorris was assigned the same task that many naval commanders had become accustomed to over the last 18 months, preventing the Japanese from reinforcing their shore bases. Brother officers had been and still were carrying out the same tasks in the South Pacific, and the only difference was the climate. But, what a difference.

March 26, 1943 was overcast and Task Group 16.6 was on a scouting mission just over a 100 miles from the Komandorski Islands. The group consisting of the flagship *Richmond*, *Salt Lake City* and Destroyer Squadron 14, *Bailey*, *Coghlan*, *Dale* and *Monaghan* was to destroy any enemy shipping encountered.

Just after 0730 when breakfast had been finished, surface radar aboard the flagship and one of the destroyers identified what appeared to be a concentration of troop and cargo ships due north. They could only be Japanese, and it looked as if the group was about to have a field day at the expense of the Imperial Japanese Navy. Within a half hour, however, elation turned to consternation. What was facing them were the *Nachi* and *Maya*, modern fast heavy cruisers accompanied by the light cruisers *Tama* and *Abukuma* and four other armed warships. In other words, McMorris was outgunned, outclassed and outnumbered. He was not however, out maneuvered, because the Japanese force commander, Admiral Hosogaya would make some rather critical judgement errors that would eventually even the odds. But, as the confrontation unfolded, the only real threat to the Japanese column was the *Salt Lake City*.

Hosogaya was transporting desperately needed reinforcements to Attu, and was not about to let this small force deter him. McMorris on the other hand opted to fight. His rough plan of attack was to engage the cruisers at long range and at the same time attempt to shoot up the transports. Even if he failed to stop the transports, he was sure that Allied aircraft that had been called for would do the job later.

So began what would become the longest and perhaps the most bizarre sea battle ever fought. It would last over three and half hours and cover nearly 80 miles! It started at 0840 when the Japanese column, which refused to go away opened fire on the *Richmond* from a distance of 20,000 yards. At 0842, the *Salt Lake City* was able to open fire and scored hits on the *Nachi* on her third and fourth salvoes. Remarkable, under any circumstance, and from this point on it was the *Salt Lake City* fighting the entire Japanese fleet with periodic attacks by the destroyers and the *Richmond* to relieve the *Swayback Maru* when the fighting overtook her.

Early in the attack, Captain Rogers of the *Salt Lake City* put the *Nachi* temporarily out of business with three 8 inch hits, yet the *Maya* was unhurt and began firing at ranges over and under nine miles. The *Salt Lake City* led a charmed life chasing salvoes until 0910 when she was hit amidships on her SOC scout plane, killing the Lt. Cmdr. Winsor Gale and Fireman James F David. Things would have been much worse had the plane's 325 pound depth charge exploded

which dropped on the deck. The wounded cruiser did not pause in her continued attack on the *Maya* and the *Nachi*. Captain Rogers and his crew were the picture of composure and confidence. The *Nachi* suffered again when a 5 inch shell from a destroyer exploded in her number one turret. Temporarily the *Nachi* was again smoking heavily and out of action. Had Hosogaya now pressed his advantage in speed he could have closed the American force and annihilated it, however, having suffered several hits from the *Salt Lake City* and company, he elected to zigzag thereby reducing the chances of being damaged further!

For the next half hour, both forces traded salvoes, often straddling one another. The blue dye in the *Salt Lake City's* 8 inch shells unnerved the Japanese who watched 100 ft purple-blue geysers of water erupt close aboard on several occasions. The *Maya* was also using blue dye shells and it was no picnic for the crew of the *Salt Lake City* to see over 200 colored geysers within 50 yards of their ship. Of course, a geyser was not a hit.

Just after 1000, the *Salt Lake City's* steering gear was hamstrung by the continued shocks from her own gunfire, and she was confined to rudder changes of less than 10 degrees for the balance of the action. This put paid to any thought that McMorris had of outflanking the Japanese and attacking the transports. Now it was time to retire, before he suffered any further abuse. It was also time to lay funnel and chemical smoke. One of the enduring photographs of World War II will always be that of the *Salt Lake City* laying smoke and retiring at best speed (30 knots) with all four of her turrets trained aft firing at the approaching enemy battle line. It will join that of the battleship *Nevada's* gallant sortie at Pearl Harbor and others such as the carrier Gambier Bay off Samar. What Task Group 16.6 lacked in resources was compensated for by bravery, determination, and the confidence of ultimate victory epitomized by the American Bluejacket.

Just after 1100, the old cruiser took another hit which flooded the engine room, yet she never stopped firing and was able to maintain fleet speed. This would soon change for the worse 45 minutes later when sea water contaminated fuel oil extinguished all burners and the ship's speed was reducing to zero. In fact, Captain Rogers hoisted "Mike Speed Zero" at 1155, and was compelled to repeat it over the radio when an enemy shell carried away the zero signal. Now bravery and confidence would no longer suffice. A miracle was needed. The Japanese line was closing on the drifting hulk which a minute before had been a first rate cruiser. The *Salt Lake City* continued firing with her after turrets as Japanese destroyers closed for a torpedo attack and the *Maya* and *Nachi* fired multiple salvoes at a range of 19,000 yards. The miracle came in three parts. The smoke screen still held and the *Bailey*, *Coghlan*, and *Monaghan* accelerated toward the Japanese cruisers to fire torpedoes. By this time, the linings in the after gun barrels of the *Salt Lake City* were protruding at least three inches, and the magazines had run out of armor piercing shells. High Capacity (HC) shells that were undyed were being trundled across open

The Salt Lake City *refuses to sink after five hours of continued pounding by gunfire and bombing. Some "Tinclad"! This view shows* Salt Lake City *being struck in the bow by a second torpedo, but she still refuses to sink.*

The 20 year old radioactive cruiser, Salt Lake City, *rolls over after being assaulted for five hours by gunfire from 25 warships, and rockets and bombs from over 400 naval aircraft. The date is May 26, 1948, 130 miles off of San Diego, California.*

Crew and observers aboard the USS Nereus *render final honors to the slain* Salt Lake City. *There were few dry eyes in the crowd as they watched the gallant ship slip beneath the waves at the end of her final voyage.*

decks from the forward magazines and fired from the aft turrets. When the HC shells exploded near the Japanese ships, Hosogaya incorrectly assumed that the clear water geysers must be from bombing attacks. Lastly, Hosogaya, a true bureaucrat, was more concerned with violating procedure by being too low on fuel and ammunition to continue. He broke off the action and retired. The *Salt Lake City* got her miracle, that of salvation.

Within a few minutes the *Swayback Maru*, who actually had shielded the task group from destruction was back up to 15 knots and steaming for Dutch Harbor. The reinforcement move had been thwarted. Seven Americans were killed (2 in the *Salt Lake City* and five in the *Bailey*). The *Salt Lake City* fired 832 eight inch shells versus 1611 being fired back by the Japanese. The behavior of the Japanese at the Battle of the Komandorski Islands left a lot to be desired, and Admiral Hosogaya found himself on the beach within a month. His flagship *Nachi* had to return to Japan for extensive repairs.

God truly was on the side of the crew of the *Salt Lake City*, and for over three hours gave his undivided attention to her on that bleak day in March 1943. The *Salt Lake City* remained in Alaskan waters until September 23, 1943, and saw the eviction of the Japanese from American soil. She sailed for Pearl Harbor with a stopover in San Francisco, arriving on October 14, 1943. The rest of the war in the Pacific would prove grueling and difficult, but was anticlimactic to her first two years at war. The tinclad had proven to be no tinclad at all.

Toward Ultimate Victory - One Atoll At A Time

The *Salt Lake City* participated in the bombardment of Tarawa, Wake Island, and again in the Marshall where she hit Wotje in early February 1944. She had made a hit and run attack just two years earlier when the war was still in doubt. Now the war was not longer in doubt, it was just a matter of when.

In April, 1944, she steamed for Mare Island

Naval Shipyard for overhaul and repair. She was given a minimal upgrade, but with the war winding down, it was not cost effective to thoroughly modernize the old cruiser.

Back in the western Pacific, she participated in one island raid and bombardment after another, and the war ended just as she was sailing for the Aleutians. She was diverted on August 11th, 1945 to Northern Honshu to cover the occupation of a major Japanese naval installation at Ominato. The end of the war found her there.

The Final Voyage - Sunk By Her Own Navy

She was assigned to "*Operation Magic Carpet*" throughout the balance of 1945, and on November 14, she became part of the 73 ship ghost fleet that would feel the effect of the twin nuclear explosions at Bikini Atoll in July of the following year.

The old cruiser was able to endure both "Gilda" and "Betty" as the July 1 and 26, 1946 atomic bomb tests were named. Although she was in the outer circle of ships, the above ground and underwater blasts hit her hard. It was absolutely amazing to anyone with any remembrance of the coy remarks made when the *Salt Lake City* was commissioned. It was said that she would never survive any form of mortal combat, yet she survived nuclear blasts, bombing and surface battles. She was eventually decommissioned on August 29, 1946, and in her final voyage, was sunk off the California coast by gunfire and bombing. She sank in deep water on May 25, 1948, and many witnesses openly wept at her loss. Today, many veterans still feel that she should have been preserved as a memorial.

The *Salt Lake City* earned eleven battle stars for action, and the Navy Unit Commendation for the efforts in the Aleutian Campaign. She also fought the only and probably final major daylight surface battle without air cover. She was a gallant ship manned by a crew that never let her down. She was faithful till the end.

The USS *San Francisco*, CA-38 "Ship of Valor"

The USS *San Francisco*, CA-38 was the first of the seven ship class of *New Orleans* class heavy cruisers. She was commissioned on February 10, 1934 at the Mare Island Naval Shipyard, located just minutes from her namesake city, the city by the Golden Gate. This cruiser was special among U.S. Navy ships as she earned 17 battle stars and one of the three Presidential Unit Citations won by cruisers.

Her origin dates back to 1929, five years before she actually plied the muddy waters of San Pablo Bay near the shipyard of her birth. On February 13, 1929, the U.S. Congress passed an act to build 15 light cruisers, five each over the next three years at an average cost of $17 million each. By the time that the *San Francisco* was actually laid down on September 9, 1931, a reinterpretation of the 1929 act had been made, and ten heavy cruisers were to be built under the auspices of the same act. By this time, cruisers had been segregated into two distinct classes, light and heavy by the London Naval Conference in 1930. In general, those ships with a main battery of 8 inch guns were designated as heavy cruisers and those with six inch guns, light cruisers. Initially, the U.S. Navy chose to build heavy cruisers to keep pace with foreign navies that were considered to be potential future adversaries.

The *New Orleans* class was the fourth of five identifiable classes of heavy cruiser built subject to the letter and spirit of the 1922 and 1930 Naval Arms Limitation Treaties. There would be eighteen heavy cruisers and nine light cruisers whose origin was wholly guided by these treaties. They would be known as treaty cruisers, but to those who built them, they were the "tin clads". To those men that fought them, the term tinclad was unacceptable, as they proved to be efficient and beautiful fighting ships. They made American naval history, and in not a few historians minds, were the backbone of victory in the early Pacific war.

The *New Orleans* class differed from it's pre-

Keel Laid Plaque of the new cruiser, USS San Francisco *CA-38, on September 9, 1931. She was one of the* New Orleans *class, and a precursor to the more modern* Baltimore *class of heavy cruisers built during World War II.*

The San Francisco *off San Pedro in April 1935. In this photo, she was the ultimate "treaty cruiser". Graceful, yet no radar, under protected and virtually without any form of antiaircraft defense. Extensive numbers of AA guns, radar and other changes would come swiftly after the war began.*

decessors, the *Pensacola, Northampton* and *Portland* classes in obvious ways that graphically showed the evolution of the cruiser. The *Pensacola's* were armed with ten 8 inch guns and more closely resembled World War I naval design thinking with boxlike fighting tops and observation platforms. By the time the *New Orleans* class was designed and launched, the bulbous clipper bow was gone and the superstructure was more pronounced. The funnels were raised higher than previous classes, but moreover, the *New Orleans* class was more contemporary looking with a more extensive bridge structure. Most importantly, the *New Orleans* class was more heavily armored than it's predecessors, yet additional protection was not enough against the concentrated fire of Japanese heavy caliber guns and the deadly "long lance" torpedo. No treaty cruiser or even their successors could stand up to the long lance.

The hull length of the *New Orleans* class was 588 feet as opposed to that of 611 feet of their immediate predecessor, the *Portland* class. The shorter length allowed greater attention to armor

protection within the 10,000 ton treaty limitation. They were handsome ships, but the boxlike hanger and catapult structure just aft of amidships did interupt their rather graceful lines.

The class consisted of the *New Orleans* CA-32, *Astoria* CA-34, *Minneapolis* CA-36, *Tuscaloosa* CA-37, *San Francisco* CA-38, *Quincy* CA-39 and *Vincennes* CA-44. The *Astoria, Vincennes,* and *Quincy* would be lost in the August 9, 1942 Battle of Savo Island, The *Minneapolis* would nearly be lost at the November 29-30 1942 Battle of Tassafaronga in the bloody contest for the Solomons, and *New Orleans* would also suffer greatly during the same battle. The only member of the class that would survive the war relatively unscathed was the Tuscaloosa, which spent much of her combat career in the European theater. The *San Francisco* would barely survive the November 13, 1942 Naval Battle of Guadalcanal. Six of the seven would meet tragedy in the bloody and violent conflict to forcibly evict the Japanese from the Solomon and nearby islands. However, through force of arms and the unparalleled brav-

ery of the crews of ships like those of the *New Orleans* class, the Japanese were defeated. As a tribute to these ships, only the carrier *Enterprise* would earn more battle stars than the *Minneapolis* and *San Francisco* at 17 each.

THE USS *SAN FRANCISCO* - A *New Orleans* CLASS HEAVY CRUISER

The *San Francisco*, like the rest of the *New Orleans* class was designed through the inspiration of Rear Admiral George Rock. Due to the length of time between design and final launching (approximately seven years), there was some dispute over the class designation. At one time the class was to be known as the *Minneapolis* class, later the *Astoria* class, but finally the *New Orleans* was settled upon as the accepted class title. These ships would depart from the earlier heavy cruiser designs and although they did not have the endurance of the earlier models, they were the precursor to the *Brooklyn* and *Cleveland* class light cruisers, and the *Wichita* and *Baltimore* class heavy cruisers. The ancestry of the modern World War II cruiser can easily be traced to the *New Orleans* class. This class was considered a breakthrough design.

Another design departure in the *New Orleans* class was the complete absence of a torpedo armament. By the time this class was being considered, Naval War College studies of the pro's and con's of cruiser mounted torpedo batteries shied away from this weapon. The Japanese were wildly successful with their torpedo batteries, yet their torpedoes were far superior to anything the U.S. Navy had during the crucial ship to ship duels during the first two years of the Pacific war. Perhaps it was all for the best, even if it was by default.

One of the other design characteristics of this class and actually of all the treaty cruisers was the tendency toward being topheavy and overweight. 10,000 ton limitation strained even the most imaginative naval architect, and by the middle of World War II, the remaining treaty cruisers were dangerously overweight with all of the new antiaircraft batteries, associated fire control and other electronics. It took the treaty breaker *Baltimore* class at 15,000 plus tons to safely and effectively carry all of the modern equipment and weapons systems necessary without worry and concern about seaworthiness.

The *New Orleans* class was characterized as in the chart on the top of the following page.

The last of the *New Orleans* class was the *Vincennes*, commissioned on February 24, 1937, three years after the lead ship, the *San Francisco* was commissioned.

The *San Francisco* was laid down on September 9, 1931 at the Mare Island Naval Shipyard in Vallejo, California. This yard was also the builder of the destroyer *Ward* DD-139 which would sound the unheeded alarm at Pearl Harbor on December 7, 1941, and of course the battleship *California* which would sink into the mud of Pearl Harbor three days after the attack.

The *San Francisco* was launched on March 9, 1933 and christened by Miss Barbara M. Bailly. The *San Francisco* was one of the first major ships that the Mare Island Naval Shipyard had built since World War I, and the citizens of Vallejo were justly proud of their achievement.

On February 10, 1934, after nearly a year of post launch fitting out, the new cruiser was commissioned and Captain Royal E. Ingersoll assumed command. For the next several weeks she went through her final fitting out period and then she was ready for her shakedown cruise. She left the muddy waters off Vallejo and went on an extended shakedown cruise that took her to South America, across to the big island of Hawaii and then back to North America where she visited Victoria, British Columbia. During her four month cruise, she even visited the Panama Canal Zone, but in late summer 1934 she arrived back at Mare Island for some needed modifications that included being readied for flagship duties and final gunnery installation.

By February 1935, she was ready to assume her role as a member of the fleet and Cruiser Division 6 based out of San Diego.

PRE-WAR OPERATIONS

As with most ships of the fleet, the *San Francisco* trained for a war that all knew would soon come in the Pacific. Only the most naive were unsure as to who the opponent would be, but no one was certain as to the time. The *San Francisco* spent much of her prewar time shuffling between the East and West coast with an occasional extended trip to the far reaches of each hemisphere.

In July 1938, she sailed for Alaskan ports and by the end of the year she was again steaming south to Peru. She had participated in the now famous Fleet Problems that endeavored to bring greater reality to war games and at the same time show the Japanese that the Pacific Ocean was not their private lake. In early 1939, she sailed for the Atlantic where she participated in Fleet Problem XX, and in March became the flagship of Cruiser Division 7, carrying Rear Admiral Husband E. Kimmel.

Kimmel would skyrocket to command the U.S. Pacific Fleet in early 1941, and just as quickly disappear in late December of the same year after the disastrous attack on the fleet and other military installations at Pearl Harbor on December 7. But in mid 1939, he flew his flag on one of the most beautiful ships in the navy's inventory as she sailed southward to visit various ports on the eastern coast of South America. The *San Francisco*, *Tuscaloosa*, and *Quincy* also transitted the Straits of Magellan on their tour and came up the west coast of South America. The straits, long feared by seafarers was not easy for the crews of the three cruisers, but the trip only took one day.

With the circumnavigation of the South American continent complete, the *San Francisco* found herself back on the east coast of the U.S. and fortuitously available to serve as Fleet Reception Ship for the World's Fair in New York City in July 1939. The world's fair was the last for several years and also was a formal plea for peace among all nations, however, Germany, Japan and Italy had other ideas. With tensions now growing in the Atlantic yet only simmering in the Pacific, the *San Francisco* and fellow cruisers, *Vincennes*, *Tuscaloosa*, and *Quincy* accompanied by the carrier *Ranger* and old battleships *Wyoming*, *Arkansas*, *New York* and *Texas* formed the Atlantic Squadron. A two ocean navy

was being created and the squadron was a mere precursor to Atlantic Fleet yet to be formed.

The first order of business after the Allied (sans the USA) September 3, 1939 declaration of war on Germany for the invasion of Poland was the formation of the Neutrality Patrol. The Neutrality Patrol was a major element of the Roosevelt Administration's "short of war" strategy to aid our prospective allies and at the same time buy time to build up the armed forces. The *San Francisco* was not ordered to the frigid north, but spent her time in the Caribbean as the flagship of a force composed of the *Tuscaloosa* and destroyers *Truxton* and *Simpson* along with other smaller patrol vessels. In January 1940, the cruiser was relieved of her duties as flagship by the *Wichita* and proceeded to Pearl Harbor to rejoin cruiser division 6.

In May 1940, after various training and patrol exercises, she was detached for an extensive overhaul in the Puget Sound Naval Shipyard. Aside from having her bottom scrapped, she was now painted in battleship grey and most of glass portlights were welded over. Also, crew space was increased to accommodate at least 300 more men. The *San Francisco* was preparing for war and shedding her peacetime niceties. In addition, she was provided an interim antiaircraft battery of four 3 inch/50 caliber guns. Two were mounted on the fantail and the other two on the aft part of the bridge so high that they were almost level with the funnel cap of the number one funnel. In addition, splinter shields were added for each 5 inch/ 25 caliber gun. These shields would prove valuable in the 1942 battles around Guadalcanal. Many of these changes were inspired by a study and consequent recommendations made by a special committee chaired by Rear Admiral Earnest J. King at the behest of the Secretary of the Navy. The "King Board," as it was known studied the existing capability of the fleet to defend itself against aircraft and found obvious deficiency in all ships. The few 50 caliber machine guns on most ships were virtually useless against modern aircraft as were the 5 inch/25 caliber guns. Even antiaircraft directors were not capable of tracking aircraft that could now fly at 300 knots or more. The antiaircraft gun crews were exceptionally well trained, but without adequate tools, their training would fall short.

The *San Francisco* now had an improved battery to repel aircraft, but it was only an in-

terim measure. Later, 20mm/40mm guns that were director controlled would close the gap, but for now, the 3 inch, 5 inch and 50 caliber machine guns would have to suffice.

In September 1940, her overhaul complete, the *San Francisco* sailed for Pearl Harbor. As 1940 wore into 1941, Pearl Harbor was becoming rapidly transformed from a pleasant anchorage to what could be dubbed a forward base. Ships and men were on a semi war footing. In order to demonstrate to the Japanese and our Pacific allies that the U.S. would not tolerate rampant militarism, the Pacific Fleet was now based out of Pearl Harbor and Husband Kimmel was jumped over several senior officers to assume command. Admiral James O. Richardson who previously held the position was removed because he opposed having the fleet at Pearl Harbor and potentially bottled up and open to Japanese attack. His politically incorrect remarks and attitude saw to his removal in February 1941.

Meanwhile, the *San Francisco* was again selected as flagship of Cruiser Division 6, flying Admiral Frank Jack Fletcher's flag. A month later, on May 1, 1941, Captain Daniel J. "Uncle Dan" Callaghan assumed command of the *San Francisco*. He had been the naval aide to President Roosevelt and was regarded as one of the better officers in the navy. Built like rock, Callaghan was well liked and respected by all who worked with him, and he was an special favorite with the crew of the *San Francisco*. Within a short period Cruiser Division Six was ordered to Long Beach much to the satisfaction of the *San Francisco's* crew. But by August, 1941, she was back at Pearl Harbor and preparing for an extensive overhaul and a period in drydock. Her bottom was foul with growth and a substantial amount of work was necessary to render her again as a top line fighting ship.

On September 11, 1941, Fletcher transferred his flag to the *Minneapolis* and a month later, the *San Francisco* left fleet availability and entered the shipyard for overhaul. She was in a partially dismantled state at 0755 on the morning of December 7, 1941.

THE ATTACK ON PEARL HARBOR FINDS THE *SAN FRANCISCO* IN PIECES

The *San Francisco* was berthed at one of the piers just down from 1010 dock, and like the straw man in the Wizard of Oz, had the stuffing out of her lying about everywhere. Her five inch guns were dismantled and her three inch guns were now removed in anticipation of new 1.1 inch machine guns being mounted. Even her fifty caliber guns were useless. But, that did not prevent the crew of the *San Francisco* from shooting back. Some grabbed rifles, others, pistols and at least two 30 caliber sub machine guns were brought into action. In desperation and rage, sailors broke into the landing force lockers and used whatever guns were available. Rage and determination replaced astonishment as the men of the *San Francisco* and other ships in the harbor began to fight back. But, the *San Francisco* was in no shape to contribute much to harbor defense.

The cruiser was preparing to enter drydock number 2 for very badly needed bottom scrapping and a new coat of paint. An enemy could not be caught with maximum speed reduced by barnacles and sea growth. She was slated to enter drydock on December 15, and in accordance with Navy policy most of her ammunition and weapons were either removed or at least immobilized. What a way to begin a war, most of the crew ashore and those aboard were sitting on dead iron without much to defend themselves. Many of the crew boarded sister cruiser *New Orleans*, moored on the opposite side of the pier and helped man their antiaircraft batteries, and 50 caliber ammunition was sent over to the destroyer *Tracy* moored nearby.

Midway into the battle, Captain Callaghan arrived and assumed command. Much to his pride, he saw an crew making a positive contribution to harbor defense without disorder and any panic. Good training, discipline and teamwork was paying dividends, but this was evident throughout the fleet. The men of the *San Francisco*, as well as thousands of others would periodically pause as some new and more horrible disaster would take place. All watched the battleship *Oklahoma* turn over just minutes into the attack as well as the explosion of the forward magazines of the *Arizona*. History will never forget that explosion which instantly killed over a thousand innocent men, nor will any ever have to be reminded of the bravery and skill of the crew of the *Nevada* as she made her abortive but courageous attempt to get to sea. Late in the battle the destroyer *Shaw* blew up in one of the most spectacular displays of fireworks in World War II, but it was equaled in emotional intensity by the slow deaths of the battleship's *California* and *West Virginia* and minelayer *Oglala*. The battle ended at about 1000, just over two hours after the first bomb hit the ramp on Ford Island. Of the 353 attacking aircraft, all but 29 returned to the six carrier task force waiting to the north. They left a swath of devastation unparalleled in warfare. No nation has ever entered a war with so smashing a victory, and ended up being so utterly devastated at it's end.

For the men of cruiser *San Francisco*, the war was just beginning, but for 2,403 others it had ended in the early morning hours of December 7, 1941. Brave deeds and violent conflict on a scale of ferocity yet unknown mankind in war would engulf this cruiser and her crew, and within one year. But, on the night of December 7, all the crew of the cruiser wanted to do was to survive,

put their ship back together and seek revenge. Some say the night of December 7, was the longest night of World War II, and for the thousands of sailors, marines, soldiers and airmen at Pearl Harbor it was understandable.

WHERE DID THEY GO AND WHAT DO WE DO?

To say there was confusion in the aftermath of the attack on Pearl Harbor is an understatement. All suspected that Admiral Kimmel would be relieved of command because punishment was now the order of the day. Preserving what was left of the Navy Yard and ships and providing sufficient defense against further attack seemed to be the most important order of business. But, there was Wake Island, Guam and the Philippines to consider. The "Rainbow" war plan was made worthless by the attack itself as was the long held belief that the battleship was queen of the ocean. Now, the carrier was queen, and the U.S. had precious few available in the Pacific.

By December 14, the *San Francisco* was again available for combat, fouled bottom and all, and on December 16, she left Pearl Harbor as a unit of Task Force 14 (*Astoria,* flagship). The *San Francisco* was part of a support force built around the carrier *Saratoga* which was to deliver Marine Squadron 221 consisting of 18 Brewster Buffaloes to Wake Island. The Buffaloes were not much to look at and certainly not a match for the "Zero", but anything would have been welcome to the Marines on Wake.

Unfortunately, indecision and fear of further naval losses caused the *Saratoga* and her screen to withdraw from the mission. At just over 400 miles distant on December 23, Admiral Fletcher ordered an about face of TF-14 citing lack of fuel oil for his destroyers. It was too late, because later that morning, the garrison surrendered and Wake Island would become the property of Imperial Japan for the next four years. Hindsight, which is always 20/20 informs us that the "Sara" and her cruiser screen could have made a high speed run to Wake on December 22, with fuel to spare including the destroyers. There they probably would have disrupted the landing and at the same time a great naval engagement would have ensued. The Japanese had pulled out the stops to take the island and even Admiral Goto, later of Cape Esperance fame was there with his force of heavy cruisers (*Aoba, Kinugasa, Furutaka,* and *Kako*) to provide support. Also available were the carriers *Soryu* and *Hiryu* recent victors at Pearl Harbor. The odds were uneven, but they were at Midway also. Who knows? In any event, the night passage back to Pearl Harbor was marked with disappointment and tears shed by the men of TF-14. Some bitterly commented that it looked like it was going to be a war between two "yellow" races.

The Marine reinforcements ended up on Midway including the misfit Buffaloes, and the *San Francisco* was detached in early January for more shepherding duty as she convoyed troops to Samoa as part of Task Force 8 with Halsey's carrier *Enterprise*. For the next several weeks the *San Francisco* operated as part of one screen after another protecting carriers *Lexington* and/ or *Yorktown*.

The San Francisco *as she is entering the Mare Island Navy Yard for extensive repairs after the November, 1942 Naval Battle of Guadalcanal. The lack of substantial armor belt protection is evident. She is painted in the dark blue, common to ships in the early stages of the war.*

On February 20, Task Force 11 made an abortive attempt to attack the Japanese bastion on Rabaul but was snooped by Japanese aircraft and had to retire. Multiple bogeys were soon sighted and the Task Force was in for a rough time as two flights of land based bombers attacked the ships. The *San Francisco* maneuvered at high speed with her four screws turning maximum knots. She provided effective antiaircraft fire that disrupted the attackers, allowing the force to retire to safety. Finally, the gunners on the cruiser had weapons to fire back and plenty of targets.

On March 7, she lost one of her SOC scout planes and after a protracted search, pilot John Thomas and radioman Otis Gannon were presumed lost. The force continued on it's way to it's planned attack on Rabaul, but on March 10, the mission of Task Force 11 was changed to raids on Salamua and Lae (New Guinea) where the Japanese had just landed. 104 planes launched from the *Lexington* and *Yorktown* made their way over the Owen Standley mountains to attack the forces at Salamua and Lae. The raid was a success.

Back to pilot Thomas and radioman Gannon. They had been missing since March 7, and miraculously, they were sighted again on March 13 by a scout plane from the cruiser *Minneapolis*. The *San Francisco* was detached to retrieve her airdales and the aircraft, and shortly thereafter all three were back aboard the cruiser. The reason for the SOC being lost: pilot error in navigation. But he and Gannon more than made up for it by rigging a sail and confidently beginning the voyage to Australia. By the time the missing SOC was discovered it had travelled 385 miles and was virtually on course the entire way. The only real serious problem developed shortly after Thomas and Gannon were certain that rescue was imminent. They broke out the pork and beans, previously being conserved, and feasted. By the time they reached the ship, both had serious cases of indigestion, but they were alive and well.

The cruiser was detached and sent to Pearl Harbor shortly after this raid, arriving on March 26, 1942. There minor upkeep was performed as well as having the new 20mm gun installed in various locations. The 20mm and

A stern view of the cruiser graphically shows the damage done to the aft superstructure and gun director by the Japanese torpedo plane that crashed on her at the outset of the Naval Battle of Guadalcanal on November 12, 1942. Fifteen were killed and 29 wounded by this first, but prophetic episode with Japanese pilots who elected to join their ancestors by crashing their damaged planes on enemy ships.

later the 40mm would replace the ineffective 50 caliber and 1.1 inch machine guns as well as the four stopgap 3 inch/50 caliber's mounted just eighteen months earlier. After a short shakedown period, the cruiser became part of an escort force watching over a convoy on its way to San Francisco. The scarred battleship *Nevada* was also part of this convoy on her way ultimately to the Puget Sound Naval Shipyard.

After a period on the West Coast, the *San Francisco* again sailed westward as escort for a troop convoy bound for Suva as well as Australia. She also visited Auckland, New Zealand

on a goodwill tour to bolster our allies confidence in the resolve of the U.S. to keep the supply and communications lines open in spite of Japanese ambitions. On May 1, 1942, another change took place, and that was the replacement of Captain Callaghan by Captain Horatio "Soc" McMorris. Callaghan had been named by the Flag Officers Selection Board meaning he would now fly his flag as an admiral. The crew was pleased for their skipper, but also would miss him. "Soc" McMorris, late of the pre-Pearl Harbor Cincpac staff was a comer, and he too would eventually fly his flag as an admiral.

The cruiser missed both the Battles of the Coral Sea and Midway. However, the *San Francisco* was to play a crucial if not critical role in a series of sea battles that have yet to be rivaled in their ferocity and strategic importance. Coral Sea and Midway were both ultimately significant victories for American arms as they prevented the continued movement of the Imperial Japanese military machine. They were decisive and stopped planned advances. In the case of the Battle of Midway, American carriers saved Midway from occupation and service as another forward Japanese arsenal. In addition, U.S. Navy pilots destroyed four carriers and their precious air groups, a blow from which the Empire never fully recovered. The IJN was forced to do something it had never done, leave the field of battle in the control of the enemy. The IJN was not planning to accommodate the Allies so easily again.

The San Francisco *is being transformed during her short stay at the Mare Island Navy Yard. Additional 20mm guns have been added along with 40mm that have replaced the less than satisfactory 1.1 inch antiaircraft guns. New radar has also been installed.*

Bow view of the San Francisco *as she enters the Mare Island Navy Yard. She had been badly damaged on "bloody Friday," the 13th of November, 1942. Most of her damage was above the waterline as the battleships she was trading shots with could not depress their main armament low enough due to the close range.*

The bow view really shows the extent that the cruiser has been modernized by February 1943 to meet the battle conditions of the Pacific war. The old bridge has been plated over and an open bridge area built to facilitate defending the ship against aircraft. The forward part of the ship also sports a number of new antiaircraft guns and directors.

Stern view of the cruiser showing a new aft director and quadruple mount 40mm located on the stern enclosed by sponsons that overhang the deck. The addition of antiaircraft guns and associated equipment caused all ships to become top heavy, consequently, items such as boatcranes were landed to conserve weight.

After director and 20mm antiaircraft platform after being hit by a damaged Japanese torpedo plane just hours before the epic surface battle fought on November 13, 1942.

Where the Japanese intended to strike was no secret to the Allies - they would seek to cut the lifeline between Australasia and the U.S. Carrier aircraft had already successfully attacked shipping and the harbor at Darwin on the continent of Australia on February 19, 1942. It was a freak raid, but it showed that the Allies could be hit hard, almost anywhere. To flesh out their slim holdings in the South Pacific and widen their opportunity, the Japanese selected a little known island in the Solomons named Guadalcanal. Not more than a fraction of the people in the world other than some astute geography teachers and a few natives had ever heard of this filthy, disease and insect infested sinkhole. However, it was strategically located and if properly developed would put an effective block to any plans the Allies had for retaking what they had lost so easily over the past few months. Accordingly, the Japanese occupied Tulagi, just opposite the "canal" on May 1, 1942 and began building a stronghold. The occupation and labor battalions generally ignored their neighbor across what would become known as Ironbottom Sound. As they were not really pestered on a regular basis by Allied visitors either by air or sea, the only visits to Guadalcanal were for meat hunting parties or recreation. Finally, the Japanese did recognize the potential value of the cleared plain just off the beach and late in June a large contingent of engineers and builders went ashore with earth moving equipment to build an airfield.

Within a few days however, an Allied B-17 reconnaissance plane took some rather remarkable photographs that changed the entire theme of the Pacific war. It also made Guadalcanal the strategic center of a bloody and expensive tug of war that made the name alone an emotion rivalling that of hatred and fear for the sailors, soldiers, marines and airmen who were forced to fight there. Until the discovery of the airfield being built near Lunga Point, Allied planners had relied on a generalized approach which called for movement up the chain of islands and eventually attacking and neutralizing the Japanese stronghold at Rabaul. The revelation of an airfield changed all of that. The strategy changed from one of movement toward Rabaul to one of stopping the Japanese cold and taking that airfield before it could do any further damage. On July 10, Allied Naval forces were notified that "Operation Watchtower" would proceed at once and Tulagi and now Guadalcanal would be secured.

On July 1, 1942, the San Francisco began preparations for what would be several months of intense fighting. All interior paint was removed as a fire hazard, and training was stepped up. By July 21, she was on her way from Pearl Harbor escorting a troop convoy that would eventually find its way to Guadalcanal. On August 2, 1942, she left Suva in the Fiji Islands for her intended destination as part of a screen for the carrier Wasp. In all, 76 ships participated in the assault on Tulagi and Guadalcanal hence the true name of the operation, "Operation Shoestring". Compared to the Invasion of Normandy, North Africa or most others in the central Pacific, this was small potatoes. But, it was our first engagement.

On August 7, 1942, eight months from the attack on Pearl Harbor, the Marines went ashore under the guns of the cruisers Quincy, Vincennes, and Astoria as well as supporting destroyers. The Marines did not meet much opposition on Guadalcanal, however the fighting on Tulagi was fierce. Both were secured, in spite of justified fear of air and surface attack. The counter attack by Japanese naval forces was less than 48 hours away. Meanwhile, the San Francisco and the distant carrier force patrolled forty miles south of the invasion beaches. A few minutes after midnight on the morning of August 9, 1942, a fast moving Japanese cruiser and destroyer force under the command of Admiral Gunichi Mikawa swept into the channel between Savo Island and Guadalcanal and within minutes sank the Australian cruiser Canberra, and American cruisers Vincennes, Quincy and Astoria, all sisters of the San Francisco. The cruiser Chicago was also damaged by a torpedo that struck her in the bow. It was a stunning victory for the IJN, and it also was the beginning of a literal hemorrhage of naval strength on both sides. Many cruisers and destroyers would either find their way to the bottom of what became known as "Ironbottom Sound" or they would limp home for repairs. Very few of the Allied navy's or IJN's front line units would escape death or mutilation. Keeping the right, title and interest of Guadalcanal and Tulagi would be much more costly than the Allies had imagined.

When all of the finger pointing stopped, the reasons became clear. The Allies were unprepared and their communication and early warning systems were deficient. They were also incredulous that the Japanese would have the audacity and boldness to sneak in under cover of darkness and catch them napping, again. Was their no honor or code of behavior that the Japanese military followed? Although this was an expensive lesson in men and material, it was not lost on Allied leaders nor the men who would fight and die in this theater. The Japanese came to win, and anything less was unacceptable - that was their code. They would do whatever was necessary to prevail and that meant butchery and willing self sacrifice. Each Imperial soldier and sailor was a weapon and the vast majority would willingly die for victory. The Allies, in particular, the sailors and marines of the U.S. Navy, discovered that civilized war was out, and the only way to win was to kill the enemy. Admiral Halsey said it best when he assumed command of the theater some weeks later, "Kill Japs, Kill Japs, Kill More Japs!" This type of raw animal passion goes against the grain of the American spirit, but during the struggle for the Solomons, it was appropriate.

As part of Task Force 61, the San Francisco remained with the carriers until late in August when she became the flagship of Rear Admiral Norman Scott who had transferred his flag from the antiaircraft cruiser San Juan. For the next two weeks and into mid September, the San Francisco provided direct support to the carrier Wasp, but on September 15, a new threat appeared in the form of submarine launched torpedoes. The Wasp was hit, and hit hard as was the destroyer O'Brien and later the battleship North Carolina. Admiral Scott ordered the Salt Lake City and San Francisco to attempt a tow, but the Wasp was too far gone and had to be sunk by friendly torpedo fire from the destroyer Landsdowne. In just over a month from the initial Solomon Islands landings, the carrier Wasp was lost along with cruisers Quincy, Astoria, Vincennes, not to mention that the cruiser Chicago, battleship North Carolina, and carrier Enterprise were forced to withdraw due to serious damage. The torpedo attack which was so costly, would have been more so, had not an alert lookout seen the tracks of torpedoes heading for the San Francisco. She altered course just in time to avert destruction.

Enough was enough. The Allies had been bombed, shelled, and torpedoed with very little loss to the enemy. Admiral Scott began to train his cruisers and destroyers for night fighting. The training in the later part of September and early October was relentless, but the Marines on Guadalcanal were desperate. Nightly, the Japanese came in by air or sea and hammered them. Japanese troops were being landed just up the coast by the "Tokyo Express", an almost regular run of destroyers or fast transports bringing in fresh supplies and reinforcements. Aside from the derailing the express, the Allies urgently wanted a victory to prop up their sagging morale and to put an end to the suspected invincibility of the Japanese navy. They would not have long to wait.

THE BATTLE OF CAPE ESPERANCE AND REDEMPTION

The Japanese wanted to evict the Marines from Guadalcanal and the strategy employed consisted of landing troop reinforcements, equipment and supplies nightly or as often as possible. Added to this was persistent harassment in the form of naval bombardment, bombing and something as annoying as the nightly arrival of seaplanes that dropped flares or small bombs. There was even an aircraft with it's engines out of synchronization that kept worn out marines from sleeping. This was "washing machine charlie", but this was nothing compared to the periodic heavy bombardment by the IJN or being greeted with hundreds of new troops each morning.

Of course, the Marines were not above such tactics and each day, Henderson Filed fliers sought out Japanese targets and did a comparable amount of destruction. They were particularly adept at disrupting the "Tokyo express", and in early October, Henderson Field was visited by swarms of Japanese bombers from Rabaul in savage retaliation. Finally convinced that the U.S. Navy and the Marine fliers on Henderson Field posed no real threat, Admiral Mikawa sent Rear Admiral Aritimo Goto with his bombardment group of cruisers and destroyers to back up a reinforcement group consisting of two seaplane carriers and six destroyers. Goto was relatively well thought of in the Imperial command. His experience included the rescue of the Wake Island invasion force assuring that the second attempt to conquer the island was successful. Goto carried his flag in the heavy cruiser Furutaka which was accompanied by sister ships Kinugasa and Aoba. The three cruisers were escorted by two destroyers, the Hatsuyuki and

Fubuki. The *Fubuki* earned her fame as the ship that identified the cruisers *Houston* and *Perth* as they attempted to run the Sunda Strait earlier that year in February. Both were sunk, but the *Fubuki* successfully sunk three friendly transports when her torpedoes missed the speeding cruisers and went into a crowded anchorage. There is justice in the world.

The night of night of October 11-12 was selected for the run, and late on the evening of the 11th, Goto was steaming deep into the slot on his way to bombard American positions on Guadalcanal. He had not reckoned with a determined force of cruisers and destroyers under the overall command of Rear Admiral Norman Scott who was flying his flag in the *San Francisco*. Scott's Task Force which actually represented the bulk of available Allied ships in the area consisted of the heavy cruisers *San Francisco* and *Salt Lake City*, light cruisers *Helena* and *Boise* and destroyers *Farenholt, Duncan, Laffey, Buchannan,* and *McCalla*. The odds were nine ships to five, but the Japanese had three heavy cruisers, and were highly experienced in night fighting. Goto had commanded this same group of ships in many past successful operations and had just completed refresher training in the Shortlands just prior to this sortie. All in all, the odds were fairly even considering every factor.

Scott was aware that a sizeable force was bent on shooting up the area having been warned on the early afternoon of the 11th by a B-17 reconnaissance plane. He just did not know exactly what the force composition was nor their expected time of arrival. Accordingly, he deployed his ships into column with three destroyers in the van, leading the *San Francisco, Boise, Salt Lake City* and *Helena*. Two destroyers brought up the rear. He began a patrol north of Cape Esperance within sight of Savo Island. The eeriness of the area was not lost on the hundreds of men waiting and coldly sweating at their battle stations. After all, just two months before in almost the same location, they had lost several shipmates when a fast moving force of Japanese cruisers swept by the outer pickets and sank four Allied cruisers. *San Francisco* sisters, *Vincennes, Astoria* and *Quincy* were three of the four. The Australian cruiser *Canberra* was the fourth. There was a difference now as Scott's force was ready for an expected attack from the sea. The men and ships had been drilled and trained for this night, so much so that the destroyer *Breese* was severely damaged after striking the *San Francisco* during a complicated night exercise. Scott was a stickler for reality, and the *Breese* had to be towed backwards to Espiritu Santo as evidence.

At 2325 the *Helena*, now carrying the most modern version of surface search radar (SG) detected a suspicious contact at 27,700 yards coming from the same direction as Mikawa had come just two months earlier. Scott on board the *San Francisco* was not so fortunate as to have an SG set, and had to rely on the older, less capable SC radar. While it was appropriate for the task force commander to hoist his flag in the *San Francisco*, it would have been more prudent to ride in the *Helena* or *Boise* which were better equipped to detect surface targets. It was 1942, however, and faith in radar was still some distance in the future. Consequently, a major advantage was lost by the American force, very nearly making the playing field level for the Japanese.

Fortunately for Scott, the Japanese were virtually asleep at the helm until they received the first salvoes from Scott's cruisers. Goto was apparently confident that no force was in his path, and his men were not at battle stations nor his guns manned. When the *Furutaka* was hit 21 minutes later, her guns were still trained fore and aft.

Scott received confusing information from the *Boise* and the *Helena*, consequently, for nearly a half hour from the first detection, no action was taken to engage the enemy. Finally, the *Helena* opened fire at 2346, followed closely by the *Boise* and other ships. Scott ordered a cease fire a minute later, thinking that his cruisers were firing at the destroyer screen, but quickly relented, and a pounding match began. The *San Francisco* opened fire with her main and secondary batteries and within minutes, the destroyer *Fubuki* and cruiser *Furutaka* were pulverized. Due to incredible luck, Scott's force had crossed the enemy's "T", and was able to bring all of it's main batteries to bear. By 0020, it was all over as the remnants of Goto's force limped out of the area. Goto had been killed by the first few salvoes, and his force badly wounded. The *Fubuki* and *Furutaka* were sunk and the *Aoba* was hit 40 times. She was out of action for several months. Unfortunately, the Japanese were able to land troops and equipment from the reinforcement group, however, two of the group's destroyers were sunk the following day by air attack. And, a scheduled bombardment was prevented - the Marines could at least get through one night without dealing with naval gunfire.

Scott had won a victory, but at a high cost. The *Boise* was very nearly sunk, and the destroyer *Duncan* was lost. The *Salt Lake City* was damaged, yet the *Helena* and *San Francisco* were spared. It was indeed lucky for Scott that Goto was unable to mount a preliminary torpedo attack. Had this occurred, the score would have been different. For the moment, however, Scott and his force were the victors, and no longer would the Japanese Navy intimidate the Allies. They could be beaten.

On the 13th of October, the *San Francisco* and *Helena* were back at Espiritu Santo awaiting new orders. The *Boise* and *Salt Lake City* were out of it, and on their way back for repairs. On the 15th, Scott sailed again aboard the *San Francisco* in company with the heavy cruiser *Chester* and *Helena*. They later joined Admiral Willis "Ching" Lee who was flying his flag aboard the battleship *Washington*. For a week they exercised together, yet on the night of October 20, their number was again reduced as the *Chester* was torpedoed. The Southwest Pacific seemed to be a jinx on cruisers!

The Naval Battle Of Guadalcanal - The *San Francisco's* Finest Hour

After shepherding transports to Guadalcanal and bombarding Japanese shore positions in late October and early November, the veteran cruiser found herself back in the lion's den. She now had a new commanding officer as "Soc" McMorris was off for promotion to flag rank. Cassin Young reported aboard on November 9. Young had just recently been promoted to Captain and was the former commanding officer of the repair ship *Vestal*. His performance during the attack on Pearl Harbor had earned him the Congressional Medal of Honor when he was successfully able to extricate his ship from alongside the mortally wounded battleship *Arizona*.

The *San Francisco* also welcomed back Rear Admiral Daniel J. Callaghan who had been designated commander of the newly formed Task Force 65, yet until it was fully composed, he was the commander of Task Force 67.4. He arrived on the *San Francisco*, his flagship on October 30, 1942. His force which now included the heavy cruisers *San Francisco, Pensacola* and *Portland*; light cruisers *Helena, Juneau* and several destroyers was designated to support Rear Admiral Richmond K. Turner's transport group. This group was slated to reinforce the Marines on Guadalcanal, and it arrived off Lunga Point at dawn on November 12, 1942. By this time, a task force under the command of Rear Admiral Scott in flagship *Atlanta* joined with Callaghan. In the early part of the afternoon, the Naval Battle of Guadalcanal began. It started with an aerial attack by 21 aircraft.

The aircraft were bent on interrupting the landing, which had fortunately been nearly completed by the time of their arrival. Instead, the aircraft attacked the transports and their escorts. The *San Francisco* and fellow heavy cruiser *Portland* attempted to use their main batteries of eight inch guns to break up the low flying torpedo planes. Gunners hoped that shell geysers would knock down the planes. One torpedo plane got through to the *San Francisco*, and after being damaged by antiaircraft fire, hit the aft superstructure of the ship. Fifteen men were killed and 29 wounded, including the executive officer, Commander Mark H. Crouter. One of the transports took off the wounded except for Commander Crouter, who begged to remain with his ship.

Intelligence received indicated that a strong force of Japanese ships was due in late that night to bombard the Marines. In fact, the Japanese command was fed up with the continuing presence of the Allies on Guadalcanal and sent a large force under Admiral Hiroaki Abe to knock out Henderson Field once and for all. Abe brought the battleships *Hiei* and *Kirishima* as well as light cruiser *Nagara* and fourteen destroyers. The battleships had a combined armament of sixteen 14 inch guns and thirty-two 6 inch guns. Besides a respectable battery of 5 inch guns, the destroyers carried many long lance torpedoes, so Callaghan was about to meet a vastly superior force. His job was to prevent them from carrying out their mission, regardless of the cost. The weary crews of Callaghan's force went to battle stations early and began their vigil opposite the Marines on shore just a few miles distant. Each was fighting their own battle, but tonight one of the deciding moments in the history of the U.S. Navy would take place. It was also the last night in the life of Admirals Callaghan and Scott as well as Captain Cassin Young and the *San Francisco's* dedicated executive officer, Mark Crouter. It was also the last night for 83 other shipmates on the cruiser.

The disposition of the task force was as follows:

Van destroyers: *Cushing, Laffey, Sterrett, O'Bannion*
Cruisers: *Atlanta* (carrying Admiral Scott), *San Francisco* (flag), *Portland, Helena* and *Juneau*.
Rear guard destroyers: *Aaron Ward, Barton, Monssen, Fletcher*.

At 0125 on November 13, 1942 later to be known as "bloody thirteenth", the *Helena* picked up a contact on her radar at a range just under 28,000 yards. Callaghan was informed and he headed directly for the contact and now both forces were closing at a combined speed of 40 knots. Again, they were in the same area as the previous two major surface battles, just off Savo Island. This time, the Japanese were at battle stations and prepared, but the battleships were ready for a shore bombardment, so their heavy caliber guns were loaded with high explosive, non armor piercing shells. Although they were unaware of any substantial force in the area, they were not going to caught off guard. At 0148 after some initial confusion, the *San Francisco* opened fire on a target at just under 4000 yards range. Callaghan relying on the *Helena* and destroyer *O'Bannion* for radar input ordered odd ships to fire to starboard and even to port. Admiral Abe was well aware of the presence of American ships and at 0150, one of his lead destroyers illuminated the cruiser *Atlanta* with a searchlight. The range was 1,600 yards, and the element of surprise had been lost. She was able to get off some rapid salvoes but was quickly drenched by shell hits and went dead in the water. Scott and his flagship were out of the fight.

Now the battle became a general street fight. The *San Francisco* had been firing with the aid of star shell, and it is possible that she hit the *Atlanta* which was burning and out of the action. Callaghan ordered a cease fire, probably in response to his fear of hitting a friendly ship, but this was quickly rescinded. What had actually happened was that his column of ships had driven right between the *Hiei* and *Kirishima* and a slug fest was taking place. Unfortunately, the treaty cruisers were now fighting well armored battleships. The *Kirishima* in particular was able to literally devastate the upper works of the *San Francisco*, and a destroyer passed down her port side shooting at everything above the waterline. In this exchange, which was not unlike a pounding match reminiscent of 18th Century ship of the line duels, the *San Francisco* lost her captain and Admiral Callaghan. Aft control was also lost due to a hit that killed Mark Crouter. His devotion resulted in his loss. All but a lucky few were killed or mortally wounded on the bridge of the cruiser. The *Helena* next in line threaded the needle of burning and twisting ships and was able to come to the aide of the *San Francisco* by spraying the offending battleship with six inch fire and at the same time shooting up a destroyer with her secondary battery. The six inch shells bounced off the armor plate of the battleship, but the intensity of fire from the *Helena* and obvious tenacity of the *San Francisco* convinced the Japanese that tonight was not the night to pursue a bombardment. The *Helena's* antiaircraft gunners even got into the act by shooting their 40mm guns at the cruiser *Nagara* which was firing at the *San Francisco*. The battle, now just over a few minutes old was effectively finished when Admiral Abe decided to pull his scarred battleships out and retire. He

had been turned, yet at a terrible cost to American ships and brave men. Among the men killed on the *San Francisco*, was a young black mess attendant, Leonard Roy Harmon.

Some people believe that all of life comes down to a few important moments. Leonard Roy Harmon, one of the men assigned to help provide first aid to wounded shipmates along with 84 of his shipmates would, in his final moments make the supreme sacrifice for their country and their ship.

Leonard Roy Harmon, born and raised in *Cuero, Texas*, enlisted in the U.S. Navy in 1939 at age 23, and as with most enlistees of color at that time promptly found his way directed to Mess Attendant rate. Later promoted to Mess Attendant First Class, Harmon was assigned to the *San Francisco*. During his final moments, amidst the carnage and destruction, he distinguished himself by assisting and evacuating the wounded on an open and exposed deck. His final act was to place himself between the murderous shell fire and a shipmate.

As a member of an aid station near the five inch batteries, he was just returning from assisting those on deck when he observed an incoming 14 inch shell probably from the *Kirishima*. Without hesitation he pushed shipmate through a hatchway into the protection of a compartment. Harmon was mortally wounded when the shell hit, but his courage did not go unnoticed. His unselfish and courageous performance resulted in his death, but as small future compensation, he was insured a permanent place in the history of the U.S. and its navy.

For his act of "extraordinary heroism", he was posthumously awarded the Navy Cross, but as a further tribute to him and his black heritage, the Navy named a warship, the destroyer escort USS *Harmon*, DE-678 after Leonard Roy Harmon. It was the first warship named for a black.

Harmon was one among many who earned a Navy Cross in the early morning hours of November 13. The ship had been hurt, and hurt badly. She was hit at least 45 times, and had 22 separate fires burning, and the 105 wounded literally overwhelmed the capabilities of medical staff. By 0300, the issue had been settled and the American force was still in possession of the waters adjacent to Guadalcanal. The cruiser *Atlanta* had been lost, the *Portland* was now out of action with her rudder jammed, and only three of the original destroyers were combat capable. The *San Francisco* was seriously damaged and the *Juneau* was hit. Only the *Helena* was unhurt except for minor shrapnel hits on her superstructure. Later on the morning of the 13th, the *Juneau* was sunk by a submarine launched torpedo in a spectacular and deadly explosion. Large chunks of the stricken ship were flung a thousand feet in the air, and many landed on the *San Francisco*, doing additional damage and wounding men. Only flotsam and a few survivors were left to mark the *Juneau's* end, and with her went five brothers of the Sullivans family.

Captain Hoover of the *Helena* had now assumed command as the senior officer of the remaining ships and the *San Francisco* was under the control of Lt. Cmdr. Bruce McCandless, the navigation officer. He conned the ailing ship out of harm's way. Incredibly, the Japanese had

Commander Bruce McCandless, former navigator of the San Francisco *receives the Medal of Honor from Admiral Earnest J. King in a ceremony held in San Francisco on December 12, 1942. McCandless assumed command as all but one other senior officer had been killed, and got the ship out of harms way.*

The destroyer escort Harmon DE-678 shortly after being commissioned. This ship was built by the Fore River Yard of Bethlehem Steel in a record time of 92 days. The Harmon served with distinction throughout World War II.

Nauita Harmon Carroll, mother of Leonard Roy Harmon, killed on the San Francisco on November 13, 1942, christens the destroyer escort, Harmon. It was the first U.S. Navy warship named in honor of a black sailor. Leonard Roy Harmon died while saving the life of another.

More evidence of the changes made in the cruiser, San Francisco. While not as modern as the Baltimore class cruiser moored off her starboard side, she was still formidable.

been stopped. They would come on again the next night, but would lose both battleships in the final hours of what would be called the "Naval Battle of Guadalcanal."

To the men of Task Force 67.4 go the same honors as those earned by John Paul Jones who defeated the Royal Navy frigate *Serapis* and the crew of the *Monitor* who turned back the CSS *Virginia* at Hampton Roads. Words are not available to describe what the U.S. Navy did during the early hours of November 13, 1942. Like Midway, it was a crucial victory. The men of Callaghan's force proved that they could meet and defeat anything sent by the Japanese, and they did. They were willing to die to win, a gift unmatched to the Marines on Guadalcanal and the American people. The *San Francisco* was granted the Presidential Unit Citation for extraordinary heroism and accomplishment.

BACK TO THE USA FOR REFIT

The battered cruiser made her way back to Mare Island via Pearl Harbor and the honors ren-

dered by CINCPAC. She arrived at her place of birth, Mare Island on December 11, 1942. For the next 2-1/2 months she underwent overhaul and modernization. This included the addition of multiple 20mm and 40mm antiaircraft guns as well as improved radar. Her bridge structure was also altered and an open platform fitted over the pilot house for better observation. Gone also were the prominent square windows that had been a hallmark of the pre-war treaty cruiser. On February 26, 1943, the modernized and revitalized cruiser made her way through the Golden Gate back to the war. The profile of the cruiser had changed, but her legacy of courage and valor would be more permanent however. A youthful Bruce McCandless was awarded the Congressional Medal of Honor for his actions following the Naval Battle of Guadalcanal. Harmon lent his name to a destroyer escort, and Admirals Callaghan and Scott were memorialized by having their names given to new destroyers as was Captain Cassin Young. Gunner's Mate Jackson Loy also was remembered for his bravery during the air attack on November 12, when a destroyer escort was named in his honor.

The *San Francisco* now became part of a different war as she reentered the South Pacific. Her constant enemy would be the aerial torpedo and bomb rather than the surface warship. In the latter more desperate days of the war, the most dreaded of all would face the Navy, the Kamikaze, something the *San Francisco* was intimately aware of having already taken one in her aft control station.

The cruiser's role had now changed. The ship versus ship duels characteristic of late 1942, were drawing to a close as the Japanese military machine was pushed off one island after another. The IJN had been beaten in the air and on the surface, and its ships were now being husbanded closer to home. Consequently, the *San Francisco* became a high speed consort to the fast carrier task forces and provided surgical bom-

An excellent shot of the San Francisco *as she loads supplies and is about ready to leave the Mare Island Navy Yard for the Pacific.*

bardment for amphibious operations. The aging cruiser would now perform the tasks that her IJN counterparts had wanted to accomplish in the Solomons, but were prevented by ships like the *San Francisco*.

VICTORY IN THE PACIFIC - ONE ISLAND AFTER ANOTHER

As most of the damage to the *San Francisco* was in her upperworks, she was back in service more quickly than most ships that had more extensive hull damage. She would now see service from one end of the Pacific to the other beginning with the Aleutians. In July 1943, she was part of the invasion force that assaulted Kiska and Attu, and in October she finally made it to Wake Island.

On October 5, 1943, nearly two years after the failed attempt to relieve the Wake Island defenders, the *San Francisco* as part of Task Unit 14.2.1 made two devastating bombardment runs on the island group, shooting up targets of opportunity. It was pay back time, and this was not the first time this would happen to the now starving Japanese defenders. Their sources of supply had been reduced to a trickle, and now Wake was to be used for target practise by passing American ships and aircraft. In reality, Wake Island was more of a liability to the Japanese and ended up not being worth the initial effort to secure it.

Next it was Makin Island and Betio and then on to the Marshalls to attack installations and shipping around Kwajalein. The cruiser ended 1943 with this operation and was back in January, 1944 to bombard the airfield at Tarao on Maloelap Atoll. This time the enemy returned fire, but ineffectively. On January 30, she encountered three fleeing cargo ships in Kwajalein Lagoon pounded them with main battery fire. After shooting up shore targets in the general area, she was detached and joined Task Group 58.2 under Rear Admiral A. E. Montgomery in the new aircraft carrier *Essex*. Next stop, Truk, a major Japanese stronghold. On January 16, at eighty miles distant from the target, carriers being screened by the *San Francisco* launched raid

after raid against what was supposed to be the Japanese Gibraltar. Truk proved not to be invincible and Japanese shipping and aircraft took a terrible beating. The carrier *Intrepid* was hit by a torpedo however, and the *San Francisco* was detailed to escort her to Majuro. They arrived on the 19th of February. The new role of the cruiser was being demonstrated - antiaircraft protection and shore target bombardment. With minor exceptions, sea battles as envisioned by pre-war planners were now a thing of the past. The great surface battles fought by desperate men nightly in the Solomons were now becoming a feature of history. It was if an era had come and gone within a few short months. The treaty cruisers had their day, and now it was time for another type of war, a modern civilian sailor technological war.

The *San Francisco* now sailed for the Palau Islands where she again was in a screen built around the fast carriers such as the *Bunker Hill*. By March 30, the cruiser had fought off eleven heavy air raids. A brief trip to the Caroline Islands for a bombardment mission in April preceded intensive training and practise exercises for her next mission, the invasion of the Mariana's. On June 6, 1944, the seasoned cruiser sailed for the invasion of Saipan as part of Rear Admiral W. L. Ainsworth's Southern Attack Force bombardment group. Thousands of miles away on the other side of the world another invasion was taking place on the French Coast of Normandy. No one could know that the war in Europe would only last another ten months, and that in the Pacific, an additional four months. But, on June 6, aboard the cruiser *San Francisco*, it was just another landing marked by the usual noise, violence and the very real possibility of death from any number of sources.

As the Allied forces drew nearer to the inner defenses of the Japanese Empire it became more evident that the war had evolved to a conflict unlike any that the western powers had ever fought or knew was conceivable. It had become a war between men who fought to die versus those who fought to live. To the Americans, life was precious not as resource to be committed to battle or for some vague promise of immortality, but for itself. This was demonstrated time and time again, but no more so than on June 15, 1944 off of Tinian. On that morning, a torpedo bomber (TBF) from the carrier *Lexington* was hit and the crew bailed out, landing close to the occupied beach. One of the *San Francisco's* scout planes was in the air, and the pilot, Ensign R. W. Gabel requested permission to land and pick up the survivors. He did and amidst heavy enemy fire and was able to rescue the crew of the downed plane. Gabel volunteered to save lives at the possible cost of his own. This incident was one of many examples of those who fought to live.

Throughout June and July, the cruiser bombarded targets in the Marianas, and on July 30, she sailed for Mare Island for overhaul and repair. Back in the war, on December 10, 1944, she sailed as part of an escort for the fast carriers as they swept in and around the Philippine Island hitting airfields and other targets. Formosa was not left out nor Hong Kong. In early 1945, she operated with the battleship *Nevada* bom-

barding Iwo Jima, and again provided support for the fast carrier strikes which were being directed at the Japanese homelands. On March 21, 1945, she was off Okinawa bombarding shore installations. The *San Francisco* like so many other major warships was all over the charts as the carriers hit anything and everything that the Japanese military owned and operated, whether far away or right at home.

During her final operations as a unit of a bombardment group off Okinawa in June and July, she would operate with a destroyer named for a beloved former captain and admiral, *Daniel J. Callaghan*, DD-792. It seemed fitting for the aging cruiser to be in company with a ship that bore the name of probably her most famous crewman. Interestingly, there is also a Admiral Daniel Callaghan Ave. in Vallejo, California that overlooks the Mare Island Naval Shipyard. It is if the two will be forever linked.

THE WAR ENDS AND THE *SAN FRANCISCO* COMES HOME

The old cruiser ended the war off China where as a part of Cruiser Division 6 under the command of Rear Admiral R. F. Good, she made sweeps near the north China coast and Korea. She also stopped at Chefoo Harbor, once a favorite port of the Asiatic Fleet. In mid September 1945, she provided support to the Seventh Fleet as it assisted in the occupation of North China. She operated out of Jinsen, Korea until November 23, 1945, when the light cruiser *Springfield* assumed flagship duties and the *San Francisco* was detached to return to the U.S. with a number of war weary marines and sailors. She entered San Francisco Bay on December 17, 1945 for her last visit. The war was over for the gallant cruiser. She went into reserve as part of the Reserve Fleet in the Philadelphia Navy Yard on January 19, 1946 and on February 10, 1947 was decommissioned. Her name was formally stricken from the navy list on March 1, 1959 along with other heavy cruisers of the treaty period, *Louisville, Augusta, New Orleans, Portland, Minneapolis, Tuscaloosa* and *Wichita*. All were sold off for scrap. The *San Francisco* was bought by the Union Minerals and Alloys Corporation of New York for $239,896.63, and towed to Panama City, Florida for dismantling. So ended an era.

The *San Francisco* earned 17 battle stars and a Presidential Unit Citation. Her battle honors were only exceeded by the carrier *Enterprise* which was the most decorated ship of World War II.

She fired 11,002 eight inch shells, 24,191 five inch, and over 150,000 antiaircraft shells. She traveled nearly 300,000 miles using over 30 million gallons of fuel oil. She suffered 267 combat casualties.

This cruiser was and will remain one of the places honored and hallowed by Americans. On her decks uncommon valor was common and when victory was needed, she was there. Although she has long since been reduced by the shipbreakers, her bridge, left over from that night in November 1942, can still be visited in *San Francisco* as it over looks the Pacific at Point Lobos. Only by visiting this monument, can one truly understand what happened so long ago.

The aging cruiser toward the end of the war. She has earned 17 battles stars only equalled by sister cruiser, Minneapolis. The San Francisco also earned a Presidential Unit Citation for her action during the Naval Battle of Guadalcanal.

The bridge wing structure of the San Francisco at Point Lobos overlooking the Pacific ocean. A plaque tells of the action on the 13th of November, 1942 and list those killed. It is a fitting tribute to a group of brave men who served on a ship that has earned a place in history with other ships as the Bon Homme Richard, Olympia, and the Enterprise.

The new battleship USS Arkansas shortly after being launched. When this photo was taken on December 16, 1913, she was the last word in American capital ship development. This would not last long, however, as a new class of more heavily armed battleships was already in the building stage.

CHAPTER III

THE BATTLESHIPS
USS *ARKANSAS* BB-33
"ANTIQUE WITH PUNCH"

The origin of the modern battleship can be traced back to the first raft used by humans that employed rocks or sticks for defense. Roman and Greek slave rowed galleys followed culminating in the sail driven ships of the line utilized by the European powers into the middle of the 19th Century. The introduction of steam power and iron plating then changed warfare at sea forever in the mid 19th Century, and the modern battleship was born.

Each maritime nation claims credit for the ultimate development of this ship type when in actuality all were responsible for the evolution of this glamorous yet legendary weapon. The famous French naval architect Dupuy de Lome is entitled to the lion's share of any credit for the origin of the battleship as it was his design that resulted in the iron plated steam driven *La Glorie* of 1858. Ugly, ungainly and squat, *La Glorie* took the world naval community by storm, especially Great Britain's Royal Navy. England quickly followed with HMS *Warrior*, an ironclad sailing ship. This offering was more graceful and could out sail the *La Glorie*, but the French had definitely stolen a march on the British Lion. From this point forward, and for the next 100 years the great navies of the world built larger and more powerful heavy gun warships. The honor for the largest most heavily armed battleship goes to the Imperial Japanese Navy which built the 70,000 ton (full load) behemoths *Yamato* and *Mushashi* that mounted nine 18 inch guns. Both were a colossal waste of Japanese material and monetary resources and were easily disposed of by concentrated air attack late in

World War II. Had they used the resources for aircraft carriers, cruisers and destroyers, then the course of the Pacific war might have been significantly different. Ironically, the battleship never really fulfilled the dreams and designs of their owners. For decades, naval officers waited for and dreamed of the ultimate clash between these titans, and it happened only sporadically. Glorious visions of battleships opposite one another separated by a few thousand yards engaged in a winner take all pounding match never really materialized. Instead, there were less than half a dozen instances where these iron monsters faced each other in open combat. Inconclusively at the Battle of Jutland in World War I, and later during the second world war, when the Bismarck made short work of HMS *Hood*. In the same war American and Japanese battleships faced off intermittently but the airplane had already sealed the fate of the obsolete floating fortress. The Royal Navy's successful torpedo plane attack on the Italian fleet at Taranto, followed by the devastating Japanese attack at Pearl Harbor in December 1941 offered painful evidence of the demise of the battleship even before it had ascended. Of course there were those diehard enthusiasts who claimed that aircraft would unfairly prevail against ships that could not maneuver, but a few days after the Pearl Harbor victory, the Japanese invalidated that argument by sinking HMS *Prince of Wales* and HMS *Repulse*. Both ships maneuvered a high speed, mounted a passable antiaircraft defense system yet were dispatched with ease by aircraft.

Today, the only remnants of the golden age of the battleship are those of the U.S. Navy, and they are either museum ships or the four *Iowa* class in reserve against a future that will likely never call upon them again. But at one time, the battleship was the monarch of the sea, and the USS *Arkansas* was a prominent member of the select few.

THE USS *ARKANSAS*: THE BATTLESHIP IN TRANSITION

The USS *Arkansas*, while classified as a battleship was actually a transition ship type. Preceding her had been a series of iron clad ship classes ranging from Ericsson's *Monitor* and her

The Arkansas *leaves New York on January 16, 1915 for the United States Fleet training ground in and around Guantanamo Bay in Cuba. The photo, taken from the Brooklyn Bridge, shows the battleship for what she is, a platform for heavy weapons. Electronics and antiaircraft defense systems would be installed over two decades later.*

later sisters employed during the American Civil War to the *Connecticut* and *South Carolina* classes of 1906 and 1910. All were ancestors to the battleship of the mid 20th Century, but the *Arkansas* class represented a significant turning point.

The two ship *Arkansas* class which included the USS *Wyoming* BB-32 was prefaced by the one of the most important American naval events of the early Twentieth Century. It was President Theodore "Teddy" Roosevelt's insistence that the U.S. Navy use it's battle force to tour the world as a show of American Naval might and a gesture of goodwill. Roosevelt, a strong supporter of the navy caused the "Great White Fleet" as the touring force was known to reach into the four corners of the world showing that the U.S. was not a second rate power, but deserved a place of equal importance among the European powers. This historic cruise was accomplished over a two year period from 1907-1909. In early 1909 as the celebrated voyage of the battleships of the U.S. Navy was drawing to a close, the President, riding a tide of pro navy sentiment was authorized by the Congress to build two battleships of steel and of domestic manufacture. The *Wyoming* was to be built at William Cramp and Sons of Philadelphia and battleship number 33 was to be built by the New York Shipbuilding Corporation of Camden, New Jersey. BB-33 was to be named the USS *Arkansas* and both ships were to be designed and built using the most modern and technologically advanced processes then known. The total budget for each ship could not exceed $6 million, exclusive of armaments and armor.

From the outset, the *Arkansas* class was built as a compromise. Her predecessor, the *Utah* class (two ships, the *Utah* BB-31 and *Florida* BB-31) had been armed with a main battery consisting of ten 12 inch/45 cal guns. This particular gun size and the arrangement of ten rifles was considered somewhat inferior, and a change in caliber and gun numbers was immediately suggested for the next or *Arkansas* class. The *Arkansas* was to be armed with twelve 12 inch/50 cal rifles arranged in an A, B, Q, R, X, Y. format. She and her sister *Wyoming* would be the last battleships designed with two barrel turrets amidships. It was envisioned that the striking power of the twelve inch gun was satisfactory providing the broadside salvo consisted of twelve guns as opposed to the ten guns available on the *Utah* class. A rather simple formula that considered shell size and numbers discharged in salvo indicated that the *Arkansas* class would prevail in a pounding match with a like sized enemy, at least in a theoretical or mathematical sense. Her predecessors of the *Utah* class would have to rely more on luck than sheer weight of shellfire. Fortunately, the designers elected to lengthen the hull to accommodate the centerline mountings rather than resorting to the more common wing mounted array. Had she been built with wing mounted batteries, she would have been embarrassingly obsolete at birth.

The *Arkansas* class just missed being armed with 14 inch/45 cal barrels but this gun size was reserved for a *New York* class, the next two ship class designed after the *Arkansas*. In fact, the 14 inch/45 caliber gun would find a home on several subsequent battleships including the

Texas, Nevada, Oklahoma, Pennsylvania, and *Arizona*. The USN would again use the 12 inch/ 50 cal gun on the short lived *Alaska* class battlecruisers *Alaska, Guam* and *Hawaii* built during World War II. The weapon found it's most valuable use aboard the *Arkansas* thirty five years after the decision to use it by a now nameless naval ordinance architect. Ironically, the weight of an armor piercing shell fired by the *Alaska* class was 1,140 pounds whereas those discharged by the *Arkansas* class topped out at 870 pounds. Similarly, the *Alaska's* could throw a shell some 38,000 plus yards at an elevation of 45 degrees, yet the *Arkansas* class had an absolute maximum of 23,500 yards at 15 degrees, at it's highest pre World War II barrel elevation.

The *Arkansas* class was also innovative as the two ships first employed the single stage shell hoisting system in a Mark IX turret. This design change made the turret to magazine relationship safer and reduced explosive hazards to a minimum.

Aside from a main battery of twelve 12 inch/ 50 guns, the *Arkansas* mounted twenty-one 5 inch/51 caliber guns as a secondary battery mostly housed in casemates. She was also armed with two 21 inch torpedoes that could be fired from apertures in her hull several feet under the waterline. This weapon was common in most capitol ships of the day, and like the casemate guns, dated these ships. Actually, no major navy ever used the hull mounted torpedo tubes for any military purpose and most subsequent refits eliminated this hypotetically useful, but actually worthless weapon. Like many secret weapons, it was no secret, and although it sounded like a good idea at the time, it was useless.

The *Arkansas* was powered by twelve coal fired Babcock and Wilcox boilers driving Parsons turbines which could generate 28,000 shaft horsepower. Not a notable amount of energy considering that modern destroyers of the late 20th Century require some 70,000 plus horsepower for their needs. Of course, the demands for electrical power and instantaneous response to mechanical needs was not required by this class of battleship.

Coal fired ships were notoriously dirty requiring a substantial commitment of human resources to ensure that they had sufficient fuel to operate. The *Arkansas* carried 2,691 tons of coal which represented just a fraction over 10% of her total displacement at 26,000 tons. Coaling was necessary every few days, and was dreaded by the engineering and deck departments who were required to labor continuously until the bunkers were topped off and the ship was again returned to her pristine condition. The greatest fear a ship's captain had was that his ship would be unable to meet her battle or operational commitments due to the lack of coal hence, coaling took place with almost a religious fervor.

From her launching on January 14, 1911 and for nearly fifteen years she used coal, and finally in 1925 her boilers were replaced with those that burned oil. Ironically, the use of coal did provide some collateral benefits to the capitol ship. Oldtimers argued that having extensive coal bunkerage added protection to the ship from shellfire and that the storage of oil reduced the stability of the ship. However, the naysayers were shouted down with the overwhelming ben-

The crew of the Arkansas *work out with a rowing machine. This was good practise for the "Arkie" held the fleet championship for rowing. As usual the officers and CPOs are watching and probably giving unnecessary advice!*

Seamen demonstrate how to wash clothing "Navy style" aboard the sister ship to the Arkansas, the USS Wyoming. *A seaman's life was not easy, but it was rewarding. Most ships of this period between the two World Wars were not equipped with bunks, and the men had to use hammocks. It wasn't until the late 1930's that improved crew habitability became a priority for the Navy. This was necessary to stem the rising number of desertions.*

efits of oil. The boiler rooms were smaller and required less than one quarter of the former engineering staff to operate the new system. This meant a savings in human and monetary resources, especially important to a navy that seemed on the verge of bankruptcy as the end of each fiscal year rolled around. Refueling was also quicker and much cleaner, not to mention that the thermal energy generated by oil was substantially greater than that of coal. On balance, converting to oil was a positive step, although unfortunately it took place many years after the dreadnought had been put into service. Aside from the engine room staff or snipes being pleased with the conversion, deck departments were satisfied with not having to remove layers of coal dust from what seemed to be every nook and cranny aboard ship.

THE *ARKANSAS* JOINS THE FLEET

The new battleship was commissioned on September 17, 1912 after having been launched on January 11, 1911. At her launching, she was sponsored by Miss Nancy Louise Macon, and her first captain was Roy C Smith. After a series of shakedown cruises, she was returned for various adjustments and repairs to her engineering and gunnery systems. Later, in October 1912, she carried President Taft who was visiting the Panama Canal Zone to view the ditch that Teddy Roosevelt had promised to dig himself if it was not finished in a timely matter. As of Taft's visit, it was yet incomplete, but well on it's way.

The new battleship served as transportation for the President again in December as she returned to the Canal Zone to take him to Key West, Florida for another visit. Finally, the *Arkansas* was released from this duty and joined the Atlantic Fleet. For months she conducted maneuvers on the east coast of the U.S. and in 1913

visited the Mediterranean. Her first combat venture was just around the corner when she was recalled and sent to the Mexican coastline to enforce a new President's views in the Caribbean. Woodrow Wilson was not about to allow the new Mexican leader, the petty brigand Victoriano Huerta to impose totalitarian rule in the western hemisphere and especially, in a country bordering on the U.S. A battle force was sent to the area with orders to provide visible encouragement to those in power that the U.S. desired a representative form of government. A dictatorship was not to be tolerated. A showdown of competing ideals finally occurred in Tampico in early 1914. This military intervention, while minor was a portent of the future role of the U.S. in world affairs. That future was played out in Vera Cruz where the battleship *Arkansas* as a major combatant along with other naval units was directed to intercept and prevent the landing of military arms and supplies to the forces supporting the Dictator Huerta. This was accomplished under the trained guns of the *Arkansas* which contributed a naval battalion of 313 men commanded by 17 officers. A major portion of the ship's complement was to be committed to this skirmish. Among the officers of the four company strong landing force was a young Lt. (jg) Jonas H. Ingram who was awarded the Medal of Honor for heroism. Ingram would again enter naval history through his efforts as commander of the Fourth Fleet which was responsible for the protection of sea lanes near South America during the Second World War.

Within days Vera Cruz was subdued through the systematic eradication of rebels and snipers that seemed to occupy every open window and alley. Two *Arkansas* men were lost during the street fighting, but by April 30, the issue was settled and the Mexican Campaign was climaxed in favor of American interests. This same scenario would be played out many times in the

The battleship, Arkansas, *passes under the Brooklyn bridge on her way to training in southern waters in 1929. The pattern of training, midshipmen cruises and regular overhauls in the Brooklyn Navy Yard was virtually an annual ritual, as the shopkeepers, barowners and girls that followed the fleet well knew. Separating a sailor from his pay was the goal of every red blooded American street walker.*

future, as the U.S. Navy acted as the bayonet point protecting American national interests abroad. An American warship, particularly a battleship loaded with professional fighting men commanded by competent officers was not something to be taken lightly.

For the next three years, the *Arkansas* operated on the east coast of the U.S. and carried out various training exercises. This would provide the ship and her crew with practical experience for the world war that would ultimately involve the U.S. On April 6, 1917, the U.S. entered the war against Germany, and July 14 of the following year, the *Arkansas* sailed for Europe to relieve the ancient battleship *Delaware* as a cooperative member of the Royal Navy's Grand Fleet. Prior to her arrival she did open fire on what appeared to be a U-boat periscope, but there is no record of any sinking.

The *Arkansas* was present at the internment of the German High Seas Fleet on November 21, 1918 at the Firth of Forth. Within a few days, she also escorted President Wilson's ship to France, and on the day after Christmas, 1918, she arrived back in the U.S., to a hero's welcome. For the next several years, the now aging battleship became a familiar sight in the fleet, operating off of the east coast and into the Caribbean. She also carried midshipmen from the Naval Academy on their summer cruises, and many ensigns owe their shipboard upbringing to the likes of the battleship *Arkansas*. Some say, she, like many of her pre World War I sisters were sailing ships without the sails. It was almost like shipping before the mast as creature comforts were not paramount on ships like the *Arkansas*.

LIFE ABOARD A BATTLESHIP: HAMMOCKS AND NO PRIVACY

Being a battleship sailor during the interwar period from 1919 to 1941 was quite different from today's service aboard a capitol ship. There were no individual bunks, air conditioned living spaces, recreation facilities or any other form of yacht like gracious living. The *Arkansas* was not a slave ship, but her crew realized that her main purpose was to fire her main battery in combat and triumph over any enemy. The guns came first, and those who served them second.

The crew used hammocks slung in various locations dependent on their job specialty. Pipe bunks were introduced in the late 1930's as an accommodation to crew morale and comfort, but in the beginning, a hammock was where you rested. If you could not sleep on your back or had difficulty tying knots, then you were in for a difficult time. Hammocks were stowed during the day, and if you were lucky you had a sleeping location that was relatively quiet and cool. Ventilation was another luxury not enjoyed by

all and the heat inside those old poorly insulated steel ships could be unbearable at times.

The food was good and there was plenty of it. Of course, the Navy served balanced nutritious meals that were not fat free nor heart smart, but bacon fat makes most foods taste better. There was no shortage of beans or cabbage either, and a good smoke along with a cup of strong coffee with your buddies seemed to make it all worthwhile and the hardships could be temporarily forgotten.

A sailor washed his clothes on deck with a brush and a bucket, and bathing was often done in the same fashion. Indoor bathing was still a generation in the future for most of the sailors in the old battleships. All in all, life aboard the *Arkansas* was not unendurable, and it did build sailors out of farmboys, clerks and former highschool seniors. Friendships that would last a lifetime were formed and the sailors learned that being a team player was all important for success in battle as well as in just simply surviving. Those who did not follow the program often found themselves off the ship, and in certain extreme cases, at night in a storm. Pogey bait was no laughing matter.

In essence, boys learned to be men and later qualified seamen aboard such ships as the *Arkansas*. Duty was rigorous, but paid off in later years. Officers learned as well as sailors. Officers were trained by old line chief petty officers, and if they listened they went on to become respected leaders. Many attained flag rank, such as Jonas Ingram and Bill Halsey. Watching a chief get the job done right without seeming to expend any effort was the final part of an ensign's education as well as learning many hundreds of other practical lessons in command. Life in the *Arkansas* and her sisters was rewarding and a necessary passage in a naval career for both enlisted men and officers alike. In fact, it was a crucial step in the naval personnel development system.

THE INTER-WAR YEARS

The interwar years from 1919 through late 1941 were similar for all major units in the U.S. Navy. Training, diplomatic visits, midshipmen cruises, drydock and occasionally, assisting a

community that had suffered a disaster. The *Arkansas* was no different as she participated in all of the above.

She provided assistance to the coastal city of Santa Barbara in early July 1925 in the wake of an earthquake that rocked the area. Her good deed done, the battleship entered the Philadelphia Navy Yard for a major refit and overhaul. She had been selected for modernization rather than scrapping as were several other major units as a result of the international naval arms limitation agreements.

She was converted from coal to oil burning. This was a major effort and caused her to reduce from 12 boilers to 4. This meant that her two funnels were trunked into one just aft of the forward superstructure. In addition, a catapult was installed on the midships situated turret (designated Q) and three aircraft were now carried abreast of the single stack. In 1927, she emerged from the yard, a modernized warship. However, no amount of modernization could change her basic design from that of a rapidly obsolecsing ship of a bygone era. She was still a pre-World War I ship with capabilities of that day.

For the next thirteen years, the *Arkansas* cruised the Atlantic and Caribbean as a training ship for graduated seaman recruits and midshipmen. She was even older than her contemporaries like the *West Virginia* and *California*, but her age really showed when battleships like the *North Carolina* joined the fleet. But age aside, she had much life left and would make a valuable contribution in the war that everyone knew was coming. She received one further major refit in 1940-41 which resulted in the addition of antiaircraft batteries and increasing the elevation of her main battery from 15 degrees to 30 degrees. This was vital to improve the range of her main armament. Her lattice mast was also replaced by a tripod. The lattice mast vibrated too much and was unsuited for the electronic gear being installed.

As she was already assigned to the Atlantic, she was one of the first ships selected along with peers *New York* and *Texas* to form the Atlantic Squadron in 1938-39. On the eve of war in September 1939, she was about to embark a group of midshipmen for a cruise when the war was

The President of the United States, Herbert Hoover, is aboard the Arkansas *as part of the October 1931 Sesqui-Centennial celebration of the surrender of British General Cornwallis at Yorktown. A squadron of flush deck destroyers can be seen in the distance fully dressed for the occasion.*

Cooks parade for inspection. At this inspection, coffee pots are being scrutinized for cleanliness. As any seaman will testify, a clean pot is essential for good coffee, and coffee was as important as fuel oil to the operation of the ship.

The coaling ship Melrose *came off second best in her bout with the* Arkansas, *but that is to be expected when a commercial ship tangles with a heavily armored battleship. The battleship did lose one of its launches as can be seen in this December 27, 1940 photograph.*

The Arkansas *receives some scratches from her collision with the collier* Melrose *off New Jersey on December 19, 1940.*

declared in Europe. Plans changed and she became a formal member of Battleship Division 5. Later, on July 7, 1941, she would join with 22 other ships to escort and carry U.S. Marine reinforcements to Iceland to replace 15,000 British Empire troops that were badly needed in other theaters where Great Britain was fighting the Axis.

Preventing the Germans from occupying Iceland was vital to Allied interest. It was said that if they had occupied that strategic point, that Nazism would have had a knife at the throat of democracy. Ships like the *Arkansas* ensured that the knife was pointed in the other direction.

Just over a month later, the *Arkansas* joined the cruiser *Augusta* which was carrying President Roosevelt to meet with Prime Minister Winston Churchill at Argentia in Newfoundland on August 10, 1941. Churchill arrived on HMS *Prince of Wales*, a ship that would four months later become a victim to Japanese bombers in the Indian Ocean. The Atlantic Charter was signed by both leaders which guaranteed a world without fear. This meant that the Axis would have to be subdued and eliminated. The U.S. had now moved to the brink of war with Germany, and it would not be long before the gloves would be removed and the slugfest would begin. After the attack on Pearl Harbor by the Japanese on December 7, 1941, the German and Italian governments declared war on the U.S. to show solidarity with Japan. The U.S. Navy had a long way to come before it could defeat the Axis in either the Atlantic or the Pacific. Ships like the *Arkansas* would have to buy time until the fleet was adequate to fight back.

THE *ARKANSAS* GOES TO WAR

The old battleship would actually fight, but she would have to wait for nearly 2-1/2 years to become an active combatant. For the first several months she served as a convoy escort and again as a training ground for the vast number of incoming men into the naval service. In mid 1944, she was included in the overall planning for the assault at Normandy. Her role as was

The Arkansas *fires away at Normany beaches on D-Day, the 6th of June 1944. She expended over 300 main battery rounds and helped pinned down Allied troops break out and get off the beach. The old battleship, actually the oldest American ship present, was finally able to use her main battery in combat.*

that of several other aging units was to provide close in bombardment and gunnery support to army units moving inland from the beachhead at Omaha Beach. The *Arkansas* was now the oldest battleship in the U.S. fleet and assumed her position some 6,000 yards off the beach. At 0530 on June 4, 1944 or D-Day, she was fired upon by German batteries and by 0552 she was replying with her ancient but effective 12 inch main battery. As part of the *Texas, Nevada, Arkansas* triad of old warriors she provided gunfire support to the tune of 350 shells. Omaha beach was no cake walk as units of the U.S. Army made attempt after attempt to scale the Atlantic Wall. Finally, destroyers moved in almost to the Wall itself and literally shot holes in the cliffs in order for the huddled troops to advance. Once this was accomplished late on D-Day, U.S. troops were able to move forward and evict the Germans from their defenses.

For nearly two weeks, the *Arkansas* provided call fire support until the army moved inland and the enemy was now beyond the range of the old battleships guns. During that two weeks, she

destroyed enemy tanks, troop convoys and even wiped out a rail-line between Caen and Cherbourg. On June 18, she returned to Portsmouth, yet her layover was brief. On June 24, she along with the cruisers *Tuscaloosa* and *Quincy*, battleships *Nevada* and *Texas* plus destroyers and two British cruisers sailed for Cherbourg. On June 25, she began dueling with German batteries, and one in particular, Battery Hamburg that was successfully able to straddle her several times. She eventually silenced the pesky guns and the port so vital to Allied supply lines was secured.

The *Arkansas* rounded out her Atlantic theater combat career by supporting the landings in Southern France August 15-17, also known as the worse kept secret of the war. Next stop, the USA for a quick overhaul, and then on to the Pacific. She provided gunfire support to the landings on Iwo Jima and later Okinawa. She stayed off Okinawa for 46 days, and unlike over 200 other Allied ships, she escaped being hit by Kamikazes. The war's end found her in Leyte Gulf.

THE MAGIC CARPET AND THEN TEST BAKER

The *Arkansas* was too old for any real further service to the Navy, except to serve as a floating transport for war weary veterans to get back home. So after four "magic carpet" trips, she was selected as a target for the upcoming Bikini Island nuclear tests, or *Operation Crossroads*.

In early 1946, she was made ready as a target ship along with 70 plus other ships found to be of no further use to the Navy. She remained at the Hunters Point Naval Shipyard for several weeks being prepared for her ordeal and finally she left for Bikini Atoll in the Marshall Islands.

Just 247 miles from Kwajalein, Bikini was selected for two atomic bomb blasts. The first,

test Able or "Gilda" would be an air burst dropped by a bomber. The second, and later the most spectacular was "Betty", was exploded sub surface. Both would devastate the ships in the lagoon and contaminate the island and most of the 70,000 onlookers. On July 1, a specially equipped B-29 bomber left Kwajalein with Gilda and later that morning the bomb was dropped. The explosion rocked the ships nearest the center, yet most survived. The *Arkansas* was a survivor, but not for long. Disappointed in the results, the observers, including project director Vice Admiral Blandy ordered the second explosion, Betty. For nearly a month the *Arkansas* and the remnants of the ghost fleet as it had become known as awaited the next test. At 0825 on the morning of July 25, 1946, it was detonated.

Within seconds the *Arkansas* was lifted several feet above the lagoon and when the geyser subsided, the old ship had gone to her grave. She was followed by another fleet favorite, the old carrier *Saratoga* some seven hours later. Many old sailors mourned the end of these gallant reminders of a now bygone era. Now the *Arkansas* rests on the bottom of Bikini lagoon and perhaps some day when the danger of radioactive contamination subsides, amateur divers will locate the old ship. In any event she disappeared from active service on July 25, and now is a page in American Naval History. Ironically, it was not until the latter half of World War II that she became of valued use to the Allies. She then proved that even an antique still had punch.

The ancient warrior in her final guise. She has been modernized and overhauled for the last time and has been declared of no further service to the U.S. Navy. Accordingly, she will join some 70 other ships as part of the Operation Crossroads *"ghost fleet." She will be a guinea pig for the world's fifth and sixth above ground nuclear detonations in the south Pacific in mid 1946.*

Perhaps the last photo of the old battleship, Arkansas. *She has just been subjected to test Able or "Gilda" and has survived with minor topside damage. As a matter of fact, most of the heavy ships survived quite well in the July 1, 1946 test. On July 25, she did not survive nor did the old carrier* Saratoga. *As the result of test baker or "Betty", both now share a place on the sandy bottom of Bikini lagoon. "Betty" was a below water burst that showed the world what nuclear power really was. To this day, the spector of that whitish mushroom of one billion tons of water and debris haunts thousands who have seen the films or were present. This was not some big bang for the entertainment of the media - it was something to fear. After all, it lifted the 26,000 ton* Arkansas *several feet out of the water and sank her immediately.*

USS *CALIFORNIA* BB-44 "THE PRUNE BARGE FIGHTS AGAIN"

WHAT'S IN A NAME?

The battleship *California* BB-40 was first authorized in a Congressional Act dated June 30, 1914 along with sisters *Mississippi* BB-41 and *Idaho* BB-42. She was to be built at the New York Navy Yard in Brooklyn, New York. This was not to be so, especially in view of the fact that a battleship named after the Golden State should at least be built there. Accordingly, after much heavy lobbying by delegations from Vallejo (location of the Mare Island Navy Yard) and officials from the state capitol in Sacramento, BB-40 was renamed the USS *New Mexico*. The next appropriation slated for 1915 accommodated officials of the Bear Republic and the BB-44 was named the USS *California*. Of course, the Navy already had a cruiser named the *California*, but she was quickly renamed the *San Diego* thus the name *California* became available. Her sister ship was the USS *Tennessee* BB-43. Construction on the *Tennessee* at the New York Navy Yard began on May 14, 1917 just six months after the *California's* keel laying on October 25, 1916. Of course, the *California* also had another name and that was the "Prune Barge". When you think of other famous warship nicknames such as the "*Mighty Mo*" (battleship *Missouri*) or the "*Big E*" (carrier *Enterprise*), the "prune barge" was not very complementary. It referred to the early 20th century view of *California* as being the prune capital of the world and Californians as prune pickers. Hence the name of it's state warship became the prune barge. She was also given a pet California brown bear cub named "Prunes" which was kept until she became more of a menace than a pet. In any event, no matter what her name, this ship performed admirably and was one of the most beautiful warships in the pre World War II U.S. Navy.

THE USS *CALIFORNIA* - A POWERFUL ADDITION TO THE FLEET

The *California* was a follow on to the *New Mexico* class and a logical step in the evolution of the battleship from the *Utah* to *Arkansas* to the *New York* to the *Oklahoma* to the *West Virginia*. Each successive class had more improved design features especially in the area of armor protection. With her flush sides and clipper bow, the *California* was practically a repeat of the *New Mexico* class and had a definite cruiser like profile. The *California* was built pursuant to the "all or nothing" concept of armor protection. This concept was based on having sufficient protection for the essential areas such as the engineering and magazine spaces, and nominal protection for all other areas. Her armor protection consisted of 8 inch tapering to 14 inches for the main waterline belt; conning tower and tube, 16 inches, and boiler uptakes 8 to 14 inches. She was also provided with a 17 foot buffer zone between her armor and her vitals that were divided into compartments that either acted as fuel bunkers or air spaces. This was designed to help protect the ship from torpedo damage. It would have worked well when she was hit by two aerial torpedoes in the early minutes of the Pearl Harbor attack, but she was virtually unbuttoned to allow for an upcoming inspection. The die was cast and she was doomed from a deliberate lack of watertight integrity.

The *California* was not a fast battleship as would be her later sisters of the *South Dakota* and *Iowa* class, but at the time of her design she was fast enough to compete with any battleship in any foreign naval inventory. Although, it was hard to believe such a sleek ship could only make 21 knots, but her shaft horsepower was only rated at 28,500. She had a turbo electric drive system with four alternating current motors. One motor coupled to each shaft. She had a wound rotor system for running and a squirrel cage winding for starting. All in all, it was complicated system, but at least the energy source was oil rather than coal. This was important as it provided for a cleaner running ship and far less human resource expense in the engine room. No stokers were needed, and above all, there were few complaints from the deck gang. The eight Bureau Express boilers used oil. The consumption rate at an optimum 17 knots was 1.07 pounds of oil per shaft horsepower per hour of operation. The two slim funnels of the *California* class was one of the distinguishing marks when comparisons were made to the *New Mexico* class. The other difference was the structure of the bridge. When the New Mexico's received their major refit in the early 1930's the classes were no longer visually comparable, and not knowing their design history, the casual viewer would swear that they were two distinctly different classes.

The *California* was armed with twelve 14 inch/50 caliber guns mounted in four triple turrets in an A, B, X and Y arrangement. This gun size was somewhat of a political compromise for there was some argument in the Navy Department over the proposed cost of the desired 16 inch/40 caliber weapon. The 16 inch gun was obviously a much more devastating weapon, but cost consciousness overcame those who were far thinking, and the *California* was armed with the 14 inch/50 caliber barrel.

This gun could fire a 1,500 pound armor piercing (A P) shell some 36,800 yards at a maximum 30 degree elevation and a 1,275 pound high capacity (H C) shell 36,600 yards at a maximum 30 degree angle. The A P shell had sufficient

The battleship California *is launched on November 20, 1919 at the Mare Island Navy Yard. In the confined channel between the City of Vallejo and the shipyard opposite there was little room. The* California *kept on going and touched the other side, but no damage was done.*

The California *being fitted out at Mare Island. She has yet to receive her 14 inch main battery. This photo was taken on April 1, 1921, nearly 18 months after her launching.*

armor penetration capability to make it a very lethal weapon. With a well trained gun crew, each barrel could maintain a firing rate of 1.5 rounds per minute. Not extraordinary by today's automatic standards, but excellent for the era in which the *California* was built. The triple barrels were housed in an armored turret weighing 897 tons. The turret face plate was covered with 18 inches of steel armor and the barbette 14 inches. Her turrets were well protected. The main battery was controlled by a Mark 9 Fire Control system.

The secondary battery consisted of fourteen 5 inch/51 caliber guns distributed seven to a side. They were located in either casemates or out in the open, but at a higher level than previous battleships. She was also armed with a paltry four semi automatic 3 inch/50 caliber antiaircraft guns and some small arms for additional defense. It was inadequate and would not be up to an aerial challenge until the latter part of World War II when she was armed with 16 five inch/38 guns,

ten 40MM quad mounts and some 60 20mm close in weapons. Late in 1943, she was a floating fortress that could survive any form of contemporary weapon, but in 1921, the year of her commissioning, she was a floating main battery destined only for a pounding match with like ships of here class, an event that only happened by accident in 1944.

She also sported two underwater torpedo tubes that could fire 21 inch torpedoes. These were removed in 1937 after being found to be of no real value.

The new battleship was christened November 20, 1919 at the Mare Island Navy Yard by Mrs. Barbara Stephens Zane, daughter of the then governor, William Stephens. The battleship slid down the ways from the yard and just kept on going to the other side of the channel until she touched the Vallejo side. She slid into the mud and was unharmed. She was immediately towed back to her proper place at the Yard and less than two years later on August 10, 1921 she was added to the Navy's growing inventory of capitol ships. Her first captain was H. J. Ziegemeier. The *California* was also a fleet flagship and had been outfitted accordingly.

THE INTER-WAR YEARS - THE BATTLESHIP NAVY

Much has been written about the "battleship navy", and all agree that the officers and men that made up this force were of a special breed. The officers were on their way up the career ladder, having only to serve their time in various assignments with hopefully ever increasing responsibilities. Often an officer would begin as an assistant in a division and transfer from one ship to another. Later he might return as a division officer, executive officer, and maybe even captain or in the best of circumstances, fly his flag as an admiral. The *California* was a flagship and she carried many men who would later attain flag rank such as Claude Block, Wilson Brown and William H. Standley. Block would figure prominently in the lack of proper defenses at Pearl Harbor on the morning of December 7, 1941, yet Husband Kimmel, the Pacific Fleet's Commander in Chief would be the one condemned.

Officers had a number of privileges during the interwar years which ceased with the beginning of the Second World War. Although the U.S. Navy did not officially sanction a caste system, this arm of the American military was the most prone to having and enforcing a definite class society. Officers were officers, chiefs were chiefs and enlisted men were enlisted men. Enlisted personnel did not socialize with the officers and vice versa. The quickest way for an officer to stop his career was to become too friendly with individual crew members, and in the worst of cases, borrow money or be seen socially with enlisted personnel. Officers had staterooms, better food, superior restroom accommodations and above all were regarded highly by civilian merchants, hotel owners and restauranteurs. Easy credit was available to officers in most establishments, and debts were generally paid with little overt collection effort. This all became a thing of the past when the war allowed thousands of reserve officers to integrate this previously closed society. They came from all walks of life, and often from the enlisted ranks. "Trade school" or Annapolis graduates quickly became a minority, and what was once a privileged class was open to anyone.

The enlisted men who served in the battleship navy were often like brothers, they too would stay with a ship for many years, many would carve out a niche that would be home during their prime working years. The *California* was no different as she had many men who had been with her for a number of years when the war broke out. Many were almost legendary such as Chief Radioman Thomas J. Reeves who earned the Medal of Honor posthumously who manned an ammunition handling line until he died on December 7, 1941. He was not alone in the battleship fleet. He like many others took great pride in the accomplishments of his ship and would not tolerate slovenliness or poor workmanship. The ship was more than gray and white painted steel, it was a home and represented the best military machine that the U.S. could put forward. The *California* and her crew were symbols of American Naval might, and in the Pacific, there was great interest in anything concerning the activities of the battle force.

Much of the two decade period between her

Sailors aboard the battleship California *man one of the 5 inch/51 caliber secondary battery guns in this 1923 phtograph. These guns were single purpose and designed to ward off destroyers or torpedo boats. Later, several of these guns removed from the older battleships were successfully used against the Japanese invaders off Wake Island in December 1941.*

The sub caliber guns of the California, *which are synchronized with the main battery, are fired in practice to conserve large caliber ammunition. A sailor can be seen in the fire control director atop the turret.*

A scout seaplane is catapulted from the aft turret of the California. *Prior to radar, the seaplanes were the eyes of the fleet.*

A detailed view of the upper top mast and cross member is depicted in this February 19, 1927 photograph. The fighting top is also shown close up. Just prior to the outbreak of the Second World War, many of the older battleships were retrofitted with 50 caliber machine guns for antiaircraft defense. Some were placed in a "birdbath" like structure attached to the fighting tops like the one shown here.

The Prune Barge enters drydock at the San Francisco Navy Yard in 1921 for her annual upkeep and repair.

The battle fleet as seen from the California. In the inter-war years, these ships represented the first line of defense for the United States.

launching and when she slowly sank into the mud of Pearl Harbor, the *California* acted as a flagship first for the Pacific Fleet and later for the Battle Force. Her duties were quite mundane, only punctuated with the periodic training exercises and fleet problems. The annual fleet problems were theoretical predicaments requiring the fleet to react to different attack scenarios. Interestingly, one was the air attack from carriers against the battle fleet at Pearl Harbor. Prophetically, the attack was a complete success. Unfortunately, little significant notice was taken. After all, the destruction of a ship the size of a battleship was not possible from the air. At least, not yet.

Although the battle force engaged in no armed combat during this period, it did act as a deterrent and as a political stick against Japanese aggression. The *California* was a successful contender for gunnery awards in 1925-26, and was one of the more battle efficient of the large ships. In 1925 she also led a number of ships on a goodwill cruise to Australia and New Zealand. It was always politically wise to show our neighbors and Allies what they could expect from the U.S. Navy.

The *California* served as a flagship which was considered a double edged sword. Always kept in tip top condition, her outward appearance was to be envied. Unfortunately, she was not always in the best material condition, and this would hurt her on the day the Japanese attacked Pearl Harbor.

She went through a minor upgrade in 1929-1930 when she replaced her antiquated anti aircraft battery with eight modern 5 inch/25 caliber guns, and again on 1936, she acquired several close in weapons in the form of water cooled 50 caliber machine guns. In her final form before the attack on Pearl Harbor, she landed her torpedoes for her submerged tubes. Like all of the other surface ships equipped with submerged tubes, the *California* also abandoned this type of armament. It was one of those ideas that sounded good at the time, but proved to be absolutely worthless. This is how the aging battleship appeared on December 6, 1941 on the eve of World War II. Like so many units of the navy, she had been transferred to Pearl Harbor as her home port. Ironically, the sailors of the fleet did not view today's tropical paradise with so much awe and charm as most tourists. The fact of the matter was that most of the fleet longed for San Pedro, Long Beach and even such places as the Fleet Locker Club in Long beach and of course, the Pike. On Saturday, December 6, 1941 most of the *California's* crew was ashore attending the "battle of the bands" and wondering what to do on Sunday. The ship had been opened up for a material inspection which meant that many of her normally dogged down spaces were open and bolts loosened in other areas. She was virtually without watertight integrity. But, Monday's inspection would come and go and she would be back to normal. Admiral William S. Pye flew his flag in the *California*, and little did he know that the following days events would cast him as the interim commander of the Pacific Fleet between the departing Husband Kimmel and the arriving Chester Nimitz. He had known disaster before as he had been the commander of DESRON 31 a part of the ill fated Destroyer

At the head of the line is the battleship California *in this May 1929 photo. She is followed by the* West Virginia, Maryland, Colorado *and* Tennessee. *Her sister ship, the* Tennessee *has just let loose a broadside. On October 25, 1944, fifteen years later all but the* Colorado *would be in a similar position, but firing on the Japanese battle line as it attempted to penetrate the Surigao Strait.*

Admiral Frank Schofield is shown making an inspection on the Prune Barge on December 12, 1930. Schofield was the commander in chief of the Battle Fleet, and the California *was his flagship.*

A landing party from the California *storms ashore in Guantanamo Bay, Cuba. This was not a pleasant duty. A* New Mexico *class battleship and a heavy cruiser can be seen in the background.*

Squadron 11 that had run aground at Point Honda in September 1923 losing seven ships. This next disaster would be the worst ever faced by the U.S. Navy.

THE JAPANESE ATTACK PEARL HARBOR: THE *CALIFORNIA* IS MORTALLY HIT

At 0805, ten minutes into the air attack by the Imperial Japanese Navy on December 7, 1941, the *California* was hit by two "Kate" torpedo bomber launched deep running torpedoes. One struck just forward of the bridge and the other below turret number 3. The torpedoes had been launched by a three plane unit coming from the southwest. By this time, the *West Virginia*, *Oklahoma*, *Arizona*, and light cruiser *Helena* had

been hit by the main body of twelve torpedo planes. The three planes that made their attack on the *California* emerged unharmed as they had fooled the anti aircraft gunners who were just getting the range. Incredibly, the *California* was slow to sound general quarters and set condition Zed. The *California* was a great ship, but at her moment of need, she was plagued with the lack of effective senior leadership and sluggish command responsiveness to the crisis. She should have survived. The explosions rocked the ship and rapid flooding began. In theory, the hits would have been damaging, but the great ship should have remained afloat and able to make minimum headway. This was not the case. Other ships such as the *Oklahoma* and *West Virginia* were hit by at least six torpedoes and succumbed.

Two torpedo hits should not have caused the *California* to sink. The six manhole covers that were removed from the double bottom and the other twelve that were loose had as much to do with the ultimate fate of the *California* as the two torpedoes that hit her. Of course, analysis after the battle cast some doubt on the importance of the opened manhole covers, yet the fact remains that the ship sank and should not have given the initial damage. The muddy waters of Pearl Harbor began to course through her spaces and she began to list to port immediately. She also lost all power due to her fuel tanks being contaminated and by 0810 she was a cold ship attempting to repulse her attackers by locally controlled guns with hand passed ammunition. Fortunately the list was corrected by the quick thinking of Ensign Edgar M Fain, a reserve officer who counter flooded. At least she would not share the fate of the *Oklahoma*, just up the line. The unfortunate *California* was hit again 15 minutes later by a 250 kilogram bomb that set off her AA ammunition killing another 53 men. Another bomb ruptured her bow plates, and flying shrapnel hit her upperworks in a number of places wounding and killing more men. By this time the ship was in bad way. She could not rely on any substantial assistance from other ships because they had their own problems as it was at the height of the battle. Finally, after a magnificent effort, power was restored and the ship was able to fight fires and fend for herself at 0855. The attack was half over by this time, but the scarred ship was ready to get underway with available power. Men had been returning to the ship which had opened the battle with many of her officers and crew ashore. Captain Bunkley had arrived back aboard and by 0910 she as ready to move. Fortune was not to smile on the ship as an oil fire on the water drifted down to surround her stern, so at 1002, fearing that his ship would be completely engulfed by fire, Captain Bunkley ordered the crew to abandon ship. This began at once as the crew swam to Ford Island just yards away. At 1015, the order was reversed and the crew ordered back aboard. This was not possible as many had just barely dragged themselves through debris and oil covered water to the relative safety of nearby Ford Island. Many were exhausted, bleeding and choking up fuel oil. The dye was now cast. The ship was leaking badly and slowly settling. Assistance was rendered by passing tugs and the minesweepers *Bobolink* and *Vireo*, but no amount of pumping could save the Prune Barge from settling into the mud. She was leaking too badly and only a concerted effort by divers with adequate equipment could have made the difference. With all the damage in the harbor, saving the *California* was not a priority; and finally, on December 10, in the late evening, the stained and blistered ship finally stopped settling. Only her superstructure appeared above the water. A callous end for a great lady.

Her human losses amounted to 6 officers, 92 men killed or missing, and 61 of her crew wounded. She fared better than most when comparing her to the other battleships that had been sunk or destroyed. Even as the battleship finally settled in the mud, another issue was settled some thousands of miles away. Added to the fact that battleships could be sunk while stationary was

Fourteen inch shells and powder are hoisted aboard the California. *Great care was exercised during ammunitioning to prevent an accidental explosion.*

The California *under siege. It is shortly after 10 AM at the height of the attack on Pearl Harbor, and hundreds of the* California's *crew are abandoning ship in accordance with Captain Bunkley's order. Oil fires on the water are drifting down from the burning* West Virginia *which prompted the abandon ship order. The order was quickly rescinded after the fires shifted, but it was too late to save the old lady. It took her two more days to settle into the muck of Pearl Harbor.*

The battlewagon encounters heavy seas in the Pacific off of San Francisco in 1939. It is no wonder that these ships were often called tubs. They could be quite wet in a seaway.

The sunken battleship has just broken water, and her main deck is now awash. A substantial effort has been made to raise this ship, and salvage experts are up to the task.

The Prune Barge emerges from Pearl Harbor on her way to the Puget Sound Navy Yard for complete modernization. Even in her reduced circumstances, she is still a handsome ship.

The California *opens fire with her 5 inch secondary battery at targets ashore on Luzon in the Philippines. Her role as a shore bombardment unit was indispensable and helped pave the way for success on the ground.*

The California *fends off repeated attacks by Kamikaze suicide planes. She was eventually hit on January 6, 1945. Forty-four men were killed, and over 150 were wounded in this attack.*

reality that they could be sunk while at high speed and attempting to defend themselves. On December 10, the Royal Navy capitol ships Repulse and *Prince of Wales* succumbed to aerial attack by Japanese aircraft. The battleship had been supplanted as the major fleet unit, and the aircraft carrier had taken it's place. However, there was still a role for the battleship as the *California* and some of her sunken sisters would prove. The *California* remained on the bottom for the next three and half months and was refloated on March 24, 1942. With almost all of her upperworks and masts removed she was floated into a drydock in the Pearl Harbor Navy Yard and by June permanent repairs had been made to much of the torpedo and bomb damaged areas. Next stop for the stripped down ship was the Puget Sound Navy Yard in Bremerton, Washington. She left Pearl Harbor on June 7, 1942 in convoy and arrived there on October 20, 1942. By this time, the battles of the Coral Sea and Midway have been fought and the struggle for Guadalcanal was underway. None of these fleet actions would have required the services of the old battleship, but her time at bat was coming soon.

BACK TO ACTION: A BRAND NEW MODERN BATTLESHIP *CALIFORNIA*

By the time the Puget Sound Navy Yard received the old battleship, a decision had been made to virtually remake her into a *South Dakota* class look a like. For the next fifteen months, thousands of yard workers crawled all over the *California* transforming her from a World War I relic to a state of the art battleship. She was stripped down to her deck level and the only remnants of her former self were the hull, engines and main armament. Everything else was modernized.

Blisters were added to her hull on both sides increasing her beam to 114 feet, thus preventing her from using the Panama canal. The added protection afforded by these blisters would help protect her from torpedoes, add greater stability and provide a base for her new five inch dual purpose guns mounted on each side. Her superstructure was rebuilt along the lines of contemporary battleships and was enclosed including the mast structure. Both funnels were trunked into one which was integrated into the conning tower and forward bridge area. She now sported a very uncrowded silhouette as opposed to the prewar eclectic look that had given her more of a yacht-like appearance. She looked more like a prize fighter now. Her armament now reflected what was necessary to fight not only surface ships but the threat from the air including the Kamikaze. She now had sixteen 5 inch/38 caliber guns housed in eight twin enclosed mounts, four to a side. They were director controlled and could put out a formidable rate of fire. To this was added a close in AA battery of ten 40mm quad mounts and sixty 20mm guns. These were placed in virtually every unoccupied space to provide maximum protection against air attack. All of this did not come without a substantial upgrade in electronics which included Mark 34 main battery directors, SK-2 radar and SP radar scanners. All of this required over 3/4 million feet of new wiring, air conditioning and auxiliary generators.

Finally, on January 31, 1944, the new *California* emerged from the yard with her new Measure 32 dazzle pattern paint scheme. She was as modern as anything built and capable of accepting her new role. She would act as a shore bombardment ship and defend ships around her with intensive AA fire as necessary. Still only rated at 21 knots, the old ship was modern looking and acting, but not capable of keeping up with the fast carriers as were the *South Dakota's* and brand new *Iowa* classes. But there was much for her to do.

BACK TO THE FIGHT

She took up her role as a shore bombardment weapon in May 1944 as the Marines attacked the Marianas. She was hit by a Japanese shore battery on Saipan on June 14, which did some minor damage and killed one and wounded nine other men. Her next stop was Guam where her main armament successfully paved the way for assault troops, and she was involved in a collision with none other than her sister, the battleship *Tennessee*. Her sister lost steering control and rammed the Prune Barge in her port bow. It took only 17 days for repairs to be made at Espiritu Santo and the battleship was back on line and fully capable. By September 17, 1944. she was able to sail for the Philippines to provide support for the landings. Here she exacted her revenge for her humiliation at Pearl Harbor. The battle was in the Surigao Strait and perhaps the last battle the world will ever witness being fought between major combatants at sea. Finally, the battleship was to perform as it was originally designed - a slugging match with ships of like size and caliber.

SURIGAO STRAIT AND THE END OF THE WAR THAT HAD BEGUN SO OMINOUSLY

The Japanese military was characterized by it's penchant for complicated operations and the series of battles fought to defeat the Allies in the Philippines in 1944 was a graphic example of this. Generally, the more complicated, the less chance an operation has for success, and the ultimate and final defeat of the Imperial Japanese Navy off Leyte confirmed this axiom of strategic planning. The battle that involved the *California* and five of her sisters was fought on the night of October 24-25, 1944 in the Surigao Strait. The Surigao Strait separated Leyte from the smaller island of Dinagat in the southern Philippine chain and opened in Leyte Gulf. Leyte Gulf is where the Imperial planners sought to catch the American Navy during its precarious amphibious phase and annihilate it. It was an all or nothing show that included massive fleet actions, diversions and near the climax, an old fashioned slug fest between opposing battle lines.

The Japanese had decided to successively attack the forces off Leyte with a number of units. The unit that attempted to penetrate the Surigao Strait consisted of Admiral Nishimura's two battleships *Fuso* and *Yamashiro*, heavy cruiser *Mogami*, and destroyers *Michishio, Asagumo, Yamagumo,* and *Shigure*. Awaiting them were Admiral Jesse B. Oldendorf's bombardment group consisting of the older battleships *Mississippi, Tennessee, California, Pennsylvania, West Virginia* and *Maryland*. With the exception of

Sailors literally man the guns as the California *enters the Philadelphia Navy Yard in December 1945. The war is over for this veteran.*

A formal ceremony takes place on the deck of the aging battleship as she is placed in the inactive reserve on August 7, 1946 at the Philadelphia Navy Yard.

the *Mississippi*, all were alumni of the Pearl Harbor attack and had a score to settle. Joining the battle line were 39 PT Boats, a variety of destroyers, and a number of heavy and light cruisers. One, the light cruiser *Phoenix* had also received the Japanese at Pearl Harbor, so several thousand American sailors were awaiting pay back time.

The reception consisted of pin prick attacks by the PT Boats followed by a concerted torpedo attack by the destroyers as Nishimura's force made it's way into the strait. Finally, at right angles or a crossed "T", the battleships would finish the job. Any remnants would be dealt with by the cruisers and aircraft the following morning.

The night was characterized by a light haze lit up by sheet lightning. The temperature was a humid 80 degrees, common to the southern Philippines. The hills on the islands reverberated with the sound of thunder, and the air was heavy with mugginess. There was very little wind movement and the sea was glossy smooth like glass. The night was almost macabre in it's effect. Just before midnight on October 24, the stillness was broken by the sound of PT Boats approaching their targets and the now alert Japanese point destroyer *Shigure* opening fire on these nuisances. The battle had begun.

There was some concern among the battleship captains as to the amount of armor piercing ammunition available. Most ships were unusually low as they had planned for shore bombardment thus their AP stock hovered at 200-300 rounds. The *California* had 240 shells, yet if correctly placed, no enemy could hope to win. The battleships had landed their aircraft ashore or stowed them in hangers to avoid the terrible mistakes made during the night battles around Guadalcanal. No one wanted to repeat the disaster of Savo Island, and although the American Navy was far more modern and the leadership much more proficient, there was always the unknown. The Japanese Navy was still a formidable foe and not to be taken lightly. Hence all preparations were made. The *California*, second in line behind the *Pennsylvania* steamed along at 10 plus knots at right angles to the strait in anticipation. At 0200 the destroyers made their initial torpedo attack, yet Nishimura kept on. By 0315, the PT Boats and

the destroyers had finished with their part of the assault, and it was time for the battle line to engage the Japanese. The destroyers had launched 47 torpedoes, and had scored five hits sinking two destroyers and ultimately the aging battleship *Fuso*. The *Mogami*, two destroyers and the *Yamashiro* came on. The *Yamashiro* was a powerful unit mounting twelve 14 inch/45 caliber guns and a secondary battery of sixteen 6 inch/50 caliber guns. She was also capable of nearly 25 knots, at least 3-4 knots faster than any of the battleships she faced. At 0323 she came in radar range of Weyland's force and he ordered the battle line to commence firing at 26,000 yards. At 22,800 yards the main battle line opened fire. The *California* was equipped with the latest in main battery fire control and along with her sisters *West Virginia* and *Tennessee* did the lion's share of the damage beginning at 0353. The Prune Barge fired 69 AP shells and the *Mogami* and *Yamashiro* were literally demolished hardly returning fire. By 0406, Olendorf ordered a cease fire and it was over for the old battleships and literally over for the Japanese. The *Yamashiro* sank soon thereafter and the *Mogami* was sunk during daylight by aircraft from nearby escort carriers. The Battle of Surigao Strait had ended and revenge had been exacted by the Americans. The *California* and her sisters were vindicated.

The war bore on for another eleven months and the *California* was engaged in shore bombardment assignments in various locations in the Philippines. She could always be depended on to support the men ashore. She was finally bloodied again by a Kamikaze on January 6, 1945. The hit caused the death of 44 of her crew and the aging ship was sent back to Bremerton for refit and repair. Back on the job in June she supported troops around Okinawa. Her last major role was that of covering the landings of the Sixth Army on Honshu in September 1945 after war's end. She left for the U.S. in October and arrived on December 7, 1945, four years after her now forgotten humiliation. She went into inactive reserve at the Philadelphia Navy Yard on February 14, 1947. Twelve years later on March 1, 1959, she was sold for scrapping to the Boston Metals Company for $860,000. Her usefulness was at an end, but she had proven that ships and men can emerge from defeat and go on to victory. The Prune Barge did fight again.

In perhaps her last photo, the California *(left) is being reduced to scrap at the Patapsco Scrap Yard in Baltimore late in 1959. Her sister, the* Tennessee *is sharing the same fate alongside her.*

USS *NEVADA* BB-36
"THE CHEER UP SHIP"

THE SHIP CHRISTENED BY A CHILD

The battleship *Nevada* was sponsored by eleven year old Eleanor Anne Seibert, niece of Nevada's governor Tasker L. Oddie. The date was July 11, 1914, just a month short of the beginning of World War I. Three quarters of a century later in December 1991, at the 50th Anniversary of the Japanese attack on Pearl Harbor, another eleven year old asked her grandfather, "Was that your ship?" She was pointing at the *Arizona* Memorial as they slowly passed by on a harbor tour boat. Next to her were several other children who could only speak Japanese. He answered "No, my ship was the *Nevada,* and she got underway and fought her way into this channel fifty years ago today." The Japanese chil-

The author's grandson, Chris, points to the only major remnant left from the Prune Barge, her ship's bell. It now resides in a quiet spot in Capitol Park in Sacramento, California.

The new battleship, Nevada, *powered by Curtis Turbines is on her way to the Brooklyn Navy Yard for some adjustments prior to builders speed trials. In the October 25, 1915 photo, her decks look quite barren compared to her profile in World War II.*

The Nevada *on speed trials in October 1915. At 21 knots, she could keep up with any contemporary battleship.*

dren could not understand the old man, but they knew enough to be silent and respectful.

The sortie of the battleship *Nevada* at the height of the battle between aircraft and antiaircraft gunners on December 7, 1941 will be forever burned in the minds of those who witnessed it. It was the finest hour for a surprised and unprepared navy which would within three years defeat the navy which had known only victory. But on that Sunday, the *Nevada's* sortie was about the only bright spot on an otherwise dismal and depressing morning. The roots of that sortie go deep and began just under three decades earlier. The date was March 4, 1911.

BUILD TWO FIRST CLASS BATTLESHIPS FOR UNDER $6 MILLION EACH

In a democracy, the people have a right to know how their tax dollars are being spent. This is especially true with expenditures for defense and the military overall. The U.S. Navy has always been scrutinized in detail as it's expenditures are large and usually in the public eye. The battleship was the backbone of the U.S. Fleet for the first 40 years of the twentieth century, and anytime one was in port, the people wanted to visit and tour this very large and prominent expenditure of their hard earned money. On March 4, 1911, the Congress of the U.S. authorized the President of the U.S. to build two first class battleships. The now forgotten congressional staff member who wrote the standard language of the act further stated that "these ships should carry the heaviest armament, have the highest speed possible and the greatest possible radius of action". Oh, and of course, should not cost more than $6 million each exclusive of armor and armament. After all, the Congress is responsible for spending the country's money and six million dollars represented a large share of the early 20th century navy's budget. The two ships would be numbers 36 and 37 and named for the states of *Nevada* and *Oklahoma*.

One would die a quick and merciful death at the outset of war, and the other would go on to become a naval legend. Both were great and wonderful ships in their own right.

The *Nevada* was to be built by the Fore River Shipbuilding Company in Quincy, Massachusetts by Bethlehem Steel workers and craftsmen. She was laid down on November 4, 1912, launched on July 14, 1914 and ultimately commissioned on March 11, 1916. It had taken five years and seven days from the authorizing legislation to visualize reality. She displaced 29,000 tons (34,000 tons full load) with a length of 583 feet overall and a beam of 95 feet (exclusive of bulges). She could make 20.5 knots which was adequate for the period in which she was built. She was the first oil fired battleship and employed six Bureau Express boilers connected to Curtiss geared turbines ultimately turning two shafts. Her geared turbines were adjustable to cruise setting allowing fuel economy similar to that experienced by reciprocating engines. Her horsepower was rated at 26,500, close to that of a Wickes class four piper destroyer of 1918 vintage. Of course, the *Nevada* could not accelerate to 35 knots yet on the other hand, a four piper could not outshoot the *Nevada*!

Her immediate predecessors were the *New York* and *Texas* and just before them, the *Arkansas* and *Wyoming*. The *Nevada* class was another graduated step in the rapidly evolving American battleship. The Nevada's represented a definitive departure from the *Texas* and *Wyoming* classes, and became the model for the future. They were oil fired as opposed to coal from the outset, a huge engineering advantage. Next, the *Nevada* class adopted the revolutionary "all or nothing" concept of armor protection. Her vitals were protected by heavy armor designed to resist penetration while other areas not considered essential to battle-worthiness were left unprotected in the classic sense. The areas protected were done so to prevent lethal projectiles from inflicting mortal wounds and thus violat-

The modern battleship, Nevada, is anchored in the Hudson River shortly after World War I. The prophetic photo correctly depicts what would emerge as the nemesis to the battleship, the airplane.

ing the integrity of the ship. No longer were such areas as the ship's stem, decks, and upper decks covered with light and medium armor as was mandated in the designs of the past.

A new school of thought had prevailed in naval design circles forcing the previously accepted practise of armoring everything with some armor to change to the "all or nothing" concept. The *Nevada* class was armored in the following way:

Belt: 8 inch lower edges and 14 inches upper
Boiler uptakes: 14 inches
Main deck: 4 inches
Conning tower/tube: 16 inches
Turrets: Face 16/18 inch/Roof 5 inch/Sides 9 (rear), 10 side

This protection was later augmented by anti-torpedo blisters, but no ship could have withstood the damage that sister ship *Oklahoma* received when she was struck by up to nine torpedoes in rapid succession on December 7, 1941. Of course, when these ships were first designed, none but the most far sighted could have predicted that these antiquated ships would have to fight the scourge of the mid twentieth century warrior - the skillfully handled torpedo plane.

The third design innovation that set the *Nevada* class apart from her contemporaries was the use of the triple barrel turrets in the 1 and 4 turrets. The superfiring positions of turrets 2 and 3 both had twin barrels, yet the triple barrel was there to stay and would be seen on the most modern of battleships, the 1940's *Iowa* class. The *Nevada* mounted a main battery of ten 14 inch/50 caliber guns controlled initially by a series of rangefinders mounted atop her bridge and aft superfirng turret. From information "borrowed" from the Royal Navy, her superfiring turrets were calibrated with large numbers to

show turret training and there is a range clock mounted on the mast. These rather crude low tech devices were designed to assist other ships in the battle line which may not be able to see the target clearly due to smoke and so forth. In any event, it was a pragmatic approach that clearly demonstrated that the fleet would act as a unit as opposed to individual ship to ship duels as was the practise in days of old.

The *Nevada* became an accepted fleet unit on March 11, 1916 when she broke her commissioning pennant under the command of Captain William S. Sims. Sims was an amazing naval officer and one of great political courage. Just fifteen years earlier when he was a young lieutenant, he boldly wrote to President Teddy Roosevelt about the poor quality of American naval gunnery, especially during the recent war with Spain. While many felt that the victories at Santiago Bay and earlier at Manila Bay were examples of high caliber gunnery, those who were realists knew that a 3 percent hit rate or a 97 percent miss score was almost criminally inadequate. Lt. Sims, prodded by other progressively minded naval officers wrote to President Roosevelt, a known supporter of all things naval, and laid out the case of improving gunnery through effective fire control. Sims had to bypass many in the Bureau of Ordnance who supported the status quo and were reluctant to rock the boat. Sims took career in hand and made the plunge. He was rewarded by having Roosevelt approve his ideas and along with Bradley Fiske and Albert Niblack, the trio quickly brought about improvement. Sims risked his career at a time when naval officers just simply did not make end runs, no matter what the cause. After his rather daring career move he rose steadily in the naval hierarchy and in 1916 assumed command of the battleship *Nevada*. In 1917, he next went to Great Britain to lay the groundwork for the covert and later open naval support to the

Allied powers. He was also credited with being a major backer of the convoy system. He was truly a great naval officer of the highest caliber when great naval officers were in short supply. Interestingly, the Navy would honor the three men who revolutionized naval gunnery by naming destroyers after them, the *Sims* DD-409, *Niblack* DD-424 and the *Fiske* DD-842. No higher tribute can be made to members of the naval service.

THE NEVADA JOINS THE FLEET, JUST IN TIME FOR WAR

After shakedown cruises and having minor repairs and adjustments made in her machinery, the *Nevada* joined the fleet on May 26, 1916. She stayed close to her east coast home port spending much of the period prior to the U.S. entry into World War I in training and exercises. She operated out of Norfolk and ranged south as far as the Caribbean on her training cruises. As the U.S. became an active participant in the "Great War", it became plain that the battleship would be needed on the other side of the Atlantic as an American partner in the British Grand Fleet. Accordingly, she sailed on August 13, 1918 for Great Britain, almost four years to the day since the commencement of hostilities. She swept through the North Sea on patrols and provided escort to various convoys carrying troops and military supplies. The war came to a close with an Armistice on November 11, 1918. The new battleship did not fire a shot in anger, but had she been called upon to engage the German fleet, she would have made a fine account of herself. Her last major role related to the Great war was to act as escort for President Woodrow Wilson when he rode the troop transport George Washington. The *Nevada* arrived back in the U.S. in late December 1918.

The war had ended before the *Nevada* was able to take an active part, but her turn was yet to come. For the next two decades the gradually obsolecsing battleship participated in the normal routine generally associated with major units of the U.S. Fleet.

WAITING AND PREPARING FOR THE WAR EVERYONE KNEW WAS COMING

The *Nevada* was one of the "mighty fifteen". She was a battleship and thus the first line of defense for the U.S. But, she and her fourteen sisters represented more than floating gray citadels of steel and men. They represented safety and security, but moreover they stood out as institutions that the average American could point to with pride. These ships were the American way of life and liberty personified. The *Nevada* was one of the "Mighty Fifteen", and wherever she sailed, it was newsworthy, and whenever she was in an American port, she was a star attraction. Only very rarely has a people embraced a military machine or organization without reservation. The "minutemen" of 1776, the Civil War Union Navy "Monitor", the "Great White Fleet" and the Marine defenders of 1941 Wake Island share a common bond with the American battleships of the interwar years.

The *Nevada* accompanied the *Arizona* BB-39 to South America to represent the U.S. at the Pe-

The port side of the Nevada *as a ship's launch comes alongside to deliver civilian visitors on July 6, 1927. Large air ventilation scoops and the starboard boat crane can readily be seen as well as excellent detail of the cage mast.*

Sailors on the Nevada *pose with children from various Hollywood film studios during a visit in July 1933. The Navy encouraged visitors to display its might.*

Crews from the Nevada, West Virginia *and* Idaho *battle for first place in cutter races in Los Angeles harbor on June 19, 1937. The* Nevada *won. Competition among battleships was often fierce in any sport from sailing to who had the best dance band.*

ruvian Centennial Exposition in July 1921, and again sailed south a year later to help celebrate the Brazilian Centennial in August 1922. This time she was accompanied by the USS *Maryland* BB-46. Thousands of visitors came aboard the *Nevada* and the comment made most often was, "with guns like that, we will always want to be friends". The South Americans had never seen such power as was contained in the 14 inch rifles of the *Nevada*. After this cruise, the *Nevada* sailed for San Diego, California and operated in Pacific coastal waters until it was decided that she should be part of as major demonstration of power.

The *Nevada* joined with sister ship *Oklahoma*, the *Pennsylvania* and a number of other fleet units to visit Pago Pago, Samoa; Melbourne, Australia and Wellington, New Zealand. The nearly 16,000 mile round trip began on March 2, 1925 and ended back in San Pedro on September 26, 1925. The voyage which was interrupted many times to allow hundreds of thousands of visitors to view the might of the American Navy served a number of purposes. It allayed the fears of our Allies down under and convinced them that we would indeed be part of any defense against Asian (Japanese) aggression. It served another purpose only noticeable to naval officers and those with a professional interest in sea power. The *Nevada* was able to sail to Australia and back with minimal refueling and reprovisioning. This accomplishment dispelled the conventional wisdom which dictated that a force of ships from the U.S. could not operate as far away from home in waters such as those near Japan. To the Japanese, the two decade old naval victory at Tsushima where the Japanese battle line had annihilated a Russian squadron was a constant reminder that an enemy fleet travelling to their waters would certainly be ripe for destruction

when it arrived. The problems of resupply, crew preparedness and equipment maintenance would be insurmountable. So it was with the Russian navy, so it would be with any other aggressor navy. The great cruise of 1925 put paid to that notion. Ships like the *Nevada* could and would be quite capable of destroying units of the Imperial Japanese Navy in their home waters. Improved provisioning, oil fired boilers and superior fighting men would make the difference. Besides, the *Nevada* did not have to rely on shore provided drinking water, she distilled a sufficient supply for all needs for the entire cruise. This was widely publicized. The cruise sent a blunt message to Japan - the U.S. considered the Pacific Ocean an international body of water and not a Japanese lake. The U.S. Navy would guarantee the freedom of the seas against any aggressor. The message was received, but not fully appreciated.

As the years wore on past the great cruise of 1925, the aging battleship entered into a peacetime routine common to all nations whose navies

were preparing for battle. Exercises, training and gunnery drills. Many men served on the slowly aging battleship for literally an entire career without knowing much beyond the railing of their own ships. In a way, this was bad. The battleship was becoming a dinosaur. Only a few, primarily those in naval aviation were vocal about their opposition to dominance of the battleship faction. The battlewagon was still the jewel of the fleet, and those who championed the cause of the battleship did so with blinders in place and tunnel vision. It was also the place where promotion was guaranteed both in the officer corps and in the enlisted ranks. So the navy moved toward the war that was sure to come on two parallel tracks. One track carried those who were determined to fight the next war with the last war's weapons and the other track carried those who knew that the next war would be fought with contemporary weaponry and tactics - the airplane. The ugly boxlike shapes in the form of the *Langley* CV-1, *Lexington* CV-2, and *Saratoga* CV-3 which always seemed to be with the fleet were constant reminders of the future. It would be the airplane, the airplane launched from a carrier that would doom the battleship. But, in the interwar years, the battleship was still in it's golden age.

The *Nevada* cost the taxpayers about 55 cents per day per man to feed, a bargain price in the early twentieth century. Of course food served was quite basic, but nutritious by then contemporary standards. The 1,500-1,600 man crew of *Nevada* consumed about 400,000 eggs per year; 45,000 pounds of coffee; 550,000 pounds of potatoes, and of course just over 40,000 pounds of

Nevada sailors eager for shore liberty line up for inspection by the officer of the deck. When the fleet was in, cities like Long Beach, Honolulu or San Francisco witnessed oceans of whitehats every weekend. Each sailor is holding out his liberty card.

navy beans. Of course, how the food was prepared meant all the difference to the crew. Legend has it that ships with bad cooks never had seagulls following them, yet the *Nevada* was not one of them. The food was good, and the cooks took pride in it's preparation.

By late 1927, it was time for an overhaul and modernization. In the *Nevada's* case, she was taken in hand by the Norfolk Navy Yard from August 1927 through January 1930. The ship shed her dated lattice masts for massive tripods and had her secondary battery re-sited a deck level higher. At least the five inch battery could now be used without fear of the gun crews being drowned. Other improvements included the addition of anti-torpedo bulges and increasing the elevation of the main battery to 30 degrees. This would augment their range. Scout plane catapults were installed on the quarterdeck and on the roof of X turret. Of course this meant large cranes were necessarily sited amidships and on the stern to recover aircraft and also for boat removal and stowage. Finally, some attention was paid to her anti aircraft battery in the form of eight 5 inch/25 caliber guns located in her waist, and a few manually operated 50 caliber water cooled machine guns atop her masts (birdbaths) and superstructure. The 5 inch guns were director controlled and designed for aircraft flying at less than 150 knots and generally below 10,000 feet in altitude. Barely functional for 1930, and wholly inadequate for what was to come in December 1941.

For the next years prior to the U.S. entry in World War II, the *Nevada* operated off the west coast and in Pacific waters. She participate in various fleet problems and in general was regarded as an excellent ship with a good record. With the exception of various upkeep periods and being prepared for the addition of 1.1 inch anti aircraft batteries, the *Nevada* began the war in the same condition as she left the Norfolk Navy Yard in January 1930. She was a World War I ship about to meet a World War II weapon.

Her survival would depend on the excellence of her crew and luck. She had both.

HER FLAG INSPIRED US ALL - THE *NEVADA* TRIUMPHS ON DECEMBER 7, 1941

In Pearl Harbor, the *Nevada* was moored behind the *Arizona* last in the line known as battleship row alongside Ford Island. It was December 6, 1941, and the quarter century old battleship was supposed to be at sea with several of her sisters. Since July of that year, the fleet had rotated with half of it's ships in harbor and the rest at sea on maneuvers. But rumors of submarine activity caused all of the major units except the carriers to be huddled in Pearl Harbor seemingly out of harm's way. Pearl Harbor was crowded that weekend with the *Arizona, Pennsylvania, California, Maryland, Tennessee, West Virginia,* and *Nevada's* sister, the *Oklahoma.* These were just the battleships, there were over 75 other ships crammed in the harbor, and shore facilities were overcrowded but making money hand over fist. Hotel Street at one end of the spectrum and the Royal Hawaiian Hotel at the other end of the social scale. It was the last night of relative peace for the U.S. and the last night of life for nearly 2,500 men and women who were to die the following morning, December 7, 1941.

Aboard the *Nevada,* the in harbor routine went on with just a couple of minor changes. In the few days prior to December 7, the *Nevada* had off loaded her main battery powder charges for new charges and heavier than standard projectiles. It seemed that all of the battle line was to trade in their powder and projectiles for projectiles that would provide for greater penetrating power. The *Nevada* was nearly out of any 14 inch ammunition and was capable of defending herself with her secondary battery only. A blessing in disguise.

The second element of luck occurred during the 2000-2400 watch on December 6, when Ensign Joe Taussig, who was to play a major role in the *Nevada's* defense the following day, ordered a second boiler lit off. The ship had been operating on one boiler as was practise to provide sufficient power for the ship to operate while moored. At 0755, the *Nevada* had two boilers on line and 60 of the required 300 pounds of pressure required to enable the ship to move. Also at this time the band had assembled near the stern to play the national anthem as the flag was raised on all ships in port. Ensign Taussig had the watch again since 0745 and was concerned about the proper size of the national ensign to be flown. A messenger was dispatched to the bow to consult with the color guard on the *Arizona's* stern just yards ahead of the *Nevada.* With that settled the ceremony began, but was interrupted by the Japanese. Just at that time, Japanese torpedo planes swooped down just feet above the channel and began launching torpedoes at the assembled ships, with the battleships being the primary targets. The resulting hits, including the one on the *Nevada* near frame 40, disproved the notion that torpedoes would dive to 75 feet before they would again come up to cruising depth of 10-15 feet. The harbor was 45 foot deep under the *Nevada,* and the torpedoes that were not supposed to work, worked quite

The battleship Nevada *in her famous sortie during the Japanese surprise attack on Pearl Harbor, December 7, 1941. She is gliding down the channel and has just been singled out for destruction by Japanese high level bombers. Her proud ensign, although tattered and burned, was an inspiration to all.*

well. The Japanese navy had fitted specially designed wooden fins on the torpedoes that eliminated the deep dive problem. The torpedo that hit the *Nevada* did some damage and opened a large jagged hole, but quick thinking prevented the ship from capsizing. She was counterflooded properly.

Lt. Cmdr. F. J. Thomas found himself in command as the battle began because Captain F. W. Scanland was ashore. Captain Scanland would fight the ship during the last 45 minutes of what would be a two hour raid. But for Thomas and his group of junior officers and experienced CPO's, it was time for action. A torpedo had just hit the ship and as the aircraft pulled out of their shallow dives, rear gunners shot up the decks and shredded the flag that just a few minutes earlier was the subject of Joe Taussig's concern. Taussig's antiaircraft crews got on target directly and began plugging away with their 5 inch/25 caliber guns, not to mention the 50 caliber close in weapons. Unfortunately the complicated gun loading and directing procedure required aircraft to behave in a more civilized and cooperative fashion. This was obviously not going to the case, so the crews loaded at peak rate and hoped that barrage fire would at least demoralize their enemy. Amazingly, the *Nevada* was spared the devastating blows of multiple torpedo hits that the *Oklahoma, West Virginia, Arizona* and *California* had to absorb. All were sunk, and two, the *Oklahoma* and *Arizona* would never return to combat.

Two minutes after the torpedo hit, the ship was subjected to at least twelve bombs, but none hit the ship. At the same time, all preparations were being made to get underway in accordance with instructions from the Navy Yard that all ships were to sortie. The *Nevada* led a charmed life for the next few minutes and as this was at the absolute height of the battle, it was by grace alone that she was spared. However, it had to end and at 0810 she was hit in the starboard antiaircraft director. Taussig, who occupied this above deck cubicle was severely wounded, but not out of the fight. Fire from his guns was maintained, and the ship escaped attention for another 20 minutes when she was hit again in the bridge area. Unfortunately smoke sifted into the engine and boiler spaces and the boilers were temporarily secured so that crews could evacuate. By 0840, she was ready to move and all that was necessary was that she be cast off from her quay. For this to happen, Chief Boatswain's Mate Edwin J. Hill and his men would have to cast loose at the quay and swim back. This done, the old battleship swung majestically out in the channel and rang up 14 knots. This was over the channel speed limit, but who cared? She glided down the channel and it seemed as if everything else stood still, and only this powerful warrior was in motion. Men wept at the sight of her tattered ensign in the wind, and when the stars on the smoke stained flag periodically came into view, grown men choked back tears of pride. Against all odds, and against the backdrop of total devastation, a lone survivor defied what seemed to be an overwhelming enemy victory. This sight inspired thousands and was forever etched in the memory of those present. It also alarmed an enemy that up to this moment had experienced complete superiority. But, oppor-

The battleship Nevada *aground near Hospital Point which was renamed Nevada Point. Fire in the forward area has gutted the ship and blistered her paint. It took the efforts of many dedicated crewmen for several hours to bring the 14 raging fires under control, but they succeeded. By Monday, the formerly devastated ship was cleaned up and ready for action - she "cheered up" those around her in the darkest of hours.*

tunity was also in the enemy's favor. A grand opportunity to sink this upstart in the channel and effectively cork the rest of the fleet in a bottle. The onslaught was about to begin, but other problems had begun to make themselves more painfully known. The old battered ship was sinking from her first hit, and the realization that her sortie was a "swinging at windmills" gesture was becoming apparent. As she moved down the channel she was repeatedly hit by bombs as the Japanese unloaded what must have been their last desperate gasp. She was hit at least six or seven times and over a dozen fires were raging all over the ship. She was directed to beach herself to avoid blocking the channel. Regrettably, her engines were stopped at 0910 and she nosed her way into the sand near Hospital Point (later dubbed Nevada Point). She was hurt, and hurt badly. Captain Scanland arrived by launch at 0915 as the Japanese planes were strafing the harbor. A new fight was about to intensify, and that was to be fought by damage controlmen rather than gunners. The ship had literally sunk on the beach was slowly being gutted by fire from the bow area back to the bridge. At least the tremendous explosion that destroyed the *Arizona* would not occur as the *Nevada* was empty of main battery powder charges.

Finally, the Japanese left just after 1000. The attack leader Commander Mitsuo Fuchida remained high above the harbor to assess damage for a few minutes after the main body had left for their carrier homes. When he was satisfied that a stunning defeat had been handed to the American navy, he too left for his carrier. He fully expected to return that afternoon and destroy the navy yard facilities and any surviving ships, but it was not be. The battle was over, and the U.S. Navy and Army were left to sift through the damage and bury the dead. By 1045, the *Nevada* was permanently grounded and any fear of her drifting into the channel was allayed. She had been hit or near missed by no less than 14 bombs and one torpedo. It was the torpedo

however, that nearly sank her, a lesson for the future. The air and sea launched torpedo was to be one the Imperial Japanese Navy's most effective weapons.

For the next several hours and into the late night fires were fought and finally brought under control an hour before midnight. Men had worked unceasingly for hours without food or water to save their ship. The light cruiser *Helena* sent over something to eat and drink in the early afternoon, but that was the only relief. The next day, Monday, December 8, inventory was taken. Fifty, including the valiant CBM Edwin Hill had perished. He was awarded the Congressional Medal of Honor as was Lt. Donald K. Ross for their heroism and valor on that day. 109 men were wounded and the rest of the crew was virtually homeless. Many had lost all of their personal items and pay records were in a shambles. For the next few weeks, many of the crew had to convince other ships and shore stations of their legitimacy and need for uniforms, shelter and food. They were homeless. It was an interesting paradox.

That following Monday, the strategic location of the *Nevada* made it imperative that she be the first line of defense against Japanese invaders who were expected at any time. Many of the *Nevada's* crew practiced "repel boarders" with broomsticks, baseball bats and the very few small arms available. What they lacked in equipment, they more than compensated for in enthusiasm.

OUT OF THE MUD AND BACK TO WORK - SALVAGE AND REPAIR

The afternoon of the 7th, the *Nevada* looked like a junk yard. She was covered with debris, human body parts, and burned and twisted metal. And, she was on fire. She had the smell of death and hopelessness about her. The following Monday morning, she was back to her old self. A metamorphosis had taken place over night. She

What the modernized battleship Nevada looked like after being updated both at Pudget Sound Navy Yard and later at the Norfolk Navy Yard. This November 1944 view shows how the old battleship looked when she took on the Japanese at Iwo Jima and Okinawa during the final year of the Pacific war.

was cleaned up and ready to fight, even if it was just with her secondary battery. She was the "Cheer Up Ship" and would fight again. It was now merely a matter of patching her and pumping some of Pearl Harbor mixed with fuel oil out of her. This began in earnest. The biggest problem was the hole made by the torpedo and the rupture on her forecastle made by bombs. Of course, the prevailing opinion on the part of many observers was that it would be too difficult to refloat her, and maybe she should just be demilitarized and cut up for scrap. This was not to be the case, and the crew and salvage professionals got to work. A wooden patch was formed using the capsized *Oklahoma* as a mold. Her bilge was identical to that of the *Nevada* as they were sisters. This would be the last event that they would share. All of the other holes big and small were patched and finally on February 18, 1942, she entered dry dock #2 for temporary repairs to enable her to return to the Puget Sound Navy Yard for modernization and permanent repair. She was a muddy and barnacled mess, but she was alive. Most of her equipment had been emersed in water, but also in fuel oil, thus salvageable. After spending two months in one of Pearl Harbor's priceless drydocks, she sailed for Bremerton, Washington arriving on May 1, 1942.

It was time for a complete facelift, and over the next several months the *Nevada* was stripped down to the bare bones of her superstructure. What emerged was a cross between the old *Nevada* and a modern *South Dakota* class battleship. She was modernized, but retained some of that old world look. During her refit she was rearmed with sixteen dual purpose 5 inch/38 caliber guns housed in eight mounts. The secondary battery was situated abreast of the upper superstructure and controlled by four high angle/low angle DCT's mounted high on the superstructure. The difference between the old 5 inch/25 caliber open mount AA battery and this new layout was to be of great value to the *Nevada* as was her new complement of eight quad 40mm mounts and forty 20mm guns. Prior to the 1942 modernization, her antiaircraft armament consisted of eight 5 inch/25 caliber guns and eight 50 caliber machine guns, a total of sixteen substandard weapons. Now she could boast 86

medium/light caliber guns that were effectively controlled and could knock down what the Japanese could throw at her.

In addition to being rearmed which gave her a more distinctive modern look, the old battleship had her superstructure built up and her masts were replaced with a stump tripod abaft her forward director and a pole just behind funnel which had a rather peculiar looking slanted cap. RDF was also added for warning and to augment gunnery control. By Mid December 1942, with a new paint job and many new hands, she was ready to rejoin the fleet. On December 19, 1942, she made the familiar journey out of Bremerton and through the Straits of Juan de Fuca to the cold waters of the North Pacific. Three thousand miles away, the *Nevada's* sister ship, the battleship *Oklahoma* quietly rested upside down, nearly forgotten. She was the tomb for approximately 400 men and work to salvage would not begin until March 1943. In the meantime, she silently and patiently waited as the war went on without her. Her sister would have to do the fighting.

BACK TO WAR - THE FROZEN NORTH

The first assignment given the "Cheer Up Ship" was to sail southward to San Pedro, which was well received by the crew. She arrived on Christmas Day, 1942. For the next few months and until April 7, 1943, the revitalized battleship engaged in various exercises and gunnery practise. She and other pre World War II battleships *Pennsylvania* and *Idaho* would spearhead Admiral Thomas C. Kinkaid's attack on Attu in the outer Aleutians. It was time to remove the Japanese from North American soil. It was none too soon for the *Idaho* and *Pennsylvania* as some of their crews had been nicknamed the "Market Street Commando's" due to the longevity of their stay in San Francisco.

The Battle of the Komandorski Islands had just been fought and won by an a smaller, but better directed American force on March 26, 1943. The Japanese had been denied access to their garrisons by the persistence of Task Force 16.6 (*Salt Lake City*, *Richmond* and four destroyers). The superior Japanese force retired, but according to the captain of the *Salt Lake City*, it

was only by the grace of God. A larger American force was now being assembled to mount the assault on Attu.

Rear Admiral Francis W. Rockwell, recently evacuated from Admiral Thomas C. Hart's tragically lost Asiatic Fleet was selected to command the amphibious assault scheduled for May 11, 1943. He was no stranger to the *Nevada* having been her skipper in 1939.

The overall force consisted of three battleships, three heavy cruisers, three light cruisers, the escort carrier *Nassau* and 19 destroyers. A formidable array of ships to take back a barren piece of ground. Weather would not be on the side of the counter-invaders, but in the far north Pacific, this was the norm. The enemy ashore was also not going to cooperate and would mount one of the most desperate suicide charges during the war.

Added to the woes of the invasion force was the relative inexperience of the amphibious landing force itself and what would become apparent, the lack of a staunch "gung ho" ground commander. The landings began on May 11, 1943 with the *Nevada* taking up position off Massacre Bay on the south end of the 35 mile long by 15 mile wide island. The enemy was at first no where to be found, but finally in Massacre Valley he came in the form of over 2,500 fanatics. For the next several days a battle was waged between the Japanese allied with the weather and the terrain against an inexperience army led by less than resolute commanders. The *Nevada* and her sister ships bombarded position after position with virtually all of their ammunition. Fortunately, the land battle climaxed on May 29, after a 1000 strong banzai charge by the remaining elements of the defending garrison. The Japanese lost all but 28 men in their overall defense of Attu. The American force triumphed, but learned a number of vital lessons, one of which was that bombardment ships should stand close to the beach to afford the greatest possible accuracy and hitting power to their comrades ashore.

THE EUROPEAN THEATER - AND BACK TO THE PACIFIC

The *Nevada* was soon detached from duty in the Aleutians and ordered to proceed to the Mare Island Nay Yard. Her engines had been causing trouble and required permanent repair. On June 7th, she left the north Pacific and arrived there later that month after 72 continuous days at sea. As June was ending, and her engines were again fully operational she was detached to the other side of the world. She entered the Norfolk Navy Yard for more extensive modernization including the addition of another quad 40mm antiaircraft battery. After this stint in the shipyard, she took up convoy duty escorting supply and troop ships from the U.S. to Great Britain. She along with hundreds of other warships guarded what was to become the men and material used in the Normandy and Southern France invasions. This accomplished she was detached to help pulverize the landing zones in France with her main armament.

On June 6, 1944, the big show began and the *Nevada* along with her elder sisters *Texas* and *Arkansas* anchored just off Utah Beach. Many of he battleship's crews feared that they were considered expendable which was the reason for anchoring them. The *Nevada* began the pre-invasion bombardment early on the sixth, and kept firing over the next several days until she had expended 2,200 rounds of 14 inch and 5,000 rounds of 5 inch ammunition. Her 40mm and 20mm heated up their barrels too as they joined the fray. The old battleship was charged with supporting the troops both at the shore line and later inland as they made their way into German occupied territory. She assisted the advancing troops with pinpoint accuracy as far inland as 17 miles and was responsible for breaking up numerous enemy formations and attacks.

Often she would be straddled by enemy fire, yet remained unhurt. Her closest encounter was at 300 yards distant. As the advancing Allies moved inland, her role was ended and she was then selected to join the force assigned to attack positions in Southern France. This began on August 15, and continued up through mid September 1944. By this time however, her main battery accuracy was diminished simply due to massive interior wear on her gun barrel linings. Before leaving however, she silenced former battleship batteries at the large French naval base at Toulon.

When there was no further need for her services, the *Nevada* sailed for the U.S. Before she could carry out her primary role of shore target bombardment, her main battery barrels needed relining. This was accomplished at the New York Navy Yard, and she subsequently returned to the Pacific. This was the last time the aging battlewagon would sail in Atlantic waters.

Her next job was Iwo Jima. As a unit of Task Force 54 ,the *Nevada* was joined by Normandy and Southern France shipmates *Texas* and *Arkansas* as well as the battleships *New York*, *Idaho* and *Tennessee*. The amphibious operation was under the overall command of Rear Admiral William H. P. Blandy, an ordnance expert. He would also command the *Arkansas*, *New York* and *Nevada* two years later at Bikini Atoll as part of the atomic bomb tests. In that operation, they would not do as well as they would at Iwo Jima. The bombardment of the Japanese host on Iwo Jima began on February 16, 1945 and continued sporadically until March 7. At times the *Nevada* would steam at 3,000 yards range from the beach to deliver gunfire support. She was asked to fire on concrete pillboxes that resisted all attempts to destroy them with high explosives. The *Nevada* responded with armor piercing shells which did the job. This was the role of the older battleship, that of mobile artillery of the heaviest sort. It had worked well in Europe and it was effective against Japanese island defenses. The *Nevada* was to perform this task once more, but in one of the grimmest campaigns in the war - Okinawa.

Still part of Task Force 54, the *Nevada* was one of nine older battleships selected to provide bombardment support to ground troops about to land on Okinawa. This time the old battleship would not fare so well. She was not alone as over 200 other ships would be damaged or sunk by the most frightening weapon yet known -the kamikaze or suicide plane.

Occasionally, the navy had encountered random acts of suicide attack by boats or aircraft

The *Nevada* *is hit by a suicide plane off Okinawa on March 26, 1945. The plane was actually intercepted above the ship, but its carcass fell on deck and damaged the number three turret. It also caused the death of eleven men.*

and banzai charges had become commonplace, but large organized masses of aircraft crashing themselves onto ships was something new. The navy had witnessed a preview of what was to come when the Philippines was attacked, but not on the scale as they approached Okinawa. This was sacred ground in home waters, and everything that could be used, was going to be brought to bear. In essence, the kamikaze was the first real form of guided missile and when the attack came in the form of a swarm of diving aircraft, defenses were overwhelmed and damage was inevitable. So it would be with the *Nevada*.

Bombardment in variety of positions began on March 25 and continued unabated. In the late afternoon of the 26th, the *Nevada* and her consorts retired after the day's work. The following morning, the group was attacked by seven kamikazes. They went directly for the battleships ignoring the escorts. One was hit just over the *Nevada* and its remains fell to the deck near turret 3. The hit effectively knocked out turret three and three nearby 20mm mounts. Eleven men were killed and 49 were wounded. One of the 14 inch barrels was even cracked from the damage.

Damage was repaired to the extent possible and the battleship continued providing fire support to the troops ashore. She was hit again on April 5, 1945 when 8 and 6 inch gun shore batteries hit her 5 times, killing 2 and wounding 16. She remained on station and continued to provide gunfire support until the war ended in mid August. She had given as good as she got and more. She like many of her sisters had risen from the mud of Pearl Harbor to defeat the most dangerous enemies ever faced by those who desire freedom. For her, the war was over, but her service life was to continue.

OPERATION CROSSROADS AND THE SHIP THAT REFUSED TO DIE

The end of World War II immediately relegated ships like the *Nevada* to the scrap heap. There would be no further need in the foreseeable future for a 30 year old battleship. This was true for hundreds of ships built before the war. The war had brought great advances in warship design and the U.S. Navy was the largest and most modern in the world. Accordingly, the *Nevada* was sent back to the U.S. to await her fate. It was not long in coming. First she participated in the transport of allied personnel back from the forward areas known as the Magic Carpet operation. This was one of the more pleasant duties assigned the old ship. This completed, she reported to the Long Beach Naval Shipyard in southern California. Here she was prepared for her upcoming role as primary target ship in the two atomic bomb tests to be carried out at Bikini Atoll in the Marshall Islands. Bikini was just 247 miles from Kwajalein, which only two years previously the Navy and Marines had to wrest from stubborn Japanese defenders.

The excitement evoked by atomic power made it imperative that the government determine if a navy was at all necessary in the future. After all, if Hiroshima and Nagasaki could be destroyed by single blasts, what would happen to ships being similarly subjected to atomic blasts? Within months of the end of the war, 73 ships and 70,000 men and women were assembled as Joint Task Force One under the overall command of Admiral William H. P. "Spike" Blandy. Their job was to prepare a "ghost fleet" of warships in a circle around the target ship, the old *Nevada*. The "Cheer Up" ship was to be ground zero in the fourth and fifth atomic blasts in human history to be held in Bikini lagoon.

Incredibly, the old ship still rides high after being battered by the 16 inch guns of the Iowa *and the combined strength of the cruiser-destroyer force.   Finally, embarrassed that surface ships could not put her down, the Navy summoned torpedo aircraft, which sank her 30 minutes after this picture was taken.*

The old warrior finally heels over and sinks stern first after enduring what many claim was the worst beating ever handed out to a ship. She now rests in 15,000 feet of water just 60 miles from where she made her famous run for the sea - Pearl Harbor.

The ships bell from the USS Nevada, *which was taken from the aging battleship and is now on display at the Nevada State Museum.*

The silver service used in the Officers' wardroom and for ceremonies aboard the battleship Nevada. *A silver service was often a token of appreciation from the state or city for which a warship was named. This service is on display at the Nevada State Museum.*

The *Nevada* was prepared for her role by specialized workers at the Long Beach Shipyard which included the installation of thermometers that could reach 3,500 degrees fahrenheit. Also, the ship was somewhat altered to allow scientists to determine the effects of the blast and radiation. Finally, she was painted an ugly reddish orange to facilitate the bombers aim from 30,000 feet. When she sailed for Pearl Harbor and then on to the Marshall Islands, few of her original crew were still aboard. To fill out her complement, naval prisoners from terminal Island had been reinstated to serve on her last cruise. She was no alone however. The battleships *New York*, *Arkansas*, and *Pennsylvania*

would also be there as well as the old carrier *Saratoga*. Joining these veterans would also be the captured Japanese battleship *Nagato* and the German heavy cruiser *Prinz Eugen*.

On July 1, 1946, all was ready and personnel were directed to leave the ships and proceed a minimum of ten miles away from the *Nevada*. The only living things were goats and mice left in various places to determine the effects of the blast and for those that survived, radiation poisoning. Later that morning a single B-29 from Kwajalein named "Dave's Dream" appeared over the lagoon and using the red dot below, dropped the weapon from 30,000 feet. This was to be designated test "Able." As planned it ex-

ploded in the air, but off target from the *Nevada*. It actually exploded about 1,700 yards away above the previously damaged light carrier *Independence*. The *Nevada* survived virtually intact and still combat capable. Test "Able" was deceiving however. It was so deceiving that many observers breathed a sigh of relief. Atomic bombs were not so destructive as rumored.

After examination of the surviving ships, it was decided to proceed with Test Baker which would be a below water burst. The bomb would be detonated at a depth of 100 feet beneath an LCI that held the device by cable. On July 25, 1946, the second bomb was detonated. This one was quite different from the first. It was terrifying and vividly demonstrated the power of the atom. The entire lagoon seemed to emerge in a huge geyser that went several thousand feet in the air. This was no loud bang like test "Able," this was raw destructive force. The *Arkansas* disappeared as did other ships. The *Nevada* was more than scorched this time. She survived, but her upper works were damaged.

It was decided that further explosions would serve no purpose and Operation Crossroads came to an end. Within weeks all that was left was a barren lagoon. Many of the test ships were towed to Kwajalein after being examined. The *Nevada*, no longer considered of any real value and highly radioactive, was decommissioned on August 29, 1946 and joined her mates anchored near Kwajalein. For two years most of the "hot" and off limits survivors quietly rode at anchor, forgotten.

In mid 1948, she was towed to an area near Pearl Harbor for one more test, a high explosive device to be detonated aboard the ship. On July 26, 1948, two years and one day after Test Baker, the secret device was exploded. The *Nevada*, predicted to sink immediately, was still drifting free. She was hurt but not going to sink. Embarrassed, the navy decide to use recently developed precision radar guided missiles. They hit 600 yards astern. So far nothing seemed to sink this ship. Bring on the destroyers. They fired hundreds of 5 inch rounds and then air launched rockets were tried. After the smoke cleared, she was still floating. She was beat up, but still there. Next it was the turn of the battleship *Iowa*. She fired her sixteen inch guns and time after time the old ship, but to no avail. Next it was the turn of the cruisers *Astoria*, *Pasadena* and *Springfield*. Still floating and for nearly a week. Exasperated, the Navy finally brought in torpedo planes. An aerial torpedo did the job and on July 31, 1948, the gallant old ship sank in 15,000 feet of water just 60 miles from Pearl Harbor. It was finally over for the *Nevada*, the "Cheer Up Ship", that helped inspire a navy and a country to ultimate victory.

USS *New Mexico* BB-40
"The Queen of Newark Bay"

In November 1947, preparations were being made for a sea battle in New Jersey's Newark Bay. The decommissioned 32,000 ton battleship USS *New Mexico* of World War II fame had been purchased along with sister battleships *Idaho* and *Wyoming* for scrapping by the Lipsett Corporation of New York City. The well known shipbreaker had chosen Newark Bay as a prime location for dismantling the ships. Railroad access to the downtown dock area made the site ideal for the year long plan to systematically dismember the ships and transport the steel to anxious buyers. However, Newark city leaders solidly backed by citizens said "absolutely not" to the idea of having these rusting old hulks being cut up in their front yard. The formally and loudly threatened to fight even to the point of engaging the *New Mexico* on the high seas to prevent her from entering the harbor! The Lipsett Corporation and the U.S. Navy now had a adversary they had not reckoned with, American citizens who wanted an attractive skyline without a wrecking yard to obstruct it.

An excellent stern view of the battleship New Mexico *shortly after she was commissioned on May 20, 1918, just months before the Armistice was signed that ended World War I. Both starboard and port accommodation ladders are attached for easy access to the ship.*

Household Appliances Versus
A Skyline

Throughout the war and into the immediate post war years, the American public had been without many of the comforts of home. Some of the new products being advertised such as improved washing machines, clothes driers, food blenders and of course a modern automobile were on every family's wish list. Unfortunately, all of these required steel and more steel, but the war had consumed nearly all that could be milled, and in 1947, demand far exceeded supply. Plastic was not yet available in quantity, so the public had to rely on the steel that could be milled or recycled. Obsolete and now forgotten warships were perfect for recycling and ultimately provided one of the greatest sources of steel. Competition for contracts to purchase these ships was stiff. The Navy was unwilling to allow many of it's ships to be broken up, especially with the sabre rattling going on in the Soviet Union, and besides, most of the fleet was relatively modern. The older, slower heavy battleship was indeed valuable to commercial interests.

The price tag on the *New Mexico* was $381,600, just over 2% of her original 1918 cost of $17,348,200. It was a double bargain for Lipsett whose corporate officers knew that the postwar steel shortage would bring top dollar and a substantial profit to the stockholders. Steel was in such demand that the mills were on a quota basis, and any stock was literally worth it's weight in gold. The three battleships would provide upwards to 65,000 tons of the much needed commodity. All that was necessary was a location to dismantle the ships and the convenience of transporting the scrap to waiting manufacturers. Newark offered the best choice, or so the Lipsett Corporation thought. But, the old battleship *New Mexico* was not just simply a source of modern conveniences for the kitchen, it was much more. In fact, she was once the queen of the seas and the best the U.S. Navy had to offer. Here is her story.

The Queen Of The Sea

The USS *New Mexico* was the namesake of a three ship class of battleships which also included the *Mississippi* and *Idaho*. These were magnificent muscular looking warships and when built during the 1915-1918 war years would have been front line ships in any navy. They followed in the footsteps of the *Pennsylvania* class, but the *New Mexico* class made use of even more improved design features than her predecessors. A far more powerful 14 inch gun main battery was installed in this next generation of battleships. The secondary battery of 5 inch guns, always the subject of controversy was finally sited a deck higher than the *Pennsylva-*

One of the four electric motors that drive the shafts of the New Mexico in her turbo electric system. These 12 foot by 12 foot motors were built and installed by General Electric and had a 7,000 horsepower capacity.

This September 6, 1919, photo shows the interior of the navigating bridge of the battleship New Mexico. Along the starboard wall are a number of voice tubes connecting the bridge to various critical locations in the ship. A hooded chart table stands behind the helmsman who is not using the traditional wheel for steering the ship, but an electrical transmitter courtesy of the General Electric Company.

nia class and the hull embrasures that were to house them were plated over during the original construction phase. This change was a major concession to experience gained with casemate gun ports that were invariably flooded during any kind of seaway thus of no value in combat. This class of battleship was also fitted with the clipper bow, a distinctive change from the straight stem cutwater bows on previous classes. The clipper bow was to remain in vogue until the North Carolina class was built some 20 years later.

The *New Mexico* was unique in that she was fitted with a turbo electric propulsion system as opposed to the more traditional geared turbine format. The electric transmission had proven to be effective and efficient aboard another ship, the *Jupiter*, later the first U.S. Navy aircraft carrier, *Langley* CV-1.

Although the turbo electric system more than fully justified it's installation, the *New Mexico* later had geared turbines installed in place of the electric system. This occurred during her major refit over the years 1931-1933. Perhaps class uniformity was more important than individual efficiency.

The *New Mexico* class was also known for improved internal protection over than used on the previous designs. The only other rather peculiar aspect of this class was that it included three ships rather two. The June 30, 1914 Congressional act that authorized the construction of this class included only two, the *Mississippi* and *Idaho* at a cost not to exceed $7.8 million each. Fortunately, other funds were made available from the sale of the older *Mississippi* (BB-23) and *Idaho* (BB-24) to the Royal Hellenic Navy of Greece. Both of these old warriors which had never known war would be sunk at

their moorings on April 3, 1941, by German aircraft which had come to the aid of the struggling and bumbling allies, the Italians. It was another example of obsolete ships attempting to compete with modern weapons.

The sale of these obsolete battleships to Greece allowed the Navy to built the *New Mexico* BB-40. But the way was not yet smooth. She originally was to be named the *California* and, later a successor ship which had been promised to a California shipyard was to be named the *New Mexico*. The *California* was to be built in New York at the New York Navy Yard, and the *New Mexico* at the Mare Island Navy Yard in Vallejo, California. After a bit of political horse trading and a return to common sense, the change was made. The *California* BB-44 was subsequently built at Mare Island beginning in 1916, and the *New Mexico* was begun a year earlier at the New York Navy Yard.

The *New Mexico* mounted twelve 14 inch/50 caliber guns in her main battery in four turrets with three barrels each. Her secondary battery consisted of twelve 5 inch/51 caliber guns and later eight 5 inch/25 caliber antiaircraft guns. In addition, there was the minimal suite of close in 50 caliber guns to be used against low flying aircraft. When the *New Mexico* was designed like all other battleships of the day, the airplane was not considered to be anything more than a nuisance, somewhat like the submarine. After

all, what could a fabric and wood fame do against the might and power of a battleship?

The three ship *New Mexico* class was armored in the "all or nothing" format. This simply meant that only the most vital areas of the ship were to be protected against weaponry of the day. Her main belt consisted of a maximum of 14 inches tapered to 8 inches. Main deck, 6-inches, lower deck 4 inches and boiler uptakes 8 to 15 inches. The turrets were protected with a 5 inch thick covering over the roof, 8 inches on the sides and an incredible 18 inches on the face plate. The conning tower and tube were protected with 16 inches. The armor protection was formed of case hardened steel, and to the casual observer, could not be detected as with earlier ships built before the turn of the century. Armor once consisted of layer upon layer of steel or iron formed over various areas, and was obvious to the naked eye. In the modern battleship, this was not true, it was hidden from view. To the untrained eye, the *New Mexico* and her sisters looked like smooth sided ships with no armor.

She was a healthy 624 feet in length and had a beam of 97.5 feet (later increased to 106.5 feet over her anti-torpedo bulges). These were fitted over her armor belt and filled with either water or oil to arrest the explosive impact of torpedoes. It worked, but not against multiple hits when the ship was in a low state of watertight integrity. This, unfortunately was the case with many of the battleships during the Japanese air attack on Pearl Harbor.

She displaced 33,400 tons (36,000 full load) and was capable of 21.5 knots developed from 40,000 shaft horsepower driving four shafts. The *New Mexico* differed from her two sisters also in that she used four White and Foster boilers instead of the six Bureau Express boilers standard in the other ships. She carried 3,277 tons of fuel oil and had a range of 10,000 miles at a moderate rate of speed. This was especially important as the fleet might at any time be required to sail for far eastern waters to combat aggression. She was also self sufficient in that she could carry food and stores satisfactory for an extended deployment, and could distill enough sweet water for the crew and ship needs.

The keel of the *New Mexico* was laid on October 15, 1915 at the New York Navy Yard, and she was launched less than two years later on April 17, 1917. Her sponsor was Miss Margaret C. Debaca, daughter of the governor of *New Mexico*. Just over a year later she was accepted by the Navy and commissioned on May 20, 1918. So would begin her rather illustrious career. After fundamental training and working out the bugs in the new battleship, she was sent along with other battleships to escort President Woodrow Wilson to the Versailles Peace talks and ultimately the Versailles Treaty. This treaty was to have paved the way for lasting peace and making the world safe for democracy - it didn't, and ships like the *New Mexico* would have to spill blood because of it.

On July 16, 1919, the *New Mexico* was honored to become the first flagship of the newly established Pacific Fleet. Admiral Hugh Rodman was the CINCPAC based at San Pedro, California. These were the golden years of the battleship, especially for the U.S. Navy in the Pacific. Whole cities, economies and social conditions grew up and changed based on the presence of the Pacific Fleet. San Pedro and Long Beach grew as navy towns catering to all of the wants and desires of the fleet's sailors. Tatoo parlors were evident on every street corner for the independent, but more often drunken spirit. Gin mills and dives of all sorts sprouted up along the waterfront such as the infamous "Shanghai Red's" in San Pedro. Anything and everything if you had enough money. Whore houses were commonplace as was what a sailor brought back from liberty - the clap and any number of other lower body ailments.

The Shore Patrol was hated, yet pitied - but not often. What was it like to be so few against so many? Payday was a big day for sailors and maybe a bigger day for waterfront businesses. After all, they ended up with most of a sailors average $20 month pay, but getting off the ship and partaking of civilian luxuries was meaningful to a sailor. Aboard ship his life was not always pleasant like the movies with Pat O'Brien and James Cagney.

Sailors washed clothing in a bucket and then themselves. Hot water came from steam pipes. A sailor simply held the bucket under the steam, and the water was quickly heated. Of course, the steam came out with considerable force, and a loosely held bucket would always get away. Water hours were often short so a sailor wanting to bathe or wash clothes had to time it correctly

or be out of luck. Being a world travelling seaman was not all that the recruiting posters portrayed. Showers were not always available, especially on the older ships. Ironing and clothing repair was the sailor's responsibility unless he could find someone that would do these chores for a minimal cost. That $20 or so per month did not go very far, and there were a number of ways it could disappear. Thievery was not a major problem as shipmates living in such close company had to trust one another. Those who broke the unwritten code were punished informally, sometimes quite harshly, and occasionally, those who broke the sailor's moral code were "accidently" lost at sea. Gambling was discouraged, but was common. On every ship there were always the smart money men who offered short term loans for exorbitant interest. They were known as the $5 for $4 men and always collected just after their client was paid. Few failed to pay on time.

Each battleship seemed to earn a nickname, in fact, nearly every ship every built has been known by a name different then that they were christened with. The carrier *Lexington* was the "*Lady Lex*", the *Langley* was the "*Covered Wagon*", yet the *New Mexico* had one of the most stately of all. She was known as the "*Queen of the Fleet*". This nickname was by no means meant to reflect humor or insult, it was given because the *New Mexico* earned so many awards for excellence in gunnery, engineering, and communications. She was the winner of the "*Big E*" for four year consecutively, and was consistently rated as the top ship in her class. She was a winner in all things.

PREPARATION FOR WAR

Just before the second world war began, the *New Mexico* and her two sisters were considered the most modern heavy ships in the U.S. Navy. All had been modernized during the early 1930's and when they emerged from their yard time, it was almost impossible to believe the before and after photos. The *New Mexico*, which received her facelift at the Philadelphia Navy Yard from March 1931 through January 1933, and her sisters went through a complete metamorphosis. Gone were the lattice masts, not to be replaced by the tripod topped by the henhouse structure most common to interwar battleship refits. The *New Mexico* had a bulky tower like bridge structure built behind her conning tower and a similar but, smaller structure built just aft of her funnel. A short pole mast was stepped at the forward end of the aft structure. Her two most aft secondary guns were removed from the superstructure, and what emerged was something completely revolutionary. She and her sisters had a powerful and purposeful looking profile that was to be the forerunner of the *North Carolina* class, the next battleships built. They almost had a European look comparable to the battleships coming out of German and French shipyards.

In addition to the radical departure from the contemporary battleship refit look, the *New Mexico* was rearmed with eight 5 inch/25 caliber dual purpose guns in open mounts. They were centrally controlled by two high angle DCT's located fore and aft. While not the best defense, it was superior to anything then available in 1934. The submerged torpedo tubes were eliminated as they had been on most of the other capitol ships, and anti torpedo bulges fitted at the waterline. Like other battleships, the *New Mexico* was also fitted with two catapults, one on the roof of turret 3 and the other on the quarterdeck. Massive cranes were also added to handle the ship's aircraft.

A 1927 overhead view of the New Mexico *as she makes her way through the Panama Canal. The upper right corner shows the canal that the French had begun, but abandoned in failure. The U.S. and President Teddy Roosevelt were not accustomed to failure or quitting in the face of adversity, so the canal was completed.*

A Chief Petty Officer demonstrates the working parts of a pistol to his men. Small arms were standard issue aboard early battleships as upwards of 200 selected crew members were expected to conduct landing operations. A sailor had to be familiar with small arms just like his ground pounding counterpart, the Marine.

The gun crew that set a world's record for the highest pointers in gunnery practise. This record, set in 1926, was never broken and was one of the reasons that the New Mexico *was nicknamed the "Queen".*

Amazingly, the turbo electric propulsion system was removed and the more common geared turbine system was installed along with the reboilering effort. The quiet and dependable operation of the electric drive would be missed.

The balance of the interwar years found the *New Mexico* as with most of the fleet in training exercises. Nothing could prepare them for what was to come, but the fleet was forever busy. Much of the time, the *New Mexico* could be found on maneuvers in the Atlantic or Caribbean, yet in October 1934, she was deployed to the Pacific, and would remain there until May 20, 1941, when she was called back to the Atlantic. Both oceans required more ships than the Navy could provide, so it became necessary to shuttle ships back and forth to meet challenges as they arose. The beginning of World War II would find the *New Mexico* a member of the Atlantic Neutrality Patrol. She and several other major fleet units had been assisting the Royal Navy in it's role of protecting merchant shipping from German submarines and surface raiders. When war was thrust upon the U.S. on December 7, 1941, we became Allies in all senses of the word and equal partner in the struggle against the Axis.

The New Mexico *has emerged from being reconditioned and modernized at the Philadelphia Navy Yard in September 1933. She is a different ship and in profile a great departure from all of the other present day battleships, with the exception of her sisters* Mississippi *and* Idaho.

THE *NEW MEXICO* AND WORLD WAR II

The *New Mexico* was anchored in Casco Bay, Maine when the news arrived that Pearl Harbor was under attack by Japanese aircraft. Feelings of rage and helplessness were felt by everyone on board, but this common on all ships. It was soon replaced by a resolve to win - something that Commander of the Imperial Japanese Combined Fleet, Admiral Isoroku Yamamoto had predicted would happen. Specifically he stated that he could guarantee success for the first year of the war, but after that he could predict nothing. His greatest fear and his earnest warning to the makers of war in the Japanese military hierarchy was that the U.S. would be filled with a courageous spirit and a terrible resolve for righteous vengeance.

On December 10, 1941, the *New Mexico* was en route to the Norfolk Navy Yard. Unfortunately, in dense fog she accidently rammed and

sank the new steamer SS *Oregon* which was on her maiden voyage. Seventeen of the *Oregon's* crew perished in this freak accident. The media was blacked out due to wartime censorship and it wasn't for several weeks that the identity of the *New Mexico* became known. The fault of the collision was with the SS *Oregon* as later determined. The *New Mexico* had some superficial damage to her hull, yet this was repaired and she was on her way to the Pacific.

Like most of the pre war battleships, the *New Mexico* was to serve in shore bombardment and convoy roles. These roles were never envisioned by the designers in 1915, but the character of war had changed greatly since the day the *New Mexico* had slid down the ways. For one thing, the aircraft carrier now was the capitol ship of choice and the battleship had been relegated to other duties in support of air or amphibious operations. The new fast battleships of the *North Carolina*, *South Dakota* and *Iowa* classes could accompany the carriers on their attacks and at

the same time defend against air and surface menaces. The 21 knot maximum speed of the older battleships was not sufficient to maintain pace with the fleet carriers.

The older battleships were less maneuverable and, at least during the first part of the war, had inadequate air defense capability. The newer battleships bristled with antiaircraft guns that were centrally controlled. They could defend themselves and other ships around them with proficiency and reliability. The older battleships however were valuable for convoy and escort duty, but moreover were priceless when it came to amphibious operations. This is where the older battleship earned its keep.

The slow heavy gunned battleship was able to close the beach and soften it up in devastating pre-invasion bombardments. Also, they could literally follow the troops inland to a distance of up to 20 miles for call fire missions. Many marines and soldiers owe their lives to battleships that were able to saturate well protected enemy positions with 12, 14 or 16 inch gunfire. The *New Mexico* was one of the leaders in effective shore bombardment operations. She bombarded the Japanese in the Aleutians in mid 1943 and later that year during the invasion of the Gilbert Islands.

In early 1944, she was in the Marshall islands hitting Kwajalein and Ebeye. She struck New Ireland in late March and was pounding Tinian and Guam in the Mariana's by mid 1944. Next it was on the Philippines to hit Leyte and later Luzon in early 1945. It was at Luzon on January 6, 1945 that she was hit and hit hard by a Suicide plane or Kamikaze.

Kamikazes were becoming more than a nuisance and a viable threat to the fleet as the Allies entered the inner ring of defense around the Japanese home islands. Suicide squadrons had been formed in the Philippines and Okinawa and were

assaulting the fleet at regular intervals. It was the *New Mexico's* turn on January 6. The kamikaze headed for the command and control center of the battleship and hit the bridge killing Captain R. W. Fleming and 29 other men. The ship continued with her pre-landing bombardment, but it was clear that she was hurt. She remained on station for another three days and then was detached to Pearl Harbor for repair.

After a short period of repair, the aging ship arrived back to the war zone for the Okinawa campaign. She began on March 26, 1945 and for the next two months her guns seemed never to be silent. They continually barked at enemy shore defenses and even suicide boats that tried to infiltrate the fleet anchorages. On May 12, in the early twilight she was again hit by a suicide plane and also the bomb from another that she had disabled with her gunfire. 54 men were killed and 119 men wounded. She left for Leyte to seek repair and the war ended as she was preparing for her next invasion bombardment role to be acted out on the Japanese home islands.

The *New Mexico* was in Tokyo Bay for the surrender ceremonies on September 2, 1945. Admiral Yamamoto's prophesy had come true, but it had taken four years and the lives of millions. Shortly after the formal surrender, thee *New Mexico*, along with hundreds of other ships began to leave for home. Some would make a number of trips carrying former prisoners of war and troops that were no longer required overseas.

The *New Mexico* left for the U.S. four days after the surrender ceremony and arrived in Boston on October 17, 1945. She had left 83 of her crew behind, the victims of Japan's last gasp, the kamikaze.

During her wartime career, she steamed over 180,000 miles and fired 12 million pounds of ammunition. Aside from pulverizing enemy ground defenses, she shot down 21 confirmed enemy aircraft. For her efforts she also won six battle stars. But, at the end of war, there was little interest in the former glories of past victories and she was quietly decommissioned on July 19, 1946. Lipsett Corporation purchased her at auction on October 13, 1947, and made preparations to tow her to Newark for scrapping. Like most of the older ships that had been decommissioned, she was to be scrapped immediately. However, controversy would take a hand in the final chapter of this grand old queen of the fleet.

NEWARK, NEW JERSEY PREPARES TO FIGHT THE *NEW MEXICO*

Less than a month after the Lipsett Corporation purchased the *New Mexico*, the shipbreaker would find itself embroiled in a major conflict that included the City of Newark and the Navy Department. The City of Newark announced that the site selected to dismantle the battleships *New Mexico*, *Idaho*, and *Wyoming* was unsatisfactory

The three ships of the New Mexico *class in formation. The* Idaho *leads, followed by the* Mississippi *and* New Mexico. *This view gives meaning to the description of these ships being dubbed "battlewagon," but also as "tubs."*

The New Mexico *framed by Mount Fujiama in one of World War II's lasting images. She was present at the surrender ceremonies on September 2, 1945 after having sailed 180,000 miles during the conflict and expending thousands of tons of ammunition.*

The New Mexico *in front shows the power and majesty of the pre-war battle line. It was no wonder the American public felt so secure when these ships hove into sight. They were indeed beautiful, and their main battery was reassuring to a public often concerned about foreign invasion.*

The battleship New Mexico *slowly steams into New York Harbor on the last day of May 1934. Seven years later, she would begin a successful struggle to defend liberty just as the symbol in the background personifies.*

Now part of the Lipsett Navy, the old battleship is on her way to Newark Harbor for dismantling with sisters, Wyoming *and* Idaho. *The people of Newark had other ideas. She broke loose from her tow but was located by the Coast Guard in the morning light of November 13, 1947.*

The proud old girl in perhaps her last profile shot before entering Newark Bay in November 1947. Her new owners have painted Lipsett on her hull, but she is still the New Mexico, *"Queen of the Fleet."*

The end result of the battle. Citizens, led by local Newark school children, welcome the old warrior, New Mexico, *to their city with a parade.*

as it would interfere with the beautification plan for the Newark waterfront (to some, a contradiction in terms). The City was spending $70 million to make improvements and the specter of three rusting hulks being torn apart and carted off like so many dinosaurs being slaughtered was simply too much. The Public Safety Commission pledged to lock arms and go to war to prevent the first ship, the *New Mexico* from entering the harbor!

The announcement of a possible sea battle between battleship and city quickly became front page news burying Truman administration advisor Bernard Baruch's controversial payroll deduction sponsored national health program. This story even rivaled that of Britain's Princess Elizabeth's upcoming wedding to Phillip. However, on November 9, 1947, the *New Mexico* set sail on her final voyage and final battle. Her first stop was New York Harbor, but not before being buffeted and tossed around by stormy seas.

The seas were so heavy that on the night of November 12th, the three tugs had to cut her loose and she drifted and became lost. Newark nearly won by default, but the Coast Guard eventually found her wallowing 35 miles off of the coast, and she was again taken in tow. But the City of Newark and it's outraged citizens had not been idly watching, they had been preparing to defend their skyline. Referring to the capsized and burned liner in New York during the war, they steadfastly declared that they did not want another "Normandie" on their hands. Taking stock of their limited arsenal, they were able to commission two aging 30 foot fireboats named the "*Michael P. Duffy*" and the "*William T. Brennan*". They were each armed with two hoses capable of 2,000 gallons per minute and a range of 400 feet. Their main battery was a bull horn in the hands of a throaty politician. The "Newark Navy" as it became known, patrolled the entrance to their bay awaiting the *New Mexico*.

Lipsett had formed its own task force which now consisted of four tugs, and additionally, the U.S. Coast Guard guaranteed a safe passage providing that legal entry was permitted. Now it looked as if there would indeed be a battle, as each side escalated the war of words. Newark's Mayor Vincent Murphy cautioned his Navy to "keep hopes high, and not to open spray until the word was passed!" Lipsett staunchly claimed that they were "coming in!"

By November 14, the old battleship had made her way to New York Harbor and awaited the tide to venture up to Newark. The tide was missed, however, and that allowed the parties a period to cool off and negotiate. The Navy Department sent Under Secretary W. John Kenney as chief negotiator, and after several marathon sessions, he was able to conclude a precarious truce between the City of Newark and the Lipsett Corporation.

The City of Newark would allow the three battleships to be dismantled, but there was to be no permanent graveyard of ships. Lipsett was given nine months to dispose of the ships, and would be forced to pay a fine of $1,000 per day beyond the deadline. All parties finally agreed, and on November 19, the *New Mexico* made her way through the Newark Channel cheerfully greeted by the City's Navy of fireboats rather than being opposed with spray and words. The old dreadnought was then saluted by school children and marching bands as she was made fast to the dock where she was to dismantled. It was a fitting end for the "*Queen*" who had done so much for her country. The "Battle of Newark Bay" ended in a victory for both sides, and one final honor for a grand old ship.

USS *NEW YORK* BB-34
"THE OLD LADY OF THE SEA"

LABOR LAW BATTLESHIPS

Shortly after the turn of the century the labor movement in the U.S. was moving into high gear and in 1910, warship construction became subject to certain new restrictions. If a shipyard wanted to build a warship under contract to the U.S. government, it had to obey the new employee welfare and protection laws being enacted by the U.S. Congress. The June 24, 1910 act that authorized the funding for the construction of the battleships *New York* BB-34 and the *Texas* BB-35 specified the following conditions: build two first class battleships exclusive of armor and armament for less than $6 million each, and in accordance with the recent act that limited daily working hours for laborers on public works jobs. These were the first two major warships built pursuant to the new labor laws that restricted employers from requiring unlimited working hours per workweek. Although industrialists and manufacturers predicted economic ruin with this degree of latitude now accorded workers, both ships were built within specified time limits and within budget. Both also went on to long and illustrious careers. The USS *Texas* still exists as a naval memorial in *Texas*, a tribute to her builders. Her sister, the *New York* persisted until mid 1948 having survived two wars and two Atomic blasts. She was finally dispatched after an eight hour pounding by gunfire and aircraft bombs. The ship named in honor of the Empire State also proved her worth in war and was a tribute to her builders skill and dedication. This is her story.

THE *NEW YORK*: FIRST BATTLESHIP WITH THE FOURTEEN INCH GUN

The *New York* and her sister, *Texas* were the first U.S. battleships built with the new 14 inch/ 45 caliber gun as their main battery. They were also the first battleships in any of the world's navies to mount the 14 inch gun. This did not last long however, as battleship design and construction was among the most fluid of overall military armaments. The rapidly changing battleship was only rivaled by progress in aeronautical design. Before the *New York* and *Texas* slid down the ways, Great Britain and Germany had already begun work on ships with larger caliber guns. The *New York* mounted ten 14 inch guns in five turrets that were sited in an A, B, Q, X and Y positions. At first, they had a maximum elevation of 15 degrees, but this was increased to 30 degrees just prior to the United State's entry into World War II. The increase in elevation was a common adjustment made to pre war battleships and improved their range dramatically. The *New York* and *Texas* were to be the last American battleships with a gun turret mounted amidships. All future designs would use either the four turret the A, B, X, and Y format or three turret A, B and Y format. The midships located battery was only one step up from the then obsolete wing mounted turrets, but was necessary to provide a sufficiently powerful broadside to compete with foreign variants. When the *New York* and *Texas* were designed, the U.S. Navy required at least twelve 12 inch guns be mounted for a competitive broadside, but the design did not provide for lengthening the ships to accommodate a six turret 12 inch battery. Consequently the battery caliber was increased to the new 14 inch/45 caliber thus only ten barrels would be required to throw the same weight as twelve 12 inch barrels. American battleships would never again employ the five turret format and all future designs would utilize a different arrangement with either four turrets or three turrets carrying two or three barrels. The next successive design after the *New*

York (*Nevada* class) would use the four turret arrangement of 3 - 2 -2 - 3 fourteen inch barrels.

The *New York* class also mounted the single purpose casemate housed 5 inch/51 caliber gun to deal with destroyers and torpedo boats. Like their predecessors, the *Arkansas* and *Wyoming*, the casemate guns proved ineffective in any kind of a sea, yet the U.S. Navy was to hold on to this concept for at least two successive designs. It would not be until the *New Mexico* class would the Navy finally abandon the lower deck casemate gun. Aside from the difficulty experienced by gun crews in serving these guns, the guns had a short range and would probably not have been of any use against the quick and elusive destroyer. The *New York* was initially armed with sixteen 5 inch/51 caliber guns, eight to a side. In addition, as an afterthought during a later re-

fit, this class was also armed with eight single 3 inch/50 caliber antiaircraft guns mounted four to a side. The initial antiaircraft defense was not in any way capable of defending the ship against aerial attack and especially not twenty five years later. Even the addition of 50 caliber machine guns did little to augment the pitiful antiaircraft defense. But, in 1915, the airplane was still a novelty and not considered to be anything more than an irritation in naval warfare. This same feeling was to persist for the next quarter century and would not be dispelled until the British success at Taranto in 1940 and of course, the Japanese victory at Pearl Harbor in December 1941. Harsh reality then set in, and the battleship would have to become a floating fortress against it's newest and most formidable nemesis, the aluminum and fabric airplane. All

An excellent view of the aft half of the battleship New York *on July 26, 1919. Her decks are relatively uncluttered, and she has virtually no superstructure. At most, she is a hull with five large turrets and two cage masts. This would change over the years as her AA battery was improved from wholly inadequate to impressive. The mushroom-like disc's that dot her deck are ventilators.*

The New York *as she appeared in 1921. She has successfully weathered World War I, and is now a part of the U.S. Fleet. She and her sister, the* Texas, *were the last battleships to be armed with five center line turrets. Future battleships would either have three or four turrets.*

in all, the battleship diehards considered it unfair and almost unsporting that something as expensive, strong and solid as the battleship would be at the mercy of something as frail and economical as the airplane.

Incredibly, the *New York* class reverted to reciprocating machinery for its propulsion system as opposed to steam turbine drive which was coming into popularity in the European Navies. Even the *New York's* immediate predecessors, the *Wyoming* and *Arkansas* had been equipped with the turbine drive as was the grandfather of all modern battleships, HMS *Dreadnought*. There were valid reasons however. The reciprocating engineering plant was desired by contemporary naval engineers and American manufacturers had little real experience in building plants that met naval specifications. The reciprocating plant was considered more economical than the relatively untried turbine system especially at cruising speeds. Thus was important for a navy that might be called upon to fight a war a long way from home (e.g. near Japan), and spent much time cruising long distances in patrolling the Pacific. Only one additional American capital ship would be equipped with reciprocating machinery and that was the battleship *Oklahoma* of the *Nevada* class.

The propulsion plants installed aboard the *New York* and *Texas* consisted of two sets of four cylinder, triple expansion reciprocating steam engines both built by the Newport News Shipbuilding and Drydock Company. Fourteen coal fired Babcock and Wilcox boilers provided steam to two engines each connected to 142 foot long shafts turning one of the two 18 foot diameter three blade propellers. The fourteen boilers would eventually be replaced by six Bureau Express oil fired boilers. Each engine was rated at 14,050 shaft horsepower for a total of 28,100 shp. This was highly satisfactory and the ship was easily driven at a top speed of 21 knots due to the shape of the hull which had been designed for up to 32,000 shp. The engine rooms were more spacious than normal at over 1,500 square feet (60 feet x 26 feet) probably due to the designers anticipating both ships being re-engined with the more space consuming steam turbine system. With all of these seeming benefits, the *New York* and her sister were dated with coal fired boilers. This would change during her refit in 1926-1927 at the Norfolk Navy Yard, but from her commissioning on April 14, 1914 until her major refit 12 years later, her crew endured the filthiest job in the Navy - coaling.

The *New York* was not armored on the "all or nothing" concept as would be the follow on class, the *Nevada*. The *New York* was armored with carbon hardened belt armor above and below her waterline ranging from 12 to 9 inches thick. The armor plate consisted of eight foot steel sections riveted to the hull. The rest of the ship was protected in the same fashion as other battleships of the day. Bulkheads were 6 to 9 inches in thickness and the main deck was just under 4 inches in thickness. The turrets were armored with six inches on the sides, 12 inches rear, four inches on the roof and 12 inches on the face plates. The barbettes were 12 inches and the conning tower and tube, 12 inches. At the time that the *New York* was designed, it was expected that a capital ship would be faced primarily with medium and large caliber shell fire at a low angle of trajectory, if not a flat trajectory. The concept of plunging fire or aerial bombs was not yet accounted for in armor design and would not until successive generations of the "all or nothing" defense.

Compartments aboard the *New York* were situated around the engine rooms and main battery turret handling spaces and magazines. Propulsion and firepower was far more important than creature comfort. Senior and junior officers as well as commissioned warrant ranks occupied the forward part of the ship under the anchor handling area. The wardroom was directly under the main deck as was the officers lavatory facilities. When a heavy or even moderate sea was running, use of the officers head must have been exciting if not downright dangerous. This class of battleship was not renowned for it's seakeeping ability nor as stable ride. Interestingly the forward most compartment in the ship underneath the officers water closet or head was the storage area for general mess supplies and more specifically cigars and tobacco products. The early and middle twentieth century navy operated on fuel oil, tobacco and good coffee. Changes in military philosophy and improved health consciousness has done away with many of the staples of the early navy and unfortunately much of the lore and legend that gave this branch of the service it's mystique and romanticism. Navy coffee was always best when a pinch of salt was added to the pot, but now there are a hundred reasons why coffee, salt and of course tobacco are not healthy or heart smart. If these items are considered hazardous to one's health as the Navy approaches the 21st Century, dieticians would be appalled at the amount of fat, starch and protein contained in the average ship's meal of a half century ago.

The captain and admiral's quarters were located just behind the conning tower and the chief petty officers lived at the after end of the ship on deck level two. The crew occupied various areas on decks two and three from the stern forward to immediately behind barbette two. Many of the crew slept in the five inch gun casemate compartments in hammocks that were slung at night and stowed during the day. More senior petty officers had spring bunks aft that by wartime grew to four deep. Mattresses were less than 3 inches in thickness, but preferable to the standard hammock. The interior bulkheads of the ship was painted white and the floors covered in red-like asphalt tile. Psychologically, the dark reddish flooring was intended to reduce the level of fear of the common sailor when men were killed or wounded in battle and blood flowed freely. Fortunately, this never occurred on the *New York*.

The *New York* was equipped as a flagship from the outset as were most capital ships. She was normally manned by crew of 1314 men during peacetime which would swell to 1530 in war. In peacetime she was crowded, and in wartime the problem was far greater. Privacy was not possible for most men except the captain and certain senior officers. Getting along in crowded conditions and maintaining high morale was always a problem for any ship, but in most cases was overcome by cooperation and organization.

In a ship like the *New York*, everything and everyone had a place, and only when something was out of order would disruption occur. Absolute organization and adhering to the rules was crucial. The *New York* was always considered a happy and taut ship.

The *New York* was 573 feet in length overall and had a 95 foot beam before the addition of torpedo bulges increased the maximum beam to 106 plus feet. She displaced 27,000 tons initially and 32,000 tons full load. Compared to the World War II *Iowa* class which displaced 45,000 tons and was nearly 900 foot in length, the *New York* was a small ship.

THE BATTLESHIP *NEW YORK* - IN TIME FOR WORLD WAR I

The *New York* was built by the New York Navy Yard, a government owned and operated shipyard. After congressional approval and funding had been granted, battleship number 34 had her keel laid on September 11, 1911. Fifteen months later she was launched on October 30, 1912. She was christened by Miss Elsie Calder, and for nearly 18 months, she was fitted out and prepared for acceptance and commissioning. She was commissioned on April 15, 1914, exactly two years before the first national income tax became effective. The *New York's* first skipper was Thomas S. Rodgers, and she went to sea for further trials. Her shakedown period was cut short however, as she was sent to Vera Cruz in July 1914 as the flagship of Rear Admiral Frank Fletcher. Democracy was being threatened by the Huerta government, and the U.S. and it's new professor president, Woodrow Wilson was not about to stand for it. The Navy was dispatched to Vera Cruz to blockade the port from arms shipments that were on their way to the revolutionary government. The blockade was a success, but not before some furious street fighting in the city that resulted in the death of several Mexican revolutionaries. With a short time, democracy was restored and the *New York* was allowed to resume her shakedown and patrol routine along the Atlantic coast. This routine was interrupted periodically by the good will of her crew for those less fortunate ashore. The *New York* earned the nickname the "Christmas Ship" when she hosted a massive Christmas party and dinner for hundreds of New York City orphans. The crew suggested this and her captain in December 1915, Hugh Rodman heartily endorsed this idea. It was to become a tradition for this ship and many other to care for the needy whenever possible. This U.S. Navy tradition has continued for many decades. Ship's crews frequently volunteer to help others with money or assistance around the world. Ships are often the most immediately available sources of aid to areas that have suffered natural disasters, and the U.S. Navy never shirks it's humanitarian obligations. So it was with the battleship *New York*.

From the Vera Cruz incident until the U.S. entry in World War I, the *New York* spent her time in training and exercises off the Atlantic coast. When war was declared she sailed for Great Britain to reinforce the Grand Fleet in the North Sea. She was the flagship of Battleship Division 9 under the overall command of former *New York* skipper Hugh Rodman, now promoted to Rear Admiral. The *New York* arrived in the Royal Navy's northern outpost of Scapa Flow on December 7, 1917 prepared to join the Allies against Germany. It was bitterly cold in Northern Scotland, but wars do not usually occur in temperate climates. The *New York* was often sent on patrol and convoy duty and the presence of a modern American force of capital ships undoubtedly inhibited the Germans from breaking out of their coastal ports as they had at Jutland. The specter of another major fleet action where battleships belching black smoke pounded each other at long range was not again to happen in World War I. Her service in World War I did not result in any shots being fired in anger, yet she did witness several surface attacks on submarines that attempted to penetrate convoy defenses. Also during her deployment as part of the Allied fleet, she was visited by much of the British nobility including *King George V* and the *Prince of Wales* who would later abdicate his throne for the love of an American divorcee. The *New York* was of great interest to many who came to see what the "colonial rebels" considered a dreadnought. European dignitaries were not the only interested visitors. In early November 1918, Emperor Hirohito of Japan then a Crown Prince and Admiral of the Imperial Japanese Navy was welcomed aboard for an inspection. No doubt his interest was more than that of a foreign dignitary paying respect to another government.

Before going back home to the U.S., the *New York* was present at one of the most dramatic of all naval events, the surrender of the pride of the German Navy, the High Seas fleet. This event took place on November 21, 1918, in the Firth of Forth just days after the Armistice was signed. A few days later these magnificent ships would be scuttled by their disenchanted crews as a show of final defiance. For this they were imprisoned for a short period but in the spirit of peace eventually freed. The hatred and bitterness still existed and again boiled over some 20 years later.

The *New York* was called upon for one final chore before sailing for home, and that was to provide escort for President Wilson on his trans-Atlantic voyage to France to participate in the formation and signing of the Treaty of Versailles. This document was to end war on the European continent and pave the way for lasting peace and ultimately the League of Nations. A noble gesture that the world was too immature to take advantage of at that time.

This done, the four year old battleship arrived back in the U.S. to take up training and patrol duties again. Her travels took her to the Caribbean along with the rest of the fleet. In late 1919 she sailed for the Pacific and joined the newly formed Pacific Fleet. She would be a part of this fleet until the mid 1930's when she would then return to the cold northern waters of the Atlantic. She did make periodic sojourns to the other side of the U.S. and on one such trip, remained at the Norfolk Navy Yard for a complete refit.

The *New York* Is Spared The Treaty Hatchet And Gets A New Lease On Life

The *New York* was over a decade old when she entered the Norfolk Navy Yard for a ma-

Gun barrels that would later turn blue with heat from firing act as benches for sailors and the cast of "Leave it to Me," a popular broadway play in 1938. Mary Martin, later of "South Pacific" and "Peter Pan" fame made her debut in this extravaganza. The U.S. Navy encouraged the public to visit its ships to prove that they were getting their money's worth in taxes. This was an extra benefit for these battleship sailors, and they had some junior officer in public relations to thank. Usually, sailors had to go looking for women ashore, not have them delivered !

jor refit. By other standards, she was obsolete compared to other battleships in the U.S. Navy's capital ship inventory and at an obvious disadvantage when contrasted with like ships in the world's major navies. She was a coal burner and her secondary battery was located virtually at sea level in an ineffective broadside arrangement. Her cage masts also identified her as behind the times and she was much slower at 21 knots than many of her potential opponents. Other ships of her genre were being selected for demilitarization or even scrapping. The *Wyoming* would become a gunnery training ship and the *Utah* was consigned to target duty in 1931. The *Utah*'s sister, the *Florida* was scrapped outright in 1931 as all of the pre-dreadnoughts had been in the 1920's. What was to become of the *New York* and her sister, the *Texas*? Fortunately, both were selected for a massive degree of modernization and refitting. Most of the rest of the fleet's more contemporary battleships would also be modernized in future years as would most of the capital ships in all of the major navies in the world. This was provided for under the provisions of the Naval Arms Limitation Treaties agreed to in 1922 and 1930. The *New York* and *Texas* were selected for upgrading and overall improvement. The *New York* would be refitted at the Norfolk Navy Yard during 1926 and 1927.

The *New York* was updated on four separate occasions during her 34 year career. Before entering the Norfolk Navy Yard she had been altered in 1919 when she landed five of her 5 inch/51 caliber secondary guns and additional 3 inch/50 caliber anti-aircraft guns were added. This

was minor compared to the job that was to be done in Norfolk.

The 14 coal burning boilers were converted to six Bureau Express oil burning boilers and the twin funnels were trunked into one just aft of the forward superstructure. This was a major achievement and set very well with a crew tired of the filth and backbreaking work of periodic coaling. Tripods were also fitted in place of the obsolete lattice masts. Atop the massive forward tripod a control tower which looked much like a henhouse was installed, and the *New York* and sister *Texas* began to bear a resemblance to the rest of the battleships in the fleet. Both also had a truss like tower built amidships that contained additional fire control as somewhat of a back up to the system atop the fore mast. This was redundancy to the extreme, but it was a naval requirement of officers fearful of not having sufficient fire control backup. Fortunately, it did not interfere with the new catapult atop "Q" turret. A second catapult was fitted on the top of "Q" turret and cranes were installed on either side of the funnel for boat and aircraft handling. Some deck protection was added, and her beam widened to 106 feet with addition of anti-torpedo bulges along the water line. Unfortunately, there was heavy price to pay for the anti-torpedo bulges. The ship, never a really excellent sea boat, became almost unstable at lower speeds, particularly in swells or quartering seas. Anchoring in the open sea without the protection of a natural or manmade breakwater also made her roll heavily. The tendency to stiffness made it ever so much more difficult to maintain an adequate level of gunfire accuracy in certain conditions, a problem for a battleship engaged in shore bombardment.

The *New York* like sister *Texas* were the beneficiaries of the Washington Naval Treaty provision that allowed up to 3,000 tons to be added to existing capital ships for defense against aerial and submerged threats. This plus other obvious improvements rendered the *New York* a relatively modern battleship when she emerged from the yard in 1927.

The *New York* would be modernized two more times and they were in 1940-41 when her main battery elevation was increased from 15 degrees to 30 degrees, and later during World War II. Experience gained in the early years of the war mandated that all ships be made capable of defending themselves against aircraft. The *New York* had the balance of her secondary battery deck guns removed and her anti-aircraft battery was increased to ten 3 inch/50 caliber guns, twenty four 40mm and thirty six 20mm guns. RDF and improved fire control were also added to augment her AA defenses. All of this eventually increased her displacement to 29,340 tons or 34,000 tons full load.

The battleship was part of the Pacific Fleet until 1937 when she was selected to carry President Roosevelt's personal representative, Admiral Hugh Rodman to England for the coronation of *King George VI*. For the next several years, the *New York* would confine her activities to the Atlantic, and act primarily as a training ship for midshipmen and newly enlisted sailors. She was also selected to test radar in 1939, only the second ship after the destroyer Leary. She was equipped with the new and improved version that the naval electronics laboratory had been perfecting over the past decade. The set installed aboard the old battleship was not as sophisticated as that commonly used in World War II and beyond, but it was great step forward.

The *New York* was a suitable test platform for radar as she was available and had adequate space aboard to accommodate the rather bulky radar installations characteristic of the early days. The tests were highly satisfactory and improved versions were introduced to other fleet units as quickly as was practical. All of the light cruisers of the *Brooklyn/St. Louis* class had radar and the battleship *West Virginia* had the trademark "bedspring mattress" antenna when she was sunk on December 7, 1941. It was not until the war was in it's second year that radar was common, and even then, many commanding officers did not trust it or understand it's potential. In any event, the first successful use of radar was on a battleship that had been judged overage in 1934, but overage or not, was destined for sterling service in World War II.

WORLD WAR II AND THE *NEW YORK*

The *New York* was ordered to safeguard the sea lanes in the north Atlantic as part of the "Neutrality Patrol". When war broke out on the European continent in September 1939, it was just a matter of time before the U.S. would be a full fledged participant. For the next 27 months the *New York* and the rest of the Atlantic Squadron (later the Atlantic Fleet) became incrementally involved in the sea war which unfolded just off

The battleship New York *lets go with a full broadside during target practise off San Nicholas Island near Los Angeles harbor. The ship is using powder that is obviously not flashless, a risky procedure in actual combat. Flashless powder was more expensive, however, and during the 1930's depression era, the Navy had to be cost conscious. Sister ship,* Texas, *just astern has fired her main battery a second or so earlier.*

the east coast of isolationist America. American destroyers were protecting Allied convoys on their way to Great Britain, and suffering in the bargain. The destroyers Kearny and Reuben James were hit by U-boat torpedoes and the "short of war" approach quickly became total war. The *New York* and other battleships like sister *Texas* and the *Arkansas* banded together to shepherd supply ships, and in July 1941, the Empire State battlewagon protected ships carrying American troops to Iceland. Duty in northern waters was harsh for sailors and further complicated by numerous submarine contacts, attacks and counter attacks. And, this was just the dawn of the new war at sea.

The peaceful invasion of Iceland by the Americans was one of the most important events of Allied military strategy prior to the official entry of the U.S. in the second world war. The Icelandic government was concerned about the possibility of the 15,000 British Empire troops which were garrisoning their homeland being withdrawn for other more pressing battle commitments. In that event, a political vacumn might be filled by Axis troops and then a knife would be pointed toward North America. Then convoys that were none too safe as things were, would be at the complete mercy of the German Navy. Enter the U.S. Navy. The U.S. provided a ground force protected by ships like the *New York* and *Texas* as well as 21 other destroyers, cruisers and battleships. They replaced the Empire troops who were quickly deployed in more critical areas. Without ships like the *New York*, this maneuver would have been impossible. Saving her from the "scrap crazed" politicians of the 1920's treaty generation proved to be an excellent decision.

The attack on Pearl Harbor on December 7, 1941 and the formal declaration of war on the Axis powers in the following days caught the now veteran battlewagon in the Norfolk Navy Yard. She was going through her third refit which was to increase her main battery elevation and augment her still inadequate AA defense. The refit was accelerated and she was back at sea convoying cargo and troop ships to Iceland and Scotland within weeks.

Her first major operation was as a unit in *Operation Torch*, the November 1942 invasion of North Africa. It was the second amphibious invasion staged by the U.S. Navy and the largest to date. The invasion of Guadalcanal just four months before had been the first attempt made by ground troops supported by the navy in attacking enemy defended shore positions.

The attack on Guadalcanal proved to be a relative success but only by the grace of God and fortune. There was little initial opposition to the landings so ground troops were in place before massive Japanese retaliation. But, there were many mistakes including poor planning, inadequate naval gunfire support and logistics and supply end in a nightmare. Fortune smiled on the Allies however, and they learned from their mistakes. The landings in North Africa benefitted from lessons learned on the other side of the world, but there was a new obstacles to overcome. For one thing, it was unclear as to whether the Vichy French army and navy, would resist, and if so, to what degree. They invasion force would soon find out.

The *New York* was ordered to provide bombardment and call fire support for the Southern Attack Group which was to attack Safi beginning on the morning of November 8, 1942. The light cruiser *Philadelphia* (flagship of Rear Admiral Lyle Davidson) and six destroyers joined the *New York* and together they mounted the attack on Safi Harbor. The *New York* was also to provide gunfire support for the destroyers *Bernadou* and *Cole* which had been detailed to enter the harbor and deliver two specially trained companies of the 47th Infantry to seize the port. Also embarked were trained naval personnel designated to assume control and begin operating port facilities. Having a fully operational port would facilitate ground operations so this task was vital. The two destroyers were ancient World War I designed four pipers that had been modified to a fast troop transport role. Their masts were removed and the superstructure's reduced in size to minimize their silhouette. This proved to be the most valuable modification of all, as the French defenders later commented that they had looked in vain for masts and by the time they recognized the destroyers, it was too late. However, neither of these ships and their brave crews could withstand the pounding of a well handled shore battery, and that is what they came up against. As they steamed into the harbor entrance with no pilot and an out of date chart, they were fired upon by a 75mm battery, but their main battery silenced this threat. They were approached and challenged by a converted Vichy tug, the *Alphonse Delanade*, but she was quickly dispatched by well handled destroyer guns. Next it was the turn of small arms and heavy machine guns all around the harbor which converged on the speeding converted troop transports. This dealt with, it looked as if the assault force was home free. It was at this juncture that the largest shore battery at Point De La Tour (four 130mm heavy caliber naval guns) opened up on the destroyers. The ships were no match for this threat. Enter the *New York* and *Philadelphia*. Both opened fire at the offending battery and within a few salvoes, the battery was silenced. The dreaded "Batterie Railleuse" could have ended the assault as quickly as it had begun, but it was no match for the *New York*. It was later learned that one of her 14 inch salvoes had struck the base of the battery which was located on a cliff and the shells had ricocheted into the observation slits destroying the range finder and killing the battery commander. For all intents and purposes, the battery was out of commission and no longer a menace to the landing force. Later, at 0700 the battery opened up on the invaders but only under manual fire control. Earlier work by the *New York* had rendered the battery incapable of accuracy and it was unable to hit either the *New York* or *Philadelphia*. Aircraft from the escort carrier Santee arrived and acted as gunfire spotters and within minutes the battery was smothered by machine gun like 6 inch gunfire from the *Philadelphia*. The *New York* remained on station until it was determined that Safi was in Allied hands and she could be released to help out at the central sector of the invasion at the Fedala landing site.

The Center Group (fire support team) which included the cruisers *Brooklyn* and *Augusta* was charged with silencing the batteries protecting the port of Fedala and insuring that units of the French navy based at Casablanca did not interfere with the landings. Both ships with their accompanying destroyers had their hands full as did the new battleship *Massachusetts* which had to immobilize the modern French battleship Jean Bart. The Jean Bart did open fire on the invaders and French cruisers and destroyers sortied from Casablanca on several occasions to do battle with the *Brooklyn*, *Augusta* and other Allied ships. The French fleet was systemically destroyed in detail and the Jean Bart was damaged to the point of being unable to return fire. The *New York* had been called from her station to the south to assist, but by the time she was in position, the issue had been settled.

Operation Torch was a success and the *New York* was there to help insure victory. It was unfortunate that so many French sailors and soldiers were forced to die on the side of the Axis, but their leaders had chosen the wrong viewpoint. It was also a shame that the cream of the French cruiser/destroyer force was annihilated, but it proved that the U.S. Navy was capable of victory at sea. It was strange however to fight an enemy who before was a friend and after defeat would again be an ally.

When the beaches were secure the *New York* was ordered back to escort duty and accompanied two convoys from the U.S. to Casablanca over the next few months. After a short overhaul period the old battleship became a main battery and escort training center for the Navy, Coast Guard and personnel from various Allied navies. From July 1943 through June 1944 she was an effective training platform for 14 inch/45 caliber gun crews and also for close in weapons. Most escort vessels coming out of American shipyards used the 3 inch/50 caliber gun and the 20mm and 40mm weapons. As the *New York* fairly bristled with these guns, she was a perfect ship for training new gunners and gunnery officers. In the year that she was in this program over 11,000 men and 750 officers participated in the training. Another battleship, the *Wyoming* was used for 5 inch/38 gun training and 20mm/40mm gun training. These old war horses has much value, even if they were not constantly on the firing line.

After her assignment as a gunnery training ship was completed, the *New York* was seconded to the Naval Academy to make three midshipman cruises from Annapolis, Maryland to Trinidad, British West Indies. Over 1,800 "middies" learned from practical experience aboard the old battleship, but in the late autumn of 1944, it was time for her to return to more serious and dangerous work. Throughout December 1944 and into January 1945, she carried out refresher training off the Southern California coast. On January 12, 1945, she rejoined the fighting navy which was on it;s way to the climax of the war in the Pacific. It would be the last hurrah for the old battlewagon.

IWO JIMA, OKINAWA AND THE LAST JAPANESE GASP

In the early days of 1945, victory was pretty much taken for granted. It was now just a matter of time before the almost defeated Axis Powers would finally succumb to the continuous Allied destruction of their military and civilian resources. To western thinking, defeating an enemy meant subverting his will to win. Unfortunately, the Imperial Japanese military machine was not bound by occidental rules of engagement and would doggedly resist to the point of complete annihilation. The battle for Iwo Jima was forecast of what might come as the U.S. Navy moved closer to the Japanese home islands. The next objective, Okinawa further became a sounding board for what would happen should the Allies attempt a landing on Kyushu, the main Japanese home island. These were not battles but rather contests between men who wanted to live and those who sought to die by killing them. It was a hideous and frightening look into the future. It could be summed up in one word - Kamikaze.

The capture and development of Iwo Jima into a fighter plane base and emergency facility for bombers was a necessary step for the strategic bombing of the Japanese homeland. Pilots needed a base near their target so that they could nurse their damaged B-29's into friendly skies at the earliest possible opportunity. It would also provide a base for some of the Army Air Force's long legged escort fighters such as the P-51 Mustang. Iwo Jima was also a milestone in the island hopping campaign. Next stop, Japan itself. The job of softening up it's formidable defenses fell to the old reliable's - battleships *Idaho*, *Tennessee*, *Nevada*, *Texas*, *Arkansas*, and of course, the *New York*.

Unfortunately, the *New York* lost a blade off of her port screw and was forced to seek repair just before the invasion began. She was in time however for the pre-invasion bombardment which began on February 16, 1945. This continued for three days. The old battleship was constantly firing at one target or another and expended 6,417 rounds of ammunition. She fired 1,037 fourteen inch shells alone and laid claim to the most spectacular secondary explosion in the campaign when one of her main battery shells hit the enemy's primary ammunition dump.

Still limping as the result of temporary repairs to the port propeller, she went on to a for-

Axis submarines and surface raiders were not the only hazards faced by the Navy in the North Atlantic. The New York *is almost dwarfed by this iceberg, and most of it is under water! Violent storms, blowing snow and ice were constant dangers to the fleet and its men, but they persevered over everything that nature and man could throw at them.*

The old battleship gently steams into New York Harbor to the cheers of sailors and well wishers. Her tripod masts, 14 inch guns, and ram like bow betray her age, but she still is a wonderful fighting lady. Updated with radar, she held sway with the best.

The New York *slides under the Golden Gate Bridge and out of San Francisco Harbor for the South Pacific. She is alone in this photo taken on May 2, 1946.*

The Empire State battleship as she passes under the Golden Gate Bridge. She carries a skeleton crew and has been stripped of her most up to date armaments. She has been prepared for Operation Crossroads *and will join some 70 other test ships in the Marshall Islands for the nuclear bombs tests scheduled for July 1946.*

The old ship has just been subjected to an air burst and an under water explosion that sunk or heavily damaged many other ships. The New York *survived virtually intact and still able to fight. The Atomic bomb was not the doom of the Navy after all. Her next stop would be back to pearl Harbor for analysis and testing,*

ward repair base at Manus for permanent restoration. This completed, she rejoined Task Force 54, the old reliable's and all steamed toward Okinawa. This fire support team had been further augmented by the arrival of the *Maryland*, *Colorado* and *West Virginia*. With the notable exception of the *Arizona* and *Oklahoma*, almost all of the pre-war battleships were present for the finale of the Pacific War. Beginning on March 27, 1945, the *New York* provided 76 continuous days of unremitting gunfire support to ground forces. She expended 4,159 rounds of fourteen inch ammunition, and a further 7,001 five inch. Her gun barrels were worn out by the time she was detached on June 11.

She was also subjected to a number of suicide plane attacks and was slightly damaged by

one on April 14, 1945. She was at Pearl Harbor having her guns relined and being prepared for the invasion of Japan when the war ended on August 15, 1945. She was now 34 years old, and obsolete by all standards. Her active military service was at an end. She made a "magic carpet" cruise with veterans from the Pacific and was greeted by singer Dinah Shore in San Pedro on September 5, 1945.

The war was over, and the Japanese had been thoroughly defeated. It had been a long and arduous journey for millions of men and women as well as thousands of ships. The old battleships were no longer of any military value as they had been eclipsed by the new capital ship, the carrier. All that was left was one of three choices; preservation as a memorial, scrapping or use as a target. The *New York* was selected for option number three - target practice.

Operation Crossroads And The End

The *New York* along with over 70 plus other ships was selected for the twin atomic bomb tests at Bikini Atoll in July 1946. She survived both blasts, much to the credit of her builders. The anti-Navy faction that predicted that the nuclear age spelled the end of navies was unnerved to see ships like the *New York* survive, virtually intact and still ready for action.

She was then towed to Pearl Harbor and the effects of the atomic bomb blasts were studied through mid 1948. On July 6, 1948, she was towed out to sea and two days later subjected to eight hours of target practise by modern aircraft and ships. Finally she succumbed and sank. The "Old Lady of the Sea" was gone and with her one of the last vestiges of an age gone by, an age when brave men made the difference rather than computer capacity.

The end of the old lady of the sea, New York, comes after eight plus hours of systematic bombing, strafing, rocket fire and gun fire from a variety of surface and aircraft. The new 5 inch rocket was tested on the old girl. She held up well, but finally, enough was enough, and late on July 8, 1946, she turned turtle and sank.

The modern battleship Oklahoma *shortly after being commissioned on May 2, 1916. Her hull housed 5 inch secondary battery casemates are open, and it is obvious that even a moderate seaway would make these guns workable.*

USS OKLAHOMA BB-37
"DEATH AT THE OUTSET"

"All Or Nothing"

The USS *Oklahoma* with sister ship *Nevada* were the first capital ships to employ the "all or nothing" concept of armor protection in the American navy. Simply stated, this meant that she was protected in those areas critical to the main purpose of her existence - a sea going movable battery of ten 14 inch/45 caliber guns. The all or nothing concept held that a warship should be able to withstand heavy caliber shell fire, and although she might be literally ripped apart, her propulsion plant and ability to continue main battery fire were to remain fully operational. With exception of an armored conning tower, small superstructure, funnel and two cage masts, her topsides were spartan. In reality, she was a low profile floating armored citadel with four massive turrets. She was designed to fight and survive in a traditional long range capital ship to capital ship pounding match. Had she been actually faced with this possibility, the *Oklahoma* would have performed exceptionally well.

There was an entire generation of capital ships built by all of the world's major navies with the same notion in mind. The majority of these ships never fulfilled their designers dreams and aspirations, although most earned respectable and important employment in war. Many ended up on the scrap pile never having fired a shot in combat, and not a few succumbed to the nemesis of the mid 20th century - the airplane. Although General Billy Mitchell overtly cheated when he demonstrated the power of bombers over large armored warships in his June 1921 exhibition of air power, his predictions were largely ignored by the diehard battleship loving community. Interestingly, the naval and military communities in other nations such as Japan accorded greater credit to the destructive power of the airplane.

It made little difference whether a battleship was protected by the "all or nothing" plan or just indiscriminately placed armor plating, the day of the battleship was over as ships like the *Okla-* homa were being born. But the naval mind set in the years immediately leading up to and including World War I was focused on bigger and more heavily armed battleships. After all, there was Jutland, and just as night follows day, there would be another war, and the battleships of the world's navies would square off against one another in the final and most valiant of all sea battles. No one dreamed that those flimsy fabric and wood contraptions that could barely escape the earth would some day be responsible for sinking the most mighty ships ever to put to sea. Such was the thinking in the U.S. Navy when the *Oklahoma* was designed. The battleship had only to fear one enemy, another battleship or perhaps a mine. The airplane and submarine were discounted. The *Oklahoma* would succumb a quarter century after being commissioned to the onslaught of nine torpedoes launched by Japanese "*Kate*" carrier borne torpedo bombers. Her "all or nothing" defense was of no value on December 7, 1941.

BEGINNINGS

The USS *Oklahoma* was authorized by a congressional act dated March 4, 1911. It was an appropriations bill that limited the cost of the ship to six million dollars less armor and armament. The First World War was three years distant when the congress authorized the navy to begin work on the *Nevada* and the *Oklahoma*. The U.S. Navy was coming of age and had been thrust on the international scene by President Theodore Roosevelt and his flaunting of the "Great White Fleet". This combined with a population that had reached all of its borders and sought further expansion as well as international respect meant that a navy was an absolute necessity. The battleships *Wyoming*, *Arkansas*, *New York* And *Texas* were in the process of being designed and built when the congress approved the construction of the *Oklahoma* and *Nevada*. The Navy's General Board must have thought that it had died and gone to heaven. The generosity of the legislature seemed unbounded especially in view of it's past record of virtually starving the navy to death. It had not been too long since the battleship *Kearsarge* had been sent with four cruisers to Europe on a state visit. Ashamed of the inadequacy of it's ships, the *Kearsarge* had been fitted with false armor and armaments made of painted canvas and wood. In reality, the pre-expansionist U.S. Navy was little more than a motley collection of obsolete warships that could only be improved through the use of canvas and wood. The congress had been finally induced out of fear or shame to augment this pitiful force with state of the art battleships, cruisers and destroyers. The cruisers and destroyers would come after the battleships, but at least the congress had heeded it's wakeup call. If the U.S. was going to play on the world stage, then it had to have a credible navy.

Things happened so fast that the navy found itself building different classes of battleships simultaneously which was generally considered to be a wartime expedient. There was an obvious overlap in battleship evolution. This trend continued throughout World War I. Just as the *Oklahoma* and *Nevada* were nearing completion, two newer classes were in process, the *New Mexico* and *Arizona* variants. There was little actual experience and experimentation with one class in advance of another being launched. Of course, the navy had to build while money was available and the sympathy of the congress was with them. The reverse would be true in the early interwar years to follow.

The *Oklahoma* was designed to carry ten 14 inch/45 caliber guns in four turrets. Turret B with two barrels would superfire over turret A which mounted three barrels. Turret Y would carry three barrels and turret X , with two barrels would superfire over turret Y. This was the first time that an American battleship would carry differing numbers of barrels per turret. Aside from the ascetic appreciation, there was a solid design rationale behind this arrangement. The all or nothing armor plan consumed much of the allowable weight of the ship, thus less was allocated for armament. This meant that a fifth turret was out of the question, yet ten guns in the main armament were specified, consequently a mixture of three and two gun turrets. As this class did not mount amidships turrets like its immediate predecessors it became a trend setter for generations of battleships to come. With the *Oklahoma* and *Nevada*, the U.S. Navy had come of age. It had literally moved through three generations of design in less than five years.

The *Oklahoma* was initially armed with twenty-one 5 inch/51 caliber guns as a secondary battery. The guns were located in casemates in the hull and superstructure. It was quickly noted however, that the lower barrels in the forward hull casemates as well the aft casemates (seven barrels) were unserviceable during any kind of a seaway and were removed during a 1918-19 refit. Antiaircraft protection was also added at that time. As with all battleships of the period, the *Oklahoma* was armed with 21 inch torpedoes which could be fired from two submerged hull apertures. These were also eliminated during a later refit.

The *Oklahoma* was powered by vertical triple expansion engines capable of a 24,800 shaft horsepower. The engines were powered by twelve oil fired boilers, also another first in American battleship evolution. Snipes aboard the *Oklahoma* did not envy engine room personnel aboard their coal burning contemporaries. Coaling and everything associated with coal fired engines were considered among the filthiest of jobs in the navy. The engines turned two shafts and the *Oklahoma* was clocked at 20.50 knots. Not sufficient speed to keep pace with a modern carrier task force, but sufficient for her role when she was launched. The day of the fast battleship was several years distant.

Her armor consisted of a main belt which encompassed the central length of the hull tapering from 14 inches to 8 inches. Her main deck was four inches in thickness, critical areas were protected with 14 inches as were the boiler uptakes. The conning tower and tube had 16 inches

as were the face plates on the twin turrets. The triple turrets had an 18 inch thickness. Both the *Nevada* and *Oklahoma* were externally bulged for torpedo defense during a later refit.

THE SOONER STATE BATTLESHIP JOINS THE FLEET

The keel of the battleship *Oklahoma* was laid on October 26, 1912, a bare twenty months since the congress had agreed to her construction. She was to be built by the New York Shipbuilding Corporation at their Camden, New Jersey facility. In the same yard, the *Arkansas* had just been commissioned a month before the keel laying and the battleship *Idaho* would follow some two years later in 1915. Sister ship *Nevada* was being built at the Fore River Shipbuilding Company and her keel was laid a week later. Although construction on the *Oklahoma* began before that on the *Nevada*, the latter ship was commissioned two months ahead of the *Oklahoma*. There had been a fire aboard the *Oklahoma* during the time she was fitting out, and this delayed her commissioning. She was launched on March 23 1914 and was christened by Miss Lorena J. Cruce. On May 2 1916 she was commissioned with Captain Roger Welles in command, a command of one of the latest capital ships which carried a crew of 55 officers and 809 men. She displaced 27,500 tons, was 583 feet in length and had a "pre-bulge" beam of just over 95 feet. She was a beautiful and graceful ship whose lines showed strength of purpose. When she fired a broadside, it was obvious that she was one of the most destructive engines of war ever to range the seas.

After a short shakedown period and trials she joined the Atlantic Fleet and along with the *Nevada* was based out of Norfolk. War had broken

out on the European Continent shortly after she was launched, but she remained close to the Atlantic seaboard for the better part of World War I. She did eventually link up with the British Grand Fleet in late 1918, but as a convoy escort. She and the *Nevada* were not summoned earlier due to the fact that there was a severe shortage of fuel oil in Great Britain, therefore none to spare for oil guzzling giants like the *Oklahoma* and *Nevada*. On the other hand, coal was plentiful hence her coal burning battleship contemporaries were welcomed with open arms. She did serve as an excellent convoy escort and was available in the North Sea to intercept any sorties by German heavy units in the closing days of the "Great War". She was then selected to escort President Wilson on his trip to Europe in December 1918 and again in June 1919.

Her postwar career was characterized by training, exercises and more training. She was a part of the Atlantic Fleet until being transferred to the Pacific side in 1921. She had undergone a refit that removed much of her less useful secondary armament and had additional antiaircraft defenses mounted just after the war, but in essence still looked the part of a pre-World War I dreadnought.

In 1925, she joined a number of ships to make the famous trans Pacific cruise to Australia and New Zealand. This cruise was to be a dramatic lesson to the Japanese that the U.S. Navy was capable of extended operations across long stretches of ocean. The Japanese home islands were not immune to American attack as was proven by this venture. Her steaming days came to end shortly after the great cruise and she went into dockyard hands for a major refit in 1927 at the Philadelphia Navy Yard. The *Oklahoma* emerged a new ship in July 1929. She had massive tripod masts topped by three enclosed observation platforms all of which replaced her light weight cage masts. Eight new boilers were added, and anti-torpedo bulges were attached to the hull which in turn increased her beam from 95 feet to almost 108 feet. She now had catapults on her stern and on turret X. At this time her torpedo capability was also eliminated. Her entire secondary armament was re-sited one deck higher, antiaircraft defenses again augmented, and her main battery was elevated from 15 degrees to 30 degrees to improve range. Sporting light grey paint and a larger funnel, she sailed for the Pacific in 1930 after a short period in the Caribbean.

For the next six years she was attached to the Pacific Fleet. This was temporarily interrupted in 1936 when she was selected to carry midshipmen on an extended European training cruise. The cruise held more for the midshipmen than common shipboard routine and periodic visits to old world countries. In 1936, civil war had come to Spain. It was no simple disagreement between political factions, it was all out war. The loyalists to the monarchy faced rebels who were well financed and supported by future axis partners Germany and Italy. The events that took place in Spain were but a portent of things to come, and on a world wide basis just a few year hence. The rebels eventually won out, but a terrible cost to the civilian population. Italy and Germany were also beneficiaries as they were able to test and refine weapons and tactics for later use.

The Oklahoma *as seen from a window of a passenger ferry. She has received her late 1920's refit as evidenced by the huge tripods, aft catapult and scout plane.*

As hostilities escalated in Spain, fear for the safety of neutral visitors became a reality. Bombs do not discriminate when exploding. The *Oklahoma* was diverted to Bilbao, Spain to recover American nationals and other refugees and transport them to Gibraltar and other ports of safety on the French coast. This was accomplished by late July 1936 without major incident. Other citizens of non belligerent nations would not be as fortunate, and it was indeed a blessing that a ship of the *Oklahoma's* stature and power was so close at hand. This accomplished, the ship steamed for the U.S. arriving on September 11, 1936. She arrived back among her Pacific Fleet colleagues on October 24, 1936.

The career of the *Oklahoma* in those last five years before the beginning of the Second World War was routine and identical to that of most other battleships. She was selected for one further update in 1941 when she received eight new 5 inch/25 anti aircraft guns which were director controlled. Now she had a barrage battery of some credibility as well as several strategically placed 50 caliber close in weapons and her four 3 inch/50 caliber guns.

Although the routine on the *Oklahoma* was seemingly unchanged from year to year, there were big changes occurring throughout the navy. The late 1930's shipbuilding programs had begun to bear fruit as new cruisers and destroyers became commonplace. Carriers of the *Yorktown* class were also becoming evident. As a matter of fact, there was increased friction between the battleship faction and the aircraft carrier supporters. The battleship community was still the dominant force, but it was obvious that this would be short lived.

Another sign of change was the dramatic increase in reservists now coming to the fleet. Many wardrooms were crowded with former bankers, teachers, CPA's and engineers. The Academy crowd still ruled, but they were becoming a minority. The enlisted ranks were also swelling with reserves, many of whom received their "crow" just out of specialty school. In the peacetime navy, earning a rate took years, and there was some envy of those who just arrived being rated within weeks of entering the naval service. But, all seemed to acclimate to the changes and in the *Oklahoma* there was very little trauma. These sailors were professional fighting men, reserve or regular.

In the last months of peace, the *Oklahoma* was involved in collision with the *Arizona* and nearly rammed the carrier *Enterprise* during an exercise. Little damage was done and Captain Edward J. Foy who was in command at the time of the collision was not held accountable. He was held in very high regard by the officers and crew and they were saddened when he left the ship for another command. The next captain, Howard D. Bode was in command when the near collision occurred during intricate night maneuvers with the *Enterprise*. He was not held in such universal esteem as was his predecessor. Interestingly, Bode would later go on to command the heavy cruiser *Chicago* during the disastrous "Battle of Savo Island" in early August 1942. There four Allied cruisers would be lost due to negligence and underestimation of Japanese intent and resolve. Captain Bode

The Oklahoma *at anchor in Cherbourg, France preparing to leave for Spain and the rescue of Americans caught up in the mid 1930's Spanish Civil War. An* Omaha *class light cruiser can be seen at anchor in the background.*

took his ship out of harm's way and escaped being destroyed. He was later severely sanctioned for this unfortunate decision, and took his own life shortly thereafter.

The *Oklahoma* entered Pearl Harbor on Friday, December 5, and was warped alongside the *Maryland* which was the inboard ship. Being outboard in the two ship nest was unusual for the *Oklahoma* as prior routine held that she was inboard. There was much grumbling from the officers of the *Maryland* who now had to cross over to board launches heading for the fleet landings. One of the quartermasters remembered that they had received a message ordering them to moor outboard. He thought this was strange, and he also noticed that many of the older ships were moored in less defensible positions. It was more of a sensation than a clear image. It just seemed peculiar. In the past the newer ships were moored outboard which would, at least in theory, enable them to get to sea quickly in any type of emergency. The obsolete minelayer *Oglala* was tied up outboard of the new light cruiser *Helena*; the *Utah* now occupied a berth typically that of a carrier; the *Nevada* was moored singly and the *Arizona* had the old repair ship Vestal alongside. The imaginative quartermaster finally shrugged this off because the relatively modern *West Virginia* and *California* were also moored in exposed locations, at least from the standpoint of defending themselves against torpedo attack. There had been submarine warnings and the threat of torpedoes was very real. Of course there was also the fact that for the first time in many months, the bulk of the battle fleet was in harbor and not on a rotation schedule. And, the carriers were absent. Add to this the fact that an Admiral's inspection was due on Monday and most of the ships were in no condition to meet an enemy air attack. Most of them were opened up and had minimal watertight integrity. For those with a conspiratorial mind, it would seem strange that all of these coincidences should collide at a time when war was imminent. There

had been one dramatic war warning just days before and the fleet was still on edge. Men in the U.S. Navy knew in their hearts that war with Japan was coming, they just did not know when. As the weekend began and sailors and officers from the fleet swarmed ashore to take advantage of the overburdened recreation facilities on Oahu, none could possibly know that nearly 2,500 of their number would never see the following Monday. For those that survived a four year war coming.

On the *Oklahoma*, the evening of December 6, passed without major incident except for the returning sailors, many of which had imbibed too much. This was normal and as the next day was Sunday, most could relax and shake off the effects of the previous night. Most of the officers were ashore and the ship was left to the relative inexperience of junior ensigns. After all, there was no real immediate threat. There had been little thought given to antiaircraft defense and even less training. Keeping the ship on precise station was considered more important than developing finely tuned antiaircraft gun crews. The gunnery officer had requested that at least a few of the air defense batteries be manned while the ship was in port, but his concerns were not taken seriously by the captain. The ready ammunition was padlocked and the keys were in possession of the officer of the deck. In any event, the *Oklahoma's* main AA defense, it's eight modern 5 inch/25 caliber guns would have been of no value. There was no compressed air for the rammers and the firing locks had been removed from the breech blocks for cleaning. Another fallout from the impending admiral's inspection. She did have some defense in her 50 caliber guns, but that was inconsequential.

The watch from 0400 - 0800 nearly passed without incident. Just five minutes before it ended at 0755, several strange aircraft were noticed in the vicinity of the anchorage. A bomb exploded on Ford Island at about the same mo-

An example of a radio message received by the Oklahoma. *One of the quartermasters to this day still contends that a message like this was received instructing the old ship to moor outboard of the* Maryland, *a strange reversal of normal routine.*

Boxing and wrestling were major pastimes for battleship sailors like most sports. This smoker, as the bouts were known, occurred just eight months prior to the day from the Japanese attack on Pearl Harbor.

The Oklahoma, *like all major warships, had sports teams that competed with other ships for various fleet championships. Occasionally, a ship would pick up a patriotic professional player who had joined the Navy. Major leaguer, Bob Feller, helped the battleship* Alabama *win fleet championship during World War II. The* Oklahoma *team was not as fortunate.*

ment. Tense and anxious Japanese torpedo plane pilots marveling at the lack of antiaircraft gunfire swooped down to just above the water and released their weapons. It was a known fact that aerial torpedoes dove to 75 feet when dropped before returning to cruising depth. Pearl Harbor was 42 feet in depth, thus aerial torpedoes would be would be useless. The Japanese Navy had specially fitted wooden fins on their aerial torpedoes that solved this problem, and before 0800, several were on their way toward defenseless targets such as the *Oklahoma*. The watch had yet to end as the planes, lightened after dropping their burdens swept up and over the tall tripods of the unwary ships on battleship row. The *Oklahoma* had just over 15 minutes to live as did 448 of her crew.

THREE BATTLES THAT FOREVER IMMORTALIZED THE *OKLAHOMA*

THE FIRST BATTLE: TORPEDO VERSUS SHIP

The "Oakie" as she was affectionately called by her crew was now to be the central character in three battles; the first of which would take minutes, the second, days and the last, months. The tragedy of her loss would be partially abated by the miraculous rescue of 32 of her crew and her eventual salvage and refloating would serve as a tribute to the efforts of men against seemingly insurmountable odds. But at 0755 on December 7, 1941, the only thought or more to the point, emotion was to get over the surprise of

being attacked from the air and man a battle station. Within in seconds of hearing explosions and a loud voice booming from the loudspeaker that an air attack was in process, men all over the *Oklahoma* began racing to their stations. Many were running to the antiaircraft batteries as instructed by the loudspeaker, but this would be to no avail. No ammunition, no air, no firing locks and no action. The five inch battery never fired a shot.

As the minute hand swept up to 0800, the battleship was struck by three "Kate" torpedo bomber launched torpedoes which hit the hull under her armor and on the unsealed port side anti-torpedo bulge. The effect of these torpedoes which hit in 15 second intervals was instantaneous. The ship took an immediate list to port of between 25 to 25 degrees and oil began gushing out of her side to form concentric circles out from the ship. The *West Virginia*, *Nevada*, *California*, *Helena*, *Utah* and *Raleigh* had also been hit and were in serious trouble. A photograph was taken at about this time from a Japanese aircraft overhead that dramatically showed the *Oklahoma* beginning to capsize in what looked like her own life's blood. This was probably the last image of this great ship still afloat and relatively upright.

With the captain being ashore, Commander Jesse L. Kenworthy, the executive officer determined that there was no real possibility of saving the ship. Counter-flooding was out of the question and air defense consisted of only two machine guns. His decision to abandon was reinforced when the wounded ship was hit by five additional torpedoes along the port side above the armor belt. The bulges that were supposed to enhance protection against torpedo attack worked in reverse as the hatches were open to the sea, and as the ship listed, Pearl Harbor flooded in worsening an already lost cause. The six inch hawsers that held the *Oklahoma* to the

Maryland began to snap and whip around the decks as the strain exceeded their capability. As the men fortunate to arrive on deck quickly surmised, the open deck was little better than a shooting gallery for trigger happy Japanese gunners. As the planes crossed over the *Oklahoma*, they strafed the white clad men as they moved from one hell to another. The decks ran red with blood and if whining bullets did not kill, then falling debris and shrapnel did. Men cringed under turret overhangs, ventilators and any space that would shield them from death. A rage of boundless proportions soon replaced fear and anguish. The ship continued to roll over to port and it became more and more difficult to keep a solid footing on the sloping, oil and blood splattered decks.

By 0815 the wonderful old ship had rolled over to port to approximately 150 degrees with her great tripods jamming in the mud thus preventing her from turning turtle. Men leaped across the widening gap to the *Maryland*, jumped overboard or simply walked their way up and over the hull. All this in full view of thousands of astonished onlookers who saw this as if in a dream state. "My God", the *Oklahoma* has just capsized", cried hundreds. It was almost impossible to believe, but there she was. Her wet and slimy hull stuck up out of the water and her starboard propeller became visible. She was gone as was the *Arizona* which had just blown up. An elderly sister, the target ship *Utah* was also gone. On that morning, the *Oklahoma*, *Utah* and old minelayer *Oglala* capsized in response to the tremendous damage done by torpedoes. Before the *Oklahoma* completely capsized, she was struck by torpedo number 9 which exploded as her port bilge keel touched the bottom of Pearl Harbor. It hit her amidships like the others almost at the main deck level below the conning tower. Incredibly, the Japanese had expended nine of their forty aerial torpedoes on the *Oklahoma*. She was hit by more torpedoes than any two other ships combined in the attack. She never stood a chance. The first battle, which lasted barely 20 minutes was over and the old ship had been killed, actually murdered at her mooring.

BATTLE NUMBER TWO: MEN AGAINST TIME

At fifteen minutes after 0800, the *Oklahoma* had ceased to be a viable fighting unit in the U.S. Navy. But, what of her crew? They may have been left without a home, but they were still her crew and still fighting men. Within minutes, many could be seen helping *Maryland* gunners in the fight to knock down the attackers. Others swam ashore to take up stations on Ford Island, and still others made to other ships to continue the fight. A few like quartermaster Bob McMahon swam to a boat, got to the Navy landing and at the height of the battle commandeered a launch to rescue sailors struggling in the oil covered burning waters near the stricken ships. Still other stayed aboard the *Oklahoma*, inside and out on the hull. Hundreds were trapped below in a world that was upside down, flooding, dark and filled with smoke. Not dark like that of night, but dark as in the complete absence of light. Terror was the order of the day, but it was

tempered with discipline. Discipline saved many who would have died in a panic.

As the ship was began to turn over, men escaped in any way that was possible. In one turret, an ensign, Francis Charles Flaherty (USNR) assisted by a Seaman, James Richard Ward stayed behind to insure that their shipmates escaped. They willingly sacrificed themselves as the turret dipped under the water. Both were later awarded the Congressional Medal of Honor posthumously. Neither had reached their twenty third birthday. Chaplin Aloysius H. Scmitt also sacrificed himself that others might escape. He was awarded the Navy and Marine Corps Medal

for valor. These were just kids that behaved in the highest traditions of the Naval Service. They were not the only valiant men that day aboard the *Oklahoma*. There were many others, especially those would remained on the hull to listen for interior noises that signified that there was still life aboard. The rescuers remained, even in view of continuous strafing, falling debris, and oil fires that were all about the harbor.

As the attack ended, men began to tap at various locations on the outer hull using blueprints brought over from the navy yard as a map to the interior. Staff aboard the neighboring *Maryland* decided that the best area to enter the ship would

Each capital ship carried a contingent of Marines. Here in this 1941 photo, the unit is being inspected by the captain. It is probably Captain Foy, a favorite among the men. A Vought scout aircraft can be seen in the background.

In this remarkable photo taken near 0800 on December 7, the Oklahoma *(lower right outboard ship) has just been hit by at least three or four torpedoes. Oil is gushing from her hull as it is also from the* West Virginia *(immediately behind her) and the* Nevada *(last in line). Both the* West Virginia *and* Oklahoma *are listing, and a recent torpedo wake can be seen just outside the oil spill next to the* Oklahoma. *The* Arizona *has not been hit as yet, but within minutes she would be struck in her forward magazine with a bomb that would destroy her and forever seal over 1,000 men in a permanent gravesite.*

The attack has ended and most of the fires are under control. The gruesome task of counting the dead and mising has begun. Men are already on the hull of the Oklahoma *listening for survivors. Thirty-two men were saved.*

Like a giant erector set, bents or wooden tripods are connected to the hulk by cables secured to Ford Island. This would be one of the most spectacular salvage jobs in the history of marine engineering.

be through the shaft alley. There was great concern that in their haste to get at the trapped men, a hole would be cut in an oil tank and more fires would begin. Cutting in the shaft alley prevented this and proved to be one of the wiser decisions of the day. Not much could be accomplished during the attack and rest of December 7, but that night, shielded acetylene torches began the work of cutting through the hull. At 0800 the following morning, December 8, six men were saved from one of the radio rooms. Shortly thereafter at 1100, another eleven men were taken out from the "lucky bag" compartment. Three hours later at 1400, five more men made it to safety from a five inch battery handling room. At 1600, eight others were pulled out. The last two were saved the following day at 0230. In all, 32 men made it out of the stricken ship. The welders and shipfitters from the yard and other ships never gave up. Regrettably, over 400 were left behind. Legend has it that tapping continued until December 23, 1941, when it stopped forever. Men who walked guard aboard the *Maryland* covered their ears in a vain attempt to shut out the noise, especially at night when all was quiet. To them, the tapping noises were the most dramatic and disturbing remembrances of the attack. Sentries wept for days in helplessness. The second battle although the most heart wrenching, was a victory for 32 fortunate men and a boost for those who never gave up.

BATTLE NUMBER THREE: THE SALVAGE THAT SEEMED IMPOSSIBLE

The last battle was that of salvaging the overturned battleship. Within months, the *West Virginia, California, Raleigh, Oglala,* and sister ship *Nevada* were being or had been salvaged. Many of the attack recipients had received repairs and sailed to the South and Central Pacific to exact revenge, but the *Arizona, Utah* and *Oklahoma* remained enigma's to the navy. All three had been damaged beyond worthwhile repair and all were memorial sites for over 1,500 men. The navy could not just simply blow them up, so another more palatable solution was needed. The *Arizona* and *Utah* would remain as permanent memorials and an attempt would be made to right the

Oklahoma and patch her up. The berthing space was valuable, but removing this ghastly vestige of defeat also influenced the decision makers. Although it was decided in May 1942 to salvage the old battleship, it would be months before an attempt was made as the call upon salvage and repair experts was at an all time high. Every week damaged ships arrived from the forward areas for repair, and this work had priority.

Working in concert with a private contractor, Pacific Bridge Company a plan was settled upon and a model created by Chief Watertender R. H. Snow was used as an exact replica of how the ship was now situated. From this, divers could access the ship and seal critical holes in order for buoyancy to be regained. This was an important step as those who worked underwater had to accustom themselves to an upside down world. After a year of preparation and sealing the holes made by the torpedoes, buoyancy was reached for 18,800 tons of the 35,000 ton hulk. There were more than just problems with sealing holes and disorientation. The ship was filled with decomposed food, clothing and of course corpses. The resulting gas was lethal and on some other jobs had killed divers. Great care had to be exercised to avoid even further tragedy. Much of the ammunition had to be removed and the propellers.

Now that the ship had positive buoyancy, the next problem was to right her so that she could be floated into a drydock for more permanent repair. Like the Lilliputians in "Gulliver's Travels", the great ship was to be righted by vertically attaching twenty-one 40 foot high frames or bents directly to the hull. These in turn were connected by cable to welded pad eyes on the starboard side of the hull. Each assembly was attached by cable to five horsepower electric winches which were bolted to concrete foundations implanted on nearby Ford Island. The block and tackle arrangement allowed for an 8000:1 ratio of pull per assembly. In March 1943, the entire rather odd looking assembly which looked more like a giant tinker toy began to work. Within a short period, the combined power of the 21 motors, winches and of course an 8000:1 ratio successfully pulled the ship to a 90 degree position. Decks and turrets which had not seen the light of day since 0815 on De-

cember 7, 1941 were again exposed to the bright Hawaiian sun. The once beautiful holystoned teak decks were covered with holes that had been made by teredos or shipworms. It was a simple task from this point forward to pull the hulk over to an upright position and after being lightened, move her to a drydock for patching. The task was elementary from an engineering standpoint, but it did take ten months. It was complicated again due to the image of the ship and all it contained. The full effect of natural and man made destruction could now be seen. The ship was a twisted mass of wreckage housing a mass of unspeakable corruption and death. Four hundred innocent souls that had been murdered had to be removed. It was a somber reckoning with the past. By this time, the war had progressed without the *Oklahoma* and with so many new battleships now available, it was decided that she was of no further service to the navy. She was then decommissioned on September 1, 1944 and sold on December 5, 1946 to the Moore Drydock Company of Oakland, California for $46,000 as scrap. In any event, the salvage of the *Oklahoma* was a triumph for salvers and engineers. It was the most spectacular job done during the war, and it was a complete success.

Her final voyage began a few months later in May 1947. She was under tow to California from Pearl Harbor and in mid May she began to take on a port list for no apparent reason. The towing firm was given permission to return to *Honolulu*, but on May 17, 1947, the list straightened out. The old battleship righted herself, not in preparation to continue the tow, but as a prelude to slipping beneath the surface of a calm evening sea. Suddenly, the crew aboard the tug felt their ship being towed backward. The *Oklahoma* was sinking and dragging them down. The line binding the two ships was cut, and the old ship disappeared from sight. In was May, 17 1947, and for her, the war was finally over.

WHAT IF THE *OKLAHOMA* HAD MOORED INBOARD OF THE *MARYLAND*?

Had the *Oklahoma* moored inboard of the *Maryland* as was the normal routine, then the fate of the *Oklahoma* would probably been that

The 21 bents connected to cables through pulleys and onto powered winches ashore have now brought the ship to a 90° angle. She has buoyancy and need only to be fully righted to be pumped out and brought into drydock.

The Oklahoma *has nearly been righted. The cables can still be seen extending out over the starboard side of the corroded and mangled ship. By this time in mid 1943, the war had long since progressed to the point that there was confidence in ultimate victory.*

of the *Maryland*, except that the *Maryland* was able to begin shooting down her attackers from the outset. She was better prepared and might have been able to ward off some of the later torpedo bombers and not capsized. Admiral Walter Anderson, who during the battle, shifted his flag from the *West Virginia* to the *Maryland* had issued standing orders that ships in his division have at least two 5 inch and two 50 caliber antiaircraft guns manned and ready day and night. He also recognized that the gunners might have to open fire instantaneously without seeking approval from a control point. His orders further instructed that as soon as a positive identification was made that enemy aircraft were attacking, then his gunners were to open fire. This they did just as the first bombs began to fall. Undoubtedly, the *Maryland* would have been struck by torpedoes, but she probably would have shared the same fate as the *West Virginia*. The damage would have been less substantial, and like the *West Virginia*, she would have returned to combat after modernization.

The *Oklahoma* would have probably not suffered severe damage during the attack on Pearl Harbor and would have been modernized like her sister, the *Nevada*. Her career would have been much like that of the other older battleships during World War II. She would have likely ended her days a target like the *Nevada*, after being subjected to the atomic blasts at Bikini Atoll in 1946. It is all conjecture however.

USS *PENNSYLVANIA* BB-38
"FLAGSHIP"

THE *PENNSYLVANIA* CLASS: SHIPS OF DESTINY

"May God protect this ship and all those who sail in her". On March 16, 1915, Miss Elizabeth Kolb spoke these words as the battleship *Pennsylvania* slid down the ways at Newport News, Virginia. Just over three months later on June 19, 1915, another christening sponsor repeated essentially the same prayer as the battleship *Arizona* first touched the waters adjacent to the New York Navy Yard. The *Arizona* and

The Oklahoma *has been stripped of her guns and cleaned up. She will be sold to the Moore Drydock Company of Oakland for $46,000. As she was being towed to Oakland from Pearl Harbor on May 17, 1947, she suddenly took on a port list, and later silently slid beneath the water. Her sister, the* Nevada, *would join her just over a year later, having been sunk as a target.*

Pennsylvania were the sisters in the two ship *Pennsylvania* class of the mid-World War I American battleship building program. The navy had become the fortunate beneficiary of pent up political and public support and battleship construction in was not unlike a feeding frenzy on public tax monies during this period. The Navy had just acquired the *Arkansas*, *Wyoming*, *New York* and *Texas*; the *Nevada* and *Oklahoma* were building and the *New Mexico*, *Mississippi*, *Idaho*, *California* and *Tennessee* were either approved or in the formative design stages. Add the *Pennsylvania* and *Arizona*, and in 1915, the U.S. Navy was in the process of training, building, designing or securing congressional approval for twelve battleships. The navy would only build another

thirteen battleships over the next thirty years, and probably for all time, so the building program during the early years of World War I was pivotal.

The U.S. Navy was quickly moving from third rate status to a first rate force, and ships like the *Pennsylvania* were to be major elements of that force for the next two and one half decades. Both ships of this class would also play major roles in American naval history, and one, the *Arizona* will be forever a part of the American experience. She would die a horrible death along with over 1,100 of her innocent crew in the early moments of the Japanese attack on Pearl Harbor on December 7, 1941. She would become the symbol that millions of citizens would

This early stern photo of the Pennsylvania *shows her aft casemate guns and cage masts. External electronics consisted of radio antenna and lighting. She was in essence a floating fortress with a main battery and little else on her decks.*

An overhead view of the Pennsylvania *taken on January 5, 1928, prior to her major overhaul. She is flying an Admiral's flag at her forward truk, and an oversized national ensign aft. She is virtually defenseless against her air attack, only armed with a small number of 3 inch/50 caliber AA guns.*

rally around to work and sacrifice until Japan was defeated. She would also become the most famous and emotion laden memorial in the U.S.

It would be for her sister and hundreds of other warships to avenge her death over the duration of World War II. Ironically the *Pennsylvania* would be present at an event that would accomplish this in a special if not predestined manner.

THE BATTLESHIP *PENNSYLVANIA* IS CONCEIVED AND BUILT

It is customary within the international naval community to keep abreast of what the com-

petition is doing. Not having adequate and accurate naval intelligence can be disastrous to a seafaring nation, consequently naval attaches and visiting naval officers spent most of their waking moments seeking information. Even idle chit chat at a Washington, London or Tokyo dinner party could reveal valuable and useful information not to be had in official channels. Every bit helped in keeping the naval design playing field level. Occasionally, one country or another would steal a march on rival nations, but overall, warship design had an international flavor. Most navies were mirror images of their competitors. When Great Britain built battleships with a 14 or 15 inch main battery, then the U.S.,

Japan, Italy and France would follow suit. This applied to battery caliber, barrel numbers, armor, and of course speed. Germany was summarily dropped, albeit temporarily from competition when she agreed to the Versailles Treaty in 1919 and the Soviet Union was not a player during the early twentieth century. That country would not have a credible navy until the late 1950's.

During the U.S. battleship expansion program of 1912-1920, Japan was also building capital ships, two of which were much like the *Pennsylvania*. They were the *Fuso* and *Yamashiro* built from the period 1912-17. They displaced 35,900 tons and mounted twelve 14 inch/45 caliber guns disposed in six twin barrel turrets. Before being modernized in the early 1930's they could make 22.5 knots. Both would clash with the a number of re-tread battleships including the *Pennsylvania* in the last major ship to ship slugging match of World War II on October 25, 1944.

The *Pennsylvania* class was considered to be an improved version of the *Nevada* class. The improvements consisted of better internal and underwater protection. Another departure from the *Nevada* class was the use of four triple barrel turrets for a total of twelve 14 inch/45 caliber guns arranged in an A, B, X, and Y format. Although her turrets housed three barrels, they were roomy and well laid out. Unlike the *Nevada* class, both the *Pennsylvania* and *Arizona* were equipped with geared turbines. The *Pennsylvania* utilized the Curtis manufactured geared turbine and the *Arizona* used that built by Parsons. The *Pennsylvania* derived power from five White Forster and one Bureau Express boilers which were oil fired. She carried up to 2,322 tons or nearly 700,000 gallons of fuel in her bunkers, and was rated highly for economy of operation. When built she and sister *Arizona* were two of the most powerful capital ships in the world and moreover, had the endurance to match. This was the second class of American battleship to be oil fired from the outset, but ironically, her source of power would prevent her from taking an active part in World War I. There was a scarcity of fuel oil in Great Britain, and the U.S. Navy could ill afford to spare any of it's very few tankers to act as a fleet train to oil fired battleships across the Atlantic. So, the *Pennsylvania* remained in U.S. coastal waters for much of the war.

A total of 32,000 SHP was generated by the *Pennsylvania's* propulsion plant which provided adequate electrical power for all needs and drove the ship through the water at 21 knots (maximum speed). She was 608 feet in length overall and had a beam of 97 feet prior to having antitorpedo bulges added. This would cause her beam to increase to just over 106 feet. Her draft with a full load was 33.5 feet. Overall, the *Pennsylvania* and *Arizona* were considered excellent sea boats and unusually stable gunnery platforms. This was vital for accurate gunfire. As with the *Nevada* class, these ships experienced difficulties with their hull mounted casemate secondary guns. These guns were unserviceable in any kind of a sea, and like their predecessors, the same solution would be sought - seal the apertures and re-site the secondary battery up to a higher deck level. As designed, she carried twenty two 5 inch/51 caliber guns to ward off

The Pennsylvania transitting the Panama Canal in late June 1927. This striking photo shows in great detail her forward fighting top, cage mast, main battery fire control director and her slitted conning tower. The crew is out and about attempting to cool off from the sweltering humidity of the region. Battttleships were not air conditioned.

Congressmen inspect the 14 inch/45 caliber gun barrels of turret "A" aboard the flagship of the U.S. Fleet, the Pennsylvania. Everything about this ship was solid and seemingly oversized. Her teak decks have been holystoned to perfection and her paint surfaces are immaculate. The barrel tips and tampions are highly polished brass. This is tax money well spent.

The Pennsylvania *is framed by two lovely ladies as she begins her exodus down the Hudson River to the sea and the Pacific in June 1934. The battleships and their crews were respected by the public. This was often true especially of the ladies who could not resist a man in uniform.*

Three sailors polish and tighten the plugs that seal the barrels of the number two turret. President Roosevelt, a staunch supporter of the Navy, spent as much time as his duties allowed aboard its ships. The sailor working on the center barrel is Douglas Lowndes, Sr., a seaman who barely missed being aboard the flagship when she was hit on December 7, 1941.

smaller ships such as the destroyer. Four 3 inch/50 caliber guns were added as an interim measure for antiaircraft defense. Two were mounted just forward of the main cage mast, and the other two on the wings of turret X. Antiaircraft defense was considered important, but not as consequential as it would eventually become.

The secondary battery was later altered to reflect increased concern for air attack, and twelve of the 5 inch/51's were landed and 5 inch/25's were mounted. These guns were highly regarded and could provide a barrage defense, primarily against dive bombers. In the years that led up to the war, it was assumed that the main air threat to the battleship would come from the dive bomber. While is true that a high level bomber caused the destruction of the *Arizona*, it is just as true that the weapon of more lethal destruction was the torpedo. In general, the navy had ignored reports and rumor of the effectiveness of the torpedo and concentrated on defenses designed to thwart the dive bomber. As a foot-

note, it was the U.S. Navy's dive bomber (Dauntless) that sank the pride of the Japanese Navy at Midway just a few months after the war began, but in truth, the Japanese torpedo did the most damage to it's opponents.

These pre-war changes occurred during periodic refits and when Japanese planes arrived overhead on December 7, 1941, the *Pennsylvania* mounted eight 5 inch/25 caliber guns that were director controlled as well as her 3 inch/50's. She also carried a number of 50 caliber close in machine guns, but they proved to be of little value, even those located in the "bird bath" structures on top of the control towers.

Her other primary weapon was the below waterline torpedo tubes designed to fire 21 inch torpedoes. This as in all other contemporary battleships was abandoned during a later refit.

The *Pennsylvania* was armored like her predecessor in the "all or nothing" format. "All or nothing" was based on the hypothesis that armoring an entire ship in either light or medium plating was unrealistic given the penetrating power of plunging projectiles and later armor piercing bombs/shells. Armor was to be limited to protecting the most vital areas of the ship to enable her to continue carrying out her mission. For example, the *Pennsylvania* was expressly armored in the following areas:

Main belt: 8 inches lower edge and 14 inches upper edge
Boiler uptakes (funnel base): 9-15 inches
Conning tower/tube: 16 inches
Turret: Face plate (18 inches), rear/sides (10 inches), roof (5 inches), and barbettes (14 inches)

The areas surrounding the engines, boilers and magazines were also heavily protected, but the rest of the ship was covered by thin shell

Signalmen aboard the Pennsylvania *prepare to hoist signal flags. A search/signal lamp is in the upper left corner of the photo. Signalmen had to know every possible means of communication ranging from semaphore to signal light.*

The crew of the Pennsylvania *man the rail in tribute to President Franklin Roosevelt who is aboard the heavy cruiser* Houston. *The fleet has just completed exercise problem XX, an annual demonstration of U.S. Naval power and effectiveness. The destroyer* Phelps, *DD-360, is in the sights of six guns of the battleship's main battery.*

Cooks aboard the Pennsylvania *prepare what seems to be an unlimited amount of mashed potatoes, and they better be good. A crew not properly fed with tasty and nutritious food is dangerous. The Army is not the only armed force that travels on its stomach. Good ship's cooks are vital to morale and the crew's well being. To a sailor, the beauty of a ship is less important than having the reputation as "a hell of a home and feeder!"*

plating only designed to protect against flying fragments and shrapnel.

When commissioned, the *Pennsylvania* carried a crew of 910 officers and men. These numbers would swell to 1,358 on the eve of World War II and as high as 2,555 at the height of the war. She was designated a flagship and for many years carried the flag of Commander in Chief, Atlantic Fleet, CIC U.S. Fleet and later CIC Pacific Fleet. She was a well respected and admired warship.

Her keel was laid on October 27, 1913 by the Newport News Shipbuilding Co. at Newport News, Virginia. Many fine ships would emerge from this yard such as the carrier *Enterprise* CV-6 and light cruiser *Boise* CL-47. On March 16, 1915 she was launched and just over a year later on June 12, 1916, she was put into commission by her first commanding officer, Captain H. B. Wilson. World War I was at it's midpoint when the *Pennsylvania* was accepted by the U.S. Navy.

WORLD WAR I AND THE INTER-WAR YEARS

As the *Pennsylvania* was not coal fired, she did not participate in the great war as an active unit of the Allied fleet. This battle force was consumed with guarding against another German sortie like what had occurred at Jutland. There was little oil available in Great Britain, consequently, the new American battleship confined her service to the East Coast of the U.S. She was outfitted as a flagship and many remarked that the habitability of the *Pennsylvania* class was much improved over previous battleship design. Of course, she was to carry an admirals flag.

Just after being commissioned, the CIC, Atlantic Fleet, Admiral Henry T. Mayo broke his flag on the *Pennsylvania*. For the next two years and until the Armistice was signed ending World War I, the new battleship was engaged in local maneuvers and training along the east coast and into the Caribbean. On December 3, 1918 she left her home waters for Europe as the guide ship for the *George Washington* which was carrying President Wilson to peace conferences in France. Shortly thereafter, she left for the U.S. and arrived in New York on Christmas Day, 1918.

For the next several years, the *Pennsylvania* was to be called upon to render honors to various dignitaries almost as a matter of routine. Admiral Mayo had been replaced by Admiral Henry B. Wilson as the Commander in Chief, Atlantic Fleet at the end of June 1919 and ultimately, the flagship made her way to the Pacific. This was like coming home for Wilson as he was her first commanding officer. She took up station in San Pedro and was homeported there from 1922 up through 1940, when the fleet moved westward to Pearl Harbor.

Over the summer months of 1925, she and the bulk of the Navy based in the Pacific made what will always be known as the "great cruise". It seemed as if the bulk of the battle and scouting fleets visited Australia and New Zealand. The force was led by the old cruiser Seattle with Admiral R. E. Coontz in command. It was a who's who in the battleship community as the *Arizona, California, Nevada, New Mexico, West Virginia, Tennessee, Colorado, Maryland, Mississippi, Idaho* and of course, the *Pennsylvania* were present. Also included were several *Omaha* class light cruisers escorted by the ever present flush deck four piper icons of the immediate post war navy. All in all it was an impressive force and a blatant lesson to the Japanese that the U.S.

Navy could range all over the Pacific. The natural defense of distance no longer applied and Japan was vulnerable to the U.S. Navy. This demonstration plus the insult of an anti-oriental immigration policy that had been adopted by the U.S. government caused escalating anger and rage among Japanese leaders. Sixteen years later they would retaliate by raping an oil rich empire in the east indies after temporarily paralyzing

131

The ship's store on the Pennsylvania. *It stocked popular items like magazines (Popular Aviation, Photoplay, Screenland, Action and Love Stories), pennants, cigarettes, watches, candy and other inexpensive articles designed to make life on a battleship more homelike. A battleship was like a city with very strict rules formed into a rigid class society. Trinkets and magazines took the edge off. Candy was known as "pogey bait," a reflection of the times and social ethics. It was a man's navy!*

The "gedunk" or soda fountain. Here sailors could order a coke or a Coca-Cola milk shake, just like the drug store fountain at home. On the bulkhead at the upper right hand of the photo, the prices are posted. A 5 cent "coke" or 10 cent soda would not break a seaman's pre-war budget and salary of $21 per month. The gedunk was a very popular place for the new recruits who had not yet been corrupted by petty officers who lived for the opportunity to break in a new man at dives like "Shanghai Red's" or any number of gin mills in San Pedro or Long Beach. Many sailors had to grow up fast, especially on December 7, 1941.

the U.S. Navy at Pearl Harbor. Their rationale for such an infamous act was to satisfy the need for natural resources to feed their burgeoning industrial economy. The true reason is more complicated and does touch on events such as the anti-immigration sentiment of the mid 1920's and the flaunting of American naval power in events such as the "great cruise". But, setting aside the international and political aspects of the cruise, it was one hell of a time for several thousand sailors. The crew of the *Pennsylvania* was no exception. They thoroughly enjoyed being honored, fed and the center of attention for thousands of well wishers, especially, the Australian and New Zealand girls. Many of the men were first introduced to heavy ale on this trip which unfortunately produces a comparably heavy hangover. It seems that there are drawbacks to everything. The "great cruise" was the highlight of many naval careers and was a real adventure for all who participated.

Back in San Pedro by late September 1925, it was time again for more serious naval training and exercises. This is what the recruiter failed to tell the innocent youth that wanted to see the world. Most of the world they would see was under steel decks or behind a gun, mop or ladling spoon. The great cruise was an exception. For the next four years the battleship participated in one exercise or problem after another as well as being the focal point for many ceremonies. The *Pennsylvania* or "*Pennsy*" was a fleet flagship and the comings and goings of important dignitaries was commonplace. By the first of June, 1929, it was time from major overhaul. Many of the navy's capital ships had already been taken in hand and were sporting the tripod in lieu of the cage masts, and enhanced antiaircraft protection was becoming more evident.

The *Pennsylvania* followed in the same pattern as the *Nevada* and had additional 3 inch/50 caliber batteries installed and her main battery increased in elevation from 15 degrees to 30 degrees. Her main battery could fire up to three shells every 40 seconds, but three per minute was average, and highly satisfactory considering that

the breech blocks were worked with hand power. Her main battery was director controlled by a Mark 23 Fire Control System

Two catapults for scout aircraft were installed. One on the stern which was accompanied by a handling crane and another on the roof of X turret. Cranes were also added amidships for aircraft and boat handling. Another major change was the construction of a multiple level superstructure behind the conning tower and just forward of the tripod. This plus a heightened funnel transformed the battleship from a pre-war archaic look to a modern post war capital ship.

Interestingly, the cost for this two year overhaul was nearly the same as her original building cost of $7.4 million, but what emerged on May 8, 1931 was a state of the art battleship. She was still rated at 21 knots and had bulky torpedo bulges, yet her AA defense had been updated to the threat existent in 1931. While it is true that ten years hence she would be no match for the aircraft and tactics of Imperial Japanese Navy, it is just as true that advances in aircraft design and development quickly out-paced the ability of any modern navy to maintain parity. In 1931, the aircraft that the *Pennsylvania* would face were still made of fabric and wood, and their bomb loads were not yet lethal to a correspondingly alert and well defended battleship. By December 1941, all that would have changed. The *Pennsylvania* and her sisters would have one final update in 1940-41 to add 50 caliber machine guns and the 5 inch/25 caliber AA battery, but by this time their opponents would be at least two generations ahead. The ships in battleship row were no match for well handled aircraft with heavy armor piercing bombs and torpedoes.

After leaving the Philadelphia Navy Yard, the *Pennsylvania* sailed for the Pacific and her homeport of San Pedro. There she remained until late 1940, however, change was evident and war was imminent. The Japanese had consolidated their hold on much of China and provoked the U.S. in 1937 by bombing and sinking the gunboat *Panay* in the Yangtze River near Nanking. The U.S. had imposed an oil and other natural

resource embargo on Japan. A war of escalating economic sanctions was quickly leading to one of bombs and bullets. On February 1, 1941, Admiral James O. Richardson was relieved as CIC Pacific Fleet due to his continued insistence that the fleet should not have been moved to Pearl Harbor in 1940. He opposed the decision which had been made by President Roosevelt and Secretary of the Navy, Frank Knox. Their reasons made good political sense and represented the finest in professional international brinkmanship. In Richardson's place, Husband E. Kimmel was appointed. He now became the Commander in Chief, U.S. Pacific Fleet and on his watch, it would be destroyed less than a year later. Whether he was culpable or could have done anything to prevent or lessen the damage is a matter for scholars to debate for decades to come. In any event, the U.S. was on track for a major war in the Pacific which could only be averted by the Japanese evacuating China and Indochina or the U.S. turning on the oil supply. Neither was likely. The Japanese industrial and war machine needed fuel and it was tantalizingly close at hand. The resource rich east indies almost beckoned for invasion. The area was lightly defended and the only major opposition would come from the U.S. and Great Britain. The U.S. Pacific Fleet had to be immobilized as would the British Far Eastern command. The U.S. Navy could be found at Pearl Harbor. Eight months after Kimmel assumed command of the fleet, the Japanese Imperial Navy began planning the Pearl Harbor strike in detail. On September 6, 1941 at a highly secret meeting of the Japanese government's Supreme War Council a plausible scheme had been formulated and the ever declining diplomatic relations with the U.S. forced the plan into reality. By mid November 1941, all was ready and preparations were made for the strike force to sail for Hawaiian waters.

Military operations of the caliber of the attack on Pearl Harbor require extensive and precise planning. This can take several months, so why the rush? The answer was simple; the Japanese oil stocks had fallen to a critical point and action was necessary before supplies would become insufficient for further aggressive action. Several officers close to Admiral Yamamoto had been studying the possibility of such an attack since the beginning of 1941, so much of the conceptual work had been completed by the time a decision was made to move forward. Excitement mounted as more naval leaders were informed of the impending attack. Finally, the U.S. would have to accept the superiority of Japanese arms and show proper respect. With great anticipation Japanese naval staff prepared for every possible contingency. There was little concern for the death and destruction which would certainly come let alone forcing the world into global conflagration. Bitterness over perceived occidental discrimination and interference in expansionist plans overcame all thoughts of what might come from such an action. Destroying the "Yankee Devils" in their lair was an all encompassing conviction. Any feeling of compassion might cause hesitation and impact the fervor of the attack. It was religious and national fanaticism at its worst.

On November 26, 1941, a strike force of six attack carriers escorted by two battleships, heavy cruisers and destroyers left a remote port in northern Japan for the trip to Oahu. They planned to be within air strike range on or about Sunday, December 7, 1941. Fortune was to smile on this force as that particular weekend would mark the first time in several months that the bulk of the battle force would be in harbor. The U.S. fleet's carriers were not available so Kimmel thought it best to retain the battleships in port as a precaution. His flagship had just entered drydock and it looked to be a quiet weekend. It would be peaceful in the harbor, but the bars and fleshpots in Honolulu would be in for quite a time. Little did anyone know that this weekend would be the last spent in peace for years to come.

Float planes from the Japanese cruisers arrived over the target area just after dawn on Sunday, December 7, to confirm the fleet's location and the presence of aircraft carriers. There was some disappointment over the vacant carrier berths, so battleships would have to do. At least

there were eight available for destruction, which was some compensation. At dawn a strike force of 40 torpedo planes (Kates), 43 fighters (Zekes) and 51 dive (Val) and 49 horizontal bombers (Kates equipped as bombers) left the carriers for the first phase of the attack. This force totaled 183 of the 353 aircraft that would eventually take part in the attack. The second wave of 170 aircraft would arrive just before 0900 or an hour after the first wave had struck. It was just before 0800 that strange aircraft appeared overhead and began their morning's work.

CAUGHT IN DRYDOCK: THE *PENNSYLVANIA* ENTERS THE PACIFIC WAR

By design or maybe fortune on December 7, 1941 the flagship of the U.S. Pacific Fleet was situated aft of two destroyers, the Cassin and Downes in drydock number 1. The *Pennsylvania* was undergoing an overhaul and her normal

berth alongside 1010 dock was occupied by the modern light cruiser *Helena* with the ancient minelayer *Oglala* moored outboard. As a matter of fact, a chart was found aboard a captured Japanese two man midget submarine that indicated the *Pennsylvania* and *Arizona* were indeed moored alongside 1010 dock. The *Pennsylvania* was often found alongside 1010 so it was a natural mistake.

The *Oglala* and *Helena* were two of the first ships attacked by incoming aircraft. Just as the *Oklahoma*, *Nevada*, *West Virginia* and *California* were absorbing torpedoes, a "Kate" swept across the channel and launched a torpedo which passed under the *Oglala* and hit the *Helena* amidships. The damage to the *Helena* was substantial but not critical. She was able to regain lost power and begin a spirited defense almost immediately and kept it up throughout the attack. The *Oglala* however was a different story. The old minelayer began to heel over to the port

Sailors take a break on the quarterdeck of the Pennsylvania *by playing in or listening to the ship's orchestra. Each capital ship had a dance band and often a full orchestra. There was keen competition among the bands periodically fought out in "battle of the bands." On Saturday, December 6, 1941, the battleship* Arizona *took the honors in the Pearl Harbor competition.*

Admiral James O. Richardson is relieved by Admiral Husband E. Kimmel as the Commander in Chief of the Pacific Fleet on February 1, 1941. Richardson would not heel to President Roosevelt's insistence that the fleet be used to bait the Japanese. Richardson paid the price of opposing your boss - dismissal.

WE WILL KEEP OPEN THESE DEFENSIVE WATERS---F. D. R.

A news magazine ran this photo and statement by President Franklin D. Roosevelt on September 12, 1941. By this time, the Japanese had settled on sinking the U.S. Pacific Fleet, including the Pennsylvania *pictured here firing a broadside.*

against the *Helena* and had to be moved around behind her to avert further damage to the light cruiser. She finally turned over from ruptured plates. The torpedo that had slammed into the *Helena* had literally sunk the *Oglala*.

The torpedo that hit the *Helena* was meant for the *Pennsylvania*, but her turn was coming. Helpless in drydock, she could however respond with antiaircraft fire. This she did from the outset of the battle. Her 3 inch guns were in action throughout the attack and along with surrounding ships kept many of the Japanese planes at bay. There were a number of misfires and duds from old ammunition. The accepted procedure was to throw the shell over the side, but the ship was in drydock. The worthless shells were stacked neatly near the guns. An intrepid shipyard worker, George Walters quickly manned the large crane above the dock and attempted to ward off the attackers. It interfered with the gunner's aim, but later served to indicate the direction from which aircraft were coming. A bomb finally stopped his contribution, but it proved that sailors were not the only one's defending their ships. Torpedo planes attempted to blow the outer locks of the drydock, but with no success. Later in the attack, Captain Charles Cooke, the stranded battleship's commanding officer purposely flooded the dock to prevent an accidental rupture that would force his ship into the two destroyers lying ahead. Unfortunately, oil fires aboard the *Cassin* and *Downes* spread as the result of the drydock being flooded. This was to cause substantial damage to the two ships.

During the first half hour of the attack, the three occupants of drydock 1 defended their position quite well. They were also virtually ignored except for opportunity strafing from attacking planes coming out of a dive on nearby Hickam Field. The *Cassin* and *Downes* initially responded with 50 caliber machine guns because their 5 inch/38 caliber main batteries were being overhauled. They were soon reassembled and began firing just before 0830.

For the first hour of the attack, the *Pennsylvania* and her two dock mates were spared but as the battleship *Nevada* steamed by the drydock on her famous, though short sortie, all hell broke loose as the Japanese determined to sink the old lady in the channel. The dive bombing Vals diverted from their planned task of destroying the *Pennsylvania* and went after the *Nevada*. Not all did so and just after 0900 an incendiary bomb exploded between the two destroyers igniting oil in nearby tanks. The raging fires quickly spread and the *Cassin* and *Downes* were doomed. Within moments, the *Pennsylvania* was also hit by a 500 pound bomb which detonated in a five inch casemate killing two officers and 16 men. This was just the beginning as bombs came like rain. Most hit the dock or the *Cassin* and *Downes*, but the fallout from one explosion did further damage to the flagship. An explosion aboard the *Downes* threw a half ton chunk of her torpedo battery onto the forecastle of the *Pennsylvania*.

Just as suddenly as it began, the attack was over. For some it had lasted a lifetime, but for others, just a few seconds. No one had ever worked so feverishly as they did from 0800 - 1000 on December 7, 1941. The *Cassin* and

Downes were a shambles. Only parts of them could be salvaged. The *Pennsylvania* was pockmarked with bomb fragments and had taken a bomb hit in one of her five inch casemates. She would have suffered much greater damage and loss of life had it not been for the effective anti aircraft fire thrown up against the Japanese. The flagship had been excused from antiaircraft drill because of her incapacitation in drydock, but this did not deter her officers and men from one of the most credible defenses on that day. They literally saved their ship and the lives of many men. This was especially significant as the ship was low in a drydock and gunner were hampered by impaired viability. Added to their troubles was the fact that power from shore was interrupted. They expended over 50,000 rounds of 50 caliber ammunition and hundreds of 3 inch. Her gunners claimed two definite kills and four probable's. They also broke up torpedo attacks and fended off wave after wave of determined attackers. The crew of the *Pennsylvania* behaved in the best traditions of the Naval Service throughout the attack.

BACK TO THE USA FOR REFIT

The *Pennsylvania* was quickly patched up, exited drydock 1 and was on her way to the Mare Island Naval Shipyard before Christmas 1941. In her place, hull repair to the critically damaged light cruiser *Raleigh* began. The old light cruiser had taken a torpedo and bomb hit that very nearly sank her. Only through skillful damage control and innovative removal of topside weight was the cruiser prevented from sharing the same fate as the upturned *Oglala*, *Utah* and *Oklahoma*.

The *Pennsylvania* remained at the Mare Island Navy Yard from December 29 until March 30, 1942. She underwent repair to the damage suffered at Pearl Harbor and was moderately modernized. Additional antiaircraft capability was finally added and partial shields were installed on her open five inch mounts. One of the earlier versions of radar had been installed prior to the attack and the classic photo of her floating among the debris in drydock number 1 clearly shows the bedspring antenna atop her fore mast. This set was improved during this refit. After leaving the yard the refitted battleship conducted training exercises off the coast of California and the presence of a capital ship did allay the fears of west coast residents who were

The Pennsylvania *shortly after the attack on Pearl Harbor had ended. She floats free in drydock while her dock mates, the destroyers* Cassin *and* Downes, *were nearly destroyed beyond recognition. The Pennsylvania was moderately damaged and was allowed to proceed to Mare Island for repairs within days of the attack.*

The battleship Pennsylvania *after being modernized. She has sixteen 5 inch/38 caliber guns in eight twin mounts that are director controlled. The catapult atop X turret has been removed, and she now carries two Kingfisher seaplanes on her fantail catapult. No longer a majestic ship, she now resembles a floating heavy gun platform. But, no matter what she looks like, she provided valuable gunfire support to troops ashore.*

expecting an invasion at any time. Besides, there was little for a slow moving battleship to do in the South Pacific and sailing to the relief of the Philippines or the East Indies was out of the question. The early days of the Pacific War had witnessed the coronation of a new monarch - the aircraft carrier. The old slow lightly defended battleship was no match for experienced naval aviators. Later classes such as the *South Dakota* and *Iowa* could hold their own, but the prewar battleship would have to find employment other than at the forefront of the battle line. Fortunately, the need for these old dowagers was at hand. The U.S. Navy in the Central Pacific under Admiral Chester Nimitz and the Army in the South Pacific under General Douglas MacArthur would need portable bombardment weapons. If territory seized by the Japanese was to be retaken, it was not enough to bomb them into submission, troops would have to assault enemy positions. They would need heavy support and the old slow heavily armed pre-war battleship was perfect for fire support.

THE SHOOTING WAR BECKONS: THE ALEUTIAN CAMPAIGN AND BEYOND

After what seemed forever, the *Pennsylvania* was called upon for active service. In other words those twelve 14 inch guns would finally be fired. The location was the far north in the Aleutians. On April 23, 1943, the old ship finally left friendly waters for the war. Being tethered to San Francisco for endless months had almost become an embarrassment to a crew that yearned for action, any action. They had watched battered ships limp in from the war zones and return to battle while they rode at anchor or were moored alongside a deserted pier. Until the Aleutian Campaign there was little work for the old battleships. The *Nevada*, *Pennsylvania* and *Idaho* were assigned to join Admiral Francis W. Rockwell's amphibious command which was slated to carry out the assault and capture of Attu Island. Under Admiral Thomas C. Kinkaid, the old battleships with three heavy and three light cruisers would provide gunfire support to the assault force. Air cover was provided by a CVE (jeep) carrier, the *Nassau*.

On May 11, 1943, the landings took place on Attu. This was one of the most desolate and forlorn spots on earth, but it was necessary to the Allied plan for reconquest of territory previously taken by the Japanese. The *Pennsylvania* and her consorts began firing their main and secondary armament in support of the troops, but he Japanese were well entrenched. The shore fire control parties constantly called for fire, especially that provided by armor piercing shells. The Japanese positions were well dug in and heavy gunfire was the solution. For the next few days, the navy provided call fire and finally on May 29, after a suicide charge that decimated the Japanese garrison, Attu was back in American hands. There were many lessons to be learned from this operation, and one involved battleship fire support.

The battleships stood unnecessarily far from shore when delivering gunfire support thus accuracy was unnecessarily handicapped. There were other mistakes as well. Logistical support was poor and army command was inept and dispirited. The victory was not won by the Americans as much as it was sacrificed by the Japanese. These mistakes would not be made in the future. Later in the war, many ships came in virtually to the surf line to deliver call fire to their brothers ashore. One destroyer even ran her bow on a reef close to shore to provide accurate gunfire. Old ways die hard, and Attu was as much a learning exercise as a victory.

Action in this theater was not just fire support for the *Pennsylvania*. She was attacked by a Japanese submarine (I-31) almost upon arrival and had it not been for the warning of a patrol plane, she would have been struck by a torpedo. Aircraft from the *Pennsylvania* also helped in strafing shore positions on Attu.

After a short period in the Puget Sound Naval Shipyard, the *Pennsylvania* was back in the north Pacific, this time for the attack on Kiska. She accompanied the assault force which on August 15, 1943 landed on Kiska unopposed. The Japanese had evacuated the island just prior to the arrival of the American force. The *Pennsylvania* remained in the area for a few days and then was reassigned to the south Pacific. It was time to begin serious island hoping, and the Gilbert Islands was chosen for an opener. The *Pennsylvania* would play an important role in the upcoming attack on the Gilberts code named Operation Galvanic. This operation was massive and a foretaste of what would come in the next two years.

ISLAND HOPING AND BATTLESHIP BOMBARDMENT

Operation Galvanic was divided into separate elements that provided for the assault of Makin Atoll and Tarawa. These were key objective in the strategy of island hoping to the Japanese home islands themselves. These islands had to be taken before others along the path could be secured. Certain Japanese bases such as Wake could be used for target practise and allowed to wither on the vine, but others had to be eliminated to avoid the danger of supply lines being disrupted from the rear. Such were places like Tarawa and Makin. The *Pennsylvania* was to be the flagship of Rear Admiral Richmond Kelly Turner who commanded the Northern Attack Force assigned to capture Makin Atoll. Rear Admiral Harry W. Hill commanded the Southern Attack Force which was to secure Tarawa. To ensure air supremacy several fast carriers were organized into four carrier groups to protect the assault force. Many of the new *Essex* class attack carriers and *Independence* class light carriers were among this force that would provide a massive air defense umbrella. The new ships would be operating with the *Saratoga* and the lucky *Enterprise* or "*Big E*". All in all 200 ships would take part as well as 35,000 plus ground troops supplied with 117,000 tons of equipment and cargo.

The Northern Attack Force arrived off Butaritari Island on the morning of November 20, 1943 and immediately swung into action. They had crept up on the Japanese held island in the night and were ready for the planned dawn bombardment. The *Pennsylvania* opened fire at just over 14,000 yards with her main battery which was quickly joined by her secondary battery of 5 inch guns.

The assault force overcame the Japanese defenders within days and Makin was secured by early afternoon on November 23, 1943. The *Pennsylvania* had shown her worth as a shore bombardment asset, something that her original designers never considered. But, when she was conceived, the *Pennsylvania* was destined to fight other battleships and not plow up coral atolls.

On the day following the capture of Makin, the crew of the *Pennsylvania* bore witness to one of war's tragedies. A huge explosion occurred just off her starboard bow as the light carrier *Liscome Bay* literally erupted. She hapless carrier had been torpedoed by Japanese submarine I-175 which had penetrated the anti-submarine screen. She lived a mere 23 minutes from the time of impact and was ripped apart by a series of explosions and fires from her own munitions supplies. She quickly sank in a steaming mass to a 12,000 foot depth. Although Makin had been secured, the enemy had not disappeared. Aircraft and submarines were a constant threat to the assault and fire support forces. On the following nights a number of attacks were made by Japanese torpedo planes, but with little effect. The next stop for the old battleship was Kwajalein Atoll in the Marshall Islands.

On January 31, 1944, the *Pennsylvania*, *Mississippi*, *New Mexico* and *Idaho* accompanied by heavy cruisers *Minneapolis*, *San Francisco* and *New Orleans* stood off Kwajalein Island and tore it to pieces with 1,340 fourteen inch shells, 400 rounds of eight inch and 5,000 of five inch. Occasionally the bombarding ships would hit Ebeye, a small island near the main island, but most of the heavy gunfire was directed to Kwajalein. Unlike the *Pennsylvania's* first time at bombardment, she stood in quite close to the beach. Some of the fire support ships came in to just over one mile, a distance almost unheard of during prior invasions. It was even said that just before the *Pennsylvania* opened up, a sailor yelled, "Reveille you sons of bitches" which was immediately punctuated with a main battery broadside. For those that lived through the tempest that was brought down, it was to be a day that none would forget.

From the air, Kwajalein is somewhat "C" shaped. The island is small, barely 2.5 miles long, and there is no point higher than a few feet. Lush with swaying palms before the attack, the terrain resembled the moon's surface after the bombardment. By the time the fast carriers strikes had been completed and the primary bombardment by the fire support force was finished, nothing was standing above ground. Mid morning on February 1, more aircraft pounded and strafed the landing sites. It was difficult to imagine that any living thing could withstand the explosions let alone the constant concussion.

The actual amphibious assault was nearly flawless as troops came ashore preceded by preparatory gunfire and followed by equipment and supplies. The capture of the island was not as easy and it would not be until February 5, that the island was secured. Apparently, several defenders had endured the bombardment and air attacks and fought back until overwhelmed by a combination of determined ground troops aided by air and sea fire support.

Interestingly, the old battleship would return to Kwajalein in late 1946 and lie quietly for 18 months before being purposely sunk in deep water. She was one of over 70 ships that comprised the "ghost fleet" Bikini Atoll. As guinea pigs, they endured to one degree or another the fifth and sixth atomic explosions on the earth's surface in July 1946. But in 1944, few outside of a research facility in New Mexico knew that such things were going to happen, and certainly no one aboard the *Pennsylvania* knew of her destiny. All that was known was that a major war was in progress and the *Pennsylvania* was to be an integral part in Allied victory. Her next stop was Eniwetok, also in the Marshall Islands. From February 17-22, she engaged in two major bombardments that seemed to merge into one continuous attack. She hit Engebi Island and then Parry Island with shell after shell from her main and secondary batteries.

The *Pennsylvania* had been rearmed during a recent refit that brought her secondary battery up to that of a more modern battleship class such as the *South Dakota*. In fact, she was now armed with eight twin 5 inch/38 caliber dual purpose guns housed in four mounts per side situated along her midships. These were director controlled and provided a formidable defense against aircraft, shore and seaborne threats. This antiaircraft armament was supplemented with what seemed to be the answer close in air attack - the 20 and 40mm antiaircraft weapon. The *Pennsylvania* was now armed with ten quad 40mm mounts and forty-two 20mm guns. All were well situated on the ship to provide optimum defense. What she might have accomplished had she been this well prepared just two years before.

Other alterations included the replacement of her tripod mainmast with a stump mast and RDF was added for air defense. The turret mounted catapult was removed and she now only had the stern catapult. Of course many of the use's of scout aircraft launched from capital ships had been absorbed by radar and carrier provided combat air patrols, so the *Pennsylvania* was not in need of it's own air force. The scout aircraft did perform many services throughout the war, but eventually they were rendered ineffectual by radar and later by the helicopter. With her new armament and other changes the *Pennsylvania* would fight on. She was never upgraded on the scale that the *California* or *West Virginia* was, but she was also less damaged and able to reenter combat at a much earlier date.

THE WAR STEPS UP: THE ALLIES CLOSE IN ON THE JAPANESE HOME ISLANDS

The *Pennsylvania* had become battle hardened and was dishing out death and destruction with clockwork regularity. After the Marshall Island campaign was finished, she spent a short period in patrol and training but in early June 1944, the assault on the Marianas commenced in earnest. The invasion of Saipan and Tinian was code named *Operation Forager*. The seizure of this territory was integral to the overall strategy of establishing bases for aircraft with reach sufficient to hit the Japanese homeland. Air bombardment on a scale only known to the Germans and the citizens of southern England was about to be visited upon a population that still believed that defeat was not possible. The overall task would consume 535 combatant and

auxiliary ships and over 127,000 ground troops which could tolerate no lack of supplies at any time. The logistics of *Operation Forager* were mind boggling, but carried out with great efficiency and effectiveness. Not the same thing could be said of the initial bombardment carried out by the fast battleships. Heavies of the *South Dakota* and *Iowa* classes began a systematic bombardment on June 13, 1944, but with very poor results. A lot of noise and dirt flying, but it would be up to the old folks to get it right. The new ships were not experienced in shore bombardment like the old reliables'.

The *Pennsylvania* was accompanied by the *Colorado*, *Maryland*, *California*, *Tennessee*, *New Mexico*, *Idaho* and *Mississippi*. It was like old home week, and on June 14, they began shooting at Saipan with their main and secondary batteries. Their scout aircraft were continuously overhead giving correction and battle damage assessment. The ships were getting hits, but when it was over, little had been done to route the defenders. They were not going to give up so easily as in the Marshall Islands.

The *Pennsylvania* fired on Saipan and Tinian for the next several days and finally, she was allowed to withdraw on June 25th, 1944. During this time the Japanese stubbornly defended Saipan and even sent a battle force to fend off the American forces. What actually resulted was the death of the Japanese naval air arm in what would be later known as the "Marianas Turkey Shoot". The Imperial Japanese Navy had never recovered from the loss of four prize carriers at the Battle of Midway, and moreover, had lost the finest of her aviators. From June 1942 until the Marianas campaign, the Japanese had endeavored to rebuild their shattered plusarm, but with little success due to continued war and attrition. The Marianas campaign was a do or die venture for the Japanese and would mark the turning point in their method of winning or even surviving. This engagement would feature the Bushido doctrine and the warrior creed in it's most blatant form but unfortunately for the Imperial Navy, will power and philosophy were no match for the skill and determination of the U.S. Navy. On June 19, 1944, the young aviators of dozen plus carriers shot the Japanese out of the sky. Suffering only 23 lost, the Americans destroyed 315 Japanese aircraft and virtually emasculated their air offensive capability. The next stage for the Japanese would be the Kamikaze.

The Marianas campaign ended when Guam was secured, and although several thousand Japanese troops were holed up in the jungle, the seabees went to work and built a new gibraltar of the Pacific. The old battleships had again proven themselves. On one of the last days of the campaign, July 21, 1944, the *Pennsylvania* came right up to the beach in support of ground troops and was pumping out nearly three salvoes per minute from her main battery. The recapture of Guam and the seizure of other islands in the Marianas was a triumph for American arms and a further testament the value of the old battleship.

After leaving the Marianas, the *Pennsylvania* took up station off Peleliu Island and provided gunfire support from September 12 -15. She fired in support of troops on that island and Anguar Island. On the latter island she devas-

tated enemy gun emplacements and literally plowed a furrow for advancing troops. On September 25, 1944, the well worn battleship was relieved and sent to a floating drydock at Manus in the Admiralty Islands. Repairs were necessary as well as a hull cleaning.

She and five sisters, the *Mississippi*, *Maryland*, *West Virginia*, *Tennessee*, and *California* became part of a battle line under Admiral Weyler and overall as a unit in the fire support and bombardment Group. This group was known as the "old battleships" under Rear Admiral Jesse B. Olendorf. In October they and several cruisers and destroyers were ordered to take part in the invasion of Leyte in the Philippines. General Douglas MacArthur was about to redeem his pledge of returning. He might have left in a plywood PT boat in 1942, but in October 1944, he returned with the most powerful navy and military machine the world had ever known.

THE *PENNSYLVANIA* CLASHES WITH HER OPPOSITE NUMBERS: THE BATTLE OF SURIGAO STRAIT

The invasion force attacking the central Philippines was a massive undertaking. The logistics problems were horrendous as the nearest permanent supply bases were many days steaming time from the objective. In the days that led up to World War II, the Japanese had much depended upon the U.S. Navy being stretched too thin and unable to supply itself for a prolonged campaign far from home. The magnificent job performed by the supply services eliminated that hope. The navy and army came to the Far East to stay until the Japanese were defeated. The supply problems might have been nightmarish, but they were solved. Many forget the value of supply and resupply, but inattention to this vital part of military operations can kill the bravest of armies and lose campaigns that were at first considered simple.

The *Pennsylvania* and her cohorts were detailed to again support amphibious landings, this time at Leyte. They arrived on October 18, 1944 and began preparations for churning up yet an another piece of enemy held real estate. She opened fire on the day she arrived and this continued into the nights until October 22. Her shore bombardment role was about to change as for the first time in her history, she and the other old battleships were about to engage the enemy not on land, in the air or under the sea, but on the surface. The Japanese were throwing in the balance of their surface navy in one last operation designed to throw the Allied forces out of the Philippines and thus out of the inner ring of home island defense. Japanese Imperial General Command headquarters was now convinced that an Allied foothold in the Philippines would enable a strike at Okinawa, the doorstep to their home islands. It was as if the Allies were reenacting the Japanese 1941-42 strategy but in reverse.

The Japanese reaction to the Allied assault, entitled the Sho-Go Plan (*Operation Victory*) consisted of a number of diverse factors including concentrated air attack with a more pronounced introduction of the suicide plane or kamikaze. This type of warfare was expected on a theoretical level, but had yet to be experienced by most ships and sailors. Fighting a man who sought to die rather than to live was a novel experience for all who faced this new and most deadly aspect of naval warfare. In essence, the kamikaze was the world's first mass produced guided weapon. Another major element of the Japanese response was to send it's navy in three separate forces to draw the Allied fleet away from the beaches thus allowing units of the fleet to disrupt the landings. This very nearly worked, but more by accident than by design. At one point during the operation, Japanese capital ships found themselves incredibly within gunfire range of several Jeep carriers or CVE's that were providing close in air support to ground troops. Fortune abandoned the Japanese however, and after inflicting moderate damage, they retired as quickly as they had appeared.

Another of the naval units attempted to force it's way into an area protected by the old battleships. Here the *Pennsylvania* and other Pearl Harbor alumni greeted and helped dispatch their Japanese contemporaries, the battleships *Yamashiro* and *Fuso*. The location was the Surigao Strait and the date was October 25, 1944 in the very early morning hours.

It was known that a force of Japanese ships including battleships, cruisers and destroyers would attempt to ram their way into the Allied backyard via the narrow Surigao Strait. In actuality, there were two battleships, *Yamashiro* and *Fuso*, both armed with twelve 14 inch/45 caliber guns; heavy cruiser *Mogami* and four destroyers. Veteran commander Vice Admiral Shoji Nishimura was in overall command of this force known as "Force C" which was to encounter the Allied defensive line. Rear Admiral J. B. Olendorf, to whom fell the honor of commanding the winning side in the last battleship pounding match probably in world history deployed his ships in a patrol line running parallel to the strait. Everyone was on the alert to avoid another Japanese victory such as occurred at the first battle of Savo Island two years earlier where the Allies lost four cruisers due to negligence.

There was some concern over the ammunition type and actual supply available as the old battleships had been prepared to bombard the enemy held Yap Island. Bombardment required high capacity (HC) as opposed to armor piercing (AP). They would have to make do, however the old girls were not alone. As the Japanese force made it's way into the strait, it would be met and fought by motor torpedo boats (PT's) first and then have to run the gauntlet of a classic torpedo attack by destroyers. The PT boats would also harass the column as it threaded through the strait and keep the rest of the Allied force informed of it's movements.

The cruiser *Mogami* and three destroyers were instructed to take the point and entered the killing zone first. They proceeded in the very early hours of October 25, and although the PT's did their best firing 34 torpedoes only one hit was made on a destroyer. It was now the turn of the first squadron of tin cans under the command of Captain J. G. Coward. His force of seven destroyers went into attack mode and as his two division made one sweep after another fired forty seven torpedoes at the approaching enemy force. He scored with five hits resulting in the sinking of three ships, including the battleship *Fuso*

The Pennsylvania *at the Hunter's Point Naval Shipyard where she is being regunned and modernized prior to the planned invasion of the Japanese homelands.*

which expired some time later. It was incredible, the textbook torpedo attack had succeeded.

Next it was the turn of other destroyers who lie waiting ahead on the flanks. Squadron's 24 and 56 engaged the force as it continued and inflicted further damage. By this time, the Japanese line was ragged and shaken up. The *Fuso* had been hit and was sinking and the *Yamashiro* had been hit. Japanese destroyers *Yamagumo* and *Michishio* had been mortally wounded and were dying. The Japanese were not the only recipients of destruction as they inflicted hits on the Allied destroyers as well. But, the trap had been sprung and it was now time for the old battleships to have their revenge.

At 0353 the battle line began to fire at the remnants of Admiral Nishimura's force that had escaped the "peter tares" and "small boys". By this time, it was only the damaged *Yamashiro* escorted by the heavy cruiser *Mogami* and the only ship to escape, the destroyer *Shigure*. The *West Virginia*, *California* and *Tennessee* which had been extensively modernized had the most modern fire control radar available (Mark 8) and thus were able to engage at long range. These three fired the most shells. Unfortunately, the *Pennsylvania* not equipped with state of the art fire control was unable to fire a shot. Her sisters more than made up for this and in company with cruisers further down the line succeeded in finishing the *Yamashiro* which capsized and sank at 0419, just 26 minutes after she encountered the old battleships. Later that morning, the *Mogami* was caught and sunk by aircraft. The battleships had wrought their revenge, and the last major ship to ship duel in World War II and probably for decades to come had ended. Olendorf had "crossed the enemy T" preceded by textbook precision torpedo attacks by torpedo boats and destroyers. Finally, the battleships had done what they were originally intended for and

with great success. For many, closure had occurred and vengeance was gratifying.

Next stop for the scarred veteran *Pennsylvania* was a return to her more mundane role as a lethal fixture that sits off a coast pounding land fortification into rubble. This she did at Santiago Island off Lingayen in the Philippines in the first days of January, 1945. The war had just eight more months before it would end, but for the *Pennsylvania* her offensive operations were ending at Lingayen. She fired a final 12 rounds at enemy vehicles ashore on January 10, 1945, and then left for the U.S. for overhaul.

LAST SHIP TO RECEIVE MAJOR COMBAT DAMAGE

The tired old warrior which now appeared to be a pre-war battleship with modern weapons grafted on her in various locations entered the Hunters Point Naval Shipyard on March 13, 1945 for a facelift and modernization. This would be her last. Her main and secondary batteries were regunned and the latest in fire control equipment was added. She now fairly bristled with 20mm and 40mm antiaircraft defenses, but traces of her heritage still remained such as the huge tripod foremast with it's large observation box. As she left San Francisco for the forward areas, many sailors probably stopped and marveled at the ancient warrior. Compared to the new *Essex* class carriers, the *Baltimore* class cruisers and of course, the *Iowa* class battleships, the *Pennsylvania* was a relic from the past. A valuable relic, nevertheless.

She left Pearl Harbor on July 24, 1945 to join the rest of the navy it seemed off Okinawa. As a matter of course, she stopped briefly to shoot up Wake island on August 1. Bombarding Wake Island was almost commonplace for American ships and planes on their way east or west. Wake

Tragedy strikes on August 12, 1945, as the aging battleship, Pennsylvania, *is at anchor in Buckner Bay. A "leaker" torpedo plane launches a torpedo that hits her near the stern doing considerable damage. She was pumped out with hoses fed down through the barrels of "Y" turret.*

The aging battleship, Pennsylvania, *just turned turtle and is about to slide beneath the waves. Just four years earlier she had helped desperate Marines wrest Kwajalein from the Japanese and now she would be resting within miles of that island.*

was just another starving Japanese outpost and served well as a place for periodic target practise.

She reached Buckner Bay in early August and anchored in preparation for her next bombardment assignment. On August 12, at 2045, she was hit by a lone air launched torpedo from one of the few remaining Japanese torpedo planes available, and was very nearly crippled by it's effect. Just 59 hours before the war was over, the *Pennsylvania* was settling by the stern and without well planned and executed damage control might still be in Buckner Bay, but on the bottom. She was hit near the starboard outboard propeller. The hit was significant as it also resulted in the death of 20 men and the injury of many others. Even the hero of Surigao Strait, Vice Admiral Jesse B. Oldendorf was injured in the attack. The ship was saved by her crew and two nearby tugs. Ironically, she was the last ship to suffer major damage in the Pacific war. On December 7, 1941, the Japanese had attempted to torpedo her in drydock by attacking the dock caissons, and as if by some twist of fate, she was hit by a torpedo in the stern in the final hours of the war. By the time the damage was contained, and the old ship was out of danger, it was all over. She could go home.

After temporary repairs were made, she sailed for Bremerton and the Puget Sound Naval Shipyard. To compound matters, her number three shaft sheered, and had to be cut loose including the propeller. She arrived in Bremerton slowly, but she arrived. Her end was in sight however. Too old to preserve and not having been modernized, she was consigned to be a guinea pig at the Bikini Atoll atomic bomb tests. She was fitted out and sent to the Marshall Islands, arriving in early July 1946. Moored some distance from ground zero, she survived both blasts, but became highly radioactive. Her service to the U.S. Navy was about at an end, and she was decommissioned on August 29, 1946.

Like so many of her contemporaries, that had survived, she was towed to Kwajalein Lagoon

for study and eventual abandonment. In 1948, she was finally towed to deep water out of the lagoon and sunk. She was rusted, corroded, but still a lady till the end. She had served as the "flagship", and had avenged her sister, the *Arizona*. On February 10, 1948, she began to settle stern first, and eventually turned turtle and disappeared from sight. She had been a great ship served by a great crew.

USS *TEXAS* BB-35
"STILL READY"

Of the fifteen pre World War II operational battleships that served in the U.S. Navy, only two were preserved after World War II. Both are well-known memorial ships. The *Arizona* quietly rests on the bottom of Pearl Harbor, sunk in the first few minutes of the Japanese air attack on December 7, 1941, and the other is preserved in La Porte, *Texas* as part of the San Jacinto Battleground Monument. She is the USS *Texas* BB-35. She is lovingly cared for and in excellent condition. In many respects, she is "still ready".

AN ALL AMERICAN DREADNOUGHT

On June 24, 1910, the U.S. Congress enacted an appropriations bill to build two first class battleships with a budget of $6 million each not including armor and armament. This was standard boiler plate language for this type of act, but there were other conditions that applied to these two ships. Both were to be built by domestic shipyards using only domestic materials (steel) manufactured only by domestic companies. In addition, they were to be built in accordance with new laws relating to wage and hours for workers. In other words, battleship number 34 (*New York*) and number 35, the *Texas* were to be all American ships. And, both were named in honor of two of the most illustrious states in the Union. In order for number 35 to use the name *Texas*, it had to be taken from another ship

A very young Miss Claudia Lyon is about to smash the traditional bottle of champagne against the hull of the brand new battleship Texas. *The* Texas, *like many of her generation, has a ram bow and submerged torpedo tubes, but as of May 18, 1912, she is the latest in naval design. Also, for a brief period, she and her sister, the* New York, *are the most heavily armed ships in the world.*

already part of the navy's inventory. She was a Spanish American War veteran best known for her bold and successful attack on a Spanish squadron commanded by Admiral Pascual Cervera. On July 3, 1898, the Texas, a unit of the American Flying Squadron took four major Spanish ships under fire with her main battery while engaging two torpedo boat destroyers with her secondary guns. All were destroyed and beached by a combination of fire from the *Texas*, *Brooklyn*, *Iowa* and *Glouchester*. What became known as the Battle of Santiago Bay was a stunning victory for an emerging power, which just a few short years before had little or no military and naval standing in the international community. The quick defeat of Cervera's fleet literally forced the door open for Spain's capitulation and the end of the war. After the war, advances in naval design began to take quantum leaps, and soon the *Texas* was obsolete. On February 11, 1911, she was recommissioned the *San Marcos* and a few months later struck from the navy list. This was not the end for the gallant old ship however. She was used a target ship in Tangier Sound in Chesapeake Bay. The "*San Marcos* wreck" as it became known was used for target practice for decades and finally after the Korean War was blown apart as a menace to navigation.

The U.S. Navy, as was the entire world naval community was impressed by the 1906 completion of Britain's newest battleship, the *Dreadnought*. This ship represented the most significant naval event in the early 20th century, yet contrary to popular belief the concept and design of the *Dreadnought* was not solely that of the Royal Navy. The U.S. Navy had prepared diagrams of an all big gun ship in 1904 which ultimately resulted in the commissioning of the *Michigan* (BB-27) and sister battleship *South Carolina* (BB-26) in 1910. The *Michigan* class was actually superior to the *Dreadnought* as it first used centerline superfiring turrets which allowed a full broadside of the entire main battery. The *Dreadnought*, while a breakthrough in warship design held on to some tradition in the form of wing mounted turrets. In any event, the world naval community saw an actual ship in the *Dreadnought* as opposed to American paper plans. Consequently credit has been accorded the British for a design wholly different from any other in the world. It also led the way to a completely new philosophy in sea warfare. The day of the all big gun battleship had arrived,

rendering the mixed battery of guns traditionally mounted on large ships obsolete. This would again change with the need for antiaircraft defense in the future, but in the years that led up to World War I, each nation began to build bigger and more powerful dreadnoughts. Fear of attack from the sky was not a major consideration until the mid point of World War I, and even then the threat was not considered anything more than a nuisance.

The U.S. Navy went through a series of battleship designs and built one class of ship after another, hardly stopping to assess the shortcomings of one class over the latest one in the builder's yards. The *Texas* and *New York* were sandwiched in between the *Arkansas* and *Wyoming* which were built 1910-1912, and the *Oklahoma* and *Nevada* built 1912 - 1916. This was a typical American approach to it's military, in particular the Navy. The U.S. government allowed it's navy to decline into obsolescence and in times of need quickly rebuilt it. This custom of indifferent congressional funding and maintenance pockmarked by rollercoaster naval construction would manifest itself throughout the Twentieth Century. But, in the years surrounding World War I, it was most pronounced. All in all, the U.S. Navy built seven separate classes of battleship (*Arkansas*, *Texas*, *Oklahoma*, *New Mexico*, *Pennsylvania*, *California*, and *Maryland*) from 1912 - 1923. And if not for the Washington Naval Arms Limitation Treaty of 1922, there would have been an eighth, the *Montana* class and two heavily armed battlecruisers. The navy had to rely on it's designers and their opinion as to the stability and relative capability of each class in lieu of hard practical evidence. Fortunately, in most instances, the designers were correct.

The *Texas* class was a logical progression from the *Arkansas* class, which was armed with a twelve gun 12 inch/50 caliber main battery.

The Navy wanted an improved version of the *Arkansas* class which meant a minimum of twelve 12 inch guns in six twin turrets. Adding the sixth turret would mean a greater length for the *Texas* class than was acceptable so another solution had to be found. There were other factors of an international nature to be considered as well. It was suspected that other nations, in particular, Great Britain would be or were secretly building battleships with heavier armament than the *Arkansas*. Consequently, it was necessary to build a viable competitor. Since additional barrels was not the answer, then greater caliber would have to do. The *Texas* class was thus selected to mount the new 14 inch/45 caliber gun in five two gun turrets. This was significant as the U.S. Navy had now graduated to the largest caliber of gun mounted on any ship in any navy. The honor of being first would not last long, but the *Texas* and *New York* were for a short time the most heavily armed ships in the world.

Like the *Arkansas* class, the main battery would be sited on the center line. Wing mounted turrets had gone the way of the horse drawn buggy. The *Texas* and *New York* mounted ten 14 inch barrels as opposed to the twelve guns in their immediate predecessors. Initially, the barrel elevation maximum was 15 degrees, but in a 1940-41 refit, this was increased to 30 degrees enabling the range to be increased to 25,000 yards. The turrets would be arrayed in an A, B, Q, X and Y order, an arrangement not repeated in successive classes. The next class, which included the *Oklahoma* and *Nevada* also mounted the new 14 inch/45 caliber gun but there was no amidships "Q" turret. The location of the "Q" or turret III just aft of the main mast also meant that it's magazine was sited between the engine and boiler rooms, which was highly undesirable due to the heat generated by the propulsion plant. Ammunition and powder storage required a

The battleship Texas *begins her slide down the launching ways at the Newport News Drydock and Shipbuilding Company on May 18, 1912. Just under her second casemate on the starboard side, two torpedo tube apertures can be seen. This launching is believed to be the first moving picture recorded event of its type in American History. over 15,000 people wished the new ship Godspeed and good hunting.*

A stern view of the Texas *in this May 11, 1915 photograph. She was commissioned on March 12, 1914, and had been active in the fleet for 14 months. Her stern mounted 5 inch 51 caliber gun is prominently shown as are her other two aft starboard casemate guns. The gun in the stern proved absolutely worthless and was a throw back to an age that had ended. This was also true, but to a lesser degree for the other casemate guns. She also has an obvious lack of antiaircraft weaponry, but this will come with time and need. However, in 1915, the* Texas *was state of the art.*

A fine view of the quarterdeck of the battleship Texas *just after her two year yard period. Her captain's gig is spotless and has woven fringes for effect. Also, evident is the truss like structure abaft the single stack that houses redundant fire control equipment. The mushroom like protrusions are ventilators.*

cooler area. However, the overall stability of the ship overrode any seemingly minor safety objections. It was considered vital to have a minimum broadside of ten 14 inch guns. Future classes used the triple barrel turret, thus eliminating the problem and still maintaining a sufficiently destructive broadside. Employing the triple barrel turret as a means to delete the "Q" turret was briefly considered as an alternative for the *Texas* class, but discarded in favor of the traditional twin turret.

The *Texas* also mounted twenty one 5 inch/51 caliber guns as her secondary battery defense against destroyers and cruisers. These were sited in hull casemates along her length. There were four near her stern, one in her extreme stern, and four more in her hull just under turret A. Ten were sited amidships in her hull (five to side) and the remaining two were located just aft of turret B at deck level. These were open mounts, the others being enclosed in casemates. As with all battleships that utilized the hull casemate housing for it's secondary battery, bitter experience caused their removal. In a calm sea, the gun ports shipped water and in moderately rough weather, the guns were completely unserviceable. Experience in the North Atlantic also convinced the navy that the open wheelhouse and bridge was not a good idea. Aside from removing some of the secondary battery as a concession to the weather, an enclosed wheelhouse was also built.

In 1918, the *Texas* lost her four most forward 5 inch/51's and of course, the ridiculous gun in her stern. At the time that these guns were removed, a minor, but significant weapon was mounted in the form of additional antiaircraft guns (3 inch/50 caliber). Two would be innovatively sited atop the two midships boat crane king posts. The *Texas* and sister *New York* would keep this caliber of gun throughout their careers, supplementing them with 20mm and 40mm close in air defense guns during World

War II. Most other battleship classes would either be retrofitted with 5 inch/25 caliber or 5 inch/38 caliber dual purpose guns to serve as their primary antiaircraft and secondary battery. When it came to the *Texas* and *New York*, funding for the new five inch dual purpose gun was not available.

The *Texas* class was also fitted with submerged torpedo tubes, two to a side located in the hull below the waterline just aft of turret A. Many battleships of the period were similarly equipped, and some years later all had this capability removed. What seemed such a good idea during World War I, was actually useless.

The *Texas* was shielded with belt armor and the protection design was not that of "all or nothing". This would come on the scene in the *Nevada* class to follow. The "all or nothing" scheme held that the ship's vitals should have the maximum protection possible leaving the rest of ship guarded against shell fragments only. The *Texas* like ships of the very early 20th century were protected throughout, but with less armor over critical areas. Her conning tower had a 12 inch thickness as opposed to the *Nevada* class which had 16 inches. Likewise, the maximum thickness on her turrets was 14 inches compared to the 16 to 18 inches in the *Nevada*. Both classes employed a belt of steel armor along the hull, but the *Texas* had a maximum of 12 inches in the lower belt down to 6 inches in the upper belt. The *Nevada* on the other hand had a continuous belt of 13.5 inches.

The *Texas* was powered by tried and true, but obsolete vertical, triple expansion reciprocating machinery instead of turbine drive which was becoming the power plant of choice in most major navies. The U.S. Navy decided to make a stand on principle with the *Texas* class as it was most concerned with endurance and economy. A modern power had to be able to defend it's possessions, trade and honor at locations all over the world, thus ships had to have a quick turn of speed, but not burn excessive coal. The Navy believed that at cruising speed, the reciprocating engine was a minimum of 30% more economical than a similar turbine power plant. As U.S. manufactures of turbine systems had been unwilling to meet Navy standards, battleships 34 and 35 were fitted with triple expansion reciprocating engines that could produce 28,100 horsepower. The engines were dependent on fourteen Babcock and Wilcox coal burning boilers supplemented with burners capable of burning oil if necessary. She carried up to 400 tons of oil for this purpose, but was not fully converted for over a decade. These were the very last American battleships to be built that depended on coal. The next class was happily oil fired from the outset, and it was not until 1926-27 when the *Texas* went through a major modernization did she too dispense with the hated coal dependency. Coaling a ship, in particular a battleship was the single filthiest duty of a crew. The *Texas* carried 2,892 tons of coal, and aside from covering the ship in coal dust, a coal dependent ship was expensive to operate and labor intensive. Converting to oil meant more than adopting a modern fuel. It meant ease of ship maintenance, upper deck cleanliness, a reduction in engine room staff (and expense), and a more efficient source of power.

The *Texas* could make up to 21.05 knots and develop 28,100 SHP turning two screws. When she did convert from coal to oil, she carried 5,200 tons of oil which gave her a range more than sufficient for extended operations (approximately 15,000 miles).

The battleship was built by Newport News Shipbuilding and Drydock Company in Newport News, Virginia, having her keel laid on April 17, 1911. Slightly over a year later on May 18, 1912, she was launched. She was 573 feet in length and had a 95.25 foot beam. Her mean draught was just under 29 feet, and she displaced 30,000 tons full load. Her complement consisted of 58 officers and 994 enlisted men. This swelled to over 1,500 in wartime. She like most battleships was fitted out as a flagship and for a brief period she was the flagship of the U.S. Fleet and also flagship of Battleship Division 1.

When the *Texas* was commissioned on March 14, 1914, she was a welcome addition to the U.S. Fleet. She was a modern, powerful warship and in a Navy that could only boast of two or at most three ships of any consequence, the *Texas* was a standout. She was also one of the most modern capital ships in any navy, and graphically represented what was to come - the most powerful navy in the world, the U.S. Navy.

CEREMONIES AND JOINING THE FLEET: THE *TEXAS* TAKES HER PLACE

The battleships *Texas* and *New York* were commissioned just as the world was entering one of the darkest periods in it's history. In August 1914, the most devastating war in human history was about to begin and the *Texas* would only be a few months old. She had been launched on May 18, 1912 with a bottle of champagne being broken on her bow by her sponsor, Claudia Lyon, the daughter of a Republican Party boss in *Texas*. The very young Miss Lyon was wearing a white formal dress and a rather large white flower covered hat for the occasion. The ceremony was recorded by one of the earliest moving picture cameras and Miss Lyon shared center stage with the new battleship. It is thought that this was the first time in history that a major ship launching was recorded on movie film. Little did the young sponsor and the 15,000 well wishers know that the massive ship would accomplish so much and 34 years later return to *Texas* soil calling the San Jacinto area her permanent homeport.

After commissioning on March 12, 1914, Captain Albert W. Grant became her first commanding officer. He too would have an illustrious career, attaining the rank of Vice Admiral. The battleship left the Norfolk Navy Yard for New York in late March, 1914 and remained at the New York Navy Yard for three weeks having her fire control equipment installed and calibrated. The fire control system in the *Texas* was a crude undertaking at this time and depended largely on the efficiency of plotting officers and accurate and rapid communications. It was far beyond individual gun laying, but an antique compared with what would become standard in World War II. At least, however, it was a vast improvement over that used just a few years before in the Battle of Manila Bay where a very low percentage of hits were registered comparative to shots fired.

An excellent bow shot of the Texas *as she plays host to 13 admirals and 20 full captains when Admiral Henry A. Wiley assumed command of the U.S. Fleet from outgoing Admiral Charles F. Hughes on November 8, 1927. Change of command ceremonies were always impressive but difficult for the crew who had to maintain the ship in a state of complete cleanliness and polish.*

The Texas *steams majestically under the Brooklyn Bridge toward the Navy Yard. Awnings cover much of her secondary armament, but she is still a formidable but beautiful warship. This photo was taken on June 27, 1928.*

The first real action that the *Texas* was involved in was that of redeeming the honor and respect of the U.S. south of the border in Mexico. Tension had grown between local Mexican officials supported by the ruling Huerta government and U.S. Navy personnel in Tampico harbor. Mexican troops had arrested a boat crew and held them for less than an hour. Apologies were demanded by the Navy and when they were not forthcoming in the exact form prescribed by Admiral Henry T. Mayo, a measured overreaction and use of excessive force was immediate. The "Tampico Incident" gave birth to the opportunity that President Wilson had been seeking to confront the anti-democratic Huerta regime. With congressional approval he sent the Atlantic Squadron to Vera Cruz to mount an expedition in order to properly retaliate for the mistreated boat crew, who now had been martyrized! On April 21, 1914 the force went ashore to seize the customs house and prevent any "contraband" arms from being unloaded. The situation escalated quickly and more warships were summoned to support troops ashore. The *Texas* sailed for Vera Cruz and arrived in Mexican waters on May 26, and remained for over two months. Finally, on August 8, 1914, the new battleship left the area and steamed for the New York Navy Yard. She was there for a brief period and then returned to Mexican waters where she patrolled and served as a station ship until November. She then returned to New York for an extended period of repairs and modifications based on experience gained in her rather unusual combination shakedown/semi-wartime cruise.

For the next two years and into early April 1917, the *Texas* participated in exercises off the east coast of the U.S. This included gunnery practice and various other fleet maneuvers. On April 6, 1917, the U.S. became a belligerent on the side of the Allies against the European Central Powers. For the *Texas*, war with Germany had begun. This unfortunately would be repeated some 24 years later when the U.S. entered World War II.

It was a matter of time before the *Texas* and other coal burning battleships would sail for Eu-

rope. As oil was not available in any real quantity in Great Britain, only those battleships that burned coal were summoned. Before leaving however, she provided training to Naval Armed Guard units selected to ride merchant ships. But, by early Autumn, 1917, Battleship Division 9 which included the *Texas* was preparing to sail for Europe. The outside date for departure was mid November. Unfortunately, the *Texas* would be delayed.

On September 27, 1917 during the mid watch, the battleship ran aground off Block Island and despite all efforts to free her by lightening the ship she remained stuck. Finally on September 30, with the assistance of three tugs, she was able to extricate herself and back free. She spent some time in the Brooklyn Navy Yard having her hull repaired and while there, her crew was detailed to scrape and paint her hull. A double dose of difficulty. Not only the embarrassment of grounding, but having to scrape and paint as well. However, she and her crew were not alone. Many capital ships find their way aground at one time or another. Just a few years later the battleship *Colorado* became part of the landscape for a short period; in 1932, the carrier *Saratoga* touched sand off Los Angeles, yet probably the most famous of all groundings was the battleship *Missouri* in January 1950. The *Texas* was not alone in her predicament.

By December 1917, the *Texas* was repaired and after participating in local maneuvers, sailed for the Royal Navy's great base at Scapa Flo arriving on February 11, 1918 to join the rest of Battleship Division 9. Here she operated with the British Grand Fleet hoping for another great and decisive sea battle. It never materialized as the bulk of the German High Seas Fleet remained tethered to port. The *Texas* did provide escort to several American minelayers as they reinforced the North Sea mine field with thousands of additional mines. By war's end, it seemed almost possible to walk across that body of water on the mines (providing one did not step on the detonating horns!). She also escorted various local convoys and occasionally relieved British capital ships on coastal blockade duty, but there was

no real naval action and would not be until the next war. That war was actually being initiated in 1918, but to the Allies and the crew of the *Texas*, another world war was the furthest things from their minds.

The war was ended with an armistice on November 11, 1918, and the *Texas* was present ten days later for the never to be forgotten scene of the German fleet shamefully sailing to surrender at Scapa flo. In a last gesture of defiance most of the fleet was scuttled by its crews. The *Texas* returned to the *New York* on the day after Christmas, 1918. The "war to end all wars" was over for her.

THE INTERWAR YEARS: TESTBED FOR NEW IDEAS

After returning to the U.S. at the end of World War I, the *Texas* was given a general overhaul plus modernization in accordance with experience gained in the war. Gone were many of the hull mounted casemate guns, the open wheelhouse and inattention to antiaircraft protection. The *Texas* like many of the other battleships in the U.S. Navy was rearmed with 3 inch/50 caliber guns to defend against threat from the air. Granted, the ship was not a antiaircraft fortress, but it was a beginning. There was another beginning as well.

The *Texas* was selected to test the flying off platform. A rather crude contraption was attached to "B" turret for the purpose of allowing an aircraft to be launched. The first airplane selected was a British Sopwith single seat fighter to be flown by Lt. Cmdr. Edward O. McDonnell. In actuality, the aircraft was not launched, it was released and rolled down the platform hopefully into the air and not onto turret "A"! Luckily, at full power with the ship steaming into the wind, the lightweight plane could take to the air quite easily. But, this first flight on March 9, 1919 from a platform on a battleship was significant. It paved the way for the catapult and eventually the use of helicopters aboard modern day warships. Other battleships were mounted with the flying off platform after the success of the *Texas* experiment, and the logical progression to the catapult, seaplane, and recovery system was not far distant. When the *Texas* was refitted over the years 1925-27, she received a catapult on her "Q" turret and one of the first aircraft she car-

The *Texas is taking on fuel from the tanker (or tank steamer)* Kanawha *off North Island in San Diego Harbor in April 1928. At sea refueling had not as yet been developed to the level that was necessary during the upcoming war.*

The *Texas moored in Balboa, Panama on February 15, 1929, after participating in fleet maneuvers designed to test the defenses of the Canal Zone. The Atlantic forces or "blue" fleet headed by the* Texas *successfully thwarted the "black" or Pacific forces. Although much heralded at the time, it was an exercise in futility because the Panama Canal was never to be a military target of value except in the Hollywood cinema.*

ried was the Loening OL-6, a three seat amphibian. By 1928, she carried the Vought 02U-1 Command aircraft, the personal plane of Admiral Henry A. Wiley when he used the *Texas* as the flagship of the U.S. Fleet. By the end of World War II, she had carried a number of scout planes, and her final aviation unit consisted of two Vought OS2U Kingfisher's. She had come a long way from that day in March 1919.

In the summer of 1919, the *Texas* sailed for the Pacific where she would remain until 1924. Also in 1919, the alpha numeric system of identifying battleships was adopted and she became BB-35.

In mid 1924, she returned to the east coast for maneuvers and carrying Naval Academy middies on a training cruise. From this she entered the Norfolk Navy Yard for a massive overhaul and modernization in accordance with the certain conditions of the three year old international naval arms limitation treaty signed in Washington D.C. Aside from having a catapult installed, there were other foundational alterations.

The *Texas*, like sister *New York* was converted from a coal fired ship to one which had six Bureau Express oil burning boilers trunked into one funnel just aft of the forward tripod. Two tripods replaced her lattice masts and a rigid framework of steel legs held up a second fire control tower just aft of her funnel.

In addition, anti-torpedo bulges were added that increased her beam to 106 plus feet, and her midships hull mounted casemates guns were resited on the main deck in sponson like structures. This solved the problem of wetness, but still prevented these guns from firing at any great range.

Her antiaircraft battery remained confined to eight 3 inch/50 caliber guns located alongside the stack and forward superstructure four to a side. This battery would see the *Texas* through

the next war. Additional armor protection was installed to provide improved protection for machinery spaces, and the four hull mounted torpedoes were removed for obvious reasons. In 1927, she came out of the Norfolk Navy Yard, a vastly improved battleship, but in reality, obsolete as a weapons system compared to two other ships also being built - the carriers *Saratoga* nd *Lexington*.

For the next decade she served in the Pacific on and off. Her routine was the same as most of the other fourteen pre-war battleships. Training, exercises, maneuvers and fleet problems. Periodic overhaul and an occasional trip to foreign ports with eager young midshipmen. Her antiaircraft battery was again augmented in 1935 when "bird bath" type structures were attached to the tops of her main and fore masts. These contained 50 caliber machine guns that were for additional antiaircraft protection. Even in combination with her eight 3 inch/50 caliber guns, her defense against aircraft was pitiful.

In 1937, she returned to the Atlantic where she evolved to become the flagship of the Atlantic Squadron, the precursor to the Atlantic Fleet. Here again, she was tapped for experimental work -testing radar. It was also obvious that she was aging and no longer considered front line battleship. There were more modern battleships in the fleet inventory such as the *West Virginia*, *Colorado* and *Maryland* with greater capability, and the new North Carolina class would cause a revolution in battleship design. As it was, the *Texas* and *New York* with older sister *Arkansas* were slowly being put out to pasture, and there was even talk of retirement. For years they had been in the backwaters of fleet operations and baring something major, they would face disposal in the early 1940's. But in 1937, when the *New York* and *Texas* were sought out as test beds for radar, they were still valuable units in the fleet, but just not for first line employment.

Radar had been under study for a number of years before a crude set was installed on the old four piper destroyer Leary. It had been developed by a number of scientists for obvious reasons. In combat, a force that is first to detect an opponent increases it's chance for victory manyfold. The navy spent millions of dollars to design high powered optical lenses and other methods of detection including underwater detection systems or hydrophonics. For many of the interwar years, the scout plane proved ideal for the purpose of seeking out an enemy beyond visual sight of the fleet. This had its limitations however in the form of darkness, foul or rough weather. Something was needed that would see in the dark and at a long range. The use of radio waves that would echo off of a solid target and reflect the image on a screen became the solution or as it became known, radar. In the U.S., the development began in 1922 at the Naval Aircraft Radio Factory in Anacostia. Technicians Leo Young and Dr. Albert Hoyt Taylor discovered what would become the principle of radar and convinced the congress to appropriate funds for further study. For 15 years, Taylor who became known as the "father of radar" and his staff experimented and finally came up with a unit that could be installed aboard a ship. The Leary was chosen. The unit was an immediate success and it caused the Navy to allow further testing, but on a grander scale. Accordingly, in early 1939 one set, a XAF was installed in the battleship *New York* and the other variant, a CXZ was mounted in the *Texas*. The unit in the *New York* proved to be far superior to that in the *Texas*. In fact, the set installed in the *Texas* was considered almost worthless. Although the captain of the *Texas* was critical of the CXZ, he whole heartily supported further development. All who observed radar, even in it's infancy knew that it would soon be perfected and quickly revolutionize modern warfare. The combination of radar and the airplane would cause the coming war to be like nothing that anyone anticipated.

NEUTRALITY PATROL: THE WAR BEGINS FOR THE LONESTAR STATE WARRIOR

Events in September 1939 ensured that the old battleships would have full employment for years to come. Just over two decades since the Germans signed the Armistice, they were again engaged in a World War. To many, it was the continuation of a war that was never really finished, but to the youth of Europe, it was a brand new experience, it was their war.

Most of the capital ships in the U.S. Navy were based at San Pedro in California. They were there as a political show of force and intent to the Japanese. For the U.S. war was anticipated in the Pacific. The older battleships in the fleet's inventory were based in the Atlantic either providing training to new sailors or carrying midshipmen on summer cruises. Since 1938, the *Texas* had been the Flagship of the Training Detachment, U.S. Fleet. On September 6, 1938, Admiral William D. Leahy, the Chief of Naval Operations established the Atlantic Squadron which consisted of seven cruisers and seven destroyers, and it was long before some real muscle was added. Without any public fanfare, Battleship Division 5 which consisted of the *Texas*, *New York*, *Arkansas* and *Wyoming* became part of the new Squadron. While Europe was hanging on to the myth of "peace in our time", the U.S. Navy was not deceived. Preparations for a renewed Atlantic war began in earnest. The Navy would guarantee safe travel for commerce and U.S. citizens by guarding the sea lanes. It would also support it's traditional allies against the emerging Axis powers. When war broke out in September 1939, the *Texas* as well as the Atlantic Squadron began patrol activity dubbed the "Neutrality Patrol".

The neutrality patrol was ordered by President Roosevelt on September 5, 1939, just two days after war began in Europe. Three days later, also in response to the war, the President also issued a proclamation of limited emergency that immediately began to strengthen the Navy. An increase from 131,485 enlisted naval personnel to 145,000 was authorized as well every available ship was to be activated for the duration of the emergency. Forty recently decommissioned destroyers were returned to service and the Atlantic Squadron became more than a paper tiger. This action by the President also saved four old battleships including the aging *Texas* from decommissioning and scrapping. All would be needed for the upcoming war at sea.

The *Texas* assumed continued duties of training, but now included were escort cruises for

Reservists board the 23 year old battleship on August 14, 1937 for a training cruise to the Virgin Islands. By this time in her career, she had been withdrawn from first line service and was on one training assignment after another.

Midshipmen board the Texas *for a training cruise in 1939. At this time, there was talk of retiring the old battleship. Her day had passed, and with the new* North Carolina *class of heavy battleship, there was little need for slow 14 inch gunned ships with obsolete AA defense and out of date electronics.*

merchant ships on their way to Great Britain. Her area of operation was bitter, ice ridden, and the seas were without pity. As 1939 became 1940 and into 1941, the Germans became more belligerent and the U.S. Navy responded in kind. By the summer of 1941, attacks were being made by both sides, and on June 20 of that year, the *Texas* was tracked by U-203 for some 16 hours. This took place between Greenland and Newfoundland and if had not been for the *Texas* obeying zig-zag procedure, she would have come within the sights of U-203 and probably taken a spread of torpedoes. This information became known after the war when German Navy records became available. The *Texas* is named in the German Submarine Command Diary of U-203 as well as the obvious disappointment of the U-

Boat commander. Of course, had the *Texas* been sunk, it might have accelerated a declaration of war on Germany.

The formal entry of the U.S. in World War II after the Japanese attack on Pearl Harbor on December 7, 1941 found the *Texas* at anchor in Casco Bay, Maine. Her crew was enjoying one of the few respites since the European War began. Within days, however, the *Texas* was back on duty as a convoy escort. Her primary function was not to fight the U-Boat, but to provide heavy gunfire support against German surface raiders. As long as there was at least a cruiser or a battleship escorting a convoy, then surface raiders remained in port. The threat of a surface raider was very real however, as the experience of the *Bismarck* was still fresh in recent memory.

For much of 1942, the *Texas* escorted various convoys to all points in the Atlantic and occasionally the Caribbean. She also patrolled off Iceland and other areas. During this period she also spent time in shipyards having her antiaircraft battery upgraded. Her 50 caliber guns were removed and numerous 20mm and 40mm guns were sited at locations all over the ship. Modern air and surface search radar was installed and by the time she was selected to participate in *Operation Torch*, the invasion of North Africa, was almost state of the art. She was an obsolete battleship, but with modern radar and effective antiaircraft defenses, she was an important asset to the fleet. *Operation Torch* would inaugurate a new role for the *Texas* and the other older capital ships in the European theater of operations - bombardment support for amphibious operations.

OPERATION TORCH: THE TEXAS PLAYS BALL

It was the turn of the Allies to move over to the offensive. Throughout 1942, they had suffered one setback after another, and the Soviets were demanding that a second front be initiated to demonstrate that the U.S. was more than just a massive supply dump. They were also demanding this action because they knew that the Germans would have to divert troop and resources away from their theater. An attack, and not just a Dieppe or St. Nazaire Commando raid was necessary. In the overall scheme of things, the Allies settled on North Africa as the place to begin winning the war. The Allied strategy was actually somewhat simple and had it's roots in ancient history. North Africa would be seized and occupied allowing an assault to be made on Italy via Sicily. Italy was the "soft under belly of Europe" as Winston Churchill named it. Later a cross channel (English) assault would be made at any of several French ports and forces driving from Italy would join with those entering through western France. In combination with the Soviet juggernaut, the Allies would literally swamp the Axis defenders. It would probably take up to ten years, but by 1952, Allied victory was assured! First, there was North Africa.

The Allied invasion of North Africa was scheduled for early November 1942 and it was one of the most tightly held secrets of the war. The U.S. would contribute a massive assault force complete with amphibious ships, heavy warships and air support. It was divided into three elements, southern, central and northern attack groups. The Northern Attack Group was under the command of Rear Admiral Monroe Kelly who flew his flag in the venerable old *Texas*. Finally, she was going into real combat as a flagship. The group also included the light cruiser *Savannah*, which would distinguish herself in this action as would a number of supporting destroyers. The old four piper destroyer *Dallas* was also in this force and she and her crew would win a Presidential Unit Citation for an incredible act of bravery and skill. She carried specially trained army *Rangers* up the Sebou River to Lyautey where they were to seize and hold the port. There was some difficulty getting up the river as it was flowing at approximately 20 knots, and the maximum speed of the old *Dallas* was 25 knots. Her

real speed over ground was only 5 knots consequently, the time she was in danger was much greater than anticipated. She finally succeeded in delivering her charges, but the experience was harrowing.

The army command was under Brigadier General Luscian K. Truscott, who would win acclaim throughout his tenure in the European theater. The assault force totalled 526 officers, 8573 men and 65 light tanks. The army units were handpicked for this task and all of their training and skill would be necessary to the success of this operation.

The hour of decision was set for 0400 on November 8, 1942. The command to open fire or commence operations was "play ball". This was dependent on the reaction of the Vichy French military forces who were known to be manning beach defenses. It was well known that there were shore batteries in the Mehdia and Port Lyautey, the area staked out for the Northern Attack Group. Whether there would be active resistance was the big question. Very early on November 8, army Rangers and other troops began to find their way ashore and with inconsequential opposition, seized their objectives. Finally at about 0600, a shore battery opened up on the destroyer *Roe* which was patrolling inshore. A ship versus shore battery duel began with no real results. At 0630, a broadcast was made from the *Texas* to the French asking them to cooperate with the Allies and join in the fight against the Axis. They did not heed the plea for sanity and resistance began to which the Northern Attack Group replied with, "play ball". The *Savannah* began shooting up one target after another with great success and the *Texas* took on an ammunition dump some nine miles inland. A short time later the *Texas* was again called upon to provide call fire. This time it was to halt the escape of a number of Vichy army vehicles near the airfield and after laying down 214 fourteen inch shells at a range of 17,000 yards, the problem was solved. No more vehicles left the area. After this incident, Admiral Kelly aboard the *Texas* again broadcast a message. This plea which included the announcement that the fort at Mehdia and the local airfield were in American hands brought no response except continued resistance. Finally at about dawn on the following day, all objectives had been taken and were secure. It had been quite a battle, and the *Texas* had been right in the middle of one of the first American amphibious victories. Much of the battle had been observed by a young news correspondent, Walter Cronkite. He left the ship just three days before she departed for home. Another soon to be famous writer, Samuel Elliot Morrison was part of *Operation Torch* as an observer aboard the light cruiser *Brooklyn*.

For the next week the *Texas* was occupied with call fire missions to support troops ashore. On November 15, her role in *Operation Torch* was at an end and she departed for the U.S. as part of a force that included the blooded cruiser *Savannah*. Interestingly, much was learned from this operation. In the South Pacific just three months earlier, the Marines had stormed ashore at Guadalcanal after a pre-invasion bombardment. Granted, it was not on the scale of bombardments in future campaigns, but it was preliminary to the landing. There was no such pre-

invasion bombardment allowed by the army in *Operation Torch* so as to preserve the element of surprise. This proved to be false precaution. Had the *Texas* and other capital ships plowed up the ground near the invasion points, then radio broadcasts might have had more effect. Later invasions would take advantage of pre landing bombardments. Pulverizing a beachhead was deemed more valuable than surprise.

The *Texas* again became a convoy escort and for most of 1943 and into April 1944 she visited ports in the Mediterranean an all over the Atlantic. She became a familiar sight for merchantmen and as long as the *Texas* was in your company, no surface raider would dare attack. But, in April this role was terminated and it was time to flex her muscles. The much heralded but secret invasion of Europe through western France was at hand and the services of *Texas* were required.

THE GREAT CRUSADE: THE BATTLESHIP TEXAS PAVES THE WAY

One of most significant moments in the history of mankind was undoubtedly the invasion of Europe code named "*Overlord*". Adolf Hitler, a tyrant and butcher had enslaved millions of people for half a decade and was also responsible for the murder of over six million Jews for none other than a political whim and inborn racial hatred. He was also directly accountable for a war that had encompassed the entire world and eventually would cost the lives of nearly 60 million souls. The invasion of Europe by the Allies was an absolute necessity in World War II. It had to occur when it did, in mid 1944. Had it been attempted in 1942 or 1943, the probability of success was less than 50%. Pinprick raids such that were mounted at Dieppe and later St. Nazaire on the French coast proved the fallacy of mounting a campaign with anything less than total commitment and overwhelming superiority of arms. In June 1944, total commitment, desire to win, combat experienced leadership, and resources were now available.

The *Texas* and the other solid, but ancient battleships *Arkansas* and *Nevada* became pawns in a power play between Admiral Earnest King, Chief of Naval Operations and the overall planners for the invasion. King felt that the Royal Navy was quite capable of providing the required fire support and all but refused to allow American battleships to be assigned for gunfire support as part of the Western Naval Task Force. He had been just adamant about landing craft availability, but this was eventually worked out. The issue of allocating battleships and destroyers was resolved only after Admiral John L. Hall, an amphibious force commander loudly voiced his complaint at a party which caused some embarrassment to the navy. The battleships were thereupon quickly reassigned to *Operation Neptune* or as it came to be more popularly known, *Overlord*.

For about seven weeks, the *Texas* prepared for her role in the largest invasion ever attempted by any nation or group of nations. She was even paid a visit by General Dwight D. Eisenhower on May 19, 1944, just two weeks before the big show was about to begin. June 6, 1944, or D-Day found the old battleship ready and willing to do her part to ensure that the Allies succeeded in this first step of the "great crusade". The *Texas* was the flagship of the bombardment group assigned to Omaha Beach. Admiral C. F. Bryant flew his flag in the old battleship and at 0400 she was about 12,000 yards off the beach near Pointe du Hoc. At 0550 she began a systematic bombardment with her main battery and her secondary battery opened fire on a nearby ravine which was pockmarked with enemy defenses. This initial bombardment lasted just over 40 minutes. The *Texas* was attempting to reduce the heavy shore battery said to exist at Pointe du Hoc. Failure to eliminate this enemy battery would mean that the beachhead would be seriously threatened with heavy gunfire. Contrary to the prevailing belief of the Army Air Forces, there were many targets that only a sea borne bombardment or determined ground troops could destroy. The battery reputed to be emplaced at Pointe du Hoc was such a target. The air force had hit it three times prior to the invasion and then it was the turn of the bombardment ships and an Army Ranger Battalion. The *Texas* fired 250 fourteen-inch shells at the target and literally churned up the soil on top and along the 120 foot high cliffs. The *Ranger*s assaulted the cliffs and during the day made it to the top. It was not until 1130 on June 8, that the American flag was seen flying above Pointe du Hoc. The *Texas* had done her part but returned during the fiercest part of the battle to supply the Rangers with food and ammunition. A combination of arms from the air, land and sea had overcome what was considered the most dangerous shore battery in "fortress Europe". Unfortunately, it was all for naught. The much feared guns were not in place and only telephone poles which simulated guns were to be found. The bravery and valor of the Rangers and the bond forged between ground-pounder and sailor will never be forgotten.

While helping to prepare the way for the *Ranger*s in the early phase of the D-Day invasion, the *Texas* was also shooting at critical Nazi defenses adjacent to an exit road at the Western end of Omaha Beach. She fired 190 rounds of 5 inch at her assigned targets, but in order to satisfactorily destroy her objective, double the amount would not have been sufficient. The Army had a mind set far different from the Marine Corps or Navy who thoroughly supported massive pre invasion bombardment. It would cost them in men and material. Throughout the day, the *Texas* and other ships were continually called up for surgical bombardment missions to help advancing troops. Destroyers such as the *McCook* DD-496, *Thompson* DD-627, and *Baldwin* DD-624 literally ran themselves on the beach to provide much of the only artillery support the desperate troops received. Many of the artillery pieces and tanks were either bogged down or lost, so the navy became a field artillery understudy.

Omaha Beach was a nightmare and the planned for call fire spotters that were to have been inland had to be replaced by Royal Air Force Spitfires that spotted for ships like the *Texas*. She was steaming at ten knots off the beach and her gunnery officer, Lt. Cmdr. Richard Derickson continually received coordinates from the low flying spit's. She interdicted and destroyed reinforcements that surely would have further hampered the beleaguered invasion troops. By the end of June 6, the *Texas* had expended 421 fourteen inch shells and 254 rounds from her ancient but still lethal five inch casemate guns.

This was to continue up through the 15th of June but particularly in the days just after the landings. The *Texas* as well as other bombardment vessels virtually prevented a German counter attack and allowed the invasion forces to breakout of their beachhead. At one point, the *Texas* even flooded her starboard blisters to give her main battery an additional two degrees of elevation to increase her 20,000 yard maximum accurate range. There was nothing this ship and the others in the bombardment group would not do for their brothers ashore. History would have been indeed different if it had not been for the ancient ships and their dedicated gunfire support. Both heavy and small ships fully justified their existence, and many a soldier owes his life to a sweating gunner or low flying RAF pilot who guided the way for the immense punishment dealt by ships like the old *Texas*. Next stop, the Port of Cherbourg.

CHERBOURG: THE *TEXAS* BECOMES THE TARGET AS THE GERMANS SHOOT BACK

By mid June 1944, the ground offensive has moved inland to a distance beyond the range of naval gunfire, but there were other significant targets within range. The next was Cherbourg and it's magnificent port. Storming the beaches at Normandy and establishing a temporary harbor was a matter of military expediency, but supplying a long term campaign was quite another. For this and future operations, a suitable port with major facilities was necessary. Cherbourg on the Normandy coast near the invasion points was ideal and had to be seized, and quickly. As it was not possible to do this simply with ground troops pivoting from their forward assault into France, it became necessary to mount another naval bombardment and render the port untenable for the German defenders. This was one of those decisions that occurred after the overall plan had been formulated. Accordingly, the *Texas* accompanied by *Arkansas*, several destroyers and minesweeping squadrons sailed for Cherbourg to take up station on June 25. Another unit consisting of the *Nevada*, cruisers *Tuscaloosa, Quincy* and Royal Navy ships was also selected to participate in this hastily conceived operation.

On June 25, 1944, the Allied Naval forces arrived to confront shore batteries that consisted of a minimum of 20 casemate enclosed guns, many of which were in the 150-280mm caliber. Also there were many 75 and 88mm mobile guns. The German ground strength was estimated to be 40,000 defenders in Cherbourg and strung out along the Cotentin Peninsula leading up to the port. The Navy was to neutralize the batteries, but for the first time since *Operation Torch*, the ships would have a relatively evenly matched contender. The guns at Cherbourg, particularly those at "Battery Hamburg" had a range of up to 40,000 yards and could fire through a wider arc. It was identified as target 2, and the plan was for the battleship *Nevada* to silence the battery while the *Texas* and *Arkan-* *sas* remained in "Hamburg's" blind side. The *Nevada* did not fulfill her end of the bargain as she had other more pressing duties. Consequently, the *Texas* and *Arkansas* blithely sailed within range of this formidable battery. The *Texas* was in the lead and nothing happened. It appeared as though the German gunners were already dead or had abandoned their posts. Before noon, the *Arkansas* began a slow bombardment and as the afternoon began, the *Texas* followed the minesweepers as they searched for mines. The Germans were not dead nor afraid nor gone. They were just waiting for an opportune moment. They began shooting at the bombardment force, not hitting the *Texas*, but making a perfect three shot straddle. They did hit the new Sumner class destroyer *O'Brien* DD-725 doing moderate damage and killing thirteen men. Her captain, William Outerbridge, formerly captain of the destroyer *Ward* DD-139, which had fired the first shot of the war on December 7, 1941, quickly retired to check the condition of his ship. At a quarter past one in the afternoon, Battery Hamburg began to get the range and then hit the *Texas* with a 280mm shell that glanced off the conning tower but killed the helmsman and wounded eleven. She was hit again later with an armor piercing shell that failed to explode. This hit was of particular interest as no one knew of it's existence until it was discovered by an officer in his stateroom resting next to his bunk. It had entered the ship unannounced and found a home without waking the landlord. The shell was removed without further incident. All in all, she was straddled or near missed 65 times during this duel and succeeded in destroying one of the four heavy guns with a direct hit that penetrated the enemy casemate. The veteran ship had fired 206 main battery shells during the confrontation. Just after 1,500, she was ordered to retire, but to her went the credit for distracting the batteries and allowing American troops to successfully attack the Germans. She arrived back in Plymouth, England for temporary repairs and within weeks sailed for the Mediterranean, and her last operation in the European theater of operations. Southern France had to be invaded and no invasion would be complete without bombardment ships like the *Texas*.

SOUTHERN FRANCE, HOME AND RETURN TO THE PACIFIC

Southern France was to be invaded primarily by American forces and the Eighth Fleet was to provide fire support. As this fleet had only light cruisers such as the *Philadelphia* to provide firepower, it was necessary to solicit the services of the old reliables, *Nevada, Arkansas* and of course, *Texas*. The area to be attacked was divided into four components, Sitka, Alpha, Camel and Delta. Overall, the Operation was code named *Dragoon* and it was to take place between the French resort area near Nice and the great Naval city of Toulon on the coast of Provence. Actually, it was in the area of the French Riviera. The date set was August 15, 1944.

The Allied force assigned to the area designated as Delta consisted of the *Nevada, Texas*, light cruiser *Philadelphia* and five cruisers of the Free French Navy. Gunfire support consisted of bombardment and counter battery fire against German defenders. Shipborne fire support lasted only just over 1.5 hours and then the famous "Thunderbirds" of the 45th Division stormed ashore. This division was primarily native American in composition and some of the finest soldiers in the army. Now they found themselves facing sporadic and dispirited resistance in the middle of Europe's playground. Quite different from the rugged terrain they were used to in other parts of Europe. The battle ended quickly with few casualties and after only two days of fire support the *Texas* left the area, eventually homeward bound. She reached New York on September 14, 1944 and underwent a period of upkeep and repair that included having her main battery barrels replaced. By November, she was on her way to the Pacific and the last great battles of World War II.

As a postscript to her service in Europe, it has rarely been said, but widely known that then Army would have not triumphed had it not been for ships like the *Texas*. As the campaigns materialized, land commanders were continually cautioned about the limitations of battleships. They were not originally designed for gunfire support, but for violent, but limited duration ship to ship combat. Their barrels wore out quickly and although they were a Godsend to troops ashore, they could only do so much. Even with their limitations they went to the extreme to ensure a successful operation. The navy did not received the formal credit it deserved for the dependable support provided by ships like the *Texas*, but every soldier trying to break out of Omaha Beach or storm Cherbourg will forever remember their comrades afloat.

Back in the Pacific, the *Texas* arrived in the Marianas in February 1945 and began an abbreviated work up for her role off Iwo Jima. On February 16, 1945, she began a rolling bombardment of selected targets on Iwo Jima in preparation for the landings that were to take place on the 19th. Unlike Europe, she did not bombard just for an hour before the troops landed, but for up to 72 hours. When the Marines went ashore on February 19th, she then took up station in a call fire mode. She remained off Iwo Jima for two weeks and provided gunfire support when needed. Her next stop was back to Ulithi to begin preparation for the Okinawa invasion. The Allies were now taking the war to backyard of the Japanese, and they were not going to allow this without a fight, and a fight to the death.

The *Texas* was again assigned to provide 14 inch gunfire support to Marine and Army units, and she began this on March 26, 1945. This time it was to be for six days prior to the actual ground assault. Off Okinawa, the *Texas* faced another threat and this was from the air. The Japanese were in the last stage of desperation and used the suicide plane or kamikaze to advantage. The *Texas* was ultimately responsible for shooting down one of her attackers and assisting in the destruction of three others.

On April 1, the ground troops went ashore, but did not meet any real resistance initially. Later, the battle to secure Okinawa was one of the most violent and bloody of the war, on land and sea. The *Texas* remained on station for two months providing support to ground units. In

The Texas *in Havana harbor just before the beginning of World War II in this 1940 photo. She now has the birdbath atop each mast with 50 caliber guns for AA defense.*

The Texas *plays host and nursemaid to a number of Italian and German prisoners captured during the invasion of Normandy on June 6, 1944. None were happy, and a few were seasick.*

mid May, she left for a minor overhaul in the Philippines and began preparations for the final assault on Kyushu, the home islands of Imperial Japan. This assault which was to be the largest attempted in the war never took place. It was intercepted by the capitulation of the Japanese government after major cities (Nagasaki and Hiroshima) were subjected to atomic bomb attacks. The Japanese surrendered on August 5, 1945, and the war was over for the *Texas* and millions of soldiers, sailors and civilians. The importance of the *Texas* as a warship was at an end also. She transported troops home from the forward areas throughout the autumn and early winter of 1945, and on January 21, 1946, she began her voyage to Norfolk and inactivation. She remained there for two years being kept out

of the fleet destined for the atomic tests in the Marshall Islands. Had she went to Bikini, she would now be on the bottom of that lagoon or at the bottom of the Pacific after being used as a target. In any event, she would not be on display. Thanks to the State of *Texas* and the State Department of Parks and Recreation, the old battleships ended up as a memorial ship at San Jacinto State Park at La Porte, Texas. On *Texas* independence day, April 21, 1948, Admiral Chester W. Nimitz, a native of Fredericksburg, *Texas* officiated at her decommissioning and dedication. There today she can be found, the oldest and boldest of the pre-World War II battleships. Her final voyage was a pleasant one, from Norfolk to La Porte, Texas. In many ways, she is "still ready".

The aging battle ship Texas *brings a large number of military personnel back from the forward areas in October 1945. She made three additional trips carrying grateful troops home. This was her last official assignment for the United States Navy.*

The Texas is being towed to her home state after being acquired by the State Department of Parks and Recreation. She left Hampton Roads on March 17, 1948 for her final voyage. She was transferred to the State of Texas to become part of the Texas Independence Monument at San Jacinto.

An excellent view of the Texas as she is being towed home to La Porte where she will exist as a memorial and the only remaining pre World War I battleship still in existence. Note the Texas "lone star" flag at her foremast.

The Texas at her permanent home in La Porte, Texas. Thousands of visitors inspect the great ship each year. She is a tribute to the American sailor and the indomitable spirit of the U.S. Navy.

CHAPTER IV

THE CARRIERS

USS *CABOT* CVL-28
"THE IRON WOMAN WHO WILL ALWAYS BE A LADY"

MEMORIAL SHIPS: IT TAKES MONEY MORE THAN LOVE

The heritage of the U.S. is preserved in a number of ways, and one very popular method is that of acquiring, housing and maintaining former U.S. Navy warships for public display. Most come from the U.S. Navy, but a few, like the former World War II light carrier USS *Cabot* CVL-28/Spanish Navy Ship (SNS) *Dedalo* are acquired from foreign owners. It is a way of allowing future generations to understand war at sea and how it has changed from the mainbrace to microchip. But, another more powerful motivation for saving these old ships is to allow veterans a second chance opportunity to rekindle that spirit that caused them to first willingly serve their country. Ironically, it is that deep nostalgic commitment that can at once produce immediate and seemingly unlimited success, yet at the same time act as a blinder to reality.

To date there are over fifty memorial ships in locations all over the U.S. ranging from everyone's favorite, the USS *Constitution* launched in 1797 and now located in Boston, Mass, to the now internationally renowned World War II Liberty ship, *Jeremiah O'Brien*. The *O'Brien* makes her home port in *San Francisco*, but the aside from the continent separating these two ships, there is a much greater gulf between them. The *Constitution* is still a commissioned ship of the U.S. Navy, and derives her financial support from the congress, yet the *O'Brien* must depend on private support. The difference between government support and private backing is vast. One requires the annual vote of the U.S. Congress, but the other demands continuous

maximum effort on the part of the foundations or non-profit organizations that have assumed responsibility for the ship. Every day is a struggle to survive, and once attainable government largesse is becoming a resource of the past. Given the choice between crime reduction and ship preservation, the average citizen will pay for increased police protection. Consequently, survival means raising and properly administering large sums of money from many personal and corporate sponsors as well as operating gift stands and developing various fund raising programs. The emphasis is on money and proper administration - if either is absent, failure is assured.

THE USS *CABOT*/SNS *DEDALO* - BACK TO THE USA

In 1989, Louisiana business people began exploring the notion of bringing an aircraft carrier to a major metropolitan center in order to sustain the ship's preservation and at the same time provide revenue to the region. The idea had some merit and heart-rending appeal and within months of the idea taking root, Spain was convinced to donate their aging fleet carrier, the SNS *Dedalo*, formerly the USS *Cabot*, CVL-28 to a syndicate in New Orleans for $550,000 to cover fuel and other costs for the ship's return voyage. A dream was about to come true. Formal approvals from the Spanish government as well as the U.S. State and Navy Department's were quickly obtained. In retrospect, securing the *Cabot* from the Spanish Navy was the easiest part of the plan, but within days of her arrival in New Orleans, the luck that brought life to the scheme evaporated. Those who had initiated the transfer saw that a fatal error had been made, and reluctantly withdrew from the project. It was simply that the *Cabot/Dedalo* had crossed the Atlantic on a thick carpet of emotional commitment and there it ended. Shortly after the welcoming ceremonies were completed and the Spanish crew had left for home, reality blinded by nostalgia came into focus, and the unpaid bills

began to mount. No one had counted on having to pay the high costs of dockage, insurance, security, public liability, office administration, and heaven forbid, repair and maintenance. The hastily formed *Cabot/Dedalo* Foundation had no long term resources to support their ship, and in desperation they looked to less than honorable sources of income. There was talk of using the ship for a gambling casino to raise revenue, but an upon hearing of this, Spain, who had graciously consented to donate the ship issued a strong protest. U.S. Marshals even seized the innocent ship to force payment of outstanding debts. Had they been living, past naval aviators and one time *Cabot* passenger, war correspondent Ernie Pyle would have cried in outraged shame.

So for a while, the rusting carrier was tied to a public dock awaiting some form of income to begin her role as a combined U.S. Navy/Spanish Navy memorial to carrier aviation. Old salts spent days and nights aboard attempting some maintenance and renovation, but the work was uncoordinated and without a solid source of funding, the ancient carrier was becoming just another rusting eyesore along the Mississippi River. To add insult to injury there were reports of pilferage, theft of artifacts, and items sold for the personal gain by some of those who purported to work on the ship. There was even an incident where some individuals masqueraded as high ranking naval officers and dressed the part. When asked about their background, one claimed that he had graduated from the U.S. Naval Academy night school degree program! Things had gotten out of control and the *Cabot* was no longer a major U.S. warship being used as a historic site - she was becoming known as the "ship of fools".

As a temporary reprieve, The U.S. Congress was convinced to appropriate $2 million from the Department of Defense budget, and this was sufficient to allow the ship to be drydocked in a local shipyard. Her hull was sandblasted and painted. The money also covered a substantial renovation including mandatory federal Environ-

The light cruiser USS Cleveland *at sea shortly after being commissioned. The light carrier* Cabot *and eight sisters of the cruiser-carrier* Independence *class were built over the hulls and power plants of the* Cleveland *class light cruiser.*

The USS Cabot *CVL-28 is launched on April 4, 1943 by the New York Shipbuilding Corporation yard at Camden, New Jersey. Her flight deck is still incomplete, and the four square funnels are visible on the starboard side.*

mental Protection Agency asbestos removal down to deck level three. As she came out of the yard, the *Cabot/Dedalo's* see/saw fortune seemed to change for the better. A Louisiana State level commission was formed to secure a permanent berthing and visitors center, and revenue was diverted ($1.5 million) from the New Orleans hotel tax as seed money. The *Cabot/Dedalo* Foundation was now under the auspices of American Legion Post 377 in Kenner, Louisiana, and the ship looked her best in years. There was renewed hope, and all that was needed was an additional $2 - 4 million to complete a dock and public access center. The Legion worked round the clock to raise money through bake sales, bingo games and anything else that would bring in revenue. If effort and commitment could be transformed into hard cash, then the American Legion and the *Cabot* veterans would have been able to support an entire carrier battle force!

Enter the Coast Guard and the Army Corps of Engineers. What Kamikazes, bombs, 50 years of rust, and financial mismanagement could not do was finally accomplished by well intentioned safety regulations. Add the fatigue brought on by a shoestring existence always one step ahead of the sheriff, and the camel's back was again broken. The location selected for the old ship was dangerous to passing river barge traffic, and if one broke loose, the public could be in danger. There was no large pot of money on the horizon, no potential source likely, and the Legion hall had been mortgaged. Reality had finally taken hold. In late June 1994, bids went out to competing scrap firms. This too was delayed pending approval of the U.S. State Department. An export license was necessary for the old ship to be taken to another country for scrapping and of course, environmental regulations forbade any transfer of a toxic ridden ship. In late 1996, the old carrier still remained in New Orleans, within sight of the French Quarter. This pathetic sad wreck of a ship which lists five degrees due to an accumulation of rain water in her bilges was not always in this state. At one time, she under construction as cruiser #79, named the USS *Wilmington*. She was one of the planned thirty six strong *Cleveland* class light cruisers of World War II. She like her sisters were being built on both coasts of the U.S. as quickly as possible to take the place of cruisers sunk or damaged in the Pacific War. There was a vital need for light cruisers as surface ship combatants, convoy escort and carrier task force protection.

The *Cleveland* class had been authorized before the beginning of World War II, and cruiser number 79 had been authorized in Federal fiscal year 1941. She had been designated a light cruiser, tentatively named for the city of *Wilmington*, Delaware. How cruiser number 79 ended up leaning against a pier in New Orleans fifty five years later and as a carrier is the story that follows.

CRUISER OR CARRIER? MAKE UP YOUR MIND!

The years leading up to World War II were fraught with indecision and argument within the Navy Department. Should the U.S. Navy concentrate on battleship construction, carriers, cruisers, destroyers, landing craft or all in a balanced plan? There were even a number of ship variations and combinations considered for multi mission use. One was the cruiser-carrier. Many planners, including then Rear Admiral Earnest J. King supported the idea of a cruiser-carrier and the concept gained momentum in the early 1930's. Details of the intended design included building a six inch gunned big light cruiser with a 200 foot long landing platform behind the forward superstructure. This ship class, known as the "flight deck cruiser" would have mounted up to nine 6 inch guns in three triple turrets forward and eight 5 inch guns ranged about the ship for antiaircraft and small surface threat defense. The conceptual design resembled a *Brooklyn* class light cruiser forward attached to one half of a *Wasp* class carrier aft. All this on 10,000 tons and a hull 600 feet in length with a 62 foot beam. Like a bad penny this idea surfaced on and off through out the years leading up to World War II. It was finally killed on the eve of war as being of minimal practicality to the U.S. Navy. The Navy opted for the real thing without compromise. Carriers and cruisers, but separately.

The Japanese Navy developed something akin to cruiser-carrier concept by rebuilding the battleships *Ise* and *Hyuga* late in the Pacific War to help replace their fleet carrier losses. The Soviet Navy also built a variation in the cruiser-carrier Kiev. None of these were successful.

The *Cleveland* class of which CL-79 or the USS *Wilmington* was included was based on an improved version of the highly successful pre-war *Brooklyn/St. Louis* class big light cruisers. These were "treaty cruisers" and the *Cleveland* class, although not strictly bound by international arms limitation treaties followed in the footsteps of this effective design. The *Wilmington* would mount twelve 6 inch/47 caliber guns in four triple turrets and twelve 5 inch/38 caliber guns in six twin mounts forward and aft of the superstructure. The *Wilmington* was powered by four Babcock and Wilcox boilers connected to G.E. turbines driving four shafts at up to 32.30 knots. Her plant generated up 109,000 shp but it was rated at 100,000 shp. She was armored with a 5 inch belt tapering to 1.5 inch (ends), 2 inch lower deck and 3 inch main deck thickness. Her armor, like all treaty cruisers was minimal and mainly consisted of shell plating designed to reduce the effects of splinters.

Her standard designed displacement was 10,000 tons and she had an overall length of 608 feet with a 64 foot beam. She could steam up to 8,640 miles at 15 knots on her 2,184 tons of fuel oil. Her crew consisted of a planned wartime total of 61 officers and 1,247 enlisted men. All in all, she was a standard light cruiser, and ultimately, twenty seven of her class joined the fleet. The *Wilmington* was laid down by the New York Shipbuilding Corporation at its Camden, New Jersey shipyard on March 16, 1942. As the light cruiser *Wilmington* she lasted until June 2, 1942 when she was redesignated CV-28, a carrier. The designation of CV was later changed to CVL, in honor of their particular class of carrier. She was the *Wilmington* for three more weeks and on June 23, 1942, she became the USS *Cabot*. A second *Wilmington*, CL-111, a Fargo class light cruiser, was begun on March 5, 1945, but this again proved to be a false start. CL-111 never became a cruiser either. With the end of World War II, worked ceased and her uncompleted hull met the scrappers torch. It seemed that no cruiser named *Wilmington* was to serve the U.S. Navy during World War II.

There were nine *Cleveland* class cruisers being built at the Camden Yard of the New York Shipbuilding Corp that would end up as light carriers. First it was the turn of the USS *Amsterdam* CL-59. She had been laid down on May 1, 1941, and much of her hull and interior work had been completed. She and eight sister *Cleveland's* were to be converted into high speed light carriers capable of embarking a small complement of fighters and bombers. With the carrier situation in the U.S. Navy and the rapid attrition of current ships, there was desperate need for fast carriers. The navy could not wait for the *Essex* class fleet carriers scheduled for delivery in late 1943, so an interim measure was needed, and fast. The Navy Department noticed the construction progress of certain light cruisers, and the solution was obvious. A fast carrier could be had in an acceptable period by installing a flight deck and other carrier features over the hull of a *Cleveland* class light cruiser. The air group would not be as hefty as that planned for the *Essex* class, and creature comforts would be at a minimum, but this was a race that had to be won. The extensive plan for building a *Cleveland* class cruiser was already out the window, and the carrier conversion time would just have to be accelerated. Ironically, the best time was with the USS *Cabot*. Twenty seven months and one week were cut off the original contracted date set for the delivery of the light cruiser, now light carrier.

One of the problems was the names of these ships. They had already been promised to various communities and civilian morale would suffer if the names were summarily changed. Thus, the name change was not immediately announced after the decision was made to convert the cruisers into a carriers. But, civilian morale aside, mechanical and engineering problems were first and foremost.

A CRUISER BECOMES A CARRIER: CL-79 TO CVL-28

The redesignated *Cabot* was still a cruiser when it was decided to finish her as an aircraft carrier. This was not to be a combination as was envisioned during the pre-war years, but it was a combination in another sense. The cruiser portion would be underneath that of the carrier. There would be no sharing of roles - the *Cabot* was to be a carrier only.

Her power plant was sufficient to provide more than enough speed for air operations and be able to keep pace with fast moving task forces. But her cruiser shaped hull could not possibly withstand a heavy and wide flight deck without danger of capsizing even in the calm water of a harbor. There was some argument over how to compensate for this and the solution was found with external blisters and minor ballasting on the port side to compensate for the island structure. A hull mounted blister with a 3.5 foot wide maximum width was attached to both sides and this did the trick. In fact, the *Cabot* rode out several of the worst storms in the Pacific in complete safety. She healed to beam ends, but remained afloat and right side up - highly desirable in a warship! Her power plant was connected to four square funnels that were fitted to the starboard side of the ship behind the island. They were braced outboard of the ship and were rather strange looking, but effective.

Weight saving aboard these ships was vital as it was in all of the *Cleveland* design's. The cruiser variations were dangerously overweight and topheavy like their cousins - what became known as the *Independence* class carriers. Even the officers staterooms did not have metal doors, they had curtains. Every bit counted.

The *Cabot* had two center mounted aircraft handling elevators on a wooden unarmored flight deck that was 573 feet by 109 feet. The ship was 622.5 feet in length but the flight deck stopped just under 50 feet from the bow. The bow areas on these ships as on all the light cruisers were not noted for strength. In fact, the bows of many light cruisers were lost or easily damaged during the war. A heavy flight deck extended out to the absolute length of the ship would have meant serious trouble. The *Cabot* and her sisters were provided with two H-IVC catapults (second added late in the war) which could launch any contemporary World War II aircraft. The hanger was partially open and measured 215 feet by just under 58 feet in width. The workshops were crowded but serviceable. There was a barber shop and even a soda stand.

She was to have been armed with four 5 inch/ 38 caliber dual purpose guns - two forward and two aft. The tie to pre-war thinking which held the possibility that the *Cabot* and her sisters might have to engage surface targets was still strong. Fortunately, the commitment to heavy guns was not strong enough and due to a number of practical considerations, she was armed with 20 and 40mm heavy machine guns. The first two of the class were temporarily armed with five inch guns, but they were quickly removed. By war's end, the *Cabot* had twenty six 40mm and fifteen 20mm guns, some radar controlled, but all exclusively for air defense. Besides, the *Cabot* and her sisters could keep up with destroyers and other cruisers which could be depended upon to provide adequate defense against anything larger than an enemy aircraft. The *Independence* class carried up to 45 operational aircraft and 100 when acting as aircraft ferries. During World War II, the *Cabot* operated 24 fighters (normally Grumman F6F Hellcats) and nine torpedo planes (TBM). The *Independence* class did not operate divebombers due to the small size of their flight decks.

In terms of her livability as a ship, the opinions ranged from tolerable to miserable. Some felt that the *Independence* class combined all of the disadvantages of both the large and small (CVE) carriers. The ships of the *Independence* class were cramped and the living quarters small, but each of the 1,315 wartime crew had a berth, and most of the 87 officers had staterooms (albeit without doors). At least there was no "hot bunk" accommodation as was common in similarly cramped ships. The crew of the *Cabot* did not seem to mind their less spacious living accommodations comparative to those aboard the more glamorous *Essex* class fleet carriers. Be-

ing able to carry a credible number of aircraft into combat and keep pace with the fast carrier task forces was the name of the game, and the *Cabot* filled the bill quite nicely. The Crew of the *Cabot* would just have to "rough it". The *Independence* class racked up a very respectable combat record during World War II. The cruiser turned carrier was a novel, and ultimately excellent idea.

A QUICK CEREMONY AND THE *CABOT* ENTERS THE ARENA

CV-28, the USS *Cabot* took to the water on April 4, 1943 when she was launched. She was sponsored and christened by Mrs. A. C. Read and continued fitting out in a nearby basin. Her designation as a CV was changed to CVL on July 15, 1943 and she was commissioned just nine days later on July 24, 1943 at the Philadelphia Navy Yard. From the time it was decided to convert her from a cruiser to a carrier till this date, fourteen months had elapsed. It was incredible. What should have taken at least two years had taken far less. There was a quick ceremony on July 24, and Captain Malcolm F. Schoeffel assumed command. Captain Schoeffel was very well liked and respected, and he was later promoted to Rear Admiral. Just before 0300 she became a fighting ship in the U.S. Navy. 1,569 officers and men would then stake their destiny and lives on this new rather odd looking ship. Over one half of the officers and crew were reserve or new to the navy. There were few officers capable of standing watches and the level of seagoing experience was not high. Most of the pilots had just finished training and many were just getting used to new aircraft, in particular, the Grumman Hellcat. The new F6F was quite different from her immediate predecessor, the F4F Wildcat. The Wildcat was forgiving and made allowances for novice pilots. The Hellcat on the other hand, demanded competence from the outset. At least the pilots had trained on a small carrier (CVE *Charger*) so a small deck was nothing new to them as they first saw the *Cabot*. New planes, new ship, new sailors, and new officers. Only the sea and the war was old. But whether she had a cruiser hull or a flat deck, the *Cabot* was a carrier and was needed. The newness would have to wear off quickly. No one at this time could know that she was destined for wartime greatness and valor sufficient to warrant a coveted Presidential Unit Citation. The commissioning crew and air groups that came aboard just hoped that she would fulfill the designers and builders expectations. The *Cabot* even had a Marine detachment that consisted of two officers and forty one enlisted men. Therefore, she must be a capital ship as well as being a carrier.

The new carrier, her paint barely dry left the fitting out basin at the New York Shipbuilding Yard in Camden for Chesapeake Bay. It was time for various trials to determine her fitness for duty. The trials were completed by mid September 1943, and she sailed for the Caribbean and the island of Trinidad.

Air Group 31 reported aboard and became the first of three groups (later Air Groups 29 and 32) assigned to the *Cabot* during World War II. It consisted of Grumman Hellcats (VF-31) and Grumman torpedo bombers (VT-31). The new

carrier operated off the British West Indies from September 20-October 6, 1943. She then sailed back to the Philadelphia Navy Yard for a short period and the addition of SK and SC-2 radar equipment. Her time on the east coast was drawing to a close and on November 8, 1943, she sailed for Pearl Harbor via San Diego, California. The carrier arrived in Pearl Harbor on December 2, 1943, just under two years after the Japanese air attack. She would not remain long and by January 15, 1944, she had joined up with Task Force 58. The day of the fast carrier task force had come with a vengeance, and the *Cabot* was to be one of the central characters of this new and destructive form of naval warfare.

THE *CABOT* AND THE FAST CARRIER TASK FORCES

The wartime career of the *Cabot* actually began with the invasion of the Marshall Islands over the period January 29-February 23, 1944. The move across the central Pacific in order to establish bases for heavy bombers to attack the Japanese home islands had begun in earnest. Securing the Marshall Islands and in particular Kwajalein was important to this overall effort. Japanese shore bases and ships in the Marshall's had been attacked before by Admiral William Halsey in February 1942 for morale and diversionary purposes. However, this attack headed by former cruiser sailor, Admiral Raymond Spruance had an entirely different goal in mind. The Japanese were to be evicted, forcibly. The *Cabot* in company with sister CVL's *Monterey*, *Cowpens*, *Belleau Wood* and *Independence* as well as the big boys, *Essex*, *Yorktown*, and *Bunker Hill* would provide air cover and wipe out any resistance offered from the ground or sea. The *Cabot's* own Air Group 31 did a highly credible job and spent many hours shuttling from the *Cabot* into action and back. This was to become the war-fighting tool of choice in the future and essentially the reason for the *Cabot* and other fast carriers existing. The fast carriers provided air superiority with the ultimate goal of air supremacy in every invasion planned during the rest of the Pacific war. Air cover and attacks by the fast carriers was integral to the success of any land or sea operation. Hitting Japanese surface ships long before they could come within range of Allied invasion forces was as important as destroying the enemy's capability in the air. The keys to this type of operation were flexibility and speed, both of which were possessed by the *Cabot* and other fast carriers.

The air battle for the Marshall Islands resulted in the first recorded enemy aircraft being shot down by a pilot from the *Cabot*. The carrier and its air group were now blooded through the fine efforts of Lt. Commander Robert Winston of Air Group 31. Now it was on to Truk atoll for a concentrated attack that would include the CVL's *Cabot*, *Monterey*, *Cowpens* and fleet carriers *Intrepid*, *Bunker Hill* and *Essex*. The force was seeking major elements of the Japanese fleet. The force had a number of escorting cruisers and destroyers including the *Wichita*, *San Francisco*, *Baltimore* and *San Diego* (CLAA). The strike on Truk was launched on February 16, 1944 and over a two day period, there was a large amount of damage done to the Japanese shore installa-

Ernie Pyle aboard the Cabot *in late 1944. This beloved and well respected war correspondent was a visitor on the* Cabot *and was enormously popular with the officers and crew. His two week visit gave him more than enough experience on a fast carrier.*

tions. On two counts there was misfortune for the American attack force. First, there were no major units of the Japanese Navy and second, the enemy was not asleep. "Bogies" broke through the antiaircraft defenses and the Intrepid was hit with a torpedo. The *Cabot* helped escort the now crippled carrier (nicknamed "*Decrepit*") back to safety. The nickname never took hold and the *Intrepid* became one of the most decorated carriers ion the Pacific.

After some respite at Pearl Harbor, the now veteran *Cabot* steamed for Japanese held Palau Islands. They were attacked over March 30-31, 1944 with excellent results. The Cabot's air group also hit Wolieai. As with the previous months raid on Truk, the Japanese maintained a spirited defense and came out looking for the carriers. On March 30, the *Cabot* deployed it's Combat Air Patrol (CAP) and it was successfully able to shoot down nine incoming enemy torpedo planes (Jills), before they were in striking range of the *Cabot*. The Japanese had honed their skills in aerial torpedo attack similar to the U.S. Navy's prowess in divebombing. If a torpedo bomber got through air and shipboard defenses, the success rate was quite high. The effectiveness of a CAP was crucial to survival as was the competence of the ship's antiaircraft gunners. The *Cabot* was in good hands.

In early mid April 1944 the *Cabot* participated in support of the Hollandia operation and on April 29-30, her air group hit Truk for a second time. On April 23 between the raids in the very early hours of the morning, the *Cabot* almost became a flaming pyre when the heavy cruiser *Wichita* strayed off course. A collision was narrowly (the cruiser passed within six feet from the carrier's bow) missed and at a combined speed of 33 knots would have demolished the gasoline laden carrier. Her history might well have ended here had it not been for a well drilled and quick thinking crew.

Her next action was during the invasion of the Mariana Islands (Saipan, Tinian, and Guam). This venture would prove quite different for the

Cabot. It would involve a large portion of Imperial Japanese naval aviation and major fleet units. The Japanese had hoped to draw out the American navy into a do or die battle. The planned outcome was for the remnants of the beaten U.S. Navy to retire in defeat and shame. The Japanese would then reverse the path that the war was now taking and return to those heady days of early 1942. What was planned by the Imperial High Command was to differ greatly from reality. The *Cabot* would play a critical part in this plan reversal.

The Allied invasion of the Marianas had a very definite purpose. Bases for long range bombers were needed and a major forward area supply facility was vital to continued operations. The 5th Fleet now renamed the 3rd Fleet was strung out far from friendly terra firma and the harbor in Guam would suit the American Navy just perfectly. For the invasion, the U.S. Navy assembled over 600 ships, a third of a million men and just under 1,000 combat aircraft. The *Cabot* was one of eight CVL's which were in company with seven fleet carriers. The Imperial Navy decided to have another showdown with the U.S. Navy and sent in five fleet and four light carriers. Unfortunately, the Japanese air groups totaled only 473 aircraft, and the pilots were not as skilled or experienced as their American counterparts. In mid June, the assault began. The *Cabot* and other carriers made numerous sweeps over enemy held territory shooting up aircraft on the ground and in the air. This was to prove crucial. The Japanese did attempt to attack the fast carriers and an aerial torpedo just missed the *Cabot*. It was the destruction of the enemy in and around their island bases that laid the groundwork for the June 19-20, 1944 "Mariana's Turkey Shoot." Admiral Ozawa, in overall command of the Japanese carrier force was relying on the honesty and truth of his

ground commanders that they had a minimum of 500 combat aircraft available that would supplement his 500 shipborne planes. With a combined total of 1,000 aircraft and the ability to shuttle from carrier to land base and into attack, the Japanese would duplicate the American victory during the Naval Battle of Guadalcanal just 18 months earlier. It was not to be. The Japanese ground commander falsely overstated his capability and the Japanese pilots were not up to the task. Believing and acting on their own propaganda was becoming a great liability to Japanese military operations. By the time the Japanese task force came within range, it was a two to one advantage for the Americans. On June 19, 1944, the Battle of the Philippine Sea or "Turkey Shoot" as it was coined by Commander Paul M. Buie of the USS *Lexington* began. By the time it was over, the Japanese had lost 243 aircraft. By the end of the following day, the score had increased to 476, including land based aircraft. In two days of concentrated fighting, pilots from fifteen U.S. carriers shot down or destroyed the backbone of Japanese naval aviation. It was one of the turning points of the Pacific War. Not only were Japanese aircraft destroyed. Avengers from the *Cabot, Monterey* and *Bunker Hill* found and hit the Japanese carrier *Chiyoda*, battleship *Haruna* and near missed the cruiser *Maya*. Between submarine actions and other aerial attacks, the Japanese also lost the carriers *Shokaku, Taiho* and *Hiyo* as well as suffering heavy damage to other ships. As Admiral Ozawa headed back to home territory he was left with 35 operational carrier aircraft and a third rate navy.

The *Cabot* as had her seven CVL sisters had played a major role in this fantastic victory, but there were some American losses. 130 aircraft and 76 aviators were lost during the two day battle, many of whom crashed near Task Force

Tere Ernie Pyle, a gentle and articulate advocate of the ordinary sailor and soldier was killed. He had been following units of the 77th Infantry Division as they captured the little island of Ie Shima. He was killed by machine gun fire in a place where little resistance was expected.

58 when looking for their home carrier. Many more would have been lost had it not been for the unorthodox decision of Admiral Marc Mitscher to light up the carriers to facilitate recovery. This saved countless lives. Carriers were also ordered to take on any aircraft from any source. The *Cabot* took on seven from other ships such as the *Wasp* and *Bunker Hill*. As darkness fell, it was difficult to determine which carrier was home, so planes landed anywhere possible to avoid ditching. Lt. E. Wood, having just attacked the Japanese flattop *Chiyoda* thought that he had selected an *Essex* class carrier for a temporary home, and was amazed to learn that he had indeed landed back aboard the *Cabot*! He had just five gallons left in his TBM. The score for the *Cabot* was 28 enemy aircraft shot down by VF-31 and three by the ships' antiaircraft defenses.

The Mariana's operation was soon concluded and next the *Cabot* sailed for raids against the Bonin Islands (Iwo Jima), Palau Islands and the Philippines. On July 4, 1944, Independence Day, the *Cabot* launched against Iwo Jima, shooting up ground installations. Next it was back to the Mariana's for ground attack and then on to Ulithi and Yap at the end of July. Early August found the *Cabot* making a strike against Chichi Jima in the Bonin Islands. It was during this raid that Task Group 58.1 found a convoy of eleven ships. Pilots from VT-31 hit and sank one of the ships, a destroyer of the *Fubuki* class. In August, 1944 the Fifth Fleet became the Third Fleet under Admiral William Halsey, and early the following month it was the turn of the Palau Islands. For the last several weeks, the *Cabot* and other fast carriers had been making hit and run raids on ground installations all over the central Pacific in preparation for future amphibious landings. Again, the optimum use of the fast carrier task force.

Ensign George Bush, later to become President of the U.S. had the distinction of becoming the youngest naval aviator in naval history at age 20. He was a TBM Avenger pilot and a soul mate of VT-31. Bush was attached to another CVL, the *San Jacinto* CVL-30 and VT-51. He was shot down over the Bonins during a diversionary raid. The raid was to fool the Japanese into thinking that a landing against the Palau Islands was not in the offing. Bush was saved from capture by one of angel of mercy rescue submarines, the *Finback* SS-230. American submarines were strung out in a configuration designed to help rescue precious air crews shot down. In Bush's case, the plan worked well, although he was more nervous aboard the sub than in his Avenger.

The next strike was against the Philippines in early September 1944 which included visits to Clark Field and attacks on shipping in and around the islands. In October, 1944, veteran Air Group 31 left the *Cabot* for the USS *Barnes*, CVE-20 yet even a smaller carrier. Air Group 31 had accomplished miracles in their short assignment aboard the *Cabot*. They had shot down 147 aircraft, sank 26 ships, and had flown 3,021 sorties (all types) from the *Cabot*. Fighter sorties totalled 861 and TBM attacks 271. They had hit everything Japanese that moved or stood still. Fighting 31 became known as the "Meat Axe Squadron", a well earned name for its many achievements. Overall, Air Group 31 was outstanding.

Air Group 29 reported aboard on October 5, 1944. Eleven days later, this group would be involved in one of the most bizarre operations in World War II - escort for "Crip Div One".

From the outset of World War II in the Pacific, Admiral Halsey had longed for one thing. He wanted to annihilate the entire Japanese fleet, preferably in one great violent aerial and surface battle. He was denied this at Midway so in October 1944, the possibility loomed again. He hoped that the Japanese would cooperate. The arrival of the Third Fleet off the Philippines and Formosa was too tempting for the Japanese to pass up. They too sought this magical armageddon at sea and hoped that the Americans had finally overextended themselves. They Imperial General Staff had never completely understood the concept of replenishment at sea so they had this fond hope that their enemy would venture beyond effective land based support. It was not to be as Halsey's forces were well provisioned and quite capable of full combat operations in any area of the Pacific.

Japanese planning took a turn back in history as they now were going to position their carriers with their depleted air groups as a tempting decoy for Halsey's undivided attention. Then the main attraction, a large surface force would enter Leyte Gulf and slaughter the defenseless transports and any warships that got in their way. Finally, the Empire's much touted super battleships the *Yamato* and *Mushashi* would earn their keep.

Admiral Halsey had been listening to Japanese propaganda in early October during and after his successful strikes on Okinawa, and the Philippines. The attacks on Okinawa had been very successful by aircraft from the *Cabot* and other carriers. Seventy five enemy ships of varying classes had been sunk as well as a number of vital shore bases demolished. Not so if the Japanese public relations effort was believed. By mid October, the Japanese had claimed the virtual elimination of the Third Fleet. As a matter of fact, Tokyo Radio claimed that nearly 30,000 American sailors had perished and 53 ships (including 16 carriers) had been sunk or damaged beyond combat capability. If the propaganda was to be accepted, the war was all but over and Japan was the victor. The reason for this outburst of lies was simple - something had to prop up civilian and military morale. The Third Fleet and it's air groups were now roving about and very close to the home islands. Unluckily, many staff officers of the Imperial Japanese Navy also believed these claims, and as a result decided it was time to finish off the invaders. Halsey too was interested in the stock placed in these wild statements about his mounting losses. Every morning he awoke and from the flag bridge of the battleship *New Jersey* he could see American warships and power from horizon to horizon.

Air fields and aircraft on Formosa were hit on October 13, to prevent the Japanese from sending aircraft to interrupt land operations in the Philippines. Japanese losses had been staggering, and American casualties were limited to downed aircraft. Luck ran out just after dark on October 13, a Friday of course, when the heavy cruiser *Canberra* CA-70 was hit by a torpedo under her armor belt. It did enough damage to warrant a tow. The light cruiser *Houston* CL-81 was ordered to take her place and a separate task unit was pulled together to protect the damaged cruiser. The very next day, the *Houston* was also struck by a torpedo by the last torpedo plane of four that attempted to break through her defenses. Now there were two badly damaged cruisers in the enemy's back yard and 1,300 miles to a friendly ship hospital at Ulithi. In some quarters it was recommended that both ships be disposed of and operations continue against Formosa. After all, they were not fleet carriers or battleships, they were mass produced cruisers, and there were plenty more on the way. However, Halsey saw a situation and opportunity that was unique. These ships were damaged and under tow. The Japanese might believe their own propaganda and seeing these pathetic "3rd Fleet remnants", might just come out to mop up. It was worth a try. Consequently it was decided to preserve these two cruisers as "bait" for the main body of the Japanese navy. Accordingly, the two clipped cruisers and a small covering force that included the CVL's *Cabot* and *Cowpens* aka Task Unit 30.3.2 or more popularly, "Crip Div 1", Cripple Division 1, or Bait Div 1 inch set sail for safety, slowly at four knots. For the next few days, the group plodded forth. Their trip was not without excitement as the Japanese did throw massive land based raids at them which resulted in another torpedo for the *Houston*.

Fighter direction was excellent from the *Cabot* and her aircraft shot down 33 attackers on October 16. Twenty seven were downed in just 15 minutes. The *Cabot* and *Cowpens* provided superb support to the two crippled cruisers and remained with them until they were out of harm's way. The Japanese fleet did come out to fight but were hurriedly frightened off by a concentrated air attack. It would take more than the "crip div" to pry the Imperial Japanese Navy from its safe harbor. The invasion of the Leyte Island in the Philippines would accomplish it easily. The Japanese knew that when the Philippine Islands were taken from them, that the door was open to the home islands. This was worth sending out the fleet.

THE BEGINNING OF THE END AND THE FINAL PACIFIC BATTLES

The invasion of Leyte took place on October 20, 1944. It was the day that thousands of Filipinos had anticipated for almost three years. It was also a day long wanted by another man, General Douglas MacArthur. He had left the Philippines reluctantly in early 1942 and had promised to return. On October 20, 1944, he did.

The *Cabot* provided support to the landings and on October 24, 1944 she was able to attack the 63,000 ton super battleship *Mushashi*. After being pounded from the air with bombs and torpedoes, the much talked about ship sank. All in all over the next few days, the Japanese Navy ceased to exist. Carriers, battleships, cruisers and destroyers were sunk in a series of air and surface battles. By the end of October, the way was clear to Japan and victory.

On October 28, 1944, the *Cabot's* air group

What combat over the light carriers looked like when the kamikazes swooped down off Okinawa. The skies were filled with black puff from five inch fire and often paths formed by thousands of water geysers marked the direction of th ekamikaze as it came in low over the water to its target. The kamikaze was a terrifying weapon - men who fought to die versus men who fought to live.

An Independence *class carrier takes a very steep roll to starboard during one of the vicious typhoons that came up in early 1945. The* Cabot *and her sisters fared well despite predictions that they would turn over in a severe blow. The CVL Langley reportedly rolled 70 degrees!*

The Cabot *has just been hit by two kamikazes (Zekes) and is burning furiously. A lone TBM Avenger sits ready for takeoff, but was incapacitated by the first hit. The day was November 25, 1945, and the time was 1254. The fleet carriers* Hancock, Intrepid *and* Essex *were also hit on that same day. The* Cabot *was ready for flight operations within hours after the hits that killed 35 men.*

now hit various airfields and other ground facilities around Manila. Three weeks later on November 19, she was back attacking the same general area. This was so with all of the fast carriers which were pounding targets wherever they could be found, especially airfield and aircraft. For the *Cabot* this would continue for the next several weeks and on into the new year. The Japanese were beginning to respond with deliberate suicide attacks from the air. Fanatic Japanese pilots (many very young and full of sake) began taking to the air with full bomb loads from bases in the Philippines, Formosa and anywhere else that was momentarily secure from the Third Fleet. Their targets were heavy ships and in particular the elevator or island structures of the fast carriers. Eventually, due to well executed anti-

aircraft defenses, the choices deteriorated to anything that could be hit. The *Cabot* was hit on November 25 by a flaming single engine kamikaze (Zeke) at 1246. The carrier had been repelling attacks from the air for a long period when one broke through. It was hit a number of times but kept on coming. It struck the ship on the flight deck port side up forward at frame 26 doing extensive damage. The 20mm gun crew never ceased firing as the flaming aircraft hit them. Two minutes later another Zeke snuck in and crashed along side the ship off the port quarter. Between the two hits, 35 men were killed and 27 were wounded. The carrier was heavily damaged. A fully loaded (four 500 pound bombs) TBF was on the forward flight deck awaiting launch when the hits occurred. It was

riddled with fragments and heavily seriously damaged. Due to the alertness of the pilot, the plane did not explode and further endanger the ship. The wounded carrier was able to keep station and maintain operations, but she was soon detached for Ulithi and repair. By December 14, she was back attacking the Japanese on the Luzon. The repair crews at Ulithi put damaged ships back in action within days and at most weeks of their arrival. This was another miracle of modern American naval warfare.

By mid January 1945, the carrier was launching strikes against China, Hong Kong and Iwo Jima. On February 9, she was visited by one of the war's most beloved correspondents, Ernie Pyle. He spent two weeks aboard the *Cabot* to get the feel of what fast carrier operations was all about. It was one of the high points for the crew to have such a man as Pyle in heir midst, and at the height of battle.

The raids continued for several weeks as the pincers of General MacArthur (South Pacific command and Admiral Nimitz (Central Pacific command) closed on Japan. After the Philippines and Iwo Jima, next was Okinawa on the plan of reconquest. The *Cabot* launched strikes on Okinawa during late March and early April 1945. The Allies were closing in on a tide of naval aviation victory after victory. In the late spring the *Cabot* finally sailed for San Francisco and a very much needed overhaul. She emerged from the Hunter's Point Naval Shipyard on June 20, 1945 and after a short period of working up sailed for Pearl Harbor and the final battles of the war. On July 12, 1945, she embarked her last wartime air group, Air Group 32. She made one last attack and that was a strike on Wake Island on August 1, 1945 and for the cruiser-carrier, active combat was now over. Her service was not however as she was selected to provide air support in the Yellow Sea operation during September and October 1945. The war might have been over, but occupation troops needed protection. The new but quiet adversary was the Soviet Union, and during this operation, *Cabot* flyers met several Soviet PBY's in the area. There were no incidents.

The *Cabot* took on a draft of passengers for the U.S. in Guam and sailed as a part of the "Magic carpet" fleet on October 21, 1945. She

The Cabot sits in drydock in Gibraltar during her assignment as a unit of NATO in the Mediterranean in 1952. Her cruiser lines are evident and her port side blister is just visible under her black waterline marker.

Another view of the Cabot in a Royal Navy dockyard drydock in Gibraltar. Large timbers are used to stabilize the ship during her hull repair and propeller replacement.

A plane crashes in the Mediterranean after a missed landing on the Cabot while she was part of a NATO submarine Hunter Killer group.

Too late! an incoming aircraft has missed an arrestor cable and is on its way to hitting the radar mast and flight deck tractor in this 1952 photograph.

This is a sequence of photos showing the incorrect way of landing on a carrier. No one was hurt.

arrived in San Diego on November 9, 1945, and subsequently left for the east coast of the U.S. She was placed in reserve and decommissioned at the Philadelphia Navy Yard on February 11, 1947. Her accomplishments were almost of legendary proportions.

During her 16 months in a combat zone she steamed 134,000 miles and flew 4,933 sorties. Two Hundred and fifty two enemy aircraft were shot down by her air groups and 96 ships sunk or damaged. She lost 27 aircraft due to enemy action and 38 pilots and air crew members were killed or missing. Twenty six of the Cabot's pilots were credited with shooting down five or more aircraft thus making them "Aces". The *Cabot* also earned the Presidential Unit Citation and nine battle stars for her service during World War II.

BACK TO SEA AND THEN INTO THE SPANISH ARMADA (NAVY)

The *Cabot* spent a very short time in mothballs. By October 27, 1948, she had been recommissioned and was now the resident training carrier at Naval Air Station, Pensacola. She operated in the Caribbean and off the east coast training reservists and new aviators in the art of carrier operations. She then was assigned a short tour as an antisubmarine carrier in a hunter killer group. There she operated as the flagship of the group during its operations as part of Nato in the Mediterranean. The Soviet Navy which had expanded its submarine force was being given a lesson. The U.S. Navy and its allies in Nato would not be intimidated by a large submarine force. Measures, including the carrier accompanied hunter killer groups were being tested at many locations around the world. It was during this period in 1952, that the *Cabot* recorded its 43,000th recovery. This ship had really been places and a lot of rubber had been left on her wooden deck over the nine years she had been in business. The CVL was again decommissioned on January 21, 1955 and placed in reserve in the Atlantic Reserve Fleet. Her days as a carrier came to an end on May 15, 1959 when she was reclassified as an auxiliary aircraft transport AVT-3.

Eight years later after being reconditioned over a 15 month period, the *Cabot* became a part of the Spanish Armada or Navy. The transfer took place on August 30, 1967 when she was inducted into the Spanish Navy as the SNS

An excellent view of the forward 40mm quad used for antiaircraft defense.

Dedalo R-01. She was their first carrier and was to carry helicopters for ASW operations. The terms of the transfer were simple. The ship would be loaned for five years and then sold to Spain if her navy so wanted. The Spanish Navy did indeed want her and the purchase occurred on December 5, 1972. For the next sixteen plus years the *Dedalo* operated in the Atlantic and Mediterranean in various exercises and as a flagship. She carried Sea king helicopters and a variation of the Harrier jumpjet, the Spanish Matador. The *Dedalo* was so successful, that a successor built much along the same lines as the *Cabot* was commissioned in May 1988. The *Principe de Asturias* was based on the perceived need for sea control ship and also carries a composite of helicopters and Harrier jets. When the *Principe de Asturias* entered the fleet, the time had come for ending the 45 year career of the world's oldest light carrier. Officials of the Spanish Navy initially decided to send the old carrier to the scrap heap, probably in Italy, but Louisiana businessmen and entrepreneurs had a different future in mind. On July 2, 1989 in Madrid, Spain a transfer contract was signed with the USS *Cabot/Dedalo* Museum Foundation, a Louisiana non profit corporation whose stated purpose was to preserve the old carrier. Spain relinquished her national interest providing that the *Cabot/Dedalo* always flew the Spanish ensign alongside of that of the U.S. and that she be operated in a dignified and proper manner. So much for promises. On August 2, 1989, the *Cabot/Dedalo* returned to the U.S. and was moored in New Orleans. There was much fanfare, and soon the flag of the U.S. was again flying over the carrier. She was back, but her stay was not to be very pleasant. Her treatment has been a national disgrace and a black eye for New Orleans. As of this writing in early 1996, her fate is still undetermined.

EPILOGUE

If the *Cabot/Dedalo* is scrapped, it will be a loss to all citizens of the U.S. as well as those of Spain, a loss that will be permanent and irrevocable. Four decades after the USS *Enterprise* of World War II fame was scrapped, many still wish that the carrier had survived the breakers torch. Old sailors are not alone as few armored vehicles of World War II survive and there are now scant numbers of Army Air Corps aircraft of the same era. The carrier *Cabot/Dedalo* like Sherman tanks and B-17 Flying Fortresses are 20th Century battlefields just like the 19th Century Gettysburg "Little Round Top". Preserving these memorials merits our best efforts, and that means more than money and sentiment. It means good management and hard headed business practise. The Iron Woman is a Lady and should be treated as such.

USS *ENTERPRISE* CV-6 "LOST, BUT NOT FORGOTTEN"

A PICTURE CAN BE WORTH A THOUSAND WORDS

Loreley Bull, a Gotham City teenager often watched one ship or another passing beneath the Brooklyn Bridge. As she stood on the bridge walkway on this 20th day of July 1949, she could expect anything. The ships passing underneath ranged from glistening luxury liners crowded with well to do passengers, to junk laden barges pushed along by chugging tugboats. She always chose the center of the bridge for the best view, but on this morning she had some competition. An International News photo journalist was also on the walkway with his camera. The two exchanged glances, neither wanting to surrender their vantage point. Fortunately, a silent truce was quickly concluded allowing both to share what was to be a historically significant sight.

The USS *Enterprise* (CV-6), America's sixth aircraft carrier was making her way to the Brooklyn Navy Yard for periodic upkeep and repair. As the dark grey ship hove into sight four of those chugging tugboats could be seen nudging her along at a respectable pace. Two other tugs, tethered to the carrier by thick lines steamed several hundred yards ahead flanking the great ship's starboard and port bow. Six tugs were required to guide this huge ship safely to the shipyard. It would not do to have this most decorated ship in the U.S. Navy go astray. Loreley could see a number of workmen and naval personnel milling about the huge flight deck as the carrier passed under the bridge. There were probably a few visitors who had always wanted a ride on this historic ship. The photographer snapped his

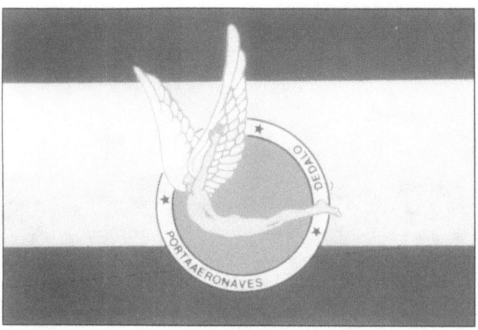

The Spanish Navy crest for the carrier SNS Dedalo *R-01. The ship was named in honor of the mythical Greek character "Daedalus." He escaped from his captors by attaching wings to his body with wax and flying away. The Spanish Navy was very proud of their new carrier and kept her in excellent condition.*

The Dedalo *at sea off Spain in the mid 1980's. She is carrying three Sea Harrier jump jets (Spanish Matador) and Sea King helicopters. The old carrier provided an excellent platform for a multi-mission presence in the Mediterranean.*

The Cabot/Dedalo *as she sits in New Orleans awaiting her fate. Both the United States and Spanish flags can be seen flying on her now deserted flight deck.*

Bunting has been hung on the bows of the Enterprise *in this October 1936 pre launching photo. No one could predict how fabulously successful this carrier would become.*

picture, but chose to include Loreley as co-star with the *Enterprise*. The image of a young girl watching the oncoming ship was too good to pass up. In fact, when the photograph was sent out to the national and international newspaper wire services, it was entitled, *"Bull - Enterprise"*. It was a sign of the times. The war had been over only four years earlier, and now the old ship was just that, an old ship sharing the limelight with a young pretty New Yorker.

Ironically, the photographer and newspaper caption editor missed more than was captured. The image that appeared on film was that of a young girl watching an old ship being towed under the Brooklyn Bridge, a sight quite common. What was omitted was the fact that Loreley was alive and free in a country that had triumphed over a cunning and well prepared adversary. The victory was made possible by that very ship and men who lost their youth and their lives serving her. They did this willingly to insure that a young girl would always be able to watch an old ship being towed beneath a bridge. The real story of that aging dark grey ship was one of vast and almost legendary proportions, but with a tragic ending. It is also one of men who were afraid, but fought with valor and courage seldom matched in American Naval History.

It is the story of the *"Big E"* as the USS *Enterprise* CV-6 was known, the most decorated ship in World War II. It all began with a new President, unemployed shipyard workers, $238 million in Public Works funds, and a self inflicted naval arms limitation treaty. The year was 1933.

NOT ANOTHER *RANGER*!: THE *YORKTOWN* CLASS IS DESIGNED

The U.S. Navy was hemmed in by lack of public funds and the Lilliputian like restraints of the 1922 Washington Naval Arms Limitation Treaty and its 1930 followup in London. The Treaty was self imposed in the naive belief that Italy and particularly Japan would play fair. They did, but not to the letter of the law. It was more to the spirit. But in the U.S., money was the real problem, and without it the Navy could not build carriers even within the tonnage allowances provided in the treaties signed with the other major naval powers. The only other nation facing the same dilemma was Great Britain. Her warship building program was on and off dependent on

what party controlled the government. At least, the U.S. Navy had a sympathizer in President Franklin Roosevelt. Besides the signatories of the naval treaties, Germany, now under National Socialist (nazi) domination was slowly unraveling the restraints of the Versailles Treaty which had ended World War I. Germany had not forgotten the humiliation and shame at having to lay down it's arms and scuttle her magnificent fleet. She was back in the military buildup business, and was about as peace loving as her future copartners in the next World War, Italy and Japan. Worst still, these countries were not currently caught up in the ravages of an economic depression as was the U.S. They were able to invest much of their national wealth into the onset of a pre-war boom in armaments, warship construction and war planes. This in itself helped to eradicate the remnants of economic depression and created a temporary, but very real industrial expansion. There was full employment for all those that wanted to work, that is work for the Axis war machine of the future. At the 1930's progressed, the U.S. was not immediately gripped by the need to stimulate its economic health with armaments production. Besides, who would pay for it? Full employment paid for by government taxation and indebtedness was not considered sound business practise. Roosevelt knew however that it was imperative for the U.S. to at least show a modicum of interest in maintaining pace with Japan. With this in mind, and the specter of 12 million unemployed men, he was successfully able to negotiate what became known as "New Deal Legislation". In the main, the sweeping legislative action was designed to provide relief to the citizens of the U.S. that had suffered so badly over the last few years. Its long reaching effect was to introduce the federal government into most aspects of modern American life, a phenomenon either hated or loved depending on one's perspective. But in 1933, this legislation was what probably saved the U.S. from abandoning its constituted form of government and reverting to fascism or overt socialism. It was an emergency on a scale not seen since the days leading up to the war between the states in 1860.

Hidden deep in that legislation was the sum of $238 million in public works funds to be distributed by under the newly created Public Works programs. Typically, these monies would have

been utilized for road, bridge and infrastructure repair and modernization, but in this instance most were earmarked for naval infrastructure modernization - new ships and planes. President Roosevelt arranged to personally oversee the expenditures made under this provision through a formal executive order (No. 6174 of June 16, 1933). This appropriation would help the thousands of shipyard workers near the coasts that were out of work, but moreover, it acted as seed money for the modernization of the U.S. Navy, a navy that would be desperately needed during the early months of the upcoming war. Had it not been for this $238 million, the remnants of the post Pearl Harbor Pacific Fleet would have suffered the same fate as the Asiatic Fleet - complete annihilation. The Imperial Japanese Navy would have ruled supreme in the Pacific and the war of reconquest would have taken several years, if fought at all. In terms of value received, this was one of the most productive expenditures of American taxpayer dollars in history.

Approximately $19 million was to be spent for one of a new class of carrier to succeed the *Ranger*. This was to be the *Yorktown* class which would include the namesake, *Yorktown* CV-5, *Enterprise* CV-6 and finally the *Hornet* CV-8, yet the unit cost was closer to $25 million. Considering that a light cruiser cost $18 million and modernizing an old battleship was figured at $8 million, the price tag was more than reasonable. The *Wasp* CV-7 was built in between the *Enterprise* and the *Hornet* to make use of the final available tonnage allowed by the treaties.

The *Ranger* CV-4 was America's first purpose built aircraft carrier, yet unfortunately the lessons learned from the *Langley* and the *Lexington* class were not strictly observed. This was due to stubborn adherence to Treaty tonnage allowance and quite simply, a continuing lack of money. Admiral Alfred T Mahan, naval guru and prophet would have turned in his grave had he known that the navy now built ships not for combat but in compromise to contemporary social and economic concepts. The Washington

Naval Treaty had allowed the U.S. an initial aircraft carrier tonnage of 81,000 tons. The *Lexington* and *Saratoga* had consumed just over 66 thousand of those tons, leaving approximately 14,500 tons available for another carrier. As a consequence, accountants were used to build the fourth American carrier, the 14,500 ton *Ranger*. She was a ship of compromise, but on the other hand, she was another carrier. The Navy craved platforms from which to fly aircraft.

The *Ranger* was slower than the *Lexington* and *Saratoga* with a maximum speed of 29 knots, and she had reverted to the *Langley* design of hinged smoke pipes. Her speed was not considered essential as she was originally destined to operate exclusively with the 21 knot battle line. She carried up to 75 aircraft in her air group, but her flight deck was thinly plated as were most of her vital areas. She was also somewhat unseaworthy and in any kind of adverse weather, she was unstable as a landing platform. All in all she was a poor advertisement for the medium size carrier built on a significantly inadequate displacement. The result did not measure up to the promise, and although the *Ranger* was not a complete failure she was in one respect, a great success. Her performance as an aircraft carrier convinced the Navy that quantity of aircraft carriers was less important than quality. The Navy had been allowed additional tonnage under the arms limitation treaty and had briefly considered building four additional carriers of the *Ranger* class. This use of treaty tonnage was quickly sacrificed in favor of a different approach. The result was the *Yorktown* class. The *Yorktown* and *Enterprise* were the next carriers built after the *Ranger*. These two ships were the beneficiaries of the *Langley* experiment, the *Lexington/ Saratoga* conversion and the *Ranger* compromise design. These ships were the result of observing the plus's and minus's of big versus small aircraft carrier design. The *Yorktown* class which also included a slightly enhanced *Hornet* was to be the finest class of carrier built before World War II and certainly was the bench-mark for all future axial deck carriers in the U.S. Navy. Aside from being more efficient and effective as airplane platforms, they were aesthetically attractive to the eye.

The *Enterprise*, nearly a duplicate of the *Yorktown* displaced 19,800 tons (25,500 tons full load), and her dimensions were initially 761feet at the water line; 809.5 feet flight deck length; 83 feet beam and 109 feet across the flight deck. She drew just under 22 feet (mean), and carried a peacetime crew of 1,889 (2,919 wartime). This included up to 306 officers.

Her flight deck was covered with six inch teak planks laid athwartships over steel plating. Her flight deck was sufficiently braced to withstand the heavier aircraft (e.g. Grumman Avengers) produced just before and during World War II, but was not armored. Even the successor class of fleet carriers *(Essex)* did not have armored flight decks. This would happen in with post war Midway class, ironically named in honor of the battle that witnessed the death of the carrier *Yorktown*. The *Enterprise* carried three centerline aircraft lifts connecting the hanger to the flight deck which facilitated aircraft transfer, a critical factor during combat flight operations. Two catapults were fitted on the flight

deck forward and one inside the hanger. It was reasoned that aircraft could be launched from three locations during emergencies. The catapult housed in the hanger was only used during wartime in Hollywood versions of naval warfare! The *Enterprise* was designed to carry 90-96 aircraft which was the published capacity, but in reality she carried 80-85 comfortably. When she was first commissioned in 1938, her air group consisted of 81 aircraft including fighters, bombers, torpedo planes and a few for utility purposes. Ninety-six aircraft was quite a large number and the logistics of plane storage and frequent respotting was nearly overwhelming. Eighty planes was optimum.

Her aircraft recovery arresting gear was prescribed by that developed and refined aboard previous carriers. It was a series of wires running across the flight deck from beam to beam, and interestingly, provision was made for landing aircraft forward from the bow. Arresting gear was installed accordingly for this purpose, but as with hanger catapult, this too fell into disuse. High capacity flight deck mounted derricks were used for boats and lifting aircraft from piers and alongside barges. One was just aft of the island and the other just abreast of the tripod foremast on it's starboard side.

The *Yorktown* class was better protected than the *Ranger* in terms of armor. In many respects this class was armored similar to other ships built under treaty mandate such as mid 1930's cruiser classes. The *Enterprise* had a tapering waterline armor belt of 2.5 inches up to 4.0 inches at the upper edge. It was sufficient to withstand the impact of a 400 pound torpedo, but the Japanese submarine launched torpedo was far more powerful. It would have taken a protection system able to resist at least 700 pounds, but that

was reserved for battleships and could not be used on the 1930's treaty bound carriers. The main deck was covered with 3 inches and the lower deck ranged from one to three inches. This was a vast improvement over the *Ranger*, but not as extensive as would be needed for survival in war, particularly an air war. The designers wanted an armored flight deck, but there simply was not enough treaty tonnage available. Sacrifice was required to honor the treaty. However, there was another form of protection and that was of extensive and well thought out compartmentalization. The *Yorktown* class was far superior to former classes in this dimension.

The *Enterprise*, like most ships that served prior and during World War II, went through a dramatic evolution in gun armament. Initially, she was armed eight director controlled 5 inch/ 38 cal guns for antiaircraft defense as well as 1.1 inch and 50 caliber close in weapons. The concept of a carrier slugging it out with enemy surface ships had now all but vanished to be replaced by increasing fears of air attack. During the war, the "*Big E*" was rearmed with 20mm and 40mm heavy machine guns and at war's end she carried eleven quad mount 40mm, eight twin 40mm mounts and numerous 20mm sited all around her flight deck and island.

Unlike the *Ranger*, the *Enterprise* was designed as a stand alone centerpiece for a fast moving strike force. Naval air warfare tactics had now evolved to the stage where the employment of hit and run carrier aviation was becoming a grudgingly accepted usage of naval resources. For this, the *Enterprise* had to depend on a propulsion plant that could drive her at sustained speeds up to a maximum of 33 knots (during her speed trials, she actually exceeded 34 knots). She was fitted with Nine Babcock and

The new light cruiser Boise *and sister to the* Enterprise, *the USS* Yorktown *flank the "Big E" as she became known in this 1938 vintage photograph. All three are in the process of fitting out. The* Boise *has yet to take on her five triple 6 inch/47 caliber turrets. All three would meet on and off, especially off Guadalcanal. The $238 million authorized by President Roosevelt's executive order was well spent on these ships and others like them.*

The Enterprise *at anchor with PBY Catalina patrol bomber taxiing behind the new carrier. The war in Europe was only two weeks old when this photograph was snapped on September 18, 1939.*

Wilcox boilers with Curtis-Parsons Geared turbines generating 120,000 shp to four shafts. She carried up to 7,366 tons of oil fuel and 186,858 gallons of high octane aviation gasoline. Unfortunately, there were serious engineering problems which necessitated the replacement of over 1,200 boiler tubes and the reduction gear machinery. This caused a delay in completing the carrier. However, this mishap had no adverse affect on her overall performance and operational readiness.

The U.S. was not alone in building improved carriers. Japan, keeping pace with the U.S. Navy took note of the *Yorktown* class, and appreciated this leap in carrier evolution. They responded with the 18,800 ton *Soryu* (34 knots, 71 aircraft capacity) and the 20,250 ton *Hiryu* (34 knots, 73 aircraft). Of course, the Japanese introduced as rather peculiar variation. The *Hiryu* had her island structure on the right side and the *Soryu*, the left side. Both carriers were designed to operate together allowing aircraft to land from both beams. This proved awkward and did not become the norm in future Japanese carrier development. Great Britain was also in the game and built HMS *Ark Royal* (22,000 tons, 31 knots, 60 aircraft capacity) and three ships of the Illustrious class, HMS *Illustrious*, HMS *Victorious*, HMS *Formidable* (23,000 tons, 30.5 knots, 52 aircraft). The *Illustrious* class was the first class of aircraft carrier with an armored flight deck, a feature that would prove itself more significant than any other means of protection.

France and Italy each built or attempted to build carriers, but their contribution was negligible in the upcoming war. Even Germany built a carrier (*Graf Zeppelin*), but it too was of no practical value. It accidently sank after the war while acting as a locomotive and industrial machinery transport to the Soviet Union. Hoarding German war booty, the Soviets overloaded the carrier and she sank.

The *Enterprise* was laid down on July 16, 1934 at the Newport News Shipbuilding and Drydock Company, and hundreds of formerly unemployed shipyard workers and artisans began to work on this new carrier. Sharing the dockyard was her sister the *Yorktown* and later the light cruiser *Boise*. Work continued apace throughout 1934, 1935, and into the early autumn of 1936. Finally, the big day arrived and on October 3, 1936, the *Enterprise* was launched. The *Yorktown* had been slid down the ways six months earlier, sponsored by the President's wife, Eleanor Roosevelt. The *Enterprise* was sponsored by Mrs. Claude A. Swanson, wife of the Secretary of the Navy. The Newport News Shipbuilding and Drydock Company had outdone themselves with the creation of the *Enterprise*. She was a beautiful and powerful addition to a navy starving for modern warships. Up through mid 1938, she was moored next to sister *Yorktown* for fitting out and final construction. Just opposite her port side, another newcomer was being completed, the big light cruiser *Boise*. All three of these ships would make their mark in naval history, but none so great as the cluttered, but organized mess called the *Enterprise*. On May 12, 1938, the watch was set and she was placed in commission under the command of Captain N. H. White.

THE *ENTERPRISE* JOINS THE FLEET AND PREPARES FOR WAR

After a period of trials, the new carrier sailed for Rio de Janeiro in Brazil. The Navy always had an ulterior motive for ship movements, and the cruise to South America was no different. Brazil would prove to be an effective ally in World War II, and her government needed to witness American naval might. Old battleships were one symbol of strength, but the versatility and futuristic might of this new weapon of war was quite spectacular. Later she joined with the *Yorktown* and they formed Carrier Division Two under the command of Commander, Aircraft, Battle Force. Carrier Division One consisted of the *Ranger, Lexington* and *Saratoga*. The old *Langley* had already been converted to a sea-

plane tender and was being assigned to duty in the Asiatic Fleet.

The *Enterprise* embarked an air group that initially consisted of 81 aircraft. It was divided into:

13 Northrop BT-1 monoplane bombers of VB-6
20 Grumman F3F fighters (biplanes) of VF-6
20 Curtis SBC-3 Scout (biplanes) of VS-6
20 Douglas TBD-1 monoplane torp/bombers of VT-6
10 Plane utility unit of various aircraft

Torpedo Squadron Six (VT-6) was created for the *Enterprise* and flew the Douglas TBD-1 from 1938 up through 1941. This squadron adopted the Great White Albatross as its emblem. Most squadrons selected a rather colorful insignia to identify their aircraft and create a sense of camaraderie. Bombing Six or VB-6 chose the wild goat and Fighting Six selected a blazing comet or shooting star. Fighting Six was armed with the agile but slow (254 mph) Grumman F3F biplane until May 1941 when it was replaced by the F4F Wildcat (334 mph) produced by the same manufacturer. This was a very fortunate upgrade as the F3F would have been a sitting duck for the Japanese Zeke or Zero fighter. As it was, the Wildcat pilots had their hands full when fighting this very superior Japanese fighter plane. Scouting Six or VS-6 had one of the more colorful in their headdress of an Aztec priest during the rite of human sacrifice.

Blue was the *Enterprise's* signature color and most tail assemblies reflected this identifier. The eclectic mixture of biplanes, and various monoplanes with fixed and folding wings would quickly be streamlined into three principal aircraft; the Grumman Wildcat fighter, Douglas Dauntless divebomber and Grumman Avenger torpedo bomber. For the time being however, a number of aircraft would come and go aboard the new carrier until the war caused some uniformity.

For the next several months and into April of 1939, the *Enterprise* operated off the east coast of the U.S. and down into the Caribbean. This was part of the traditional working up plan for new ships. In late spring she sailed for the Pacific, briefly stopping in San Diego. Subsequently, she steamed northward to San Francisco Bay. In July, she spent time in San Francisco anchored off Treasure Island. This was a 400 acre man made island dedicated to the 1939 Golden Gate International Exposition. The island also provided landing and hanger space for Pan American Airlines long range China clippers.

The bay current that flows past the island is strong and can change direction or strength without notice. The *Enterprise* was anchored just off the island adjacent to the main entrance, and was a beautiful sight for thousands of visitors from all over the world. It is no doubt that many photographs were taken by Japanese and German tourists that found their way into military intelligence briefings. On the opposite coast, the World's Fair in New York was claiming the lion's share of national attention and it seemed that most of the U.S. Navy was anchored in the Hudson River. In fact, ships that were detached and deployed to the Pacific carried crews bitter

The USS Enterprise *on September 20, 1939 with her port anchor in the water. Launches are tethered to the giant carrier; and on her deck, the distinctive "E N" identifies her. She is a new carrier, and her air group obviously needs updating from biplane to monoplane aircraft.*

over having missed the event. All was not lost as the Exposition on Treasure Island was one of the most beautiful sights created by man and there was plenty of action in the Bay area for sailors, both cultural and temporal. Some sailors experienced too much culture and suffered the effects of the following morning. What better treatment for a suspected hangover than a small boat ride and a little painting. Such was the prescription for two *Enterprise* sailors obviously in need of fresh air and light work. They were assigned a small punt and a can of grey (what else) paint and instructed to touch up the eyes of the ship where rust appeared. Not fully recovered from the previous night's marathon drinking bout, they tied the boat to the anchor chain. A few moments later, the Boatswain decided to let out a few more feet of anchor chain to compensate for the current. This had the double effect of taking boat, painters and equipment down several feet under the water off Treasure Island. The only thing injured was pride, but at least the hangovers disappeared.

Ships are made of steel, wood, leather, oil, paint, but above all, men. The *Enterprise* could have been a dismal failure or a complete success dependent on the men who served in her. She became a great success and a tribute to her men. Legends like the anchor chain incident become part of the ship's character. From the outset, the *Enterprise* was special and destined for greatness. Even in jest, she and her crew excelled.

It was not long before the carrier was summoned to Pearl Harbor, 2,400 miles closer to future combat. For the next several months, the ship and her squadrons were engaged in one training exercise after another. There was no breathing room as it was certain that war was imminent with Japan. The question was how soon? The carrier and her escorts rarely spent

time at Pearl Harbor, and as the autumn of 1941 became the winter, training intensified. On November 28, 1941, the *Enterprise* and her task force left Pearl Harbor to transport and deliver twelve F4F-3 Wildcat fighters to Wake Island. A week later, on December 4, Marine VMF-211 flew off to land at Wake. Their intended purpose was to defend the island outpost against Japanese attack and await the arrival of PBY Catalina's and other patrol planes. Wake Island had been selected as a forward patrol facility to provide intelligence and early warning about Japanese air and ship movements. This role was never to be and within days, they were in action. The efforts of 12 obsolecsing fighter planes and a spirited ground defense thrilled the nation starved for any sign of victory over the Japanese. During the days leading up to the ultimate capture of Wake Island by an overwhelming force of crack troops, one of the finest chapters of heroism was written in Marine Corps history.

It was while the *Enterprise* and her escorting task group were making their way back to Pearl Harbor that the Japanese staged their attack. She was some 200 miles out, and launched Bombing Six with instructions to land at Ford Island. The Japanese attacking force had hoped to catch the *Enterprise* and other carriers in the harbor, but they had to settle for battleships, cruisers and other craft. Had any or all of the American carriers been present in Pearl Harbor, the Pacific war would have had an entirely different complexion. As it was, aircraft from the *Enterprise* did participate in the attack, being shot at by the Japanese as well as excited friendly antiaircraft crews. Douglas SBD's arrived at the height of the attack and although most were able to get down safely, this was not so for returning search planes that night. Thirteen SBD's were sent out at about noon to search for the elusive Japanese

task force, but nothing was sighted. Five made it back to the *Enterprise* after dark, but of the remaining eight, two were brought down by enemy aircraft, two successfully landed, and tragically four were shot down by friendly, but undisciplined antiaircraft batteries. At sea in the *Enterprise*, Admiral William Halsey became enraged that he was not able to participate in the battle and launched virtually everything that could fly in a vain attempt to search out and destroy the enemy. In a small way, his failure to engage Admiral Nagumo's six carrier strike force saved the *Enterprise* from destruction. She was one lone carrier against six that had over 350 exhilarated veteran pilots and well armed planes. The *"Big E"* could have mustered at best only 21 Wildcats and no more than 22 torpedo bombers. Her divebombers were having difficulties of their own over Pearl Harbor, and her available antiaircraft protection was wholly inadequate.

The *Enterprise* entered Pearl Harbor at dusk on December 8, 1941, and upon seeing the ruin of what was once the battle fleet, "Bull" Halsey vowed that only in hell would the Japanese language be spoken. Her turnaround time for fueling and re-provisioning was rapid and just before first light on December 9, she hurriedly departed. As the task force left the harbor and thousands of troubled sailors viewed the smoking ships, a sense of determination slowly began to overtake that of uneasiness. Halsey and Company were not about to suffer the same fate as the battleships. The war had begun in earnest for the *Enterprise*.

THE LEGEND BEGINS:
SCRATCH ONE SUB!

The *Enterprise* was assigned the rather dubious task of hunting submarines around Oahu. It was correctly suspected that one of the principal elements of the overall Japanese attack was to station her ocean cruising submarines off Hawaii to pick off any stragglers that escaped from Pearl Harbor. The *Enterprise* was sent out to rid this menace, and one of her patrolling SBD's found one. The I-70 was surfaced and surprised by a plane piloted by Lt. (jg) Edward Anderson. He did enough damage to prevent the sub from submerging and later that day, Lt. Clarence Dickinson administered the final rites. This was certainly not the only encounter as the *Enterprise* and her hunter-killer group attacked many more contacts by air, depth charge and even gunfire from the cruiser *Salt Lake City*. By December 15, the show was over and the task force returned to Pearl Harbor. The air groups flew to Ford Island and the ships moored in the relative protection of the harbor. The first ship sunk by the *Enterprise* was a submarine, but it was certainly not to be the last.

THE FIRST WEEKS: WHAT IS THE NEXT
MOVE FOR THE U.S. NAVY?

War Plan Orange,the pre December 7, 1941, blueprint for war in the Pacific was now on the bottom of Pearl Harbor. Of course there would be a delaying action fought in the Philippines, but no triumphant battle fleet would sail to the rescue and defeat the Japanese Navy in one all inclusive slugging match. Nothing remotely resembling World War I's Battle of Jutland was about to happen. The U.S. Navy had been shorn of its first line of defense, its battleships. What remained were three carriers, a number of treaty cruisers and several relatively modern destroyers. The submarine force was also still in tact and eventually it's effort would dramatically improve our chances for ultimate victory, but at this stage in the war, it was up to the carriers.

The Navy had to develop a strategic plan and quickly. It was too late to save the Philippines and the oil rich east Indies, so the life line to Australia had to be preserved. Panama and its vital link to the Atlantic must also not be forgotten in the revised plan. In addition, the American island possessions that formed the outer ring of defense for the west coast had to be protected. The fear of a coastal invasion was constant for the first few months of 1942, and a repeat raid on Pearl Harbor was expected at any moment. The remnants of the U.S. Navy had to be employed for in a protective role. Defensive fighting was not a popular choice for the fleet, especially for men like Admiral Halsey, but practical logic overrode revenge. This did not mean that the Navy would sit and await the Japanese. It did mean that fast moving carrier strike forces would have to attack and neutralize current Japanese bases in the Marshall Islands from which attacks on Samoa and Fiji were expected. Samoa had already been bombarded from the sea on January 11, 1942, and if this region was captured, then a vital communication and supply line to Australia-New Zealand would be breached.

With the capture of Wake Island and Guam in the Marianas Islands, the primary tactical objectives of the fleet would be to protect Midway Island (still in American hands), as well as Fiji and Samoa. It was known that there were substantial Japanese bases in Marshall Islands, and in order to interrupt further advances toward Fiji and Samoa, a raid was necessary. The carriers *Enterprise* and *Yorktown* were selected for this first major strike of the Pacific War. The old *Saratoga* had been temporarily immobilized by a submarine launched torpedo, so two carriers would have to do the job.

The Enterprise *moored in Pearl Harbor in early 1942. She now has been fitted with 20mm guns in the bow and stern areas. She also sports the bedspring CXAM-1 radar antenna. Radar would be vastly improved as the war progressed, and heavy ship commanders began to rely on its effectiveness. The foremast of the still sunken Pearl Harbor attack victim, battleship* West Virginia, *can be seen in the distance.*

FEBRUARY 1942: THE *ENTERPRISE* ATTACKS THE MARSHALL ISLANDS

Task Force 8, centered on the *Enterprise* was comprised of the cruisers *Salt Lake City*, *Northhampton* and *Chester* accompanied by six destroyers sailed for the Marshalls from Samoa on January 25, 1942. The *Yorktown* group commanded by Rear Admiral Frank Jack Fletcher (TF-17) also left Samoa for the same purpose but was assigned to attack the southern most islands. On February 1, 1942, both were in place. The *Yorktown* was in the enemy's back yard, and the *Enterprise* was at the front door.

Task Force 8 was divided into three separate attack units. The heavy cruiser *Chester* accompanied by one destroyer as well as the *Salt Lake City* and *Northhampton* also with destroyers pealed off to bombard Taroa Island and Wotje respectively. The *Enterprise* began launching aircraft at 0443 and within minutes, nine torpedo bombers, 37 divebombers and a number of Wildcat fighters were on their way to various targets

on and around Kwajalein. Eventually 59 aircraft were winging their way toward preselected targets and any that happened to be fat and juicy. The results were different for each area attacked. The attack on Kwajalein Lagoon was a resounding success as a transport and subchaser were sunk and six other ships damaged. Eighteen aircraft were hit on the ground. The attacks on Roi and Wotje were satisfactory, and the Japanese quickly retaliated with an air attack that did some minor damage. The short lived attack consisted of three bombers that arrived shortly after lunch, one of which attempted a suicide attack. The fanatic was diverted through quick maneuvering and the timely action of Bruno Gaida who hit the plunging aircraft with 30 caliber machine gun fire. By February 2, 1942, the *Enterprise* and her charges were safely on their way to Pearl Harbor. They had scored a major victory and although there were some aircraft losses, morale was vastly improved. Perhaps this war could be won.

For the next several weeks and on into mid March 1942, the *Enterprise* and company visited Wake and Marcus Islands hitting them hard. The Japanese were not being left alone. On March 13, 1942, the well worn carrier returned to Pearl Harbor for repairs and painting. She had been constantly steaming from one side of the ocean to another, and simulating different task forces was quickly taking it's toll. Initial war experience also proved that her antiaircraft battery was wholly insufficient. Even massed 50 caliber machine guns would not bring down modern well built aircraft. Something heavier was necessary, and during her hurried overhaul the carrier was armed with additional 20mm guns forward and aft. Forty millimeter guns would have been better, but there were precious few mounts available in the navy at this time. Within months thousands would come of the assembly lines, but for now 5 inch/38 caliber guns assisted by 20mm and 50 caliber would have to suffice. The February raid on the Marshalls had been a

shot in the arm for the navy, but the continuing series of reverses in the Atlantic and Pacific had reduced the confidence of the American public to a dangerous low. Something spectacular had to happen, and soon. From this need, the Army-Navy raid on Tokyo was born.

DOOLITTLE'S RAID: THE *ENTERPRISE* WAS THERE AS WELL

As early as January 1942, the Chief of Naval Operations, Admiral Earnest J. King, had been searching for some method of practical retaliation for the Pearl Harbor raid. The idea of launching Army Air Force bombers from carriers had een suggested by the chief of the Army Air Forces, General Henry A. "Hap" Arnold. However his idea was not Japan as a target, but North Africa. Japan being a target came from Captain Francis S. Low, King's Operations Officer in Washington. Within days a few other people were consulted including Lt. Colonel James Doolittle and Captain Donald Duncan, King's air officer. From these early brain storming sessions, the plan originated. The navy would provide a carrier and suitable escort for sixteen Army North American B-25 medium bombers that would be launched within striking distance of a selected number of cities in Japan. Douglas B-23's were considered as they met the one ton bomb capacity and 2000 mile range, however the B-25 had a shorter wingspan. On the narrow confines of a carrier flight deck, this made the B-25 a natural choice. Of course, if any navy aircraft could have remotely matched the B-25 Mitchell, then it might have been a navy show all the way. As it was, the magnificent cooperation between the services helped to guarantee success.

Volunteers were accepted from the 17th Bomb Group and 83rd Reconnaissance Squadron which were not only equipped with B-25's, but were on active anti-submarine patrol off the Oregon and Washington coasts. After a short period of training at Elgin Field in Florida, the aircraft and their crews, who were still in the dark about the mission, flew to Mather Field in Sacramento. They had been taking off from a remote part of the Florida base from a strip that had various distance markers, one of which was quite intriguing. It was at 400 feet, and the navy training officer was somewhat adamant about the planes being lifted off by the time they reached this marker. On April 1, 1942, the planes and crews arrived over their final destination at the Alameda Naval Air Station and saw a small postage stamp like ship docked next to the landing field. Incredibly, B-25's were being lifted onto her flight deck. The ship was the USS *Hornet* CV-8, and the confused crews were vaguely reminded of the marked off strip at Elgin Field. It looked much like the flight deck of that very same carrier.

Throughout the first day of April, Army aircraft and crews were welcomed aboard the *Hornet*. She was actually a step sister to the *Enterprise* and *Yorktown* as she was slightly larger. The crazy scheme concocted by Navy and Army brass just weeks before was coming to fruition. On the following day, the *Hornet* and cruiser destroyer escorts sailed for the north Pacific. For just under two weeks, the task force sailed northwestward hoping to avoid any air or sea traffic, and of course any Japanese snoopers. The *Hornet* was virtually defenseless as her air group had been struck below in every conceivable spot. The sixteen B-25's took up most of the deck just aft of the island. If the group were to encounter any enemy opposition, then the army planes would either have to fly off or be pushed over the side. The ships would then have to defend themselves as best possible. On April 13, 1942, a beautiful sight was beheld by the *Hornet* task group. Task Force 16 with the fully functioning *Enterprise*, two heavy cruisers and destroyers appeared. The force could now defend itself with some credibility. Now the total force consisted of two major carriers, four cruisers, eight destroyers and two fleet oilers. As a footnote, it is important to realize how significant this raid was considered to be. The highest levels of government had pulled two fleet carriers out of the line to attack a few Japanese cities with light bombs and incendiaries. The actual damage was expected to be minor, and it was. However, the psychological affect was overwhelmingly positive for the Allies and at the same time caused despair and apprehension in Japan. The gamble was well worth the risk.

On April 17, the force refueled from the oilers USS *Sabine* and USS *Cimmarron*. The carriers and cruisers left the tin cans and slow tankers behind, and began their run in for the launch. The plan called for the attackers to be launched within 500 miles of their target, but in the very early morning hours of April 18, the force was discovered by picket boats. They were operating nearly 600 miles from their homeland and by 0500 had sent a warning. The American force had no way of knowing that the warning had little effect, but caution was the by word. The task force commander, Admiral Halsey in consultation with Doolittle decided that it was prudent to launch rather than abort the entire mission. The *Hornet* was still 668 miles from Tokyo, and the additional 1093 miles to potential safety on

the Chinese mainland was cutting the safety margin to less than 200 miles! Turning back now would have been more demoralizing than the failed Wake Island Relief expedition and the surrender of Bataan together. At 0725, Lt. Colonel Jimmy Doolittle (soon to the Brig General Doolittle) took off the plunging deck of the *Hornet*. He was not the first to fly a B-25 off her deck however. The whole project might have been scrapped had it not been for Ist Lt. John E. Fitzgerald who had secretly been launched from the *Hornet* off Norfolk on February 2, 1942. It could be done, and it was, sixteen times on April 18, 1942 Less than an hour after Doolittle took off, the last being piloted by Lt. William G. Farrow. Farrow and his crew were captured and amid much sickening fanfare were tried and convicted of war crimes. Farrow and his gunner, Sgt. Harold A. Spatz were executed by firing squad. Plane number 16's other crew members were Japanese POW's until liberated.

The raiders hit Tokyo, Nagoya, Kobe and Yokohama. The damage to industrial and military facilities was light, but the raid was a great success. Eighty Army air crew took part as did 10,000 U.S. Navy personnel in the task force. Seventy one of the raiders survived this remarkable incident, one that will always adorn American history. All of the planes were lost or grounded, yet most of the men survived. Doolittle was awarded the Medal of Honor and the other 79 men received the Distinguished Flying Cross. They earned their awards.

Having launched the strike, Halsey beat a hasty retreat from the area at 25 knots. Aircraft from the *Enterprise* encountered sixteen different patrol boats which they took great pleasure in shooting full of holes. Several sank and one even surrendered to the cruiser *Nashville*. The Japanese crew that surrendered to the *Nashville* almost became pets to the cruiser's crew, but they were still POW's and as such were herded ashore and imprisoned when Task Force 16 arrived back in Pearl Harbor on April 25, 1942. It had been quite a spectacular and momentous affair. President Roosevelt told the press that the raiders had come from "Shangri-la", but half the navy knew that they came from the *Hornet*. Unfortunately, most forgot that the *Enterprise* was also a major part of this operation. She was also there and without her diligent air cover, the outcome would surely have been different. The Halsey-Doolittle Raid or "Thirty Seconds over Tokyo" had been an Army Navy affair. There was something brewing that concerned Midway, the Imperial Japanese Navy and code breaking on an unprecedented scale. This was to be an all navy affair.

THE BATTLES OF THE CORAL SEA AND MIDWAY: AMERICAN AND JAPANESE PREPARATIONS

The Japanese had suffered a loss of face due to the Halsey-Doolittle Raid in April, but this was a mere blip on the screen of their onslaught. The balance sheet showed that as of May 1, 1942, the Japanese had lost 23 warships (largest being a destroyer), 67 merchantmen and a few hundred aircraft. On the credit side, the Imperial forces had sunk or damaged two carriers (HMS *Hermes* and USS *Saratoga*), 10 battleships, and numerous Allied cruisers and destroyers. To this

was added many thousand tons of merchant shipping and hundreds of Allied aircraft. Even the most optimistic among Allied planners were now asking not when the Japanese could be stopped, but if! The period from December 7, 1941 up through May 1, 1942 had been a disaster of vast and mounting proportions.

The Japanese Planning Staff had remained close to their pre-war strategy of capturing the resource rich Netherlands East Indies and then establishing a series of defensive rings around their conquests. That meant denying access to the U.S. Navy. By early spring, 1942, the target areas had been secured and it was time to consolidate and fortify the outer defense ring. For this, Port Moresby in New Guinea as well as Tulagi in the Solomon Islands would have to come under the protective Imperial umbrella. These areas in Japanese hands would prevent the American Navy from threatening the Coral Sea region. The Aleutians and Midway Island were also slated to become part of the Japanese outer defensive ring. They knew that a thrust in either direction would draw the remaining elements of the U.S. Navy into a major battle. Suffering from the effects of what was becoming known as the "victory disease", it was automatically assumed that the U.S. Navy would soon find its way to the bottom of the Pacific Ocean or Coral Sea. The notion that any of his imperial majesty's navy would suffer the same fate was not considered.

It was in this context that the Battle of the Coral Sea was fought over the three day period from May 5-8, 1942. They had massed a large invasion and carrier covering force and were met by Task Force 17 composed of the carriers *Lexington* and *Yorktown* supported by American and Australian cruisers as well as a number of destroyers. After a series of air battles, the result was that the Japanese were prevented from immediately occupying Port Moresby and lost their first carrier, the CVL *Shoho*. They were successfully able to secure Tulagi, but the cost was unusually high. Ironically, they would have right, title and interest for just a few months. In August, the Allies would come back, this time with amphibious forces. At Coral Sea, the U.S. Navy lost the carrier *Lexington*, the destroyer *Sims* and the oiler *Neosho*. To the pessimistic, it was another Allied loss, but strategically, it was the first time that the Japanese were halted in their plans. Both sides withdrew after the battle. The sole surviving American carrier, the *Yorktown* was damaged and sailed for Pearl Harbor and repair.

On May 1, 1942, the *Enterprise* and her escorts were ordered to steam at flank speed for the Coral Sea to provide support, but long before they could reach the battle, it was over. War exclusively between carriers without either force coming within visual range had begun. The *Enterprise* returned to Pearl Harbor on May 26, 1942. During her time at sea, a change was made in the identification markings on her aircraft. The red star surrounded by the light blue and white was replaced by a single white star surrounded by a field of white. The red star in the center of the insignia could be deceiving during combat, so a more simple marking was selected. From a larger standpoint, this minor change represented a graduation from pre-war naval aviation to that which was war tested. The old days had come to an end.

A B-25 begins her roll down the flight deck of the Hornet *on April 18, 1942. Destination: Tokyo and other major cities. The* Enterprise *was providing naval air coverage for the entire operation.*

A translated copy of the April 19, 1942 issue of the Japan Times and Advertiser newspaper. Their version was somewhat different from the facts, a problem with most media reporting.

Although the Japanese withdrew from the Port Moresby operation, they had yet to suffer a serious setback or any credible losses. The plan to attack and occupy the Aleutians and Midway was not interrupted by the Coral Sea standoff, and on they came. Midway was situated some 1135 miles from Pearl Harbor and considered to be part of the Hawaiian chain. They Japanese, contrary to popular belief were not interested in using Midway as a spring board to occupy the Hawaiian Islands and then on to the west coast of the U.S. They wanted Midway to use as their furthest outpost and a base for staging nuisance raids on Pearl Harbor. The U.S. Navy was not certain of their strategy, but was not about to allow another Wake Island. Midway was going to be held. The Japanese had other ideas and were so confident of another victory, that the fleet post office in Tokyo was notified to forward one air group's mail to Midway after early June! This belief in the superiority of Japanese manhood over their American opponents would prove disastrous in the first days of June 1942.

Defense of Midway was to be from land based aircraft and what carriers that could be mustered. The *Enterprise* and *Hornet* were available and ready to fight. The *Hornet* had an inexperienced but eager air group. But a third carrier was vital. It had to be the *Yorktown* and she required at least one and a half months in a shipyard to repair the damage sustained at Coral Sea. When she arrived in Pearl Harbor on May 27, 1942, over 1,400 skilled and dedicated yard workmen treated her injuries. She emerged 48 hours later on May 29, and sailed for Midway on May 30, 1942. Her regeneration was analogous to that of a severely beaten prize fighter who is obviously hurt, but doctored enough to score a knockout in the final round. There were now three carriers. Unfortunately, the logical leader for the American response, Admiral Halsey was stricken with a skin disease, probably the result of six months of unbelievable strain. In his place, Rear Admiral Raymond Spruance, a cruiser sailor was appointed as task force commander. Spruance was not an aviator nor had he commanded air operations. He did have the confidence of the Commander in Chief of the Pacific Fleet, Admiral Chester Nimitz, and the blessing of Admiral Halsey. Besides, Captain Miles Browning, a Halsey devotee was assigned as a battle advisor to Admiral Spruance. There would be a Halsey influence after all.

Admiral Spruance was in command of Task Force 16 which was composed of the *Enterprise* and *Hornet* with supporting cruisers and destroyers. TF-16 was then part of the larger Carrier Striking Force under Rear Admiral Frank Jack Fletcher who carried his flag in the *Yorktown*. American warship resources totalled 3 carriers, 8 cruisers, 19 destroyers, and 19 submarines. The combined carrier air groups consisted of 79 Wildcat fighters, 112 SBD divebombers, and 42 torpedo planes, which totalled 233 combat capable aircraft. The ground based air defenses at Midway consisted of 32 PBY Catalina patrol planes, 27 Buffalo and older Wildcat fighters and a sprinkling of divebombers and torpedo planes. The U.S. Army also contributed 23 bombers (4 B-26 medium bombers and 19 B-17 Flying Fortresses). Midway even had its own mosquito fleet of eight motor torpedo boats of MTB

Squadron 1, and of course there was the 6th Marine Defense Battalion should the Japanese make it to the beaches. There was one other major if not the deciding factor in favor of the American defenders. A few unruly, undisciplined, but extremely persistent men had broken the Japanese codes and were deciphering important message traffic. They discovered the Japanese timetable and what was to be expected from the Imperial Japanese Navy. This leveled the playing field.

The Japanese, confident in their ultimate success in capturing Midway were also very much looking forward to destroying any American Carriers brave enough to attempt any opposition. For this operation, Admiral Yamamoto who rode in his flagship, the 63,000 ton battleship *Yamato* deployed the following forces:

Carriers: 5 (*Akagi, Hiryu, Soryu, Kaga* and *Zuiho*)
Battleships: 4 (*Haruna, Kirishima, Kongo,* and *Hiei*)
Cruisers: 12
Destroyers: 23
Submarines: 16

In addition, there were other heavy units being sent to attack the Aleutians, and a very large fleet train which included transports, cargo ships and oilers. The occupation force originated in the Marianas and the super battleship *Yamato* with two other battleships and the light carrier *Hosho* was to the rear of the carrier striking force. The Japanese carrier striking force had 272 first line aircraft that could be brought into battle. The odds facing the U.S. Navy were appalling.

THE BATTLE OF MIDWAY - FORTUNES CHANGE IN JUST MINUTES

Orders from Nimitz were simple. "Hold Midway and inflict maximum damage on the enemy by strong attrition tactics". The battle began on June 3, 1942 when Midway based aircraft bombed Japanese transports. A PBY patrol plane had discovered two Japanese forces at about 700 miles distant from their objective. Shortly after a frantic message was received at Midway, B-17 bombers were on their way to bomb the Japanese force. Bombs were dropped in late afternoon with no hits. Subsequently, in the very early morning hours of June 4, 1942, PBY *Catalina's* armed with torpedoes tried their luck. One torpedo hit one of the oilers in the fleet train. Later that day, Navy pilots would have better luck.

On June 4 at 0430, the four Japanese carriers launched a balanced strike of 108 aircraft that could deal with ships, ground facilities and any American aircraft that rose to the attack. Between 0630 and 0715 the Japanese did their work and then left. They had lost approximately 30-35 aircraft in this first raid, but they had hit Midway quite hard.

The Americans retaliated, and aircraft from the *Hornet* and *Enterprise* searched for the elusive Japanese carriers. Much of the Hornet's air group (divebombers and fighters) had to land at Midway after missing the Japanese. This left the Torpedo Squadron 8 to go into the attack after locating the Japanese. It was a slaughter.

Japanese Zero fighters descended to wave level to attack the slow moving Devastators and those of Lt. Cmdr. John C. Waldron's squadron that persisted were quickly shot down by escorting destroyers and cruisers. By 0930, Torpedo Eight was history with the exception of one lone pilot who landed in the water. Ensign George H. Gay was in for the show of a lifetime. Bobbing about in the sea he was about to witness a miracle. The continued use of obsolete torpedo bombers and defective torpedoes came into question as a result of this attack. The Grumman TBF soon replaced the old TBD and torpedoes were made more effective. A pilot and crew that withstands a curtain of flack and defending fighter planes deserved at least a fighting chance of hitting the target and survival.

The Japanese were jubilant over their easy victory. But, the battle was not over. The *Akagi, Kaga* and *Soryu* had been dodging torpedo planes from all three American and had not been able to launch aircraft during this phase of the battle. In addition, their combat air patrols were at deck level and not up over the formation as they should have been. Jubilance was replaced by terror as Dauntless Divebombers from the *Yorktown* and *Enterprise* began coming down. Ensign Gay who watched the show from the best seat in the house - the water, later stated that the Dauntless's came down screaming with dive brakes retracted. It was a full speed dive bombing attack born out of excitement or design, but it worked. Lt. Cmdr. Clarence W. McClusky led 37 divebombers into a lethal attack on the *Kaga* and *Akagi*. Within minutes both of the battlecruisers converted to large carriers were burning furiously. *Enterprise* delivered bombs had hit their loaded flight decks and petrol filled hanger decks. In a twelve minute period from 1016-1028, pilots from the *Enterprise* hit the *Kaga* with four bombs and the *Akagi* with two bombs. It was enough. The carrier *Soryu* was also hit and mortally wounded in the same 12 minutes by divebombers from the *Yorktown*. The *Hiryu*, several miles away from her three sisters, escaped unharmed for the time being.

It was incredible. Through determination and simply force of circumstance, aircraft from underdog carriers had destroyed three large Japanese fleet carriers. Of course, the Japanese still had one fleet carrier available, and there were not about to leave knowing that one or more American carriers were in the vicinity.

Admiral Nagumo, victor at Pearl Harbor was forced to leave the *Akagi* and transferred tactical command to Rear Admiral Hiroaki Abe. The position of one or perhaps two enemy carriers was known and Admiral Abe directed the undamaged *Hiryu* to launch everything capable of flying. Within 15 minutes of the smashing victory over the *Akagi, Kaga* and *Soryu*, 18 divebombers and six Zero's were winging their way to what was the *Yorktown*. Shortly thereafter another group of torpedo bombers and fighters followed the first wave toward the *Yorktown*.

The combat air patrol over the *Yorktown* shot down half of the attackers but she took three bombs in very critical areas. Shortly after the first raid at half past 1400, the torpedo planes arrived. Every gun in the task force including the main batteries of the several of the heavy

cruisers opened fire on the incoming "Kate" torpedo planes. Four got through and two hits were registered on the carrier's port side. Within 30 minutes, it became obvious that the situation was hopeless, and abandon ship was ordered. As luck would have it, aircraft returning from the *Yorktown* spotted the *Hiryu* and radioed its position to the *Enterprise*. She then launched a strike that included planes from the *Yorktown* and at 1600 or one hour after the abandon ship order on the *Yorktown*, the *Hiryu* was hit with four bombs. The following morning at 0900, she too joined her three dead sisters. With her went the dreams and aspirations of a nation, with 272 planes and most of their pilots. Admiral Yamamoto had told his staff that after the successful attack on Pearl Harbor, he would more or less run unchallenged for a year. He overestimated by six months.

The Japanese assault force had no choice but to retreat and during its retirement it was harassed by aircraft from Midway and the *Hornet* and *Enterprise*. There was still some lingering concern that all of the Japanese carriers were gone, so caution was exercised. Spruance did not want to lose another carrier. The Japanese had no carriers to lose, but two cruisers, the *Mikuma* and *Mogami* were severely mauled first by Midway based aircraft and then by divebombers from the *Hornet* and *Enterprise*. The *Mikuma* finally succumbed late on June 6, 1942. For the Japanese, the battle was all but over.

The *Yorktown* had been abandoned and drifting when it was decided to save her. At this time she was being towed by a small old ocean going tug, *Vireo ATO-144* with three escorting destroyers. A select crew of volunteers was transferred from the destroyer *Hammann* which lashed herself alongside and they began the work of saving this priceless ship. The Japanese had other plans for the carrier and after stalking the *Yorktown* for 24 hours, the submarine I-168 put three torpedoes into her and the *Hammann*. That finished the carrier and the *Hammann*. The *Yorktown* rolled over and sank the following morning at 0600. The Battle of Midway was over.

The scorecard showed that the Americans lost one carrier, one destroyer and just under 140 aircraft. Over thirty percent of the aircraft losses were torpedo planes. The Japanese lost four first line carriers, one heavy cruiser and a fleet submarine. Of greater significance was the loss of 272 aircraft and veteran pilots many of whom ditched after their homes were sunk. The Imperial Japanese Navy had suffered the first true defeat in it's history. It never recovered. The *Enterprise* had worked miracles, and for a reward she was allowed a short period of rest and overhaul. She sailed from Pearl Harbor on July 15, 1942 for the South Pacific as a member of Task Force 61. The Allies were going to begin reclaiming stolen property from the Japanese. The *Enterprise* would be needed to provide air cover for the upcoming invasion of the Solomon Islands.

THE SOLOMONS: THE "BIG E" TAKES HER FIRST HIT

For many it was still difficult to understand what had taken place at Midway. We had lost the *Yorktown*, but the Japanese were now without the core of their carrier aviation program. Moreover, the U.S. Navy would be commissioning many *Essex* class fleet carriers and *Independence* class light carriers within a year. The Japanese navy had no such massive building program underway. Thousands of naval aviators were being trained at facilities all over the U.S., and again no such large scale programs were in effect in Japan. Ships like the *Yorktown, Lexington, Hornet, Saratoga* and *Enterprise* were holding the line until joined by modern powerful carriers with well trained air groups. That these five carriers would also wipe out the pride of Japanese naval aviation was an added bonus. The war was not over yet. There was still the matter of defeating the rest of the Japanese military machine. Attention was now switched to the Solomon Islands and in particular a small strip of real estate on Guadalcanal.

The Allies spearheaded by the U.S. Navy and Marine Corps suddenly appeared between Guadalcanal and Tulagi on August 7, 1942. Within hours assault troops were ashore forcibly taking back territory seized by the Japanese just months earlier. The Allies were mainly interested in a partially completed air field on Guadalcanal. Whosoever controlled this airfield threatened an area for hundreds of miles in any direction. The Allies were not about to allow the Japanese this advantage. U.S. Marines quickly overcame the defenders most of whom temporarily fled into the jungle. They then named the field after a Marine flyer who had been killed at Midway. Henderson Field became one of the most famous air strips in World War II, and also one of the most hotly contested. The Japanese wanted it back, and desperately.

Less than three weeks after the Allied invasion, the Japanese followed up their spectacular surface ship attack of August 9, 1942. On that night they had swept into the channel between Savo Island and Guadalcanal and sank four Allied cruisers. It was a disgrace. Now on August 24, 1942, they were back, this time with three carriers, three battleships and many cruisers and destroyers. Of the three carriers, two were the *Shokaku* and *Zuikaku*, which were the remaining two survivors of the Pearl Harbor raid. The other four had been sunk at the Battle of Midway. The third flattop was the light carrier *Ryujo*. The Japanese had successfully carried off a hit and run night raid, but now it was time to throw the Allies out of the Solomons. Seven hundred hand picked army troops were being transported in to eject the Marines. Task Force 61 commanded by Admiral Frank Jack Fletcher in the carrier *Saratoga* included the *Enterprise* (TF-16 under Rear Admiral Thomas C. Kinkaid) and the *Hornet* (TF-18 under Rear Admiral Leigh Noyes). This force would oppose the Japanese thrust.

The battle that ensued on August 24 was somewhat confused, for both sides. The Japanese were again hoping to repeat their Midway strategy, but this time successfully. They placed the light carrier *Ryujo* in a position where it could be discovered and used for bait. This worked. Shortly after noon, after receiving a number of sightings, the *Enterprise* launched a strike of 23 aircraft sent out with orders to locate and engage. By early afternoon, the *Saratoga* too had

launched a large number of aircraft with the same instructions. Obviously enemy carriers were in the vicinity, but where and how many? *Enterprise* pilots located the *Shokaku* in mid afternoon and attacked her. She was slightly damaged in the attack. Later they found the *Ryujo* and missed her with torpedoes. Just after the abortive attack by planes from the *Enterprise*, a large force from the *Saratoga* found the unlucky "bait" carrier and disposed of her. Finally, the *Saratoga* which had been the butt of jokes for months had engaged the enemy and sunk a carrier. It nay have been a light carrier, but it was still a carrier. It was time for the Japanese to retaliate.

In the late afternoon, the two Japanese fleet carriers launched full strikes against the last reported position of the American carriers. This force, hungry for American blood arrived saw it's quarry at half past 1600. Everything that could fly was in the air to repulse the attack, but at 1641, the Japanese began attacking in earnest, quite willing to penetrate the curtain of fire being lifted to greet them. The "*Big E*" took three direct hits and four near misses in a matter of moments. She was hit twice near her aft elevator and once on the flight deck near the island. Fragments opened holes in her side and she took on a slight list (3 degrees). Seventy four men were killed and 95 wounded during this attack. As soon as it began it was over. Fortune smiled on the *Enterprise* as she later became incapacitated with a jammed rudder, but no torpedo planes found her in this condition. And, unlike her sister the *Yorktown*, no prowling Japanese submarines were able to hit her when she was in trouble. By seven in the evening, she was able to steam at 24 plus knots and her rudder was

free. Damage control had won this battle. Her air group was sent to Henderson Field and the damaged carrier was detached for repairs at Pearl Harbor with the cruiser *Portland* and four destroyers. The scorecard for what became known as the Battle of the Eastern Solomons was muddy. The Japanese had lost the carrier *Ryujo* and suffered some damage to other ships, but the *Enterprise* was now out of action. Many thought that a more diligently pressed attack would have resulted in the complete destruction of the Japanese force and permanent relief for the Marines on Guadalcanal. The lack of information and intelligence had protected both forces, but this would have to be changed if the Allies wanted to win. Lessons were learned from this battle that would prove valuable in the future. For the *Enterprise* and crew, both were long overdue for rest. They arrived in Pearl Harbor on September 10, 1942.

The battle scarred carrier was to have remained in the yard for some period, but on August 31, the *Saratoga* was hit by a torpedo for the second time in eight months and again put out of action. Just two weeks later on September 15, the carrier *Wasp* was hit by submarine launched torpedoes and had to be sunk by her escort. This left the *Hornet* as the only combat available in the Solomons Area. In less than one month, the U.S. Navy had lost three quarters of its carrier strength. At least, the pilots and most of the planes could make it to Guadalcanal. There they were quickly "shanghaied" into the "cactus airforce".

With the losses of carrier strength in the South Pacific, the yard was ordered to hurry repair and get the *Enterprise* back to work. She entered

Dauntless SBD divebombers are being readied for attack in early June 1942. Divebombers from the Enterprise *would sink two carriers (*Akagi *and* Kaga*) and damage two others during the short, but decisive Battle of Midway. An eyewitness to the attack indicated that the Dauntless' took their loads down without dive brakes and pulled out of their dives just above the ocean suuface.*

These are six frames from a navy news reel taken during the bombing of the *Enterprise* in the Battle of Eastern Solomons. This news reel footage is among the most unusual to come out of World War II.

Frame #1: Men running toward the hit on the aft elevator.

Frame #2: Crew aware of a bomb about to hit just aft of the island.

Frame #3: Precise moment of a bomb exploding on the flight deck.

Frame #4: Damage controlmen working on both hits.

Frame #5: Massive hole in the flight deck from second hit.

Frame #6: Steel patch over hole and flight operations under way.

drydock without unloading ammunition and other dangerous stores and although a fire broke out on her hull, work continued around the clock. The fire had the effect of cleaning the hull of barnacles and sea growth. No matter what happened to this carrier it turned out alright. A large consignment of 40mm quad mounts had arrived from the mainland and these were taken straight from the transport ship to the deck of the *Enterprise*. Her 1.1 "Chicago piano" four barrelled AA guns were removed and the deadly 40mm Bofors were emplaced. The *Enterprise* was one of the few ships to have these new guns, and they would provide quite a surprise for the Japanese who depended on poor performance of the 1.1's and the Browning 50 caliber machine guns. Now armed with the 20mm oerlikon and the 40mm heavy machine gun, her antiaircraft defense was downright dangerous. She was able to remain in the yard until October 16, 1942, but she was vital to the next operation and she sailed back to the South Pacific.

ATTACK, ATTACK, ATTACK: "BUT THE PAINT IS NOT EVEN DRY YET"

The battles on and around Guadalcanal were not going very well for the Allies. Nimitz suspected two problems, lack of aggressive spirit and low morale. His prescription was quick - Admiral Bill Halsey. His slogan and fundamental instruction to his men was simple and to the point, "Kill Japs, Kill Japs, Kill More Japs". Halsey assumed command from Admiral Robert L. Ghormley on October 18, 1942 while the *Enterprise* was en route. She arrived in the area on October 24, 1942 and was accompanied by the new battleship, USS *South Dakota*. She was also known as "battleship X" or the "big bastard". To the Japanese, she was the latter. She too was heavily armed with a very large number of the new 40mm antiaircraft weapon. Her crew was especially well drilled in gunnery and took great pride in this. On the other hand, the *South Dakota* was not known for a spit and polish attitude and to some she resembled a Singapore junk manned by pirates, but after the upcoming Battle of the Santa Cruz Islands, her crew was forgiven for any violations of the white glove police.

Admiral Halsey was recharged when he saw his old friend the *Enterprise*. Now, the Allies stood a fighting chance. The Japanese were simply not going to allow the Allies to retain Guadalcanal. The Imperial General Staff was convinced, and rightly so, that losing this area would begin a reversal of fortune that would not be stopped until the U.S. Navy was anchored in Tokyo Bay. The significance of Guadalcanal was critical to both opponents, consequently in late October, another big push was to be inaugurated.

The Japanese would be deploying 4 carriers, 5 battleships, 14 cruisers and 44 destroyers in the event the American carriers and other sea forces came within range of Guadalcanal. Admiral Yamamoto himself, aboard the super battleship *Yamato* anchored at Truk was exasperated with the Imperial Japanese Army's failure to wrest Henderson Field from the Marines and threatened to withdraw his naval forces for lack of fuel. On the other hand, not wanting to admit defeat, the Imperial Army kept promising victory at any moment. The Japanese fleet mean-

The Enterprise *has just been hit during the Battle of the Eastern Solomons. Quick and efficient damage control would save this icon of naval history time and time again.*

dered at about 300 miles north of the ground battle and now the *Enterprise*, and *Hornet* with escorting *South Dakota* and an number of cruisers and destroyers were poised with effective strike range on October 26, 1942. Halsey was then clear with his intentions, "Attack, Attack!" At 0500, the *Enterprise* launched a 16 plane strike of Dauntless's armed with 500 pound bombs. On hour and forty minutes later at about 200 miles distance from their ship, the carrier *Zuiho* was located and then hit on her flight deck with two 500 pound bombs. In the interim, the Japanese had also launched a strike from the carriers *Zuikaku* and *Shokaku*. They were on the way to hit suspected American carriers. Both strikes passed with sight of one another some 60-90 miles from one another's carriers. Although a dogfight would have been quite satisfying, both groups had other fish to fry. The *Enterprise* attack force was intercepted and mauled by enemy fighter planes ("Zekes"), but the *Hornet's* aircraft made it the target - the *Shokaku* and *Zuikaku*. After for what seemed an eternity, some of the divebombers were in position for the attack. The *Shokaku* was the recipient of at least three 1,000 pound bombs that put her out of the war until mid 1943. Of course, the Japanese aircraft were also in position to attack the American force, and attack they did.

The *Enterprise* was able to avoid the initial Japanese strike due to the fortuitous appearance of a rain squall. Mother nature was still the best defense against non radar guided weapons. The *Hornet* was fair game and 20 minutes before her brood of bombers even found the *Shokakau*, she had been hit by four bombs, two torpedoes, two damaged bombers turned kamikazes and one

near miss. She was hit and hit very hard. Now it was the time for the *Enterprise*. She had emerged from the rain squall, and was met by 43 aircraft that had been launched from the Japanese carriers. The air defense put by the *Enterprise* and escorts was quite different from that around the *Hornet*. The pirates aboard the *South Dakota* and the rapid firing 5 inch twin mounts on the *San Juan*, an antiaircraft light cruiser began to knock down the surprised Japanese planes in droves. They were accustomed to the lackluster performance of the 1.1's and 50 caliber close in guns, the new 40mm and five inch guns were something again. The screen ships and the *Enterprise* were able to dispense with most of the attacking aircraft, but the "Big E" was hit by three bombs. Two hit the flight deck and the third, a very near miss opened a number of holes in the hull. Damage control took over and quickly brought the situation under control. Her forward elevator was damaged which caused some difficulty until permanently repaired, but the ship was able to soldier on. The *Enterprise* lost 44 men killed and 75 wounded during this attack. The *South Dakota* had outdone herself shooting down 26 aircraft. She was hit by a bomb on her forward turret that did no damage, but the battleship accidentally turned toward the *Enterprise* and had it not been for alert lookouts and helmsmen, the *South Dakota* might have done more damage to the carrier than the Japanese.

The *Hornet* was mortally wounded and eventually sank on October 27, 1942. On October 26, American destroyers *Mustin* and *Anderson* fired sixteen torpedoes of which nine hit. The *Hornet* still refused to sink and next the destroyers resorted to gunfire. They pumped 430 rounds into the burning ship. It was still no go, so fearing Japanese surface ships, they departed at high speed. The *Hornet* would have to sink on her own or the Japanese would have to do the job. Just before midnight, the Japanese did appear and then took great delight in firing more torpedoes and ropping bombs on the brightly lit hulk. At 0135, the last sister of the *Enterprise* sank. It had taken at least 13 torpedoes, many bombs and 400 plus medium caliber shells to do the job. She was a tough old girl, and her place in history was secure. No one will ever forget the April raid on Tokyo.

The U.S. Navy was without another major carrier in the Pacific and its most veteran ship, the *Enterprise* had been hurt again. The Japanese had been stopped, but they would soon be back. The luxury of another Pearl Harbor refit was not possible. The Allies could not afford to have the *Enterprise* out of action for more than a few days. She sailed for Noumea, New Caledonia for repairs and arrived four days after the battle. She was carrying a number of *Hornet* aircraft in addition to her own depleted air group. She was allowed just twelve days to have her flight deck patched, not enough to fully repair her forward elevator, but the Japanese were considerate of her needs. The USS *Vestal*, AR-4, of Pearl Harbor fame made an all out effort to bring the carrier back to maximum fighting capability even to the extent of allowing her skilled repairmen to accompany the ship as she left for the next battle. If she could launch aircraft and was maneuverable, than she had to steam for battle. This time, the Imperial Japanese Navy was going to make an all out effort and in so doing would shed much American blood. The name of the upcoming battle was the all inclusive "Naval Battle of Guadalcanal", and it began on November 12, 1942.

This time, the Japanese brought up two carriers, the Junyo and the Hiyo, but they played a vary minor role in this battle. This battle was primarily a series of night surface engagements between heavy ships. The Japanese were intent on routing the Marines from the rather tenuous toehold on Guadalcanal and the Allies were not about to leave, at least without a major fight. For this massive assault, the Imperial Navy brought up battleships *Hiei, Kirishima, Kongo* and *Haruna*. These battleships served as escorts for the carriers and the *Hiei* and *Kirishima* were to be used for shore bombardment. The Japanese also brought a number of cruisers and destroyers, but interestingly, the *Yamato* remained at Truk as a floating palace for Admiral Yamamoto. Had this over-sized heavy gunned tub lent her support to the bombardment force, the outcome might have been different. The axiom that a fleet in harbor is no fleet at all was proven in this battle.

The early morning hours of Friday the 13th or "bloody Friday" witnessed a major clash between the Japanese bombardment force and a pick up squad of American cruisers and destroyers. The U. S. Navy lost six ships, and the Japanese, two destroyers and the Hiei was critically hit. The following morning, what was left of both forces limped away, but the Japanese were still in danger of air attack. The fact that Henderson Field was still in business completely vindicated the heavy naval loses suffered just hours before.

The *Enterprise* sent a strike searching for enemy carriers, but they were too out of range. Barring this, several of the carrier's aircraft were placed at the disposal of the Marines at Henderson Field. At 1020, torpedo planes found the *Hiei* and hit her. Three hours later *Enterprise* and Henderson Field aircraft returned to see their quarry steaming in circles. She was then bombed, torpedoed and literally shot to pieces by aircraft from every base in the area. Even B-17's from Espiritu Santo got into the act, and finally at dusk the bomb resistant battleship slid stern first to join a number of other famous ships on the ocean's bottom near Guadalcanal.

Next it was the turn of seven troop and equipment filled transports to die. The *Enterprise* and fast working Henderson Field air crews kept aircraft bombing and strafing transports until seven were dispatched at sea and four had to be beached. On the following day (November 15), Henderson Field and *Enterprise* aircraft shot up the beached ships and literally wiped out the supplies and troops in the area. By the end of this attack, they could claim the elimination of 11,000 troops out of the 13,000 sent to reinforce the Japanese forces ashore. It was also the end for any further serious reinforcement attempts. It was not the end for the phenomenal accomplishments of naval air during this contest. Hungry pilots from the *Enterprise* also found the heavy cruisers *Kinugasa, Chokai* and *Maya*. Their attack resulted in the sinking of the *Kinugasa*, damage to the *Chokai, Maya* and light cruiser *Isuzu*. The *Enterprise* was ordered back to Espiritu Santo on November 15, 1942. Her presence had

made the difference. She had helped to sink or damage sixteen ships.

The battle was not yet over, for on November 14-15, 1942, the American battleships *Washington* and *South Dakota* fought it out with the Japanese battleship *Kirishima* and her escorting heavy cruisers and destroyers. The *South Dakota* was mauled during the confrontation, but the *Kirishima* was sunk by gunfire from the *Washington*.

The Naval Battle of Guadalcanal paralleled the Battle of Midway in it's importance to Allied victory in the Pacific. The Japanese had been stopped in their thrust toward the Hawaiian Islands at Midway. This thrust was motivated to a certain degree by revenge born out of the military's embarrassment over the Halsey-Doolittle Raid on their homeland. The Imperial Navy desperately wanted a clash of titans to vindicate their hurt pride but there was also a desire to strengthen their outer ring of defense against Allied retaliation. Conversely, the Naval Battle of Guadalcanal was born out of the absolute strategic imperative to eject the Allies from a piece of real estate that was pivotal to winning the war. Admiral Yamamoto and all of the Imperial General staff were keenly aware of the value of the Solomons. If the Allies continued to have an airfield on Guadalcanal, then it would just be a matter of time before they would begin to move toward the Japanese homeland. This was the rational behind both sides committing so much of their resources. The Allies triumphed by early 1943, and in both the Battle of Midway and Guadalcanal, the *Enterprise* was there to make a significant if not decisive contribution. Had

The October 26, 1942 Battle of the Santa Cruz Islands witnessed the end of the last sister to the Enterprise, *the carrier* Hornet. *She had been a fellow traveler on the Halsey Doolittle Raid just six months before. Here she is about to be hit by an early version of a kamikaze. Seconds later, she took the hit on her aft island and funnel structure.*

The Enterprise *and her crew are awarded the Presidential Unit Citation by Admiral Chester W. Nimitz at Pearl Harbor on May 27, 1943.*

this ship, her crew and air crews never did anything more in World War II, then they still would have accomplished more than any ship in the history of the U.S. Navy. The *Enterprise* was truly a legend in her own time. Often when she entered any Pacific port, men would stop whatever they were doing to view with pride and awe this remarkable ship. The course of the Pacific war and world history had been altered by the effort of this carrier.

THE WAR ENTERS A NEW PHASE: THE *ESSEX* AND *INDEPENDENCE* CARRIER CLASSES JOIN THE *ENTERPRISE* ON THE FRONT LINE

The victorious but very well worn carrier remained at Noumea for just over two weeks and then it was back to sea for training. She was engaged in one last combat mission before returning to Pearl Harbor and that was the Battle of Rennell Island where she attempted to protect the sinking heavy cruiser *Chicago*. Despite her valiant efforts and the high number of Japanese attacking planes that were shot down, the lightly armored treaty cruiser sank late on January 30, 1943.

From here the *Enterprise* spent some time off Espiritu Santo and in late May 1943, she entered Pearl Harbor where on May 27, Admiral Nimitz presented the Presidential Unit Citation to the ship and her officers and men. It was quite an occasion as the *Enterprise* was the first carrier to receive this high honor.

From Pearl Harbor she sailed for the Puget Sound Naval Shipyard for a major overhaul and upgrade. She entered one of the yard's drydocks on July 20, 1943 and there she remained for three months. A protective blister was added to her hull and her flight deck expanded. The ship had grown from 809 feet in length to 827 feet and the beam had changed from 109-114 feet. She now displaced 21,000 tons and her 5 inch and 40mm batteries were improved with radar assisted fire control direction. Fourteen new 20mm guns were added as well as twenty-two 40mm guns. She was now about as well defended against air attack as was possible at this stage of the war.

Her air group was also updated with the newest version of the Avenger and the F4F Wildcat had been replaced by the F6F Hellcat. The Hellcat was more than a match for the Zero, a painful lesson learned by the Japanese throughout the rest of the war.

The war had taken a new direction during the time that the *Enterprise* was being modernized. The new *Essex* and *Independence* class carriers were entering service and pilots and planes by the thousands were emerging from the shipyards and flight training facilities all over the U.S. The day of the lone wolf carrier acting the part of an entire carrier task force was luckily now over. The task force headed by the fast carrier was the weapon of choice now for Pacific commanders. The more fleet carriers, the better. When the "*Big E*" returned to battle she would join many new sisters who would now share some of the boldest but grimmest days of the war. The overriding difference now was that the Allies were confident of not losing and the Japanese were not confident of winning.

Aside from taking on new aircraft, being modernized, and having some fast moving sister carriers, the *Enterprise* was to take on a new role which would prove vital in the air battles to come. The first demonstration of this new tactic was during the invasion of the Gilbert Islands in late November 1943. The *Enterprise* was operating off the invasion front and on November 26, was called upon to deal with Japanese twin engine "big butt" Betty's as they were known to the Allies. Torpedo laden Betty's had been heckling the task force for two solid nights, and a remedy was sought on the third. The *Enterprise* was able to test her new "bat" team which consisted of two specially trained F6F Hellcats guided by radar equipped TBF torpedo bomber. One of the Hellcats was piloted by none other than Lt. Commander Edward H. "Butch" O'Hare, a Congressional Medal of Honor winner. The Japanese sent in thirty Betty bombers from Rabaul to attack the carriers and other heavy ships of the task force, so this was no nuisance raid as before. Although there was some initial difficulty with the new tactics, the night fighters shot down two attackers. With the American fighters being in and amongst the attacking formation, the Japanese became confused and the raid was aborted. Unfortunately, one of the Betty's took station with the returning "Bat team", and during the ensuing exchange of gunfire, O'Hare was shot down and lost. It was a great loss of a fine pilot and shipmate, but it was also a successful demonstration of how night fighting could be employed. A large raid of torpedo bombers had been driven off and the task force was unmolested that night.

The *Enterprise* next hit Kwajalein on December 4, with a devastating raid that hit shore installations and shipping. She had been there before in February 1942. In February 1944, just two years later, her pilots found themselves in the enemy's backyard at Truk. It was to be another night operation, but not defensive.

On February 17, 1944, twelve night tactic trained TBF's of Torpedo 10 under the command of Lt. Commander William L. Martin were launched from the *Enterprise*. Unluckily, Martin had to remain behind nursing a broken arm, but his every thought was with his men and the theory of night bombing that they had practiced. They came in at 500 feet to avoid radar detection and began dropping their 500 pound bombs on sleeping merchant ships. Eight ships were destroyed and five damaged by this first night radar guided bombing attack. The hit rate was exceptional - over 60,000 tons of shipping. Now the Japanese were fair game, night or day.

The *Enterprise* left Task Force 58 for a series of raids against Jaluit Atoll and next provided air cover for the late March landings on Emirau. The Japanese were quickly becoming introduced to daylight and nighttime precision raids on all of their formerly untouched outer fortifications. Yap, Ulithi, Woleai and Palau were hit into early April 1944, and then it was on to Hollandia, New Guinea and another visit to Truk on April 29-30. The next operation was the invasion of the Marianas and a "turkey shoot".

The Japanese had again decided to draw the American fleet out into the open for another cataclysmic, winner take all confrontation. This time Vice Admiral Jisaburo Ozawa was in command of essentially what was left of Japanese naval air power in the region. He was able to bring together five fleet carriers, four light carriers and a healthy number of cruisers and destroyers. He even had five battleships. His aircraft strength totalled 473 aircraft of which 222 were fighters, 113 divebombers, 95 torpedo planes and 43 were float planes. Against this, the U.S. Navy brought up seven fleet carriers, eight light carriers and a hefty number of other warships. In terms of aircraft, the carriers had 475 fighters or one for each of all aircraft in the Japanese inventory. To this formidable force was added 232 divebombers and 184 torpedo bombers. The navy also had some 65 float planes available for a grand total of 956 or 2:1 odds! It was Midway, but in reverse.

The Japanese may have been inferior in numbers but hoped to make it up with tactical advantages. It now was they who had airfields on well defended islands (Guam, Rota, and Yap), while the U.S. Navy had to rely solely on its carriers. The Japanese hoped to accomplish the same as had the *Enterprise* when using Henderson Field during the final phase of the November 1942 Naval Battle of Guadalcanal. The three island bases would act as three stationary carriers thus leveling the playing field. The Japanese also had the natural advantage of the wind. They could launch and recover while cruising toward the objective in the wind. The Americans would have to turn from the objective. Finally, Japanese aircraft, bereft of armor plate and self sealing fuel tanks were more long legged and could fly to greater ranges than their opponents. These advantages, while impressive were quickly trampled by major problems. First, the 500 planes supposedly on the island aircraft carriers had been destroyed, but Admiral Ozawa believed his own propaganda. No help from the islands! Next, his pilots were ill trained and incapable against their counterparts in the U.S. Navy. Finally, American leadership was practical and not prone to believing everything put out by the media and public relations. Admiral's Spruance and Mitscher were grounded in reality. The battle for Saipan, just miles from Guam in the Marianas began on June 15, 1944. It proceeded according to plan, but the big air show was not to open until June 19.

The "Great Mariana's Turkey Shoot" as it has become known or more properly, the Battle of the Philippine Sea began on June 19, 1944. Both the American and Japanese forces were to the southwest of Guam. The Japanese position had been betrayed by American submarines and the clash began at 0300 and lasted to mid afternoon at about 1500. Admiral Ozawa sent out strike after strike to attack the American fleet for a total of four major raids. The vast majority of enemy aircraft were intercepted far from their intended targets and summarily dispatched. In fact, by day's end, over 300 American planes had engaged the enemy and shot down or destroyed 315 precious Japanese aircraft. In battles past, it was the loss of pilots that was crucial, but not this time. The Japanese pilots were simply no match for the American defenders. U.S. Navy losses totalled 23 shot down and six operational losses. On no front in any theater of the world war was there ever such a day when so many aircraft had been destroyed. It was total victory and the pilots from the *Enterprise* shared in it, but the victory was not yet complete. There was still the matter of the floating homes from which the enemy had come. While the turkey shoot was underway several thousand feet above, the submarine *Albacore* torpedoed the new Japanese flattop *Taiho* and the SS *Cavalla* sank an old nemesis of the *Enterprise*, the *Shokaku*. The following day, the slaughter continued with a general mopping up of what was left of Japanese naval aviation. The carrier *Hiyo* was also destroyed and the one survivor of the Pearl Harbor attack, the *Zuikaku* was badly mauled by aircraft from the *Enterprise*. By the end of the working day on June 20, the U.S. Navy had virtually defeated the Imperial Japanese Navy. Three carriers, 476 total aircraft of which 426 came from the carriers and 445 pilots were forever denied continued service to the Emperor. As a reward for the good and faithful service of American naval aviators, Admiral Marc Mitscher turned on the fleet's lights to allow his shot air crews and planes back aboard their mother ships. By midnight, June 20, 1944, it was all over.

The *Enterprise* continued to provide support in the immediate area of Guam and the other Mariana's and after a brief respite in Pearl Harbor, she was back at work hitting the Bonin Islands and Yap as autumn began in 1944. Her next job was that of providing support to the invasion of the Philippines at Leyte Gulf in October 1944. Up through late November, the *Enterprise* hit a number of targets in the area, primarily in and around Manila. She also hit Yap. She was back in the Philippines in early 1945,

the last year of the war. Now the fears of losing the war were over, it was just a matter of time for the Japanese to be defeated. Everyone knew that the Japanese would not willingly surrender so the country would have to be utterly destroyed before the war would be finished. For the crew and aviators of the *Enterprise*, the many other carriers and ships heading for Japan, it would be more of the same until the end. Run in, hit the enemy and retire. Run in, hit the enemy, stay and hit him again. So became the ritual until the Allied navies sailed at will within the inner ring of Japan's defense. The Japanese formally initiated a new method of fighting. The suicide plane or kamikaze. It was the world's first guided missile and if it got with close range of a carrier, it did not often miss. The *Enterprise* had been wounded by a bomb hit on March 18, 1945 while operating off Japan, but she was put back into shape at Ulithi in short order. The *Enterprise* was going to be there at the end as she was at the beginning, so by April 5, 1945 she was steaming back to action, this time off Okinawa where she was damaged by a kamikaze on April 11. Her luck seemed to be on the ebb. She was back in action on May 6, 1945, and eight days later her war fighting days ended.

Along for her final combat ride was no less a character than Admiral Mitscher. The *Essex* class carrier *Bunker Hill* had been the flagship up through May 11, 1945 when she was hit by two well placed kamikazes that put her put of the war and killed nearly 400 of her crew. Mitscher moved his flag to the *Enterprise*. The "Big E" now had a date with a young inexperienced, but lucky samurai pilot that had drawn a Zero as his tomb and vehicle to enter heaven. In his fighter loaded with a large bomb Tomi Zae lifted off a local airfield with 25 other planes bent on sacrificing themselves on the deck of a U.S. Navy ship, hopefully a big carrier. Nineteen of the incoming warriors were intercepted and downed by combat air patrol and six were accounted for by antiaircraft gunnery. This just left pilot Tomi Zae. He hit the *Enterprise* at 0656 just abaft the forward elevator. Suicide pilots and those that used to simply drop bombs were always in-

An aviators shot! This photo was taken by the rear gunner in a Douglas Dauntless divebomber aircraft which has left the deck of the "Big E."

Damage to the forward elevator on May 14, 1945. The engine, pilot and bomb plunged downward and detonated below.

The Enterprise *in all of her glory is on her way to the Atlantic after six tough years in the Pacific. This time she is to be a floating hotel for 10,000 GI's wanting to come home from Europe.*

The veteran carrier is at rest in preparation for the October 17, 1945, Navy Day celebration in New York. President Harry S. Truman would personally congratulate this wonderful ship and her valiant crew.

Pipe bunks are being welded aboard the Enterprise *for her duty as a troop transport.*

The Enterprise *takes it on the chin, and so do over 5,000 returning soldiers on board. In this December 1945 photograph, she is riding in rough seas, and has been for nine days. Seasickness was only abated by thoughts of home.*

structed to hit a carrier's elevator. A simple hole in the flight deck can be mended locally, but a sick elevator required a yard job. Zae knew what he was doing, and did it well. He, his bomb, and engine kept going through the deck and the resulting explosion sent the forward elevator half the length of the *Enterprise*, but straight upward. The elevator resembled a flat iron missile being launched, but the effect was deadly. Fires immediately broke out but were soon contained. Thirteen men were killed and sixty eight wounded. The *Enterprise* was out of the war. Admiral Mitscher bade one of his favorite ships farewell the following day and transferred to the new fleet carrier *Randolph*. It was a great run, but it was now over.

BACK TO THE USA, AND SADLY, THE "BIG E" LOSES HER LAST BATTLE

The *Enterprise* left the combat area for repair and overhaul at the Puget Sound Naval Shipyard and arrived on June 7, 1945, a beautiful time of year in Bremerton, Washington. The war ended while she was under repair. Her next duty was to ferry over 1,000 former POW's from Pearl Harbor to the continental USA. She then par-

ticipated in the Navy Day celebration in New York, the biggest event of its kind in history. She was known to be the most decorated ship in the U.S. Navy and an obvious candidate for preservation, only rivalled by the old frigate, *Constitution*. From this huge celebration she sailed for the Boston Navy Yard where she was fitted with thousands of pipe berths and became a huge passenger liner for soldiers anxiously returning from Europe. She carried upwards to 10,000 men in this last effort as part of her service in World War II. On January 18, 1946, she entered the New York Navy Yard for mothballing and reserve status. She was decommissioned on February 17, 1947. She was awarded 20 battles stars and one class "B" star for antisubmarine action on December 10, 1941. She was commanded by fifteen historically fortunate men from May 12, 1938 through February 17, 1947. In early 1947 she was part of the Atlantic Reserve Fleet and its flagship. Periodically she would emerge for overhaul and during mid 1949, just such occurred when young Loreley Bull watched her pass beneath the Brooklyn Bridge. But what does a country do with a chronologically new but technologically obsolete ship? There was talk of converting her to an antisubmarine ship

Berthing areas where divebombers, fighters, and torpedo planes once lived.

and after being redesignated as an attack carrier (CVA) in 1952, this was then changed to CVS or ASW Support Aircraft Carrier in 1953. Unknowingly, time was running out for the proud ship. There was an early bid by a consortium in San Francisco to moor her at Treasure Island as a floating educational ship, but financial resources could not be mustered. It was too soon after the war for this kind of thing and there was no money.

New York Harbor on January 14, 1946. This is the last trip for the old carrier, Enterprise. She has brought home a contingent of 3,557 grateful veterans including 212 Army WAC's.

Loreley Bull watches the famous carrier pass beneath the Brooklyn Bridge on July 20, 1949.

August 21, 1958, just over nine years after Loreley Bull watched the Enterprise sail beneath the Brooklyn Bridge. The now doomed carrier heads for her fate - the scrapper's torch.

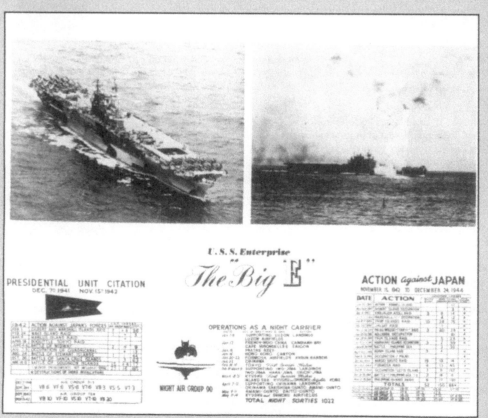

This is the real story of the Enterprise - what she did for the United States and her citizens. She and her crews deserved every honor a grateful nation could bestow.

Enterprise's bell at the entrance to Bancroft Hall at the U.S. Naval Academy. The class of 1921 provided the mounting.

By 1956, the navy indicated that there was no further use for this ship and asked congress for permission to scrap her along with dozens of other World War II veteran warships. No date was set for her disposal. On October 8, she was declared surplus and to be sold for $1 million in scrap value. Again, no date was set. Time was provided to allow the Enterprise Association to raise the money necessary to preserve the ship, but not enough time. On July 1, 1958 she went to Lipsett Incorporated for just over one half million dollars to join past ships like the battleships *Wyoming, Idaho* and *New Mexico*. By March 1960, she was totally gone, and sadly one of the greatest losses in American history. It may have been more fitting had she joined her two sisters *Hornet* and *Yorktown*. At least they died at the hand of the enemy. The *Enterprise* CV-6 was a wonderful, beautiful and historically significant warship that was lost, but will never be forgotten.

THE USS *LANGLEY* CV-1, AV-3 "SENSELESS LOSS"

The USS *Langley* was many things to many people. To the fledgling naval aviation program she represented a victory over the hide bound capital ship traditionalists. To post World War I old line naval leadership, she was a tolerable and necessary evil. To young and often reckless naval aviators, she was both a challenge and a sign of acceptance. To the Japanese, she was a threat. To her last commanding officer her loss and his hastily written sinking report nearly resulted in career disaster, and to 16 crewmen, she will be an eternal haven. To a 14 year old girl whose father was part of her crew, she was a beautiful and wonderful ship that over a half century later still provided her with treasured memories.

But, officially and historically, she was simply a rivetted steel warship built by the Mare Island Navy Yard and launched as the USS *Jupiter* AC-3 on August 24, 1912. Less than a year later on April 7, 1913 she was commissioned and went about her duties as a fleet collier for the next seven years until she was decommissioned on March 24, 1920. The *Jupiter* was stricken from the navy list but not for the purpose of scrapping or being sunk as a target. She had been selected for conversion as the first aircraft carrier in the U.S. Navy and would be renamed the *Langley* in honor of Samuel Pierpont Langley, a noted scientist and airplane enthusiast. She had been a successful collier with a distinguished record, and on March 20, 1922, just under ten years from her launching, she was commissioned as CV-1, the USS *Langley*. She was the test tube for the Navy's carrier aviation program and would be so until joined by the *Saratoga* and *Lexington*, both considered full size attack carriers. Her career spanned fifteen years until selected for a more mundane role. After being modified for service as a seaplane tender she emerged from her place of origin, the Mare Island Navy Yard as the USS *Langley*, AV-3 on April 21, 1937. She was later transferred to the Asiatic Fleet, and the beginning of the Second World War found her moored in Manila Bay. For the next three months she tended her flock of seaplanes and performed other duties as required

A 1945 photograph of the human resources necessary to maintain, launch and recover a carrier aircraft. When the Langley *witnessed her first aircraft launching in 1922, only a fraction of the men pictured were needed. Many tasks, now considered essential for flight operations were pioneered and refined aboard the* Langley.

The Navy collier, Jupiter, *anchored in San Francisco Bay before the U.S. entrance into World War I. The collier was as important to the fleet as the oil tanker of World War II. Without fuel, a navy remained in port, a collection of armed barges. The colliers were designed to enable specially designed railroad coal cars to be lifted and dumped directly into their coal holds. Derricks aboard the collier assisted in loading ships that were unable to seek coal at a land coaling station.*

for the quickly disintegrating Far East command and on February 27, 1942 she was hit by Japanese bombers and had to be sunk by her escorting destroyers. She had lived as three ships for three decades. So the story of the first aircraft carrier in the U.S. Navy ends.

Operational history is factual but cares little for the human side of the Navy, it's ships and the men and women who serve in and near them. This is true of all ships, but in particular for the *Jupiter* AC-3 turned *Langley* CV-1, AV-3. Here is the real story.

THE USS *JUPITER*, AC-3, FLEET COLLIER

In 1908, the U.S. Navy used bunker coal to fuel it's ships. This had been so since the first

warships had been converted from sail power to steam. Coaling was considered one of the worst jobs imaginable for a warship. Coal dust covered everything and made a pristine and bristol fashion ship look like tramp steamer too long without overhaul. The entire crew turned out for the event which meant the transfer of hundreds of tons of coal from either a specially rigged shore facility or a collier like the *Jupiter*. The best design possible was selected for the *Jupiter*, but she was still a collier. Imagine the difficulty that her crew must have experienced keeping her reasonably clean.

The construction of the *Jupiter*, a Neptune class fleet collier was approved by the U.S. Congress on May 13, 1908. She was one of two ships in that congressional appropriations bill,

Sailors assigned to the fire room shoveled coal to feed fire boxes that heated the ever hungry boilers. This was the filthiest and most difficult chore aboard ship. It was also where apprentice engineers began their careers. Oil eventually replaced coal as the fuel of choice in the U.S. Navy. Aside from being a more efficient source of power, there was an immediate 25% savings in manpower.

A homely Eugene Ely, the first true U.S. carrier pilot, sits at the control of his Curtiss pusher aircraft being readied for take off from the wooden deck of the armored cruiser Pennsylvania. Only a barnstormer and daredevil could attempt and succeed at such a feat. Ely was both. To many, he is the father of carrier aviation.

the other being the *Cyclops*. Like her sister, the *Cyclops* had a tragic ending, but much earlier and far more mysterious. The *Cyclops* literally disappeared without a trace sometime shortly after March 4 1918 in the Caribbean. Her loss and that of her entire 280 man crew is still one of the great unsolved riddles of the sea. Some even say that she was a victim of the "Bermuda Triangle", but in any event her disappearance has never been explained. The theory that makes most sense is that her cargo shifted during the night and before any of her crew could make it to lifeboats or rafts, the collier turned over and sank. No one will ever really know.

The cost of the *Jupiter* was not to exceed $1.8 million, a large amount of money in 1910. Her keel was laid at the Mare Island Navy Yard on October 18, 1911, and sponsored at her launching on August 24, 1912 by Mrs. Thomas F. Ruhm. The 19,360 ton 542 foot long ship was commissioned on April 7, 1913, and shortly thereafter joined the Pacific Fleet. She was a welcome addition to the fleet which was always in need of coal. The *Jupiter* was also the first warship fitted with Melville-McAlpine Electric Drive and experience with this system caused its use to be expanded to capital ships built later. Her propulsion plant developed 5,000 shp driving two shafts at a maximum speed of 15 knots. She carried 2,300 tons of fuel which gave her a range of 12,260 miles at ten knots. After her shakedown cruise and trial period her first task was to join American Naval forces which were enforcing the will of President Wilson in Mexican waters. An incident had taken place where American sailors had been temporarily detained and the Mexican government's apology was not sufficient nor satisfactory. The "Tampico Incident", perhaps similar to other events in recent history such as the "Tonkin Gulf Incident" in August 1964 resulted in an armed confrontation in Vera Cruz. The *Jupiter* provided fuel and support to ships on patrol in the region. Although armed with four 4 inch guns, they were not put to use during this event. In October 1914, she departed from the Vera Cruz area as the crisis dissipated and sailed for the east coast

of the U.S. The *Jupiter* was the first major ship to transit the new Panama Canal from west to east. This was to the first of many "firsts" in this ship's history. Her World War I service included cargo trips to France and coaling duty for troop ships that were transporting American doughboys back home at war's end. She almost met disaster off France when a German U-boat fired two torpedoes at her as she was entering the Gironde River on June 5, 1917. The torpedoes missed. Less than a year after the First World War ended, the *Jupiter* was selected for conversion to an aircraft carrier or flying on and off platform.

In 1919, no one was really certain what an aircraft carrier was, should do or look like. Most designers and pilots recognized that an airplane carrier should have a deck, a storage area and be able to move through the water, but that was about as far as conventional wisdom took carrier enthusiasts. It was for the *Langley* to lead the way.

The *Jupiter* ended her days as a collier on August 24, 1920 having been selected for conversion to an aircraft carrier on July 11, 1919. She then entered the Norfolk Navy Yard and on April 21, 1920 she became the *Langley*. For nearly two years yard workmen labored on this novel looking ship and on March 20, 1922, she was recommissioned as the USS *Langley*, CV-1. The entire conversion cost less than $500,000 and what emerged was a rather odd looking ship that resembled "covered wagon" or pioneer prairie schooner. The name stuck and she affectionately became known as the "Covered Wagon" to all who served in the navy.

USS *LANGLEY* CV-1: DESIGNED AND CREATED FROM THE IMAGINATION

Naval aviation had it's formal beginning with the commissioning of the *Langley*, but a solid foundation had been established long before the new carrier made her shakedown cruise. It began when sailors dreamed of flying from a ship, and first took form during the Civil War on August 3, 1861. John La Mountain ascended in a stolen balloon from the Union Navy steamer "Fanny" which was named as such for reasons best known only to the navy department. He spotted Confederate troop concentrations and artillery batteries at Sewell's Point near Hampton Roads and reported this to Admiral commanding who in turn notified the Union ground forces. This was the first use of naval aviation for military purposes and so impressed the Federal Army that a "balloon carrier" was immediately demanded for future engagements. The ship's name probably also gave rise to the phrase that many naval aviators "fly by the seat of their pants"!

Naval aviation, limited to tethered balloon rides went on hiatus after the Civil War. It did not become a serious military option until after the turn of the century and the development of the heavier than air machine powered by the internal combustion engine. On October 13, 1910, the Secretary of the Navy recognized that Naval Aviation should be explored and detailed two officers to examine and study it's possibilities. Just a month later, from a wooden platform attached to the scout cruiser *Birmingham* CL-2, Eugene Ely gunned his Glenn Curtiss built string,

The collier, Jupiter, *is no more. The mock up aircraft carrier,* Langley, *is on her way to completion. She was essentially a hull with a wooden flight deck supported by hundreds of interlocking girders. There were no standards or previous models, so she is more or less emerged from the imagination and willpower of her dedicated supporters, Cmdr. Kenneth Whiting and Lt. Cmdr. "Chevy" dec Chevalier.*

A *"Ready Room" aboard the* Essex *class carrier, Yorktown, in 1955. The* Langley *did not initially have ready rooms for her pilots and their squadrons. This was developed after years of experience, but the concept came from the* Langley *as did most carrier procedure. The early* Langley *pilots did not even have hard helmets. They used the soft leather skull covers fashionable during that era.*

The Langley or *"covered wagon" conducting early flight operations. The carrier is anchored and taking a biplane aboard. During flight operations, a crash boat was ready to be launched or in the water and a seaplane with a flight surgeon was available nearby. The men of the* Langley *were confident, but not that confident.*

fabric and wood pusher plane and successfully executed a take off from a warship. Another leap forward had been made. Ironically, Ely's feat took place very near the location where La Mountain's balloon flight had occurred a half century earlier. Within two months on January 18, 1911, former barnstormer and aerial daredevil Ely was back at the controls and successfully landed and took off from a platform attached to the armored cruiser *Pennsylvania* ACR-4. This time it was on the West Coast in San Francisco Bay. There was standing room only for this demonstration, and was attended by a number of naval officers and observers that would have been justified in their opinions had Ely crashed. This was not to be, at least not on this occasion. Unfortunately, Ely was killed later that year but earned a Distinguished Flying Cross for his bravery as a naval aviation pioneer. The

Navy allowed an additional $25,000 for further study into the possibilities of having a mix of ships and aircraft.

Events were moving more quickly now and on April 12 1911, Lt. T. Gordon Ellyson, USN became "Naval Aviator Number One" having successfully completed training at the Glenn Curtiss Aviation Center in San Diego. On May 8th of the same year, naval aviation was formally inaugurated with the awarding of a contract to Glenn Curtiss for two naval aircraft. Over the next few years, naval aviation moved in various directions. Much of it was confined to seaplane operations and experiments with catapults and flying off platforms mounted on large ships. World War I accelerated the development of naval aviation and even produced the first American naval flying ace. Lt. David Ingalls, while attached to the Royal Air Force shot down five

enemy aircraft. World War I caused substantial rethinking of the future of Naval Aviation and how is would best serve the U.S. It was plain that seaplanes were important to coastal defense and of value to operations that took place within 100-200 miles of a calm body of water. However, military campaigns notoriously failed to accommodate the wants and wishes of it's commanders. Thus the seaplane, later launched from capital ships had limitations, even as a scout. But, the redoubtable seaplane persisted as a rescue craft and for other duties until July 12, 1968 when the last, a P-5 Mariner was retired. They had been eclipsed by the rotary wing aircraft or helicopter, but they gave over half a century of excellent service.

But as naval aviation rapidly diversified, bigger, faster and more lethal aircraft would be built that would outclass even the most capable pontoon and land based aircraft. Another solution had to be found for naval aviation to flower and surmount all that sea warfare would entail in the future. Great Britain had already taken a step forward in the development of shipboard aviation by the conversion of the battlecruiser HMS *Furious* into a crude mockup of what would be the future aircraft carrier. Subsequently in 1918 the HMS *Argus* a flush deck model was built on the hull of a former Italian passenger liner. The Royal Navy quickly followed up with HMS *Hermes*, launched in 1919. It was time for the U.S. Navy to join Great Britain because a serious threat from the east was developing in the form of the Imperial Japanese Navy. They too desired entrance to the carrier club and joined in late 1922 with the IJN *Hosho*, which ironically was one of the few ships in the Japanese navy's inventory to survive World War II. The *Hosho* also represented aviation pioneering in its own right. This was the smallest carrier ever built at 7,470 tons, and light and mirror landing aids were first employed as a means of directing incoming aircraft. The USN would not use this or a similar system for at least three decades.

Various plans were put forward for a carrier or aeroplane carrying platform. One, in 1919 called for a 700 foot model that would displace 15,000 tons, have automatic hanger to flight deck elevators, aircraft with folding wings and make 30 knots. This was nothing compared to the plans advanced by General Billy Mitchell of the Army. At one time he suggested that the nation needed three carriers, two for bombers and one for fighters. They would have a 40-50 knot top speed, 1,000 foot long by 300 foot wide flight decks and be purchased with Army appropriations. Of course the Navy would cease to exist and a unified air force under one central command would be the nation's first and only line of defense. When the collier *Jupiter* was converted into the *Langley* she must have been quite a disappointment!

Naval aviation was further advanced by the influence of three separate but interrelated events. The Bureau of Aeronautics was created in August 1921, and in the same year the Naval Arms Limitation Conference was opened in Washington D.C. on November 11. The third and possibly the most influential were the series of Army and Navy bombing tests. Older warships were subjected to controlled bombing runs which proved that ships could be successfully attacked from the air. This alarmed the farsighted into intensified action yet, incredibly made more firmly resolute those who did not see a future in military aviation. Added to this was the continuing specter of rising militarism in Japan, and the result was greater tolerance and even grudging support for naval aviation. Not to the degree that battleships would assume second or an equal place with the aircraft carriers, but the die was cast. It was now time for the USN to build its first real aircraft carrier.

The *Jupiter* was ideal for conversion to a small aircraft carrier. She was relatively modern, having been completed in 1913. There were large holds, substantial headroom, and very little

superstructure to remove. She also required very few personnel to get underway and operate. One drawback was her limited speed of 15 knots, but other than that she proved a worthy candidate for conversion. Another drawback was the simple fact that she was still a valuable asset to the fleet. A large but dwindling number of warships still depended on coal so there was some reluctance to sacrificing her to this new and untried aspect of the naval service. That was not the only objection however. Many senior officers had great disdain for allowing any precious taxpayer dollars or resources to be wasted on what seemed to be a hopeless and valueless venture. With the end of World War I, and powerful forces of world pacifism at work, there was little anticipated use for any military let alone a collection of heavy and gluttonously expensive warships. There was very little money and it had to be rationed in accordance with tradition and need. In the years that immediately followed the Armistice, destroyer commanders had to ration fuel and crews had to serve on two or more ships on a rotating basis just to keep them active. Naval appropriations were paltry and difficult to justify, so a $500,000 expenditure for converting a coal barge to an experimental laboratory for a bunch of irrepressible and sometimes irreverent aviators was hard to swallow. Even at the last minute Secretary of the Navy, Josephus Daniels overruled Admiral William S. Benson's order countermanding the conversion. On July 11, 1919, the decision was made - convert the *Jupiter*. But, convert it into what? Seeking overt assistance from the Royal Navy was not possible. Ostensibly an ally, Great Britain was still a competitor and was very secretive where carrier design and naval aviation were concerned. The U.S. Navy would have to do the best it could with what was available in technology and wing it! There were very few examples to use as a basis for creating the *Langley*, so the Navy Yard at Norfolk began, albeit in some confusion. The yard, not hard pressed on other projects still kept the *Jupiter* conversion at the lowest priority.

Work began and what eventually emerged was due to the persuasive powers of Commander Kenneth Whiting (Naval Aviator 16), her prospective executive officer and Commander Simmers of the Navy Construction Corps Lt. Cmdr. Godfrey "Chevy" dec Chevalier, (Naval Aviator 7), was also part of the initial team that kept the yard working, despite their continued objections. Interestingly, the prospective commanding officer, Captain Stafford H. R. "Stiffy" Doyle, a card carrying member of the "gun" club did not put in an appearance during conversion nor even attend the commissioning on March 20, 1922. This was too bad because he probably would have had a good laugh when he saw the commissioning pennant nailed to a mop handle fixed to the flight deck. There were no masts on the ship as yet so the pennant had to go somewhere, even if on a stick. Doyle's refusal to acknowledge the ship spoke reams about the regard in which naval aviation was held at this time. However, with or without Doyle, work continued. During his assignment in command of the *Langley*, he displayed virtually no interest in aviation or the problems inherent during the infancy of carrier operations. It was Doyle's attitude and aviation illiteracy that forced Whiting to ask friends in Washington D.C. to pass a public law requiring aviator qualification for any and all officers given a command responsibility over ships primarily involved with naval aviation. A general line officer had to earn wings of gold before contemplating leadership in naval aviation, and well it should be.

The first effort in the conversion was to raze the upper works of the *Jupiter* and install a flat end to end wooden platform over the entire structure. The wooden flight deck was to be 534 feet by 64 feet and have height of 56 feet above the water. The flight deck was not angled or curved, it was a perfect rectangle. Every square inch of landing surface was to be used for handling aircraft. It had five expansion joints to absorb the ever changing movement of the ship. The former cargo and coal holds were converted to store air-

A Landing Signal Officer (LSO) helps direct an incoming aircraft aboard his carrier. Approach speeds were kept as slow as possible for pilot and carrier safety in the early days. The origin of the LSO can be traced directly to Cmdr. Kenneth Whiting who used to stand on the deck edge of the Langley *and help guide pilots during recovery. He often waved his arms frantically.*

The light and mirror landing system used for automatic landings. This concept was pioneered by the Japanese in the 1920's aboard their first carrier, the IJN Hosho. They were seeking a method for recovering aircraft at higher speeds than currently in practice. The system was never perfected. The light and mirror method employed on American carriers is highly effective and indispensable to high speed jet aircraft recovery.

Lt. Cmdr. Godfrey "Chevy" dec Chevalier has just landed his Aeromarine 39B aboard the Langley on October 26, 1922. This is the first landing on the carrier and was wildly celebrated later at the Norfolk Yacht and Country Club (inauguration of Tailhook?). In this photo Chevalier is taking off in his Aeromarine as the carrier rides at anchor.

What the Langley has brought into the right knit world of the United States Navy. A very early model torpedo plane flies over the battleship Idaho just after the Langley was commissioned. The torpedo plane would spell the doom for the undefended battleship in just a few years at Taranto, Pearl Harbor, and off Singapore.

craft, petrol, and ammunition. One of the holds near the center of the ship was used to house lift machinery for an elevator leading from below deck stowage to the flight deck. Traveling three ton capacity overhead cranes in the hanger or aircraft assembly area moved dismantled aircraft from lower deck cargo storage to the hanger deck for assembly. After reassembly, the complete airplane was then allowed on the lift for elevation to the flight deck. The *Langley* carried up to 55 aircraft that could be stowed in the cargo holds. At the time, this was the largest number of aircraft embarked on a "fleet type" carrier. Other navies in the international carrier club had air groups of 34 or less aircraft. On the *Langley*, just under 30 aircraft could be parked on the after end of the flight deck to not interfere with launching operations. During the bulk of her career, the *Langley* normally carried 34 aircraft which consisted of 12 fighter or "chasing" planes, 12 scout or spotter planes, 4 torpedo planes and 6 torpedo capable seaplanes. The seaplanes were serviced by boom cranes with a 35 foot reach were provided on either side of the carrier amidships.

Even catapults were fitted on deck that could be used to launch the heavier aircraft such as the torpedo carrying aircraft. These could be accelerated to 60 mph in just 60 feet, quite an accomplishment. Stopping an airplane was indeed a major consideration and the new carrier was eventually fitted with cross deck arresting gear, a purely American Naval invention. This system enabled a landing at 60 mph to be stopped in 40 feet, without major injury to pilot or plane. This was truly amazing, and the bravery required for pilots to inaugurate these new ideas cannot be overstated. The first arresting system which resembled a complicated wire mesh quickly gave way to the cross deck wire system. Much experimentation was performed to perfect various methods that would later find their way to larger and more sophisticated fleet carriers.

One of the primary problems that faced carrier designers and was only solved with nuclear power. This was the dispersion of gases or smoke from the ship's power plant. It often caused difficulty for air operations and always was a nui-

sance. The *Langley* made use of a rather ingenious system that allowed exhaust smoke to be funneled through two interconnected tubes that on the port side led to hinged stacks, one of which could be lowered to allow the smoke to theoretically mix with sea spray. It seemed to work and having stacks that could be lowered prevented a hot pilot from crashing into them. A ship with a power plant as limited as that of the *Langley* could utilize this type of an exhaust system, but 30 knot plus carriers with nearly 200,000 shp required a massive funnel or funnels to discharge gases. This became apparent with the next two ship class of carriers, the *Saratoga* and *Lexington*.

The *Langley* was a flush deck carrier that had to be navigated from a structure in the bow area but under the flight deck. Her jackstaff was lowered during flight operations as was her stern flagstaff. There was even a pigeon loft in the stern that was built as a home for carrier pigeons (no pun intended), but the pigeons were obviously mentally retarded and failed to carry out their missions. A secondary use was found and they provided many fine dinners in the wardroom! Many changes were made in tradition.

The *Langley* was not only a ship designed from creative ideas, but also from bartering, kumshaw and outright thievery, but on March 20, 1922, the *Langley* was commissioned as the first aircraft carrier in the U.S. Navy. She became CV-1 and the "*Covered Wagon*". From her date of commissioning thru September of 1922, the carrier was modified and further refined. Finally, she put out sea for trials and on October 17, 1922, what she was built for finally occurred.

THE *LANGLEY* BECOMES AN AIRCRAFT CARRIER, AND THE REAL WORK BEGINS

On October 17, 1992, the first of many events that marked the *Langley* as an aircraft carrier came to pass. Lt. Virgil C. Griffin, piloting a Vought VE-7SF was launched from her deck. The aircraft had a 180 hp Wright engine that could pull the 2,100 pound aircraft to a top speed of 117 miles per hour! The *Langley* was at a standstill, but it was an experiment. Nine days

later, on October 26, 1922, Lt. Cmdr. Godfrey dec Chevalier landed an Aeromarine 39B on the slowly moving carrier (6 knots into a 30 knot head wind). In actuality, the plane was nearly at a relative standstill when it arrived over the *Langley* and then unceremoniously dropped onto the deck. He did this with no assistance, no landing signal officer, no guidance and no practise. What a way to begin! Unfortunately, he was killed on a routine flight sometime later.

Both aircraft had been custom selected for the tests. The VE-7SF was more powerful and lighter than the Aeromarine which weighed 2,520 pounds and developed 100 hp for a top speed of 68 mph. Both tests were successful, although Chevalier won the award for the first upending of a plane and nicking the deck with his propeller. The fore and aft deck mounted arresting and cross deck wires successfully snagged the aircraft, but it was clear that some other method of stopping a plane from going off the forward end of the flight deck had to be devised. Besides, there was no shock absorbing system in use on the aircraft. The plane simply stopped (or dropped) in a controlled crash. Automatic hydraulic beam to beam arresting gear was not far off and would be a vast improvement. This was indeed a learning adventure.

Cmdr. Whiting was also a pilot as well as being the ship's executive officer. There was no way that he was going to remain on board while others did the hard work. On November 11, he was launched in PT Liberty 12 torpedo seaplane that had a 400 hp engine that powered the three and half ton aircraft. He was sent into the air by catapult, another first. He also crashed when landing because he had lost his undercarriage and one of the pontoons. The PT had been modified for catapult launch using a crudely fashioned carriage and it failed, another first! Whiting almost became the FIRST casualty, but he successfully landed the plane alongside and both were saved and returned to the *Langley*. The major firsts were now over and the time for refining this new naval weapon was at hand. There would be other innovative experiments, but take offs, landings and catapult launchings were possible, and with no prior experience.

The Navy was not home to an unlimited supply of aviators, and in fact there were only 314 in the Navy at the time the *Langley* took to the water. Almost all were seaplane aviators and had little or no experience with land based aircraft. The *Langley* was no place for training so Carlstrom Field at Fort Meyers, Florida was used as a substitute. Later, Long Beach Airport in Long Beach, California became another alter ego to the *Langley*. A duplicate outline of the carrier complete with landing nets was created for training on the west coast. As pilots became qualified in land plane or wheeled aircraft operations they were allowed to further hone their skill on the real thing. Whiting, a fanatic for doing it right began filming landings from the outset. Eventually, he had quite a collection of landings, mostly all bad and some fatal. These were known as the disaster movies. But pilots and flight deck personnel were learning and learning fast.

Whiting and the early aviators deserve much praise. They were not only naval aviation pioneers, but test pilots for aircraft and carrier flight operations. All things had to originate somewhere, some by design and others simply by accident. When the *Langley* began flight operations, ships boats were manned and made ready for launching, a yard tug would trail the ship, and a doctor detailed as a flight surgeon hovered in a seaplane. The plane guard destroyer would be the outgrowth of this early practise of providing reasonably effective pilot rescue services as would the helicopter and flight deck emergency medical people. This was by design, but a practise that conceived by accident was the landing controller. It evolved from Cmdr. Whiting's involuntary hand movements to actual hand signals and ultimately to someone using flags to guide an incoming aircraft safely aboard. Added to this was the red flag that signified landings forbidden to a white flag allowing the planes back aboard. The origin of naval aviators having notoriously raucous parties probably can be traced to the first celebration of a safe landing. The party, which some considered rather boisterous, even for the "roaring twenties" was held at the Norfolk Yacht and Country Club on October 31, 1922, honoring Lt. Cmdr. Chevalier. By the middle of November he would be dead, a great loss to naval aviation. Lt Virgil "Squash" Griffin assumed Chevalier's duties and within a few weeks the *Langley* left for Pensacola, which would become the home of naval aviation. It was hot and humid, but the weather was more stable and year round flight operations were possible. Now the flight deck crews and pilots could get down to serious training and perfecting carrier operations. It became patently clear that one of the most important aspects of carrier warfare was the ability to launch, land, rearm, refuel and again launch aircraft in the shortest period of time. By 1926, just three years later, the crew of the *Langley* reduced the take off interval from minutes to 15 seconds and the landing interval from a several minutes to 90 seconds. This was a major accomplishment, given the crude systems then available.

For the next two years, the *Langley* conducted one training exercise after another, and her pilots and flight deck personnel became experts. The *Langley* was an designated an experimental ship and everything in the navy's aircraft inventory with wheels found its way to her deck at one time or another. Launching was not the problem - landings were. If a pilot could walk away from an airplane still capable of flight, then it was a good landing. If not, then more experience was necessary for the pilot and the plane, providing both were repairable.

On November 17, 1924, her designated experimental days came to an end as she became a unit of the Battle Fleet. She sailed for the Pacific and arrived in San Diego on November 29, 1924. Of course there were a few more "firsts", one of which was the first night carrier landing carried out by Lt. John Dale Price on April 8, 1925. Landings in all sorts of weather became the norm and the *Langley* assumed her role as part of the fleet. She took part in various fleet problems or major exercises that now included limited air operations. Her first was in the spring of 1925. Her aircraft were sent to scout for one of the opposing fleets and the results were spectacular. Naval aviation in a more practical sense had been witnessed by senior officers in the fleet and one of the age old problems of determining an enemy's movements over the horizon had been solved. A mobile aircraft carrier that could operate far out at sea was the answer. The *Langley* and carrier aviation had taken a major step forward. In fact, many senior officers were so encouraged that they could scarcely wait for the *Lexington* and *Saratoga* to become operational.

The apex of her career as a carrier occurred in 1928 during Fleet Problem VIII. It was the "flour bomb" attack on Hawaiian military installations. Military targets were subjected to flour sack bombings which was quite embarrassing for the recipients, especially those who considered naval aviation as just a passing fad. The surprise air attack was an unqualified success and a portent of an event that would occur some 13 years later, but with far greater devastation than flour and embarrassment. She was not so fortunate during Fleet Problem X in 1930. The *Langley* and *Saratoga* were surprised by aircraft from the *Lexington* and judged destroyed by exercise referees. Naval aviation now had the capability of determining major fleet operations, a lesson not lost on anyone who observed.

The sunshine days of the *Langley* came to an end with the commissioning of the two aircraft carrier giants, the *Lexington* and *Saratoga*. It was an interesting twist that the U.S. went from a slow small carrier with limited capability to what amounted to two of the largest carriers built by any nation. These two giants would be among the world's largest for years to come, but much of what they achieved was founded on the experiments through trial and error aboard the *Langley*. Because of the *Langley*, these two ships were "ready to use" carriers. The *Langley* and pioneer pilots, Whiting and Griffin who had been assigned to the *Saratoga* had done the navy a great service. The old "covered wagon" would now find the backwaters of naval aviation and although she would persist as a carrier well into the mid 1930's, her days as a fleet carrier had ended. She would play host to the Navy's first rotary wing aircraft, an Autogiro piloted by Lt. A. M. Pride On September 23, 1931, but on September 15, just five years later she was summarily transferred to the Base Force as a seaplane tender. She had proved her usefulness as a carrier and put naval aviation on the fast track to success.

THE NAVY'S BEST SEAPLANE TENER: THE LAST ROLE OF THE *LANGLEY*

The *Langley* arrived in the Mare island Navy Yard on October 25, 1936, that also being the last day that aircraft ever flew from her deck. She remained in the yard for conversion until February 26, 1937. She was modified to her new role, seaplane tender. Some 40% of her forward deck was removed leaving just over 300 feet available for storage for seaplane repair and upkeep. An open signal bridge was built up on the assembly deck just ahead of where the flight deck had been removed and a proper mast was erected. Signal flags in the more traditional sense could be flown and the ship actually guided from an area with adequate visibility. Her holds that had been used for aircraft were converted to storerooms and supplemental living quarters. Fueling points were placed along her main deck, and what emerged in the spring of 1937 was a first class seaplane tender and the best in the Navy.

In this May 5, 1927 photograph the Langley *is being warped to her mooring by two navy tugs. Some of her aircraft are ranged on deck. She has a 55 plane capacity but rarely operates more than 34. Both of her telescoping masts are rigged thus flight operations are suspended.*

Her accommodations were spacious and she earned an excellent reputation for service and crew morale. Her two forward and two aft mounted 5 inch/51 caliber guns were left for defense against destroyers or torpedo boats. This seemed patently absurd, because the entire existence of the *Langley* over the last fourteen years had been to establish carrier aviation as the threat of the future. Later she shipped a variety of other weapons including four flight deck mounted and sandbag surrounded 3 inch/50 caliber AA guns, but nothing would be sufficient when she met the Japanese aerial threat five years and one day in the future. She was now designated AV-3, and left Mare Island on May 27, 1937. She cruised under the Golden Gate Bridge which had just been erected and made her home wherever

her assigned flock of seaplanes needed her. She operated out of Sitka, Alaska, Pearl Harbor, T.H., San Diego and Seattle. Sitka was probably the worst as it was so barren. Aside from the *Langley* there were fish and fishing boats, and little else. Leaving the frozen north was not regretted by any of the *Langley's* crew. She served on the east coast for a brief period and made an appearance at the World's Fair in May 1939 in New York. She was quite an attraction and was visited by many people who were fascinated with the U.S. Navy and it's now historic first aircraft carrier. By this time she had served for 27 years and it was now again time for her to find the backwaters of the Navy - the Asiatic Fleet. She arrived in Manila on September 24, 1939. She had a little over two years left.

The Monkeys Have No Tails In Zomboanga: Philippine Duty

A familiar song to anyone who served in the Asiatic Fleet or appreciates film director John Ford's war movies is:

"Oh, the Monkeys have no tails in Zamboanga,
The Monkeys have no tails in Zamboanga,
They were bitten off by whales,
Oh the Monkeys have no tails in Zamboanga"

This was a familiar piece of music to all in the Asiatic Fleet and is still known in naval circles. Of course the Asiatic Fleet no longer exists in the U.S. Navy. But while it existed, it served a number of useful and occasionally unorthodox purposes. It was generally composed of older ships and aircraft that were no longer considered suitable for front line Pacific or Atlantic Fleet operations. Most, like the *Langley* could not keep pace with modern fleet maneuvers. Her top speed had dropped from 15 to 13 knots, and she was only suitable for limited operations. Of course this did not prevent her from carrying out various flag showing exercises. The *Langley* was still a large warship and had five inch guns, therefore she looked the part. The natives were always suitably impressed, but those with any military savvy knew better. The heaviest ship in the fleet during the 1930's was first the heavy cruiser *Augusta* and in the final days, the *Houston*. The old light cruiser *Marblehead* was also a major unit as were a number of ancient World War I vintage four piper destroyers. There were a few relatively modern submarines; fleet train and support ships and of course, four seaplane tenders including the *Langley*. It was a paper fleet at best. Aside from being the Navy's attic of relics, the Asiatic Fleet had the reputation for career warehousing and not a few officers and men found their way there via court of inquiry or under some cloud of misconduct or undesirability. On a positive note however, the officers and sailors of the Asiatic Fleet were among the best fighting men in the U.S. Navy. They would prove this many times

Aircraft were not the only modes of transportation stored on the assembly or hanger deck of the Langley. *Automobiles belonging to the officers could also be found there along with ship's launches.*

Aircraft were assembled on the hanger or assembly deck of the U.S. Navy's first carrier and then moved to the elevator by the three ton overhead crane shown above in this photo. It was a complicated process to assemble, fly, disassemble and store aircraft. The Navy was learning quickly that safety, speed and efficiency were the bywords of naval aviation opeations.

The crew is assembled on the hanger deck for what appears to be a change of command ceremony. Eventually, the crew of a carrier became distinct and separate from its air groups. A line was drawn, but not in anger or mistrust. Each needed the other or both would be lost in combat.

in the few months following the Japanese attack on Pearl Harbor on December 7, 1941.

The Asiatic Fleet represented the U.S. Navy and the American government in Asia. The ships individually or in company protected American commercial, social and religious interests in China and any other area that the American flag or its citizens ventured. It had existed for decades and was either loved, despised, but always tolerated. The ships provided protection and the crews provided a continuous source of revenue to bars, whorehouses and dives of all sorts from Shanghai to Manila. As the Japanese overwhelmed China in the late 1930's, the fleet was moved to the Philippines and established its homeport in Manila Bay. There were satellite ports at Subic Bay and Cebu, but the Navy concentrated its fleet repair facilities and headquarters at the Cavite Navy Yard in Manila Bay.

It was also at Cavite where many officers and men had their families and dependents housed. It was pleasant duty, as most ships rarely strayed too far from Cavite and generally could be found moored or anchored nearby. It was so with the *Langley*. From the Navy's first carrier, she had become its most comfortable seaplane tender and now was located in Manila Bay. She was there for two years from late 1939 through December 1941. One of the people who best remembers the old carrier turned seaplane tender was a young girl, the daughter Henry "Hank" Mummy, MMC, USN.

Henryette "Mummy" Coker lived with her family near the shipyard in a brick building that had once been used as a barracks for the Spanish Army in the days that led to 1898 Spanish American War. Like all good Navy wives, Chief Mummy's wife followed her husband from one duty assignment to another. The Chief had been aboard the *Langley* since her golden days as a carrier in 1931 and Manila was to be the last for the Mummy family which besides Henryette, now included five children. The family shopped at the base commissary and occasionally in the local barrio which is the Philippine equivalent of a village. There, stooped shouldered old women (probably less than 50) gummed cigar like cigarettes that smelled like burning hemp rope and sat on their haunches trading gossip. Balut sellers peddled putrid duck embryos as a great delicacy and every once in a while a cart driver would fall to the ground in a sodden heap. He was undoubtedly full of tooba, an fermented coconut liquor reputed to intoxicate, but not reach it's designed effect until the drinker was blind. Binnie Boys picked fights using agile billy singh knives and stabbing was the desired way to settle a disagreement. Girls learned to grip a half coconut husk with one foot and a rag with the other to polish the floor. Laundry was done outdoors at a local river and there was no delicate cycle as everything was beat on river rocks and then twisted until dry. Of course, American families had servants and domestic life was made much easier with a house maid, cook and gardener. All for a nominal sum. Chiefs and officers never had it so good.

Life on a naval station in the Philippines or the P.I. was interesting, diverse and everyone experienced some difficulty coping with customs that clashed with those of California, New York,

One of the Langley's *aircraft takes off to entertain onlookers in New York City in late 1927. Safety nets are in evidence for the deck crew to use when an aircraft decided to misbehave. As usual, the ship is at a standstill. Fast carrier operations began with the giants* Saratoga *and* Lexington. *Both could steam at 33 plus knots, far out-pacing the* Langley's *best speed of 15 knots.*

Texas or Nebraska. When not in a well chaperoned and strict girls Catholic school Henryette spent as much time as possible with her father and his shipmates on and off the *Langley*. The ship was more than steel plates, diesel oil, and gray paint. It was a home for hundreds of men and a symbol of everything that the U.S. Navy held dear. It was invariably clean, maintained in an immaculate fashion and well ordered. The food was good and there was always plenty of it. A favorite, for reasons only known to Mrs. Coker was the combination of lunch meat, canned peaches and navy coffee. The coffee was arguably the best, but only if it was brewed with a pinch of salt. Many of her days were spent sitting on the seawall and watching the grand old lady of naval aviation riding at anchor. The *Langley* was ungainly and to some ugly, but to 14 year old girl, the half carrier was a sight to behold and representative of her father. Taking the ferry from Cavite to Manila to sample the more cosmopolitan life of one of the major far eastern cities was always an adventure, even if enlisted men under the rank of CPO had to ride down below. Rank determined level in society and the boundaries were never crossed. This was one of those customs that was inherent in the Navy and even more so on foreign soil.

Henryette, her mother and the other five children had to leave Cavite, the *Langley* and her father long before the Japanese paid their unwelcome call, but the eight months she spent there were memorable and provide a valuable clue as to what life was like in the final salad days of the *Langley*. A few dependents refused to leave and unfortunately became civilian prisoners of war after the Japanese occupied the is-

lands. A world of privilege complete with a race based caste system was about to undergo a very dramatic change. With change came another realization. The Asiatic Fleet was no match for the Imperial Japanese Navy. All this became apparent in the days following December 8, 1941.

THE GRAND OLD LADY JOINS THE ORPHAN FLEET

Soon after the news was received that the Japanese had bombed Pearl Harbor, aircraft sporting the red ball and rising sun were soon sighted over American military installations on Luzon, the main island of the archipelago. Admiral Thomas C. Hart, Commander in Chief of the Asiatic Fleet thought better of subjecting virtually defenseless ships to determined attack by Japanese bombers. Accordingly, he dispatched the *Langley*, and fleet oilers Trinity and Pecos to the southern Philippine Islands to seek the temporary safety of being out of Japanese aircraft range. They left just in time and avoided destruction. The navy yard at Cavite was bombed and reduced to rubble on December 10, 1941, as were most of the nearby facilities.

The *Langley* and the other three seaplane tenders, *Childs, Heron* and *William B. Preston* would have to care for Patrol Wing 10 elsewhere than in their customary harbors in and around northern Luzon. The PBY's had been well serviced by these tenders, and of all the *Langley* was the favorite. She had spacious accommodations and good food. The *Heron* was a small tender and the others were converted flush deck four piper destroyers.

The carrier at speed in the Pacific. One of her smoke funnels is in its horizontal position, and the other is coming up. Both were kept down during flight operations to prevent a wayward pilot from hitting them.

The Langley *all decked out at North Island in San Diego Harbor in the early 1930's. As can be seen, she is just a hull with a wooden deck supported by a maze of steel girders. To those that loved her, she was beautiful.*

The Japanese quickly established air superiority and within weeks, air supremacy. This meant that Allied ships, men and equipment traveled in daylight at their own peril. Patrol Wing 10's aircraft, or what was left of the original 28 PBY's and utility craft were ordered to the Netherlands East Indies. There was nothing to be gained from losing the entire wing and its trained personnel.

Traveling south with the *Pecos* and *Trinity*, the *Langley* was attacked by a Japanese submarine that fired two torpedoes at her. The submarine claimed credit for sinking the *Langley*, but the torpedoes missed (the ones fired by a German submarine in 1917. Ironically, it would be American torpedoes that would finally sink the old carrier three months later.

On December 13th 1941, the Manila Bay escapees rendezvoused with Admiral William A. Glassford's Task Force 5, a composite group of the most capable American ships in the area, which included heavy cruiser *Houston* and the light cruiser *Boise*. The *Boise* had been shanghaied by Admiral Hart after the new light cruiser had been detached from escort duty in late November. She had modern weaponry and radar. Unfortunately, her availability to the rapidly shrinking Asiatic Fleet ended within weeks. She struck an uncharted reef and was detached to the U.S. for repair.

The American force arrived in Balikapapan and remained for a short period before being divided into different units. Task Force 5 became the Asiatic Fleet striking force and the *Langley* and other seaplane tenders found various coves and deserted inlets to provide service to the dwindling number of PBY's in Patrol Wing 10. The Patrol Wing was actually based out of Surabaya yet its aircraft found their tenders in some of the remotest areas on the Malay barrier. The tenders and their charges were constantly on the move to avoid the spreading octopus of Japanese air power. One PBY after another was lost or damaged beyond repair. By new years day 1942, there were just eight serviceable aircraft available. Eleven more aircraft were flown in from Pearl Harbor, but in just 23 days, the Japanese had culled naval aviation in the Asiatic Fleet

to less than half of its original number. By March 1, 1942, only ten of the total force of 44 PBY's were left and the utility squadron was down to one plane. Patrol Wing 10 had fought a desperate battle against overwhelming odds, but the same story was true for all of the units in the Asiatic Fleet. The fleet was being dispersed and in essence, it ships and units were becoming orphans. Every home they sought was bombed or gutted by the Japanese.

The *Langley* ended up in Australia and eventually Fremantle on the western coast of the country. She should have remained there. Much of January 1942 was spent moving army aircraft from one location to another as the old seaplane tender had become an aircraft ferry. Her commanding officer, Captain Felix Stump was transferred to the staff of Admiral Thomas Hart as air intelligence officer. Cmdr. Robert P. McConnell became her next and final commanding officer after relieving Captain Stump. The executive officer was Cmdr. Lawrence Divoli, who was highly regarded and well liked by the crew. The *Langley* was a very successful ferry and could carry a large number of assembled aircraft on her spacious flight deck. Thus she was selected for what was to become her final assignment. This was to load and transport Army P-40 fighters directly to Java to enable continued defense against the seemingly unstoppable Japanese juggernaut. It was a foolish decision motivated by political pressure and a complete lack of appreciation of the military situation in the theater. Sadly, the *Langley* and many of her crew would have to pay the price for command negligence. It was to be a "senseless loss".

THE *LANGLEY* BECOMES A CASUALTY OF A POLITICAL GESTURE

The combined command of American, British, Dutch and Australian forces was identified as ABDA. It was a hastily assembled command organization that covered all Allied military forces in the far east. Formed in mid January 1942, ABDACOM or the senior officer was British Field Marshall Sir Archibald Percival Wavell, headquartered in central Java. Naval forces were

under the command of Admiral Hart, ABDAFLOAT. He had a title, but no actual authority to direct and control all units assigned. The British operated in one area and the Dutch in another. The Australians supported the remnants of the American Asiatic Fleet which was formally disbanded on January 27, 1942. Its few and diverse fragments became an element in the newly created Southwest Pacific Command. It was the same organization commanded by Hart, but Hart's former deputy, Admiral William Glassford was it's new commander. It was confusing to all who took the time to decipher the organization. In any event, Hart was eventually ordered back to the U.S. and the position of ABDACOM was filled by Dutch Admiral Conrad E. L. Helfrich on February 14, 1942. He inherited a command that was worn out, fatigued and not worthy of the Japanese challenge. Within two weeks it would be destroyed in detail by a vastly superior and well coordinated Japanese force. This occurred quickly after the devastating defeat in the Battle of the Java Sea on February 27, 1942. Java was now completely open to Japanese occupation and the combined Allied command would have to regroup and reorganize in the comparative safety of Australia. On the same day, but not in the climatic Java Sea battle, the *Langley* also met her end.

From the outset of the war in the Pacific, the Dutch government in exile requested aircraft, in particular fighters to defend their colonies the Netherlands East Indies. They had an air force, but much of it was obsolete and no match for Japanese "Zero" fighters. In fact, there were no aircraft in the far east that could effectively deal with the Zero. It was a fast and maneuverable aircraft quite capable of defeating the American P-40 Warhawk and Royal Air Force Hawker Hurricane. To make matters worse, Japanese pilots were well trained and had combat experience. They were winning and this too was a factor, a major factor in their meteoric success. The Dutch deployed 70 odd American produced Brewster Buffalo fighters first to help defend Singapore and next to hamper the Japanese advances in Borneo. The Buffalo was no match for the Japanese. All but seven were destroyed either on the ground or in the air. The Japanese captured seven and later used them in propaganda films, but their assessment of the Buffalo's performance was simple - easily defeated. If this what the Allies considered a first line fighter, then the war would be over by mid 1942. By February, 1942, the Netherlands East Indies Army Air Corps had its back to the wall in Java and was desperately seeking relief from any Allied source.

The Allied command made two concerted efforts to supply the Dutch Air Force with P-40 fighters and other aircraft suitable for combat service, but in both instances ferrying the planes by air resulted in huge losses. The last attempt was made during the period from January 29, up through February 11, with the transfer of three full but unfortunately inexperienced squadrons. The loss rate was 60%, a figure much higher than even could be expected in combat during a similar period. The effort brought the Army fighter strength in Java up to a pathetic 26 aircraft. The Dutch considered this unacceptable and demanded more support and quickly. Constant pleas from the Dutch influenced Allied planners who were now undoubtedly pressured by political considerations. On one hand the Dutch and uncoordinated remnants of the ABDA command were attempting to prevent the Japanese from overrunning their homeland and precious oil resources. On the other hand, much of the Allied command was moving to Australia and relative safety. There were no overt departures, but the flight to safety was on. This was irksome to the Dutch so they insisted on fighters be brought in to make a final stand against the Japanese invasion. This the Dutch command wanted immediately. Unlike Winston Churchill who refused to supply Royal Air Force fighter squadrons to France during her final hour, the Allies decided to send a shipload of precious P-40s and irreplaceable pilots to Java. The *Langley* and a cargo ship, *Sea Witch* were selected for this hopeful but futile gesture.

The *Sea Witch* was loaded with 27 disassembled fighters in her holds and on her deck. The *Langley* was loaded with 32 ready to fight P-40s and had embarked 33 pilots and a limited number of supporting air crew. The aircraft were flown in from across Australia and moved through city streets to the loading dock. They were individually towed by trucks with the aircraft tail tied to the truck beds. When they got to Java, streets would also have to be cleared and men used to pull the vital fighters to the airstrip. Of course there was no airstrip when the decision was made to bring in fighters so one was being hastily crafted near the city of Tjilatjap. Even had it been completed, it was highly doubtful that P-40's could effectively use it. The P-40 required a proper air field as it was a high performance aircraft. It was too bad that the Langley's flight deck had been shortened or she might have been able to launch the fighters some distance from her destination. History might have been altered in a major way. But, on February 22, 1942 she and the *Sea Witch* were loaded and sitting in Fremantle Harbor awaiting final sailing orders. A convoy was being formed which would include the *Langley, Sea Witch* steamers *Duntroon* and *Katoomba*. All four were to be escorted by the modern American light cruiser *Phoenix*. She, like the *Boise* mounted

The Langley *with most of her aircraft on deck. Her fore mast is stepped and smoke pipes in upright position signalling no flight operations. Within a half hour this could change, and she could be launching aircraft.*

This excellent bow shot of the Langley *shows in detail the safety netting rigged on each side of the ship. This was an absolute necessity as many new pilots landed on other parts of the ship rather than the flight deck.*

fifteen 6 inch guns and had a director controlled antiaircraft battery of eight 5 inch/25 caliber guns. With the Pearl Harbor survivor *Phoenix*, the convoy was in good hands. As a footnote, the *Phoenix* would soldier on for another four decades and be sunk by a British submarine! In 1982, she was a flagship in the Argentine Navy and was sunk during the short Falkland Islands War won by Great Britain.

The *Langley* was to have loaded up to 300 officers and enlisted men as part of the aircraft shipment, but this never happened. She embarked only a fraction of that number. There was rampant confusion, lack of coordination and indecision at all levels of the Allied command. But, on February 22, 1942, the *Langley* and *Sea Witch* left Fremantle destined for Tjilatjap, Java. They were to take a course designed to keep them from harm's way by sailing far to the southwest of Java and then steaming back to Tjilatjap. The plan was soon abruptly changed. Admiral Helfrich of the Dutch Navy had assumed command of ABDAFLOAT replacing Admiral Hart. On February 23, he ordered the *Sea Witch* and *Langley* to proceed directly to Java and arrive on the morning of February 28, 1942. Admiral Glassford sanctioned the decision. To compound matters, revised instructions were received directing the *Sea Witch* to remain under the protection of the convoy and the *Langley* was to proceed at best possible speed alone. The height of command stupidity had been reached. There was no longer a probability or even a strong possibility of success. It had dropped to the level of hoping and praying that the old carrier would safely arrive in Java. The Japanese were about to overrun Java; there was no airfield; no method to transport aircraft to the airfield that didn't exist; and the ship bringing the aircraft did not stand a chance against the Japanese. Of course, a promise was a promise and the fighters were on the way, but even Don Quioxti would have abandoned this as a complete folly.

The *Langley* was armed with four 3 inch/50 caliber AA guns placed on her flight deck in relatively strategic locations. They were surrounded by sand bags. She also had various smaller weapons for close in defense including 50 caliber machine guns and even a sprinkling of hand held Browning Automatic Rifles (BAR). The old carrier also had her four 5 inch/51 caliber deck guns, a remnant from the past, but they too were of no value against even the slowest aircraft. Matters were to become complicated and more confused, but there was no turning back.

In the early afternoon of February 26, 1942, two flying boats were sighted. They were identified as Dutch PBY Consolidated patrol planes that had come to share a bit of good news. An escort had been provided and though it was only the small lightly armed 1,300 ton minelayer *William Van der Zaan*, it was welcome. The sea was lonely and there was some strength in numbers. Unfortunately, the minelayer was experiencing engine trouble and her reduced speed was actually handicapping the *Langley*. The Dutch minelayer was using oil from Borneo, and her burners were not adapted for its thin viscosity. Captain McConnell had been directed to arrive at Tjilatjap by 0930 the following morning, and it would be impossible if he had to remain with his slow escort. He thus decided to go on alone. Later that evening, his decision was reversed and he was instructed to allow the minelayer and the two PBY's to act as escort. Accordingly, he reversed course to rejoin them. Another change of orders was received just as the minelayer hove into sight and the *Langley* was directed to rendezvous with the destroyers *Whipple* and *Edsall* some 200 miles distant. Having destroyers for an escort was considered far better than a broken down and unreliable minelayer. Of course both the *Whipple* and *Edsall* had been in action for several weeks and were virtually worn out, but you take what you get. Both had hull damage and were not capable of sustained high

The Langley *parades with other elements in the fleet during this 1934 review. By now she has been relegated to the fleet train due to her lack of speed and overall value. An air group, spawned by this great old lady flies overhead.*

speeds. At 0720 the following morning, the destroyers were sighted, however there was a suspected submarine contact in the area. It was not until 0900 that the ships were able to begin assembling into a defensive convoy, but it was too late. An unidentified aircraft, which was undoubtedly a Japanese reconnaissance flying boat (*Kawanishi*) discovered the ships and radioed his find to a local land based attack force. Imagine the pilot's excitement, an American carrier and two light cruisers (four piper destroyers were often mistaken for *Omaha* class light cruisers, especially by the over exuberant). It was already a beautiful day with light cloud cover and with these prime targets, this would be a banner day for Japanese naval aviation.

Knowing what was about to happen, McConnell begged Admiral Glassford for fighter cover, but there was none to spare. *Langley* and company would have to fight this one alone and try to steam the last 130 miles to Java without being sunk. Just over two and one half hours later at 1140, nine twin engined bombers arrived over the force at an altitude of 15,000 feet. They were Mitsubishi G4M1 "Betty's" which were highly capable medium bombers. They carried 20mm cannon, machines guns and nearly a ton of bombs. More importantly, they had an exceptional endurance and a ceiling of 29,000 feet. They could remain over the *Langley* for hours and out of her antiaircraft defense range. On their first pass they lazily took a long look at the old carrier. The *Langley* was beginning to take what evasion maneuvers that were possible by zig zagging. At 13 knots, this was a vain gesture as was the barrage put up from the ancient 3 inch guns. It would be a matter of minutes before the green and brown mottled colored bombers would begin the days work.

The first bomb salvo hit the water just off the port bow and fragments slashed thru her hull and ripped the bridge structure apart. No one was hurt as yet, but if near misses could do this, what would happen when bombs hit the grand old lady? Avoidance tactics by the ship delayed this knowledge and the bombers were fooled, but not enough to waste bombs. There would not be third time. The Japanese planes went into what appeared to be a huddle and in anticipation of the ship's movements, salvoed their load. This time the ship was hit five times and directly. Three near misses also did substantial damage, two of which straddled the ship. It was not an equitable match, and the *Langley* was outclassed. World War II technology overwhelmed War World I tactics and weapons. She never stood a chance.

Her deck was a shambles and there were burning P-40's everywhere. Four of the bombs hit on or near the flight deck destroying aircraft, boats, the port aft elevator, and staff quarters. One hit aft abreast of the port funnel supports. Near misses ripped holes in her side and combined with the damage topside, the ship was done for. She was slowly sinking and her gyro compass was put out of action. The nine bombers were subsequently joined by six fighters which immediately attempted a concentrated strafing attack. This was broken up by effective close in AA defense from resolute gunners standing amidst the burning wreckage on the flight deck. Miraculously, the attack ended as quickly as it had begun but it had taken 90 minutes. Fires were raging at many locations made worse by the buildup of paint over the years. Some areas had up to one inch of paint, an extreme fire hazard. McConnell conned the ship to a point where there was very little wind thus helping the fire

fighters, but great damage had been done to her old hull plates from near misses. She was quickly filling with water, and the pumps were not keeping pace. McConnell now realized that bringing his ship and what aircraft were left to Tjilitjap was hopeless. The *Langley* was riding too low in the water and would surely run aground in the channel leading to Tjilitjap, so he decided to take the old ship to the closest point on the Javanese coast, thus allowing his men a fighting chance for survival. This plan was quickly discarded because by early afternoon water had entered and filled the electric motor pits and the propulsion system was about to fail. At 1345, the order to abandon ship which was now listing 17 degrees was given, and by 1400 all except the captain a few others had left the ship. A few men had already found their way into the water before the order was given, but there was much confusion and communication was difficult. Sixteen did not make it and remained with the ship for eternity. Captain McConnell attempted old fashioned chivalry by expressing his desire to remain with the ship, but he was passionately dissuaded by his crew. He then left the ship. The *Edsall* and *Whipple* efficiently retrieved the survivors which amounted to 464. The *Whipple* was carrying 308, and the *Edsall* had the remainder. The destroyers did an excellent job in rescuing the *Langley's* survivors and there was only one task left, scuttling the old ship. The *Whipple* fired nine 4 inch shells into her and added two torpedoes. The old carrier that had witnessed and nurtured naval aviation refused to sink. The destroyer captains were desperate to leave the area to avoid further air attacks, but they could not just leave the *Langley* to burn and drift. Finally, patience wore thin and the destroyers left the *Langley* to her own fate. She was later reported by a passing Dutch patrol plane to have sunk later that night, just 75 miles from her intended destination .

It was over for the old carrier. One of the most significant ships in the history of the U.S. Navy had been destroyed through political foolishness and a lack of appreciation for the true state of affairs in the southwest Pacific theater. The Netherlands East Indies was virtually no more and sending a defenseless seaplane tender with fighter planes for a region soon to be invaded was criminally negligent. Unfortunately, the saga of the *Langley* was not over. The grand old girl was now at the bottom of the Indian Ocean, but her 468 surviving crew members were not safe and would have to face one ordeal after another.

JUST WHEN YOU THINK YOU ARE SAFE; YOU'RE NOT

After hearing the news that the *Langley* had been abandoned and was sinking, Admiral Glassford ordered a search for survivors. This included sending what was left of the local units of the Asiatic Fleet to sea. This included the gunboat Tulsa and minelayer *Whippoorwill*. Neither had a any credible AA weaponry, but at least a demonstration of concern was made. The *Edsall* was ordered to Tjilitjap to bring the rescued Army flyers to Java for possible work in air defense. They would be handy in case the aircraft from the *Sea Witch* were assembled. The

Sea Witch had made it without incident and then safely returned to Australia. A strange twist of fate.

Before leaving for Java, the *Edsall* and *Whipple* met with the fleet tanker *Pecos* off Christmas Island. The destroyers were to transfer the *Langley* survivors sans the Army personnel to the old tanker and then she would proceed to Australia. This plan was interrupted by three twin engined "Bettys" that bombed nearby shore installations. It was appropriately decided to leave the area quickly as it too was becoming untenable. A submarine was also sighted. This reinforced the decision to proceed. Soon after first light on March 1, 1942, the transfer of survivors was completed and the ships parted company. The *Edsall* sailed for Java, unaware that it had been overrun. She and her Army flyers never arrived, a mystery until after the war ended. Captured Japanese movies showed the silhouette of a four piper destroyer being successfully shelled and sunk by the battleships *Hiei* and *Kirishima*. There were no survivors, and even though the American naval command was abandoning Java, Glassford had failed to countermand his order directing the *Edsall* to Tjilitjap and certain doom.

The *Pecos* steamed for Australia on a course that hopefully would keep her out of harm's way. This was not to be and she was spotted by a Japa-

The Langley *has become an aircraft tender and is operating out of Manila Harbor as part of the Asiatic Fleet. She was the best tender the fleet ever had. She was spacious, had excellent accommodations and always a welcome sight to tired Patrol Wing 10 PBY crews.*

This Independence *class CVL (light carrier),* Langley, *CVL-27, in war paint on duty in the Pacific. This carrier also distinguished herself by helping to avenge the death of her namesake. She earned a Navy Unit Commendaiton for her service against the Japanese.*

One of the last photographs taken of the Langley. *All of the survivors had been rescued by the destroyers* Whipple *and* Edsall. *The* Edsall *is just behind the listing old seaplane tender. Nine 4 inch shells and one torpedo were fired at the sinking ship by 1428. The* Whipple *fired a second torpedo at 1445 on the afternoon of February 27, 1942. The destroyers then left the ship to her own devices. She sank a few hours later, just 75 miles from her objective.*

The new airplane carrier, Saratoga, *being fitted out after launching. This view shows that huge derrick used for liting seaplanes on and off the ship and the 8 inch guns of "B" turret. The starboard 5 inch/25 caliber antiaircraft guns are swung out over their supporting sponson, and the armor belt (blister) is easily seen at the waterline in theis November 5, 1927 photograph.*

nese scout plane just hours after parting company with the *Edsall* and *Whipple*. Just before noon, the now terrifying sight of Japanese aircraft appeared in the form of dive bombers. They were from the carrier *Soryu* which earlier had a role in the Pearl Harbor attack. Until 1530 or late in the afternoon, the bombers attacked the old tanker. Her AA defense that consisted of two 3 inch/50 caliber guns and a mixture of four 30 and 50 caliber guns were no match for the onslaught. The Japanese pilots dropped fifty bombs and only hit the *Pecos* directly with five. Poor average, but sufficient to do the job. By 1600, the old tanker, another relic of the Asiatic Fleet upended and went bow first down to her grave. The carnage on her decks was horrible. The Japanese had bombed and strafed a defenseless ship for four hours. It was legalized murder, not war.

The *Langley* survivors were again without a ship and many were attempting to stay alive in oil covered water. Some died, but for those that lived for another four hours, a beautiful sight came up on the horizon - the USS *Whipple*. She had responded to the call for help and had steamed at full speed to the rescue. Just before dark at 1930 she began a second rescue attempt. This went on for the next two hours, but in the end had to be terminated due to a firm submarine contact. A conference was held with Destroyer Division 57 commander, Commander E. M. Couch and the commanding officers of the *Whipple*, *Pecos* and *Langley*. It was decided to leave the area and seek safety. All concurred and with 232 survivors, the destroyer headed for Australia. Only 146 of the *Langley's* crew were aboard. Four hundred and thirty four officers and men had been killed aboard the *Pecos* or had been lost at sea. No one will ever be certain.

The *Whipple* arrived in Fremantle on March 4, 1942. The saga of the *Langley* was almost over. Commander McConnell would suffer a three month period in purgatory for his lack of report writing skills. His original hastily and poorly worded report of the Langley's loss was accepted by Admiral Glassford but forwarded with negative comment. Three months later, the comment was reversed in Washington by Admiral Earnest King, the Chief of Naval Operations. McConnell had done all that he and his men could have done to save the old ship. It was the ineptitude of the Allied command and its futile gesture that had caused the loss of the *Langley* and most of her crew, not McConnell. He was exonerated, and he eventually attained the rank of Rear Admiral. It was finally over.

USS SARATOGA CV-3
"A SEVEN HOUR STRUGGLE WITH DEATH"

"THE LAST THING I SAW WAS THE NUMBER THREE"

The old Chief Aviation Machinist Mate had been in the navy for almost thirty five years, and had witnessed a revolution in naval warfare. This was his final trip and when *Operation Crossroads* was completed he had promised to settle in the midwest far away from anything remotely resembling the U.S. Navy. He often joked with the younger men that he would tie an anchor on the radiator of his car and when someone far inland asked what it was, then he would be home. He had one last job to finish and that was to watch his old home, the carrier *Saratoga* CV-3 go to her final resting place. Regrettably, she had been selected as a test ship for the twin atomic blasts at Bikini Atoll in the Marshall Islands being held in July 1946. The atomic bombs dropped in Japan at Nagasaki and Hiroshima just eleven months before had destroyed both cities and killed hundreds of thousands of people. It was now important to see how a fleet of common ordinary warships would fare against these nuclear monsters. Besides, it would provide an excellent opportunity to demonstrate the sheer amount of destructive power now in the possession of the American military. For this, observers from most nations were invited and in particular, those from the Soviet Union. It was vital to ensure that our Russian Allies know what they might receive should we become active belligerents rather than silent protagonists. The veteran Chief was not really concerned with international politics, he was there to say goodbye to an old friend.

He had been among the commissioning crew after being reassigned from the carrier *Langley* in early 1927, a year before the *Saratoga* went to sea on here shakedown cruise. The *Langley* was the only training ground available for the new super carriers *Lexington* and *Saratoga* and what a difference between the two classes of aircraft carrier. The *Langley* was slow, small and box-like, the *Saratoga* was fast, powerful and could accommodate any type of aircraft. The U.S. Navy had moved from one end of the carrier aviation spectrum to the other in less than half a decade.

The Chief had witnessed the rise of naval aviation from a novelty to that of the central theme in late twentieth century naval warfare. The mobility and striking power of carrier borne naval aviation now reflected the ability to fulfill national policy abroad. It was the weapon of choice for superpowers and those that could no longer afford to maintain fleet carriers would slip to second place in international stature. The battleship, once the queen of the sea, had been relegated to a subordinate role eclipsed by the new capital ship, the aircraft carrier. The Chief had also watched his country move from an inferior naval power to super power status largely based on the accomplishments of naval aviation during World War II. Now 19 years after his first glimpse of the *Saratoga*, he stood in awe of the two atomic blasts that had smothered the seventy odd ships in Bikini Lagoon. The first explosion was an air burst, and it had done very little actual damage. To many, the July 1 test was a dismal failure. Just a loud bang and a few fires aboard ships nearest the center of the blast. His old friend, the "Sara" looked unhurt and even one of her aircraft, a Grumman TBF torpedo plane was still in it's pre-blast station at the rear of the flight deck. So much for nuclear power. The second and final detonation on July 25 was different. This bomb was suspended 100 feet under a small landing craft (LCI) and when it was triggered, the result was devastating. The decades old battleship *Arkansas* was literally lifted out of the water and immediately sank. Other ships were likewise damaged, but not all were vaporized as had been predicted. Most survived, but with extensive topside damage. The *Saratoga* was smoking and obviously damaged but still on an even keel. She had been just 500 yards from the epicenter and the blast was ulti-

mately lethal to the old battlecruiser turned aircraft carrier. She sank just seven and one half hours later. Salvage crews were prevented from saving the wounded giant because of excessive radioactivity. In the early afternoon, she plunged stern first into the depths of the lagoon. There she joined the *Arkansas* and the twisted remains of other ships. Today, she sits upright in the lagoon and in decades to come she will undoubtedly attract amateur divers who will marvel at this fine specimen of American Naval history. For the old chief, now gone himself, the last thing he saw through his tears, was the number three. As the ship slid stern first, her bow momentarily tilted upward. The number "three" was plainly visible for a minute and that image was the captured on film, the last of this gallant ship. The number represented the third aircraft carrier in the U.S. Navy, CV-3. What follows is the saga of her origin and accomplishments. She was conceived as a battlecruiser, yet born as a huge aircraft carrier.

A GIANT-KILLING TREATY PRODUCES TWO GIANTS BY DEFAULT

In the years immediately following the end of World War I, there was a general demand for arms reduction by the citizens of the civilized world and in particular the U.S. Post war dreams of having a "navy second to none" were gradually replaced by Navy Department satisfaction at having a navy at all. It had been just three short years before that the U.S. Navy was on track to becoming the most potent and destructive seaborne force ever to cruise the oceans of the world. By late 1921 and into 1922, its ships were being laid up in droves, some actually being launched only to be immediately placed in reserve or even scrapped. Much of the problem lay with a country shouting pacifism in the wake of the most catastrophic international war in human history. However, a national budget shrunk by lack of bonded credit and tax revenues also played a part. The people of the U.S. had begun to express an unwillingness to indebt themselves for the sake of maintaining a high degree of military preparedness. Anyway, preparedness for what? Japan was 10,000 miles to the west; Germany was defeated; Italy and France were not real threats and Great Britain was nearly bankrupt. Two oceans separated the U.S. from potential enemies, and neighbors Canada and Mexico were friendly. With the exception of periodic banana republic upheavals and the overnight ascent and descent of third world military dictators, the U.S. was insulated from conflict.

Yet, there was a honeymoon period with the military in the immediate months that followed the Allied triumph in Europe, and most Americans had not yet fallen under the spell cast by fanatics of "peace through total disarmament". President Woodrow Wilson, a man of peace and one of the architects of settling international disagreements through the auspices of an international organization still recognized the need for a strong navy. Following on the 1916 legislation that had provided for a massive shipbuilding program, in 1919 he proposed further expansion. Accordingly, construction began on the

The new carrier Saratoga *is being nudged by tugs shortly after being commissioned on November 16, 1927. The huge funnel seems to overshadow everything about this ship and would be her trademark for nearly two decades.*

This aft view of the Saratoga *graphically depicts her 8 inch gun main battery. These guns would prove useless and were just so much dead weight to be carried until 1942.*

This view shows the island structure and the immense 79 foot high funnel. Dispersing smoke and gasses from the 180,000 shp propulsion plant required a funnel this large. Carriers built by other nations used hinged smoke pipes and side mounted funnels, but none were as successful as those aboard the Lexington *and* Saratoga. *Besides, the funnels gave these ships character and majesty.*

battleships *Colorado, West Virginia, South Dakota, Iowa, Montana, North Carolina, Indiana* and *Massachusetts.* In addition, six battlecruisers, also authorized in 1916 were laid down. Two of these 40,000 ton monsters were the *Lexington* and *Saratoga.* However, the honeymoon soon ended and the building program came to an abrupt halt within months. By 1921, construction was allowed to continue only on the *West Virginia, Colorado* and the two battlecruisers. It was time to pay the piper.

Economic woes had already struck Great Britain whose navy had been forced to scrap 38 battleships, two battlecruisers, 87 light cruisers and 300 destroyers! It was incredible. What had been scrapped seemingly overnight represented a powerful navy in itself. The only classes of ship not sent to the junkyard were aircraft carriers and submarines.

The U.S. would soon follow suit. This was not solely due to public outcry although it was becoming more pronounced. The American public, especially those living in the midwest were certain that war was the outgrowth of international arms races. The concept of deterrent through the maintenance of superior arms was not acceptable, and most citizens supported the wholesale elimination of weapons. However, there were other more compelling reasons for ratcheting down the proliferation of arms. There was a rising national security concern due to the increasing expansion of the Japanese Navy and its influence in the Pacific. Japan may have been 10,000 miles distant from the west coast of the U.S., but her navy could quickly overcome the natural defense of distance. It seemed that every time a new class of American battleship was laid down, Japanese shipyards followed suit. It was unnerving, especially in view of the fact that the Nipponese economy was strong and quite capable of sustaining a naval arms race. Japan committed a major proportion of its gross national resources into its military machine, a phenomenon impossible in a peacetime democracy.

A method had to be sought to at once placate the American public, reduce defense spending, help out British Allies and level the playing field with Japan. President Wilson's concept of a League of Nations as a body to limit arms in accordance with international peace mandates had failed, but his successor in the White House attempted a different approach.

As an American President and world leader, Warren G. Harding, successor to Woodrow Wilson has not been treated well by history. He was tainted by one scandal after another, but his administration was responsible for convening a naval arms limitation conference in late 1921. On November 11, 1921, delegates from Great Britain, France, Italy, Japan, the U.S., Belgium, Netherlands, Portugal, and China met in Washington D.C. The purpose of the conference was to hammer out an international agreement limiting naval armaments. The concept had been sponsored by Senator William Borah who in June of the same year had arranged for full congressional support from both chambers. His reasoning was simple and naive; no arms races, no war. For the Harding administration, the conference was a political Godsend. For the U.S. Navy, it appeared to be a disaster of immense proportions. For Great Britain, it allowed an economic breathing space. A continuing arms race would quickly cripple her weak economy and shake confidence in her place in the world. A controlled arms race would be tolerable. For Japan, there was grudging recognition of its growth as an international force, but little else. Besides, her military would only pay lip service to this contrived western hobbling of her plans of future conquest.

Unlike most international conferences, this one was distinctive for two reasons. First, the delegates concluded their business in near record time. From inception to treaty agreement the elapsed time was 88 days. Secondly, there was a concrete agreement and a plan that all could abide by, at least on the surface. What emerged was the Washington Naval Arms Limitation Treaty.

In summary it provided for:

1. Total capital ship tonnage was allowed based on a formula of 5 USA: 5 UK: 3 Japan :1-3/4 Italy: 1-3/4 France.
2. Sixty capital ships were to be scrapped or demilitarized.
3. Ten Year Moratorium on capital ship construction
4. Various clauses for cruisers/destroyers and land base fortifications.
5. The American battlecruisers *Lexington* and *Saratoga* could be rebuilt as carriers with a similar allowance for Great Britain and Japan.

The primary purpose of the conferees was to restrict and regulate the construction of battleships then considered the most lethal of all warships. The U.S. Navy was forced to suspend work on seven new ships and sink or scrap four existing battleships. Work on all battlecruisers was to cease save two, the *Lexington* and *Saratoga.* They were to be rebuilt as aircraft carriers but were limited to 27,000 tons in accordance with the treaty. Savvy American horse trading permitted an increase ultimately to 36,000 tons. The treaty which was intended to kill giants, allowed two of the biggest carriers in the world to be built. Japan was allowed to convert two capital ships (*Akagi* and *Kaga*) to heavy carriers as was Great Britain with the battlecruisers turned carriers, Courageous and Glorious. Unknowingly, a new queen of the sea had been christened - the aircraft carrier. In the years that followed the signing of the Washington Naval Arms Limitation Treaty, the carrier would emerge from its vague role to the capital ship of choice. The Treaty had encouraged the development of the aircraft carrier, but in the spring of 1922, its purpose was still unclear. The heavy caliber gun remained the gauge of fleet power, and the carrier was unproven. That would come later.

FROM BATTLECRUISER TO AIRCRAFT CARRIER

The *Saratoga* and *Lexington* were originally designed as high speed heavily armed capital ships to compete with any built by any nation. The 1916 congressional appropriation allowed for six battlecruisers, and although not stated publically, the purpose was evident - outclass the Royal Navy. Initially, these brutes were to displace a whopping 43,500 tons with an armament

The Imperial Japanese carrier Akagi. *She was one of two capital ship conversions allowed by the Washington Naval Arms Limitation Treaty, an exception similar to that allowed the United States and Great Britain. The U.S. navy built the* Lexington *and* Saratoga *while Great Britain converted the smaller* Courageous *and* Glorious. *The 34,000 ton* Akagi *and half sister, 33,000 ton* Kaga, *were both lost at the battle of Midway on June 4, 1942.*

of ten 14 inch guns. The secondary battery was to be at least five inch in caliber and perhaps six inch. These ships would develop over 150,000 shp generating a top speed of 33 knots. Sixteen boilers were to be situated on two levels and seven funnels were planned. This concept did not last long. Fourteen inch guns were insufficient compared to heavier calibers already being forged in Great Britain and Japan. The original design was subsequently modified to allow for a heavier caliber gun (eight 16 inch barrels in four twin turrets) and a reduction of seven funnels to five. The fascination with a fast heavily armed, but lightly armored (7 inches on the belt) super battlecruiser was amazing and addictive.

The battlecruiser was designed to act as a scout that could visually detect an enemy battle line, and with its superior speed outrun its slower, but better armored adversaries. Unfortunately, the battlecruiser was the embodiment of "speed is armor", which turned out to be a false promise. As with most limited purpose designed ship classes, the battlecruiser never carried out the scouting role. Instead, they accompanied heavily armored capital ships into slugging matches, and when they did, they suffered. The image of power was quickly dispelled when shells easily penetrated the thin armor of these ships.

The sheer size of the planned *Lexington* class battlecruiser was remarkable considering the fact that the next largest size of warship in the U.S. Navy was to be the 32,000 ton *Maryland* class battleship, the ostensible queen of the sea. Of course, it was only important to out-displace the British. The *Hood* class was known to displace 41,200 tons, have a maximum speed of 31 knots and a main battery of eight 15 inch guns. Clearly, the *Lexington* class battlecruiser was superior. These ships might have been actually built had the World War I German U-boat not proved to be such a menace. As a consequence, American shipbuilding facilities and resources were devoted to destroyer construction. The battlecruisers would have to wait. This combination of events was actually fortuitous for the U.S. Navy. Had the six battlecruisers been built, they too might have shared the fates of HMS *Hood* (sunk by the German battleship *Bismarck*) and HMS *Repulse* (sunk by Japanese aircraft.) In any case, in later years they would have been relegated to second place behind the aircraft carrier - a dubious use of taxpayer dollars. Building the six battlecruisers would have also dramatically impacted the navy's aviation program. Each year beginning with 1918, the navy asked for an appropriation to built a large carrier(s). Each year the congress rejected their request, and in all probability this trend would have continued into the late 1920's. Political events provided two hulls that could be successfully converted to the large carriers the navy needed at a much reduced cost in taxpayer dollars and goodwill.

With the end of World War I work on the battlecruisers should have begun in earnest, yet this was not to be due to the Washington Naval Arms Limitation Treaty. The treaty caused the cessation of work on four of the battlecruisers, but allowed the partially built *Lexington* and *Saratoga* to be converted to aircraft carriers. Of all six, these two were furthest along in overall construction so they became the logical candidates for conversion. The treaty, with last minute amendments specified that these two ships were allowed to displace up to 36,000 tons, the final three thousand tons for anti-torpedo blisters and/ or flight deck protection. This grew to 39,000 tons when they were fully loaded. Less than half a year after the treaty, the *Saratoga* was formally reclassified CV-3. The battlecruiser was now an aircraft carrier.

Converting a battlecruiser to an aircraft carrier was no small or simple task. The *Langley* provided some clues as to what a proper aircraft carrier should be and there was some information available on the Royal Navy's building program, but for the most part, the designers were on their own. Both Japan and Great Britain were also converting unfinished battlecruisers and battleships to large carriers, but their initial offerings were easily outclassed by American counterparts. The Imperial Japanese and Royal Navies opted for multiple flight decks forward for aircraft launching thus constricting their air group capacities to less than 70 aircraft. They also utilized an inadequate smoke dispersion system of side mounted or hinged smoke pipes. The Americans were novices from a design and building standpoint, yet the *Lexington* and *Saratoga* were far beyond the experimental or novelty stage. When completed, they were the finest carriers in the world, and would be for many years to come. However, they were not perfect. When they were launched, the evolution of carrier warfare had not yet progressed to point where aircraft were considered the carrier's main battery. This would be a long and exasperating battle. In fact, the delegates at the Washington Naval Conference were more concerned with the caliber of guns aboard the new carriers than the size of the carriers. It had taken 2,000 pound bombs to sink one of the targets ships (former German capital ship *Ostfriesland*) during military air advocate General Billy Mitchell's bombing tests. As no aircraft conceived could lift off a carrier deck with such a load, the delegates were convinced as were many other lead-

History being made as Lt. Cmdr. Marc Mitscher makes the first landing aboard the new fleet carrier Saratoga *on January 11, 1928. The cumbersome wire "spider web" arresting gear is still being used and will not be replaced for some time. Mitscher as well as the* Saratoga *were both destined for greatness.*

Within months after the first landing aboard the Saratoga, *she now has a full air complement. Pilots and flight deck personnel had been well trained by the* Langley *people. From the outset, the* Saratoga *was a first line fleet carrier. The only problem was that many were unsure as to her ultimate usefulness to the fleet.*

ing naval leaders - the 8 inch gun would be the maximum size weapon allowed on the two new carriers. This was in part based on the reasoning that the two battlecruisers turned carriers were certainly faster than any capital ship in existence or planned, but there was that possibility of an enemy eight inch gunned cruiser catching one of them at night or by accident. Consequently, the *Lexington* and *Saratoga* were armed with eight 8 inch 55 caliber guns arranged in four twin turrets. Two were sited in a superfiring format in front of the island and the other two in similar fashion aft of the enormous funnel. This

kind of firepower could deal with any single cruiser, providing it remained on the starboard side of the carrier. Firing across the deck to port was discouraged for obvious reasons. The eight inch guns were never fired in anger, thankfully.

Aside from the eight inch main battery, both ships were armed with twelve 5 inch/25 caliber dual purpose guns to counter enemy destroyers or aircraft. There were no "close in" weapons such as the 50 caliber gun provided when these ships were built. This weapon was finally added years later for light AA defense. The main threat was expected from the surface or from dive bombers. The five inch guns would provide a barrage defense against the dive bombers and the main battery would account for any surface ships encountered.

The engineering plant in the *Saratoga* consisted of sixteen White and Foster boilers providing power to General Electric turbines driving four shafts. When built this propulsion plant was the most powerful in the world with a rated shaft horsepower of 184,000 and able to drive the huge ship at a trial maximum speed of 33.25 knots. As a tribute to her engineering plant, she reached 97% of her designed speed or 32.25 knots only using 85% of her designed power. She carried 8,884 tons of oil fuel which was consumed at the rate of 2,000 tons per 24 hour period when under full power. One of the distinguishing features of the *Saratoga* was the massive funnel structure that was nearly eighty feet in height. This huge structure housed four funnels. These funnels were large for a very good reason. A plant that generated 209,000 shp at full power required a substantial gas dispersion apparatus - a large and high stack for escaping smoke. By comparison, the carrier *Langley* was able to utilize two small hinged smoke pipes, but her power plant generated only 5,000 shp, less than 3 percent of that available in the *Saratoga*!

The ship was founded on electrical power and there were over 1,000 electric motors aboard performing nearly all mechanical tasks. Her electrical systems were centrally controlled in one location, a feature that nearly proved disastrous when she was damaged by a submarine launched torpedo in late 1942. The severe shock of the explosion caused electrical short circuits in her main system which immobilized her entire propulsion plant for several hours.

The power generated by the *Saratoga's* systems could generate up to 3.26 million candlepower, a extraordinary capacity for a early 20th century warship. This capability to furnish electrical power was graphically demonstrated by sister carrier *Lexington* when she provided emergency generating power for the city of Tacoma, Washington in December 1929. The city was dependent on hydro electric power which had been severely reduced by continuous drought. During the month when the *Lexington* was connected to the city's system, she more than compensated for the loss of power from local sources. In actuality, she provided a staggering 4.25 million kilowatt hours during her stay.

The *Saratoga* was armored in accordance with the original battlecruiser design. Her side belt was a maximum of six inches in thickness and there was one inch of armor under her wooden flight deck. Bulkheads were seven inches and the main deck over the belt was two inches. She was externally bulged to mitigate torpedo damage. She was plated from her hull to the flight deck yet the armor protection did not extend beyond the hull.

The side plating up to her flight deck was punctuated in several locations by large openings that allowed room for boat stowage and minimal ventilation and access to the hanger areas. The *Saratoga* had a two level hanger deck and access to the flight deck was via two "T" shaped lifts. One was opposite the forward island superstructure and the other opposite the funnel. Her 888 foot by 130 foot (maximum) flight deck was planked and approximately 60 feet above the waterline. This carrier was huge compared to the *Langley*. She was also unusually spacious compared to other major warships in the Navy. A sailor had only to compare her hanger deck with the casemate gun deck of a battleship to see the difference. The *Saratoga* and *Lexington* had cross deck landing nets or mesh (later a more sophisticated arresting format) that extended 100 feet from the un-recessed aft portion of the flight deck. Experience with the *Langley* had been of great benefit to the *Saratoga* and her sister, the *Lexington*.

The *Saratoga* also had a derrick located just forward of turret A (8 inch) which could be used for lifting the heaviest seaplane unto the deck and vice versa. For launching heavy aircraft, a catapult was available forward that could thrust virtually any size contemporary aircraft to flying speed in just 60 feet of travel. Most aircraft were launched without the aid of the catapult, but on the other hand, most pre-jet age aircraft were light enough to take off unassisted.

The *Saratoga* embarked up to 72 aircraft normally yet was rated at 90 full load. In this respect both the *Lexington* and *Saratoga* were superior to their rivals (IJN *Kaga* and *Akagi* and RN *Courageous* and *Glorious*). The initial price tag for the battlecruiser, exclusive of armor and armament was $16.5 million. By the time she was completed as an aircraft carrier (including aircraft) costs had risen to just over $45 million, a bargain for the U.S. and unknowingly a giant step forward for the navy. All in all, the *Saratoga* was a modern fully operational carrier. She and the *Lexington* even had an enclosed or hurricane bow, a feature abandoned for many years until mid-1950's carrier modernization programs. In many ways, these two ships were technologically ahead of contemporary naval strategy - a long way ahead. It would take many years to silence criticism that seemed to come from every nook and cranny in the naval establishment, but these two ships more than proved their worth.

NOVEMBER 16, 1927: THE *SARATOGA* BECOMES PART OF THE FLEET

Eleven years from the original congressional authorization in 1916 for battlecruiser CC-3, the aircraft carrier *Saratoga* was commissioned on November 16, 1927. Her keel had been laid on September 25, 1920 at the New York Shipbuilding Company at Camden, New Jersey. Work began on the battlecruiser *Saratoga* and continued until a formal decision was made to convert her uncompleted hull into a large carrier. Accordingly, on July 1, 1922, she was redesignated, CV-3 and after some debate congress passed a separate act to fund the conversion in accordance with the treaty they were so relieved to oblige. She was launched just under three years later on April 7, 1925. Captain Harry E. Yarnell commissioned this majestic giant of a ship on November 16, 1927. It was a mutual love affair. In contrast to the first captain of the USS *Langley* CV-1 who failed to attend the commissioning ceremonies, Yarnell was definitely present as the commissioning pennant was broken on the *Saratoga*.

Harry Yarnell was an outspoken naval aviation enthusiast and proudly wore his "wings of gold". He rose to flag rank and commanded carriers in their first successful attack (mock) on Pearl Harbor on a lazy Sunday morning in 1932. The ease of which this was accomplished was certainly noted by the Japanese who carried out the "real thing" nine years later. Captain Yarnell was the embodiment of naval aviation leadership and a perfect match for the first major fleet carrier in the U.S. Navy. The "Sara" predated the "Lady Lex" which was commissioned a month later on December 14, 1927. This year marked another significant event in naval aviation as the USS *Ranger* CV-4 was authorized for construction. Unlike her three predecessors, the *Ranger* would be a "from the keel up" aircraft carrier

Even as the great ship became an active unit in the fleet, nagging questions about her use persisted as did with carrier aviation in general. What was her true role to be? A scout for the battle fleet? Providing air cover for the battle line against opposing air forces? Independently attacking enemy shore installations or locating and destroying enemy battle fleet units? Locating and destroying opposing carriers? Initially, it was determined that carrier aviation would simply exist to support the battle line. The use of the carrier as a capital ship on its own was not to be until the beginning of World War II. The battleship "gun and hunt club" was going to retain the carrier in a secondary role and as long as there was no war, there was no reason to change. The carrier would act as a scouting unit and to defend the battle line against opposing scout aircraft and bombers. Accordingly, the *Saratoga* and the *Lexington* became floating mobile airfields for "Aircraft Squadrons, Battle Fleet".

By 1928, the *Saratoga* had embarked five squadrons to form her total air group. It consisted of fighting, bombing, scout and torpedo squadrons with a three or four plane capacity utility unit. All of her first aircraft were biplanes, the most popular being the Boeing F2B1 fighter bomber (31 embarked) which had a maximum speed of 160 mph. She also carried up to 24 Martin torpedo planes to fill out her complement. Pilots were interchangeable as the Navy could ill afford the luxury of specialists in bombing, scouting, pursuit and other tasks.

Economic considerations seemed to be at the forefront of any planned training or exercises involving the new carriers and naval aviation overall. The notion that naval aviation would be an inexpensive method of defending the country was quickly dispelled by reality. Aircraft required continual servicing and were all but worthless after 18 months of hard use. Unlike ships which had a 20-40 year service life, aircraft became obsolete in less than three years. Flight operations aboard the carriers was also severely limited due to fuel costs. The *Sara* and the *Lady Lex* were required to accelerate to a speed sufficient to allow aircraft to be launched and recovered several times during a day, and this consumed huge amounts of fuel oil. Accordingly, air groups spent much of their time at local naval air stations where costs could be kept down.

Penny pinching became worse as the years

One of the only photos of the three U.S. navy carriers moored together for yard work in 1931. This was the total of American carrier strength and was comparable to any that Japan and Great Britain could muster.

Aircraft warm up aboard the Saratoga in preparation for launching. The smaller fighter-bombers are in the foregound and the torpedo planes at the stern. In the distance off the port side a four stack, flush deck destroyer acts as plane guard. Countless pilots were rescued by these guardians. The "small boys" were required to conform to the movements of the carrier, which frequently changed due to the wind across the deck requirement.

A female well wisher waves farewell to the Saratoga as she leaves New York on June 18, 1934. The public was always welcome to visit these ships and were suitably impressed by American carrier air power, even in the early 1930's.

wore on into a new decade and a new low was reached in 1933 at the onset of the economic depression. Many in the Naval Academy graduating class did not receive their commissions that year, and the navy suffered an overall 15% pay cut. This for a service that could barely keep ships at sea and planes in the air. 1928 seemed like the good old days for naval aviation by the early 1930's.

There was one bright spot in the final year of the "roaring twenties" for the Saratoga and naval aviation in general. It had already been established that the carrier existed as a servant to the battle line, yet during Fleet Problem IX in January 1929 an extraordinary discovery was made. The Saratoga was allowed to proceed independently escorted by a single cruiser to a point near the Panama Canal and launched a pre-emptive strike on the canal locks. This she did with great success. Her sixty-six plane attack force hypothetically immobilized the defending aerodrome and its aircraft and destroyed two of the canal's locks. The attack from the Saratoga also evaded patrolling aircraft from the Lexington and the much vaunted scouting fleet of cruisers and destroyers which were deployed in a traditional defensive posture. This was significant for a number of reasons. Primarily, a carrier without the protection of the ponderous "Nelson like" battle line had penetrated a heavily defended area and launched a successful air strike. Secondly, it was evident that the navy possessed a heretofore unknown weapon that could deliver mass destruction to a target well over a hundred miles distant and within hours of selecting the target. Land based facilities, at least those near

the ocean, were no longer immune from a fast hit and run carrier strike. By extension, the same was true of any slow moving battle line, although most battleship admirals were unwilling to concede the veracity of this revelation. Nothing was safe from those flimsy fabric and wood contraptions carted around the seas by those ungainly box like ships. The Saratoga was sunk at least three times theoretically by defending aircraft from the Lexington on January 26, 1929, the same day of the Panama Canal attack, but the point had been made. The fast paced carrier task force commanded by creative and daring leadership was the weapon of the future. The following year's exercise witnessed the destruction of the Langley and Saratoga by aircraft from the Lexington, further proof of the value of carrier tactics. Another nail had been driven into the coffin containing the battleship and its hidebound supporters.

Naval aviation enthusiasts had attempted nearly every possible method of securing needed resources to expand the carrier force, but unfortunately the country was beginning to suffer great economic woes. Appropriations from congress were almost exclusively reserved for reconstruction and modernization of the existing battleships in accordance with clauses in the international naval arms treaties. Another conference had been held in London in 1930 which further refined various previously agreed to restrictions. Naval aviation was still a stepchild.

In 1931, a new tact was taken. This time, one of naval aviation's most flamboyant fliers and supporters, Lt. Cmdr. Frank W. "Spig" Wead, USN (Ret) was asked for assistance. Wead had distinguished himself in a number of ways, not the least of which was his miraculous comeback from being completely paralyzed and then becoming a successful writer. He had been retired from the navy due to disability and had gone to work for Metro Goldwyn Mayer studios to write a screenplay on,"of all subjects", aircraft carrier operations. The result was "Helldivers", starring Wallace Beery and first time actor, Clark Gable. The leading lady was the *Saratoga*. The movie featured a number of scenes that realistically depicted flight operations aboard the *Saratoga* in her early days. The "secret" arresting gear which now consisted of nine cross deck retractable wires was partially censored to prevent the Japanese or others from knowing how this system worked, yet careful inspection showed the details quite clearly. The film was an instant success and the public loved it, as did the Imperial Japanese Navy. Publicity was more important than security at this point. The cause of naval aviation was now in front of the American public, and a new and dashing hero created, the carrier pilot. Not all looked like Clark Gable, but the navy didn't complain. The movie also captured the essence of early naval aviation. Aircraft squadrons were tight knit units that spent much time at shore installations (e.g. North Island, Alameda, and Pensacola) and rotated with one of three carriers. There was intense competition among the squadrons and maneuvers were as realistic as possible. Cameras were substituted for guns, sacks of flour for bombs, and tallies kept of bombing and shooting. However, squadron rivalry was matched by loyalty and dedication to naval aviation in general. Carriers such as the *Lexington* and *Saratoga*, now distinguished from her sister by a wide black vertical stripe on her funnel, as well as the slow and diminutive *Langley* were regarded with reverence and fondness. Many bar room fights erupted between battleship sailors and those from the carriers. A negative comment about the *Saratoga* came with a heavy price such as broken nose or black eye.

Aviators came from a number of sources. Most from the Academy and other officer pools. However, there were a number of enlisted pilots that eventually became officer pilots. The navy made use of all resources possible to keep its carrier aviation program on track. The aircraft they flew steadily improved in quality and quantity. Many had very colorful markings such as red, green and yellow tail assemblies. This helped in squadron identification and also was easier for rescuers to spot when an aircraft was down in the sea. The *Saratoga* and *Lexington*, major beneficiaries of lessons painfully learned on the *Langley* now used flag waving landing signal officers that carefully guided incoming aircraft onto the deck. Flight deck crews had been organized into specialties and the phrases such as "pilots man your planes" or "clear the flight deck" became part of carrier life and later legend. Groundwork was being laid for the greatest naval air armada in history, and on the decks of three American carriers still shunned by much of the naval hierarchy. World War II, which was almost at hand, would confirm the value of the fleet carrier.

The *Saratoga* spent the decade between 1931 and 1941 in one training exercise after another, yet probably the most significant occurred in 1932. Harry E. Yarnell, her commissioning commanding officer was a rear admiral and in command of both the *Lexington* and the *Saratoga* as

the major components of Aircraft, Battle Force. One Sunday morning, while participating in general exercises around Hawaii, aircraft from both carriers arrived unannounced over Pearl Harbor and virtually wiped out the land, sea and air forces present. How many hints did the U.S. Navy have to provide? This same pattern was repeated in the spring of 1938 when the *Saratoga* successfully launched a surprise air attack on Pearl Harbor, and repeated the same over Long Beach, Mare Island and Alameda at other times.

For all but the utmost diehards, the day of the carrier had arrived.

Another significant step for carrier warfare, and ultimately the solution to supply problems inherent during extended operations was the development of underway replenishment. Off the west coast, over June 11-13, 1939, the *Saratoga* and the fleet oiler *Kanawaha* AO-1, successfully carried out underway fuel replenishment. The age old problem of being tethered to a shore installation or having to moor next to a fleet auxil-

The "boys of summer" practise aboard the Saratoga *in preparation for fleet baseball championships. No other class of ship provided such an opportunity. Try to imagine this aboard a destroyer!*

Sister carrier, Lexington, *passes under the Golden Gate Bridge in San Francisco, California. It appears as of her foremast was just able to clear the lower span. The* Lexington *was lost during the Battle of the Coral Sea, but not before the Japanese were prevented from continuing their seemingly unchecked advance in the Pacific. Within weeks of her loss, she was avenged at the June 1942 Battle of Midway where four first line Japanese carriers and their precious pilots and planes were lost.*

The battle fleet takes a break from an exercise in this May 12, 1937 photograph. Three carriers (Saratoga, Lexington and Ranger) are anchored in Lahaina Roads off Maui in the Hawaiian Islands. Early in the morning of December 7, 1941, Japanese cruiser scout planes checked this anchorage for the fleet and specifically the carriers. Had they been located there in this fashion, all probably would have been lost.

The Saratoga and Lexington are anchored off Waikiki Beach in this late 1941 photograph. They were missed by Japanese raiders on December 7, 1941. The Lexington was at sea and the Saratoga was just entering San Diego harbor as Japanese aircraft began launching torpedoes at battleship row.

have to wait until after the war had begun. A partial modernization was hurriedly completed in late April 1941, and she left the yard on April 28, for the western Pacific. She was now one of three fleet carriers available in the Pacific as the last summer and autumn ended.

AT FIRST, ONLY A BRIDESMAID: THE "SARA" GOES TO WAR

The word "unfortunate" characterizes the early wartime career of this great ship. Through one set of circumstances or another she was always where the action was not. This dilemma would end, but for the first few months it was disconcerting. For the "Sara" it began in San Diego.

The attack on Pearl Harbor by the Japanese on December 7, 1941 put the battleship navy out of business as the focal point of any future offensive naval strategy. Most of the obsolecsing battleships damaged or sunk at Pearl Harbor would be renovated and serve a useful purpose in the war, both in the Atlantic and the Pacific. But, it was up to two and at most three fleet carriers accompanied by cruisers to bear the brunt of the early fighting. Ironically, it was in these early days that set the stage for the defeat of the Imperial Japanese Navy.

On December 7, in the Pacific, the *Lexington* was at sea as was the *Enterprise*, CV-6, one of the new *Yorktown* class carriers. The third and only other carrier in the Pacific was the *Saratoga*. She was just coming into San Diego harbor with her escort of a light cruiser and three destroyers. She was there for minor repairs, but according to the Japanese attack force, she was definitely at Pearl Harbor and moored where in actuality, the *Utah* was quietly sitting. In her place the *Utah* absorbed torpedo hits which caused her to turn turtle within eleven minutes and there she remains as a memorial. The planks on the *Utah*'s deck deceived excited Japanese attackers into believing that they had sunk the famous *Saratoga*.

The *Saratoga* left San Diego on December 8, with a hastily assembled escort force. She arrived at Pearl Harbor just a week later to witness the still smoking remains of the battle line. Her first assignment was to provide air cover for a relief column headed for Wake Island. Marine defenders on Wake had been continually pounded from the air and a second landing by hardened Japanese assault troops was imminent. Speed was crucial if the defenders were to saved. A task force was built around the *Saratoga* and *Tangier*, a seaplane tender which was to transport the relief force. Cruisers *Minneapolis*, *San Francisco*, *Astoria* were to provide escort along with a number of destroyers. The *Tangier* and fleet oiler *Neches* left for Wake a day before the *Saratoga* arrived, and after being refueled the *Saratoga* sailed on December 16. Time was running out and in truth was being lost due to faulty intelligence, lack of command coordination, and just plain bad luck. No one from Washington to Wake Island knew where the Japanese carriers were lurking and showy bravado was tempered with fear.

On the 17th of December, the *Saratoga* and her escort sighted the *Tangier* and her slow consort, the 13 knot oiler *Neches*. For the next few

iary to take on fuel and supplies was resolved. Unknowingly, this demonstration was a portent of one of the most important and significant advantages that the U.S. Navy would possess in the upcoming Pacific war. Continued sustenance of a carrier task force at sea allowed an aspect of sea warfare never before envisioned. The concept of a periodic fleet actions was replaced by the capability of relentlessly pounding and hounding the enemy from on, under and above the sea. It was one of many innovations that would prove disastrous to the Japanese.

By January 1941, the *Saratoga* was long past due for a major overhaul and modernization. The Puget Sound Naval Shipyard in Bremerton,

Washington welcomed the 14 year old carrier with open arms. By this time, the three ship *Yorktown* class of large carrier was the most modern in the fleet and had somewhat supplanted the gentle giants, *Lexington* and *Saratoga*. The enormous funnels and four ancient 8 inch turrets dated these ships and an upgrade was necessary to prepare for the Pacific war that was long overdue. The planned overhaul was budgeted at $7.5 million and was to accomplish a number of objectives including the widening of her deck forward, increased antiaircraft protection and a blister on her starboard side. There was also serious consideration given to the removal of the eight inch battery, but that would days, the Task Force 14 took station on the wallowing oiler and on the 22nd it was decided to fuel some of the destroyers. This proved to be fateful. The very next day Wake Island and her desperate garrison was overrun. The *Saratoga* eventually came within 425 miles of the island, but it was now in the hands of the Japanese. Dejected and ashamed the task force turned for safer waters. Pilots aboard the *Saratoga* broke down and wept as the final furtive messages from the island were received. For the want of a command decision, hundreds of men were now consigned to three years of brutal Japanese prison life.

For the next few weeks, the *Saratoga* and Task Force 14 operated in Hawaiian waters and on January 11, 1942, her luck turned even more sour. She was struck by a submarine launched torpedo which flooded three fire rooms and killed six of her crew. She made it to Pearl Harbor under her own power, and after having her eight inch gun main battery removed, she left for Bremerton and extensive repairs. With the temporary absence of the *Saratoga*, Task Force 14 was also broken up and her units distributed into other commands. This Task Force had accomplished little during its short life, but all of its ships would help win the war in the Pacific in the months and years to follow.

The *Saratoga* received a rather extensive refurbishing at the Puget Sound Naval Shipyard which included the addition of four twin mount 5 inch/38 caliber dual purpose guns. They were located at the sites formerly occupied by their useless eight inch predecessors. These new guns were director controlled, a vast improvement in antiaircraft defense. Also added were a number of 20mm heavy machine guns. The *Saratoga* now also carried CXAM-1 radar and an SC set as well. Her flight deck was extended to 901 feet at its maximum, and gone was the old fashioned tripod foremast. It was replaced by a pole mast. Only her huge funnel now betrayed the secret of her age. It was during her final days in Bremerton that her exact twin, the *Lexington* died after being bombed by Japanese carrier aircraft during the Battle of the Coral Sea. Raging fires that took hold after the attack doomed the *Lexington*. The *Langley* had died in late February near Java, and now there was just one of the original three carriers.

On May 22, 1942, she left the yard for San Diego where she was again detached to carry aircraft to another potentially threatened mid Pacific garrison - Midway Island. She arrived at Pearl Harbor just days after the pivotal battle of the Pacific had been won by aircraft from carriers, *Enterprise*, *Yorktown* and *Hornet*. The *Saratoga* had missed *Coral Sea* and *Midway*, she was still a bridesmaid.

NO LONGER A BRIDESMAID: GUADALCANAL AND BEYOND

The Imperial Japanese Navy was relentless in its drive to conquer territory in the Pacific, and for the first few months of the war, it appeared that nothing could stop octopus like spread. The Battles of the Coral Sea and Midway prevented a wholesale rout of Allied forces, but now it was time to reverse the trend of unopposed conquest. Guadalcanal in the Solomon

Islands was chosen as our first major attempt to oust the Japanese from territory they had captured. The Japanese were building an airstrip that would threaten Allied supply lines and at the same time serve as an outer defense perimeter for the ever expanding Japanese Empire. The *Saratoga* was selected to provide air cover and support for the landing force.

The date of the assault was August 7, the eight month anniversary of the Pearl Harbor attack. Under the overall command of Rear Admiral Frank Jack Fletcher, the carriers *Saratoga*, *Wasp* and *Enterprise* provided support and air defense to the landing force. The *Saratoga* remained on station for two days helping to intercept and knock down a series of Japanese air raids by aircraft coming in from Rabaul. As the fears of additional raids diminished, she withdrew for fueling out of harms way. As she was refueling, a fast moving force of Japanese surface ships arrived off Guadalcanal and surprised the Allied force that was supposed to protect the beachhead. The August 9, 1942, Battle of Savo Island as it became known was a complete and utter defeat for the Allies who were then basking in the warmth of glory resulting from the successful landings on Guadalcanal and Tulagi.

Vice Admiral Gunichi Mikawa, in command of the Eighth Fleet at Rabaul was not pleased with the desperate reports he was receiving from local commanders at Guadalcanal detailing the Allied invasion. Very quickly he assembled a force comprised mostly of heavy cruisers and pointed them toward Savo Island. Guns would be used to eliminate the Allied troop and cargo transports and break up this impertinent landing. His force arrived between Cape Esperance and Savo Island just after 0130 and made their run amongst the unsuspecting defenders. By 0230 they were speeding back home having inflicted mortal hits on the American heavy cruisers *Quincy*, *Vincennes,* and *Astoria*. The Australian cruiser *Canberra* was also hit and sunk later in the morning. The Japanese escaped unscathed and taught the Allies a priceless lesson. Never let down your guard and never underestimate your enemy. Having a constant cover of carrier aircraft might have prevented this defeat, but given the level of tactical and command experience at this time, it is doubtful.

The Japanese were elated at their victory and kept up the pressure with continuous land based air attacks. By late August Japanese capital ships were brought into action and substantial reinforcements were on the way to counter the Allied hold on Guadalcanal. Leading the Japanese attack were the veteran carriers *Shokaku* and *Zuikaku* accompanied by battleships, cruisers and destroyers. The light carrier *Ryujo* was also in attendance but incredibly as a diversion. What unfolded was to become known as the Battle of the Eastern Solomons beginning on August 23, 1942.

Intercepting the Japanese response was Task Force 61 which was composed of the carriers *Saratoga*, *Enterprise* and the *Wasp* with supporting cruisers, destroyers and the battleship *North Carolina*. The *Saratoga* was the flagship of Task Force and carried Admiral Frank Jack Fletcher. On the afternoon of the 23rd, the *Saratoga* launched a strike consisting of 31 SBD "Dauntless" dive bombers and 6 TBF torpedo planes to

Grumman "Avenger" torpedo bombers in echelon. These aircraft were part of the Saratoga's *air group when she attacked and sank the Japanese 13,000 ton carrier* Ryujo *during the August 1942 Battle of the Eastern Solomons.*

locate and sink the transports and their escorts. Unfortunately, their search was fruitless and they had to spend the night at Henderson Field on Guadalcanal, guests of the "cactus airforce" as the constantly harassed land based force was known. The following morning, the group took off looking for trouble and just after being recovered aboard the *Saratoga*, they were launched against reported enemy carriers. They found and engaged the light carrier *Ryujo* and after hitting her with at least four 1,000 pound bombs and a torpedo, she was left sinking. The 13,000 ton carrier which was foolishly used as "bait" for the American force finally disappeared beneath the waves four hours before midnight. The Japanese were still smarting over their defeat at Midway and knew it was vital to eliminate carrier air capability in the area. Now they had lost another carrier, and even though she was not a fleet type carrier, she was still on a par with the new *Independence* class CVL.

On the following afternoon (August 24), the Japanese retaliated with a carrier strike from the main body. Radar aboard the American ships detected the incoming raid and all available aircraft were scrambled and sent to intercept the Japanese onslaught. On board the *Saratoga*, five TBF's and two Dauntless divebombers were ordered into the air to help defenders from the *Enterprise*. Without benefit of directions or charts they were immediately launched. They helped engage the enemy which was boring down on the carriers. The Japanese had only one objective - total destruction of American carrier airpower. Ironically, less than a decade before, naval leaders everywhere scoffed at the possibility of the very event that was unfolding that afternoon. Incredibly, the lone seven plane pickup squad from the *Saratoga* stumbled on elements of the powerful Japanese advance force and another prime Japanese target, the seaplane

Dauntless divebombers arrive back aboard the Saratoga *after lunch on November 5, 1943. They had just come from a successful raid on the Japanese stronghold at Rabaul. This was a brilliant air strike from the old girl and the light carrier* Princeton.

No raid is without some loss. Here Cmdr. Henry Caldwell, who was one of the strike leaders, leaves the cockpit of his Avenger which crash landed back aboard the Saratoga. *A tribute to the Grumman Company and the skill of Caldwell, the plane was recovered with only one wheel, no radio, and no flaps or ailerons. His photographer was killed and the gunner wounded.*

tender *Chitose*. The five torpedo planes struck out, but the two dive bombers were able to severely damage the seaplane tender with near misses.

The *Enterprise* had been damaged by the Japanese attack force, but owing to bad weather, the *Saratoga* was spared any harm. All in all, it had been another hard won, but unfortunately an incomplete victory for the American carriers. The Japanese were forced to withdraw after losing more of their precious pilots and planes, but their two fleet carriers were still a menace. The war of attrition was slowly crippling the capability of the Japanese Navy to wage an effective naval air war, but it was taking its toll on the U.S. Navy as well. For the American Navy, the temporary loss of the *Enterprise* was a very small price to pay for what could have been a major defeat. The Gods of weather provided unplanned for protection.

The *Saratoga* retired from this action with a crew replete with the knowledge that the jinx was surely over. From now on, the old carrier was destined for one glorious victory after another. The dream soon faded. On August 31, 1942, she was patrolling southeast of Guadalcanal, and a submarine contact was made in the early morning hours. I-26, a 2600 ton cruiser submarine was in the vicinity and when her periscope was raised, her captain and crew were rewarded with a beautiful sight - the USS *Saratoga*. Although hounded by the destroyer *MacDonough*, she launched a spread of six torpedoes just after 0700 when her target's crew was sitting down for breakfast. The *MacDonough* even brushed against the hull of the submerged I-26, but she escaped to fight on for another two years. The *Saratoga* swung to avoid the reported torpedoes, but her wide turning radius prevented her from completely avoiding all torpedoes. One hit her on the starboard side just under her island. Regrettably in some instances it only takes one bomb or torpedo to put a carrier out of business. After the gusher of oil and water subsided and the cheering of the Japanese submarine crew died out, damage was being assessed aboard the *Sara*. There was little actual damage and only twelve men were injured, but the vibration from the explosion literally disabled the ship. Her main control room was engulfed in smoke from an related electrical fire and both main generators were automatically shut down. The much vaunted power plant that could develop such a high capacity of power was now useless and the *Saratoga* was a drifting hulk. For hours her engineering crew did what they could to restore power, but the result was an unnerving speed of 12 knots.

The *Sara's* commanding officer, Captain Dewitt C. Ramsey wisely decided to fly off the air group to a shore station. Eventually, the bulk of the *Sara's* air strength found its way to Henderson Field and now not as guests, but now as paid up members of the "cactus air force". The *Saratoga*, with some assistance from the cruiser *Minneapolis*, made it to the relative safety of a nearby anchorage, and thence to Pearl Harbor for permanent repairs. This completed in November 1942, she was assigned duty to fly cover for various backwater operations in the eastern Solomons. This continued for many months. Modern, heavily armed and powerful

Here Captain John "Hopalong" Cassady and helms-men steer the veteran carrier Saratoga *in the Pacific. The carrier has more than made up for the bad luck that seemed to plague her in 1942.*

A quarter view of the Saratoga *on October 30, 1944. She has aircraft spotted all over her flight deck. She also has a number of life rafts attached to her funnel, which fortunately were never used. Her forward five inch barrels are pointed skyward in anticipation of a surprise Japanese air attack. Once the American Navy entered the inner defense perimeter of Japan, air attacks became commonplace and a part of daily life.*

carriers were emerging from American shipyards such as the *Essex's* and the light carrier version *Independence* class. Although the usefulness of the *Saratoga* was unquestioned, she was out of sight, out of mind. She reemerged in the sunlight of the war with the Royal Navy carrier HMS *Victorious* and CVL-23, *Princeton* in October 1943 where they provided air cover for the critical landings on Bougainville. Her next stop was Rabaul and one of the most spectacular carrier strikes in World War II.

THE JAPANESE CRUISER THREAT IS ELIMINATED AT RABAUL

In November 1943, the Japanese island fortress at Rabaul was still formidable, but leary of the obvious Allied thrust toward the Philippines. If the Allies were to be checked, powerful naval reinforcement was imperative. Consequently a force of seven heavy cruisers were sent in. This force included such veterans as the *Chokai, Mogami, Maya, Chikuma* and *Atago*. They were supplemented with a light cruiser and four capable destroyers. It should be recalled, that just 16 months previously, a force of approximately the same power swept into American dominated waters off Savo Island and easily dispatched four Allied heavy cruisers. In fact, the *Chokai* was an alumni of that very night back in early August 1942. This new threat could disrupt and even shatter Allied plans if allowed to break out. Enter the *Saratoga* and light carrier *Princeton*.

The two carriers were principal units of Task Force 38 under the command of Admiral Frederick C. Sherman and included two antiaircraft light cruisers, *San Diego* and *San Juan* with nine destroyers. Air Group 10 was aboard the *Saratoga* and had been chomping at the bit for just such an assignment - attacking moving warships. The task force sped through bad weather to a point 230 miles southeast of Rabaul and began the day's work at 0900 on November 5, 1943. They had yet to be observed, thanks to rain squalls and overall inclement weather.

A total of 23 torpedo planes (Avengers), 22 dive bombers (Dauntless's) and 52 modern fighters (Hellcats) were launched and headed for their

The Saratoga *had escaped major damage since August 1942, but on February 21, 1945, her good luck expired. Under the shield of cloud cover, six enemy aircraft hit the old carrier with five bombs. Two hours later just before sundown, she was again hit by a single bomb.*

target - warships at Rabaul. Just after 1100, they arrived and in precision form went into the attack. Rabaul stood out in bright sunshine yet the American force was still under heaven sent overcast. The Japanese were completely surprised and in the ensuing battle only shot down or damaged 10 total aircraft which failed to return home. In exchange for this loss, the Japanese suffered an irreversible beating. Heavy cruisers *Maya, Atago, Takao,* and *Mogami* were disabled by hits or near misses. Light cruisers

Agano and *Noshiro* were damaged as well as two hapless destroyers. The threat of any Japanese surface power was ended and the way was clear for continued Allied advance. A major threat had been eliminated and in many ways, it was the crowning achievement of this aging but still valuable carrier. Task Force 38 escaped unscathed but as usual was reported destroyed by the Japanese press. In reality, the only destruction occurred when a Japanese aerial strike force was sent in pursuit of the *Saratoga* and com-

An artist rendering of the successful Japanese air attack on the Saratoga *off Iwo Jima on February 21, 1945. She lost 123 of her crew and many score were wounded.*

The wounded giant moved slowly ahead as smoke seeps from her flight deck and hanger areas. For a while, the fired nearly consumed the forward part of the great ship, but superior damage control brought them under control. Fire had consumed her twin sister, the Lexington, *just after she was hit by bombs during the Battle of the Coral Sea.*

pany, yet attacked a PT boat and a small landing craft. Neither was sunk, but PT-167 was elevated to "sunken" American carrier status. The result was a victory of "flying over lying!"

After nearly a year of steaming and one operation after another, the *Saratoga* was detached and ordered to the San Francisco Naval Shipyard for a major overhaul. From December 9, 1943 until January 3, 1944, fast paced shipyard workers swarmed all over the ancient ship and

when she emerged she had a rather homely camouflage paint job designed just for her. She resembled a giant zebra in repose, but she was also now reinforced with sixty 40mm guns that now supplanted and supplemented her close in battery of thirty six 20mm guns. Her updated antiaircraft battery was formidable, and had the now lost carriers from the early days been likewise armed, they too might still be alive.

The veteran carrier stood out from the

Golden Gate on January 3, 1944, and steamed for Pearl Harbor, now far to the rear of the Pacific war. For the next two months she provided support to forces attempting to take the Marshall Islands from stubborn Japanese defenders, but in early March, she assumed a new role. She was detached to join forces with British Eastern Fleet with the carrier HMS *Illustrious* at its head.

THE *SARATOGA* BECOMES PART OF AN INTERNATIONAL FORCE

In concert with the Royal Navy which had been operating in the Indian Ocean, the *Saratoga* became part of a multinational force destined to initiate the reclamation process in the Dutch East Indies. This group was further augmented by the Free French battleship *Richelieu*, and they then began the systematic reduction of Japanese holdings in that region. For two years the Japanese had held sway over this territory having mercilessly wiped out the Allies during January through March 1942. Now the conquered returned to take back that which had been stolen.

First it was necessary to soften defenses and reduce the ability of the oil rich Indies to provide sustenance to the Japanese war machine. After all, one of the major reasons leading to the war was the Japanese need for a dependable supply of oil and other natural resources. This had to be interrupted. The port at Sabang in Sumatra was first hit and hit hard on April

19, 1944. American pilots acted as mentors to their Royal Navy counterparts and with these new skills, the raids were quite successful. The following month on May 17, 1944, aircraft from the *Saratoga* and HMS *Illustrious* attacked Surabaja in Java. This raid must have heartened local Dutch civilians and loyal Javanese who had endured Japanese occupation for so long. As was the pattern established by the Axis, air attack preceded a land assault, and this was not too far distant. Her work finished with the British Eastern Fleet, on May 18, the *Saratoga* steamed for the Puget Sound Naval Shipyard in Bremerton, Washington for repair and overhaul. This time she emerged with a more modern air and surface search radar system and an enlarged elevator for handling aircraft. The old "T" shaped elevator had to be updated and enlarged to accommodate contemporary aircraft. She remained there up through September and then sailed for Pearl Harbor to join with the next oldest carrier in the navy, the USS *Ranger* CV-4.

TRAINING, FINAL WAR DAMAGE AND BOWING OUT GRACEFULLY

The *Saratoga*, still less than 20 years old was now obsolete by late World War II standards. She was armed with sixteen 5 inch/38 caliber guns and over one hundred 20mm and 40mm guns as well as employing modern radar, but she was tired and fatigue was beginning to set in. Fleet carriers of the *Essex* class were continuously sliding down the ways and many were spearheading carrier raids all over the Pacific. There were even three 45,000 ton super giants, the *Coral Sea, Midway* and the *Franklin Roosevelt* being built. The *Saratoga*, still the largest of all U.S. carriers was also the most antiquated, and rapid advances in overall ship and especially carrier development had left the *Saratoga* far behind technically. The old carrier joined a shipmate, the *Ranger* in the autumn of 1944 and in truth the autumn of their service lives. Both were used to develop night fighter tactics that soon would be vitally needed in the upcoming drive into waters adjacent to the Japanese home islands. She and the *Ranger* carried out experiments and developed methods into mid January 1945. Then the *Saratoga* was requested to join with another old veteran, the *Enterprise* to establish a night fighter defense in the Iwo Jima operation. Apparently, there was still a important combat role for the *Saratoga*. This mission came to an abrupt end on February 21, 1945, when six Japanese aircraft finally hit the old girl with five bombs. Later that day, she was hit again by one more bomb, but finally damage control parties brought fires under control and she was able to depart the area under her own power. The shooting war was over for the grand old lady of U.S. Naval aviation. The damage was enough to disable and send her back home for repair. The attack also cost the lives of 123 men

After repairs in Bremerton she briefly trained pilots and when the war was over, joined the "magic carpet" fleet and brought thousands of veterans back home to the USA. When this duty was complete, she was not placed in reserve, but was slated for atomic bomb testing. She may have been the largest carrier in the navy, but her

age had finally caught up with her. Her huge funnel bespoke the truth of her age as did the thousands of rivets in her hull. There was no reprieve for the old carrier, and she was sent to Bikini Atoll to be subjected to the July 1946 twin Atomic blasts code named *Operation Crossroads*.

THE *SARATOGA* DIES A STATELY BUT AGONIZING DEATH

Watching the old carrier being deluged by the tidal wave of debris and water vapor after the second blast was painful for those who remembered and loved the *Saratoga*. He funnel was

Even though the Saratoga *was hit by six bombs, she was able to recover aircraft within hours. This was a victory for damage controlmen.*

Fires still rage on the Saratoga *as anxious gunners scan the skies for more attacks. She had been torpedoed twice in 1942, but the aerial bombs did the most damage and caused the greatest number of casualties.*

knocked down on the deck and she was slowly sinking. There was no possibility of plugging the holes and saving her. The radioactivity level was lethal and it was best to let her go. It was a seven and one half hour struggle but finally she succumbed and slipped beneath the calm water of the lagoon. She had been a majestic ship and the pride of American Naval Aviation for nearly two decades. The old Chief was sad, but quietly pleased to be present at her end and proud to have been a part of the life of this great lady.

Crewmen study the score board showing the victories of the great carrier. Dozens of aircraft have been shot down or destroyed as well as many ships sunk or damaged. This is a record of which to be proud and fully justified the Saratoga's existence. One of the records not shown is a lifetime total of 98,549 landings.

The old girl has survived the first atomic bomb test at Bikini. The air burst did little damage, and she looks as if she could recommence flight operations. A TBF Avenger still sits on her after deck, apparently unharmed. The next test would yield far more devastating results.

The gentle giant, Saratoga, slips beneath the lagoon's surface on July 25, 1946. She was hit hard by an underwater blast detonated just 500 yards from her location in the anchorage. When the water vapor subsided, her funnel was lying across her deck, and she was obviously in a bad way. Seven and one half hours later, she sank to the bottom, 180 feet down. The last of the converted naval treaty battlecruisers, ws now gone, and with her, the end of an era.

BIBLIOGRAPHY

I. Primary Materials

A. Private Papers - Manuscript/Photo Files
Armada de Chile files on USS *Brooklyn/ O'Higgins*, 1989

Bonner, Kermit H. Sr., Lt. Commander, USN(Ret) 1995

Photos of the USS *Boise*, USS *Arkansas* Bonner, Kermit H. Jr., Private Collection

Call Bulletin Newspaper Files, 1995, Treasure Island Museum

Coker, Henriette, 1994, USS *Langley*

Dennis, Jess, 1994, USS *Pennsylvania*

First Shot Naval Veterans, USS *Ward* Collection, Russell Reetz, Secretary, 1994

Jaekel, H. H., 1995, USS *Salt Lake City* photos

La Flame, Arthur L., 1994, USS *Hobson* disaster

McMahill, Thomas A. Jr., 1992, USS *Brooklyn* photos/files

McMahon, Robert, Lt. Cmdr., USN(Ret), 1994, Photos of the USS *Oklahoma*

Merrill, A. Philip, 1995, USS *Belet*

Parr, John S., 1994, USS *Concord*, private collection

St. Pierre, Paul, 1993, USS *Langley* History

Transfer Contract of Aircraft Carrier *Dedalo* from Spain to the *Cabot/ Dedalo* Museum Association. 1989

U.S. Navy Photo Collection, Treasure Island Naval Station

U.S. Naval Institute Photo Collection

USS *Enterprise* Association, 1994, Photos and ship history

USS *Wasp* unofficial report of sinking the USS *Hobson*, April 28, 1952 and approved press releases

B. Interviews

Anderson, Bill, 1996, *Cabot/Dedalo* Association

Austin, Warren E., 1991, USS *Helena*

Bean, Harold, 1994, USS *California*

Blahnik, Ted, 1992, USS *Helena*

Boggs, Clair, 1991, USS *Brooklyn* at war

Bonner, Kermit H. Sr., Lt. Cmdr., USN (Ret), 1991, 1994, Life aboard the USS *Boise*, USS *Arkansas* and the pre-war U.S. Navy

Brady, Will, 1991, USS *Helena*

Brown, Clinton, 1991, USS *Boise*

Bukrey, Edward, 1993, USS *Ward* at Pearl Harbor

Bunker, Bill, 1991, USS *Helena*

Clark, Curt, CWO3, USN, Ret, 1994, The Four Stack APD Veterans in World War II

Clark, John A., 1992, USS *Helena*

Clark, Salome Springer, 1990, Sponsor of the USS *Boise*

Darby, Joe, "The Times Picayune", *New Orleans, Cabot/Dedalo*

Dascher, Vernon G., 1994, USS *New Mexico*

Deforest, Ary, 1991, USS *Helena*

Dubose, Dorse, 1992, USS *Brooklyn* at War

Dvorak, Theodore, 1990, USS *Brush* remembrances

Fazio, Anthony J., 1993, USS *William D. Porter*

Fey, Stanley W., 1993, Sinking of the USS *Hobson* by the USS *Wasp*

Fox, Al, Cmdr. USN (Ret), 1991, The USS *Boise* at the Battle of Cape Esperance

Gruening, D. W., 1993, USS *Ward* at Pearl Harbor

Hall, Omer David, 1991, USS *Brooklyn*

Hammergren, Nelson, 1992, USS *William D. Porter*

Himes, H. G., 1994, USS *Concord* at War

Holbrook, Heber, 1994, USS *San Francisco*

Jaekel, H. H. "Jake", 1995, USS *Salt Lake City*

Lockhart, Lester, 1994, USS Concord

Lusky, Tom, 1994, USS *Concord* at War

Mason, Robert, 1991, USS *Brush* DD-745

Moran, Moore, 1992, Son of Captain Mike Moran of the USS *Boise*

Mullican, Denver, 1996, *Cabot/Dedalo*

Nolde, Raymond, 1993, USS *Ward* at Pearl Harbor

Olson, A., 1995, USS *Enterprise*

Panarese, Adam, 1994, USS *Concord* at War

Peick, John Patrick, 1993, USS *Ward* during World War II

Potter, Bob, Major USAF, 1994, Radiation Testing - Pentagon Spokesperson

Reimer, Bulldog and Audrey, 1992, USS *Nashville* as part of the Halsey-Doolittle Raid

Reynolds, H. R. "Shorty", 1995, USS *New York* in World War II

Showen, Anderson V., 1991, USS *Brooklyn*

Swaney, Ed, 1995, USS *Nevada*

Ulmer, Frederick, 1994, USS *Ward* during World War II

Van Watts, Lt. Cmdr. USN (Ret), 1994, "The Anchor Chain Catastrophe"

Weisgall, Jonathan M., 1994, Effects of Radiation at Bikini and Kwajalein Atolls 1946

Wells, Alfred, 1991, USS *Brooklyn*

Westcamp, Clarence, 1994, USS *Concord*

Yoshida, Akihiko, Captain, JMSDF (Ret), 1992

Imperial Japanese Navy records on the Solomon Islands naval engagements

C. U.S. Government Documents

U.S. Naval War College, "The Battle of Midway, including the Aleutian Phase June 3-14, 1942, Strategical and Tactical Analysis", NavPers 91067, 1948

U.S. Navy, "The Story of the USS *Helena*" October 23, 1943

USS *William D. Porter*, Loss Report, June 18, 1945

II. Secondary Materials

A. Books, Monographs, Treaties

Terzibaschitsch, Stefan, "Aircraft Carriers of the U.S.Navy", Naval Institute Press, 1978

Wickland, John J. Jr., "All the Queens Men", Goretske *Enterprises*, 1992

Ewing, Steve, "American Cruisers of World War II", Pictorial Histories Publishing, 1984

Sweetman, Jack, "American Naval History", Naval Institute Press, 1984

Preston Antony, "Aircraft Carriers", Brompton Books Corp, 1979

Beigel, Harvey M., "Battleship Country", Pictorial Histories Publishing Co., 1983

Mason, Theodore C., "Battleship Sailor", Naval Institute Press, 1982

Power, Hugh, "Battleship *Texas*", Texas A and M University Press, 1993

Karig, Walter/Kelley, Welbourn, "Battle Report, Pearl Harbor to Coral Sea"/ "The Atlantic War"/"End of an Empire", Farrar and Rinehart Inc., 1944

Friedman, Norman, "Carrier Air Power", Naval Institute Press, 1981

McNeil, "Charleston's Navy Yard", Cokercraft Press, 1985

Office of Naval History, U.S. Navy, "Dictionary of American Naval Fighting Ship", all volumes, U.S. Government Printing Office, 1969

Cohen, Stan, "East Wind Rain", Pictorial Histories Publishing Co., 1981

Maas, Jim, "F2A Buffalo in Action", Squadron Signal Publications, 1987

Holbrook, Heber A., "History of the USS *San Francisco* in World War II, Pacific Ship and Shore, 1978

Morison, Samuel Elliott, "History of U.S. Naval Operations in World War II", all volumes, Atlantic Little Brown and Co., 1962

Andrews, Phillip, "Navy Yearbook", Duell, Sloan and Pierce, 1944

Swaney, Edwin S., "Operation Crossroads (USS *Nevada*)", Sutherland Publishing, 1986

Hoyt, Edwin P., "Pacific Destiny", W. W. Norton and Company, 1981

Messimer, Dwight R., "Pawns of War", Naval Institute Press, 1983

Miller, John Grider, "The Battle to Save the *Houston*", Naval Institute Press, 1985

Winslow, W. G., "The Fleet the Gods Forgot", Naval Institute Press, 1982.

Hoyt, Edwin P., "The Lonely Ships", David MacCay and Co., 1976

Wright and Logan, "The Royal Navy in Focus, 1930 - 1939", "Vol II, The Royal Navy in Focus, 1940 - 1949", Maritime Books, 1981

Chant, Christopher, "Sea Forces of the World", Bryant Trodd Publishing House Ltd., 1990

Chesneau, Roger, "The World's Aircraft Carriers 1914-1945", Arms and Armour Press, 1986

Young, Stephen Bower, "Trapped at Pearl

Harbor, Escape from Battleship *Oklahoma*", North River Press, 1991

Melhorn, Charles M., "Two Block Fox, the Rise of the Aircraft Carrier, 1911-1929", Naval Institute Press, 1974

Friedman, Norman, "U.S. Destroyers", Naval Institute Press, 1982

Friedman, "U.S. Cruisers", Naval Institute Press, 1984

Larkins, William T., "U.S. Navy Aircraft 1921-1941", Aviation History Publications, 1961

Miller, Nathan, "U.S. Navy, an Illustrated History", American Heritage Publishing Co., Inc., 1977

Friedman, Norman, "U.S. Naval Weapons", Naval Institute Press", 1985

McMahill, Thomas A., "USS *Brooklyn* CL-40, Just a Touch of the Sea", Personally Published, 1988

Hudson, J Ed., "USS *Cabot* (CVL-28): A Fast Carrier in World War II", Personally Published, 1986

Ewing, Steve, "USS *Enterprise* (CV-6), The Most Decorated Ship of World War II", Pictorial Histories Publishing, 1982

First Shot Naval Vets, "USS *Ward* Fires First Shot of WWII, Organizationally published, 1983

Jentschura, Hansgeorge/Jung, Dieter, "Warships of the Japanese Navy, Naval Institute Press, 1970

Angelucci, Enzo/Matricardi, "World War II Airplanes, Vol II", Rand McNally and Co., 1976

Bailey, Dan E., "WWII Wrecks of Kwajalein and Truk Lagoons", North Valley Diver Publications, 1989

B. Articles

Johnson, Edwin L., "Fly on...Fly Off...The First American Floating Aerodrome: USS *Langley* (CV-1)", Nautical Research Journal, January, 1981

Schwartz, Robert L., "The Night the Hobson Died", December 1955, Argosy Magazine

Tate, Jackson, Rear Admiral, "We Rode the Covered Wagon", U.S. Naval Institute Proceedings, October 1978 Vol 104

Pictorial: "*Oklahoma*: Up from the Mud at Pearl Harbor", Naval Institute Proceedings, December 1975, Vol 101

Lumb, Fred A., "WWII's Last Shot, V F W Magazine, August 12, 1945

C. Unpublished Works

Lewis, H. Seward, 1944, "Hot, Straight and Normal", USS *William D. Porter*

McMahon, Robert, Lt. Cmdr., USN(Ret), 1994, "In Dawn's Early Light" (USS *Enterprise* CV-6)

USS *Brush* DD-745 Association, unk ear, "History of the USS *Brush* DD-745 inch

USS *Concord* CL-10, Navy Day 1945 Book

D. Newspapers

Shipmate, May 1990, "Cape Esperance and Murphy's Law, Leonard F. Baird, Capt. USN (Ret)

The Cincinnati Enquirer, August 22, 1970, "Narrow Escape by FDR on Battleship is Recalled", Staff writer

The Daily Gazette, August 25, 1993, Schnectady, New York, "Oldest Living sailor from the Battleship USS *New York*", William Urbaetis.

The Idaho Evening Statesman, March 14, 1952, USS *Boise* and Salome Springer Clark, Staff writer

The Sacramento Bee, November 14, 1993, "Don't Shoot, we're Republicans", Kit Bonner

The Times Picayune, June 25, 1994, "Museum Ship Goes Down the Drain Due to Money", *Cabot/Dedalo*

E. Other

Argentine Embassy, Naval Attache Office, 1991, USS *Boise/Argentine* "9 de Julio".

Chilean Embassy and Naval Attache, 1994

City of Helena, 1991, USS *Helena*

Cruise Book, USS *Cabot*, 1952

Dinkins, David, Mayor New York City, 1990, USS *Brooklyn*

Guadalcanal Campaign Veterans, 1992, USS *Helena*

Metro Goldwyn Mayer, from a story by Lt. Cmdr. Frank W. "Spig" Wead, "Helldivers", 1931

Nationwide Radiological Study: Republic of the Marshall Islands, 1994

Newport News Shipbuilding Public Relations: USS *Boise* and USS *Enterprise*

Office of Navy Information, East 1990 on USS *Brooklyn*

Statements of Harry J. Pettengill, U.S. Dept of Energy, Professor Merril Eisenbud, Bill Graham, Billiet Edmond Mayor Rongelap (Marshall Islands), Jonathan M. Weisgall, Attorney, February 24, 1994, Congressional subcommittee on Oversight and Investigations

USS *Boise* Reunion Newsletters

USS *Brooklyn* Association, Newsletters, files and papers

USS *Brooklyn* Launching Program

USS *Cabot* CVL-28 Association

USS *Concord* CL-10, Minutemen Association

USS *Enterprise* Association

USS *Helena* Association, Battle Honors and Reports

USS *Hobson* Memorial Society

USS *Oklahoma* Survivors

USS *Nevada* Association

USS *Salt Lake City* Association Newsletters, various.

USS *Salt Lake City* Cruise Book

USS *San Francisco* Newsletter, October 1993

USS *Texas* Memorial

USS *Wasp* Association

Robbins, L. M., 1943/1944, Life aboard the USS *Brooklyn* in 1943 and 1944

Texas State Department of Parks, State of Texas, 1995

Photo right: The Brooklyn *and* Phoenix *in reserve at the Philadelphia Navy Yard. Within two years of the end of World War II, other ships such as the* Honolulu, Philadelphia, San Francisco *and many batttleships and destroyers would also be members of the ghost fleet. They lay asleep until recalled for sale, scrapping, activation or in some rare cases, renovation as museum ships.*

Photos above and below: Sailors love to tell tall tales whether aboard the Union Navy warship USS Richmond *in 1860 or aboard the* Saratoga *in October 1935.*

A night bomber pilot sits ready in a TBM in March 1945. He will soon be launched off the Enterprise, *which has specialized in radar guided night attack work. The* Enterprise *has already demonstrated her prowess in this work with fighter interception and other attacks. His destination is Kyushu.*

The trip through the Canal Zone in autumn 1945 was not so bad when visitors like these came aboard.

The brand newly renovated battleship Texas *at anchor in the Hudson River in April 1927. She now has the look of a modern battleship and is respected by all, especially children who dream of going to sea and women who admire the navy and its fighting men.*

The Nevada *leaves Pearl Harbor for the Pudget Sound Navy Yard and complete modernization and repair. It only took salvage experts three months to plug holes and move her into dry dock #2 in Pearl Harbor. By May 1942 she was in the hands of stateside shipyard workers and on her way to full recovery.*

The new Sumner *class 2,200 ton "big destroyer"* Brush *slides down the ways on December 28, 1943, just over two years since the Japanese attack on Pearl Harbor. The* Brush *and her sisters were purposeful looking warships that looked less graceful than the* Fletcher *class, but far more muscular.*

Index does not include Bibliography.

January 23, 1972, the Mexican destroyer California is damaged beyong any hope of redemption and has been abandoned. Her captain has disappeared, and only the tourists are left to mourn her loss.

Printed in the USA
CPSIA information can be obtained
at www.ICGtesting.com
JSHW060052150824
68134JS00032B/2717